OXFORD STUDIES IN EUROPEAN LAW

Reflexive Governance in EU Equality Law

OXFORD STUDIES IN EUROPEAN LAW

Series Editors

Paul Craig, Professor of English Law at St John's College, Oxford
Gráinne de Búrca, Professor of Law at New York University School of Law

The aim of this series is to publish important and original research on EU law. The focus is on scholarly monographs, with a particular emphasis on those which are interdisciplinary in nature. Edited collections of essays will also be included where they are appropriate. The series is wide in scope and aims to cover studies of particular areas of substantive and of institutional law, historical works, theoretical studies, and analyses of current debates, as well as questions of perennial interest such as the relationship between national and EU law and the novel forms of governance emerging in and beyond Europe. The fact that many of the works are interdisciplinary will make the series of interest to all those concerned with the governance and operation of the EU.

OTHER TITLES IN THE SERIES

Enhanced Cooperation and European Tax Law
Caroline Heber

Legal Pluralism in European Contract Law
Vanessa Mak

Europe's Passive Virtues
Deference to National Authorities in EU Free Movement Law
Jan Zglinski

Accountability in EU Security and Defence
The Law and Practice of Peacebuilding
Carolyn Moser

Accountability in the Economic and Monetary Union
Foundations, Policy, and Governance
Menelaos Markakis

Official Secrets and Oversight in the EU
Law and Practices of Classified Information
Vigjilenca Abazi

Risk Regulation in the Internal Market
Lessons from Agricultural Biotechnology
Maria Weimer

EU Health Law & Policy
The Expansion of EU Power in Public Health and Health Care
Anniek de Ruijter

The Horizontal Effect of Fundamental Rights in the European Union
A Constitutional Analysis
Eleni Frantziou

EU Powers Under External Pressure
How the EU's External Actions Alter its Internal Structures
Christina Eckes

Reflexive Governance in EU Equality Law

EMMA LANTSCHNER

OXFORD
UNIVERSITY PRESS

OXFORD
UNIVERSITY PRESS

Great Clarendon Street, Oxford, OX2 6DP,
United Kingdom

Oxford University Press is a department of the University of Oxford.
It furthers the University's objective of excellence in research, scholarship,
and education by publishing worldwide. Oxford is a registered trade mark of
Oxford University Press in the UK and in certain other countries

First Edition published in 2021

Impression: 1

Published in the United States of America by Oxford University Press
198 Madison Avenue, New York, NY 10016, United States of America

British Library Cataloguing in Publication Data

Data available

Library of Congress Control Number: 2021940643

ISBN 978–0–19–284337–1

DOI: 10.1093/oso/9780192843371.001.0001

Printed and bound by
CPI Group (UK) Ltd, Croydon, CR0 4YY

Series Editor's Preface

The principle of equality and the prohibition of discrimination are by now core features of European Union law, and indeed ever more important features at a time of rising xenophobia and illiberalism. An extensive body of legislation, case law and primary law govern the scope, application and enforcement of EU anti-discrimination law, including provisions of the EU Treaties, the Charter of Rights and the Gender Equality as well as the Race Equality and Framework Employment Equality Directives. At the same time, EU law has an extensive body of case law governing the effectiveness of remedies, and the equality and anti-discrimination directives contain provisions governing their enforcement. Individuals can bring domestic actions based on EU law equality guarantees, and the European Commission can use its powers to bring infringement proceedings against Member States in which EU anti-discrimination law is not being adequately observed.

In this thoroughly interdisciplinary book, Emma Lantschner examines the implementation of the Race Equality Directive and the Framework Employment Equality Directive over the years (more than two decades since their initial adoption), using multiple case studies of 'older' and 'newer' member states, including Austria, Belgium, Bulgaria, Germany, Ireland, and Romania. She looks at both judicial mechanisms and non-judicial mechanisms, focusing on the role of multiple institutions including not just national governments, legislators and courts, but also NGOs, equality bodies and institutions and other civil society actors. The book contains a valuable comparative review of the transposition and implementation in practice of provisions of the two key EU anti-discrimination directives of 2000. Lantschner carefully synthesizes the results of this comparative review, and identifies a range of good practices as well challenges in the implementation of these measures.

The book also examines mechanisms of compliance used in relations with non-member states in the pre-enlargement process, focusing on the example of Croatia's process of alignment with the EU's anti-discrimination *acquis*. The author uses this process-tracing case study of the implementation of EU anti-discrimination law in Croatia to examine her central hypothesis that a strategy of conditionality is likely to be a less successful one for bringing about compliance with EU law than a reflexive, experimentalist, learning-based approach focused on cooperation between all relevant actors. Despite her normative preference for the latter, she finds a lack of strong commitment to the reflexive approach as well as limited practical realization of this approach in the Croatian context, particularly with regard to the facilitation of civil society participation, as well as with regard to pooling and sharing of best practices, benchmarking and ongoing monitoring. The author uses these findings from her case study to make a series of recommendations and to propose a set of indicators for existing as well as future member states.

This book is a rigorous and original work. It contains valuable theoretical analysis and synthesis, as well as novel empirical material on the implementation EU anti-discrimination directives as well as EU approaches to enforcement and compliance both in its member states and with prospective member states. It should be of interest to all those who are concerned with EU equality and non-discrimination law, and to legal academics as well as political science scholars who are interested in theories and practices of EU governance, implementation and compliance.

Paul Craig
Gráinne de Búrca

Preface

Research on this book started in early 2015 and reached a preliminary end in mid-April 2021. It has been a long journey and its end is only preliminary as the subject of equality and non-discrimination will continue to attract me, for several reasons. One is the academic interest in observing how legal norms in this policy field and their practical implementation will further evolve. Announcements at European level have been made (as they have been in the past), but it remains to be seen if and how they materialize. It will also be interesting to observe how courts at national and European levels will interpret the legal framework, as an increasing number of discrimination cases reaches also the Court of Justice of the European Union (CJEU), with the latter sometimes handing down quite controversial decisions. Another reason is the high relevance which the issue of inequalities and discrimination on various grounds, existing for a long time and partly systemic, will continue to play in our societies in the future. The issue itself is not new of course, but with the global pandemic that we have witnessed since early 2020, these inequalities have become more visible. Another reason for continuing to work in this field, and to me the most heartfelt reason, is connected to the massive respect that I have developed while doing the interviews for this research for the many people working in their daily practice with and for individuals that have become the victims of discrimination on various grounds. The personal, and in some cases financial, commitment with which they do this deserves great appreciation. Each and every one of us can contribute to making our societies more equal and, in the spirit of Marie Curie's famous observation: 'You cannot hope to build a better world without improving the individuals. To that end each of us must work for his own improvement, and at the same time share a general responsibility for all humanity, our particular duty being to aid those to whom we think we can be most useful', I try to contribute my share with this book.

Considering the above, it is these human rights defenders and lawyers, civil society activists, Equality Board members, and all my other interview partners to whom I would like to extend my first expression of gratitude. This book benefits enormously from the first-hand experience that they have contributed and I hope that some of what is said in the book will help them to support their case, or lend force to their claims.

A sincere thanks also goes to my academic teachers and mentors, first and foremost Professor Joseph Marko and Professor Wolfgang Benedek. They were there for engaging and insightful discussions and support throughout the work on this book (and way beyond) which constituted an important step in my tenure track process. I am also grateful to my colleagues at the University of Graz, in particular Fynn Heckert, for his research assistance.

Many thanks also to the series editors of Oxford Studies in European Law, Paul Craig and Gráinne de Búrca, for accepting the book into the series, and to Brianne Bellio and Luise Wilde, the Oxford University Press editors guiding the publication process with their support and encouragement.

The biggest thanks goes to my husband, for his moral support, his technical advice when I was struggling with my reference management system, and his never-ending patience. Thank you so much, Simon.

I would like to end this Preface with another line from Marie Curie that applies to the production of the book as well as for its subject matter: '*I was taught that the way of progress was neither swift nor easy*.' Time is more than ripe for tangible progress in making the promise of equal treatment become a reality, and improving compliance with the EU acquis relating to equality and non-discrimination.

Emma Lantschner
Graz, April 2021

Contents

List of Tables

List of Abbreviations

ACFC	Advisory Committee on the Framework Convention for the Protection of National Minorities
ADA	Antidiscrimination Act (Croatia)
BUG	Büro zur Umsetzung von Gleichbehandlung e.V. (Germany)
CERD	Committee on the Elimination of Racial Discrimination
CFCF	Chance for Children Foundation (Hungary)
CFR	Charter of Fundamental Rights of the European Union
CJEU	Court of Justice of the European Union
CoE	Council of Europe
CPAD	Commission for Protection Against Discrimination (Bulgaria)
CRPD	UN Convention on the Rights of Persons with Disabilities
CSO	civil society organization
CVM	Cooperation and Verification Mechanism for Romania and Bulgaria
EA	Equality Authority (Ireland)
ECJ	European Court of Justice
ECRI	European Commission Against Racism and Intolerance (CoE)
ECSR	European Committee of Social Rights (CoE)
ECtHR	European Court of Human Rights
EEA	Employment Equality Act (Ireland)
EED	Council Directive 2000/78/EC of 27 November 2000 establishing a general framework for equal treatment in employment and occupation (or Employment Equality Directive)
EELN	European network of legal experts in gender equality and non-discrimination (or European Equality Law Network)
EIGE	European Institute for Gender Equality
ENAR	European Network Against Racism
EP	European Parliament
Equinet	European Network of Equality Bodies
ERRC	European Roma Rights Centre
ETA	Equal Treatment Authority (Hungary)
ETC	Equal Treatment Commission (Austria)
EU-MIDIS	EU Minorities and Discrimination Survey, carried out by the Fundamental Rights Agency in 2009 (EU-MIDIS I) and 2017 (EU-MIDIS II)
EUMC	European Monitoring Centre on Racism and Xenophobia
FADA	Federal Anti-discrimination Agency (Germany)
FRA	European Agency for Fundamental Rights
GANHRI	Global Alliance of National Human Rights Institutions
GETA	General Equal Treatment Act (Germany)

GOHMR	Government Office for Human Rights and Rights of National Minorities (Croatia)
GPR	General Policy Recommendation (of ECRI)
ICERD	UN Convention on the Elimination of all Forms of Racial Discrimination
IHRC	Irish Human Rights Commission
IHREC	Irish Human Rights and Equality Commission
IHRECA	Irish Human Rights and Equality Commission Act
LGBT(I)	Lesbian, Gay, Bisexual, Transgender (Intersex)
NCCD	National Council for Combating Discrimination (Romania)
NGO	Non-Governmental Organisation
NHRI	National Human Rights Institution
OHCHR	UN Office of the High Commissioner for Human Rights
OO	Office of the Ombudsperson (Croatia)
PADA	Protection Against Discrimination Act (Bulgaria)
para.	paragraph
RED	Council Directive 2000/43/EC of 29 June 2000 implementing the principle of equal treatment between persons irrespective of racial or ethnic origin (or Racial Equality Directive)
SCA of GANHRI	Sub-Committee on Accreditation of the Global Alliance of National Human Rights Institutions
SLG	Starting Line Group
UNAR	Ufficio Nazionale Antidiscriminazioni Razziali (National Office Against Racial Discrimination, Italy)
Unia	Equality Body of Belgium, formerly known as Centre for Equal Opportunities and Opposition to Racism, and Interfederal Centre for Equal Opportunities and Opposition to Racism and Discrimination
WRC	Workplace Relations Commission (Ireland)

Introduction: Aim and Scope of the Book and Its Structure

When French president Emmanuel Macron addressed the German Bundestag on 18 November 2018 he spoke about a Europe being at a crossroads: It either plunges, as has happened in the past, 'into the abyss of fascination for ... nationalism without memory and for fanaticism without values. Or it remembers the unique accomplishments of progress and starts a new era from which all humanity can benefit.' He advocated a stronger Europe, a pooling together of decision making on policies such as foreign affairs, migration, and development as well as a common defence strategy. He called on Europe to overcome taboos and habits.[1] While he was addressing the global challenges that Europe found itself exposed to, including the question of how to deal with migration flows, with the rise of nationalist parties in several Member States, and the threats to the European values of democracy, rule of law, and fundamental rights, he indirectly spoke at so many levels to the topic that is at the centre of the present research: the right to equality and non-discrimination.

Much about the status in which a society finds itself can be seen in how it deals with the weakest parts of it (like those belonging to national minorities), how it deals with phenomena that do not represent the mainstream or 'traditional' values (like different sexual orientations or gender identities), or with persons that do not fit (any more) into the performance-driven society (like the elderly or disabled). The rising nationalism in several European countries alluded to by Macron in his speech, be they members of the European Union or aspiring to become members in the future, has led to a situation in which it has become more and more normal to openly attack persons who, for various reasons, are 'different'. Political leaders in an increasing number of countries stir fears and resentment against such individuals or groups. Faced with challenges that appear to be more pressing or important, like financial crises, Brexit, or global terrorism, issues such as equality and non-discrimination risk slipping from the agenda. Macron's speech has been overtaken by a global pandemic that broke out in early 2020 and represents yet another such challenge. The Covid pandemic has exacerbated pre-existing discrimination and disparities in our

[1] The full speech of President Macron in German translation is available on the website of the German Bundestag, at https://www.bundestag.de/dokumente/textarchiv/2018/kw46-volkstrauertag-577158. Author's translation.

Reflexive Governance in EU Equality Law. Emma Lantschner, Oxford University Press.
DOI: 10.1093/oso/9780192843371.003.0001

societies.[2] Furthermore, the Black Lives Matter movement, emerging after the death of George Floyd as a result of brutal police action, has contributed to heightened awareness of persistent racism, not only in the US but also in Europe.

Faced with such challenges, it is all the more important that there are actors who do not tire of raising awareness about discrimination persisting or even increasing in society, informing others about the rights and means of redress, supporting victims of discrimination in getting redress and trying to influence public policy on the matter and public discourse surrounding various discrimination grounds. These actors are first and foremost the civil society organizations working in the interests of those who are exposed to discrimination, as well as Equality Bodies. Both these actors have been given a prominent role in the fight against discrimination at EU level by being assigned important functions by the two Directives that will be studied in depth in this book: Council Directive 2000/43/EC of 29 June 2000 implementing the principle of equal treatment between persons irrespective of racial or ethnic origin (hereafter: Racial Equality Directive or RED), and Council Directive 2000/78/EC of 27 November 2000 establishing a general framework for equal treatment in employment and occupation (hereafter: Employment Equality Directive or EED). The development of this EU non-discrimination regime is introduced in Chapter 1.

There is one message from Macron to the deputies of the German Bundestag that applies not only to these actors, but probably even more so to political decision makers: We must overcome taboos and habits. Such taboos and habits exist also in the way in which the 'problem' of discrimination has been perceived, understood, and interpreted so far and the kinds of solutions to the problem different countries have come up with. How can this be achieved? The adoption of common European rules in the form of Directives can be seen as just a first and important step in this direction, the next being the transposition into national legislation. But at this point we are only half way there, if that.[3] According to Article 288 of the Treaty on the Functioning of the European Union (TFEU), Directives are binding 'as to the *result* to be achieved' (emphasis added). In addition to transposition, this requires a strong focus on implementation in practice.

All these issues are relevant in the context of EU Member States but they also have a bearing in the context of countries currently negotiating to become members of the EU. This book is, therefore, guided by *two overlapping aims*. The *first* is to investigate how implementation and compliance with norms and policies relating to equality and non-discrimination adopted in the course of EU enlargement could

[2] Steering Committee on Anti-Discrimination, Diversity and Inclusion (CDADI), 'COVID-19: An analysis of the anti-discrimination, diversity and inclusion dimensions in Council of Europe member states' (17 July 2020) CDADI(2020)9.

[3] On the different stages in the lifecycle of a norm, see Martha Finnemore and Kathryn Sikkink, 'International Norm Dynamics and Political Change' (1998) 52(4) International Organization 887; Thomas Risse, Stephen Ropp, and Kathryn Sikkink (eds), *The Power of Human Rights: International Norms and Domestic Change* (CUP 1999); and Thomas Risse, Stephen C Ropp, and Kathryn Sikkink (eds), *The Persistent Power of Human Rights: From Commitment to Compliance* (CUP 2013).

be improved, and the likelihood of sustainability (or continuation) of reforms after accession be enhanced. Ultimately, this is a matter of finding out which mode of governance may be most effective in addressing the policy field of equality and non-discrimination, before accession but also with regard to current (and future) Member States.

In trying to find an answer to this question, Chapter 2, laying out the theoretical foundations of the present research, reviews explanatory models of rule adoption of Europeanization, policy transfer, and diffusion literature, and the conditions they identify for a successful transfer of norms and ideas. It argues that the external incentives model, using a strategy of reinforcement by reward, might best explain the likelihood of rule adoption, but if the ultimate goal is that rules are applied and enforced, learning-based approaches have to be strengthened in the enlargement process. Different approaches to reflexive governance,[4] all focusing on the conditions required for a learning process to be successful, are presented claiming that they offer ideas that merit being studied more closely to establish their potential in improving the performance in the EU enlargement process and beyond.

The central hypothesis of this book is thus that the concept of reflexive governance is well suited to capture all the actors involved in framework regulation as in the case of the transposition of binding directives, which offer the states some leeway in implementation by defining just the broad goals to be reached by them or by proposing different policy options to choose from.[5] While this might be more readily acceptable in the context of EU Member States, it might be counterintuitive in the context of accession negotiations. This book sets out to show that conditionality alone, with its focus on external incentives and rule adoption, based on a theory or liberal intergovernmentalism,[6] does not do the trick and needs to be backed up by a stronger emphasis of elements of reflexive governance already in the pre-accession process, as this has the potential of improving compliance and preventing backsliding after accession. It strengthens EU-oriented epistemic communities (such as the above-mentioned civil society organizations and Equality Bodies and their respective transnational networks) and contributes to building up domestic resonance, both conditions for social learning or lesson-drawing to be successful.[7] The concept of reflexive governance is thus grounded in the multilevel governance theory of European integration.[8]

[4] Olivier de Schutter and Jacques Lenoble (eds), *Reflexive Governance: Redefining the Public Interest in a Pluralistic World* (Hart Publishing 2010).

[5] Oliver Treib, Holger Bähr, and Gerda Falkner, 'Modes of Governance: Towards a Conceptual Clarification' (2007) 14(1) Journal of European Public Policy 1, 15.

[6] Andrew Moravcsik and Frank Schimmelfennig, 'Liberal Intergovernmentalism' in Antje Wiener, Tanja A Börzel, and Thomas Risse (eds), *European Integration Theory* (3rd edn, OUP 2019).

[7] Frank Schimmelfennig and Ulrich Sedelmeier (eds), *The Europeanization of Central and Eastern Europe* (Cornell University Press 2005) 18–25.

[8] Liesbet Hooghe and Gary Marks, *Multi-level Governance and European Integration* (Rowman & Littlefield Publishers 2001); Simona Piattoni, *The Theory of Multi-level Governance: Conceptual, Empirical, and Normative Challenges* (OUP 2010).

In order to test the hypothesis, a case study on Croatia has been carried out. By means of process tracing[9] the plausibility of the argument is assessed. Furthermore, the case study serves to highlight where this particular governance approach would still need to be strengthened. In particular, it emerged that there is a need for more consistent, informed, and transparent monitoring. Furthermore, pooling of results and the drawing of conclusions from such results, which is a decisive criterion for the success of a reflexive governance system, is given too little room and attention, in particular by the Commission and candidate countries.

The *second aim* of this research, constituting a natural consequence of working on the first aim is therefore, to make a contribution to both these issues. On the basis of a comparative review of transposition and practical implementation of selected parts of the RED and the EED in EU Member States, it will undertake such a pooling of results, by identifying good practices and challenges in the implementation and enforcement of the selected policy options. Drawing from this experience, especially focusing on implementation and the impact on rights holders, indicators will be proposed, on the basis of which the Commission can evaluate progress in the transposition and practical implementation of the EU acquis in the field of equality and non-discrimination during the pre-accession phase. In doing so, it is hoped that this research will make a contribution to improve benchmarking and monitoring and support thinking out of the box, thereby stimulating mutual learning processes and ultimately, improved implementation of the EU non-discrimination acquis.

The use of indicators is not uncontroversial but their increasing relevance is shown by the attention given to this tool by the United Nations (UN) in the framework of the monitoring of its human rights treaties, or by the use made of indicators in the work of the EU Fundamental Rights Agency. To address the criticisms of the concept, Chapter 3 is dedicated not only to an analysis of the purposes for which indicators can be used and the related advantages, but also to a discussion of the limitations and pitfalls connected with their use. The main purpose of the indicators developed in the framework of this research is to support consistent monitoring of the transposition and implementation of the EU non-discrimination acquis. As such they can reinforce the accountability of the duty bearer but also serve as a tool for advocacy and political dialogue in the triangle of actors composed of the Commission, the civil society sector, and the state authorities. They can, however, also be used to analyse the situation with regard to equality and non-discrimination in a specific context on the basis of which new legislation or policies can be proposed.[10] Importantly, this chapter also introduces the division between

[9] Andrew Bennett and Jeffrey T Checkel (eds), *Process Tracing: From Methaphor to Analytical Tool* (CUP 2015); Paul Collier, 'Understanding Process Tracing' (2011) 44(4) Political Science and Politics 823.

[10] Todd Landman, 'Measuring Human Rights: Principle, Practice, and Policy' (2004) 26(4) Human Rights Quarterly 906, 909; Todd Landman and Edzia Carvalho, *Measuring Human Rights* (Routledge 2010) 4–6.

structural, process, and outcome indicators, that measure the progress of implementation in different phases of the implementation process. Finally, it looks at the use that the Commission makes or does not make of indicators in pre-accession monitoring to show that there is, so far, a rather inconsistent use of the concept.

Part II then sets out to pool the results of about more than fifteen years of implementation of RED and EED and to derive from this comparative analysis indicators to be used in the monitoring process. This exercise is carried out with the aims of providing current candidate countries with an analysis of which options have worked and which have not in the attempt to achieve the results expected by the Directives, and of making a contribution to improved monitoring in the pre-accession phase. However, the findings should also be useful to current Member States in reconsidering the legislative choices they have made. The comparative review further reveals that some form of monitoring or dialogue about the practical implementation of legal choices is necessary also for current (old and new) Member States.

Chapters 4 and 5 look at the reaction to discrimination, while Chapter 6 deals with the promotion of equality and the prevention of discrimination. Therefore, the book does not cover the whole range of provisions contained in the two Directives. It does not deal with the substantive provisions regarding the concept and scope of discrimination or individual discrimination grounds. Rather, it focuses on the enforcement and promotion of the right to equality and non-discrimination and the various actors and institutions involved in this context. It is intended to investigate how different actors and institutions and their relationships contribute to the functioning of the non-discrimination system as a whole. The actors and institutions concerned involve, next to governmental authorities and the legislator, primarily the judiciary, when it comes to access to judicial complaints mechanisms (Chapter 4), and Equality Bodies, when it comes to the access to quasi- or non-judicial complaints mechanisms (Chapter 5). Although such Equality Bodies are not foreseen by the EED, the majority of countries have established bodies that cover not only discrimination related to race and ethnic origin (and gender, as such Bodies also have to be established under Directives 2004/113/EC and 2006/54/EC) but also at least some of the grounds covered by the EED, sometimes going even further. An important role in the defence of rights is further played by associations or organizations which have a legitimate interest in ensuring compliance with the Directives (Chapter 4).

When it comes to promotion and prevention also, it is the state authorities (Chapter 6.1), the Equality Bodies (Chapter 6.2) and the civil society organizations (Chapter 6.3) which are given important roles by the Directives and which are therefore analysed in detail.

The decision to focus on enforcement and promotion, which puts these actors in the forefront, has been taken because these are the actors the Commission can engage with and support pre- and post-accession. They are also the actors that can make the best possible use of the legal framework that has to be put in place, even if governmental efforts to make it work remain, for whatever reason, limited. It is therefore all the more important to consider the impact the legal choices have on the ways in which these actors can play their role, whether the state is making an effort in translating legal rules into practice and if not, to consider how the Commission could react to such circumstances. A final reason why these enforcement and promotion related issues were chosen for analysis is that it has been found elsewhere[11] that the reasons for the divide between the law in the books and practice in this area are, at least partly, related to lack of support by civil society organizations and weak Equality Bodies, to a continued lack of awareness, and to reluctance of states to aim at substantive equality by making use of positive action.

All issues will be addressed by going through the whole policy cycle, from the formulation of the rule at EU level, to the legal transposition in the EU Member States, and their practical implementation in selected countries. In doing so it will be possible to assess whether unsatisfactory outcomes are related to the mode of legal transposition or to their application. The analysis of all issues is structured in the same way: adopting and combining a legal-dogmatic with a structural-functional approach, they start with an introduction which clarifies central concepts, which will be done on the basis of the norm contestations[12] in the Council during the adoption of the respective provision of the Directives, of the infringement proceedings commenced by the Commission in the years following the transposition dates, and, to the extent it exists, of the jurisprudence by the Court of Justice. These parts serve to explicate the contested meaning and the objective of the respective provision. They are followed by a comparative analysis of the legal transposition in all twenty-seven EU Member States plus the UK. The main sources for this part have been the yearly reports provided by the legal experts of the European network of legal experts in gender equality and non-discrimination (hereafter: European Equality Law Network or EELN) as well as scholarly research. For the comparative analysis of the practical implementation, case studies have been carried out in most chapters from a legal-sociological perspective. The point at issue was to find out whether, in order to make an impact on the rights holders, the decisive criterion was the inclusiveness of the legislation, or whether and under which circumstances more narrow and less permissive legal choices can also have an impact. The cases selected for the

[11] Gerda Falkner and Oliver Treib, 'Three Worlds of Compliance or Four? The EU-15 Compared to New Member States' (2008) 46(2) Journal of Common Market Studies 293, 304–06; Fundamental Rights Agency, 'Opinion of the European Union Agency for Fundamental Rights on the situation of equality in the European Union 10 years on from initial implementation of the equality directives' (2013) 1/2013.

[12] Antje Wiener, *A Theory of Contestation* (Springer 2014); Joseph Marko, 'Law and Sociology: The Constructivist and Interpretative Turn' in Joseph Marko (ed), *Human and Minority Rights Protection by Multiple Diversity Governance: History, Law, Ideology and Politics in European Perspective* (Routledge 2019) 162–74.

case studies[13] therefore range from very permissive (in line with the logic of appropriateness) to minimalist (following the logic of consequentialism) forms of transposition.[14] The case studies are based on in-depth interviews with relevant actors, reports and studies produced by national and international organizations, and academic research. They highlight the challenges and good practices encountered in transposition and practical implementation and also allow us to draw some conclusions as to where not only the national regulations could be amended to better achieve the objectives of the Directives but also where the framework rule at EU level (the two Directives) would need to be reconsidered.

This approach then makes it possible to achieve the second purpose of Part II of this book, which is the elaboration and proposal of structural, process, and outcome indicators, that will help to strengthen and improve the monitoring of the EU non-discrimination regime in the pre- and in the best of cases also in the post-accession phase (in the sense of all EU Member States).

The final chapter draws conclusions about the level of reflexivity present in the interplay between the different actors, its value for an effective enforcement and promotion of equality and non-discrimination law, and the role it can play in preventing backsliding and creating resilience. It concludes with an assessment of what can be drawn from these findings with regard to the main theoretical explanations of European integration.

From this introduction of the overall research and its structure it will have become clear that, while acknowledging that a legal-dogmatic approach is necessary to get a proper grasp of the core concepts and objectives of the different provisions under consideration, the main interest guiding this research is to study both the enlargement process and the transposition and practical implementation of the two EU non-discrimination Directives to understand on one hand the impact of different legal choices on the rights holders, as well as on the other hand, how the accession process could be strengthened with the aim of avoiding backsliding after accession. This requires approaching the problem not only *de lega lata* but also *de lege ferenda*. Therefore, when studying the norm contestations in the processes of transposition and implementation, the judgments of national and supranational courts are analysed not only as a source of authoritative decision making from the perspective of legal-dogmatic analysis, but also for the empirical effect they shall and can have from a legal-sociological perspective for the particular kind

[13] Ran Hirschl, *Comparative Matters: The Renaissance of Comparative Constitutional Law* (OUP 2014); Donatella Della Porta and Michael Keating (eds), *Approaches and Methodologies in the Social Sciences* (CUP 2008).

[14] James G March and Johan P Olsen, 'The New Institutionalism: Organizational Factors in Political Life' (1984) 78(3) American Political Science Review 734; James G March and Johan P Olsen, 'The Institutional Dynamics of International Political Orders' (1998) 52(4) International Organization 943; Thomas Risse and Stephen Ropp, 'Introduction and Overview' in Thomas Risse, Stephen C Ropp, and Kathryn Sikkink (eds), *The Persistent Power of Human Rights: From Commitment to Compliance* (CUP 2013).

of transposition and implementation. Like the doctrine of the *effet utile* in public international law and the teleological method used by the Court of Justice of the European Union (CJEU), this approach makes the conceptual development of EU law and national law in the field of the right to equality and non-discrimination visible and therefore contributes to the understanding of the heuristic value of legal-dogmatic analysis. With the translation of the results of the comparative and legal-sociological analysis into structural, process, and outcome indicators, the book finally also pursues a legal policy objective, which is to contribute to a more transparent, consistent, and systematic evaluation not only of correct legal transposition but also effective implementation. Finally, as the conclusions will show, this book also makes a contribution to the existing literature on European integration theories.

PART I

THE RELEVANCE OF REFLEXIVE GOVERNANCE FOR EU EQUALITY LAW

1
The Development of the EU Non-Discrimination Regime

This chapter introduces the development of the EU non-discrimination regime which has led to the adoption of the two Directives that are at the centre of this book: the Racial Equality Directive (RED) and the Employment Equality Directive (EED). It does so first, by tracing the historical discussions and legislation from the founding of the European Economic Community (EEC) back in 1957 up until today. Development at the level of policy programmes and institutions will also be covered. Secondly, from a substantive point of view, the evolution of the jurisprudential interpretation of the concept of non-discrimination used in the two Directives will be analysed.

1.1 From a Human Rights and (Almost) Equality-Free Zone to an EU Non-Discrimination Law and Policy

When the EEC was founded in 1957, the EEC Treaty did not contain any reference to human rights,[1] or a broad provision on equality or non-discrimination. The creation of an area focusing on free trade was not expected to impact on human rights.[2] Nevertheless, one could have expected a reference to an intention to fight racial and religious intolerance, considering the 'European integration's historical motivation as a legacy of the Second World War'.[3] The only two grounds on the basis of which discrimination was prohibited by primary law from the beginning were the grounds of nationality and gender, the latter restricted to equal pay for women and men.[4] The reason for including these grounds of discrimination was, however, not primarily related to considerations of fundamental rights protection but was primarily seen 'as contribution to the common market'.[5]

[1] Christopher McCrudden and Haris Kountouros, 'Human Rights and European Equality Law' in Helen Meenan (ed), *Equality Law in an Enlarged European Union: Understanding the Article 13 Directives* (CUP 2007) 87 ff.

[2] Fundamental Rights Agency and ECtHR, 'Handbook on European Non-Discrimination Law' (2018) 20.

[3] Mark Bell, *Anti-Discrimination Law and the European Union* (OUP 2002) 55.

[4] Art 119 EEC (now Art 157 TFEU) and Art 48 EEC (now Art 45 TFEU).

[5] Olivier de Schutter, 'Three Models of Equality and European Anti-Discrimination Law' (2006) 57(1) Northern Ireland Legal Quarterly 1, 5. De Schutter further mentions that the equal pay provision of ex-Art 119 EEC had an economic justification, as highlighted by the Court of Justice in *Defrenne*

Reflexive Governance in EU Equality Law. Emma Lantschner, Oxford University Press. © Emma Lantschner 2021.
DOI: 10.1093/oso/9780192843371.003.0002

Faced with cases brought before it alleging the violation of human rights caused by Community law, the Court of Justice began to develop the 'general principles' of Community law which it derived from national constitutions and human rights treaties, in particular the European Convention on Human Rights (ECHR). The scarce primary legislation was supplemented by secondary legislation in the form of Regulation 1612/68/EEC on free movement for workers within the Community. As a consequence of 'a combination of political and judicial interventions in the 1970s'[6] three Directives were adopted in the field of gender discrimination: the first specified in more detail the principle of equal pay,[7] the second extended the prohibition of discrimination to all aspects of an employment relationship,[8] whereas the third aimed at achieving progressive implementation of the principle of equal treatment for men and women in matters of social security.[9] It was on the basis of these legal norms that the Court of Justice steadily improved the understanding and interpretation of some of the core concepts of non-discrimination law which later where integrated into the Directives dealing with other grounds.

The origins of the EC policy regarding the issue of racism can be traced back to the mid-1980s.[10] The debate was led in the framework of the community policy on migration and the internal market. The Commission adopted Decision 85/381/EEC setting up a prior communication and consultation procedure on migration policies in relation to non-member countries. Some Member States sought to annul the decision and the Court, while upholding those provisions where it could establish a connection between migration policies and the EC labour market, declared invalid those provisions relating to the cultural integration of immigrants. Around the same time, the European Parliament established a 'Committee of Inquiry into the Rise of Fascism and Racism in Europe'. Its report, presented in

(*Gabrielle Defrenne v Société anonyme belge de navigation aérienne Sabena* [1976] ECLI:EU:C:1976:56) para 9: 'to avoid a situation in which undertakings established in States which have actually implemented the principle of equal pay suffer a competitive disadvantage in intra-Community competition as compared with undertakings in States which have not yet eliminated discrimination against women workers as regards pay'. On the transition of non-discrimination from economic right to fundamental human right, see further Catherine Barnard, 'The Contribution of Anti-discrimination Law to European Integration: The Added Value of the EU Level' in Olivier de Schutter and Violeta Moreno Lax (eds), *Human Rights in the Web of Governance: A Learning-Based Fundamental Rights Policy for the EU* (Bruylant 2010) 224–28.

[6] Bell, *Anti-Discrimination Law and the European Union* (n 3) 43.

[7] Council Directive 75/117/EEC on the approximation of the laws of the Member States relating to the application of the principle of equal pay for men and women.

[8] Council Directive 76/207/EEC on the implementation of the principle of equal treatment for men and women as regards access to employment, vocational training, and promotion and working conditions.

[9] Council Directive 79/7/EEC on the progressive implementation of the principle of equal treatment for men and women in matters of social security.

[10] For an analysis of the discourses that moved from an anti-racism agenda to eventually focus on anti-discrimination, see Terri E Givens and Rhonda Evans Case, *Legislating Equality: The Politics of Antidiscrimination Policy in Europe* (OUP 2014) 48–72.

1985, 'identified serious problems of racism and xenophobia in the Member States and recommended action by the Community . . . including a new EC Treaty competence on racial discrimination'.[11] In response, the Council, the Parliament, and the Commission signed in 1986 a Joint Declaration against racism and xenophobia in which they acknowledge that the 'respect for human dignity and the elimination of forms of racial discrimination are part of the common cultural and legal heritage of all the Member States'.[12] The Council, however, did not want this declaration to be understood as a 'starting point for concrete action'.[13] In fact, in the period between 1985 and 1990, racism was repeatedly raised as an issue by the European Parliament and the Commission[14] but constantly blocked by the Council, based on a lack of competence. As Bell put it 'the question of competence became a kind of filter mechanism, a device to keep off the agenda issues the Council did not wish to address'.[15]

In the 1990s the Council's opposition shifted to support, for three main reasons: 'the development of cross-border racism; spillover effects from EU immigration and asylum policies; and the establishment of an effective EU lobby against racism'.[16] Regarding the last point, the role of the Starting Line Group needs to be highlighted.[17] Upon the initiative of a few human rights organizations, a number of legal experts developed already in 1992 a draft Directive on the 'prohibition of discrimination based on race, colour, descent, nationality, or national or ethnic origin across a wide range of fields'.[18] Although the proposal gained the support of over 250 non-governmental organizations (NGOs) and the European Parliament, the Commission did not accept it because of a lack of competence. The Group thus shifted its focus to making a proposal that would provide the Community with the necessary competence by an amendment of the EC Treaty. This time the proposal, supported by almost 300 NGOs and the European Parliament, also gained the support by the Commission.[19]

[11] Bell, *Anti-Discrimination Law and the European Union* (n 3) 60–61; European Parliament, 'Committee of Inquiry into the Rise of Fascism and Racism in Europe: Report on the Findings of the Inquiry' (December 1985).

[12] Joint Declaration on racism and xenophobia, 11 June 1986, OJ C158/1.

[13] Bell, *Anti-Discrimination Law and the European Union* (n 3) 61.

[14] For instance through the Commission's 'Communication to the Council of the fight against racism and xenophobia', 1988 and the Parliament's second Committee of Inquiry on Racism and Xenophobia, which published its report in 1991.

[15] Bell, *Anti-Discrimination Law and the European Union* (n 3) 63.

[16] ibid 63.

[17] For some discussion of its role in more detail, see Rhonda Evans Case and Terri E Givens, 'Re-engineering Legal Opportunity Structures in the European Union? The Starting Line Group and the Politics of the Racial Equality Directive' (2010) 48(2) Journal of Common Market Studies 221; Isabelle Chopin, 'The Starting Line Group: A Harmonised Approach to Fight Racism and to Promote Equal Treatment' (1999) 1(1) European Journal of Migration and Law 111; Isabelle Chopin, 'Possible Harmonisation of Anti-Discrimination Legislation in the European Union: European and Non-Governmental Proposals' (2000) 2(3/4) European Journal of Migration and Law 413.

[18] Bell, *Anti-Discrimination Law and the European Union* (n 3) 68.

[19] Commission of the European Communities, 'Communication on racism, xenophobia and anti-semitism and proposal for a Council Decision designating 1997 as European year against racism' (13

Further support for such a Treaty amendment came through the so-called Kahn Commission,[20] a 'Consultative Commission on racism and xenophobia' set up by the Council on the initiative of France and Germany and composed mainly of representatives of Member States. In its final report, issued in 1995, it concluded, after '[h]aving considered the matter carefully', that 'amendment of the Treaty to provide explicitly for Community competence must be regarded as an essential element in any serious European strategy aimed at combating racism and xenophobia'.[21] Furthermore, based on the experience in the area of discrimination on the ground of sex, it recommended the adoption of legislation to combat 'discrimination on grounds of race, religion or ethnic or national origins'.[22]

The approval by the Council of the Commission's proposal to designate the year 1997 as 'European year against racism' as well as the creation in the same year of the European Monitoring Centre on Racism and Xenophobia (EUMC) can be seen as a result of the Kahn Commission's proposals. After the Council identified majority support (with the exception of the UK) for the inclusion of a general prohibition of discrimination in the EC Treaty, including on grounds of race and religion, the path was free for the elaboration and eventually (after a change in the UK government) the adoption of Article 13 EC through the Amsterdam Treaty in 1997. Article 13 (today Art 19 TFEU) reads as follows:

> Without prejudice to the other provisions of the Treaties and within the limits of the powers conferred by them upon the Union, the Council, acting unanimously in accordance with a special legislative procedure and after obtaining the consent of the European Parliament, may take appropriate action to combat discrimination based on sex, racial or ethnic origin, religion or belief, disability, age or sexual orientation.

As just mentioned, this development is partly due to the strong lobby of the Starting Line Group for the inclusion in the Treaty of the prohibition of discrimination on the basis of race, ethnic origin, and religion. Similar support for the ground of disability was provided by the European Disabled People's Parliament. The inclusion of sexual orientation was more surprising as it did not benefit from a similar lobby. Regarding this ground, the European Parliament played an important role, inter alia, through the 1994 Roth report,[23] which was followed by a

December 1995) COM(95) 653 final; see also Bell, *Anti-Discrimination Law and the European Union* (n 3) 68.

20 For more details on the Kahn Commission see, Givens and Evans Case (n 10) 60–66.

21 Consultative Commission on Racism and Xenophobia, 'Final Report' (23 May 1995) Ref 6906/1/95, 57.

22 ibid 59.

23 European Parliament, 'Report for the Committee on Internal Affairs and Citizens Rights on Equal Rights for Homosexuals and Lesbians in the European Community' (1994) A3-28/94.

Resolution of the European Parliament,[24] calling upon the Commission to submit a draft Recommendation to the Council with the aim of eliminating discrimination of homosexuals in criminal and civil law, in labour relations, as well as in areas such as partnership and adoption law. Although the report and the resolution shone a light on the deeply differing views on the subject within the Parliament and even caused an intervention by the Pope,[25] it placed the issue firmly on the European agenda. While sexual orientation as a suspect ground of discrimination appeared and disappeared in the draft of the amending Treaty several times, in the end 'no state apparently wish[ed] to be seen as openly objecting to anti-discrimination measures for any of the grounds in the draft Article', including sexual orientation.[26]

At this point, considering the unanimity requirement of (then) Article 13 EC, one could not have expected any legal measures to be taken quickly on a topic which had proved to be controversial over the previous years. It was therefore remarkable that only a year after the entry into force of the Amsterdam Treaty in 1999,[27] two Directives were adopted by the Council: Council Directive 2000/43/EC of 29 June 2000 implementing the principle of equal treatment between persons irrespective of racial or ethnic origin, and Council Directive 2000/78/EC of 27 November 2000 establishing a general framework for equal treatment in employment and occupation, covering the grounds of religion or belief, disability, age, and sexual orientation.[28] The material scope of application of the former is much wider as, in addition to employment and occupation, it also applies to social protection, including social security and health care, social advantages, education, and access to goods and services (including housing). In 2008, the Commission proposed a Directive extending this scope of application also to the grounds of religion and belief, disability, age, and sexual orientation,[29] but over a decade later the Member States could not agree on adopting this so-called horizontal Directive. On the other hand, the legislative development of the EU non-discrimination regime continued,

[24] European Parliament, 'Resolution on equal rights for homosexuals and lesbians in the EC' (8 February 1994).

[25] He criticized the proposed resolution as not only rejecting unjust discrimination against persons with homosexual tendencies but as an attempt to legitimize a moral disorder. See Bell, *Anti-Discrimination Law and the European Union* (n 3) 105.

[26] ibid 106–07.

[27] Among the reasons for the swift adoption of these Directives was the entry into government of the extreme right-wing FPÖ in Austria and the attempt to give a European answer to that by the adoption of these two Recommendations in the field of non-discrimination. See on this, for instance, Mark Bell, 'The Principle of Equal Treatment: Widening and Deepening' in Paul Craig and Gráinne de Búrca (eds), *The Evolution of EU Law* (OUP 2011) 618.

[28] For a detailed account on the processes that led to the adoption of the Race Equality Directive, see Givens and Evans Case (n 10) 73–91. Furthermore, see Elspeth Guild, 'The EC Directive on Race Discrimination: Surprises, Possibilities and Limitations' (2000) 29(4) Industrial Law Journal 416; Siobhan McInerney, 'Equal Treatment between Persons Irrespective of Racial or Ethnic Origin: A Comment' (2000) 25 European Law Review 317.

[29] Commission of the European Communities, 'Proposal for a Council Directive on implementing the principle of equal treatment between persons irrespective of religion or belief, disability, age or sexual orientation' (2 July 2008) COM(2008) 426 final.

with the adoption of the Gender Goods and Services Directive in 2004[30] and the Gender Equality Directive (recast) in 2006.[31] As a result, the scope of application of the various Gender Directives remains also more limited than that relating to the ground of racial or ethnic origin.

To give the full picture of the legal development one must not forget, of course, the proclamation of the EU Charter of Fundamental Rights in 2000 and its elevation into the status of primary law by the entry into force of the Treaty of Lisbon in 2009. Its Chapter III (Arts 20–26) is dedicated to equality. Article 21 on non-discrimination states that '[a]ny discrimination based on any ground such as sex, race, colour, ethnic or social origin, genetic features, language, religion or belief, political or any other opinion, membership of a national minority, property, birth, disability, age or sexual orientation shall be prohibited' and thus extends the principle to further grounds beyond those covered by the above-mentioned Directives. Since 2009, the principle of equality, next to respect for human dignity, freedom, democracy, the rule of law, and respect for human rights, including the rights of persons belonging to minorities, is further included among the values on which the European Union (EU) is founded. Article 2 of the Treaty on European Union (TEU) goes on to state that '[t]hese values are common to the Member States in a society in which pluralism, non-discrimination, tolerance, justice, solidarity and equality between women and men prevail'. Finally, at the level of primary law the mainstreaming duty contained in Article 10 of the Treaty on the Functioning of the European Union (TFEU) has to be mentioned. It is another change introduced by the Lisbon Treaty and foresees that '[i]n defining and implementing its policies and activities, the Union shall aim to combat discrimination based on sex, racial or ethnic origin, religion or belief, disability, age or sexual orientation'.[32]

The emergence of a legal non-discrimination framework was flanked by a number of support programmes and institutional developments. The adoption of the two Directives in 2000 came along with the adoption of a five-year Action Programme,[33] by which research and awareness-raising as well as the building of

[30] Council Directive 2004/113/EC of 13 December 2004 implementing the principle of equal treatment between men and women in the access to and supply of goods and services.

[31] Directive 2006/54/EC of the European Parliament and of the Council of 5 July 2006 on the implementation of the principle of equal opportunities and equal treatment of men and women in matters of employment and occupation (recast).

[32] On further details about the integration of the principle of equal treatment with the Treaties see Bell, 'The Principle of Equal Treatment: Widening and Deepening' (n 27) 629–31.

[33] Council Decision 2000/750/EC of 27 November 2000 establishing a Community Action Programme to Combat Discrimination (2001 to 2006). For a detailed analysis see Gráinne de Búrca, 'EU Race Discrimination Law: A Hybrid Model?' in Gráinne de Búrca and Joanne Scott (eds), *Law and New Governance in the EU and the US* (Hart Publishing 2006) 97; Mark Bell, *Racism and Equality in the European Union* (OUP 2008) 75–81; Katrin Wladasch, Marta Hodasz, and Barbara Liegl, 'Reflexive Governance in the Public Interest: Anti-discrimination' (2008) Working paper series: REFGOV-FR-24, 161–72. A separate Action programme was set up in respect of gender. Bell, *Racism and Equality in the European Union* (n 33) 75.

NGO capacity was supported. The Year of Equal Opportunities for All[34] was set up in 2007 with similar objectives as the Action Programme and with the aim to 'lend fresh impetus to supporting Member States efforts to implement Community legislation on equal treatment and non-discrimination'.[35] After the end of the Action Programme, in the period 2007–13 its goals were further pursued by the social policy programme PROGRESS, which dedicated 23 per cent of its budget to the fight against discrimination and promotion of diversity and 12 per cent to the promotion of gender equality.[36] This programme was followed by the Rights, Equality and Citizens Programme, set up for the period 2014–20.[37] Furthermore, between 2001 and 2008 the EQUAL initiative, that comes under the European Social Fund as part of the European Employment Strategy, funded projects dedicated to the fight against discrimination on the grounds covered by EU Directives.[38] As of 2021, the Citizens, Equality, Rights and Values Programme includes one strand dealing with Equality, Rights, and Gender Equality and supports civil society organizations engaging for European values.[39]

With regard to the institutional dimension, various levels can be identified: national, European, as well as attached to or within the European institutions themselves. At the level of Members States, the RED as well as the Gender Directives call for the establishment of Equality Bodies supporting victims of discrimination, undertaking surveys and research into issues related to discrimination, and making recommendations. These Equality Bodies, that in many countries have been given a broader mandate to cover also grounds beyond racial or ethnic origin and gender, are closely cooperating at European level within the European Network of Equality Bodies (Equinet), financially supported by the European Commission.[40] According to its Statute, the network was created to 'effectively combine their [the Equality Bodies'] capacities and their functions to strategically push for changes to and respect for the principles of equality, diversity and nondiscrimination' as well as 'to allow the individual member organisations 'to benefit from their mutual experience and expertise in their continual effort to optimize the implementation of laws, policies and practices relating to equal treatment and to guarantee that the pro-equality organizations which are united in Equinet are heard on a European level'.[41]

[34] Decision No 771/2006/EC of the European Parliament and of the Council of 17 May 2006 establishing the European Year of Equal Opportunities for All (2007)—towards a just society.

[35] Recital 9.

[36] Valérie Amiraux and Virginie Guiraudon, 'Discrimination in Comparative Perspective: Policies and Practices' (2010) 53(12) American Behavioral Scientist 1691, 1695; Bell, *Racism and Equality in the European Union* (n 33) 75.

[37] Regulation (EU) No 1381/2013 of the European Parliament and of the Council of 17 December 2013 establishing a Rights, Equality and Citizenship Programme for the period 2014 to 2020. See de Búrca, 'EU Race Discrimination Law: A Hybrid Model?' (n 33) 103.

[38] Amiraux and Guiraudon (n 36) 1695.

[39] The respective Regulation was expected for April 2021.

[40] For a reflection on Equinet's role see Wladasch, Hodasz, and Liegl (n 33) 93–98.

[41] Equinet Statutes, Art 3.

Through the above-mentioned programmes, the Commission is further funding networks of NGOs regarding the different suspect grounds.[42] Regarding racial discrimination, for instance, it has supported the establishment and functioning of the European Network Against Racism (ENAR). In the disability field, it funded one umbrella organization in addition to five smaller organizations dealing with specific disabilities.[43] In the field of sexual orientation, the Commission supports the function of ILGA-Europe and in the field of age discrimination the European Older People's Forum-AGE.[44]

At the level of EU institutions, in 2006 the European Institute for Gender Equality (EIGE) was established[45] and a year later the EUMC has been transformed into the Fundamental Rights Agency (FRA),[46] giving it a broader mandate. The Agency has the mandate to provide EU institutions and Member States with assistance and expertise regarding fundamental rights. It does so, for instance, by collecting, analysing, and disseminating objective, reliable, and comparable information, carrying out scientific research and surveys, and formulating opinions.[47] It operates on the basis of a multiannual framework, the thematic areas of which 'must include the fight against racism, xenophobia and related intolerance'.[48] The current Multiannual Framework, covering the period 2018–22, includes 'equality and discrimination based on any ground such as sex, race, colour, ethnic or social origin, genetic features, language, religion or belief, political or any other opinion, membership of a national minority, property, birth, disability, age or sexual orientation, or on the grounds of nationality'.[49] The Agency has carried out two large-scale surveys on the discrimination of minorities[50] (with a focus on Roma,[51] Muslims,[52] and migrant women[53]) as well as on

[42] On the role of different umbrella organizations see Wladasch, Hodasz, and Liegl (n 33) 71–93.

[43] Bell, *Racism and Equality in the European Union* (n 33) 79.

[44] Gráinne de Búrca, 'Stumbling into Experimentalism: The EU Anti-Discrimination Regime' in Charles F Sabel and Jonathan Zeitlin (eds), *Experimentalist Governance in the European Union: Towards a New Architecture* (OUP 2010) 223–24.

[45] Regulation (EC) No 1922/2006 of the European Parliament and of the Council of 20 December 2006 on establishing a European Institute for Gender Equality.

[46] Regulation No 168/2007/EC establishing a European Union Agency for Fundamental Rights.

[47] Regulation No 168/2007/EC, Arts 2 and 4.

[48] Regulation No 168/2007/EC, Art 5.

[49] Council Decision (EU) 2017/2269 of 7 December 2017 establishing a Multiannual Framework for the European Union Agency for Fundamental Rights for 2018–2022, Art 2(b). Comparing this list to previous multiannual frameworks, the current one is the most extensive one. The first one (2007–12) focused only on the grounds covered by the Directives of 2000 as well as gender, the second (2013–17) included all other grounds listed in Art 21 of the Fundamental Rights Charter that in the meantime became a binding instrument, and in the last one, the ground of nationality was added.

[50] Fundamental Rights Agency, 'EU-MIDIS Main Results Report' (2009); Fundamental Rights Agency, 'EU-MIDIS II: Main Results' (2017).

[51] Fundamental Rights Agency, 'EU-MIDIS Data in Focus Report No. 1: The Roma' (2009); Fundamental Rights Agency, 'EU-MIDIS II: Roma—Selected Findings' (2016).

[52] Fundamental Rights Agency, 'EU-MIDIS Data in Focus Report No. 2: Muslims' (2009); Fundamental Rights Agency, 'EU-MIDIS II: Muslims—Selected Findings' (2017).

[53] Fundamental Rights Agency, 'EU-MIDIS II. Migrant women—Selected Findings' (2019).

LGBT[54] and the experiences and perceptions of antisemitism.[55] Furthermore, it published an opinion 'on the situation of equality in the European Union 10 years on from initial implementation of the equality directives'.[56]

Until December 2014, the Commission financed two networks of legal experts: the European Network of Legal Experts in the Non-discrimination Field and the European Network of Legal Experts in the Field of Gender Equality. Since then, the two bodies have been merged into the European Network of Legal Experts in Gender Equality and Non-Discrimination (EELN).[57] Its main task is to provide independent and reliable expert information on legal developments in the Member States including relevant case law and it regularly publishes comparative and thematic reports.

The Commission has further established High Level Groups composed of representatives from the Member States. The first was the Governmental Expert Group in the field of non-discrimination (2008–13),[58] established as part of its 'renewed commitment' for non-discrimination and equal opportunities which came along with the Commission's proposal of the above-mentioned horizontal Directive. The group's aim was 'to examine the impact of national and EU-level non-discrimination measures, validate good practice through peer learning and develop benchmarks to evaluate the effectiveness of non-discrimination policies'.[59] The Governmental Expert Group was followed by the High Level Group on Non-Discrimination, Equality and Diversity, established in 2015. Its mandate is, inter alia, to 'deepen cooperation and coordination between Member States' relevant authorities and the Commission on questions relating to achieving diversity and full equality in practice, and eliminating discrimination; in particular through the exchange of experiences and good practices on related issues of common interest to be defined by the Group and the establishing, when appropriate, of common policy objectives'.[60] The network holds two meetings per year to which it invites

[54] Fundamental Rights Agency, 'EU-LGBTI II. A Long Way to Go for LGBTI Equality' (2020); Fundamental Rights Agency, 'EU LGBT Survey. European Union Lesbian, Gay, Bisexual and Transgender Survey: Main Results' (2014).

[55] Fundamental Rights Agency, 'Young Jewish Europeans: Perceptions and Experiences of Antisemitism' (2019); Fundamental Rights Agency, 'Experiences and Perceptions of Antisemitism. Second Survey on Discrimination and Hate Crime against Jews in the EU' (2018).

[56] Fundamental Rights Agency, 'Opinion of the European Union Agency for Fundamental Rights on the situation of equality in the European Union 10 years on from initial implementation of the equality directives' (2013) 1/2013.

[57] See the website at https://www.equalitylaw.eu/.

[58] Commission of the European Communities, 'Decision setting up a non-discrimination governmental expert group' (2 July 2008) C(2008)3261 final.

[59] Commission of the European Communities, 'Communication from the Commission to the European Parliament, the Council, the European Economic and Social Committee and the Committee of Regions: Non-discrimination and equal opportunities: A renewed commitment' (2 July 2008) COM(2008) 420 final, 9.

[60] European Commission—Directorate-General Justice and Consumers, 'High Level Group on Non-discrimination, Equality and Diversity. Mandate' (2015) pt 3.

NGO representatives as well as Equinet and the Fundamental Rights Agency (FRA).[61]

This overview of the historical development of a growing concern within the European Union for the protection from discrimination and the promotion of equality has shown that today there exists a comprehensive package of legally binding norms combined with a range of financial support mechanisms and institutions aimed at ensuring compliance with EU objectives in this field.[62] In the years 2020 and 2021, the Commission has adopted a number of strategies and action plans in different fields, some for the first time ever, like the LGBTIQ Equality Strategy 2020–25[63] and the EU anti-racism action plan 2020–25,[64] others where renewed, like the EU Roma strategic framework on equality, inclusion and participation[65] and the Strategy for the Rights of Persons with Disabilities 2021–30,[66] or upgraded, like the Gender Equality Strategy 2020–25.[67] They can be seen as a contribution to President von der Leyen's commitment to a Union of Equality, which finds expression also in the nomination of the first-ever Commissioner for Equality.[68] When announcing these various strategies, it was mentioned several times that, following the evaluation of the implementation of the RED in 2021 and of the FED in 2022, legislative amendments might be proposed, inter alia, with the aim of strengthening the legal framework with respect to law enforcement and the position of Equality Bodies.

[61] In the October 2017 meeting of the High Level Group, Equinet representatives were, for instance, invited to present the network and in particular its work on standards for Equality Bodies. See http://ombudsman.hr/en/all-news/discrimination/discrimination-article/1185-equinet-ovi-standardi-o-tijelima-za-jednakost-predstavljeni-clanicama-eu-2. Issues presented by the FRA were related to standards for Equality Bodies, advancing equality for lesbian, gay, bisexual, trans, and intersex people, as well as equality data. See http://fra.europa.eu/en/event/2017/eus-high-level-group-non-discrimination-equality-and-diversity-meets. Following this discussion, the High Level Group initiated a subgroup on equality data (led together by the Commission and FRA), which started its work in January 2018 'with the objectives to facilitate the exchange of good practices in equality data collection'. See http://ec.europa.eu/newsroom/just/item-detail.cfm?item_id=612778. The subgroup has developed 'Guidelines on improving the collection and use of equality data', a 'Compendium of Practices on Equality Data' as well as a 'Diagnostic mapping tool'; see https://fra.europa.eu/en/themes/equality-non-discrimination-and-racism/about-compendium.

[62] Amiraux and Guiraudon (n 36) 1695.

[63] European Commission, 'Union of Equality: LGBTIQ Equality Strategy 2020–2025' (12 November 2020) COM(2020) 698 final.

[64] European Commission, 'A Union of equality: EU anti-racism action plan 2020–2025' (18 September 2020) COM(2020) 565 final.

[65] European Commission, 'A Union of Equality: EU Roma strategic framework for equality, inclusion and participation for 2020–2030' (7 October 2020) COM(2020) 620 final.

[66] European Commission, 'Union of Equality: Strategy for the Rights of Persons with Disabilities 2021–2030' (3 March 2021) COM(2021) 101 final.

[67] European Commission, 'A Union of Equality: Gender Equality Strategy 2020–2025' (5 March 2020) COM(2020) 152 final.

[68] See President Ursula von der Leyen's mission letter to the Commissioner for Equality, Helena Dalli, of 1 December 2019, at https://ec.europa.eu/commission/commissioners/2019-2024/dalli_en and the statement on the webpage of the Commissioner for Equality, on 22 December 2020, at https://ec.europa.eu/commission/commissioners/2019-2024/dalli/announcements/union-equality-first-year-actions-and-achievements_en.

In the present research, the role of institutions at national and European level in enforcing the legal regime, the cooperation and coordination amongst them, and their aspiration to exchange good practices and learn from one another will be of central importance. From the brief description of the mandate of some of the above-mentioned institutions it is already clear that mutual learning and the collection of good practice is central to their mandates. As will be explained in more detail in Chapter 2, this is indeed one of the distinguishing features of the EU anti-discrimination regime as it has been developed in the post-Amsterdam period and is one of the cornerstones of the idea of reflexive governance.

This research sets out to make these ideas fruitful on one hand to improve the accession process of candidate countries to the European Union but at the same time also to improve enforcement of Directives within Member States. The focus of the work will be on the two Directives adopted in 2000, namely, the Racial Equality Directive and the Employment Equality Directive. The Gender Directives will not be considered in detail. However, taking into account that all four Directives are built on the same principles, the findings of this research can also be made use of in the context of gender discrimination. This is particularly so in the chapters dealing with Equality Bodies, considering that the FED does not even require the establishment of such bodies (most countries do, however, extend their mandate also to the grounds covered by this Directive) while the Gender Directives do. Furthermore, as will be seen in the next chapter, some of these principles have first been developed under the much older jurisprudence relating to gender discrimination and are now applied also in the context of discrimination on the basis of race or ethnic origin, religion or belief, disability, age, or sexual orientation.

Before entering into further analysis, a conceptual clarification is required: what is to be understood by the terms non-discrimination and equality. The following chapter will try to provide an answer to this question by analysing the jurisprudence of the apex courts of the European Union and the Council of Europe to see how they influenced each other and the impact this has had on the principle of equality as contained in constitutional law.

1.2 From Non-Discrimination to Substantive Equality

All post-Second World War constitutions, and later the constitutions of the new democracies, Greece, Portugal, and Spain, as well as the former communist countries, contain a common constitutional principle of equality. Almost every Constitutional Court in Europe defined the meaning of the principle of equality as treating like cases alike and different situations differently, according to the 'Aristotelian' formula. As such, the principle is extremely broad and can be raised in all policy areas. Each norm can be scrutinized on this basis and public authorities must be able to explain why they have or have not differentiated in a specific circumstance. As such, equality is frequently invoked before all Constitutional Courts in Europe, even though rarely successfully. This is related to the fact that the criteria for deciding whether the distinction made is based on a good justification have to be found in the context outside the equality principle itself. And the evaluation of this context depends on the values that inspire the legal system in question, the legislator, or the judge. Because of this breadth and emptiness of the equality principle, Constitutional Courts have been rather deferential to the choices of the law makers and have only in recent decades become more activist.[69]

This trend is arguably also related to the development of the anti-discrimination regime at the level of the European Union and the Council of Europe. This regime, decisively formed by the jurisprudence of the respective apex courts, has led to a significant legal change in Europe.[70] In the following, the development of the understanding of the concept from anti-discrimination to full and effective equality will be traced to see how this development impacted on European constitutional/legal systems.

The core provision of the ECHR is contained in Article 14 which reads as follows:

> The enjoyment of the rights and freedoms set forth in this Convention shall be secured without discrimination on any ground such as sex, race, colour, language, religion, political or other opinion, national or social origin, association with a national minority, property, birth or other status.

It thereby grants protection from discrimination only with respect to rights and freedoms set out elsewhere in the Convention. It was only with Protocol No 12 that the principle of non-discrimination became a self-standing right applicable across the board.[71] In the Belgian linguistic case, the European Court of Human Rights (ECtHR) was called upon for the first time to give an interpretation of Article 14 ECHR. Considering that the wording of the French and English versions of the text differed, the judges had to determine the meaning of the term discrimination. The French version spoke of 'sans distinction aucune', whereas the English version used the formulation 'without discrimination'. The judges thus had to clarify whether the provision had to be understood in the broad sense insinuated by the French version of forbidding every difference in treatment. The judges found, however, that

[69] Bruno de Witte, 'From a "Common Principle of Equality" to "European Antidiscrimination Law"' (2010) 53(12) American Behavioral Scientist 1715, 1715–18; see also Christa Tobler, *Indirect Discrimination: A Case Study into the Development of the Legal Concept of Indirect Discrimination under EC Law* (Intersentia 2005) 19–24. For a comparison of the principle of equality under Austrian constitutional law with equal treatment in labour law and anti-discrimination under EU law, see Magdalena Pöschl, 'Verfassungsrechtliche Gleichheit, arbeitsrechtliche Gleichbehandlung, unionsrechtliche Antidiskriminierung' [2013] DRdA 467.

[70] de Witte (n 69) 1718.

[71] It entered into force in 2005 after ten ratifications, with twenty ratifications today, amongst them only ten EU Member States, as well as all the Western Balkan (potential) candidate countries.

this would lead to 'absurd results' as in such case every administrative provision, which does 'not secure to everyone complete equality of treatment in the enjoyment of the rights and freedoms recognized' would have to be qualified as contrary to the Convention. The judges went on to find that '[t]he competent national authorities are frequently confronted with situations and problems which, on account of differences inherent therein, call for different legal solutions; moreover, certain legal inequalities tend only to correct factual inequalities. The extensive interpretation mentioned above cannot consequently be accepted.'[72] In defining the criteria which allow to establish whether a difference amounts to discrimination or not, the Court, drawing from the 'principles which may be extracted from the legal practice of a large number of democratic States, holds that the principle of equality of treatment is violated if the distinction has no objective and reasonable justification'. Such a justification is given if the different treatment pursues a legitimate aim and if there is a 'reasonable relationship of proportionality between the means employed and the aim sought to be realized'.[73]

The judges have thereby established that there is a difference between 'distinction' and 'discrimination': distinctions in rule making and rule applications which can be reasonably and objectively justified do not constitute discrimination. Most importantly, however, by their references to 'situations and problems which, on account of differences inherent therein, call for different legal solutions' and by their finding that 'certain legal inequalities only tend to correct factual inequalities', they established a *duty to differentiate*. This opened the door for the concept of 'effective equality' to be achieved by affirmative/positive action and clearly went beyond the narrow understanding of the principle of non-discrimination 'just' aiming at formal equality.[74]

While the ECtHR thus clarified the more procedural aspect that there is no absolute prohibition to make distinctions and elaborates on the standard of judicial review for an evaluation of whether such distinctions amount to discrimination or not, it does not say anything on the content of the concept of discrimination, in other words, on which behaviour amounts to discrimination.

It was the European Court of Justice, which in the meantime developed in its case law related to nationality and sex discrimination the concept of indirect

[72] ECtHR, App No 1474/62; 1677/62; 1691/62; 1769/63; 1994/63; 2126/64, Case 'Relating to certain aspects of the law on the use of languages in education in Belgium' v Belgium, judgment of 23 July 1968, para 10.

[73] ibid.

[74] Joseph Marko, 'Against Discrimination: The Right to Equality and the Dilemma of Difference' in Joseph Marko (ed), *Human and Minority Rights Protection by Multiple Diversity Governance: History, Law, Ideology and Politics in European Perspective* (Routledge 2019) 311–13; Joseph Marko, 'Five Years After: Continuing Reflections on the Thematic Commentary on Effective Participation. The Interplay between Equality and Participation' in Tove Malloy and Ugo Caruso (eds), *Minorities, their Rights, and the Monitoring of the European Framework Convention for the Protection of National Minorities. Essays in Honour of Rainer Hofmann* (Martinus Nijhoff Publishers 2013) 111–13,

discrimination,[75] which was later laid down in secondary EU law with the RED and EED in the year 2000, albeit (as will be shown below) in a different way as compared to the developed jurisprudence of the Court of Justice.

In *Sotgiu*,[76] a case decided in 1974,[77] the Court had to decide whether a rule granting a higher separation allowance to workers who had their residency in Germany at the time of their initial employment as compared to workers who, at that time, had their residency abroad amounted to discrimination. The Court first established, that the rules regarding equal treatment contained in primary and secondary legislation 'forbid not only *overt* discrimination by reason of nationality but also all *covert* forms of discrimination which, by the application of other criteria of differentiation, *lead in fact to the same result*. It may therefore be that criteria such as place of origin or residence of a worker may, according to circumstances, be tantamount, as regards their practical effect, to discrimination on the grounds of nationality, such as is prohibited by the Treaty and the Regulation.' On this basis, the German regulation was found to be discriminatory, unless 'the scheme relating to such an allowance takes account of *objective differences* in the situations of workers according to whether their residence at the time when they take up their employment is within the territory of the State concerned or abroad'.[78]

This judgment thus outlined two important characteristics of indirect discrimination: first, it is an effects-based concept in the sense that even if a norm or policy is formulated neutrally, thus, without explicit reference to the suspect ground, it has a detrimental effect on a specific group. The norm or policy is therefore in fact not neutral. Second, however, such a measure does not amount to discrimination, if it can be shown that it may be objectively justified.

In the area of equal pay for men and women, the *Jenkins* case[79] was the first in which the Court of Justice made reference to indirect discrimination. The case

[75] For an in-depth analysis of the concept and the jurisprudence of the Court of Justice, see Tobler, 'Indirect Discrimination: A Case Study into the Development of the Legal Concept of Indirect Discrimination under EC Law' (n 69). Schiek discusses the concept also beyond the context of the European Union in Dagmar Schiek, 'Indirect Discrimination' in Dagmar Schiek, Lisa Waddington, and Mark Bell (eds), *Cases, Materials and Text on National, Supranational and International Non-Discrimination Law* (Hart Publishing 2007).

[76] *Sotgiu v Deutsche Bundespost* [1974] ECLI:EU:C:1974:13.

[77] A precursor from the US, considered a landmark case relating to racial discrimination, was *Griggs v Duke Power Co.*, decided by the US Supreme Court in 1971. As Tobler states, referring also to Schiek, the common law systems in the US, UK, and Ireland have decisively influenced the development of the concept of indirect discrimination on the European continent. Christa Tobler, *Limits and Potential of the Concept of Indirect Discrimination* (European Network of Legal Experts in the Non-discrimination Field 2008) 23.

[78] *Sotgiu v Deutsche Bundespost* (n 76) paras 11–13. Emphasis added.

[79] *Jenkins v Kingsgate* [1981] ECLI:EU:C:1981:80. For a detailed discussion of the case see JM Barrett, 'Part-time Workers and Equal Pay: The Case of Jenkins v. Kingsgate' [1981] The Human Rights Review 174; Ian Snaith, 'Two More Equal Pay Cases from the United Kingdom' [1981] European Law Review 193; Erika Szyszczak, 'Differences in Pay for Part-time Work' [1981] Modern Law Review 672; Tobler, 'Indirect Discrimination: A Case Study into the Development of the Legal Concept of Indirect Discrimination under EC Law' (n 69) 141–46.

raised the question of whether a difference in the level of pay for part-time work as compared to the same work carried out full-time amounts to discrimination, when it appears that it is predominantly or exclusively women who work on a part-time basis. In principle, the Court found that 'the fact that part-time work is paid at an hourly rate lower than pay for full-time work does not amount *per se* to discrimination ... in so far as the difference in pay between part-time work and full-time work is attributable to factors which are objectively justified and are in no way related to any discrimination based on sex'.[80] In the case in point, the policy was allegedly introduced to ensure that the expensive machinery in the factory was being used to its fullest extent and to ensure greater productivity. The Court, however, noted that 'if it is established that a *considerably smaller percentage* of women than of men' work full-time, the inequality in pay will be discriminatory 'where, regard being had to the difficulties encountered by women in arranging to work that minimum number of hours per week, the pay policy of the undertaking in question *cannot be explained by factors other than discrimination based on sex*'.[81] In fact, in the case in point there was only one man who worked on a part-time basis, while all the other part-time workers were women. By reference to the 'considerably smaller percentage', the Court already alluded to the relevance of statistics in providing facts from which discrimination might be presumed to have taken place. The Court left it to the national court 'to decide in each individual case whether, regard being had to the *facts of the case, its history and the employer's intention*', such a pay policy is in reality discrimination based on the sex of the worker.[82] This wording implies that the Court at this point still understood indirect discrimination as being intentional discrimination albeit in a hidden form.[83]

This approach already shifted five years later, when the Court decided the *Bilka* case.[84] The case regarded a pay policy, which excluded part-time workers from the occupational pension scheme on the ground that it seeks to employ as few part-time workers as possible. The measure was thus construed as necessary to make full-time work more attractive.[85] The Court stated, along with the Commission, that it is 'not sufficient to show that in adopting a pay practice which in fact discriminates against women workers the employer sought to achieve objectives other than discrimination against women' but the employer must show 'that the means chosen for achieving that objective correspond to a real need on the part of the

[80] *Jenkins v Kingsgate* (n 79) para 11.

[81] ibid para 13. Emphasis added.

[82] ibid para 14. Emphasis added.

[83] de Schutter, 'Three Models of Equality and European Anti-Discrimination Law' (n 5) 9.

[84] *Bilka v Weber von Hartz* [1986] ECLI:EU:C:1986:204. For a detailed discussion of the case see Anthony Arnull, 'Sex Discrimination in Occupational Pension Schemes' [1986] European Law Review 365; Vivien Shrubsall, 'Article 119, Pensions and Part-time Workers' [1987] Industrial Law Journal 52; Tobler, 'Indirect Discrimination: A Case Study into the Development of the Legal Concept of Indirect Discrimination under EC Law' (n 69) 146–50.

[85] *Bilka v Weber von Hartz* (n 84) para 33.

undertaking, are appropriate with a view to achieving the objective in question and are necessary to that end'.[86] This judgment thus made clear that it is not for the complainant to demonstrate that the measure was taken to discriminate against women but it is for the employer to show the economic necessity of the measure, 'once a disparate impact on women is identified'.[87]

This line of argumentation continued in a number of other cases and eventually conflated into Council Directive 97/80/EC on the burden of proof in cases of discrimination based on sex. Article 2(2) of the Directive contained a provision on indirect discrimination with was defined as a situation 'where an apparently neutral provision, criterion or practice disadvantages a *substantially higher proportion* of the members of one sex unless that provision, criterion or practice is appropriate and necessary and can be justified by objective factors unrelated to sex'.[88] The definition thus relied on the collection and analysis of statistical data to show a disparate impact of a specific measure on one sex. Considering that getting hold of such data could be quite burdensome or even impossible for victims of discrimination, the Commission proposed an alternative wording when the RED and EED were tabled.

Article 2(2)(b) RED for instance reads:

> [I]ndirect discrimination shall be taken to occur where an apparently neutral provision, criterion or practice would put persons of a racial or ethnic origin at a *particular disadvantage* compared with other persons, unless that provision, criterion or practice is objectively justified by a legitimate aim and the means of achieving that aim are appropriate and necessary.[89]

The shifting of the burden of proof applies to both direct and indirect discrimination under both Directives. According to the preambles, national rules 'may provide in particular for indirect discrimination to be established by any means including on the basis of statistical evidence'.[90]

The intention of the Commission, as shown in its explanation on the provision regarding indirect discrimination, was to facilitate the task of the victim by not obliging it to collect statistical data but to allow a victim, in case such data is unavailable, to demonstrate 'by any other means ... that a provision would be intrinsically disadvantageous for the person or persons concerned'.[91] However, as a result of discussions within the Council, it now remains within the discretion of

[86] ibid paras 35–37.
[87] de Schutter, 'Three Models of Equality and European Anti-Discrimination Law' (n 5) 10.
[88] Emphasis added.
[89] Emphasis added.
[90] RED, preamble, 15th recital; EED, preamble, 15th recital.
[91] Commission of the European Communities, 'Proposal for a Council Directive establishing a general framework for equal treatment in employment and occupation' (25 November 1999) COM(1999) 565 final, Explanatory Memorandum.

the Members State to allow or not to allow a victim to rely on statistics to establish a presumption of discrimination.[92] This narrows down the scope of the principle as it makes it difficult to challenge practices which, although apparently neutral, have a disparate effect on a particular group. Requiring to show that the measure puts a group at a 'particular disadvantage' compared with others, 'remains implicitly indebted to an understanding of discrimination which sees it as necessarily intentional'.[93]

De Schutter anticipated another difficulty related to the requirement to show a particular disadvantage compared with others: Could a person still complain about a measure which created a disadvantage, if he or she could have avoided it by adopting a certain behaviour? The example he gives is that a person could have sacrificed a specific dimension of his or her ethnicity or renounced one aspect of his or her freedom to express a religious belief. While acknowledging that it would be unacceptable to expect the abandoning of one of the defining traits of an ethnic or religious minority, he pointed to borderline cases, 'where a specific practice is not central to one's ethnicity or religion'.[94]

A case in point might be the judgment of the Court of Justice in *Achbita*,[95] and even more than the judgment, the opinion of Advocate General (AG) Kokott. In this case, a company had a rule prohibiting employees to wear visible signs of their political, philosophical, or religious beliefs in the workplace for reasons of neutrality. Although there are strong grounds for arguing that the Court could have found this practice to constitute direct discrimination, both the AG as well as the Court ruled out this option and found that the measure could amount to indirect discrimination. When evaluating the proportionality of the measure the AG made the following statement:

> However, unlike sex, skin colour, ethnic origin, sexual orientation, age or a person's disability, the practice of religion is not so much an unalterable fact as an aspect of an individual's private life, and one, moreover, over which the employees concerned can choose to exert an influence. While an employee cannot 'leave' his sex, skin colour, ethnicity, sexual orientation, age or disability 'at the door' upon entering his employer's premises, he may be expected to moderate the exercise of his religion in the workplace, be this in relation to religious practices, religiously motivated behaviour or (as in the present case) his clothing.[96]

[92] de Schutter, 'Three Models of Equality and European Anti-Discrimination Law' (n 5) 13–16.
[93] ibid 17.
[94] ibid 18.
[95] *Samira Achbita and Centrum voor gelijkheid van kansen en voor racismebestrijding v G4S Secure Solutions NV* [2017] ECLI:EU:C:2017:203. For further references and a detailed discussion of the case see Chapter 5.4.3.1.
[96] *Samira Achbita and Centrum voor gelijkheid van kansen en voor racismebestrijding v G4S Secure Solutions NV—opinion of the AG* [2016] ECLI:EU:C:2016:382, para 116.

For Kokott, religion can thus be treated differently from other protected characteristics as she conceives it more as a question of choice that can lawfully be restricted by an employer. While the Court did not enter into this discussion in its judgment, it still found that the pursuit of a policy of neutrality is a legitimate aim justifying a measure that could otherwise amount to indirect discrimination, as long as the measure is appropriate and necessary (requirement of proportionality) to achieve that aim. For the Court, the measure (prohibition on wearing religious symbols) is appropriate to achieve the aim (neutrality) as long as it is 'genuinely pursued in a consistent and systematic manner'. Regarding the necessity, this is achieved for the Court if the measure is restricted to employees who have contact with customers and if the company offers those employees insisting on wearing religious signs a position not involving visual contact.[97] Thus, the Court applied a very lenient justification test, which has been heavily criticized in the scholarly literature.[98]

Another interesting case when it comes to identifying the Court's approach in specifying the meaning of an objective justification in indirect discrimination cases is *CHEZ*.[99] The case regarded the complaint by a non-Roma woman regarding the placement of electricity meters at an unusual height in a Roma district, allegedly to avoid fraud. The Court recognized that preventing fraud and abuse and protecting individuals against the risks to their life and health which such conduct could entail, can be considered as a legitimate aim.[100] It stresses, however, that it is not enough to identify the theoretical legitimacy of the aim. The Court made it clear, that the 'company has the task at the very least of *establishing objectively*, first, the *actual existence and extent* of that unlawful conduct and, second, … the precise reasons for which there is, as matters currently stand, a major risk in the district concerned that such damage and unlawful connections to meters will continue'. The Court went on to state that the company 'cannot merely contend that such conduct and risks are "common knowledge", as it seems to have done before the referring court'.[101] When discussing the proportionality of the means, the Court took into consideration, inter alia, 'the legitimate interest of the final consumers of electricity in having access to the supply of electricity in conditions which do not have an offensive or stigmatising effect'.[102] While taking into account these dimensions

97 *Samira Achbita and Centrum voor gelijkheid van kansen en voor racismebestrijding v G4S Secure Solutions NV* (n 95) paras 40–43.

98 See, for instance, Erica Howard, 'Islamic Headscarves and the CJEU: Achbita and Bougnaoui' (2017) 24(3) Maastricht Journal of European and Comparative Law 348, and further references in Chapter 5.4.3.1.

99 *'CHEZ Razpredelenie Bulgaria' AD v Komisia za zashtita ot diskriminatsia* [2015] ECLI:EU:C:2015:480. For a discussion of the case see Sara Benedi Lahuerta, 'Ethnic Discrimination, Discrimination by Association and the Roma Community: CHEZ' (2016) 53(3) Common Market Law Review 797; Christopher McCrudden, 'The New Architecture of EU Equality Law After CHEZ: Did the Court of Justice Reconceptualise Direct and Indirect Discrimination?' [2016] European Equality Law Review 1. For more references and a discussion, see Chapter 5.3.3.2.

100 *'CHEZ Razpredelenie Bulgaria' AD v Komisia za zashtita ot diskriminatsia* (n 99) paras 113–14.

101 ibid paras 116–17. Emphasis added.

102 ibid para 124.

in a case related to discrimination of Roma is to be welcomed, it is not to be expected that the Court will in the future address only practices that are humiliating and stigmatizing, nor that it understands such practices as being at the core of anti-discrimination law.[103]

While the Court of Justice thus has a long, albeit not always linear, tradition of taking indirect discrimination into account, the integration of this concept in the jurisprudence of the ECtHR started relatively late with the case of *Thlimmenos v Greece*.[104] The case concerned a member of Jehovah's Witnesses who had been criminally convicted for refusing on religious grounds to wear a military uniform. Although he came second in a competition for the appointment of twelve chartered accountants, he was refused the position on the ground of his criminal conviction. The applicant complained about the fact 'that in the application of the relevant law no distinction is made between persons convicted of offences committed exclusively because of their religious beliefs and persons convicted of other offences'.[105] In this context, the Court held that '[t]he right not to be discriminated against in the enjoyment of the rights guaranteed under the Convention is also violated when States without an objective and reasonable justification fail to treat differently persons whose situations are significantly different'.[106] Considering that, 'unlike other convictions for serious criminal offences, a conviction for refusing on religious or philosophical grounds to wear the military uniform cannot imply any dishonesty or moral turpitude likely to undermine the offender's ability to exercise this profession' the Court concluded that '[e]xcluding the applicant on the ground that he was an unfit person was not, therefore, justified'.[107]

The Court thus looked carefully at the factual context of the underlying situation and emphasized the duty to differentiate, already developed in the Belgian linguistic case. While some consider this being the first case in which the ECtHR has found indirect discrimination, Marko argues that the 'factual *group-related effect* of allegedly "neutral" provisions' required by definition for indirect discrimination is missing in this case. In *Thlimmenos*, an individual was discriminated against because the Greek courts had not taken into account the factual difference, in violation of the duty to differentiate inherent in Article 14 ECHR.[108]

In *Chapman*[109] the Court developed a 'special duty to protect' doctrine, implying a positive obligation on a contracting state not only to respect but also to protect and promote diverse identities.[110] In fact, '[t]he Court observes that there

[103] If this were the case, McCrudden would qualify this as 'far from progressive'. See McCrudden, 'The New Architecture of EU Equality Law After CHEZ: Did the Court of Justice Reconceptualise Direct and Indirect Discrimination?' (n 99) 9–10.

[104] ECtHR, App No 34369/97, *Thlimmenos v Greece*, judgment of 6 April 2000.

[105] ibid para 42.

[106] ibid para 44.

[107] ibid para 47.

[108] Marko, 'Against Discrimination: The Right to Equality and the Dilemma of Difference' (n 74) 316.

[109] ECtHR, App No 27238/95, *Chapman v UK*, judgment (Grand Chamber) of 18 January 2001.

[110] Marko, 'Against Discrimination: The Right to Equality and the Dilemma of Difference' (n 74) 316.

may be said to be an emerging international consensus amongst the Contracting States of the Council of Europe recognising the special needs of minorities and an obligation to protect their security, identity and lifestyle (see … in particular the Framework Convention for the Protection of National Minorities), not only for the purpose of safeguarding the interests of the minorities themselves but to preserve a cultural diversity of value to the whole community'. The Court also acknowledged that 'the vulnerable position of Gypsies as a minority means that some special consideration should be given to their needs and their different lifestyle both in the relevant regulatory planning framework and in reaching decisions in particular cases … To this extent, there is thus a positive obligation imposed on the Contracting States by virtue of Article 8 to facilitate the Gypsy way of life.'[111] The duty to protect, however, still resembles the duty to differentiate in that it requires authorities to take the factual context of a person or the impact for a disadvantaged group into account, in the latter case coming close to the meaning of indirect discrimination under EU law. In any case, the duty to protect does not encompass a duty to take positive measures. In fact, the Court ruled out the finding that the number of Gypsies is statistically greater than the number of caravan places available would justify the imposition of an obligation on the state 'to make available to the Gypsy community an adequate number of suitably equipped sites. The Court is not convinced, despite the undoubted evolution that has taken place in both international law, as evidenced by the framework convention, and domestic legislations in regard to protection of minorities, that Article 8 can be interpreted as implying for States such a far-reaching positive obligation of general social policy … .'[112]

Further steps in the integration of the definition of indirect discrimination in the case law of the ECtHR were taken in the cases of *Hugh Jordan v the UK*[113] and *D.H. v the Czech Republic*.[114] In the first case the applicant complained, inter alia, of discrimination considering the high number of killings of Northern Irish Catholics by security forces in combination with the low number of prosecutions and convictions. The Court argued that '[w]here a general policy or measure has disproportionately prejudicial effects on a particular group, it is not excluded that this may be considered as discriminatory notwithstanding that it is not specifically aimed or directed at that group'.[115] It did not, however, accept that 'statistics can in themselves disclose a practice which could be classified as discriminatory within the meaning of Article 14'.[116] While the Chamber judgment in the *D.H.* case followed the same argumentation, the Grand Chamber determined that statistical

[111] ECtHR, *Chapman*, paras 93 and 96.
[112] ibid para 98.
[113] ECtHR, App No 24746/94, *Hugh Jordan v UK*, judgment of 4 May 2001.
[114] ECtHR, App No 57325/00, *D.H. v Czech Republic*, judgment (Chamber) of 7 February 2006 and (Grand Chamber) of 13 November 2007.
[115] ECtHR, *Hugh Jordan*, para 154.
[116] ibid.

evidence is allowed. Recapitulating the main principles to be applied in the case concerning the disproportionate placement of Roma children in special schools, the Grand Chamber stated that in the more recent cases of *Hoogendijk*[117] and *Zarb Adami*,[118] in which the applicants alleged a difference in the effect of a general measure or de facto situation (thus 'indirect discrimination') 'the Court relied extensively on statistics produced by the parties to establish a difference in treatment between two groups (men and women) in similar situations'.[119]

The above quoted decision of the Court in *Hoogendijk* was not only meaningful in establishing that statistics are allowed as evidence but it also went on to describe the consequences for the burden of proof. The Court stated that 'where an applicant is able to show, on the basis of undisputed official statistics, the existence of a prima facie indication that a specific rule—although formulated in a neutral manner—in fact affects a clearly higher percentage of women than men, it is for the respondent Government to show that this is the result of objective factors unrelated to any discrimination on grounds of sex. If the onus of demonstrating that a difference in impact for men and women is not in practice discriminatory does not shift to the respondent Government, it will be in practice extremely difficult for applicants to prove indirect discrimination.'[120]

The ECtHR had thus integrated in its jurisprudence on Article 14 ECHR all main elements of the definition of indirect discrimination as contained in the RED and EED as early as 2000. In particular, in the Grand Chamber judgment in *D.H.*, the ECtHR elaborated its framework for the analysis of the case at hand by referring to the RED, its definition of direct and indirect discrimination, its rule regarding the reversal of the burden of proof, and related case law.[121]

The ECtHR, however, went a step further in the case *Oršuš and Others v Croatia*[122] in which it 'developed and applied a full-fledged doctrine of a *positive duty* to take *special positive measures* on behalf of minorities'.[123] As in *D.H.*, the case

[117] ECtHR, App No 58641/00, *Hoogendijk v Netherlands*, decision on admissibility of 6 January 2005.
[118] ECtHR, App No 17209/02, *Zarb Adami v Malta*, judgment of 20 June 2006.
[119] ECtHR, *D.H. (Grand Chamber)*, para 180.
[120] ECtHR, *Hoogendijk*.
[121] ECtHR, *D.H. (Grand Chamber)*, paras 81–91.
[122] ECtHR, App No 15766/03, *Oršuš and Others v Croatia*, judgment of 16 March 2010. For a discussion see Andrea Grgić, 'Recognizing Formal and Substantive Equality in the Oršuš Case' (2012) 9 European Yearbook of Minority Issues 327.
[123] Marko, 'Against Discrimination: The Right to Equality and the Dilemma of Difference' (n 74) 323. De Schutter interprets the *Oršuš* judgment not as implying an obligation to take positive measures but simply as confirming that states are not prevented from taking such steps. He substantiates this interpretation with the explanatory report to Protocol 12 ECHR, which, at para 16, states as follows: 'The fact that there are certain groups or categories of persons who are disadvantaged, or the existence of de facto inequalities, may constitute justifications for adopting measures providing for specific advantages in order to promote equality, provided that the proportionality principle is respected. . . . However, the present Protocol does not impose any obligation to adopt such measures. Such a programmatic obligation would sit ill with the whole nature of the Convention and its control system which are based on the collective guarantee of individual rights which are formulated in terms sufficiently specific to be justifiable.' Olivier de Schutter, *The Prohibition of Discrimination under European Human Rights Law. Relevance for*

regarded the enrolment of Roma children in special classes. In *Oršuš* these classes were situated in regular primary schools and the reason for placing them there was related to their allegedly poor command of the Croatian language. The measure was thus construed as a sort of positive action. The Court stated that a temporary placement in separate classes for the mentioned reason does not automatically amount to discrimination. 'However, when such a measure disproportionately or even, as in the present case, exclusively, affects members of a specific ethnic group, then appropriate safeguards have to be put in place.'[124]

With regard to the alleged poor command of the Croatian language among the pupils concerned, the Court found that

> the State ... had the *obligation to take appropriate positive measures* to assist the applicant in acquiring the necessary language skills in the shortest time possible, notably by means of special language lessons, so that they could be quickly integrated into mixed classes.[125]

Considering a drop-out rate as high as 84 per cent of Roma pupils before completing primary education the Court further clearly stated that

> such a high drop-out rate ... called for the implementation of *positive measures in order*, inter alia, *to raise awareness* of the importance of education among the Roma population *and to assist* the applicants with any difficulties they encountered in following the school curriculum. Therefore, some *additional steps were needed* in order to address these problems, such as active and structured involvement on the part of the relevant social services.[126]

The transition in the jurisprudence of the ECtHR from formal to substantive equality, eventually picking up its judgment in the Belgian linguistic case, was thereby completed. Apart from the fact that subsequent judgments again caused a backlash against the Court's jurisprudence,[127] Marko asserts that this development of jurisprudence still fails to reach the participatory, let alone transformative dimension of equality. This final stage of equality, which he calls 'institutional

the EU Non-Discrimination Directives—An Update (European Network of Legal Experts in the Non-discrimination Field 2011) 31.

124 ECtHR, *Oršuš*, para 157.
125 ibid para 165, emphasis added.
126 ibid para 177, emphasis added.
127 Marko refers in this context to the cases *Yordanova and Others v Bulgaria*, App No 25446/06, judgment of 24 April 2012, and *Ciorcan and Others v Romania*, App No 29414/09 and 44841/09, judgment of 27 November 2015. Marko, 'Against Discrimination: The Right to Equality and the Dilemma of Difference' (n 74) 324. For a discussion of *Ciorcan* see also Sandra Fredman, 'Emerging from the Shadows: Substantive Equality and Article 14 of the European Convention on Human Rights' (2016) 16(2) Human Rights Law Review 273, 285–87.

equality' would be required in order to trigger structural change thereby addressing systemic discrimination and institutional segregation, which is 'the result of the failures of social and system integration … following from a lack of effective political participation'.[128] When referring to participatory and transformative dimension of equality, he follows the typology proposed by Fredman, who distinguishes between the redistributive dimension (aiming at redressing disadvantage), the recognition dimension (addressing stigma, stereotypes, prejudice, and violence), the participatory dimension (facilitating participation), and the transformative dimension (accommodating difference, including through structural change).[129]

This categorization coincides with de Schutter's models of equality. He arrives at these models by distinguishing on one hand according to the aim pursued by non-discrimination legislation. Is the aim to seek to protect individuals from being discriminated against (formal equality) or is it to ensure equal representation of diverse social groups in different sectors of society and a roughly equal distribution of social goods among these groups (substantive equality)? On the other hand he asks whether the suspect characteristic is visible or not, or, in case it is not visible, if efforts are undertaken to make the characteristic explicit while respecting requirements of privacy.[130]

Combining the two questions he arrives at three models of equality. The first is the simple prohibition of discrimination (formal equality) where the aim is to protect from discrimination and the assumption is that shielding suspect characteristics from the view of others will contribute to protecting them from discrimination. However, this is first, not always possible (think for instance of gender, age) and the approach could therefore be that it is better to recognize that these (and other) characteristics may play a role in decision making. If, besides formal equality, the approach to equality remains a negative one, the focus will be on prohibition of discrimination, including indirect discrimination. This is the second model of equality. In the third model, which he calls 'affirmative equality', not only are suspect characteristics taken into account but there is also a move to a positive approach to equality. The aim under this model is 'not only to avoid instances of discrimination, but also to make progress towards a fair share of social goods among the different segments of the population … [and] to improve the representation of certain groups in the areas or at the levels where they are underrepresented'.[131] To put it in the words used by the

128 Marko, 'Against Discrimination: The Right to Equality and the Dilemma of Difference' (n 74) 310. For a chart showing the relationship and interrelatedness of equality and representation/participation see, ibid 166. Fredman too concludes that the Court is cautious in relation to transformation and structural change. See Fredman, 'Emerging from the Shadows: Substantive Equality and Article 14 of the European Convention on Human Rights' (n 127) 301.

129 See Fredman, 'Emerging from the Shadows: Substantive Equality and Article 14 of the European Convention on Human Rights' (n 127) 281–84.

130 de Schutter, 'Three Models of Equality and European Anti-Discrimination Law' (n 5) 1–3.

131 ibid 3–4.

Framework Convention for the Protection of National Minorities (FCNM), the aim is to achieve 'full and effective equality'.[132]

The participatory dimension in Fredman's typology and adopted also by Marko, and the affirmative equality model of de Schutter therefore overlap. The means to achieve this form of equality is in both cases affirmative action,[133] which in the framework of the Equality Directives is called 'positive action', whereas the FCNM speaks of 'adequate' or 'special measures',[134] a terminology which has been unified under the term 'positive measures' by the Advisory Committee of the FCNM.[135] Considering the wording used by the ECtHR in the *Oršuš* case (obligation to take appropriate positive measures) one could be led to think that what Fredman coined as participatory and transformative dimension has already been reached in the jurisprudence of the court. The question is however, what is the aim of these positive measures: do they aim to create equality of opportunity or equality of result? The wording of paragraph 40 of the Explanatory Note of the FCNM seems to imply that only the former is meant. In fact, this paragraph explains that '[n]o separate provision dealing specifically with the principle of equal opportunities has been included in the framework Convention ... as the principle is already implied in paragraph 2 of this article [4]'. However, to achieve full and effective equality, as required by the FCNM, it might be required to aim beyond establishing equal opportunities. To successfully counter systemic structural discrimination it might be required to aim at equality of results, for instance, by the introduction of a quota for specific underrepresented groups. Fredman, in line with Marko's idea of 'institutional equality' pushed the meaning of substantive equality in a direction that included not only the aim to redress disadvantage or address stigma, stereotypes, prejudice, and violence, but also to enhance voice and participation, accommodate difference, and achieve structural change.[136]

132 FCNM, Art 4(2). For the interpretation given to this provision by the Advisory Committee on the Framework Convention for the Protection of National Minorities (ACFC) see Adela Schmidt, 'Artikel 4' in Rainer Hofmann and others (eds), *Rahmenübereinkommen zum Schutz nationaler Minderheiten. Handkommentar* (Nomos 2015); Barbara Wilson, 'Commentary of Article 4 of the Framework Convention for the Protection of National Minorities' in Rainer Hofmann, Tove H Malloy, and Detlev Rein (eds), *The Framework Convention for the Protection of National Minorities. A Commentary* (Brill 2018).

133 For an in-depth discussion about the concept see 'The concept and practice of affirmative action: Final report submitted by Mr. Marc Bossuyt, Special Rapporteur, in accordance with resolution 1998/5 of the Sub-Commission for the Promotion and Protection of Human Rights' (17 June 2002) UN doc E/CN.4/Sub.2/2002/21; Christopher McCrudden, 'Rethinking Positive Action' (1986) 15(1) Industrial Law Journal 219.

134 FCNM, Art 4(2) and Explanatory Report, para 39.

135 See ACFC, 3rd opinion on Germany (2010) fn 10.

136 In addition to Fredman already quoted, 'Emerging from the Shadows: Substantive Equality and Article 14 of the European Convention on Human Rights' (n 127), see also Sandra Fredman, 'Substantive Equality Revisited' (2016) 14(3) International Journal of Constitutional Law 712; Catharine A MacKinnon, 'Substantive Equality Revisited: A Reply to Sandra Fredman' (2016) 14(3) International Journal of Constitutional Law 739; Sandra Fredman, 'Substantive Equality Revisited: A Rejoinder to Catharine MacKinnon' (2016) 14(3) International Journal of Constitutional Law 747; Catharine A MacKinnon, 'Substantive Equality Revisited: A Rejoinder to Sandra Fredman' (2017) 15(4) International Journal of Constitutional Law 1174.

De Schutter put it quite clearly that the EU anti-discrimination regime belongs to the first of his three models of equality, while Member States should be incentivized to espouse also the second. However, problems regarding the third model, the affirmative equality model, persist and they relate on one hand to uncertainties regarding the protection of personal data and on the other hand to the understanding of the equal treatment principle under EU law.[137] In fact, positive action is not required under EU law, but it is also not openly prohibited. Already before the inclusion of a cautious provision in this sense by Article 5 RED and Article 7 EED, the Court of Justice had the opportunity to scrutinize affirmative action measures for women regarding their compatibility with the Gender Equality Directive.[138] In particular, the Court was called to decide whether quotas were compatible with Article 2(4) of Directive 76/207/EEC, which provided that the Directive 'shall be without prejudice to measures to promote equal opportunity for men and women, in particular by removing existing inequalities which affect women's opportunities'.

The first case in this context was *Kalanke*.[139] In that case, the Court had to address the question whether Article 2(4) of Directive 76/207 would cover a norm, which provided that equally qualified women had to be given automatic priority in appointments in sectors where they were underrepresented. This was, as Advocate General Tesauro put it, 'certainly not a trivial one [question]'. The Court's judgment made reference to Council Recommendation 84/635/EEC of 13 December 1984 on the promotion of positive action for women, which encouraged Member States to adopt positive measures, inter alia, 'to eliminate or counteract the prejudicial effects on women in employment or seeking employment which arise from existing attitudes, behaviour and structures based on the idea of a traditional division of roles in society between men and women'.[140] Without calling it such, this Recommendation clearly addressed the problem of structural discrimination. Among the possible measures states could take, Recommendation 4 lists also the 'recruitment and promotion of women in sectors and professions and at levels where they are underrepresented'. The Court, however, found (by using what Marko refers to as the 'rule-exception structure' of the then Art 141 Treaty establishing the European Community (TEC) and today's Art 157 TFEU[141]) that '[n]evertheless, as a derogation from an individual right laid down in the Directive, Article 2(4) must be interpreted strictly' and therefore '[n]ational rules which

[137] de Schutter, 'Three Models of Equality and European Anti-Discrimination Law' (n 5) 3–4.

[138] de Witte (n 69) 1724.

[139] *Kalanke v Freie Hansestadt Bremen* [1995] ECLI:EU:C:1995:322. For a discussion of the case see Eva Brems, 'European Court of Justice, case C-450/93, Eckhard Kalanke v. Freie Hansestadt Bremen, 17 October 1995' [1995] Columbia Journal of European Law 172; Erika Szyszczak, 'Positive Action After Kalanke' (1996) 59(6) Modern Law Review 876; Dagmar Schiek, '"Kalanke" und die Folgen - Überlegungen zu EG-rechtlichen Anforderungen an betriebliche Gleichstellungspolitik' (1996) 44(4) Arbeit und Recht 128.

[140] Council Recommendation 84/635/EEC of 13 December 1984 on the promotion of positive action for women, Recommendation 1(a).

[141] Marko, 'Against Discrimination: The Right to Equality and the Dilemma of Difference' (n 74) 329.

guarantee women absolute and unconditional priority for appointment or promotion go beyond promoting equal opportunities and overstep the limits of the exception in Article 2(4) of the Directive'.[142]

The decision of the Court was criticized for 'making the concept of "substantive equality in practice" ineffective'.[143] In a Communication from the Commission to the European Parliament and the Council, the European Commission gave its interpretation of the judgment of the Court in *Kalanke.* In the view of the Commission, the judgment cannot be interpreted as dismissing the possibility of justifying any quota system. The 'only type of quota system which is unlawful is one which is completely rigid and does not leave any possibility of taking account of individual circumstances. Member States and employers are thus free to have recourse to all other forms of positive action, including flexible quotas.'[144] The Commission even recommended an amendment of Article 2(4) of Directive 76/207 in this sense.

The Court of Justice was confronted with a similar case in *Marschall.*[145] The case differed from *Kalanke,* however, in that the provision under scrutiny provided for a so-called 'saving-clause'. The Court took account of this difference by stating:

> Unlike the rules at issue in Kalanke, a national rule which, as in the case in point in the main proceedings, contains a saving clause does not exceed those limits [of the exception in Article 2(4) of the Directive] if, in each individual case, it provides for male candidates who are equally as qualified as the female candidates a guarantee that the candidatures will be the subject of an objective assessment which will take account of all criteria specific to the individual candidates and will override the priority accorded to female candidates where one or more of those criteria tilts the balance in favour of the male candidate.[146]

Most importantly, the Court adds to this that 'it should be remembered that those criteria must not be such as to discriminate against female candidates'.

To reach this conclusion, the Court again made reference to Recommendation 84/635/EEC and acknowledged that 'it appears that even where male and female candidates are equally qualified, male candidates tend to be promoted in preference

[142] *Kalanke v Freie Hansestadt Bremen* (n 139) paras 21–22.

[143] Marko, 'Against Discrimination: The Right to Equality and the Dilemma of Difference' (n 74) 330.

[144] Commission of the European Communities, 'Communication from the Commission to the European Parliament and the Council on the interpretation of the judgment of the Court of Justice on 17 October 1995 in Case C-450/93, *Kalanke v Freie Hansestadt Bremen*' (27 March 1996) COM(96) 88 final, 10.

[145] *Marschall v Land Nordrhein-Westfalen* [1997] ECLI:EU:C:1997:533. For a discussion of Kalanke and Marschall see Dagmar Schiek, 'Sex Equality Law After Kalanke and Marschall' (1998) 4(2) European Law Journal 148; on *Marschall* see further Oliver Suhr, 'Grenzen der Gleichbehandlung: Zur Vereinbarkeit von Frauenquoten mit dem Gemeinschaftsrecht' (1998) 25(5–6) Europäische Grundrechte-Zeitschrift 121.

[146] *Marschall v Land Nordrhein-Westfalen* (n 145) para 33.

to female candidates particularly because of prejudices and stereotypes concerning the role and capacities of women in working life and the fear, for example, that women will interrupt their careers more frequently, that owing to household and family duties they will be less flexible in their working hours, or that they will be absent from work more frequently because of pregnancy, childbirth and breast-feeding. For these reasons, the mere fact that a male candidate and a female candidate are equally qualified does not mean that they have the same chances.' A rule like the one under scrutiny 'may counteract the prejudicial effects on female candidates of the attitudes and behavior described above and thus reduce actual instances of inequality which may exist in the real world'.[147]

In *Badeck and Others*[148] the Court reiterated its position that a quota which does not give automatic and unconditional priority to equally qualified women does not constitute a violation of Article 2(4) of Directive 76/207. However, in that case it found a system that 'does not fix an absolute ceiling but fixes one by reference to the number of persons who have received appropriate training' as being compatible with Community law, as this 'amounts to using an actual fact as a quantitative criterion for giving preference to women'.[149] Furthermore, the Court found it to be in line with EU law when 50 per cent of training places with a view to obtaining qualifications with the prospect of subsequent access to trained occupations in the public service are reserved for women, when the state does not have a monopoly on the training and therefore training places are available also in the private sector, and when, 'despite appropriate measures for drawing the attention of women to the training places available', there are not enough applications from women, in which case men can be assigned more than half of the training places.[150] Finally, a national rule which guarantees, where male and female candidates have equal qualifications, that women who are qualified are called to interview, in sectors in which they are underrepresented, is not considered to go beyond the exception of Article 2(4) as the provision 'does not imply an attempt to achieve a final result—appointment or promotion—but affords women who are qualified additional opportunities to facilitate their entry into working life and their career'.[151]

All these provisions are understood by the Court as contributing to equality of opportunities for women but not as aiming at equality of results as the latter would go beyond what is covered by EU law. This explains why the Court is willing to accept even absolute priority for women when it comes to measures that 'just' improve opportunities, such as access to training or calls to job interviews.

[147] ibid paras 29–31.

[148] *Badeck and Others* [2000] ECLI:EU:C:2000:163. For a comment see Peter Köhler, 'Promotion of equal opportunities between the sexes, selection of the best, merit system' (2000) 1(1) The European Legal Forum 63.

[149] *Badeck and Others* (n 148) para 42.

[150] ibid paras 51–53.

[151] ibid paras 56–63.

De Schutter further argues that the Court has so far considered legitimate only measures that can be understood as tools to remove actual inequalities, but not measures thought to compensate for past discrimination of the group concerned (backward-looking) or measures aiming at proportionate representation or diversity (forward-looking).[152] In fact, the Court in all the above cases states that Article 2(4) 'is specifically and exclusively designed to authorise measures which, although discriminatory in appearance, are in fact intended to eliminate or reduce *actual instances* of inequality which may exist in the reality of social life'.[153] This might have been justified in times where secondary EU legislation spoke of 'removing existing inequalities' as was the case with Article 2(4). The approach could have changed however, already with the amendment of Article 141 TEU (now Art 157 TFEU) to include 'measures providing for specific advantages in order to make it easier for the underrepresented sex to pursue a vocational activity or to *prevent or compensate for disadvantages* in professional careers'.[154] The formulation 'prevent or compensate'—which was taken over by all Equality Directives adopted in the 2000s—would have allowed already in *Badeck* for an interpretation including both the backward as well as the forward-looking justification for the adoption of affirmative action measures.[155]

This review of case law has shown that it took the ECtHR quite a while to take on board the concept of indirect discrimination. This is related to the fact that non-discrimination, as the other rights granted under the Convention are understood as individual rights so that the group-oriented dimension inherent to the concept of indirect discrimination was usually ignored.[156] On the other hand, the *Oršuš* judgment can be interpreted as an opening towards the idea of a positive duty to take special measures which, however, remains to be confirmed by further case law.[157]

While the Court of Justice was quick in understanding the need to subsume also 'covert' forms of discrimination under the interpretation of relevant provisions of primary and secondary legislation, it remains the case that positive action to achieve equal opportunities is allowed but equality of results appears to be excluded from this permission. Also, EU norms cannot be interpreted as imposing a duty on states to take positive action to combat discrimination.[158]

To what extent have the developments of the anti-discrimination law at European level influenced national legal systems? As described at the beginning

[152] de Schutter, 'Three Models of Equality and European Anti-Discrimination Law' (n 5) 45.
[153] *Kalanke v Freie Hansestadt Bremen* (n 139) para 18; *Marschall v Land Nordrhein-Westfalen* (n 145) para 26; *Badeck and Others* (n 148) para 19. Emphasis added.
[154] Emphasis added.
[155] de Schutter, 'Three Models of Equality and European Anti-Discrimination Law' (n 5) 45.
[156] Marko, 'Five Years After: Continuing Reflections on the Thematic Commentary on Effective Participation. The Interplay between Equality and Participation' (n 74) 111.
[157] Marko, 'Against Discrimination: The Right to Equality and the Dilemma of Difference' (n 74) 332.
[158] ibid.

of this chapter, the principle of equality, albeit existing throughout the Western countries, was a broad and empty concept at the same time. The jurisprudence of European courts contributed to reducing this emptiness by developing meanings and interpretations of equality, which were later codified in secondary EU legislation. This was done on one hand by introducing new suspect grounds, such as age, religion, and sexual orientation, and on the other hand by developing (through the just described case law) the prohibition of indirect discrimination.[159] As this chapter has shown, an obligation for states to adopt positive measures is still not part of EU non-discrimination law[160] and also the jurisprudence of the ECtHR requiring such measures cannot, for the time being, be considered as being prevailing. The approaches of different constitutions and Constitutional Courts, therefore, also vary and change over time.

In Slovakia, the provision of the law transposing the RED which provided for the possibility to adopt positive measures has been challenged by the government before the Constitutional Court, which in 2005 declared such measures unconstitutional 'on the grounds of vagueness and that the Constitution did not allow for the provision of positive measures on the grounds of race or ethnic origin.'[161] In 2008, the Anti-Discrimination Act was amended and now provides for the possibility of taking positive measures on the grounds of, inter alia, social and economic disadvantages,[162] thereby avoiding reference to race and ethnic origin. The Cypriot Supreme Court, in a judgment of 2015, reversed its practice of declaring unconstitutional any law that introduced positive measures, when it rejected a claim that a

[159] de Witte (n 69) 1720–21.

[160] See however Commission of the European Communities, 'Communication from the Commission to the European Parliament, the Council, the European Economic and Social Committee and the Committee of Regions: Non-discrimination and equal opportunities: A renewed commitment' (n 59) 7–8, where the Commission first reiterates that EU legislation does not prevent states from maintaining or adopting positive action measures but then goes on to state: 'There is a rapidly growing appreciation of the role positive action can play to redress the lack of substantive equality in societies . . . Some Member States . . . have introduced provisions making it a duty for public authorities to promote equality as a core objective of all their activities. The Commission will use the permanent dialogue with Member States to promote the full utilisation of the possibilities for positive action, in particular in access to education, employment, housing and health care.' The Commission thus signals its sympathy for a more consistent use of positive action measures.

[161] Slovak Constitutional Court, PL ÚS 8/04 of 18 October 2005. Quotation from ECRI, 'Report on Slovakia (fourth monitoring cycle) adopted on 19 December 2008' CRI(2009)20, para 20. For a discussion of the Constitutional Court's decision see Alexander Bröstl, 'Positive Action and the Principle of Equality: Discussing a Decision of the Constitutional Court of the Slovak Republic' (2007) 5 European Yearbook of Minority Issues 377. While the decision of the Constitutional Court was still pending, the ACFC gave its opinion about the issue in its 2nd opinion on Slovakia, (2005) para 38: '[S]pecial measures are not only legitimate but may even be required under certain circumstances in order to promote full and effective equality in favour of persons belonging to national minorities. Provided they are in conformity with the proportionality principle, such measures shall therefore not be considered an act of discrimination. The Advisory Committee is of the opinion that without such measures being taken, it is extremely difficult to reach full and effective equality between persons belonging to vulnerable minorities and those belonging to the majority.'

[162] ECRI, 'Report on Slovakia (fourth monitoring cycle) adopted on 19 December 2008' (n 161) para 20.

law imposing a quota for persons with disability in public employment was unconstitutional. The Croatian Constitutional Act on the Rights of National Minorities provides for proportionate representation of persons belonging to national minorities in the state and local administration and the judiciary and Article 74(7) of the Judiciary Act stipulates that '[i]n the appointment of judges account shall be taken of the representation of judges belonging to national minorities, in accordance with the provisions of the Constitutional Act on the Rights of National Minorities'. When this provision was challenged before the Constitutional Court, it found that such special positive measures aim at eliminating factual inequalities without being automatic and unconditional and that they are not discriminatory as long as they were justified and proportionate.[163] Disability is the ground for which most positive measures, mainly in the form of quotas in (public) employment are already in place.[164]

De Witte presents four more elements that show the impact of European anti-discrimination regime on the legal landscape in Europe. One is related to the access to justice. Constitutional equality clauses, because of their vagueness and the lack of specific enforcement mechanisms, were generally underused by the groups concerned. EU anti-discrimination law introduced an increased attention to securing procedures and remedies that contribute to the effective application of the rules on non-discrimination and equality. The RED as well as the Gender Directives, require, for instance, the designation of one or more bodies for the promotion of equal treatment, that—amongst other tasks—are supposed to provide independent assistance to victims of discrimination. Furthermore, all Directives require that NGOs must be allowed to support victims of discrimination in any judicial and/or administrative procedure aiming at the enforcement of the Directives. A 'new demand for judicial enforcement' was thereby created, and required from national legal systems to adapt concepts that were hitherto unknown to them.[165] Considering the language used in the RED and EED for the scope of action of these institutions, states were given considerable leeway in transposing these provisions and this provides ample room for mutual learning and exchange of practice. Large parts of the present research are therefore dedicated to an analysis of how these provisions were translated into the national legal systems and how they play out in practice.

Another element by which the impact of the EU anti-discrimination regime on the nation legal systems becomes evident is related to the fact that European countries have generally been reluctant to recognize a horizontal effect to constitutional

[163] European network of legal experts in gender equality and non-discrimination, 'A comparative analysis of non-discrimination law in Europe 2017' (2017) 79, making reference to Constitutional Court Decisions No U-I-2767/2007, 31 March 2009 and No U-I-402/2003 and U-I-2812/2007, 30 April 2008.

[164] ibid 81–83.

[165] de Witte (n 69) 1721–22.

rights, in other words, to recognize that they also directly bind private persons. The widely used approach is to leave it to the legislator to decide what kind of norms to adopt in acting against violations of fundamental rights committed by private actors. The EU anti-discrimination regime has considerably limited the choice of the legislation by the horizontal extension of the equal treatment obligation. While gender equality in private employment relations was already horizontally applied since the Equal Treatment Directive of 1976, the grounds and areas of social life to which the principle of equality had to be applied horizontally was considerable enlarged with the adoption of the RED and EED.[166]

Because of the direct effect and the primacy of EU law within the national legal orders, national (including constitutional) courts have to use EU legislation as a standard against which they review their own legislation. The possibility for the Commission to bring infringement proceedings before the CJEU in case a state fails to comply with the obligations deriving from EU law, adds to the strength of the European anti-discrimination regime. The European law compliance system is thus another factor that shows the impact of EU anti-discrimination regime on the legal landscape in Europe.[167]

And finally, the impact of EU rules on non-discrimination and equality on the national legal systems also becomes evident in 'the way in which the constitutional equality rules of European states are currently understood and applied' in those areas that are not covered by the scope of EU anti-discrimination laws in terms of protected grounds and fields of application. De Witte gives the example of the Belgian Constitutional Court finding that an upper age limit for membership of church councils was a form of age discrimination in violation of the constitutional principle of equality, and this although the facts of the case were not covered by the EED (church council members not being employed by the church councils). He therefore concludes that 'the directive was clearly instrumental in leading the court to interpret Belgian constitutional law in a different way than it would otherwise have done'.[168]

The development of the non-discrimination regime at European level, both through the development of the legal framework as well as though the jurisprudence of the CJEU and the ECtHR has, therefore, 'modified the traditional understanding of equality law in Europe and [is] giving "teeth" to the abstract principle of equality'.[169]

Having introduced the legal norms that are at the centre of the present research, the next chapter will present the theoretical approach underpinning it.

166 ibid 1722.
167 ibid 1722–23.
168 ibid 1723.
169 ibid 1715.

2

Theoretical Foundations: Reflexive Governance, EU Enlargement Process, and Non-Discrimination

2.1 Introduction

By combining approaches and concepts of political science, legal philosophy, and governance studies, this chapter provides the theoretical framework which is used in approaching the problem addressed by the present research: how can post-accession compliance with the EU non-discrimination acquis be improved?[1] Political science literature on Europeanization, policy transfer, and diffusion is highly relevant in explaining why candidate countries adopt the EU acquis. These fields of study provide explanatory models for rule adoption and specify the conditions which have to be present in order for these models to be successful. The focus is thus on the transposition phase. The newest strand of Europeanization literature looks at the performance of new Member States a couple of years into their membership. This research has shown that new Member States continue to be quite effective in transposing EU law, including the acquis related to the protection from discrimination. However, when it comes to application and enforcement they have huge problems, resulting in an enormous gap between the at times very advanced legislation and practice.

The present research argues that the external incentives model, using a strategy of reinforcement by reward might best explain the likelihood of rule adoption but if the ultimate goal is that rules are applied and enforced, learning-based approaches have to be strengthened in the enlargement process. It further argues that reflexive governance offers ideas for what could be done in the pre-accession process to improve compliance after accession and thus to come out from what has been called by Falkner et al the 'world of dead letters'.[2]

The hypothesis is thus that a stronger focus and more consistent use of elements of reflexive governance has the potential to improve performance. This is not to

[1] The following is based on a revised, restructured, and updated version of Emma Lantschner, 'Reflexive Governance in the EU Enlargement Process' (2015) 98(2) Kritische Vierteljahresschrift für Gesetzgebung und Rechtswissenschaft 130.

[2] Falkner and Treib, 'Three Worlds of Compliance or Four? The EU-15 Compared to New Member States', *Journal of Common Market Studies* (2008), 46(2): 293; Gerda Falkner, Oliver Treib, and Elisabeth Holzleithner (eds), *Compliance in the Enlarged European Union: Living Rights or Dead Letters?* (Ashgate 2008).

Reflexive Governance in EU Equality Law. Emma Lantschner, Oxford University Press. © Emma Lantschner 2021.
DOI: 10.1093/oso/9780192843371.003.0003

say that better compliance *can be secured* by reliance on reflexive governance but, as Schuppert put it, those governance structures should be favoured that have *the potential* of coordinating the actions of self-interested actors so that their contributions are channelled to conflate eventually on the millwheel of the common good.[3]

After spelling out the problem statement in more detail, this chapter will place the concept of reflexive governance in context with Europeanization, policy transfer, and diffusion literature (2.2) to elaborate on the advances it makes vis-à-vis these studies with the concept of reflexive governance (2.3). It then elaborates on the appropriateness of this concept in the enlargement process (2.4) and with regard to the EU anti-discrimination regime (2.5). It goes on to empirically test the hypothesis using the example of Croatia (2.6) and then draws conclusions on how to further pursue the present research (2.7).

2.2 From External Incentives to Compliance: An Unfinished Road?

2.2.1 Explanatory Models of Rule Adoption in Europeanization, Policy Transfer, and Diffusion Literature: The Transposition Phase

The domestic impact of the EU on its Member States is regularly referred to as 'Europeanization'. One strand of this literature has focused on studying this impact on candidate countries. The research on the Europeanization of candidate countries and more recently of new Member States has rapidly grown over the past fifteen years. The main research question guiding studies on the Europeanization of candidate countries is 'under what conditions are the EU's attempts to influence candidate countries effective?'[4] The questions asked are thus, whether the EU has any domestic impact and by which factors this impact can be explained. Lacking empirical evidence for the application and enforcement phase, the focus of the research on Europeanization of candidate countries was initially on the transposition phase, the translation of EU law into domestic legislation.

Different explanatory models for rule adoption in the pre-accession phase have been elaborated, most authoritatively for instance by Schimmelfennig and Sedelmeier.[5] Their elaboration of a theoretical framework of analysis is

[3] Gunnar Folke Schuppert, 'Governance—auf der Such nach Konturen eines "anerkannt uneindeutigen Begriffs"' [2008] Politische Vierteljahresschrift 13, 32.

[4] Ulrich Sedelmeier, 'Europeanisation in New Member and Candidate States' (2011) 6(1) Living Reviews in European Governance <http://www.europeangovernance-livingreviews.org/Articles/lreg-2011-1/> 9.

[5] Frank Schimmelfennig and Ulrich Sedelmeier, 'Introduction: Conceptualizing the Europeanization of Central and Eastern Europe' in Frank Schimmelfennig and Ulrich Sedelmeier (eds), *The Europeanization of Central and Eastern Europe* (Cornell University Press 2005) 8–25.

representative for most of the literature on the Europeanization of candidate countries, which is situated within the debate between rational choice and constructivist/sociological neo-institutionalism in international relations and comparative politics.[6] Schimmelfennig and Sedelmeier distinguish between two dimensions. The first one asks whether the change is EU or domestically driven. The second considers the logic of action, which can be a logic of consequences, following thus a rational choice approach, or a logic of appropriateness of the constructivist approach. If a rule change is EU driven and follows a logic of consequences the explanatory model for rule adoption is labelled as the 'external incentives model'. If rule adoption is EU driven but follows the logic of appropriateness this results in 'social learning', where the government concerned adopts EU rules if it is persuaded of its appropriateness. Finally, if there is domestic discontent about a status quo and the rule change is thus home driven, this results in both institutionalist variants in 'lesson-drawing'. When it derives from a logic of consequences, simple learning takes place (changing means, not the ends), whereas when it is based on a logic of appropriateness, complex learning takes place (modification of underlying goals). In borderline cases, according to Schimmelfennig and Sedelmeier, the external incentives model can explain the rule adoption, but the lesson-drawing model explains the choice of specific rules.[7]

This can be the case when the EU rule is quite flexible and allows for different ways of adapting to it. In the typology of modes of governance in the policy field, established by Treib et al, this would be the field of framework regulation, which remains within the realm of binding law (eg in the form of directives) but offers states more leeway in implementation.[8] The EU Non-Discrimination Directives can serve as an example in this respect. For instance, the Directives call for the establishment of Equality Bodies without establishing binding rules on exact mandate, composition, and functioning.

Most of Europeanization literature seems to share the conclusion of Schimmelfennig and Sedelmeier that the external incentives model using conditionality as its main strategy and being based on a rationalist institutionalist approach is the dominant mechanism of the EU's domestic impact. In fact, these studies have found that 'the main rationale for adopting the acquis was the benefits of full EU membership rather than the intrinsic benefits of EU models in the various policy areas'.[9]

For the purpose of this research, it is relevant to recall the main conditions under which the external incentives model deploys its effectiveness.[10] The most

[6] Sedelmeier, 'Europeanisation in New Member and Candidate States' (n 4) 7.

[7] Schimmelfennig and Sedelmeier, 'Introduction: Conceptualizing the Europeanization of Central and Eastern Europe' (n 5) 21–22.

[8] Treib, Bähr, and Falkner, 'Modes of governance: towards a conceptual clarification', *Journal of European Public Policy* (2007), 14(1): 1.

[9] Sedelmeier, 'Europeanisation in New Member and Candidate States' (n 4) 6–7.

[10] For the following see Schimmelfennig and Sedelmeier, 'Introduction: Conceptualizing the Europeanization of Central and Eastern Europe' (n 5) 12–17.

important precondition for the success of this model is the credibility of the reward, that is, of EU membership. Credibility is important also in other respects. It is for instance relevant to look at whether a policy is consistently pushed forward by different EU institutions or whether there exist internal conflicts. Credibility is increased if the monitoring of a specific policy area is consistent and the legitimacy of the rule to be adopted is supported by parallel or additive conditionality stemming from other international organizations. The most relevant aspect of credibility is, however, that the EU is willing to *and* capable of paying the promised reward of membership. Connected to this sizeable reward (also size influences effectiveness) is the speed at which it comes about: a very distant (or even moving further) perspective of being paid the reward can have a negative impact on rule adoption. And finally, the adoption costs are another decisive factor influencing the success of the external incentives model: adoption costs must not be prohibitively high or endanger the power base of governing elites.

An in-depth study on the practical impact of conditionality on the elements of democracy and rule of law of the political Copenhagen criteria was carried out by Kochenov back in 2007 and regarded the fifth and sixth enlargement wave. His findings are also relevant for the present research. While he acknowledges the potential of conditionality to improve the way enlargements are negotiated, he found that it totally failed in the fields of democracy and the rule of law. Among the major drawbacks he identified were a '[c]omplete lack of clarity about the standards that candidate countries were expected to comply with', which made an assessment of pre-accession democracy and rule of law 'extremely difficult, if at all possible'; '[p]oor analysis quality provided by the Commission, including random choice of issues, unreliable conclusions, [and] numerous contradictions'; and a '[l]ack of clarity about the benchmarks to determine compliance', which led to a situation in which often no distinction was made between 'genuine reforms and legislative window-dressing'. Finally, he also found '[u]njustified differentiated treatment of the candidate countries at all stages of the pre-accession process'.[11] While the approach of the Commission in dealing with issues related to the core values of democracy, rule of law and fundamental rights has certainly improved in the current enlargement wave,[12] the criticism raised towards the consistency and transparency

[11] Dimitry Kochenov, *EU Enlargement and the Failure of Conditionality: Pre-Accession Conditionality in the Fields of Democracy and the Rule of Law* (Kluwer Law International 2008) 311; Dimitry Kochenov, 'The Aquis and Its Principles: The Enforcement of the "Law" versus the Enforcement of "Values" in the EU' in András Jakab and Dimitry Kochenov (eds), *The Enforcement of EU Law and Values: Ensuring Member States' Compliance* (OUP 2017) 15.

[12] Starting with the negotiation framework for Croatia of 2005, a new Chapter 23 has been introduced dealing with the judiciary and fundamental rights, as well as a new Chapter 24, dealing with justice, freedom, and security. It was only with the enlargement strategy 2011, however, that the Commission decided to open these chapters at the very beginning of negotiations and to keep them open until the end, which has become known as the 'fundamentals first' approach. With the enlargement strategy of 2006, the concept of benchmarks has been introduced. On the criticism raised towards the application of this concept see 2.6.3.1. In February 2020, the Commission announced a revised methodology, which is supposed to make accession negotiations more credible, more predictable, more dynamic, and

of monitoring, at least in parts, still holds true, as will be shown in the case study below on Croatia (see in particular 2.6.3.1). In more general terms and for the still ongoing enlargement, Bieber also vigorously calls for 'internal clarity and consistency', in addition to broad societal and elite support as well as committed governments, as conditions to overcome what he calls 'formal Europeanisation that is undermined by simultaneous de-Europeanisation'.[13]

In terms of explanatory models for rule adoption, social learning and lesson-drawing are considered by Europeanization literature as complementary to the external incentives model.[14] Social learning is more likely to take place in situations where rules and processes through which they are established and transferred enjoy a high level of legitimacy; when there is a high level of identification of the target government and/or society and the community which has set up the rules; and where there is domestic resonance, either because of a lack of domestic rules on the issue or dissatisfaction with their functioning.[15] While ideally these conditions exist both with regard to the governing elite in a country and societal groups and organizations, it could also be that only the latter are persuaded about the appropriateness of the EU legal norm. In such cases it will be important for the EU to empower these actors domestically.

Policy transfer[16] and diffusion literature[17] share with Europeanization literature the concern for how 'knowledge about policies, administrative arrangements,

guided by a stronger political steer. This includes, amongst other things, to better define the conditions set for candidates to progress, as these conditions must be objective, precise, detailed, strict, and verifiable. European Commission, 'Enhancing the Accession Process—A Credible EU Perspective for the Western Balkans' (5 February 2020) COM(2020) 57 final. The formal inclusion of values in the Treaty text 'could be characterized as one of the key legacies of EU enlargements in the field of EU constitutionalism'. Kochenov, 'The Aquis and Its Principles: The Enforcement of the "Law" versus the Enforcement of "Values" in the EU' (n 11) 15–16, referring to Wojciech Sadurski, *Constitutionalism and Enlargement of Europe* (OUP 2012).

[13] Florian Bieber, 'Conclusion: Rethinking Europeanisation' in Jelena Dzankic, Keil Soeren, and Marko Kmezić (eds), *The Europeanisation of the Western Balkans: A Failure of EU Conditionality?* (Palgrave Macmillan 2019) 240.

[14] See for instance Judith Kelley, 'International Actors on the Domestic Scene: Membership Conditionality and Socialization by International Institutions' (2004) 58(3) International Organization 425, 257, who argued, for instance, that 'conditionality motivated most behavior changes, but that socialization-based efforts often guided them'.

[15] Schimmelfennig and Sedelmeier, 'Introduction: Conceptualizing the Europeanization of Central and Eastern Europe' (n 5) 18–22, referring inter alia to Jeffery T Checkel, 'Why Comply? Social Learning and European Identity Change' (2001) 55(3) International Organization 553 <http://www.jstor.org/stable/pdfplus/3078657.pdf?acceptTC=true> 562–63.

[16] David P Dolowitz and David Marsh, 'Who Learns What from Whom? A Review of the Policy Transfer Literature' (1996) 44(2) Political Studies 343; David P Dolowitz and David Marsh, 'Learning from Abroad: The Role of Policy Transfer in Contemporary Policy-Making' (2000) 13(1) Governance 5; Richard Rose, *Learning From Comparative Public Policy: A Practical Guide* (Routledge 2005); Russell Prince, 'Policy Transfer as Policy Assemblage: Making Policy for the Creative Industries in New Zealand' (2010) 42(1) Environment and Planning A 169; David Benson and Andrew Jordan, 'What Have We Learned from Policy Transfer Research? Dolowitz and Marsh Revisited' (2011) 9(3) Political Studies Review 366.

[17] Tanja Börzel and Thomas Risse, 'From Europeanisation to Diffusion: Introduction' (2012) 35(1) West European Politics 1.

Table 2.1: Explanatory models of rule adoption in Europeanization (E), policy transfer (P), and diffusion (D) literature

	Logic of consequences	**Logic of appropriateness**	**Logic of arguing**
EU driven/direct	E: External incentives P: Conditionality D: Legal coercion D: Manipulation on utility calculations (pos/neg incentives, capacity building)	E: Social learning D: Socialization by normative pressure	D: Persuasion through reason giving
Domestically driven/indirect	E: Lesson-drawing P: Lesson-drawing (perfect, bounded rationality) P: Voluntary transfer driven by perceived necessity D: Lesson-drawing D: Competition	E: Lesson-drawing D: Mimicry	

institutions and ideas in one political setting (past or present) is used in the development of policies, administrative arrangements, institutions and ideas in another political setting'.[18] They are all quite similar in classifying explanatory models for rule change within their field of study, no matter the diversity of terms used to describe these phenomena. As shown in Table 2.1, it is possible to classify the different explanatory models distinguishing between logics of action on the one hand (with diffusion studies adding the logic of arguing[19]) and the directly EU driven or domestically driven pathways on the other. The three strands of literature slightly differ in the definition of scope conditions which are expected to lead to a successful transfer of norms and ideas.[20] While learning is a central element of all three strands, none of them, however, goes really deep in trying to understand how this learning comes about, or how the conditions for the learning operation could

[18] Dolowitz and Marsh, 'Learning from Abroad: The Role of Policy Transfer in Contemporary Policy-Making' (n 16) 5.

[19] Within a logic of arguing, 'actors try to persuade each other about the validity claims inherent in any causal or normative statement'. Börzel and Risse (n 17) 8; see also Thomas Risse, '"Let's Argue!" Communicative Action in World Politics' (2000) 54(1) International Organization 1, 2–7.

[20] For a discussion of these differences see Lantschner, 'Reflexive Governance in the EU Enlargement Process' (n 1).

be expanded such that its effectiveness as normative process is ensured. As will be shown, this is the contribution of reflexive governance approaches.

2.2.2 About Compliance in New Member States

By finding that the external incentives model best explains the likelihood of rule adoption the respective literature does not mean to claim that it is also the best to ensure application and enforcement. Rational cost-benefit calculations about accession which are typical for a rational-choice institutionalist approach 'may inform legal changes in candidate countries, but this does not necessarily mean that legal changes are underpinned by successful socialization into European norms or indeed will promote such a normative and behavioural change'.[21] Schimmelfennig and Sedelmeier have indeed found that '[r]ules that are transferred through social learning or lesson-drawing are much less contested domestically. Implementation is more likely to result in behavioural rule adoption and sustained compliance, while external incentives primarily privilege formal rule adoption as the least costly form of rule adoption.'[22]

This assessment was made at a point in time when ten[23] Central and Eastern European (CEE) countries had just acceded to the Union. It is thus interesting to look into empirical findings of the performance of new Member States a couple of years into their membership in order to establish the success of the external incentives model, both in terms of continued transposition but primarily also in terms of application and enforcement. This is indeed what the newest strand of Europeanization literature does. It conceives the research on Europeanization of new Member States not simply as part of Europeanization of Member States[24] but

[21] Gwendolyn Sasse, 'The Politics of EU Conditionality: The Norm of Minority Protection During and Beyond EU Accession' (2008) 15(6) Journal of European Public Policy 842, 856.

[22] Frank Schimmelfennig and Ulrich Sedelmeier, 'Governance by Conditionality: EU Rule Transfer to the Candidate Countries of Central and Eastern Europe' (2004) 11(4) Journal of European Public Policy 661, 674.

[23] The ten countries which acceded to the EU in 2004 were the Czech Republic, Cyprus, Hungary, Estonia, Latvia, Lithuania, Malta, Poland, Slovakia, and Slovenia.

[24] On compliance studies in the context of Member States see, for instance, Tanja Börzel and others, 'Obstinate and Inefficient: Why Member States Do Not Comply with European Law' (2010) 43(11) Comparative Political Studies 1363; Oliver Treib, 'Implementing and Complying with EU Governance Outputs' (2014) 9(1) Living Reviews in European Governance 1. From his review of academic literature in the field, Treib has derived the conclusion that literature has thus far 'focused heavily on transposition of EU directives, while comparatively little is known about issues of enforcement and application of both directives and regulations' and that 'more energy needs to be devoted to systematic research on the phase of practical implementation'. More in general on compliance, see Checkel, 'Why Comply? Social Learning and European Identity Change' (n 15); Harold Hongju Koh, 'Why do Nations Obey International Law' (1997) 106 The Yale Law Journal 2599; Thomas Risse, Stephen C. Ropp and Kathryn Sikkink (eds), The Persistent Power of Human Rights: From Commitment to Compliance (Cambridge University Press 2013); and Malte Brosig, 'No Space for Constructivism? A Critical Appraisal of European Compliance Research' (2012) 13(4) Perspectives on European Politics and Society 390.

as a continuation of Europeanization of candidate countries. As such it tries to establish how sustainable the EU's pre-accession endeavours are.[25]

Parts of this literature are more concerned about continued transposition performance or with the question, whether states have dismantled institutional change carried out in the pre-accession phase, both as a reaction to the changed incentive structure after accession. Sedelmeier has found, for instance, that 'continuity in government partisan preferences or the presence of veto players can lock in conditionality-induced institutional change after accession'. If, however, there is a change in government orientation and if there are no veto players, such institutional change can also be reversed.[26] At the same time, he points out that such a direct and open dismantlement of institutional change might not even be necessary. States which follow a 'more cost-efficient strategy' decouple their 'institutional practice and formal rules'.[27] In other words the institutional change remains formally in place but application and enforcement is deficient.

In this context, an insightful study in the non-discrimination field has been carried out by Falkner and Treib. Going beyond the transposition phase, they also evaluate enforcement and application of, inter alia, two Equality Directives in Hungary, Slovenia, Slovakia, and the Czech Republic. They found that the transposition record of these four countries was 'considerably better than that of the EU-15' and that transposition efforts did not significantly decrease after accession. In fact, they tentatively concluded that new Member States 'even perform systematically better than old ones'.[28] However, when it comes to the application and enforcement of EU directives, all countries analysed have huge problems which results in an enormous gap between the at times very advanced legislation and what happens in practice.[29] In their quadripartite categorization of 'worlds of compliance', the authors have classified this group of countries into the 'world of dead letters'.[30] This world is characterized by rather good transposition into domestic laws (which can be marked by political battles between parties and interest groups), 'but

[25] Sedelmeier, 'Europeanisation in New Member and Candidate States' (n 4) 6; Börzel and Risse (n 17).

[26] Ulrich Sedelmeier, 'Is Europeanisation through Conditionality Sustainable? Lock-in of Institutional Change after EU Accession' (2012) 35(1) West European Politics 20, 34.

[27] ibid 23.

[28] Falkner and Treib (n 2) 303 and 307. Sedelmeier reaches the same conclusion in Sedelmeier, 'Is Europeanisation through Conditionality Sustainable? Lock-in of Institutional Change after EU Accession' (n 26) 23–24.

[29] Falkner and Treib (n 2) 303.

[30] The other worlds are: 1) the world of law observance (compliance goal typically overrides domestic concerns, well considered and adapted laws, application and enforcement typically successful, non-compliance rare, remedied fairly quickly); 2) the world of domestic politics (obeying EU rules is at best one goal among many, main obstacle to compliance is political resistance at transposition stage, once transposed, implementation and enforcement not problematic, as administration and judiciary function well); 3) the world of transposition neglect (compliance with EU law is not a goal in itself, administrative inefficiency, inactivity, negligence is characteristic at the transposition stage, not at the implementation stage).

then these countries lack proper institutions and processes for turning these laws into action.'[31]

For the purpose of this research, three things need to be highlighted. Conditionality and the external incentives model do indeed seem to be effective in the transposition phase. It even seems that candidate countries have internalized the adaptation pressure and continue with transposition after accession at a level which bears comparison with old Member States or might even go beyond them. The lack of application and enforcement is, however, alarming and consideration must be given to how this shortcoming of the external incentives model can be overcome. Sedelmeier hypothesized that the lack of enforcement could be an unintended consequence of the application of pre-accession conditionality. He reasons that although the EU institutions have continuously emphasized the need for the appropriate administrative and judicial structures for the correct application and enforcement of EU legislation, pre-accession conditionality might have placed too much focus on fast and correct legal transposition, as this is easier to monitor.[32] One could therefore ask whether a stronger focus on social learning and lesson-drawing would improve this situation and if so, how this could be achieved in the pre-accession period and what could be done in the post-accession period.

Second, Falkner and Treib have found that the 'world of dead letters' is not only composed of new Member States but old Member States also fall within this category. It can thus be presumed that whatever the lessons learned from an enhancement of the learning process for candidate countries are, can be fruitfully used by and applied to old Member States as well.

The third set of considerations that requires highlighting is connected to the explanations offered by the authors for the implementation gap in the non-discrimination field. One problem was the lack of litigation from below, which accounts on one hand for a lack of knowledge among the potential victims of discriminations of their rights and on the other hand for a lack of litigation culture among citizens of formerly socialist countries. Connected to that, the authors also found that court proceedings are rather lengthy in some of the countries which can also be a deterrent for a victim of discrimination to go to court. A second problem was detected in the lack of support by civil society actors. In fact, the procedures for involving organizations with a legitimate interest in ensuring the compliance to the Equality Directives in judicial or administrative proceedings (as provided by the Equality Directives) have remained 'at a rather minimalist level in most countries'.[33] A third reason for the enforcement gap was found in the so far rather toothless Equality Bodies, which often struggle with a lack of visibility, institutional standing, and resources. Finally, the authors have found that labour inspectorates

[31] Falkner and Treib (n 2) 310; see also Falkner, Treib, and Holzleithner (eds) (n 2).
[32] Sedelmeier, 'Europeanisation in New Member and Candidate States' (n 4) 27.
[33] Falkner and Treib (n 2) 305.

often place too little attention on equality issues. Inspectors often also lack the expertise in this field of law.[34] Section 2.5 will assess how these problems could be addressed by resorting to reflexive governance approaches.

2.3 How to Complete the Road: Reflexive Governance?

To summarize what has been said so far before introducing the hypothesis for how the identified challenges could be met: It is acknowledged that the external incentives model based on a conditionality strategy is the dominant mechanism explaining rule adoption. A look into application and enforcement in the field of non-discrimination shows however, that there is a huge gap between the law in the books and in practice. If it is true that rules that have been adopted on the basis of social learning and lesson-drawing suffer less from domestic contestation at the application level, it is only logical to ask whether there is room for more such learning in the enlargement process and how this learning can be organized so as to be successful.

The reason why it makes sense to shift the focus from the rationalist to the constructivist perspective lies not only in the fact that it is assumed that enforcement results are somewhat better[35] but also in the fact that the most important condition for the external incentives model to be successful seems to have lost force in the context of the enlargement to the Western Balkans and Turkey: the credibility of the membership award.[36] It is therefore useful to think of ways in which the enlargement process could be reconsidered with not only successful transposition but also compliance in mind as its ultimate goal.

It is appropriate here to introduce the idea of *reflexive governance*. This can be understood as a model of governance that

[34] ibid 304–06.

[35] See Schimmelfennig and Sedelmeier, 'Governance by Conditionality: EU Rule Transfer to the Candidate Countries of Central and Eastern Europe' (n 22) 674. In the context of this research this proposition will be empirically tested with regard to the non-discrimination acquis compliance in Croatia (see 2.6).

[36] David Phinnemore, 'Beyond 25—The Changing Face of EU Enlargement: Commitment, Conditionality and the Constitutional Treaty' (2006) 8(1) Journal of Southern Europe and the Balkans 7, 8; Sedelmeier, 'Europeanisation in New Member and Candidate States' (n 4) 31. When he first took office, the previous president of the European Commission Jean-Claude Juncker made it clear that he intended to freeze EU enlargement during his term, ie at least until 2019. The Western Balkans strategy of early 2018 has set 2025 as the date from which the EU could possibly embrace new members, giving a new impulse to the credibility of the enlargement process. See European Commission, 'A Credible Enlargement Perspective for an Enhanced EU Engagement with the Western Balkans' (6 February 2018) COM(2018) 65 final. The current Commission published a revised methodology in March 2020, emphasizing again the credibility of the membership perspective. See European Commission, 'Enhancing the Accession Process—A Credible EU Perspective for the Western Balkans' (n 12). A positive development was in any case the 2020 Council decision to open negotiations with North Macedonia and Albania.

> involves the establishment of institutions and processes which facilitate the actors within a domain for learning not only about policy options, but also about their own interests and preferences.[37]

Lenoble and Maesschalck present a continuum of four approaches to reflexive governance, which continuously expand the conditions for the success of the learning operations such that, from the point of view of expectations of actors involved, their effectiveness as normative processes is ensured.[38]

The starting point is the neo-institutionalist economic approach. The next step is the collaborative-relational approach, which has been alluded to by diffusion studies by reference to the logic of arguing. The two pragmatist approaches, one best represented by Sabel, Dorf, and Zeitlin (experimentalist governance)[39] and one represented by Schön and Argyris[40] further expand the conditions for the success of the learning operation. The maximum of expansion is reached by the concept of a genetic approach to reflexive governance developed within the Centre for Philosophy of Law at the Université catholique de Louvain, in particular by Lenoble and Maesschalck.[41] Each of these approaches has a different conception of reflexivity. They all share the learning imperative but differ in the way they conceive the conditions for success of a learning operation. In this respect 'they lie on a continuum. [They] reflect increasingly expansive conceptions of the conditions that must be satisfied to ensure the success of the learning operation.'[42]

After discussing the different approaches of reflexive governance in more detail, it should be possible to answer the question, whether these theoretical thoughts about how learning can be improved can be used in the enlargement process in the context of the non-discrimination field.

What sets the *neo-institutionalist approach* apart from the other three approaches is the fact that learning (in other words: change) is triggered by an external incentive (externalist conception of learning and governance). New solutions can be generated only through an outside incentive. Any expansion of behaviour does not emerge from a learning operation but from an external factor.[43] The external incentives

[37] Jacques Lenoble and Marc Maesschalck, 'Renewing the Theory of Public Interest: The Quest for a Reflexive and Learning-based Approach to Governance' in Olivier de Schutter and Jacques Lenoble (eds), *Reflexive Governance: Redefining the Public Interest in a Pluralistic World* (Hart Publishing 2010), quoting Scott, 'How Reflexive is the Governance of Regulation?', paper presented at the annual meeting of the Law and Society Association, Berlin, 2007.

[38] ibid 7.

[39] Michael C Dorf and Charles F Sabel, 'A Constitution of Democratic Experimentalism' (1998) 98(2) Columbia Law Review 267; Charles F Sabel and Jonathan Zeitlin (eds), *Experimentalist Governance in the European Union: Towards a New Architecture* (OUP 2010).

[40] Chris Argyris and Donald Schön, *Theory in Practice: Increasing Professinal Effectiveness* (Jossey Bass 1974); Chris Argyris and Donald Schön, *Organisational Learning: A Theory of Action Perspective* (Addison Wesley 1978); Chris Argyris, *Knowledge for Action. A Guide to Overcoming Barriers to Organizational Change* (Jossey Bass 1993).

[41] Jacques Lenoble and Marc Maesschalck, *Democracy, Law and Governance* (Ashgate 2010).

[42] Lenoble and Maesschalck, 'Renewing the Theory of Public Interest' (n 37) 7.

[43] ibid 11–12.

model in Europeanization studies and its analogues in policy transfer and diffusion studies follow this logic. The following approaches to reflexive governance sharpen the lesson-drawing and social learning variants of explanation on the issue of the 'organization of the learning operation with respect to decentralized interaction'. They share a commitment to 'internalizing' the conditions for the success of the learning operation.[44]

The *collaborative-relational (deliberative) approach* is based on Habermas' theory of communicative action.[45] Learning is the result of the organization of a dialogue between various actors, who have to provide good arguments for their positions and who have to engage with the viewpoints of the other participants. The widest possible range of views should be heard and the consensus reached between the actors involved should be based on rational arguments. According to this approach, it is necessary to act on the organization of decentralized interaction. The problems related to this participatory and deliberative reflexive approach appear to be first, that there exists a lack of trust in relation to these processes and second, that actors' capacities might need to be reinforced. The focus here, different to the following reflexive approaches, is on the strengthening of capacities for argumentation. This implies that actors must have or be able to acquire the relevant knowledge and understanding to engage in argumentation and the development of methods of debate.[46]

Whereas this is how far the deliberative approach goes for Lenoble and Maesschalck, Risse conceives it as a 'truth-seeking discourse', in which actors 'must be prepared to change their own views of the world, their interests, and sometimes even their identities'.[47] This goes already in the direction of one of the two versions of the *pragmatist approach*. They are pragmatist in the sense that they 'posit that true learning can only occur by a revision of the very presuppositions that guide us in action, and those we fall back upon and make explicit when we have to defend our choices against external critiques'.[48]

Sabel's theory underlines the necessity to organize the negotiation in an *experimentalist* manner. This means that

[44] ibid 13.

[45] Jürgen Habermas, *Theorie des kommunikativen Handelns* (Suhrkamp 1982).

[46] Lenoble and Maesschalck, 'Renewing the Theory of Public Interest' (n 37) 14–15.

[47] Risse (n 19) 2. For Risse, in addition to social constructivism and rational choice there is a third logic of action: argumentative rationality. This is reflected in Table 2.1. See Risse (n 19) 2–7.

[48] Olivier de Schutter and Jacques Lenoble, 'Introduction: Institutions Equipped to Learn' in Olivier de Schutter and Jacques Lenoble (eds), *Reflexive Governance: Redefining the Public Interest in a Pluralistic World* (Hart Publishing 2010) xvii–xix. According to de Schutter and Lenoble they are pragmatic also because they accept 'that innovation ... can only emerge from actors' engagement with concrete controversies. Learning is therefore not a theoretical enterprise, and it is not an abstract calculation of the pros and the cons of different scenarios. It is necessarily embedded: linked to problem-solving in specific settings.... And finally, they acknowledge the open-ended nature of the inquiry: ... "New solutions tend to generate new problems." ... In that sense, learning is a continuous process ...'.

> actors must be engaged in a process of joint inquiry in order to 'allow themselves' to be taught by the results of an experimental encounter between existing solutions and new problems requiring solution.... This 'expansion' of the conditions for success of the learning operation is reflected ... in the requirement that three new conditions be fulfilled in building systems of governance: co-design (and thus collaboration among those who define policy and those responsible for implementing it), benchmarking and monitoring.[49]

Experimentalist governance is a recursive process in which framework goals/rules are defined by a combination of central and local units, the target countries implement them as they best see fit taking their local circumstances into consideration, agree to report on their performance, undergo peer review, share their knowledge with others, and exchange good practices which ends up in a re-evaluation and, if necessary, reformulation of the framework rule.[50] Experimentalist governance can thus be described as decentralized problem solving combined with the pooling of results.[51] For de Búrca, the two most crucial features for an experimentalist governance system to succeed in addressing a problem are first, 'the broadest degree of stakeholder participation compatible with effective decision-making', and second, 'effective and informed monitoring'.[52] In the EU context, for both these features a triangle of actors, composed of EU institutions, state institutions, and other stakeholders, including civil society organizations, has to be considered. The strong focus on participation and cooperation moves this governance model away from a classical top-down or principal–agent approach towards an equal partnership and a forward-looking or dynamic accountability.[53] It clearly resonates also with Fredman's participative dimension of equality which 'requires decision-makers to hear and respond to the voices of groups sharing a protected characteristic rather than imposing top-down decisions' and requires the state to ensure that 'those affected have the capacity to participate meaningfully'.[54]

The second version of the *pragmatist approach* (Schön and Argyris) has revealed the weakness within the first version consisting in this approach obscuring that the actors' spontaneous capabilities may not suffice. It is thus more radical in the enhancement of actors' capacities. It highlights defensive strategies which prevent actors from forming appropriate representations of new problems and finding solutions (repetition compulsion). From this it follows that organized reflexivity, in

[49] Lenoble and Maesschalck, 'Renewing the Theory of Public Interest' (n 37) 16.

[50] Charles F Sabel and Jonathan Zeitlin, 'Experimentalism in Transnational Governance: Emergent Pathways and Diffusion Mechanisms: Paper presented at the panel on "Global Governance in Transition", annual conference of the International Studies Association' (Montreal, 16 March 2011) 1.

[51] de Schutter and Lenoble, 'Introduction: Institutions Equipped to Learn' (n 48) xviii.

[52] Gráinne de Búrca, 'New Governance and Experimentalism: An Introduction' [2010] Wisconsin Law Review 227 <http://wisconsinlawreview.org/wp-content/files/De-Burca-Final.pdf> 235.

[53] For more on this, see 2.4.

[54] Sandra Fredman, 'Emerging from the Shadows: Substantive Equality and Article 14 of the European Convention on Human Rights' Human Rights Law Review (2016), 16(2): 273.

the sense of actors returning over their pre-existing frames, is necessary. In the view of these pragmatist authors, an incentive suffices in order to start this reflexive process. However, it is questionable whether the capacity to transform one's frames can be taken for granted.[55]

This then is the contribution of the *genetic approach*. It asks

> how the actors involved in collective action and problem-solving can be supported in operating a revision of the assumptions guiding both their description of the problem, and their choice of solutions. It posits that such revision can be triggered by requesting from these actors both an exercise in reconstruction and an exercise in political imagination.[56]

The reconstruction exercise takes account of the understanding that our past experiences and the social norms we have internalized shape our desires and expectations. It further acknowledges the psychological tendency to adjust one's preferences to one's situation. The genetic approach aims at creating the background conditions to support the actors in questioning these preferences 'by an explicit examination of their genesis', and in questioning the role each actor seeks to play for himself. The term 'genetic' is intended to take account of two factors: 'on one hand, the set of conditions for production (that is, engenderment) of actors' capacity to carry out the "reflexive" return required for the success of the learning operation; and on the other hand, the setting up of institutional conditions likely to guarantee effective implementation of the actors' commitments'.[57]

This approach is similar to the capabilities approach of Sen and Nussbaum[58] in that it emphasizes the need to ensure that actors are equipped with the resources required to effectively participate in collective action and in that it acknowledges that the ability of actors to use these resources varies depending on their specific situation. It differs from the capabilities approach in that it postulates that 'what actors need is not just to be equipped with the required capabilities: they must be prepared to question their very representation of their role and, ultimately, of their identity'.[59] They must be ready to understand that it is not only their past knowledge which is inadequate but their past positioning.[60]

Directed into the future, political imagination implies that actors accept to 'get rid of institutional fetishism' and instead are open to political imagination as 'it is unrealistic to expect that all problems can be solved appropriately within

[55] Lenoble and Maesschalck, 'Renewing the Theory of Public Interest' (n 37) 16–19.

[56] de Schutter and Lenoble, 'Introduction: Institutions Equipped to Learn' (n 48) xix.

[57] Lenoble and Maesschalck, 'Renewing the Theory of Public Interest' (n 37) 10.

[58] Amartya Sen, *Commodities and Capabilities* (North Holland 1985); Martha Nussbaum, *Women and Human Development. The Capabilities Approach* (CUP 2000).

[59] de Schutter and Lenoble, 'Introduction: Institutions Equipped to Learn' (n 48) xxi.

[60] ibid.

institutions as they are given'.[61] The genetic approach thus suggests that learning-based theories of governance are 'complemented by an approach focused on the capacities of the actors'.[62]

Common to these approaches is the reflexivity. The conception of it varies in that they show a

> growing recognition of the need to progressively expand the conditions to be put in place to ensure the success of the reflexive operation. [The four currents] are complementary and reflect an increasingly acute understanding of the precise nature of the conditions required for the success of this operation.[63]

From this introduction to the idea of reflexive governance it becomes clear that it is based on the concepts of lesson-drawing and social learning and develops them further regarding the question of how this learning process should be organized in order to ensure the success of the learning operation. From the action theoretic perspective, it is situated within a logic of appropriateness and a logic of arguing. The epistemological position taken, especially of the pragmatist and the genetic approaches, is clearly one of interpretivism/constructivism,[64] in that it is emphasized that our understanding and/or explanation of phenomena that we observe and problems that arise as well as how we react to them is determined by the interpretation we give to these phenomena and problems on the basis of mental concepts or models deriving from our past experiences and the social norms we have internalized.

Reflexive governance is in line with Antje Wiener's theory of contestation,[65] which she herself qualifies as a 'reflexive approach'.[66] In fact, the theory of contestation starts from the assumption that norms 'are contested by default [as] their meanings evolve through interaction in context'.[67] It thus posits that the understanding of a norm is dependent on its 'meaning in use'. In other words, the interpretation and application given to a norm in a specific social context is decisive for its meaning. This meaning in use can evolve over time, as the norm has to be

[61] ibid xix–xxi; Olivier de Schutter, 'A New Direction for the Fundamental Rights Policy of the EU' (2010) Working paper series: REFGOV-FR-33, 2; Olivier de Schutter, 'The New Architecture of Fundamental Rights Policy in the EU' [2011] European Yearbook on Human Rights 107.

[62] de Schutter and Lenoble, 'Introduction: Institutions Equipped to Learn' (n 48) xix–xxi.

[63] Lenoble and Maesschalck, 'Renewing the Theory of Public Interest' (n 37) 5.

[64] See Jonathon Moses and Torbjørn Knutsen, *Ways of Knowing: Competing Methodologies in Social and Political Research* (Palgrave Macmillan 2012).

[65] Antje Wiener, *A Theory of Contestation,* (Springer 2014). See also Antje Wiener, 'The Dual Quality of Norms and Governance beyond the State: Sociological and Normative Approaches to 'Interaction'' (2007) 10(1) Critical Review of International Social and Political Philosophy 47; Antje Wiener, *The Invisible Constitution of Politics: Contested Norms and International Encounters* (CUP 2012).

[66] Antje Wiener, 'Contested Compliance: Interventions on the Normative Structure of World Politics' (2004) 10(2) European Journal of International Relations 189, 200.

[67] Antje Wiener, 'Making Normative Meaning Accountable in International Politics' [2007] WZB Discussion Papers, 4.

applied to changing circumstances. It further depends on the cultural context in which the norm is set and on the individual experience of the persons putting a norm into practice.[68] The references to the cultural context and individual experience are well reflected also in the just described reflexive governance approaches—which have thus to be situated within sociological neo-institutionalism—and are relevant in the enlargement context.

In fact, in a transnational context like the EU, where different legal cultures and traditions come together, norm contestation can be more pronounced than in purely domestic contexts. The different approaches to reflexive governance take account of such circumstances in various ways: the collaborative-relational and the experimentalist approaches put emphasis on deliberative, argumentative, and experimentalist processes, during which diverging approaches and understandings can be detected and ways to deal with these found. Contestation understood as 'allow[ing] citizens to critically engage with the norms that govern them'[69] coincides with the experimentalist approach that seeks the broadest stakeholder involvement compatible with efficient decision making.[70] Access to regular contestation (as opposed to ad hoc contestation) has been seen as 'key condition to enhance legitimacy in global governance'.[71]

The pragmatist approach as well as the genetic approach on the other hand called into question the internalized norms and behaviours of a specific legal culture, asking whether the problems to be solved can be appropriately addressed by sticking to established institutions and norms. Reflexive approaches, including the theory of contestedness, thus require the actors involved to think out of the box.

2.4 Reflexive Governance and Enlargement

Europeanization, policy transfer, and diffusion studies are highly relevant in explaining *why* rules are adopted. The contribution of reflexive governance is to offer ideas for *how* the current performance in the enlargement process *could be improved* to come out from the 'world of dead letters'.[72] The tools it offers can be divided into procedural and psychological. Collaborative-relational ideas and the experimentalist governance approach have their strength (although not

[68] Sonja Schirmbeck, 'Normerosion: Zur Schwächung von Tabus in den internationalen Beziehungen. Nukleares Tabu und Folterverbot' (Dissertation, Johann Wolfgang Goethe Universität Frankfurt 2013) 80.

[69] Antje Wiener, 'A Theory of Contestation—A Concise Summary of Its Argument and Concepts' (2017) 49(1) Polity 109, 112.

[70] de Búrca, 'New Governance and Experimentalism: An Introduction' (n 52) 235.

[71] Wiener, 'A Theory of Contestation—A Concise Summary of Its Argument and Concepts' (n 69) 114–15.

[72] Falkner and Treib (n 2); Falkner, Treib, and Holzleithner (eds) (n 2).

exclusively) in the former, while the pragmatist approach of Schön and Argyris as well as the genetic approach concentrate on the latter.

Sticking to the example of transposing EU (eg Equality) Directives into domestic law, the procedural side highlights the importance of effective participation of all stakeholders in deliberation about how they are translated into national legislation. In fact, in experimentalist thinking, agenda-setting and problem-solving are opened to a wide range of actors, particularly from civil society. '[T]he broadest possible degree of stakeholder participation compatible with effective decision-making' has been identified as one of the most important factors for an experimentalist governance system to succeed.[73] The procedural side of reflexive governance also addresses the scope condition of empowerment of domestic actors highlighted by both Europeanization and diffusion studies. Indeed, 'effective participation' in the sense of the collaborative-relational approach implies a transparent negotiation process and a public information campaign providing all stakeholders with the necessary knowledge to participate in argumentation and thus avoiding information asymmetries between the government and civil society actors. The procedural side thus not only enhances the ownership of the process but also addresses problems of 'uninformed, incomplete or inappropriate transfer', identified by policy transfer literature as impediments for the success of learning from abroad.[74] In fact, the risks connected to a lack of information about the policy to be transferred, how it operates, what its crucial elements for success are and what kind of socio-economic, political, and ideological context it presupposes can be reduced if a government engages in the first place in finding and providing extensive information about it and is ready to involve a wide spectrum of partners from civil society in the reflections of how to approach a new uncertainty arising from the need to adapt to the EU acquis. As will be seen below in the case study, the Commission is paying increasing attention to the establishment of structures and procedures of stakeholder involvement in decision making. It can thus exert pressure on candidate countries to organize such national consultations or be proactive in empowering relevant stakeholders. In this context, the financing priorities of the Commission are of great relevance.

Of further importance is the technical assistance provided in the framework of TAIEX and Twinning projects. The idea of these project lines is to bring together experts from Member States' administrations with experts from candidate countries' administrations with the aim of supporting the latter in their institutional adaptations and capacity building in a specific policy field. The success of this endeavour will depend, inter alia, on the approach of those involved: a twinning adviser could perceive his/her role as 'teacher' and simply provide an input by

[73] de Búrca, 'New Governance and Experimentalism: An Introduction' (n 52) 235.

[74] Dolowitz and Marsh, 'Learning from Abroad: The Role of Policy Transfer in Contemporary Policy-Making' (n 16) 17.

presenting a solution to a specific policy problem considered as good practice in their own Member State. Or he/she understands his/her role as facilitator who, on a par with the counterparts from the candidate country, reflects on the most suitable solution for the specific context and is ready to 'learn something from the everyday work on the reforms in a candidate country'.[75] Through such projects, the counterparts in the receiving countries may be supported in redefining the perception of their role, in reconsidering the ways in which they have approached the issue so far (both in terms of description of the problem and the kind of solutions accepted), and in political imagination. The example of twinning projects is thus not only a playground for testing collaborative-relational and experimentalist approaches but also the strand of reflexive governance focusing more on psychological aspects.

Learning from good practice already at work elsewhere, be it in legislative processes or capacity-building endeavours such as twinning, does not necessarily make the exercise one of experimentalist governance. For that there needs to be some sort of recurrence of the process. In the framework of current EU enlargement design one element in this recursive process consists of the monitoring by the Commission and peer reviews. In fact, according to de Búrca without 'effective and informed monitoring' an experimentalist system will fail to address the problem.[76] Peer reviews, similar to the twinning projects, are thought to provide an opportunity for exchange of experience between experts from Member States and experts from candidate countries. Peer review reports contain an assessment of the state of implementation in a specific policy field and a set of recommendations which need to be translated by the beneficiary administration into specific action plans. The results of this peer review process also then feed into the regular monitoring of the Commission. The idea behind the peer reviews is one of horizontal transfer of knowledge.[77] A closer look into empirical practice would reveal whether this approach could be strengthened.

Another way to enhance the mutual learning and experimentalism and thus reflexivity in the current enlargement round would be to provide for possibilities for countries of the Western Balkans to confront themselves over specific policy issues. Böhmelt and Freyburg have found, for instance, that spatial interlinkages have some relevance in explaining variance in the compliance with the EU accession criteria. As a result of their research, they suggest that the EU might want to pay 'more attention to trans- and intergovernmental cooperation and exchange in policy-specific networks that bring together candidate countries with varying

[75] Elsa Tulmets, 'Experimentalist Governance in EU External Relations: Enlargement and the European Neighbourhood Policy' in Charles F Sabel and Jonathan Zeitlin (eds), *Experimentalist Governance in the European Union: Towards a New Architecture* (OUP 2010) 310.

[76] de Búrca, 'New Governance and Experimentalism: An Introduction' (n 52) 235.

[77] Vitalis Nakrošis, 'Policy Transfer in the Pre- and Post-Accession Period: Experience of the New EU Member States' [2004] Lithuanian Political Science Yearbook 113, 122–23.

levels of compliance'.[78] A step in this direction is the possibility given to candidate countries to take part in the activities of EU agencies and committees, which allows them to become acquainted with the internal functioning of the EU.[79]

In the end, a specificity of the experimentalist approach deserves to be highlighted for its relevance in the enlargement context: this approach dissolves the distinction between conception and execution and, connected to that, the principal–agent relationship which results in a different form of accountability. The recursive experimentalist process consisting of agreement on framework goals, implementation by local actors as they best see fit, and comparative review and monitoring that results in the revision of local plans and central goals, means that 'the implementation becomes the conception'.[80] In such a context the principle recognizes that the goals 'are reshaped by the agent's efforts at implementation'. In terms of accountability this means that the agent is not simply supposed to follow instructions that prescribe how to realize the goal but he/she is obliged 'to explore possibilities for attaining the goal and even the advisability of modifying it, [to] diligently and responsibly engage ... in this kind of exploration, making at least adequate, and preferably optimal, use of all the information and experience available for doing so'.[81]

Sabel and Zeitlin call this 'forward-looking or dynamic accountability' to distinguish it from the rule-following form typical for principal–agent regimes.[82] In the context of enlargement this new understanding of accountability could be emphasized at two levels: first, in the relationship between the EU and the candidate countries and second, in the relationship between candidate country and its administration and other stakeholders, including civil society organizations (CSOs). As mentioned above, this kind of approach in the enlargement process, including the triangulation of actors (EU—state authorities—local stakeholders including CSOs) would lead to a shift from a top-down approach towards a more participatory approach of equal partnership.

As has been seen, the current enlargement mechanisms contain elements of reflexive governance. The question is how they are actually used, what kind of impact they have, and whether it would make sense to strengthen them.

The enlargement process as a whole can be seen as a mix ranging from neo-institutional to genetic approaches to governance. The external incentive of getting EU membership as reward for legislative and institutional reform no doubt has a powerful driving force. However, when it comes to the specific choice of a rule, and

[78] Tobias Böhmelt and Tina Freyburg, 'Diffusion of Compliance in the 'Race towards Brussels?' A Spatial Approach to EU Accession Conditionality' (2015) 38(3) West European Politics 601, 621.

[79] Tulmets (n 75) 310–11.

[80] Charles F Sabel and Jonathan Zeitlin, 'Experimentalism in the EU: Common Ground and Persistent Differences' (2012) 6 Regulation & Governance 410, 411.

[81] ibid.

[82] ibid; see also Gráinne de Búrca, Robert O Keohane, and Charles F Sabel, 'Global Experimentalist Governance' (2014) 44(3) British Journal of Political Science 477.

especially to the application and enforcement phase, it could make sense to provide more space for reflexive processes. Even if it is the case that, at the level of law making, rational choice, that is, the attempt to maximize utilities, should outweigh the readiness to redefine roles and identities, it is still imaginable that at the level of application, when it comes to making most of what is there, reflexive approaches would fall on fertile ground. If, for instance, an Equality Body is determined to make the non-discrimination legislation work in the best possible way for potential victims of discrimination, to provide it with the opportunity to learn in a reflexive process could be a step further towards full and effective enjoyment of the right to equality and non-discrimination. Thus, while some of the elements of reflexive governance might appear more readily applicable within the EU, many of its elements are present also in the pre-accession phase. The case study on Croatia will show which use was made of them and which elements should be strengthened in order to improve the outcome.

When situating the reflexive governance approach within the dominant European integration theories it becomes clear that the theories of federalism and neo-functionalism are not able to capture the processes and actors that play a central role in the enlargement context. Neo-functionalism does emphasize, for instance, the role of supranational institutions, such as the Commission, but leaves us in the dark with regard to the 'relevance and role of (varying) domestic actor constellations and structures in the applicant countries'.[83] Liberal intergovernmentalism, an application of rationalist institutionalism, considers that supranational institutions have limited importance in the integration process (more in the form of supportive structure for states) and that national governments are the key actors of integration. The use of theories of preference formation, bargaining, and institutionalization are clear expression of the rationalist approach taken by liberal intergovernmentalism.[84] This theory is certainly well suited to explain the main substantive and institutional outcomes in the integration process (both in terms of widening and deepening the EU).[85] However, it appears to pay too little attention, especially in the enlargement context, to the role of the Commission and local stakeholders (including CSOs).

Reflexive governance thus appears to be best reflected in the multilevel governance theory.[86] It argues that the 'authority and policy-making influences are

[83] Arne Niemann and Philippe C. Schmitter, 'Neofunctionalism' in Antje Wiener and Thomas Diez (eds), *European Integration Theory* (2nd edn, OUP 2009) 62–63. For a more recent account of neofunctionalism see Arne Niemann, Zoe Lefkofridi, and Philippe C Schmitter, 'Neofunctionalism' in Antje Wiener, Tanja A Börzel, and Thomas Risse (eds), *European Integration Theory* (3rd edn, OUP 2019).

[84] Andrew Moravcsik and Frank Schimmelfennig, 'Liberal Intergovernmentalism' in Antje Wiener, Tanja A Börzel and Thomas Risse (eds), European Integration Theory (3rd edn. Oxford University Press, 2019).

[85] Andrew Moravcsik and Frank Schimmelfennig, 'Liberal Intergovernmentalism' in Antje Wiener and Thomas Diez (eds), *European Integration Theory* (2nd edn, OUP 2009) 80–83.

[86] Liesbet Hooghe and Gary Marks, Multi-level Governance and European Integration (Rowman & Littlefield Publishers 2001); Simona Piattoni, *The Theory of Multi-level Governance: Conceptual, Empirical, and Normative Challenges* (OUP 2010); Simona Piattoni, 'Multilevel Governance' in Klaus Detterbeck and Eve Hepburn (eds), *Handbook of Territorial Politics* (Edward Elgar 2018). It should be

shared across multiple levels of government—subnational [regional and local authorities and civil society organizations], national and supranational' and that subnational actors work in 'both national and supranational arenas, creating transnational associations in the process'.[87] Reflexive governance is very explicit in requiring cooperation between these three different levels in different constellations in the different stages of the policy-cycle. Also, as will be seen below, the emergence of transnational networks of non-state actors is particularly relevant in the non-discrimination policy field and fits well the multilevel governance approach. Furthermore, multilevel governance has been considered as central in understanding the implementation of EU directives[88] and therefore puts much focus also on the implementation phase which is also central to the present research.

2.5 Reflexive Governance and Non-Discrimination

Can these theories about how learning can be improved in the enlargement context be used for the equality acquis? An experimentalist approach requires, for instance, that the local actors (in the context of enlargement the candidate countries) have some leeway in implementing the framework provided by the centre (the EU). The equality acquis is perfectly compatible with this as the norms to be transposed are founded in directives which leave the countries some flexibility in transposition.

At this point it is useful to briefly recall the explanations given by Falkner and Treib for the huge gap between the law and the practice in their comparative analysis of transposition and enforcement of two Equality Directives in four CEE countries: the lack of litigation from below, the lack of support by civil society actors, rather toothless Equality Bodies, and problems related to labour inspectorates. These issues touch on some of the distinctive features of the EU anti-discrimination regime: the role of non-state actors and transnational networks, as well as a focus on dialogue, information, and alternative dispute resolution.[89] It could therefore be asked whether performance could be improved by a stronger integration of reflexive thinking.

The problems related to a lack of litigation from below and a lack of support by civil society actors will be addressed together. If there was stronger support from the civil society sector, this would presumably have an impact on the willingness of

noted that multilevel governance is understood by some not as a theory but rather as a 'descriptive metaphor ... that subsumes nearly all possible political interrelationships found in the EU'. Moravcsik and Schimmelfennig, 'Liberal Intergovernmentalism' (n 84) 68.

[87] Hooghe and Marks (n 86) 2–4.

[88] Brainard Guy Peters and Jon Pierre, 'Governance Approaches' in Antje Wiener and Thomas Diez (eds), *European Integration Theory* (2nd edn, OUP 2009).

[89] Gráinne de Búrca, 'Stumbling into Experimentalism: The EU Anti-Discrimination Regime' in Charles F Sabel and Jonathan Zeitlin (eds), Experimentalist Governance in the European Union: Towards a New Architecture (Oxford University Press, 2010), 221–25.

victims of discrimination to actually go to court and thus also address the problem of a lack of litigation from below. It is, however, submitted that there are a number of other factors that influence the readiness to bring a discrimination case before the court.[90]

The Equality Directives assign a variety of roles to a range of non-state actors. Associations, organizations, or other legal entities with a legitimate interest in ensuring compliance with the Directives may engage in judicial or administrative proceedings.[91] As evidence from the four CEE countries reviewed by Falkner and Treib has shown, the specific design chosen by the countries to implement this possibility has remained quite minimalist. An *actio-popularis* claim, for instance, is foreseen only in *Hungary* under certain conditions.[92] From a pragmatist (in the sense of the word used by Schön and Argyris) and even more so from a genetic point of view, one would need to question the defensive strategies of decision makers against such an option 'by an explicit examination of their genesis' and encourage them to undertake an 'exercise of political imagination'. They can be supported in doing so on one hand by partners in the EU (Member States, Commission). On the other hand an informed civil society sector can try to shape the discourse during the deliberation about how to transpose the Equality Directives, arguing for such a possibility, founded on the experience with this instrument in other countries. This would also be in line with the feature of the non-discrimination regime emphasizing the state–non-governmental organization (NGO) dialogue. The involvement of the biggest possible number of stakeholders in the legislative process is a central element of the collaborative-relational as well as experimentalist governance approaches. It should be assessed whether there would be room for improvement, both domestically (on the side of the state and the civil society) and how the Commission deals with it in the course of negotiations and monitoring.

A lack of activity from the civil society sector in making use of existing possibilities (for instance, to support individuals in legal proceedings if not to act on their behalf) could further be addressed by reflexive mechanisms, both procedurally and psychologically: first, relevant NGOs, but also potential victims of discrimination, have to be empowered in the sense of fully informing them of the possibilities offered by the legal framework. They could be provided with good practice examples from other countries and supported, for instance, in the identification and preparation of strategic litigation cases. Second, civil society actors could be encouraged to exercise their imagination in the sense of questioning the role they can play in bringing discrimination cases to court. The idea of actively intervening

[90] Falkner and Treib mention for instance lack of rights awareness, fear from victimization and a lack of litigation culture. Falkner and Treib (n 2) 304. In addition, lengthy and costly court proceedings can be mentioned.

[91] See for instance Art 7(2) of Council Directive 2000/43/EC of 29 June 2000 implementing the principle of equal treatment between persons irrespective of racial or ethnic origin.

[92] Falkner and Treib (n 2) 305.

on behalf of or in support of a victim of discrimination might not have been part of their understanding of their role. They could be supported in reconsidering this role in light of the possibilities introduced by transposed EU directives and of the experiences collected by other NGOs in this context.

Problems related to the establishment and functioning of Equality Bodies has also been identified as a factor explaining the gap between law and practice. Here too, states have room for experimentation. The directives requiring their establishment are broadly framed, which allows for diverse approaches in transposition. In terms of their practical performance, Falkner finds that Equality Bodies are 'promising babies with teething problems . . . plagued by a lack of visibility, institutional standing and resources'.[93] Ombudspersons' offices have often been the beneficiary institutions of twinning projects. It would thus be instructive to evaluate the successfulness of the learning process through such twinnings in the non-discrimination field to find out which approach the twinning advisers have taken and how it has been received by the beneficiary administration, how the ownership of the process has been enhanced or could still be improved, and what the concrete results in terms of application and enforcement of the non-discrimination regime have been.

Further, it is also interesting to look at the role played by transnational networks, like the European Network of Equality Bodies (Equinet),[94] the Fundamental Rights Agency (FRA), or the various umbrella organizations[95] in the mutual learning process and the exchange of good practice.[96] Noted above was the possibility of learning from within by allowing candidate countries to participate in EU agencies to get acquainted with their functioning even before accession. Such a possibility is provided by Article 28 of the Council Regulation establishing the Fundamental Rights Agency. According to this rule the Commission can propose that the Council invite all countries with which a Stabilisation and Association Agreement (SAA) has been concluded to participate in the Agency as an observer. This option has been used so far with regard to Croatia before it became a full member, and more recently North Macedonia, Serbia, and Albania have gained observer status within the FRA. The Agency produces country or thematic studies in which

[93] ibid.

[94] Equinet brings together the national Equality Bodies required to be established under the anti-discrimination directives.

[95] European Network Against Racism (ENAR), European Disability Forum (EDF), International Lesbian, Gay, Bisexual, Trans and Intersex Association (ILGA-Europe), European Older People's Forum (AGE).

[96] Defenders of a logic of contestedness call for the establishment within supranational organizations such as the EU (where contestedness is typically particularly pronounced) of fora in which the different interpretations given to specific norms can be discussed in order to avoid a clash of incompatible interpretations. See Schirmbeck (n 68) 81. This fits perfectly with the thinking of an experimentalist governance approach, which conceives the advantage of such fora not only in the avoidance of incompatible interpretations but also in mutual learning and deliberation on how the framework initially provided could be improved on the basis of the collected experiences.

it includes only members or observers. Such studies are a useful source of comparison and review for the candidate countries in their endeavour to align with EU law. Therefore, the Commission could consider making broader use of such proposals to the Council to invite SAA countries.

Another element of the current EU anti-discrimination regime is that harassment and victimization are now clearly prohibited.[97] Still, its definition remains rather loose. In this respect the Directives leave room for local experimentation and it would be instructive to comparatively assess how states have made use of it in the transposition stage, but even more so in the application and enforcement stage which gives a clearer picture of the understanding different actors have of their role in interpreting the existing provisions.

De Búrca has found that the EU anti-discrimination regime clearly resembles an experimentalist governance regime:

> The legislation is clearly designated as 'framework' only, the regulatory norms are broad and open-ended, a range of different social actors are specifically allocated various roles in promoting equality, implementing the norms, raising awareness, providing information, assistance, and reporting back.... Finally, in the text of the various Directives, the Commission has undertaken to review and revise the legislation in the light of periodic reports on its implementation received from the Member States.[98]

Therefore, the EU non-discrimination regime constitutes an appropriate policy field to study further the potential of reflexive governance in securing adequate transposition and improving compliance in the post-accession phase. The respective EU Directives are broadly framed so that they allow for different solutions in the transposition and implementation. Such framework regulation is one of the elements of an experimentalist governance approach. Reflexive governance, especially the experimentalist governance approach with its focus on participation, seems to be particularly appropriate to enhance the participative dimension of equality.[99]

The following case study on Croatia investigates whether a higher level of compliance can be found in situations where the focus in the pre-accession phase was on elements of reflexive governance. It will also show where shortcomings persist which negatively influence the deployment of the full potential of reflexive

[97] See, however, the Commission report which found that protection from victimization seems to be limited in practice in a few Member States. European Commission, 'Report on the application of Council Directive 2000/43/EC implementing the principle of equal treatment between persons irrespective of racial or ethnic origin ('the Racial Equality Directive') and of Council Directive 2000/78/EC establishing a general framework for equal treatment in employment and occupation ('the Employment Equality Directive')' (Brussels 19 March 2021) COM(2021) 139 final, 9.

[98] de Búrca, 'Stumbling into Experimentalism: The EU Anti-Discrimination Regime' (n 89) 221–26.

[99] Fredman (n 54) 282–83.

governance approaches. Procedural as well as psychological elements will be taken into consideration. Especially regarding the latter, and considering that the conceptualization of reflexive governance is still at an early stage, the exact ways to achieve this form of reflexivity are not yet very clear.[100]

2.6 Case Study: Croatia

2.6.1 Introduction

The purpose of the empirical analysis of the Croatian case is to establish whether elements of reflexive governance have played a role in the pre-accession phase in the anti-discrimination field and if so, whether a causal link between the use of such an approach and the level of application and enforcement can be made. The aim is to learn something for the still ongoing enlargement process. If the plausibility of a cause–effect relation can be established, more weight should be given in the future to such elements of reflexive governance, thereby contributing to the solidification of reforms. The results of this analysis will also inform the further path of the current research.

Croatia has been considered as particularly suitable for this purpose, as the same conditionality and the most similar procedural strategy[101] was applied to it as to the current candidate countries. It was, for instance, the first country to which opening and closing benchmarks were applied. Furthermore, it is most similar with the current (potential) candidate countries in terms of historical past and legal culture.[102] For these reasons it is expected that lessons learned from the prototypical Croatian case[103] are more likely to be applicable to the countries which are part of the ongoing enlargement process, than lessons that could be learned from any other new Member State.

Adopting a historical institutionalist perspective, in terms of methodology this case study sets out, by way of process tracing,[104] to test the plausibility of the

[100] James Lawless, 'Book Review: Reflexive Governance' (2011) 17(3) European Law Journal 429.

[101] It is acknowledged that the Commission fine-tuned the strategy in 2011 with the 'fundamentals first' approach, thus only at the very end of Croatia's negotiation process. Furthermore, since 2015 the Commission is committed to making the yearly reports more clearly comparable and is attempting to promote the role of civil society. European Commission, 'EU Enlargement Strategy' (10 November 2015) COM(2015) 611 final. Finally, in February 2020, the Commission announced a revised methodology which is supposed to make accession negotiations more credible, more predictable, more dynamic, and guided by a stronger political steer. European Commission, 'Enhancing the Accession Process—A Credible EU Perspective for the Western Balkans' (n 12).

[102] For a comparison of the approaches of Western European countries and CEE post-communist countries to the issue of equality and non-discrimination, see Barbara Havelková, 'Resistance to Anti-Discrimination Law in Central and Eastern Europe—A Post-Communist Legacy?' (2016) 17(4) German Law Journal 627–56.

[103] Ran Hirschl, Comparative Matters: The Renaissance of Comparative Constitutional Law (Oxford University Press 2014), 256–60.

[104] Kyriakos Moumoutzis and Sotirios Zartaloudis, 'Europeanization Mechanisms and Process Tracing: A Template for Empirical Research' (2016) 54(2) Journal of Common Market Studies 337;

argument that a stronger focus on approaches of reflexive governance in the pre-accession phase contributes to solidify reforms also beyond the accession date. Process-tracing has been considered to be the appropriate method for this within-case analysis based on qualitative data. At the beginning of each of the following subsections (2.6.3.1–2.6.3.4) the evidence that should be observable, if the argument that there is a correlation between reflexive governance and enhanced implementation is correct, will be laid out. This will be followed by a detailed empirical description of developments to verify whether this causal nexus is given.

Among the sources used to test the plausibility of the above argument were twelve in- depth individual face-to-face interviews carried out in October 2015 and two Skype interviews carried out in July and October 2018. A final check on the results of the process was carried out in March/April 2021 through either interviews or other sources. Interviewees were drawn from NGOs, academia, the judiciary, members of parliament as well as representatives of government institutions, of the Office of the Ombudsperson (OO) and the Office of the Ombudsperson for Gender Equality. In addition, official EU and national documents related to the enlargement process and the post-accession phase concerning the anti-discrimination field, NGO publications, as well as the relevant academic literature on the issue were analysed.

Before entering into an analysis of the reflexive governance mechanism at play in the Croatian context and thus the *processes* of legal transposition and practical enforcement, the *substance* of the Croatian implementing legislation, mainly contained in the Antidiscrimination Act (ADA) of 9 July 2008[105] will be briefly summarized.

2.6.2 Croatia's Alignment to the EU Non-Discrimination Acquis

The Constitution of the Republic of Croatia lays down in Article 3 that '[f]reedom, equal rights, national and gender equality, peace-making, social justice, respect for human rights, … are the highest values of the constitutional order of the Republic of Croatia.' The section of the Constitution on the protection of human rights and fundamental freedoms starts with a common provision in Article 14 according to which everyone 'shall enjoy rights and freedoms, regardless of race, colour, gender,

Andrew Bennett and Jeffrey T. Checkel (eds), Process Tracing: From Methaphor to Analytical Tool (Cambridge University Press 2015). Ibid.; Paul Collier, 'Understanding Process Tracing', Political Science and Politics, (2011), 44(4): 823; Jeffery T Checkel, 'It's the Process Stupid! Process Tracing in the Study of European and International Politics' [2005] ARENA Working Paper.

[105] Official Gazette 85/08, entered into force on 1 January 2009, as amended by the Act of 28 September 2012, Official Gazette 112/12.

language, religion, political or other conviction, national or social origin, property, birth, education, social status or other characteristics', thereby leaving the list of discrimination grounds open. Before the adoption of the ADA, the core legal instrument adopted in the context of aligning to EU anti-discrimination regime, anti-discrimination provisions were scattered over various norms, among them the Constitutional Act on the Rights of National Minorities,[106] the Labour Act,[107] the Act on Same-Sex Communities,[108] the Civil Servants Act,[109] and the Criminal Code.[110]

In addition to the discrimination grounds mentioned in the Constitution, the ADA also protects against discrimination on grounds of trade union membership, marital or family status, age, health condition, disability, genetic heritage, gender identity and expression, or sexual orientation. Thus the discrimination grounds cover not only those contained in the EU directives but go far beyond them. This raises questions regarding the interpretation of certain of these grounds and their practical impact. An early commentary on the ADA suggested applying a hierarchy between the different discrimination grounds. The authors were of the opinion that 'it would be highly undesirable if the courts started to equally apply prohibition on all of the mentioned grounds of discrimination because it would produce immeasurable consequences for practical functioning of a society'.[111] As an example they mentioned the collapse of the progressive tax system if the antidiscrimination rules would be applied to the ground of property equally as on grounds of ethnicity. According to these authors, the highest level of protection is to be granted to the discrimination grounds contained in the EU directives. They argue that these grounds, unlike other grounds contained in the ADA, have a history of systematic discrimination which places persons associating with these grounds in a particularly unfavourable position within society.[112] While this might be true for all grounds covered by EU directives, this could, however, also be claimed for persons who are discriminated against on grounds of their language or social origin. The consequence for these grounds getting a lower level of protection would be that a 'milder form of prohibition of direct discrimination' would be applied, and that indirect discrimination would be included only if used to hide a discriminatory intent.[113] It is, however, accepted that the absence of a discriminatory intent does not preclude the finding that indirect discrimination has occurred. As neither

[106] Official Gazette 155/02.

[107] Official Gazette 38/95, 54/95, 65/95, 17/01, 82/01, 114/03, 142/03, 30/04, 137/04—consolidated text.

[108] Official Gazette 116/03.

[109] Official Gazette 92/05, 142/06, 77/07, 107/07, and 27/08.

[110] Official Gazette 110/97, 27/98, 50/00.

[111] Goran Selanec and Tena Šimonović Einwalter, 'Scope of the Anti-Discrimination Act' in Tena Simonovic Einwalter (ed), *A Guide to the Anti-Discrimination Act* (Government of the Republic of Croatia Office for Human Rights 2009) 24.

[112] ibid 24–25.

[113] ibid 25.

the arguments for making a distinction between discrimination grounds based on an alleged 'history of systematic discrimination' are convincing, nor the proposed consequences covered by the text of the ADA, the construction of such a hierarchy among discrimination grounds seems rather problematic. This is, however, not to say that it will indeed be difficult to rely on some of the discrimination grounds in a meaningful way.

In addition to a wide range of discrimination grounds, the law also provides for a very wide scope of application, going beyond EU requirements also in this respect. Besides the areas foreseen by EU law, the ADA applied to the areas of science and sports, judiciary and administration, public information and the media, membership and activities in trade unions, civil society organizations, political parties or any other organizations, as well as to access to participation in cultural and artistic creation.

The drafters of the ADA have been quite progressive in including, in addition to direct and indirect discrimination, discrimination by association in Article 1(2), although at the time of drafting the law this concept had not yet been developed at EU level. It was only later in the same year that the European Court of Justice (CJEU) for the first time found such form of direct discrimination in the *Coleman* case.[114] While this case related to discrimination on the ground of disability within the scope of employment, the Croatian ADA extends this concept to all the grounds and areas covered by the law.[115] It also covers discrimination by assumption,[116] and has duly incorporated the concepts of harassment (explicitly regulating sexual harassment),[117] of victimization,[118] and of reasonable accommodation.[119] Encouragement to discrimination shall be deemed to be discrimination only if conducted intentionally. Depending on the way Croatian courts interpret the requirement of intent, this restriction could be contrary to EU law. In fact, EU directives do not require intent for an instruction to discriminate to be considered discrimination.[120] In addition to these forms of discrimination, the ADA explicitly stipulates that segregation shall be deemed discrimination[121] and qualifies

[114] *S. Coleman v Attridge Law and Steve Law* [2008] ECLI:EU:C:2008:415. In this case a women considered herself as discriminated against by her employer due to her son's disability. For a comment see Gabriel N Toggenburg, 'Discrimination by Association: A Notion Covered by EU Equality Law?' [2008] European Law Reporter 82; Monika Schlachter, 'Benachteiligung wegen besonderer Verbindungen statt Zugehörigkeit zu einer benachteiligten Gruppe' [2010] Recht der Arbeit 104–09.

[115] Selanec and Šimonović Einwalter (n 111) 29.

[116] Art 1(3) ADA.

[117] Art 3 ADA.

[118] Art 7 ADA.

[119] Art 4 ADA.

[120] Goran Selanec, 'Forms of Discrimination' in Tena Simonovic Einwalter (ed), *A Guide to the Anti-Discrimination Act* (Government of the Republic of Croatia Office for Human Rights 2009) 56.

[121] Art 5 ADA. The definition of segregation given in the Act has been criticized for cumulatively requiring the existence of a 'forced and systematic separation of persons on any of the grounds referred to' in the Act. As such, segregation which is not the result of force but of social behaviour, prejudice, or the acceptance of certain practices as normal is thereby excluded from the definition. See Nada Bodiroga-Vukobrat, Mario Vinković, and Antonija Petričušić, 'Legal Protection Against Discrimination in

multiple, repeated, and continued discrimination as more serious forms of discrimination.[122] Positive action does not amount to discrimination if it aims 'to improve the status of ethnic, religious, language or other minorities or other groups of citizens or persons discriminated on the grounds referred to' in the ADA.[123] While thus all groups protected by the ADA are covered by this provision, the legislator apparently thought it important to mention positive action in favour of ethnic, religious, and linguistic minorities explicitly.

The ADA provides for the possibility for (inter alia) civil society organizations dealing with the protection of the right to equal treatment to intervene in a judicial proceeding in support of an individual plaintiff and to act on behalf of a group of persons in cases where a discriminatory behaviour affects a larger number of persons associated by one of the prohibited grounds or there is no identifiable victim (joint legal action).[124] The EU directives request that Member States shall ensure that such bodies may engage 'either on behalf or in support of the complainant'.[125] The Croatian legislation is thus quite comprehensive and goes beyond what is strictly required by the Directives, as it allows discrimination claims to be brought by associations where there is no identifiable victim. Before the adoption of the ADA, the tool of a 'joint legal action' (Art 24 ADA) was known within the Croatian legal system only with regard to the protection of consumer rights. In this latter case, however, the organizations authorized to bring such action were narrowed down by a list issued by the government.[126] Also in this sense the ADA represented substantial progress as it opened up the possibility for over 270 CSO to engage for victims of discrimination in court proceedings to over 270 civil society organizations in Croatia who deal with the protection of human rights and the rights of specific groups.[127] A ruling in a joint legal action case determining discrimination (not a ruling rejecting the claim) has prejudicial effects for future individual disputes, in which damages could be sought by members of the group in question. In such cases, the court would not need to reconsider the question of discrimination but just whether the plaintiff is a member of the group in question. A ruling on a prohibitional claim would oblige the perpetrator to abstain from such behaviour in all future cases.[128] This shows the broad impact of collective complaint cases.

Croatia' in Barbara Liegl (ed), *Legal Protection against Discrimination in South East Europe: Synthesis Report* (Centre for South East European law school network (SEELS) 2016) 194.

[122] Art 6 ADA.
[123] Art 9(2)(2).
[124] Arts 21 and 24 ADA.
[125] Art 7(2) Race Directive, Art 9(2) EED, Art 8(3) GD, Art 17(2) recast.
[126] Interview, Professor of Procedural Law, University of Zagreb, 13 October 2015.
[127] Alan Uzelaz, 'Proceedings Before the Court' in Tena Simonovic Einwalter (ed), *A Guide to the Anti-Discrimination Act* (Government of the Republic of Croatia Office for Human Rights 2009) 103.
[128] ibid 107–08.

The above-mentioned possibilities are open not only to civil society organizations but also to the OO, which in Article 12 ADA has been assigned the role of 'central body responsible for the suppression of discrimination'. It is assigned the competence to provide information about rights and obligations to victims of discrimination and to assist them by engaging in their support in judicial proceedings or by bringing a joint legal action, as well as to investigate cases of discrimination brought before it and to take actions required for the elimination of discrimination.[129] According to Article 12(2)(5) ADA it falls further within the scope of the Ombudsperson's activities to conduct mediation with the parties' consent. Furthermore, the OO has the responsibility to engage in preventive actions, such as the collection and analysis of statistical data, the provision of annual and extraordinary reports to the Croatian parliament on the occurrence of discrimination, and the conduct of surveys and giving opinions and recommendations on appropriate legal and strategic solutions to the government. The independence in carrying out its tasks, a requirement of the EU directives, is entrenched in Article 93 of the Constitution, which foresees that the 'Ombudsperson shall be autonomous and independent in his/her work'. Next to the Office of the Ombudsperson, the Croatian law has created special ombudspersons for gender equality, disabled persons, and for children.

The heading 'Social dialogue and co-operation with civil society organisations' of Article 15 ADA is similar to that of Articles 11 and 12 RED and Articles 13 and 14 EED, but whereas the Directives envisage this cooperation between the state on the one hand and social partners and civil society organizations on the other, the ADA puts the Ombudsperson under the obligation to consult these actors when drawing up reports, opinions, and recommendations. In particular Articles 11 RED and 13 EED thus remain uncovered by the ADA.

The ADA was adopted after an extensive public debate which will be discussed in detail below. In the parliamentary debate the framework law was generally welcomed. However, some speakers expressed an outright denial of the existence of discrimination which confirmed the concern of other speakers that there is a lack of awareness within society at large of the problem of discrimination in general, of what constitutes discrimination, and what can be done about it. There was also considerable scepticism regarding the likelihood of proper implementation. In this respect, several speakers highlighted the importance of increasing the capacities of and the funding for the OO, considering that this office was assigned the role of central Equality Body. Likewise, it was emphasized that intensive training for the judiciary will be necessary in order to make judges acquainted with the (procedural) novelties introduced by the Act, such as the joint legal action and the shifting of the burden of proof. Some members of parliament

[129] See Art 12(2)(2)–(3).

also raised the issue of the reluctance of victims of discrimination to go to court because of doubts that such a proceeding would be successful. In this respect, hopes were expressed regarding the newly introduced possibility for NGOs to intervene in such proceedings. On the other hand it was also highlighted that the OO and the courts cannot fight alone against discrimination, alluding to the fact that reactive measures have to be complemented by preventive ones. One speaker mentioned in this context the importance of including civil education in the school curriculum. Another speaker expressed his hope that the law would be adopted for Croatian society generally, and not for the EU alone. Reference to experience with the implementation of the EU anti-discrimination regime existing already elsewhere and that it might be useful to learn from such experience was made only sparingly.[130] One can therefore conclude that the idea of exchanging experiences and of mutual and collective learning had not occurred to the members of the Croatian Sabor.

Only two months after the ADA was passed, the National Plan to Combat Discrimination 2008–13 was adopted. It selectively addressed a couple of discrimination grounds and some of the areas covered under the ADA but it was not harmonized with the law. The National Plan was criticized in terms of process for not having been elaborated in an inclusive way. In terms of content, civil society organizations especially found that the objectives and measures for the elimination of discrimination were not well thought through and it did not contribute to the coordination of activities of various public bodies charged with the implementation of anti-discrimination policies. They raised the further criticism that the measures proposed in the National Plan were insufficiently monitored. They condensed their critique in a document in which they analysed the National Plan and made recommendations for its improvement in the subsequent cycle.[131]

This brief overview of the substance of the ADA shows that several parts are quite progressive and go beyond the strict minimum required under the Directives. Problematic aspects are related to the probably too broad and undefined approach when it comes to discrimination grounds. Furthermore, the state–CSO dialogue remains uncovered by the law. The next section will delve into the question of whether elements of reflexive governance have played a role in the adoption and implementation phase of this law during the accession process, what use has been made of such elements, and whether they have had an impact beyond the accession date in the sense of having contributed to a solidification of pre-accession reforms.

130 Parliamentary debate, 28 May 2008.

131 Ljiljana Božić Krstanović and Sara Lalić, 'How Much Equality? Monitoring the Implementation of the Legal Aid Act and of the Anti-discrimination Act' (Centre for Peace, Nonviolence and Human Rights—Osijek, Centre for Peace, Legal Advice and Psychosocial Assistance—Vukovar, Serbian Democratic Forum, in cooperation with Centre for Peace Studies—Zagreb 2013), containing in an appendix 'Umbrella against discrimination: analysis of design of the National Plan for Combatting Discrimination and Recommendations for Improvement' 63 ff.

Where such elements have not been used to their fullest extent this will also be highlighted.

2.6.3 Elements of Reflexive Governance in Action

As has been mentioned above, the success of the *experimentalist approach* is dependent on three conditions: co-design, benchmarking, and effective and informed monitoring. These three conditions are broken down into a recursive process in which framework rules are defined by the central and local units together, the target country implements these rules as it sees fit, it reports on performance, undergoes peer review, shares knowledge with others, and exchanges good practice which leads to a re-evaluation and maybe even reformulation of the national and/or the framework rule. An important characteristic of the *experimentalist approach* and of the *collaborative-relational* is furthermore the level of stakeholder involvement in the drafting of legislative and policy measures as well as in their evaluation.

The lack of the condition of co-design in the enlargement context potentially has a detrimental effect on the success of the learning operation but can be tempered by the fact that a candidate country has generally accepted that it will adapt its legislation to the acquis as a condition for acquiring EU membership. Furthermore, due to the recursive process, the perspective of co-design is there for the period after accession. Due to the lack of this element in the accession process, the focus of the empirical research will be first on the benchmarking and monitoring, second on the stakeholder involvement, and third on the aspect of knowledge sharing and exchange of good practice.

To study the first item (at 2.6.3.1.), the European and Accession Partnerships, the results of the screening, the benchmarks set for the relevant negotiation chapters, and the regular country reports will be analysed. The research seeks to establish whether these instruments have been properly used and whether this has contributed not only to correct legal transposition of the anti-discrimination acquis but also to a satisfactory level of implementation at the moment of accession and beyond.

Section 2.6.3.2 will then look more closely at stakeholder involvement during law and policy making, implementation, and evaluation. As will be seen, there was quite substantive involvement of civil society at various points in the process. The questions to be answered are what opportunities for stakeholder involvement have been created through the accession process, what efforts have been undertaken to build the capacity of the stakeholders to be effectively and meaningfully involved, the roles played in this context by the Commission and Croatia respectively, and the effect this has had on the quality of the legal alignment and the level of implementation.

Section 2.6.3.3 analyses the measures set in the pre-accession phase for the purpose of sharing knowledge and exchanging good practice to find out about their long-term impact on implementation.

The *pragmatist and genetic approaches* imply that actors engage in reflection upon the way they represent a problem, the kind of solutions they come up with, and the role they play in the whole process. Section 2.6.3.4 explores whether such reframing has taken place in the case of Croatia, and if so, with regard to which actors and how it was triggered.

2.6.3.1 Benchmarking, Monitoring, and the Relevance of Indicators

In the framework of accession negotiations benchmarking takes the form of priorities set in the European and Accession Partnerships as well as opening and closing benchmarks for each negotiation chapter. For Chapters 23 (Judiciary and fundamental rights) and 24 (Justice, freedom, and security) in addition, interim benchmarks are set. Monitoring instruments are the screening reports on the individual chapters, taking stock of the situation at the beginning of negotiations, peer reviews as well as the annual country reports.

European and Accession Partnerships 'guide the countries' reform efforts and indicate the concrete actions needed to achieve progress through the road-map. They identify the short and medium-term priorities for each particular stage of the pre-accession process.'[132] As such they are an important instrument for the Commission in setting specific targets to be met in specific areas and constitute the main reference documents in the intensified political dialogue on those key priorities.[133] Benchmarks were first used vis-à-vis Croatia and Turkey. In the Enlargement Strategy of 2006, they were described as

> a new tool introduced as a result of lessons learnt from the fifth enlargement. Their purpose is to improve the quality of the negotiations, by providing incentives for the candidate countries to undertake necessary reforms at an early stage. Benchmarks are *measurable* and linked to key elements of the acquis chapter. In general, opening benchmarks concern key preparatory steps for future alignment (such as strategies or action plans), and the fulfilment of contractual obligations that mirror acquis requirements. Closing benchmarks primarily concern *legislative measures, administrative or judicial bodies*, and a *track record of implementation* of the acquis.[134]

As has been discussed elsewhere, 'the idea of introducing benchmarking procedures in the realm of ... human rights is a quite challenging undertaking.'[135] Benchmarking requires the reliance 'on clear concepts, objectives, and transparent time tables'. This means that 'a clear ex-ante definition of what is meant by the central concepts

[132] European Commission, '2005 Enlargement Strategy Paper' (9 November 2005) COM(2005) 561 final, 11.

[133] European Commission, 'Enlargement Strategy and Main Challenges 2008–2009' (5 November 2008) COM(2008) 674 final, 6.

[134] European Commission, 'Enlargement Strategy and Main Challenges 2006–2007' (8 November 2006) COM(2006) 649, 6. Emphasis added.

[135] Raffaella Del Sarto, Tobias Schumacher, and Erwan Lannon, 'Benchmarking Democratic Development in the Euro-Mediterranean Area: Conceptualising Ends, Means, and Strategies' (EuroMeSCo Report, October 2006) 17.

of … human rights, and which key features they comprise, is imperative'.[136] As the right to equality and non-discrimination constitutes a part of human rights, these findings can be applied also to this right and in the context of enlargement. As the above discussion of the meaning of equality has shown, the interpretation of this concept is all but uncontested, which makes benchmarking a challenging task.

The authors of the same study differentiate between naïve and intelligent benchmarking. They state that

> all benchmarking models require an ex ante decision as regards the measurement methods, the units to be measured, the chosen and appropriate (quantitative and/or qualitative) indicators, and the preferred data collection method. Eventually, this somewhat determines whether the process in question can be considered as naïve benchmarking or as intelligent benchmarking. Whereas the former is characterised by intuition and superficial comparisons, which can be easily misinterpreted and—depending on how seriously they are taken—have problematic and sometimes even socially damaging implications, the latter, i.e. intelligent benchmarking, is much more concrete, systematic and holistic.[137]

In order for an experimentalist governance approach to deploy its full potential (in the sense of leading to a successful learning operation) it is reasonable to expect that intelligent benchmarking is applied, including the establishment of clear benchmarks and the ex ante identification of clear indicators, on the basis of which the achievement of the benchmarks can be measured and consistently monitored. In the following, the priorities and benchmarks set in the Croatian accession process with respect to the area of non-discrimination and equality will be analysed and assessed on whether they fulfil the above criteria for intelligent benchmarking, whether they have been properly monitored, whether they have been met, and where there would be room for improvement.

Box 2.1 Process tracing: What evidence should be observable if the argument that there is a correlation between reflexive governance (here with a focus on experimentalist governance) and enhanced implementation is correct?[138]

Benchmarking and monitoring →	Intelligent benchmarking: • clear benchmarks • clear indicators • consistent monitoring →	Enhanced implementation

[136] ibid.
[137] ibid 15.
[138] Pascal Vennesson, 'Case Studies and Process Tracing: Theories and Practices' in Donatella Della Porta and Michael Keating (eds), *Approaches and Methodologies in the Social Sciences* (CUP 2008) 238.

The 2004 European Partnership[139] and the 2006 and 2008 Accession Partnerships[140] with Croatia focused on the improvement of respect for minority rights and especially of the situation of Roma, inter alia, through anti-discrimination measures aimed at fostering employment opportunities. In the 2008 document the implementation of the Constitutional Law on the Protection of National Minorities was qualified as a key priority. Further, the cooperation with the OO had to be improved. Finally, legal alignment with the EU legislation in the fields of gender equality and anti-discrimination had to be continued, a comprehensive anti-discrimination strategy adopted and implemented, and the related administrative and enforcement structures strengthened.

In June 2008, negotiations on Chapter 19 began, while negotiations on Chapter 23 were started only in June 2010. The anti-discrimination relevant closing benchmark for Chapter 19 was the adoption of a comprehensive anti-discrimination law. The closing benchmarks for Chapter 23 were to establish a track record of implementing anti-discrimination and hate crime legislation, as well as raising the capacity of the OO. They further requested that the protection of minorities be strengthened, including the effective implementation of the Constitutional Law on National Minorities. While the adoption of a law can be easily measured, it is less clear how to measure a 'track record of implementation' of a law as well as the raising of the Ombudsperson's capacity.

Were these priorities and benchmarks consistently monitored, and if so, how? And were they met at the moment of accession? The priorities and benchmarks related to the improvement of the respect for minority rights and the implementation of the Constitutional Law on the Protection of National Minorities were constantly subject to detailed comments in the annual Commission reports. In the comprehensive monitoring report of 2012, the Commission stated that the situation continued to improve, however challenges remained in the field of equal representation in the administration, the judiciary, and in employment in general, as well as regarding the situation of the Roma. It also stated that Croatia needs to take measures to protect those who may still be subjected to discrimination, hostility, and violence.[141] In the last monitoring report before

[139] Council Decision 2004/648/EC of 13 September 2004 on the principles, priorities and conditions contained in the European Partnership with Croatia.

[140] Council Decision 2006/145/EC of 20 February 2006 on the principles, priorities and conditions contained in the Accession Partnership with Croatia and repealing Decision 2004/648/EC; Council Decision 2008/119/EC of 12 February 2008 on the principles, priorities and conditions contained in the Accession Partnership with Croatia and repealing Decision 2006/145/EC.

[141] European Commission, 'Comprehensive Monitoring Report on Croatia's State of Preparedness for EU Membership' (10 October 2012) COM(2012) 601 final, 4 and 11.

accession, it took note of the adoption of a National Strategy for Roma Inclusion 2013–20 and of legislative amendments in the field of combatting certain forms and expressions of racism and xenophobia by means of criminal law. The only explicit request for further efforts regarded the primary and secondary education of Roma children.[142] Comparing this last report with the opinion of the Advisory Committee on the Framework Convention for the Protection of National Minorities, it becomes clear that problems previously addressed by the Commission in its monitoring reports continue to exist but are no longer explicitly mentioned in the final report.[143]

Legislative alignment in the fields of equal treatment and anti-discrimination were regularly monitored in the progress reports. The comprehensive ADA and the Gender Equality Act were adopted in July 2008 with amendments made to the ADA in 2012 due to criticism from the Commission in its monitoring reports. A National Plan to Combat Discrimination had been adopted to cover the period 2008–13. A National Policy on the Promotion of Gender Equality was already in place for the period 2006–10. A new National Policy for Gender Equality for the period from 2011–15 was elaborated after a process of public consultation[144] but has not been mentioned in the 2011 Progress Report. In 2013 the Commission thus came to the conclusion that 'Croatia has completed legal alignment in the fields of anti-discrimination and equal opportunities'.[145]

As part of the strengthening of implementation structures, another set of priorities and benchmarks circulated around the cooperation with, and the strengthening of capacities of, the OO. The role of the Ombudsperson and specialized ombudspersons in human rights protection was regularly evaluated in the progress reports and their strengthening in terms of funding, personnel, authority, and outreach recommended. In the last monitoring report the Commission still found that '[c]ontinued attention needs to be paid to ensure that the Ombudsman's recommendations are followed up.... There continues to be a need for further strengthening the Ombudsman offices [including] adequate financing and office premises.'[146]

Regarding the track record of implementation of the ADA and legislation on hate crimes, the comments of the Commission focused on the application of

[142] European Commission, 'Monitoring Report on Croatia's Accession Preparations' (26 March 2013) COM(2013) 171 final, 9.
[143] For a more detailed analysis of the Commission's monitoring see Wolfgang Benedek and others, 'Mainstreaming Human and Minority Rights in the EU Enlargement with the Western Balkans' (European Parliament, Directorate-General for External Policies, Policy Department 2012) 67–68.
[144] For details on this plan see DG for Internal Policies, 'The Policy on Gender Equality in Croatia, Update 2013' (2013) 6–10.
[145] European Commission, 'Monitoring Report on Croatia's Accession Preparations' (n 142) 10.
[146] ibid 9–10.

dissuasive sanctions, the provision of training to police officers on the suppression of hate crimes, and the legislation on free legal aid. While the dissuasive sanctions were not broached in the last monitoring report, the Commission found that training activities had been stepped up and that the draft amendments to the Legal Aid Act aimed at facilitating access to legal aid and at fostering the role of NGOs as legal aid providers. It further noted that there had been consultations with relevant stakeholders on these draft amendments and they were supposed to be adopted before accession.[147]

In the Commission's language in its monitoring reports, a shift can be seen from observing legal alignment *and* practical implementation to a stronger focus on correct legal transposition. In the negotiation framework with Croatia of 2005 the Commission underlined that 'Croatia's correct transposition *and implementation* of the *acquis, including effective and efficient application through appropriate administrative and judicial structures,* will determine the pace of negotiations'.[148] Up until 2009, the Commission was of the opinion that the level of protection against discrimination in practice and its judicial prosecution was not in line with EU standards and also in the following years it dedicated a large number of its comments to the implementation. What seemed to count in the end was the finding that 'Croatia has completed *legal alignment* in the fields of anti-discrimination and equal opportunities'.[149] Benchmarks such as 'improving' the protection of minorities or 'raising the capacity' of the Ombudsperson's office are not as easily measurable as the adoption of a law, in particular in the absence of clear indicators. Also, the establishment of a track record of implementation leaves a lot of room for interpretation. The benchmarks are formulated so that they constitute open-ended targets. This leaves room for a political decision at the end of the process. However, this raises the question of whether this formulation is appropriate if the claim is to constitute incentives to bring about sustainable reform. The criticism raised by Kochenov in his 2007 study regarding lack of clarity of standards that candidates are supposed to comply with and benchmarks to determine compliance[150] is thus still valid.

Used in this way, benchmarking and monitoring will not be able to deploy their potential in terms of elements of a reflexive governance regime either. Two things could be considered in order to improve the situation: first, benchmarking and monitoring have to be reconsidered, and second, monitoring continues after accession.

[147] ibid 10.

[148] Negotiating Framework for Croatia, Luxembourg, 3 October 2005, para 27. Emphasis added.

[149] European Commission, 'Monitoring Report on Croatia's Accession Preparations' (n 142) 10. Emphasis added.

[150] Kochenov, *EU Enlargement and the Failure of Conditionality* (n 11) 311.

In the viewpoint of a member of the Croatian parliament, benchmarks as they are now 'are easy to be fulfilled without changing anything in the substance'.[151] While acknowledging the difficulty of benchmarking in the human rights field, it would be all the more important to do it in an 'intelligent' way. As mentioned above, this requires benchmarks to be developed with clear concepts, measurement methods, indicators, data collection methods, and time frames in mind, as only this allows for effective and informed monitoring, considered a precondition for experimentalist governance to be successful. A central element to all this is the development of indicators. This would require making very clear the meaning of anti-discrimination, breaking it down into its constitutive elements and developing structure, process, and outcome indicators.[152] Indicators would make it clear what exactly the Commission is monitoring and would allow for consistent monitoring over time.

The Commission might be reluctant to accept such an approach as it could be perceived as limiting its room for manoeuvre. The 2015 enlargement package could be seen as an attempt to improve the monitoring, with some impact also on the benchmarking. In particular, progress reports as of 2015 are supposed to provide 'clearer guidance for what the countries are expected to do in both the short and long term' in order to meet their targets. The revised methodology announced by the Commission in February 2020 is yet another step towards making accession negotiations more predictable. The document reiterates the Commission's benchmarks approach and makes clear that it is important 'that Member States share a clear understanding of what exactly is requested from the candidates'. For that purpose, '[t]he Commission will better define the conditions set for candidates to progress, in particular through its annual reports. These conditions must be objective, precise, detailed, strict and verifiable.' While this wording is coming close to the idea of indicators in the context of intelligent benchmarking, the Commission does not seem to change its approach in the formulation of benchmarks nor to develop indicators. Rather, it announced the use of 'third party indicators where relevant to provide Member States with the broadest possible base for their decisions'.[153]

It thus appears that the Commission is sticking to its rather vague benchmarks and leaving it to the states (in consultation with the Commission) to develop the details in the framework of Action Plans. Such Action Plans are foreseen as an opening benchmark for Chapters 19 and 23, the chapters relevant for the

[151] Interview, Member of the Croatian parliament, President of the Serb National Council, 13 October 2015.

[152] See OHCHR, 'Human Rights Indicators. A Guide to Measurement and Implementation' (2012) <http://www.ohchr.org/Documents/Publications/Human_rights_indicators_en.pdf>; Gauthier de Beco, 'Human Rights Indicators for Assessing State Compliance with International Human Rights' (2008) 77(1–2) Nordic Journal of International Law 23. The idea of structure, process and outcome indicators is further introduced below in Chapter 3.2.

[153] European Commission, 'Enhancing the Accession Process—A Credible EU Perspective for the Western Balkans' (n 12) 5.

non-discrimination field. While the screening reports do not prescribe in detail how these Action Plans should look, they usually set out strategic objectives and concrete activities planned to meet these objectives, which are linked with the institutions required to put in place the activities, timeframe, and financial costs. Indicators are regularly part of these Action Plans. However, in the view of the experts of a peer review mission on minority rights in Serbia, these indicators focus too little on measuring the actual impact of activities on the rights holders and the actual fulfilment of their rights.[154]

Another aspect which would improve the effectiveness of benchmarks and which could be seen as strengthening the collaborative-relational as well as the experimentalist side of reflexive governance, would be the immediate publication of opening, interim (if they exist), and closing benchmarks on the Commission's website. As the experience of Croatia has shown, a negotiating government could easily hide behind the fact that the benchmarks are documents produced by EU institutions and it thus has, technically, no authority to disclose them. This constitutes an obstacle for civil society organizations to systematically and independently monitor the performance of the government, which would be particularly relevant for such benchmarks as the establishment of a track record of implementation of certain legislation.[155]

The risk (also, or even more so) with clear benchmarking combined with indicators is that it may take a country too long to meet the benchmarks. If EU accession as the reward for accepting domestic costs for undertaking reforms is too remote, the reformative fervour might well fizzle out. The second proposal is thus to have proper benchmarking and monitoring before accession, to accept that implementation cannot be perfect at the moment of accession—as, incidentally, the Commission has acknowledged with regard to the benchmark of raising the Ombudsperson's capacity, but with no consequences—and continue monitoring after accession on the basis of the same indicators used in the pre-accession phase.[156] However, this would (and this has been emphasized by many

[154] Emma Lantschner and Stéphanie Marsal, 'Expert Report regarding the protection of minorities and cultural rights in the Republic of Serbia' (Peer review expert mission to Serbia on Chapter 23—Judiciary and fundamental rights, focussing on interim benchmarks on protection of minorities and cultural rights, 24 March 2017) 5.

[155] Marina Škrabalo, 'Transparency in Retrospect: Preliminary Lessons from Croatia's EU Accession Process' (Discussion paper commissioned by the Greens/EFA in the European Parliament 2012) 6–7; see also Igor Vidačak and Marina Škrabalo, 'Exploring the Effects of Europeanization on the Openness of Public Administration in Croatia' (2014) 14(1) Croatian and Comparative Public Administration 149. Currently, the opening benchmarks, contained in the screening reports, are readily available on the Commission's website. However, for instance, the EU Common Position on Chapters 23 (adopted with regard to both Montenegro and Serbia), containing the interim benchmarks for these chapters is not available on the Commission's website, but information about them can be found online.

[156] Dimitrova and Buzogány have shown that the existence of such a monitoring framework could be made use of also by NGOs in the post-accession phase. See Antoaneta Dimitrova and Aron Buzogany, 'Post-Accession Policy-Making in Bulgaria and Romania: Can Non-State Actors Use EU Rules to Promote Better Governance?' (2014) 52(1) Journal of Common Market Studies 139.

interviewees) render new Member States second class members, if old Member States, which often have a similarly bad if not worse record on anti-discrimination issues, are not also submitted to such monitoring. The way out would thus be general human rights (including anti-discrimination) monitoring for all Member States. For this purpose, the FRA's mandate could be extended.[157] However, this idea has so far not found support among the Member States.[158]

To extend monitoring beyond accession would also be a condition for the experimentalist approach to deploy its full potential. As mentioned above, this approach is characterized by its circularity, by the recursive process of rule formulation, implementation, monitoring, and sharing of experiences, potentially leading to a re-evaluation of the rule. While there is nothing that prevents Member States from exchanging experiences and in fact, as described in Chapter 1.1, a number of institutions have been established for that purpose, the monitoring element of the recursive process, in the sense of a country-specific, regular review of legal and practical compliance with the objectives of the Directives, is stopped at the moment of accession.[159]

[157] Toggenburg and Grimheden state that after the revision of Art 7 by the Treaty of Nice, the Commission concluded that 'it was now entitled to introduce a regular monitoring of the Member States in order to assess their adherence to the values laid down in Article 2 TEU.... However, such a more permanent and explicit EU monitoring framework has yet to be set up. The role and the contribution of the FRA to such a monitoring also remains to be defined.' Gabriel N Toggenburg and Jonas Grimheden, 'Upholding Shared Values in the EU: What Role for the EU Agency for Fundamental Rights' (2016) 54(5) Journal of Common Market Studies 1093, 1094–95. For a summary of the main proposals as to how to ensure that values are enforced, see Kochenov, 'The Aquis and Its Principles: The Enforcement of the "Law" versus the Enforcement of "Values" in the EU' (n 11) 17–25.

[158] On this point see eg Viktoria Wagner and Manfred Nowak, 'Monitoring the Protection of Human Rights in the European Union: An Evaluation of Mechanisms and Tools' in Olivier de Schutter and Violeta Moreno Lax (eds), *Human Rights in the Web of Governance: A Learning-Based Fundamental Rights Policy for the EU* (Bruylant 2010) 156–57. On the attempts of the European Parliament to introduce an inter-institutional pact on democracy, rule of law, and fundamental rights (rejected by the Commission), see Sergio Carrera, Elspeth Guild, and Nicholas Hernanz, 'The Triangular Relationship between Fundamental Rights, Democracy and Rule of Law in the EU—Towards an EU Copenhagen Mechanism. Study Prepared for the European Parliament' (CEPS Commentary 2013); Judith Sargentini and Aleksejs Dimitrovs, 'The European Parliament's Role: Towards New Copenhagen Criteria for Existing Member States?' (2016) 54(5) Journal of Common Market Studies 1085; Petra Bárd and others, 'An EU Mechanism on Democracy, the Rule of Law and Fundamental Rights' (CEPS Paper in Liberty and Security in Europe, April 2016); European Commission, 'Follow up to the European Parliament resolution with recommendations to the Commission on the establishment of an EU mechanism on democracy, the rule of law and fundamental rights, adopted by the Commission on 17 January 2017' (17 February 2017) SP(2017)16. On the rule of law debate more generally, in the context of which fundamental rights also play a role, see the Special Issue, edited by Dimitry Kochenov, Amichai Magen, and Laurent Pech, 'The Great Rule of Law Debate in the EU' (2016) 54(5) Journal of Common Market Studies 1045; and Werner Schröder (ed), *Strengthening the Rule of Law in Europe: From a Common Concept to Mechanisms of Implementation* (Bloomsbury 2016).

[159] The five-yearly reports by the Commission on the application of Directives 2000/43/EC and 2000/78/EC, foreseen by Art 17 RED and Art 19 EED, cannot be considered as country-specific regular monitoring reports. In these reports the Commission makes an overall assessment of the application in all EU Member States without formulating any recommendations to individual Member States. See European Commission, 'Joint Report on the application of Council Directive 2000/43/EC of 29 June 2000 implementing the principle of equal treatment between persons irrespective of racial or ethnic origin ('Racial Equality Directive') and of Council Directive 2000/78/EC of 27 November 2000 establishing a general framework for equal treatment in employment and occupation ('Employment

As has been indicated in the above box, in order for benchmarking and monitoring to be able to enhance implementation and compliance it is necessary that benchmarks are clear, that the progress towards reaching a benchmark is measurable over time by the use of indicators, and that this progress is consistently and continuously monitored. Consistent monitoring in this case means also that there is a continuous focus on both legal alignment *and* practical implementation, which would be guaranteed by the use of structural, process, and outcome indicators. These conditions were not in place with regard to Croatia. Also, it was shown that open, transparent, and participatory mechanisms were not in place during the monitoring phase. All these issues should therefore be considered seriously in the ongoing enlargement process and, as is suggested here, even beyond.

2.6.3.2 Meaningful Stakeholder Involvement

De Búrca has identified 'the broadest possible degree of stakeholder participation compatible with effective decision-making' as one of the most important factors for an experimentalist governance system to succeed.[160] In her article responding to the critique about the ineffectiveness and top-down approach of the international human rights regime, she shows the relevance of the involvement of the civil society sector in countering these tendencies, both in the formulation of legislation and policies as well as in their monitoring. In fact, from a review of a range of empirical studies, she concludes that there exists 'a clear correlation between human rights treaty ratification and improvement in human rights standards where there is a reasonably active civil society within the states in question'.[161]

This chapter thus explores the role civil society has played in the adoption of the ADA and the National Plan for Combatting Discrimination as well as their monitoring and implementation. The conceptual framework for this analysis borrows from the 'usages' approach of Jacquot and Woll[162] which distinguishes between opportunities, usage, and impact. The creation of opportunities is a necessary but not

Equality Directive')' (Brussels 17 January 2014) COM(2014) 2 final and before the separate reports Commission of the European Communities, 'The application of Directive 2000/43/EC of 29 June 2000 implementing the principle of equal treatment between persons irrespective of racial or ethnic origin' (30 October 2006) COM(2006) 643 final and Commission of the European Communities, 'The application of Directive 2000/78/EC of 27 November 2000 establishing a general framework for equal treatment in employment and occupation' (8 July 2008) COM(2008) 225 final/2.

[160] de Búrca, 'New Governance and Experimentalism: An Introduction' (n 52) 235.

[161] Gráinne de Búrca, 'Human Rights Experimentalism' (2017) 111(2) American Journal of International Law 277, 299 and 301.

[162] Sophie Jacquot and Cornelia Woll, 'Usage of European Integration—Europeanisation from a Sociological Perspective' (2003) 7(12) European Integration online Papers (EIoP); Cornelia Woll and Sophie Jacquot, 'Using Europe: Strategic Action in Multi-level Politics' (2010) 8(1) Comparative European Politics 110.

sufficient precondition for actors to seize them. And even if actors intentionally make use of them to reach their goal, this does not necessarily mean that the final outcome corresponds to the initial objective.

This approach goes well together with reflexive governance with its emphasis on the enhancement of actors' capacities. In fact, reflexive governance acknowledges that even if stakeholders are involved in decision-making and policy-formulation processes, the success of this involvement depends, first, on whether these actors had the capacity to be involved, both in terms of resources and information, as well as in terms of thinking out of the box. Second, even if they had the capacity, this is a necessary but not sufficient requirement for this involvement to be meaningful, as this requires that their voices are heard. This would already cover the opportunity-usage-impact sequence. Some authors refer in this context to the empowerment of civil society.[163] But this empirical section is interested in yet another dimension, and that is the role stakeholders continue to play in the implementation and the monitoring of the legal and policy framework in place. In fact, de Búrca's finding on the importance of an active civil society for improving human rights standards strongly focuses on its role during the monitoring phase regarding the implementation of human rights treaties and its dialogue with the state and treaty monitoring bodies.

This section will thus analyse the opportunities created by the accession process for stakeholder involvement and their use, the efforts undertaken to build the capacity of the stakeholders to be effectively and meaningfully involved in the transposition of the acquis and related policies, and whether their involvement has had any impact on the final outcome. Furthermore, their role in the implementation phase will be looked at, in terms of implementation, monitoring, and awareness raising. In all these fields, the role played by the Commission will be questioned, as well as where there is room for improvement in the ongoing enlargement process.

[163] On the various meanings of empowerment see Lauren Bennett Cattaneo and Aliya R Chapman, 'The Process of Empowerment: A Model for Use in Research and Practice' (2010) 65(7) American Psychologist 646. Wunsch has done extensive research on the issue in the context of enlargement. See, for instance, Natasha Wunsch, 'Beyond Instrumentalisation: NGO Monitoring Coalitions in Croatia, Montenegro, and Serbia' (2015) 31(4) East European Politics 452; Natasha Wunsch, 'Right Goals, Wrong Tools? Civil Society Empowerment in the EU Accession Process' (February 2015). DGAPanalyse 2; Natasha Wunsch, 'Coming Full Circle? Differential Empowerment in Croatia's EU Accession Process' (2016) 23(8) Journal of European Public Policy 1199; Natasha Wunsch, 'Unpacking Differential Empowerment: Civil Society Mobilisation in the EU Accession Process' (PhD thesis in Political Science, University College London 2016); Natasha Wunsch, *EU Enlargement and Civil Society in the Western Balkans: From Mobilisation to Empowerment* (Palgrave 2018); as well as Adam Fagan and Natasha Wunsch, 'Fostering Institutionalisation? The Impact of the EU Accession Process on State–Civil Society Relations in Serbia' [2018] Acta Politica 1.

Box 2.2 Process tracing: What evidence should be observable if the argument that there is a correlation between meaningful stakeholder involvement and enhanced implementation is correct?

Meaningful stakeholder involvement →	• Opportunities created in accession process • Stakeholders making use of them • Building capacity of stakeholders • Impact of stakeholder involvement • Stakeholders' role in implementation, monitoring, awareness raising →	Enhanced implementation

First, as shown in the above box, it will be asked what opportunities for stakeholder involvement were created through the accession process and what efforts were made to build their capacity, in particular by the Commission but also by Croatia. It can be anticipated that the Commission's approach has gradually developed from focusing on capacity building of individual organizations and using NGOs as its local watchdogs[164] to declaring civil society participation as 'a key factor in ensuring good quality comprehensive legislation and in developing sustainable policies that reflect people's needs and are accepted by those most concerned by them'.[165] That this latter approach has started to take effect only when Croatia had already become an EU Member State might help to explain why, as we will see, the role of civil society organizations after accession was vulnerable when the political climate was in flux.

The Negotiation Framework of October 2005 did not contain any reference to transparency and inclusiveness in the negotiation process,[166] but the Commission included allusions in this direction in its subsequent strategy documents. In the Enlargement Strategy 2007–08[167] the Commission announced for instance the introduction of a 'facility to further the development of civil society, notably through capacity-building and exchange projects'.[168] With these activities it aimed at 'strengthening the fabric of democracy across civil society' in the candidate countries and at fostering mutual knowledge, understanding, and dialogue between the citizens of EU

[164] Wunsch, 'Coming Full Circle? Differential Empowerment in Croatia's EU Accession Process' (n 163) 1212.
[165] European Commission, 'Guidelines for EU support to civil society in enlargement countries, 2014–2020' (14 October 2013).
[166] Škrabalo (n 155) 2 and 6.
[167] European Commission, 'Enlargement Strategy and Main Challenges 2007–2008' (6 November 2007) COM(2007) 663 final.
[168] ibid 4.

Member States and the enlargement countries. The so-called Civil Society Facility, launched in 2008, supported national and multi-beneficiary projects with the goal to strengthen the role of civil society bodies in the political process, enhance their capacity to develop cross-border projects and networks, and to familiarize them with EU affairs. Among the covered sectors were also human rights and gender equality.[169] This initiative indicated the increasing emphasis placed by the Commission on the development and capacity building of civil society and its involvement in political processes, both at the moment of law making but also at the stage of implementation, monitoring, and evaluation of public policies. The ensuing Instrument for Pre-accession Assistance (IPA) 2008 programme with the title 'Enhancing the capacities/roles of CSOs in the monitoring of the implementation of the EU acquis in the field of the comprehensive anti-discrimination strategy' clearly showed the Commission's interest in building the capacities of CSOs for monitoring the implementation of this part of the acquis and enhancing the role of CSOs in this context.

Only in 2013, thus when Croatia had already acceded to the EU, the Commission went a step further with the 'Guidelines for EU support to civil society in enlargement countries, 2014–2020', which focus on 'enabling and stimulating participatory democracy'.[170] This implies the creation of an environment conducive to civil society activities, the provision of structures and mechanisms to ensure their participation in law making and the development of policies, and the capacity building of CSOs in order for them to be 'effective and accountable independent actors'.[171] The Commission Guidelines envisage both political support and financial assistance to reach these goals. According to the Guidelines, an expected result is that '[p]ublic institutions recognise the importance of CSOs in improving good governance through CSOs' inclusion in decision making processes'.[172]

During Croatia's accession process, however, this approach had not yet been formulated in such a clear manner. In fact, as Wunsch points out 'political support by the European Commission for civil society inclusion remained largely restricted to regular, but superficial observations in its annual progress reports. At no point

[169] ibid 14–15.

[170] European Commission, 'Guidelines for EU support to civil society in enlargement countries, 2014–2020' (n 165) 1.

[171] Capacity building is understood by the Guidelines as improving CSOs' 'autonomy, representativeness and accountability by strengthening their membership base, by higher internal governance standards, … monitoring and evaluation, financial management, transparency, geographic outreach and cooperation'. Effectiveness can be increased by 'increasing their capacity for analysis, monitoring and advocacy as well as networking, partnership, coalition-building and active involvement in the policy and law making processes'. ibid 1–3.

[172] ibid 9. New Guidelines for the period 2021–27 are currently being drafted, having the following three objectives: a) achieving an environment that is conducive to civil society operation and activities; b) strengthening relations between CSOs and IPA beneficiary authorities/institutions; and c) reinforcing the capacity and resilience of CSOs to be effective and accountable independent actors. The Draft Guidelines are planned to include clear benchmarks and results indicators on the basis of which the progress in achieving the agreed objectives can be measured. See DG NEAR, 'Guidelines and Strategic Directions for EU Support to Civil Society in the Enlargement Region 2021–2027—Working Draft' (19 February 2021) 6.

during the negotiations was the issue of effective inclusion presented as a priority, much less a potential obstacle to eventual accession. Instead, the absence of formal benchmarks for civil society inclusion made it difficult to move beyond a soft approach to the issue, with EU officials limiting themselves to encouraging their negotiating partners to improve cooperation with CSOs, but leaving the precise form and degree of such involvement up to them.'[173]

Notwithstanding this lack of clear political support by the Commission, an 'authentic civil society'[174] active in the non-discrimination field managed to make itself visible and to push issues on their agenda with certain embassies who, for their part, supported these issues vis-à-vis the Commission's delegation. The Commission started having regular meetings with civil society organizations and asked them for their opinion before writing the progress reports.[175] Thus the government knew that it was important to involve civil society in order to get positive comments in the progress reports.

This might explain why, although the adoption of the ADA in 2008 was done through an urgent procedure which would have made it possible to skip a consultative process,[176] the government decided to set up a Working Group composed of the relevant ministries, specialized bodies (such as a representative of the OO) as well as representatives of civil society and academia. Apart from being elaborated in this Working Group, the draft was debated during a public discussion, organized by the Working Group, with NGOs and other relevant stakeholders. From the procedural point of view, the drafting of the ADA was thus comparatively inclusive and transparent.[177] It was only in 2009 that Croatia adopted a Code for NGO Consultations.[178] It lays down the minimum standards for consultations, including amongst other things the involvement of stakeholders in the drafting of legislation through Working Groups, online consultations, and the organization of public discussions.[179] Consultation coordinators were installed in all ministries and governmental agencies and training programmes financed by the EU's financial assistance

[173] Wunsch, *EU Enlargement and Civil Society in the Western Balkans: From Mobilisation to Empowerment* (n 163) 45.

[174] Interviews, Jagoda Novak, 13 October 2015. Also Deputy Ombudsperson for Gender Equality, Croatia, 12 October 2015 (especially regarding women's rights); Professor of Political Science, University of Zagreb, 13 October 2015.

[175] Interview, Executive Board Member of Centre for Peace Studies and NGO activist, 13 October 2015. For candidate countries in general Wunsch, 'Coming Full Circle? Differential Empowerment in Croatia's EU Accession Process' (n 163).

[176] At the peak of negotiations, 87 per cent of all legislation was adopted through the urgent procedure. Škrabalo (n 155) 9.

[177] The government decided against the same inclusive process when the amendments to the ADA were discussed in 2012, as it did not want to risk opening discussion on the whole law.

[178] Code of Practice on Consultation with the interested Public in Procedures of Adopting Laws, other Regulations and Acts, Official Gazette no 140/2009. On its 'troubled course of adoption' see Škrabalo (n 155) 10.

[179] Bulgarian Center for Not-for-Profit Law, Participation of NGOs in the Process of Policy- and Law-Making. Comparative Analysis (2008) 20–21 https://www.icnl.org/post/analysis/participation-of-ngos-in-the-process-of-policy-and-law-making.

instruments.[180] The drafting process of the ADA thus somewhat anticipated the procedure laid down a year later in the Code for NGO consultation.

The first National Plan for Combatting Discrimination, covering the period 2008–13 (NP 2008–13), on the other hand, was adopted without any stakeholder involvement. As mentioned by several interview partners both from the governmental side and the NGO sector, this document never came to pass. Upon the initiative of some NGOs and with the financial support by the Commission, the NP 2008–13 was evaluated and recommendations for improvement formulated. When the work on the new NP supposed to cover the period 2015–20 started in 2014, these recommendations were taken as a starting point for the discussions. In addition, the Government Office for Human Rights and Rights of National Minorities (GOHMR), responsible for drafting the document, involved a broad range of people in the Working Group in order to substantiate the new NP, including representatives of NGOs[181] and the Equality Body. Focus groups with forty NGOs were organized to cover all the grounds included in the ADA. Regional meetings were organized in order to reach out to organizations throughout the country.[182]

It was exactly in this period, where the Civil Society Facility of the Commission started to deploy its first effects. While the capacity building of the Commission thus had no impact on the drafting of ADA, it was very important in the context of drafting the National Non-Discrimination Plan. The Zagreb-based Center for Peace Studies implemented a project under the above-mentioned IPA 2008 Programme.[183] The project called 'Stronger civil society for efficient implementation and monitoring of anti-discrimination policies in Croatia' was carried out between April 2011 and July 2013. Among the most important results achieved by this project was the publication of a monitoring report on the implementation of the ADA and the Free Legal Aid Act as well as the just mentioned evaluation of the National Plan for Combatting Discrimination 2008–13 including recommendations for its improvement. This result has been achieved by joining forces with another IPA-funded network of NGOs led by the Osijek-based Center for Peace, Nonviolence and Human Rights. Cooperation between these NGOs continued beyond the duration of the IPA projects. Beyond strengthening their capacity of being meaningfully involved in policy formulation, the goal of creating sustainable networks has thus also been reached. This example is in line with the finding of a study on the role of Croatian CSO in the EU accession process, according to which

[180] Igor Vidačak, 'Impact of Europeanization on Interest Groups Access and Representation in the Policy Making Process in Croatia' [2011] Etudes européennes La revue permanente des professionnels de l'Europe, 9.

[181] Center for Peace Studies and Croatian Law Center.

[182] Interview with a former official working at the GOHMR, October 2015.

[183] The programme was entitled 'Enhancing the capacities/roles of CSOs in the monitoring of the implementation of the EU acquis in the field of the comprehensive anti-discrimination strategy'.

there is an above-average continuation of cooperation between NGOs that have started working together during an EU-funded project.[184]

The pushes from both the Commission and civil society might have been necessary but not enough for the process of drafting the ADA and the NP to become an inclusive one. It also depended a lot on the acceptance by the GOHMR that it did not have enough of its own experience and resources to draft these two documents without outside support and the openness and willingness of decision makers within this office to set up broadly constructed Working Groups. The ice was broken by a Progress project which was dedicated to the raising of awareness of and capacities among all relevant stakeholders in the anti-discrimination field. This was the starting point of the cooperation of the GOHMR with the OO and civil society organizations, which continues until this very day. In the words of one interview partner: 'This project helped building a partnership among people and institutions who would normally not work together.'[185] The openness of officials in governmental institutions was instrumental in the Croatian case, but is helpful only if they also enjoy political backing. In fact, other research has shown that there is 'a gap in responsiveness between civil servants, who are generally open to collaboration, and political appointees who remain reluctant to opening up the hierarchical model of policy-making to outside actors'.[186]

The question is thus, whether—even if stakeholders are involved in the drafting of legislation or strategic documents and they are equipped with the necessary capacities—their voices are really heard and their viewpoints and objectives are reflected in the final outcome. According to the information provided by interview partners both with governmental and NGO backgrounds, civil society representatives and representatives of the OO *did* have a say in the drafting processes. For instance, the representative of the Ombudsperson in the Working Group for the drafting of the ADA was an expert in the anti-discrimination field who heavily influenced the substance of the law. The part concerning judicial protection was essentially drafted by an expert in procedural law from the University of Zagreb.

When it comes to the National Plan on Combatting Discrimination, the picture is mixed. It was due to the above-mentioned concerted efforts of civil society organizations that an evaluation of the first plan was undertaken and the recommendations coming from this evaluation could serve as a basis for work on the new plan. Several of the recommendations were taken into account.[187] Information gathered

[184] Croatia 45.7 per cent, EU countries 32.1 per cent, IPA countries 22.1 per cent), see Irena Đokić and Marijana Sumpor, 'The Role of Croatian Civil Society Organisations in the European Union Accession Process' (Technical Assistance for Civil Society Organisations Croatia Office, International Swedish Institute for Public Administration, Zagreb June 2013) 4 and 34–35. 49 per cent of respondents of this study further indicated that the quality of partnerships improved as a result of the accession process. ibid 34.

[185] Interview, staff member at the GOHMR, 12 October 2015.

[186] Fagan and Wunsch (n 163) 3–4.

[187] Božić Krstanović and Lalić (n 131) 67.

through focus groups and regional meetings with NGOs working on different protected grounds, was also taken into consideration when drafting the Plan. By the end of 2015, a final draft for the National Plan for Combatting Discrimination was thus drafted in a way in which stakeholders were not only involved in the drafting processes but also managed to influence the outcome.

However, the document was not adopted until the end of 2017. In the meantime, Croatia had two elections, in November 2015 and September 2016, and the incumbent conservative governments did not have the fight against discrimination high on their agenda. A first redraft of the National Anti-discrimination Plan was done in the first half of 2016 and put out for public discussion. But with the next elections already coming up in autumn 2016, this plan was not adopted, even if it was 'part of the activities to meet ex-ante conditionality from the EU's Operational Program Competitiveness and Cohesion 2014–2020'.[188] With the new government in office, the GOHMR started redrafting the National Plan under the coordination of the deputy prime minister in February 2017. NGOs with the best track record in working on non-discrimination issues, such as the Centre for Peace Studies, were not included in the Working Group—although such expertise is a requirement for being selected for the Working Group in the course of a public call—while NGOs with a more conservative agenda were admitted.[189] As a result of these two redrafting processes, several measures relating to LGBT rights, gender identity, and the protection of reproductive rights were deleted from the Plan. However, due to the intervention of the OO and of the Ombudsperson for Gender Equality (both represented in the Working Group), most of these measures could be brought back into the version of the Plan that was finally adopted in November 2017 for the period 2017–22. The reintegration of these measures was partly also related to the pressure built up by NGOs in the Croatian media and—to a more limited extent—through their interventions with different embassies and the EU representation in Croatia.[190]

These developments are related to the generally shrinking space for civil society organizations, contrary to the Commission's proclamation of a conducive environment for civil society organizations in its strategic document of 2013.[191] It could thus be concluded that the Commission's emphasis on involvement of stakeholders in the formulation of legislation and policy documents has come too late in the

[188] Nives Miošić-Lisjak, 'One Step Forward, Two Steps Back: Anti-Discrimination Policy in Croatia 2011–2016' (Centre for Peace Studies, October 2017) 4–5.

[189] ibid 5.

[190] Interviews, Executive Board Member of Centre for Peace Studies, Zagreb, 1 August 2018 and staff member at the OO, 26 October 2018. In fact, both concurred in their impression, that the Commission dedicated limited interest to the issue as formally Croatia complied with the EU Directives considering that it had the anti-discrimination law in place and had designated an Equality Body.

[191] European Commission, 'Guidelines for EU support to civil society in enlargement countries, 2014–2020' (n 165).

Croatian case to be able to be properly institutionalized by the time of accession. Institutionalization, as defined by Fagan and Wunsch, means in this context the full implementation of 'a mechanism enabling the effective and transparent integration of a diverse range of civil society actors into processes of policy development'.[192] They presume 'that the more fragile political environment prevalent in EU candidate countries requires such formalised procedures at least in the intermediary period in order to provide a recognised framework regulating interactions between state and civil society actors'.[193] Instead, what can be observed in the Croatian context can either be described as façade-implementation, where consultative mechanisms are only formally implemented, or even reversal, where new practices established are reversed at a later stage.[194] As a CSO representative mentioned in an interview, CSO representatives involved in Working Groups are 'there to be there'. Furthermore, comments of CSOs with a focus on human rights or non-discrimination on draft documents are rarely accepted and the elaboration on the reasons for rejection is scarce or even non-existent. Compared to the situation in the early 2010s, where the acceptance rate was higher and explanations for rejections more abundant, the situation has thus deteriorated.[195] While structures have changed and new procedures have been introduced, the authors of a study on the role of Croatian civil society organizations in the EU accession process also expressed concern about the tendency among public administration officials to perceive civil society involvement as the fulfilment of formal requirements and thus as an exercise legitimizing their actions and not as a way to improve the quality of policies. As such, involvement is not truly participatory.[196]

It can therefore be concluded that the Commission would do well to invigorate its support for civil society organizations in candidate countries, but also to grant sustained financial and political support to NGOs after accession. While financial support appears vital in a situation where NGOs in many European countries suffer from serious funding cuts, it is even more important that the EU insists vis-à-vis the Member States—as it does in its Guidelines for EU support to civil society in enlargement countries—on a 'conducive environment' for NGOs, including an appropriate legal and financial environment as well as the institutionalization of their involvement in decision-making processes.

[192] Fagan and Wunsch (n 163) 5.

[193] ibid. Also Chhotray and Stoker write that 'for participatory governance to last, it must be institutionlised'. Vasudha Chhotray and Gerry Stoker, *Governance Theory and Practice: A Cross-Disciplinary Approach* (Palgrave Macmillan 2010) 186.

[194] Fagan and Wunsch (n 163) 6. Chhotray and Stoker, reviewing a number of studies evaluating the experience of participatory projects, also identify 'a ritual of participation that is not substantiated in reality' among the problems revealed. Other problems relate to 'elite capture of participatory spaces/forums' and 'the marginalization of possibilities by which the poorest and most vulnerable sections of a community may be represented'. Chhotray and Stoker (n 193) 188.

[195] Interview, Executive Board Member of Centre for Peace Studies, Zagreb, 1 August 2018, confirmed by interview with staff member at the OO, 26 October 2018.

[196] See Đokić and Sumpor (n 184) 22.

The last question to be asked, as shown in the above graph, is what role stakeholders continue to play in the implementation phase, for instance in terms of judicial protection, independent monitoring, and awareness raising. At the outset it is fair to admit that one cannot expect the involvement of stakeholders in law and policy making, as well as in monitoring implementation, to be a panacea for all implementation-related challenges. These challenges remain high also in the Croatian context. But in terms of ownership and awareness raising, as well as keeping the issue of non-discrimination on the agenda, which are all key to ensure sustainability of reforms, the approach of involving stakeholders is certainly more promising than working behind closed doors.

As a matter of fact, such ownership might be lacking within the judiciary. Asked about the biggest challenges related to implementation, most interlocutors mentioned the application of the ADA by the courts. As in other new Member States, only a limited number of discrimination cases is brought before the courts.[197] The reasons for this are the victims shying away from the lengthy proceedings, the uncertain outcome of the case, and the risk, in case of defeat, of having to pay the cost of the proceedings. The outcome is felt to be uncertain because there were a few cases reported in the media, where one could reasonably have expected the plaintiff to win but this was not the case. This, in turn, is connected to the fact that judges are rarely confronted with discrimination cases, they lack experience in dealing with them, and sometimes have difficulty in applying some of the concepts newly introduced by the ADA. This is why, as will be further discussed below, training on anti-discrimination legislation and the relevant European courts' practice should be compulsory and should take place on a regular basis. In order to increase the number of cases brought to court, it would be useful if the OO and NGOs made greater use of the opportunities offered by the ADA to support a victim of discrimination by an intervention or by bringing a joint legal action.[198] If a couple of leading cases were brought before the courts, this would draw attention to problems of discrimination, make it possible to establish a court practice on discrimination cases, and thus render the outcome more predictable. In this context, NGOs as well as the Equality Body may not yet have made extensive use of the opportunities provided by transposing the Directives.

Among the reasons why both OO and NGOs are reluctant in using this option is, similarly to victims of discrimination, the financial risk. The ongoing discussions at the level of the European Parliament and the Commission to support litigation and in particular strategic litigation is thus a welcome development.[199]

[197] The number of criminal discrimination cases remains fairly low. The number of civil discrimination cases was even decreasing for a number of years, while in 2019 it has remained at approximately the same level as in 2018. See EELN, Country Report Croatia, 2020, 78.

[198] In 2015, the OO has engaged an individual with the task of identifying cases suitable for such strategic litigation. It is currently involved in one case relating to discrimination on the ground of age.

[199] See, for more on this, Chapter 4.4.

However, as one should not always look only at European sources, such funding could and should be made available also at the level of Member States. In Croatia, such funding could, for instance, be taken over by the National Foundation for Civil Society Development.[200]

More than in judicial protection, civil society organizations see their role in the independent monitoring of the implementation of anti-discrimination related policies and in raising awareness about discrimination more generally. In the pre-accession phase, the Commission financed a number of IPA projects aimed at strengthening the capacities of civil society organizations in these fields.[201] This funding made it possible to set up the Croatian Equality Forum,[202] to elaborate a toolkit on the application and enforcement of the anti-discrimination law and policy for Croatian civil society, to implement awareness-raising activities among media, political stakeholders, and the public at large on the importance of a strong anti-discrimination policy, and to create networks of Zagreb-based NGOs with organizations in other parts of the country. As mentioned above, the evaluation of the ADA and of the first National Anti-Discrimination Plan was a result of the joint efforts of these networks.[203] In 2019, following a recommendation of the Ombudsperson,[204] the government established a Working Group for Monitoring the National Plan for Combatting Discrimination 2017–22, including the Osijek-based Centre for Peace, Non-violence and Human Rights. A side-effect of EU-funded projects enhancing the capacity of civil society organizations in the anti-discrimination field is that many of the individuals involved in the projects on the CSOs' side have later moved to state institutions, which means they also bring with them their knowledge and experience.

These examples show that civil society organizations did use the opportunities offered by the pre-accession process and make it reasonable to expect that they will also play a role in the future when it comes to independent monitoring and awareness raising.

The Croatian experience has also revealed where there is room for improvement regarding the Commission's approach in enhancing stakeholder involvement, including through capacity-building measures. On a more practical note, beneficiary institutions were often confronted with planning problems due to the late

[200] See the Foundations webpage at https://zaklada.civilnodrustvo.hr/en.

[201] Five projects were granted to networks of civil society organizations under IPA 2008 and four under IPA 2010.

[202] The forum funded under IPA 2008 did not survive in its initial conception. However, through funds of the National Foundation for Civil Society Development, a new Equality Forum was created which built on the membership of the previous one. Interview, representative of the Croatian Law Centre, 13 October 2015.

[203] The most recent evaluation of anti-discrimination policy in Croatia, published in October 2017 by the Centre for Peace Studies, was financed by the Commissions Rights, Equality and Citizenship Programme and co-funded by the Office for cooperation with NGOs of the Croatian Government. Miošić-Lisjak (n 188).

[204] Ombudswoman of the Republic of Croatia, 'Annual Report 2018' (2019) 13.

implementation start. IPA 2008 projects only started in 2011, IPA 2010 projects in 2013. Activities they had planned when submitting their proposal had in some cases already been accomplished by the time implementation started. People that were planned to be involved were no longer available. A quicker decision on the granting of funds would therefore be desirable. In terms of exchange of experience, it would be good for all beneficiaries of one IPA generation to meet and inform each other about the activities of their project work. This would help to avoid duplications and create synergies between different projects.[205] Such meetings could also be used to bring in foreign experts who could share their experience. Such linkages between projects could be created not only at national but also at regional level as a contribution to strengthening civil society in the region.[206] A limitation of EU-funded activities is the fact that only a small number of NGOs, mostly based in the capital, were stable enough to apply for projects and get funding. This reduces the territorial coverage of these activities. The civil society funding schemes recently adopted in the context of the Multiannual Financial Framework 2021–27[207] should take into consideration these limitations.

More strategically, the Commission's shift from 'mere' capacity building, to emphasizing the need for inclusive policy making[208] is to be welcomed. Support in this sense should start at the earliest possible stage in the accession negotiation to make it more likely that by the time of accession inclusive and transparent procedures have become institutionalized and are not only a façade.[209] This way, it is suggested, backsliding with regard to serious stakeholder involvement as described above could be prevented. In any case, continued financial and political support for a conducive environment for NGOs also post-accession, in fact for all EU Member States, appears essential.

2.6.3.3 Knowledge Sharing and Exchange of Good Practice

Knowledge sharing and the exchange of good practice is a typical element of the recursive process within the experimentalist governance approach. By learning from the experience of other actors in the implementation of the co-designed framework rule, not only can the individual actors adapt their own way of handling the issue but it can eventually also lead to a reformulation of the central rule. By looking at

[205] Interview, representative of the Croatian Law Centre, 13 October 2015.

[206] On transnational learning with regard to civil society organizations see Natasha Wunsch, 'Transnational Learning and Civil Society Empowerment in the EU Enlargement Process' [2018] Journal of Common Market Studies 1.

[207] For more on the Multiannual Financial Framework 2021–27 and the possibilities for NGO financing in the framework of the Justice, Rights and Values Programme, see Chapter 6.3.3.

[208] European Commission, 'Guidelines for EU support to civil society in enlargement countries, 2014–2020' (n 165), followed in 2015 by European Commission, 'Guidelines for EU support to civil society in enlargement countries, 2014–2020' (June 2015), and currently in the process of being strengthened in the context of the Guidelines for the period 2021–27, DG NEAR (n 172).

[209] Wunsch, 'Coming Full Circle? Differential Empowerment in Croatia's EU Accession Process' (n 163) 1212–13; and Fagan and Wunsch (n 163) 5–6.

how others have approached the same problem and what kind of solutions they have found the ground for *reframing* (discussed at 2.6.3.4) can be prepared. The pooling of results and finding out about good practices, as well as the challenges that have been encountered during the implementation of the framework rule, is therefore of the utmost importance in achieving the objectives of the rule.

In the framework of enlargement, twinning arrangements are an important forum for knowledge sharing. Twinning is conceived as a peer-to-peer assistance programme, in which officials from Member States 'share with colleagues in public administrations of beneficiaries in enlargement … regions, their experience and know-how, the complexities of EU legislation and best practice related to its implementation'.[210] But the various networks created by the EU non-discrimination regime also play an important role in the exchange of good practice and mutual learning. In the present case study, the role of the Equinet and FRA will be briefly discussed.

An important element in order for knowledge sharing and exchange of good practice to result in a substantial and sustainable impact is local ownership. Simmons pointed out in relation to compliance with human rights treaties that even if processes of change take place with outside help, it is important that it is the locals who 'make decisions about what is culturally appropriate in their society and how best to deploy limited resources in order to realize the greatest benefits'. The most important policy advice she derives from her study is thus 'domestic ownership'.[211] Local ownership goes hand in hand with equal partnership. While it is the candidate country that has to adapt to the EU acquis it is not excluded that there are already procedures and practices in place from which the incoming peer can learn, thus making it a mutual learning process. The best knowledge-sharing exercise will most likely be in vain if there is not the political will and backing inside the beneficiary institution to reconsider the solutions that have so far been found for a particular problem. This links to the issue of reframing, dealt with at 2.6.3.4. It might therefore be possible to find differences with respect to the success of the learning exercise depending on whether the beneficiary institution is a public administration or an independent institution. Apart from bilateral settings of knowledge sharing, such as in the case of a twinning, the exchange of experience should take place also at European level, involving all actors concerned by the framework rule, which are all in search for solutions to the common problem.

[210] European Commission, TAIEX and Twinning Activity Report 2014, 2015, 1.

[211] Beth Simmons, *Mobilizing for Human Rights* (CUP 2009) 371, 378: 'One of the lessons that follows from the research in this book is the crucial role that domestic actors play in their own human rights fate. Rights stakeholders around the world have actively made decisions about when and how to employ the norms contained in human rights treaties to influence practices on the ground in their countries. Sometimes they have done this with outside help, but the locals are the ones who carry the ball and take the risks. They also make decisions about what is culturally appropriate in their society and how best to deploy limited resources in order to realize the greatest benefits from the promises of the human rights treaties their governments have signed.… The most important policy advice that comes from this study … is domestic ownership. Human rights treaties matter where local groups have taken up the torch for themselves.'

Box 2.3 Process tracing: What evidence should be observable if the argument that there is a correlation between knowledge sharing and exchange of good practice on one hand, and enhanced implementation on the other is correct?

knowledge sharing and exchange of good practice →	• local ownership • equal partnership • political will – reframing • participation in national and European networks →	Enhanced implementation • improved procedures • increased awareness • sustainability beyond end of project

Croatia has implemented a twinning project, financed under IPA 2009, under the title 'Establishing a comprehensive system for anti-discrimination protection'.[212] The twinning adviser in this case was not the public administration of a Member State (as is usually the case), in this case Austria, but a mandated institution: the Ludwig Boltzmann Institute of Human Rights, based in Vienna. The beneficiary institutions were the Croatian Government Office for Human Rights and Rights of National Minorities and the OO, who is the designated Equality Body.[213] Implementation started in November 2011 and ended in June 2013, so just before Croatia acceded to the EU on 1 July 2013.

The project had three components. Within the first component, the capacity of key actors active in the implementation of the ADA was supposed to be raised. This included the staff of the OO, judges, state attorneys, and civil servants. The aim of the second component was to set up a system for the collection and monitoring of discrimination complaints, data on court cases on discrimination, and equality data. The last component aimed at the development of a system of assistance to potential victims of discrimination.

Activities under the first component consisted mainly of training for various stakeholders. For this purpose the training needs of each target group were identified and curricula developed. In terms of long-term impact, a distinction can be made between first, training provided to staff of the OO and second, training provided to judges, state attorneys, and key actors in the administration (county coordinators for human rights, coordinators for gender equality, commissioners for ethics from state administration[214]). In the first case the staff

[212] A project description and some of its outcomes can be found at http://bim.lbg.ac.at/en/croatia-establishing-comprehensive-system-anti-discrimination-protection-twinning.

[213] As mentioned above, the ADA assigns certain activities to 'Special Ombudsmen' (the ombudsmen for gender equality, disabled persons, and for children). The OO is the central Equality Body.

[214] European Commission, 'Twinning Review Mission Report' (January 2015) 5.

who underwent training remained fairly stable following the end of the project[215] and all those who participated in the project's training activities were later grouped in a specialized anti-discrimination department established in the course of a reorganization of the Office after the end of the project. Due to their type of work they are also in a position to apply their newly acquired knowledge regularly. The impact can thus be considered to be high.

In the second case, the long-term impact might have been more limited, at least at first sight. There is no doubt that the judiciary is a cornerstone when it comes to enforcement of the anti-discrimination legislation. It is further undisputed that due to a number of innovative elements in the Anti-Discrimination Act (such as joint legal action, the role of NGOs, the shifting of the burden of proof, but also the definition of the various forms of discrimination) as well as the necessity to take the jurisprudence of European courts into consideration when taking decisions in discrimination cases, there is a strong need to providing in-depth and continuous training for judges and state attorneys. These issues have been raised repeatedly in the parliamentary debates about the ADA, in which MPs of different political parties have underlined this need and urged for the provision of necessary funds for that purpose. The question is, however, how to achieve this goal.

Anti-discrimination legislation and the procedural specificities are neither part of the compulsory university curriculum[216] nor of the initial training programme of the Judicial Academy, where it would be a compulsory subject for future judges and state attorneys. In the framework of twinning, fifty judges and twenty state attorneys received a one-day training on anti-discrimination issues. The impact in terms of reaching out to the target group might therefore be considered to be rather limited.

However, building on the partnership established during the twinning project between the OO and the Judicial Academy, six further training sessions on discrimination issues were organized after the end of the project in 2014, gathering a total of seventy-four judges and state attorneys.[217] Furthermore, based on the curriculum developed during the twinning, the Judicial Academy continued to offer a one-day training course on the application of the ADA as part of its optional programme for the continuing education of judicial officials.[218] However, to date, only a limited number of discrimination cases have

[215] ibid. More than seven years after the end of the project the workforce has remained stable and those involved in training during twinning are still working there, with one exception. Interview, staff member at the OO, 26 March 2021. Lack of stability and continuity resulting from personnel changes has been identified as one problem for the long-term effects of twinning projects. See Malgorzata Fuszara, 'The OMC, Gender Policy and the Experience of Poland as a New Member State' in Fiona Beveridge and Samantha Velluti (eds), *Gender and the Open Method of Coordination. Perspectives on Law, Governance and Equality in the EU* (Ashgate 2008) 112.

[216] And could not be requested as such as part of the National Plan for Combatting Discrimination, due to the autonomy of universities.

[217] European Commission, 'Twinning Review Mission Report' (n 214).

[218] Interview, staff member at the GOHMR, 12 October 2015.

come before the courts, so a long period may elapse before a judge, who participated in a training course on non-discrimination legislation, is faced with a discrimination case. A one-day training course dating back a long time might not therefore have the impact one would wish for.

On a positive note however, the cooperation between the OO and the Judicial Academy has remained stable since the implementation of the twinning project and the training methodology developed in the course of twinning has been replicated in the framework of other training activities jointly organized by the two institutions. After Croatia's accession to the EU, the network of Croatian partners involved in the anti-discrimination twinning, including the OO and the Judicial Academy, has been granted a project under the EU's Rights, Equality and Citizenship Programme,[219] which picked up on the results of the twinning project and developed them further. It continued working, for instance, on the education of lawyers, judges, and state attorneys regarding anti-discrimination legislation in general, and hate speech and hate crime in particular. In the framework of this project, e-learning materials on anti-discrimination issues have been developed as part of the regular (but still optional) programme for serving judges. Furthermore, in the preparation of its annual educational programme, the Judicial Academy regularly consults the OO for input regarding the content, which can be considered an improvement in the relations between the two institutions.[220] While of course this development cannot be attributed solely to their cooperation regarding the twinning project, it has certainly contributed to solidifying cooperation between the OO and the Judicial Academy.

Even if the immediate impact of the twinning project in terms of raising awareness among judicial officials about anti-discrimination issues might have been limited at first sight, an assessment of its long-term impact should not neglect the continuing existence of the network of partners, which continues working towards the same aim.

The second component focused on the establishment of databases on discrimination cases reported to the OO and cases brought to court (established at the OO) as well as on equality data (established at the GOHMR). With regard to the latter, the project team produced a handbook, with the aim to 'provide public institutions as well as regional and local units of self-government with information and guidelines on how to collect equality data ... contain[ing] information for describing, analysing and assessing conditions and issues of equality in a society'.[221] The

[219] The project was led by the Centre for Peace Studies, the partners were: Ludwig Boltzmann Institute for Human Rights, Office for Human Rights and the Rights of National Minorities (Croatia), Ombudsman of the Republic of Croatia, Judicial Academy (Croatia), Serbian National Council (Croatia). See the project website at the Boltzmann Institute: Mind the Gap: Measuring (In)equality in Croatia, at https://bim.lbg.ac.at/en/project/completed-projects-projects-antidiscrimination-diversity-asylum-projects-antidiscrimination/mind-gap-measuring-inequality-croatia.

[220] Interview, staff member at the OO, 26 October 2018 and 26 March 2021.

[221] Theodora Manolakos and Monika Mayrhofer, 'Handbook on how to collect equality data targeting public institutions, regional and local units of self-government which collect equality data'

beneficiary institutions agree that the twinning project was very useful for the setting-up of the databases. The interlocutor from the GOHMR mentioned for instance that the experience from other Member States was useful in defining what kind of data the equality database should contain, how they should be structured, etc.[222] After the end of the twinning, filling the databases, especially the one on equality data, proved challenging. One of the reasons was that a majority of institutions did not collect data broken down by the grounds contained in the ADA (eg ethnicity). However, the process of filling the database was considered to be a process of changing the way the state administration collects data.[223] Initial criticism has been raised by other interview partners of the limited use made of the data available to the OO and the GOHMR. The OO in particular was encouraged to make use of the data for awareness-raising and advocacy and not only for reporting purposes.[224]

More than seven years after the end of the project, the databases continue to be in use and the one established within the OO has served as a template for the setting up of a general database for the whole Office. The data are mainly used for reporting purposes to the Parliament, the FRA, and UN monitoring bodies. Flowing from an analysis of the data and the identification of problems, the OO is also addressing warnings and recommendations to different institutions. Furthermore, working with the equality database established within the GOHMR has revealed that certain data are missing, especially with regard to certain particularly vulnerable groups. This led to another twinning project in which baseline data were collected regarding Roma in various areas of life, such as employment, housing, and health care. The data collected in this context were used to evaluate the existing Roma strategy and to feed into the new national policy on Roma integration.[225]

It can thus be concluded that the establishment of the databases during the twinning was instrumental in systematically collecting data both at the level of the OO and within governmental institutions (with regard to the latter, this has played out positively mainly with regard to Roma). The data are used to inform recommendations to decision makers and have triggered intensified data collection regarding Roma. The results of the twinning have thus had an impact way beyond the end of the project.

Within the third component of the twinning regarding the improvement of the assistance to victims of discrimination, in addition to setting up two regional offices,

(Twinning Project: Establishing a comprehensive system for anti-discrimination protection, Zagreb January 2013) 5.

[222] Interview, staff member at the GOHMR, 12 October 2015.
[223] ibid.
[224] Interview, Executive Board Member of Centre for Peace Studies and NGO activist, 13 October 2015.
[225] Interview, staff member at the OO, 26 October 2018.

a telephone hotline has also been established as a way to improve the outreach, visibility, and accessibility of the OO. Notwithstanding the recommendations made in the framework of the project, the OO cannot offer this service free of charge. For the time being only one person, instead of a small team as recommended, is in charge of answering these calls. The number of regional offices has, since the end of the project, been increased to three and these are instrumental in particular when it comes to reaching out to Roma communities living in the respective areas.[226]

And finally, the external experts coming in through the twinning helped to reflect on the way discrimination complaints are handled within the OO and provided opportunities for sharing views among the staff members of the Office. This led to the formulation of rules on complaints handling, including a standardized procedure as well as more direct links and exchange between the discrimination victim and the case worker handling his/her complaint. The rules have been continuously developed since the end of the project and continue being applied not only within the specialized anti-discrimination department but throughout the OO.[227] The twinning has thereby not only contributed to more efficient procedures in discrimination cases but has also strengthened the capacity of the body with regard to the rest of its mandate.

Although twinning as an instrument has been criticized,[228] this specific twinning experience was perceived as positive and successful both by the beneficiary institutions as well as the twinning adviser.[229] The Twinning Review Mission Report came to the conclusion that 'it appears the project fed an internal reflection and evolution which were pre-existing within the Beneficiary Administration. The project, facilitated, supported, boosted the institutional changes occurred in the field of anti-discrimination policy over the last few years. In a schematic way, we could tell the project somehow fed the change more than it created the change from scratch.'[230] A favourable factor for the success of the twinning was thus that it fell on fertile ground. Interview partners agree with the Twinning Review Mission Report on the point that there was a strong ownership of the project. This can be related on the one hand to the fact that the project objectives were genuinely identified and expressed by the beneficiary institutions and not imposed from above.

[226] ibid.

[227] European Commission, 'Twinning Review Mission Report' (n 214); and interview, staff member at the OO, 26 October 2018.

[228] See eg Fuszara (n 215) 111–13, where she found that 'twinning projects were not based on the assumption of mutual learning'. Rather, they 'were formed around the idea of the "old" member state teaching the candidate state about the ways and methods employed in the EU'. In practice she recognized that a mutual learning process took place since the EU experts were in most cases unaware of the institutions, traditions, and regulations existing in the receiving country but 'there was no expectation that the models from the candidate countries would be copied, even if they were considered to be in fact better'.

[229] Interviews with representatives of the beneficiary institutions as well as the resident twinning adviser in 2015 and again in 2018 and 2021.

[230] European Commission, 'Twinning Review Mission Report' (n 214).

On the other hand the resident twinning adviser managed to maintain this ownership by conceiving her role as a facilitator of reflection and reform rather than as a promoter of a Member State's practice. Unlike in other twinning projects, the partnership was perceived as equal with a very strong desire on the part of everyone involved to get the best out of the project. The beneficiary institutions also appreciated the flexibility of the twinning adviser to make use of pre-existing experiences, expertise, and materials, to build on the outcomes of previous projects, and on the existing networks. In fact, another factor mentioned as being key to success was that all the Croatian partners involved in the twinning had already worked together in a Progress project. Whereas with regard to the GOHMR most of twinning activities were targeting other stakeholders and not their own capacity, seven years after the end of the project it can be concluded with regard to the OO that the twinning sustainably strengthened its professional functioning, its visibility and outreach, as well as its position in the overall landscape of institutions dealing with issues related to discrimination.[231]

Twinning is not the only means by which knowledge sharing has taken place in Croatia's pre-accession phase, in particular when it comes to the Equality Body. As described above, the exchange of practice and learning from the experiences of others is one of the goals of Equinet. According to its strategic plan 2019–22 it pursues, inter alia, the objective to 'facilitate knowledge exchange, sharing of good practices and peer-to-peer support among equality bodies'.[232] The network is co-funded by DG Justice and is also open to accession countries. Its proactive role, already during the pre-accession phase, has been perceived by Croatian interview partners as very positive.[233] Staff of member institutions are involved in various Working Groups, elaborating comparative reports, guidelines, and toolkits. Peer-to-peer visits take place so that staff may learn from each other.

Whereas within Equinet, institutions from Member States and accession countries meet on an equal footing, within the FRA, candidate countries can only be awarded observer status. Croatia was awarded this status in May 2010. Both the focal point as well as the state administration have seen this possibility of being involved in the FRA's activities as a useful learning tool. They had the feeling that through the questionnaires received by the FRA on a yearly basis, the research they

[231] A review of a similar project in Serbia concluded that the implementation of the project with the Commissioner for the Protection of Equality (the independent Equality Body) 'was very successful and the institution has demonstrated its willingness to continue working on this direction after the closure of the project.... In contrast, the implementation in the OHMR [the governmental Office for Human and Minority Rights] was not that successful because of the particular position of this institution within the government structure, which does not allow for much independent actions and active involvement in all activities. However, the project definitely created a space for stakeholders to have peer-to-peer work that may continue after the closure of the project.' Lorena Diz Conde, 'The Impact of EU-funded Projects on Minority Protection in the Republic of Serbia' (Master thesis, University of Graz 2018) 86.

[232] Equinet, 'Strategic Plan 2019–2022' (2019) 5.

[233] Interviews, Deputy Ombudsperson for Gender Equality, Croatia; and staff member at the GOHMR, 12 October 2015.

had to do, and the fieldwork they had to carry out, they achieved a better understanding of the way how human rights issues in general and anti-discrimination issues in particular are framed in the EU. It was also considered a subtle reminder of the data that were still missing and of areas that need to be worked on.[234] On the other hand, the data published in FRA reports could be made use of in the drafting of policy documents, for example, the National Plan for Combatting Discrimination and the National Plan on Gender Equality. It is therefore a positive development, that next to North Macedonia, that has observer status since October 2017, this status has also been granted to Serbia in July 2018 and to Albania in December 2020.

In conclusion, it seems that under the above described circumstances, twinning as an element of experimentalist governance can be a successful tool for the exchange of experience between Member and candidate States and extend its impact into the post-accession period. This is the case especially for institutions such as the independent Equality Bodies which, if the requirement of independence is respected, have greater leeway in adapting their approaches and procedures if felt appropriate than governmental institutions, that might be limited by political considerations. However, considering the central importance of Equality Bodies in the overall enforcement of the equality regime, this is of no less importance. Their participation in national and Europe-wide networks, such as Equinet, is also an important element in achieving enhanced implementation and compliance. For governmental institutions, the observer status at the FRA could play an equally relevant role.

2.6.3.4 Reframing?

As mentioned in the introduction, *pragmatist and genetic approaches* require actors to engage in reflection upon the way they represent a problem, the kind of solutions they come up with, and the role they play in the whole process. Have actors reconsidered their pre-existing frames? Have they undertaken an exercise of reconstruction and an exercise in political imagination? And if so, how was it triggered?

The present empirical research suggests that no such processes have taken place among the political elite. Reforms were undertaken because they were a precondition for joining the EU, without reflecting on their appropriateness, thus following exclusively a logic of consequences. Becoming a member of the EU was almost considered a second recognition. This helped to overcome high domestic costs, like the extradition of war criminals to the International Criminal Tribunal for the former Yugoslavia (ICTY),[235] but resulted in what has been labelled by Boduszynski as

[234] Interviews, staff member at the GOHMR; and representative of the Croatian Law Centre, 13 October 2015.

[235] Interview, Professor of Political Science, University of Zagreb, 13 October 2015.

'simulated transition':[236] changing legislation without intention to change anything in practice. Although the Commission pledged that legal alignment is not enough and that substantive progress in implementation is required, what counted in the end was legal alignment. Several interlocutors concurred in their view that the lack of interest by the Commission in the faith of legislative reforms and their implementation after accession sends out the signal to current candidate countries that 'simulation' is enough. This brings us back to the idea of continued monitoring discussed above. Such continued monitoring was felt to be all the more important as it has been also generally accepted that the short time span before accession makes it almost impossible to ensure consistent implementation. The 'fundamentals first' approach, by which the important Chapters 23 and 24 are opened at the very beginning of negotiations and kept open until the end, can be seen as an improvement but might not be able to resolve the problem. But even if there is no continued monitoring, the question is whether the Commission can plant the seeds for appropriate implementation in the pre-accession phase among the key actors when it comes to application and enforcement: the judiciary, specialized bodies, as well as civil society organizations.

At the level of enforcement the central actor is the judiciary.[237] The empirical research has led to the conclusion that changes introduced by the ADA, in substantive and in procedural terms, trickle down only very slowly to the broad range of judges. Notwithstanding all the training provided to the judiciary in the framework of Progress, twinning, or other projects, continued efforts are required to substantially improve the capacity of judges to handle discrimination lawsuits and to break the formalism and bureaucratic way in which laws are very often interpreted and applied. It appears that European courts' practice is taken into consideration only if a judge is personally motivated. According to several interview partners, prejudices against persons who are victims of discrimination because of particular grounds (especially belonging to certain minorities, or LGBT) persist. The Judicial Academy, although increasingly offering courses on non-discrimination, also in cooperation with the Equality Body, continues dealing with the non-discrimination field in a marginal way.

An exercise of reconstruction and of political imagination can be said to have taken place within the OO, the designated Equality Body. As mentioned above, the twinning project has been used as a tool of reflection over the kind of institution it wants to be, the way certain things are done, how it is structured, etc. This reflection has led to a reorganization of the Office and a change

[236] Mieczysław P Boduszyński, *Regime Change in the Yugoslav Successor States: Divergent Paths toward a New Europe* (Johns Hopkins University Press 2010).

[237] Ott questions whether Croatia managed to avoid the Cooperation and Verification Mechanisms because it did a better job (inter alia, regarding the judiciary) than Bulgaria and Romania or because the EU became aware of questionable effects of this tool. Katarina Ott, 'Croatia and the EU: The Catch-Up Issue' (CEPS Commentary, 28 June 2013) 2.

in procedures, which have also been implemented by departments other than the one involved in anti-discrimination issues.

Civil society has taken up the challenge of revising its role in the anti-discrimination field throughout the pre-accession phase. It has managed to make use of the funding possibilities provided through the process. It has lobbied with the embassies of EU Member States and the Commission's delegation to influence the way the Commission reported about the issue. It also managed to create synergies out of various EU-funded projects and has tried to influence national decision-making processes on strategic documents. Within its financial capabilities, it has also tried the new role of acting in court in support of or on behalf of victims of discrimination. Bigger organizations are also engaged in transnational networks. With the pressure put on them in terms of financial cuts and reduced spaces for participation, they appear, however, to be pushed back to engaging more in their traditional roles of awareness raising, training, and monitoring, and less in litigation.[238]

It appears that working together on projects financed through the instruments of pre-accession assistance has contributed to new forms of cooperation such as between the Governmental Office for Human and Minority Rights, the OO, and CSOs. One could thus claim that this has also been the effect of targeted EU funding. While cooperation between the OO and CSO has become institutionalized over the years, the cooperation with the GOHMR appears to depend more on the personal motivation of those involved as well as the political backing or lack thereof received by officials of the Office.[239] CSO representatives also deplore the fact that notwithstanding fruitful cooperation on an individual basis, governments of all colours still do not consider civil society actors as a partner, or its critique as a constructive input to political processes.

2.6.4 Impact of Reflexive Governance Approaches in the Croatian Context

In this chapter, different approaches to reflexive governance have been presented claiming that they offer ideas that merit being studied more closely to establish their potential for improving compliance with the EU acquis also after accession. To that end, the theoretical considerations have been empirically tested in the case of Croatia and the policy field of equality and non-discrimination. The case study

[238] Ombudswoman of the Republic of Croatia (n 204) 27.

[239] Đokić and Sumpor found in their study dating back to 2013 that 31.4 per cent of NGOs indicated that the relationship between CSOs and the state/public sector has remained unchanged. 25.7 per cent find that this relationship has slightly improved, whereas 18.6 per cent are of the opinion that it has significantly improved. The overall rate finding that the relationship has improved is, therefore, at 44.3 per cent. Đokić and Sumpor (n 184) 37. It can be assumed that a similar study carried out today would show a deterioration of the CSO-state relationship.

has shown that elements of reflexive governance, especially of experimentalist governance, are in use in the pre-accession phase, with varying degrees of impact both on transposition and implementation of the relevant acquis. If one looks again at the implementation problems identified by Falkner et al and compares them with the situation in Croatia, the following conclusions can be drawn:

The first problem identified by Falkner was related to the lack of litigation from below which we have dealt with jointly with the second problem, the lack of support by civil society organizations. Croatia is no exception to the finding that only a limited number of discrimination cases end up being decided by a court. The preconditions for civil society organizations to bring discrimination cases to court are, however, better compared to the ones in the countries studied by Falkner. Unlike other legislation, the Croatian ADA foresees joint legal action and does not require more from organizations who want to bring such an action to court other than that they have a justified interest in protecting the collective interests of a certain group or that within the scope of their activities they deal with the protection of the right to equal treatment. It is hard to prove that this very open provision was included in the law *exactly* because of the broad stakeholder involvement in the drafting of the ADA, even if, as a matter of fact, the wording was proposed by an independent professor of procedural law who undertook a cursory review of European practice before proposing this text. In terms of implementation, exactly this open provision could help to overcome the lack of litigation from below, as it might help to address some of the reasons why people shy away from bringing their cases to court. The creation of a body of court decisions could make outcomes more easily predictable. NGOs could provide psychological support to victims of discrimination throughout the proceedings. Although NGOs would generally be willing to support victims in this way, they are reluctant because of the risk of having to pay the legal costs.[240] The Commission should therefore pursue the idea of encouraging NGOs in candidate and Member States to engage in such activities by financially supporting strategic litigation activities. It could further exert pressure on Judicial Academies to integrate courses on anti-discrimination legislation in its compulsory curriculum both for candidate judges as well as for the continuing education of incumbent judges. Further problems concerning the judiciary are of a more general nature and have to be resolved in the framework of an overall reform of the judiciary.

From the above one cannot, however, derive a lack of support from civil society. Quite the contrary: it was upon the initiative of NGOs that the NP 2008–13 was evaluated and recommendations for improvement made. It was also thanks

[240] In its 2018 Annual Report, the Croatian Ombudswoman found that the decline in NGOs being active in collective judicial protection is less connected to a drop of interest but rather to objective circumstances preventing them from acting. She therefore called for a financial strengthening of such NGOs. Ombudswoman of the Republic of Croatia (n 204) 27.

to the pressure built by NGOs in the media (as well as to the intervention of the Equality Bodies), that a substantial watering down of the current NP 2017–22 was prevented. Civil society organizations continue to monitor the implementation of non-discrimination policies in Croatia and organize awareness-raising measures for the general public, inter alia by attempting to include civic education (with an anti-discrimination component) into the general school curriculum. These activities have profited from pre- (and post-)accession EU funding, which helped to create networks surviving the accession date.

However, the case study has also shown that the involvement of civil society actors in decision-making processes has suffered some backsliding and civil space in general is shrinking in Croatia (as in many other European countries). The Commission should therefore thoroughly pursue its political and financial support to civil society, in enlargement countries but also in Member States. Otherwise, an important actor required to make reflexive governance work would be missing, considering that broad stakeholder participation has been identified as being one of the crucial features for experimentalist governance to be successful.

The third problem referred to by Falker et al regarded the relative weakness of Equality Bodies. Twinning has been mentioned as an example of experimentalist governance where knowledge sharing and exchange of good practice can take place, which can lead to a reconsideration of the solutions so far applied to certain problems (genetic approach). The twinning experience between the Croatian GOHMR and OO on the one hand and the Boltzmann Institute on the other has helped to identify the preconditions under which such peer-to-peer learning can be successful: it is essential that the beneficiary institutions have strong ownership of the project, which is the case if they genuinely identify with and express the project objectives without imposition from above. This ownership can be maintained if the resident twinning adviser conceives his/her role as a facilitator of reflection and reform rather than as a promoter of a Member State's practice. It is further important that the partnership is perceived as equal. Both ownership and equal partnership can be strengthened by a flexible approach of the twinning adviser being ready to make use of pre-existing experiences and expertise, to build on the outcomes of previous projects, and on the existing networks. The training provided to the staff of the OO (which has remained fairly stable), the input from external experts feeding into the ongoing reflections within the Office, and taking account of pre-existing experience have all helped the OO to reconsider its organization and work processes. From the point of view of the OO, the learning operation can be considered a success. The impact on potential victims is more difficult to measure. The positives are the better accessibility and visibility of the Office through the telephone hotline and two (by now three) regional offices, a professionalized complaints handling service including personal contact with the victim, and the establishment of an equality database which triggered a process of reconsidering the way in which state administration is collecting data. If Falkner has described the

Equality Bodies analysed in her study as toothless, the twinning might not have made an acrimonious tiger out of the OO but the teeth have definitely grown.

2.7 Conclusions

The empirical case study on Croatia has shown that many elements of the reflexive governance approach are present in the pre-accession process. Although the analysed mechanisms have not managed to address fully the implementation-related problems, the results they have achieved deserve serious attention as it seems plausible that a stronger focus on approaches of reflexive governance in the pre-accession phase might contribute to solidify reforms.

It has also shown that with regard to some of the elements, their full potential has not been achieved as their use has only been half-hearted or processes have been interrupted half-way. This is the case in particular for benchmarking and monitoring, which require further consideration by the Commission. In order for benchmarking to become more 'intelligent' and monitoring more transparent and informed, it is considered necessary to strengthen benchmarking by the use of indicators and to establish some form of post-accession monitoring of the implementation record, including all Member States, thereby creating the recursive process envisaged by experimentalist governance.

The case study on Croatia has further shown that CSOs have contributed to an advanced transposition of the Directives, carried out important monitoring activities of non-discrimination policies, and contributed to preventing a watering down of the current National Plan for the fight against discrimination. To some extent they have also played a role in the enforcement of the right to equality and non-discrimination. In order to secure the positive potential of these stakeholders, their involvement needs to be better entrenched in the pre-accession phase and sustained financial and political support be granted to NGOs also after accession.

The example of twinning has shown not only that it can deploy a sustainable impact way beyond the end of the project, but also that it can trigger a return over pre-existing frames, a reconsideration of past knowledge and positioning, and thus of the solutions so far found for a specific problem. The EU non-discrimination regime provides for a number of avenues in which such reframing could be triggered. Government representatives can exchange experiences in the framework of the High Level Group, but regrettably, candidate countries are not regular members of the Group.[241] Equality Bodies of member and candidate countries are successfully connected through Equinet, CSOs can collaborate and learn from each other in the

[241] See, however, European Commission—Directorate-General Justice and Consumers, 'High Level Group on Non-discrimination, Equality and Diversity. Mandate' (2015), pt 4(f).: 'Participants from additional countries may be invited by the Commission to participate in the Group, if it is found relevant. This will be decided on a case by case basis.'

framework of umbrella organizations at European level. The EELN experts provide yearly reports about the transposition in all the Member States as well as comparative reports. However, it appears that the different actors (Commission, government level, NGOs, perhaps to a lesser extent the Equality Body) are not making use of the existing resources and institutions. In the terminology used by experimentalist governance, the pooling of results and the drawing of conclusions from such results is given too little attention.

The following chapters therefore pursue two objectives: On the basis of a comparative review of the transposition and practical implementation of the two Directives under consideration, it will first, undertake such a pooling of results, by identifying good practices and challenges in a number of selected fields. On this basis, it will, second, develop indicators that can be used by the Commission to transparently and consistently evaluate progress in the transposition and practical implementation of the EU acquis in the field of equality and non-discrimination during the pre-accession phase, and ideally also beyond accession for all Member States. In doing so, it is hoped that this research will make a contribution to improve benchmarking and monitoring (thereby also addressing the still valid critique of Kochenov, concerning the lack of clarity and differentiated treatment of candidate countries[242]) and support thinking out of the box, thereby stimulating mutual learning processes and ultimately, improved implementation of the EU non-discrimination acquis.

242 Kochenov, *EU enlargement and the Failure of Conditionality* (n 11) 311.

3
Indicators as a Tool for Strengthened Monitoring

3.1 Introduction

The previous chapter proposed that benchmarks be combined with indicators as a tool to make benchmarks measurable and thus strengthen pre-accession monitoring and make it more effective and informed.[1] While it is hoped that such monitoring would make backsliding after accession less likely, it is further proposed that regular and comprehensive monitoring of fundamental rights be established for all current Member States, which could be extended to a monitoring of adherence to the values enshrined in Article 2 of the Treaty on European Union (TEU). This would eventually end the 'double standard' of yearly monitoring in the pre-accession phase, followed by a relative neglect once a country has become a member of the EU.

Indicators are receiving increased attention by various EU bodies (including the European Parliament, the Commission, and the Fundamental Rights Agency). Before embarking on the pooling of results and the development of indicators in Part II, this chapter discusses why and for what purposes indicators are useful as well as their limitations (3.2) and what role they currently play in the pre-enlargement context, mainly focusing on the issue of non-discrimination (3.3). On this basis, section 3.4 will then outline the criteria for the subsequent development of indicators in the area of enforcement and promotion of equality and non-discrimination.[2]

[1] Parts of this chapter have been previously published in Emma Lantschner, 'Indicators for Monitoring Implementation of EU Equality Directives' (2020) 45(4) Review of Central and East European Law 444.

[2] A large majority of the European Parliament accepted in October 2016 a legislative own-initiative report on an EU mechanism on democracy, the rule of law, and fundamental rights (DRF-Pact). See European Parliament, 'Report with recommendations to the Commission on the establishment of an EU mechanism on democracy, the rule of law and fundamental rights (2015/2254(INL))' (10 October 2016) A8-0283/2016, rejected by the European Commission, 'Follow up to the European Parliament resolution with recommendations to the Commission on the establishment of an EU mechanism on democracy, the rule of law and fundamental rights, adopted by the Commission on 17 January 2017' (17 February 2017) SP(2017)16.

Reflexive Governance in EU Equality Law. Emma Lantschner, Oxford University Press. © Emma Lantschner 2021.
DOI: 10.1093/oso/9780192843371.003.0004

3.2 Definition, Purposes, and Limitations of Indicators

For the definition and purposes, we borrow from work carried out in the past twenty years by various authors and institutions regarding human rights indicators. Maria Green defines a human rights indicator as 'a piece of information used in measuring the extent to which a legal right is being fulfilled or enjoyed in a given situation'.[3] Gauthier de Beco understands the term human rights indicators as 'indicators that are linked to human rights treaty standards, and that measure the extent to which duty-bearers are fulfilling their obligations and rights-holders enjoying their rights'.[4] Paul Hunt, who served as UN Special Rapporteur on the right to health, distinguished a health indicator from a *right to* health indicator by the fact that the latter 'derives from, reflects and is designed to monitor the realisation, or otherwise, of specific right to health norms, usually with a view to holding a duty bearer to account'.[5] In this context Hunt points out that '[t]he relationship between indicator and norm has to be reasonably close and precise'.[6] The institution dealing most extensively with human rights indicators in the past fifteen years is the UN Office of the High Commissioner for Human Rights (OHCHR). In its documents it defines human rights indicators as 'specific information on the state of an event, activity or an outcome that can be related to human rights norms and standards; that address and reflect the human rights concerns and principles; and that are used to assess and monitor promotion and protection of human rights'.[7] The EU Fundamental Rights Agency (FRA) in its work on indicators relies on this definition.[8]

What is common to these definitions is that they all understand indicators as being rights-based, in the sense of a 'reasonably close and precise'[9] link with a specific norm. In this context, the area of non-discrimination is relevant in a double sense. First, non-discrimination is a cross-cutting human rights norm which 'is at the heart of all work on human rights'.[10] As such, it has to be taken into consideration in the development of indicators for every single human right, typically

[3] Maria Green, 'What We Talk About When We Talk About Indicators: Current Approaches to Human Rights Measurement' (2001) 23(4) Human Rights Quarterly 1062, 1065.

[4] Gauthier de Beco, 'Human Rights Indicators for Assessing State Compliance with International Human Rights' Nordic Journal of International Law (2008), 77(1–2): 23.

[5] Paul Hunt, 'Interim report of the Special Rapporteur of the Commission on Human Rights on the right of everyone to enjoy the highest attainable standard of physical and mental health, Mr. Paul Hunt' (UN General Assembly, 2003) A/58/427, para 10.

[6] ibid para 11.

[7] OHCHR, 'Report on Indicators for Monitoring Compliance with International Human Rights Instruments' (11 May 2006) HRI/MC/2006/7, para 7; OHCHR, 'Human Rights Indicators. A Guide to Measurement and Implementation' (2012), 16.

[8] Fundamental Rights Agency, 'Annual Report 2014. Fundamental rights: challenges and achievements in 2014' (2015) 14.

[9] Hunt (n 5) para 11.

[10] OHCHR, 'Human Rights Indicators. A Guide to Measurement and Implementation' (n 7) 13, and also 38–41. See also OHCHR, 'Report on Indicators for Promoting and Monitoring the Implementation of Human Rights' (6 June 2008) HRI/MC/2008/3, para 5.

by the disaggregation of data collected to populate an indicator in relation to prohibited grounds of discrimination.[11] With Green, the right to non-discrimination understood as a cross-cutting norm can also be labelled a 'procedural right'.[12] Secondly, non-discrimination has to be considered as a self-standing human right, for which specific indicators can be developed. In the EU context, the question arises, to which legal norms do such indicators have to be related. There is no doubt that the Directives adopted in this field are the main basis. In the context of the present research, the focus is on the Racial Equality Directive (RED) and on the Employment Equality Directive (EED). Of course the Treaties too (Art 2 TEU and Art 19 of the Treaty on the Functioning of the European Union (TFEU)) as well as the Fundamental Rights Charter (Arts 20–23 dealing with the issues of equality and non-discrimination) should be reflected in the indicators. Furthermore, indicators should also relate to international standards accepted by Member States or, as in the case of the UN Convention on the Rights of Persons with Disabilities, by the EU.[13] Both non-discrimination as a procedural right and as a self-standing right, can be divided into a substantive part, dealing for instance with the question of whether a specific behaviour constitutes direct or indirect discrimination, and a procedural part. The latter refers to mechanisms of enforcement, by which to react to alleged violations (eg access to different complaints mechanisms) and preventive and promotional mechanisms (eg positive measures). The indicators developed in the present research focus predominantly on this procedural part.

A further commonality of the above-mentioned definitions is that indicators are supposed to measure not only the commitment of, and efforts made by, the duty bearers to meet their legal obligations but also the extent to which the rights holders enjoy their rights. From a methodological point of view this has been translated into a configuration of structural, process, and outcome indicators.[14] *Structural indicators* measure the commitment of a state to implement the human rights standards accepted with the ratification of a human rights treaty, or in case of EU law, the commitment of Member States to transpose a directive. Structural indicators allow for the evaluation of the legal, policy, and institutional framework. They inform about legislation in place, adopted action plans and guidelines, and the existence of complaint and support mechanisms. *Process indicators* provide information about the efforts made by the duty bearer to transform their formal

[11] OHCHR, 'Human Rights Indicators. A Guide to Measurement and Implementation' (n 7) 38–41.

[12] Green (n 3) 1071.

[13] Fundamental Rights Agency, 'Annual Report 2014. Fundamental rights: challenges and achievements in 2014' (n 8) 14.

[14] See Hunt (n 5) para 15. This approach has been taken up by the OHCHR, 'Report on Indicators for Monitoring Compliance with International Human Rights Instruments' (n 7); OHCHR, 'Report on Indicators for Promoting and Monitoring the Implementation of Human Rights' (n 10); OHCHR, 'Report of the United Nations High Commissioner for Human Rights to the Economic and Social Council' (26 April 2011) E/2011/90; OHCHR, 'Human Rights Indicators. A Guide to Measurement and Implementation' (n 7).

commitment into concrete results. They focus on policy implementation as well as the effectiveness of established complaints mechanisms and support systems. This also involves budgetary allocations for the effective implementation of legislation and action plans. *Outcome indicators* capture the situation on the ground. They provide information about the level of enjoyment of a right in practice and the impact of the efforts undertaken by the state. They capture for instance the actual awareness of rights or the actual occurrence of violations.[15] Going back to Fredman's categorization,[16] it could be said that outcome indicators provide information about the level at which legal commitments and practical efforts have managed to satisfy the redistributive dimension, the recognition dimension, the participative dimension, and the transformative dimension of equality. All these dimensions, especially the participative one, clearly have a bearing on how commitment and efforts are framed.

Even if, in principle, non-discrimination is a right that should not be subject to progressive realization, both its substantive part as well as procedural part are, in reality, realized over time and thus require monitoring tools which allow for the measurement of progress over time. The structural-process-outcome indicators model is well suited for this purpose and will thus serve as the basis for the development of indicators for the procedural part of the right to equality and non-discrimination.

When it comes to different purposes, for which indicators can be useful, the primary purpose according to the above-mentioned definitions is monitoring, 'usually with a view to holding a duty bearer to account'.[17] The OHCHR includes in its definition the point that indicators are 'used to assess and monitor promotion and protection of human rights'.[18] In fact, the Office started its work on indicators in response to a request from the inter-committee meeting of the UN treaty monitoring bodies to prepare a background paper on the possible uses of indicators for the monitoring of UN human rights treaties. However, the OHCHR pointed out that 'the demand for appropriate indicators is not only for monitoring the implementation of the human rights instruments by States parties, but indicators are also seen as useful tools in reinforcing accountability, in articulating and advancing claims on the duty-bearers and in formulating requisite public policies and programmes for facilitating the realization of human rights'.[19] The FRA

[15] OHCHR, 'Human Rights Indicators. A Guide to Measurement and Implementation' (n 7) 34–38; Fundamental Rights Agency, 'Annual Report 2014. Fundamental rights: challenges and achievements in 2014' (n 8) 15.

[16] Sandra Fredman, 'Emerging from the Shadows: Substantive Equality and Article 14 of the European Convention on Human Rights', Human Rights Law Review (2016), 16(2): 273.

[17] Hunt (n 5) para 10.

[18] OHCHR, 'Report on Indicators for Monitoring Compliance with International Human Rights Instruments' (n 7) para 7; OHCHR, 'Human Rights Indicators. A Guide to Measurement and Implementation' (n 7) 16.

[19] OHCHR, 'Report on Indicators for Monitoring Compliance with International Human Rights Instruments' (n 7) para 3.

takes this latter idea further and sees a role for indicators in supporting 'relevant actors in policy evaluation and design'. To assess whether specific measures have reached their goal by the use of indicators could, in the view of the FRA, 'facilitate a better understanding of drivers and barriers in policy implementation. From a fundamental rights perspective, this will allow for better law making and render policymaking more transparent while also holding policymakers accountable for their actions. In the long run, this will strengthen democratic legitimacy and entrench a fundamental rights culture in whatever the EU does.'[20] In the view of the Council of Europe's Congress of Local and Regional Authorities' Monitoring Committee '[h]uman rights indicators are useful tools for both analysing the situation of human rights in a given state and communicating best practices and institutional solutions that can be of interest to local and regional authorities within the state and between member states'.[21] A European Parliament-commissioned study on Human Rights Benchmarks for EU's External Policy recommends developing human rights benchmarks and indicators in-house to guarantee consistency. It stresses that it is 'highly recommended that the EU applies the *same human rights indicators and benchmarks for its internal as well as external human rights policy* [to] increase the credibility of EU's external policies in general and legitimate the EU institutions in asking for human rights compliance vis-à-vis third countries'.[22]

To sum up, indicators are a useful tool for:

- consistent monitoring, with a view to reinforcing the accountability of the duty bearer;
- advocacy and political dialogue[23] between international monitoring bodies and the civil society sector on one hand and states on the other;
- evidence-based law and policy making: indicators can play an important role in supporting relevant actors in evaluating the status quo and, based on these findings, designing laws and policies;[24]
- analysing the human rights situation in a specific context and identifying good practices and institutional solutions others can learn from.

[20] Fundamental Rights Agency, 'Annual Report 2014. Fundamental rights: challenges and achievements in 2014' (n 8) 11–12.

[21] Council of Europe, Congress of Local and Regional Authorities, Monitoring Committee, 'Developing indicators to raise awareness of human rights at local and regional level' (6 October 2011) CG(21)10, quoted in Fundamental Rights Agency, 'Annual Report 2014. Fundamental rights: challenges and achievements in 2014' (n 8) 14.

[22] Anja Mihr, 'Human Rights Benchmarks for EU's External Policy' (European Parliament, Directorate-General for External Policies, Policy Department 2011) PE 457.059, 5.

[23] Todd Landman, 'Measuring Human Rights: Principle, Practice, and Policy', Human Rights Quarterly (2004), 26(4): 906; Todd Landman and Edzia Carvalho, Measuring Human Rights (Routledge 2010), 4–6. Landman identifies six different purposes for measuring human rights: 1. contextual description and documentation; 2. classification; 3. monitoring; 4. mapping and pattern recognition; 5. secondary analysis and policy prescription; 6. advocacy and political dialogue.

[24] See also Klaus Starl and others, 'Human Rights Indicators in the Context of the European Union' (Deliverable within the FP7 Project 'Fostering Human Rights among European Policies', ETC Graz, 24 December 2014) 17.

While the indicators developed in the following chapters are particularly suitable to achieve the first two purposes, they are also capable of covering the other two. They certainly allow for informed and consistent monitoring, with a view to highlighting where the duty bearer still does not live up to its obligations to achieve the objective of the Directives. As such, they can be used as a monitoring tool by the Commission, but also as a framework for analysis for the country reports written in the context of the European Commission's Network of Legal Experts in Gender Equality and Non-Discrimination. As monitoring should, however, be understood as a cooperative process, with the aim of educating, and eventually leading to an improved enjoyment of rights, the indicators will also serve as a tool in the political dialogue between the Commission, the civil society sector, and states. They can also be used by legislators or other actors to analyse the status quo regarding the right to equality and non-discrimination and deduce from such analysis further legislative or policy measures.

Notwithstanding the potential usefulness and benefits of indicators, it is also important to recall the limitations and points of critique, in particular related to the use of indicators for consistent monitoring.

A first issue is related to the fact that countries and regions within countries have different social, economic, and political points of departure and attainment levels with regard to the realization of human rights. As a result, it might be difficult to devise indicators that are applicable universally, or in our context, throughout the EU and acceding countries. In the view of the OHCHR it would still be relevant to monitor the core content of rights universally while, depending on circumstances, contextually specific indicators might be needed in addition.[25]

To focus on core aspects of rights could lead to a second problem: the risk of defining indicators on the basis of a superficial consensus on a basic set of indicators, also for the sake of making monitoring a manageable task.[26] If this task was cut down to become feasible, it risks reducing the substantive rights to something too superficial and too narrow. Monitoring states' performance in human rights protection through a limited set of indicators could, thus, risk 'oversimplifying the situation and could lead to a failure to capture future trends'.[27] The challenge of developing indicators is thus to transform the standards into a matrix of structural-process-outcome indicators without losing anything of the substance. In order

[25] OHCHR, 'Human Rights Indicators. A Guide to Measurement and Implementation' (n 7) 44.

[26] For an illustration of the potential problem it is useful to refer to the work on indicators carried out by the FRA in recent years. Since the EU acceded to the Convention on the Rights of Persons with Disabilities (CRPD) in 2010, the FRA has developed indicators for the monitoring of Art 29 CRPD, related to political participation of persons with disabilities. For this article alone, the FRA has developed a set of twenty-nine structural-process-outcome indicators. Fundamental Rights Agency, 'The right to political participation of persons with disabilities: human rights indicators' (2014).

[27] Wouter van Ballegooij and Tatjana Evas, 'An EU mechanism on democracy, the rule of law and fundamental rights. Interim European Added Value Assessment accompanying the Legislative initiative Report (Rapporteur Sophie in 't Veld)' (European Parliamentary Research Service, European Added Value Unit, April 2016) 13.

to achieve this, it is necessary to find the right balance between quantitative and qualitative indicators.

The OHCHR's methodological framework expresses a clear preference for fact-based statistical indicators.[28] Notwithstanding the merits of quantitative indicators, it is useful to consider the probably excessive expectations vis-à-vis this type of indicators and the methodological problems connected with it.[29] Quantitative indicators are understood to have the following advantages: 'they render complex data simple and easy to understand; they can be designed to demonstrate compliance with obligations, fulfilment of rights, and government efforts toward these goals; and they are capable of capturing progress over time and across countries'.[30] Behind these expectations stands a trust in numbers, which are putatively objective and as such more reliable than the judgement of a human being. Neither is completely correct. According to Rosga, the 'presentation of neatly tabulated numbers [just] erases the means and messiness of their own generation. It obscures evidence of the human judgment involved in statistical production.'[31] Besides, objectivity (understood as disinterested, honest, reliable, impartial[32]) is not necessarily obstructed by the involvement of the human mind and of human judgement. Furthermore, quantitative studies might miss out the gradual dialogic change taking place with respect to certain issues.[33]

Another challenge for the use of quantitative indicators is the availability of data[34] and the above-mentioned comparability over time and across countries. Both are key to quantitative indicators being able to deploy their potential strength. The availability of appropriately disaggregated data is of particular concern when it comes to the right to equality and non-discrimination, as has been recognized by various monitoring bodies.[35] Lack of comparability of data is connected to

[28] OHCHR, 'Human Rights Indicators. A Guide to Measurement and Implementation' (n 7) 16–19, in particular 19.

[29] Sally Engle Merry, *The Seductions of Quantification: Measuring Human Rights, Gender Violence, and Sex Trafficking* (University of Chicago Press 2016).

[30] AnnJanette Rosga and Margaret L Satterthwaie, 'The Trust in Indicators: Measuring Human Rights' (2009) 27(2) Berkeley Journal of International Law 253, 255. For a discussion of the benefits of quantitative indicators for treaty bodies, states, as well as individuals and advocacy organizations, see Judith V Welling, 'International Indicators and Economic, Social, and Cultural Rights' (2008) 30(4) Human Rights Quarterly 933–58, 940–47.

[31] Rosga and Satterthwaie (n 30) 283.

[32] ibid 284.

[33] Debra J Liebowitz and Susanne Zwingel, 'Gender Equality Oversimplified: Using CEDAW to Counter the Measurement Obsession' (2014) 16(3) International Studies Review 362; Christopher J Fariss, 'The Changing Standard of Accountability and the Positive Relationship between Human Rights Treaty Ratification and Compliance' (2018) 48(01) British Journal of Political Science 239.

[34] On the kind of data needed to populate human rights indicators generally, see de Beco (n 4) 34–38. He suggests the use of event-based data, socio-economic data, household perceptions, and expert judgements, and discusses the advantages and downsides of each of these.

[35] See, for instance, ACFC, 'Thematic Commentary No. 3: The Language Rights of Persons Belonging to National Minorities under the Framework Convention' (24 May 2012) ACFC/44DOC(2012)001 rev, para 19 et seq; and ACFC, 'Thematic Commentary No. 4: The Framework Convention: a key tool to managing diversity through minority rights' (2016) ACFC/56DOC(2016)001, para 66.

diverging data collection methods across countries.[36] On a defensive note, the OHCHR pointed out that the lack of available data (and the same goes for their comparability) does not discredit the use of indicators altogether; at best, it will simply delay their use until the required data become available.[37] Within the EU, it is part of the FRA's mandate to collect objective, reliable, and comparable information on the development of the situation of fundamental rights and to 'develop methods and standards to improve the comparability, objectivity and reliability of data at European level'.[38] In order to enhance comparability, the FRA does not rely on secondary data collected by Member States but collects its own primary data.[39] In the 2015 Annual Report, it still found that '[a]cross the EU, there is a lack of comparable and disaggregated data on manifestations of ethnic discrimination, racism and related intolerance'.[40] It has therefore launched a second wave of its European Union Minorities and Discrimination Survey (EU-MIDIS) with the aim of assessing progress made since the first EU-MIDIS survey in 2008. This survey also serves to populate core indicators for measuring progress in the implementation of the EU Framework for National Roma Integration Strategies and selected indicators on immigrant integration.[41] To work with indicators is, thus, a further attempt of the FRA to live up to its mandate to 'develop methods and standards to improve the comparability, objectivity and reliability of data at European level'.[42] Former FRA Director Morten Kjaerum expressed his hope that the existence of an indicator framework also makes it more likely that, in addition to its own primary data collection carried out by the FRA, the data collected by Member States will also become more comparable over time.[43] The development of indicators should, thus, not be guided by the availability of comparable data. Conversely, the existence of indicators can support the generation of the required data.

[36] For instance, target groups might be differently defined. While in one case a survey on violence against women covers only women of child-bearing age, another survey might look only at domestic violence. FRA Factsheet, FRA research: Providing robust, comparable data and analysis, 2011, available at http://fra.europa.eu/sites/default/files/fra_uploads/1717-FRA-Factsheet_Methodology_EN.pdf.

[37] OHCHR, 'Human Rights Indicators. A Guide to Measurement and Implementation' (n 7) 21 and for details about data disaggregation, 68–70.

[38] Council Regulation (EC) No 168/2007 of 15 February 2007 establishing a European Union Agency for Fundamental Rights, Art 4.

[39] FRA Factsheet (n 36).

[40] Fundamental Rights Agency, 'Annual Report 2014. Fundamental rights: challenges and achievements in 2014' (n 8) 50.

[41] Information taken from the EU-MIDIS Project website at http://fra.europa.eu/en/project/2015/eu-midis-ii-european-union-minorities-and-discrimination-survey. For the main results of the first survey see Fundamental Rights Agency, 'EU-MIDIS Main Results Report' (2009), and for the second survey see Fundamental Rights Agency, 'EU-MIDIS II: Main results' (2017).

[42] Council Regulation (EC) No 168/2007 of 15 February 2007 establishing a European Union Agency for Fundamental Rights (n 38) Art 4.

[43] Fundamental Rights Agency, 'Developing indicators for the protection, respect and promotion of the rights of the child in the European Union. Summary Report' (2009) 5.

Analysing the indicator documents developed so far by the FRA, it becomes clear that it relies on both quantitative and qualitative indicators.[44] In its 2015 Annual Report, which dedicated its special focus to the subject of indicators, the Agency pointed out that indicators should be populated with qualitative evidence, such as the analysis of legislation, case law, strategies or action plans, and quantitative data.[45] Outside the frame of the FRA's work with indicators, the first EU Anti-Corruption Report issued by the European Commission in 2014 is mainly built on qualitative assessment.[46] The authors of the Report acknowledged that it might be difficult to get 'to the core of corruption problems' by the relying primarily on quantitative indicators.[47]

The approach of these examples will be followed by the present research. Quantitative indicators are useful to express the magnitude of a phenomenon, but for their appropriate interpretation, they also require qualitative indicators, which allow for contextual analysis and accurate interpretation of the numbers and statistics.[48] This is also necessary in order to reduce the risk that states aim to demonstrate success in the form of improving numbers related to a given indicator rather than improving the enjoyment of the human right itself.[49]

Another point to be made regards a potential strength but also potential limitation of indicators and is related to the importance of participation in the development and use of indicators.[50] Earlier work of the OHCHR seemed to start from the assumption that universally applicable indicators could be developed by experts at the international level. However, the OHCHR report on indicators published in 2008 already had a much more participatory approach, both in terms of selection of indicators and their use.[51] After a number of years of working on the

[44] The aim of the child rights indicators, for instance, is to move beyond a purely quantitative approach towards a qualitative assessment of the 'effects of legal, policy and institutional measures on children's lived experiences'. See, for instance, Fundamental Rights Agency, 'Developing indicators for the protection, respect and promotion of the rights of the child in the European Union' (November 2010) 14, but also 20, 21, 93, 134.

[45] Fundamental Rights Agency, 'Annual Report 2014. Fundamental rights: challenges and achievements in 2014' (n 8) 14. This has also been the approach followed by the Agency when it developed and populated indicators on the right to political participation of persons with disabilities. Even if many of the chosen indicators could be expressed quantitatively (eg the number of cases considered by non-judicial complaints bodies), the analysis provided did not only include a short analysis of the cases found but also highlighted promising practice. See eg Fundamental Rights Agency, 'The right to political participation for persons with disabilities: human rights indicators' (2014) 62–64. The population of indicators thus fulfilled the double function of assessing the state of affairs in EU Member States as well as identifying good practice other states can learn from.

[46] Petra Bárd and others, 'An EU mechanism on Democracy, the Rule of Law and Fundamental Rights' (CEPS Paper in Liberty and Security in Europe, April 2016), 10.

[47] European Commission, 'EU Anti-Corruption Report' (3 February 2014) COM(2014) 38 final, 39–40.

[48] Starl and others (n 24) 18.

[49] Rosga and Satterthwaie (n 30) 286.

[50] ibid 313–14.

[51] See ibid 297, referring to OHCHR, 'Report on Indicators for Promoting and Monitoring the Implementation of Human Rights' (n 10) para 11. See also OHCHR, 'Human Rights Indicators. A Guide to Measurement and Implementation' (n 7) 40.

development of indicators in various settings, the FRA has spelled out, among its lessons learned, that 'indicators have to be agreed through a deliberative process with the actors who will be assessed through their application. These would be primarily "duty bearers", namely EU institutions and Member States, but also other stakeholders representing the "rights holders", such as social partners and civil society, to ensure a wide consensus through informed participatory processes.'[52] Fredman's participatory dimension would thus be duly taken into account.

Participation understood as a cross-cutting human right could also be narrowed down as an unintended consequence of the use of indicators, if specific policy choices themselves are turned into indicators. The challenge in the enlargement context, but also within the EU, is therefore to give acceding and Member States detailed enough guidance as to what is expected from them in their effort to bring legislation and practice in line with EU standards without limiting the possibility to choose the policy option which is best tailored to their needs and circumstances.[53]

In the course of drafting its legislative own-initiative report on a Pact on Democracy, Rule of Law and Fundamental Rights (DRF) the European Parliament commissioned two papers[54] which, amongst other things, assessed the need and possibilities for the establishment of a DRF scoreboard, tackling in this context also the question of practicability and usefulness of indicators. The authors took quite a critical stance towards the use of indicators. In their view, the assessment through numerical indicators should not constitute the core method but should rather be one element. With regard to the concepts of democracy and (even more so) the rule of law they found that they are fluid and have 'to contain a share of vagueness in order to accommodate [their] very nature'.[55] To turn the rule of law 'into a shopping list of elements ... [e]liminating vagueness entirely' for them would profoundly undermine the usefulness of the concept itself. Therefore, they recommended using benchmarking and indicators only sparingly.[56] They even called

[52] Fundamental Rights Agency, 'Annual Report 2014. Fundamental rights: challenges and achievements in 2014' (n 8) 14. Serban too, having analysed the Cooperation and Verification Mechanism vis-á-vis Romania, comes to the conclusion that indicators are rejected 'if there is no domestic ownership in either their construction or use'. Mihaela Serban, 'Rule of Law Indicators as a Technology of Power in Romania' in Sally Engle Merry, Kevin Davis, and Benedict Kingsbury (eds), *The Quiet Power of Indicators: Measuring Governance, Corruption, and Rule of Law* (CUP 2015) 217. An impressive example of how seriously the FRA is taking this lesson is provided by the Working Group that has developed the Roma integration indicators. It was composed of officials from the European Commission (from the Directorate-General for Justice and Consumers and the Directorate-General for Employment, Social Affairs and Inclusion), Eurostat, Eurofound, the World Bank, the UN Development Programme, the OSCE, the Council of Europe, EEA and Norway Grants, and Open Society Foundations, in addition to seventeen EU Member States. When the Working Group started to test populating the indicators it further involved national statistics offices to identify methods to generate the required data. This working party had seven meetings between 2012 and 2015. Fundamental Rights Agency, 'Annual Report 2014. Fundamental rights: challenges and achievements in 2014' (n 8) 16.

[53] Rosga and Satterthwaie (n 30) 306–12.

[54] Bárd and others (n 46); Laurent Pech and others, 'An EU Mechanism on Democracy, the Rule of Law and Fundamental Rights' (European Parliament, European Added Value Unit, April 2016).

[55] Bárd and others (n 46) iii–iv.

[56] ibid iv.

the use of indicators in this context 'a rather dubious exercise that can easily be attacked as politically or ideologically biased'.[57]

Their judgement seems to be based on the assumption that the indicators would mainly be 'numerical'. While scepticism towards overreliance on numbers without taking the specific context into account is shared, and one can agree with the allegation that the selection of indicators (just as any qualitative assessment) can be politically or ideologically biased, the present research starts from the assumption that both quantitative *and* qualitative indicators are needed, and that in order to be able to interpret what the indicators actually indicate a contextual assessment is needed. Along the lines of Rosga's findings after critically discussing the inappropriateness of a blind trust in numbers, it is understood that monitoring states' compliance with human rights obligations by using indicators means that 'monitoring will always be context-dependent, that it will involve the function of judgment, and that it will never be a purely technical exercise'.[58]

The allegation of Bárd et al with regard to political or ideological bias is actually exactly what the European Parliament has tried to address with its DRF Pact by proposing a monitoring framework which would be 'objective, impartial, evidence-based and applied equally and fairly to all Member States as well as to the institutions of the Union'.[59] One tool to reach this goal could be the use of common and objective indicators. In his follow-up study to the European Parliament's Resolution of 2015 on the situation of fundamental rights in the EU, de Schutter supports this view. He writes: 'Indicators allowing to examine the situation of democracy, the rule of law and fundamental rights should ensure that the principles of objectivity, non discrimination and equal treatment are complied with, and that the monitoring is performed in a non-partisan way and is based on sound evidence.'[60] Accepting all the limitations and challenges inherent in the use of indicators discussed above, they still display one clear advantage, especially in the context of EU internal and external monitoring: they contribute to the transparency and predictability of monitoring and, because they are applied equally to all states, they lose at least part of their potential of being politically or ideologically driven.

[57] ibid. As a matter of fact, what in the draft DRF Pact had been called 'indicator' and had been listed separately for each of the three sectors, democracy, rule of law, and fundamental rights, was called 'aspects' in the adopted document without further dividing between the three areas. The subsequent list, however, remained the same, with some additions. As a result, the 'aspect' of equality before the law and non-discrimination was proposed to be part of the DRF Report (that had replaced the Scoreboard) accompanied by country-specific recommendations. See European Parliament, 'Report with recommendations to the Commission on the establishment of an EU mechanism on democracy, the rule of law and fundamental rights (2015/2254(INL))' (n 2).

[58] Rosga and Satterthwaie (n 30) 311.

[59] European Parliament, 'Report with recommendations to the Commission on the establishment of an EU mechanism on democracy, the rule of law and fundamental rights (2015/2254(INL))' (n 2) 15, point 1.

[60] Olivier de Schutter, 'Follow-up to the European Parliament's Resolution of 8 September 2015 on "The situation of fundamental rights in the European Union (2013–2014)"' (European Parliament, Policy Department for Citizens' Rights and Constitutional Affairs, Brussels 2016) 35.

3.3 The Current Use of Indicators in the Enlargement Context

So far, the Commission has been rather reluctant to use indicators in its pre-accession monitoring. The benchmarks that were introduced with the Enlargement Strategy 2006[61] came without indicators. If they were used, such as in the context of monitoring progress in the framework of the Commission's Instrument for Pre-Accession Assistance,[62] their development suffered from methodological flaws and could not be considered clear and transparent. The Indicative Strategy Paper for Serbia for the period 2014–20, for instance, identified fundamental rights as one key priority for Serbia and thus as one of the areas for which EU assistance will be granted under the Instrument for Pre-accession Assistance (IPA) II. The expected results included 'consistent implementation of anti-discrimination policies and measures'. The indicator supposed to measure progress in this sub-sector is 'Progress made towards meeting accession criteria' and the source mentioned to populate this indicator is the yearly Progress Report published by the Commission.[63] External indicators were used as sector indicators in the Strategy Paper for Serbia as amended in 2018.[64] However, they are not related to the 'consistent implementation of anti-discrimination policies', which continues to be listed as an expected result, but only to the freedom of press.[65]

In February 2020, the Commission announced a revised methodology, which is supposed to make accession negotiations more credible, more predictable, more dynamic, and guided by a stronger political steer.[66] In terms of predictability, the Commission announced that it would 'better define the conditions set for candidates to progress, in particular through its annual reports. These conditions must be objective, precise, detailed, strict and verifiable. The Commission further announced [the use of] third party indicators where relevant to provide Member States with the broadest possible base for their decisions.'[67] The first reports

[61] European Commission, 'Enlargement Strategy and Main Challenges 2006–2007' (8 November 2006) COM(2006), 649.

[62] The IPA regulation for the period 2014–20 is very explicit in establishing how progress over time towards achieving the specific objectives of reform and development are to be monitored: this shall be done 'on the basis of pre-defined, clear, transparent and, where appropriate, country-specific and measurable indicators'. Regulation (EU) No 231/2014 of the European Parliament and of the Council establishing an Instrument for Pre-accession Assistance (IPA II) 11 March 2014.

[63] European Commission, 'Instrument for Pre-accession Assistance (IPA II). Indicative Strategy Paper for Serbia (2014–2020)' (19 August 2014); European Commission, 'Annex to the Commission Implementing Decision amending Commission Decision C(2014)5872 of 19.8.2014 adopting the Indicative Strategy Paper for Serbia for the period 2014–2020' (10 August 2018) C(2018) 5064 final.

[64] European Commission, 'Annex to the Commission Implementing Decision amending Commission Decision C(2014)5872 of 19.8.2014 adopting the Indicative Strategy Paper for Serbia for the period 2014–2020' (n 63).

[65] The whole area of fundamental rights is evaluated on the basis of the composite indicator derived from the Freedom House and Reporters Without Borders Indices.

[66] European Commission, 'European Commission, Enhancing the Accession Process—A Credible EU Perspective for the Western Balkans' (5 February 2020) COM(2020) 57 final.

[67] ibid 5.

following this new methodology were published in October 2020, but do not appear to be more specific or detailed and contain no reference to third party indicators under Chapter 23. It is still to be seen what role indicators play in the new programming period of IPA.

Indicators are also used in National Action Plans adopted by candidate countries. However, structural—and especially process—indicators figure much more prominently for instance in the Serb Antidiscrimination Action Plan as compared to outcome indicators.[68] While the indicators used in these Plans might be useful for policy evaluation at national level, it is questionable whether they are also helpful for the Commission's monitoring, where a greater level of abstraction as well as a stronger focus on outcomes is required.

While the Commission has clearly committed itself to monitor progress towards achieving the objectives under its financial and technical assistance instrument (IPA II) through clear, transparent, and measurable indicators, it has so far not developed such indicators but is referring to its own Progress Reports which are themselves not drafted on the basis of indicators. To end this self-referential approach, the Commission would need, at some point, to develop such indicators for its own monitoring. Such indicators could then, in the framework of national Action Plans, be adapted to the specific national context and thereby make the overall assessment of progress more consistent and transparent.

3.4 Conclusions

This chapter has explained the advantages connected with the use of indicators but has also highlighted their limitations. Any development of indicators needs to take these limitations into account. It has further shown that for the time being, the Commission makes limited use of indicators in its pre-accession monitoring and where indicators are used, their development has methodological flaws or serves a purpose different from the Commission's monitoring. However, in order to strengthen the benchmarking approach used by the Commission (intelligent benchmarking) and for monitoring of the Commission, as part of a cooperative and reflexive process, to be effective and informed, the development of indicators is considered to be necessary.

On the basis of the above described purposes and limitations, the following criteria for the subsequent development of indicators in the area of equality and non-discrimination have been established:

[68] Republic of Serbia, 'Action Plan for the Implementation of the Strategy for Prevention and Protection againgst Discrimination for the Period 2014–2018' (2 October 2014). See also Emma Lantschner and Stéphanie Marsal, 'Expert Report regarding the protection of minorities and cultural rights in the Republic of Serbia' (Peer review expert mission to Serbia on Chapter 23 – Judiciary and fundamental rights, focussing on interim benchmarks on protection of minorities and cultural rights, 24 March 2017).

- The indicators developed by this research should mainly allow for the monitoring of pre- and post-accession compliance with the non-discrimination acquis. As such, they can be used by various actors: the Commission, the Network of Legal Experts in Gender Equality and Non-Discrimination, or national or transnational non-governmental organizations (NGOs). It should be added here, that monitoring in this context should not be understood as a top-down exercise but as part of a recursive cooperative process, which has the aim of contributing to mutual learning and eventually leading to an improved enjoyment of rights.
- Therefore, the indicators can also be used as a tool in the political dialogue between the Commission, the civil society sector, and state authorities. They can also be used by legislators or other actors to analyse the status quo regarding the right to equality and non-discrimination and deduce from such analysis further legislative or policy measures.
- This research deduces indicators from a comparative review of legal transposition and practical implementation of the RED as well as the EED. In other words it sets out to pool the results of experiences in the implementation of the EU non-discrimination acquis in the past two decades, identifying good practices and challenges. On the basis of this comparative analysis, indicators are devised. It should be underlined that although the Gender Equality Directives are not the focus of the present research, the findings as well as the indicators are applicable also to them, as there is an overlap in the formulation of the norms analysed.
- The indicators do not intend to limit policy options but should facilitate an understanding of what the state has done to transpose *and* effectively implement the Directives in practice, *and* whether this has had an impact on the ground. For this purpose, structural, process, and outcome indicators will be developed.
- Quantitative and qualitative indicators will be identified. The explanatory power of numerical indicators derives from their being placed in relation to each other and contextualized.
- The availability of data to populate the indicators will not be taken as a limiting criterion for the selection of indicators as it is expected that the existence of indicators will contribute in the long run to the improvement of data collection.[69]

[69] See also Marta Hodasz, Katharina Köhler, and Barbara Liegl, 'Indicators and Monitoring Systems as Preventive Tools in the Area of Ethnic and Religious Discrimination' in Julia Kozma, Manfred Nowak, and Roland Schmidt (eds), *Indicators and Monitoring Systems as Preventive Tools for Ensuring Peace and Security and Respect for Human Rights in External Policy-Making of the EU: Proceedings of the COST Workshop 'Human Rights, Peace and Security in EU Foreign Policy'* (NWV, Neuer Wissenschaftlicher Verlag 2009) 94.

- The issue of participation in the development of indicators is not addressed by the present research. The indicators developed should therefore be understood as a proposal, derived on the basis of the comparative research. If the proposed indicators were to be used in a specific context, they should serve as a point of departure and be adapted to the specific context in order to become meaningful.

PART II

POOLING OF RESULTS AND DEVELOPMENT OF INDICATORS

'Learning-based theories of governance posit that learning should take place without teaching: the solutions are not to be imposed from above, they must emerge from below. However, that is not to say that the actors should not be supported in their ability to learn'.[1]

Reflexive governance, however, is not satisfied with equipping actors to learn but also aims at triggering a revision of actors' self-representation. Decentralized problem solving, followed by a pooling of results is the way in which experimentalist governance in particular expects to generate innovation. It is expected that each unit 'will have to redefine its policies, and improve on them, in the light of the successes and failures of others'.[2] While this does not necessarily lead to the more radical revision of the understanding of the role an actor wants to play, such comparison with experiences of others does have the potential to trigger such a revision.

This part of the book thus has a dual purpose. First, in carrying out a pooling of results it aims to support various actors in looking at the range of possible answers given to the same problem. This may start a reflection process around whether the solution they have found for this problem is the most appropriate or could be reconsidered. The comparative review carried out for this purpose does not aim to find the one and 'best' possible way of transposing and enforcing the Equality Directives. Rather, it highlights potential benefits of possible solutions and challenges related to them, on the basis of which, we can evaluate what the most appropriate solution could be in a specific context.

All issues will be addressed by going through the whole policy cycle, from the formulation of the rule at EU level, to its legal transposition in the EU Member States and their practical implementation in selected countries. It is only by pooling results and experiences in the implementation phase, and closing the loop by feeding

[1] Olivier de Schutter and Jacques Lenoble, 'Introduction: Institutions Equipped to Learn' in Olivier de Schutter and Jacques Lenoble (eds), Reflexive Governance: Redefining the Public Interest in a Pluralistic World (Hart Publishing, 2010), xxii.

[2] ibid xviii and xxii.

these results back into a learning process, thus potentially starting a new policy cycle, that the system can improve. In doing so it will not only be possible to assess whether unsatisfactory outcomes are related to the way the legal framework is designed (at central and peripheral levels), or rather to the way in which this framework is applied. This approach will also allow us to achieve the second purpose of this part of the book, which is the development of proposed indicators that will help to strengthen and improve the monitoring of the EU anti-discrimination regime in the pre- and, ideally, also in the post-accession phase (in the sense of: all EU Member States, not just new Member States). As has been mentioned above, the intention is to develop structural, process, and outcome indicators. By looking at how Member States have legally transposed the Directives it will be possible to derive structural indicators. Looking into the efforts that states have undertaken to transform their commitment into concrete results, as well as the outcomes produced by a specific choice of solution, it will also be possible to derive process and outcome indicators.

The selection of fields for the pooling of results and development of indicators has been guided by the factors identified elsewhere[3] that prevent more effective implementation of the Equality Directives. One of the reasons for the gap between the objectives of the Directives and their impact on the ground is related to obstacles in the access to justice as a *reaction to discrimination*, through either judicial or quasi- and non-judicial mechanisms, that result in underreporting and a lack of litigation from below. The factors that contribute to this situation include the rules on legal standing of interested organizations and the opportunities for them to engage in individual or collective judicial disputes regarding discrimination. Chapter 4 thus focuses on the role of non-state actors in judicial dispute resolution. Another reason for the discrepancy between the law on the books and the situation on the ground has been found in the rather toothless Equality Bodies. Chapter 5 will therefore comparatively assess how Equality Bodies of different types have contributed to providing access to justice in discrimination cases.[4]

While these aspects are related to the reaction to a violation of the right not to be discriminated against, some other reasons for the gap between the Directives' objectives and the situation on the ground are more related to the *prevention* of such violations and the *promotion* of the principle of equality. Chapter 6 will look at the way in which the state authorities, Equality Bodies, and civil society organizations (CSOs)

[3] See eg Gerda Falkner and Oliver Treib, 'Three Worlds of Compliance or Four? The EU-15 Compared to New Member States', Journal of Common Market Studies (2008), 46(2): 293, 304–6; Fundamental Rights Agency, 'Opinion of the European Union Agency for Fundamental Rights on the situation of equality in the European Union 10 years on from initial implementation of the equality directives' (2013) 1/2013.

[4] Further concerns with regard to the reaction to discrimination relate to the victims' fear of retaliation as well as to the low and diverging levels of compensation. See European Commission, 'Report on the application of Council Directive 2000/43/EC implementing the principle of equal treatment between persons irrespective of racial or ethnic origin ("the Racial Equality Directive") and of Council Directive 2000/78/EC establishing a general framework for equal treatment in employment and occupation ("the Employment Equality Directive")' (Brussels 19 March 2021) COM(2021) 139 final.

have contributed to raising the awareness of rights holders and duty bearers about the existing rights and obligations. Furthermore, the advisory role of Equality Bodies will be looked at as well as the CSOs' involvement in law and policy making.

By focusing the comparative research on the aspects that appear to hamper effective implementation it is hoped that attention will be concentrated on these problematic areas and performance improved progressively.

In analysing the legal transposition and practical implementation (ie commitment, efforts, and results) the following methodology will be applied. Each chapter will be introduced by an analysis of the drafting history of the relevant provision[5] and the clarification of central concepts by way of studying relevant infringement proceedings and case law of the Court of Justice of the European Union (CJEU). Thereafter, it will be explored how the twenty-seven EU Member States (plus the UK) have transposed the relevant provision into their national legislation. The main sources for this part are the yearly reports provided by the legal experts of the European network of legal experts in gender equality and non-discrimination (EELN) as well as scholarly research. For the comparative analysis of the practical implementation, case studies have been carried out in most chapters. The point of this was to find out whether, in order to make an impact on the rights holders, the decisive criterion was the inclusiveness of the legislation, or whether and under what circumstances, more narrow and less permissive legal choices can also deploy an impact. The cases selected for the case studies therefore range from very permissive to minimalist forms of transposition.[6] In a few chapters it was considered more appropriate to try to cover the practical implementation more broadly, either because there was no such apparently diverging legal transposition or because the provisions of the Directives have seen hardly any legal transposition at all. The parts on the practical implementation are based on semi-structured in-depth interviews with representatives from the European Commission, Equality Bodies and their Europe-wide network, representatives of civil society organizations, and independent experts on non-discrimination issues. The interviews were either carried out face-to-face or via Skype, often followed up by obtaining further clarifications via e-mail. In addition to the interviews, scholarly literature as well as reports and studies carried out by various national or international institutions have informed the part on practical implementation.

The sections on the legal transposition and practical implementation are followed by a summary of the challenges and good practices encountered. This allows us also to draw some conclusions not only as to where the national

[5] This will be done on the basis of a comparison of the Commission's initial proposal, the Starting Line Group's proposal (the grouping of nearly 400 NGOs, trade unions, churches, and independent experts that was quite influential in the drafting phase) and the final Directives as well as the existing literature.

[6] Ran Hirschl, Comparative Matters: The Renaissance of Comparative Constitutional Law (Oxford University Press 2014); Donatella Della Porta and Michael Keating (eds), Approaches and Methodologies in the Social Sciences (Cambridge University Press 2008).

regulations could be corrected to achieve the objectives of the Directives, but also where the framework rule at EU level (the two Directives) should be reconsidered. This sequence of analysis will then make it possible to achieve the second purpose of this part of the book, which is the proposal of structural, process, and outcome indicators.

4

Reaction to Discrimination by Judicial Mechanisms

The Role of Non-State Actors in Judicial Dispute Resolution

As de Búrca has pointed out, one of the innovative features of EU's anti-discrimination regime introduced with the Directives starting in 2000 is the fact that they assign a variety of roles to non-state actors. When it comes to reacting to discrimination, the Directives most importantly lay down that

> Member States shall ensure that associations, organisations or other legal entities, which have, in accordance with the criteria laid down by their national law, a legitimate interest in ensuring that the provisions of this Directive are complied with, may engage, either on behalf or in support of the complainant, with his or her approval, in any judicial and/or administrative procedure provided for the enforcement of obligations under this Directive.[7]

This chapter will look at this opportunity created for non-governmental organizations (NGOs) (and in some countries also for Equality Bodies, to be dealt with in Chapter 5) to participate in the application and enforcement of the anti-discrimination legal framework. As has been acknowledged elsewhere, the legal mechanisms through which these actors can access national courts to enforce the right to equal treatment and non-discrimination have rarely been studied so far.[8] Even the most recent report of the European Commission on the application of the two Directives gives it surprisingly little attention, although it acknowledges that according to some Member States 'the organisation's legal standing plays a decisive role in cases of collective discrimination harming people who are not directly or immediately identifiable'.[9]

[7] Art 7(2) RED; Art 9(2) EED.

[8] Claire Kilpatrick and Bruno de Witte, 'Introducing the Role of Collective Actors and Preliminary References in the Enforcement of EU Fundamental Rights Law' in Elise Muir and others (eds), *How EU Law Shapes Opportunities for Preliminary References on Fundamental Rights: Discrimination, Data Protection and Asylum* (European University Institute, EUI Working Papers 2017) 2.

[9] European Commission, 'Report on the application of Council Directive 2000/43/EC implementing the principle of equal treatment between persons irrespective of racial or ethnic origin ("the Racial Equality Directive") and of Council Directive 2000/78/EC establishing a general framework for equal treatment in employment and occupation ("the Employment Equality Directive")' (n 4) 7–8.

Reflexive Governance in EU Equality Law. Emma Lantschner, Oxford University Press. © Emma Lantschner 2021.
DOI: 10.1093/oso/9780192843371.003.0005

The first section (4.1) will analyse the part of the article which allows Member States to lay down, by national law, the criteria on which legal entities are considered to have a legitimate interest in ensuring compliance with the Directives and, on that basis, are permitted to engage in support or on behalf of victims of discrimination (legal standing). The second section (4.2) will look at collective redress mechanisms that are neither prescribed nor precluded by the Directives and which have been introduced by a number of countries. These sections will undertake a conceptual clarification and map the legal solutions adopted by Member States regarding these two issues.

The third section (4.3) will then look into the effects in practice of the legislation on the legal standing of NGOs, and the practical implementation of NGO engagement in individual and collective litigation. It will identify efforts undertaken by Member States and NGOs to put this into practice. It will further assess the impact of NGO support on the individual and societal levels (in terms of raising awareness, improving reporting behaviours, clarification of legislation, and changes in policies and practices, as well as societal perceptions).

NGO engagement in individual and collective litigation is relevant in the context of the findings of previous research[10] that found two of the reasons for the implementation gap are the lack of litigation from below as well as a lack of support from civil society actors. This chapter thus sets out to understand the experience so far of implementation of these provisions and attempts to identify good practices and challenges (4.4). This pooling of results should help to trigger a reconsideration of legislative and policy choices at Member State and EU levels.

Finally, on the basis of the findings of this chapter, the last section (4.5) will propose a limited number of structural, process, and outcome indicators.

4.1 Legal Standing of Associations

4.1.1 Introduction and Conceptual Clarification

The way in which civil society actors have been formally brought 'into the governance regime as part of the law-making and law-application process' has been described as one of the distinctive new features of the EU anti-discrimination regime.[11] In the context of law application, the core provisions are Article 7(2) of the Racial Equality Directive (RED) and Article 9(2) of the Employment Equality Directive (EED). Considering the role attributed to civil society actors through these provisions has been new in this field,[12] some effort requires from them in

[10] Falkner and Treib (n 3) 304–06; Fundamental Rights Agency, 'Opinion of the European Union Agency for Fundamental Rights on the situation of equality in the European Union 10 years on from initial implementation of the equality directives' (n 3).

[11] Gráinne de Búrca, 'Stumbling into Experimentalism: The EU Anti-Discrimination Regime' in Charles F Sabel and Jonathan Zeitlin (eds), Experimentalist Governance in the European Union: Towards a New Architecture (Oxford University Press, 2010), 222.

[12] The litigation strategies NGOs are allowed to put in place through the Directives were known, however, (in some countries at least) for the Gender Equality Directive of 1976. See Bruno de Witte,

redefining their role. Depending on how the states have transposed the relatively loose framework given by the Directives, they were given more or less opportunities to react to cases of discrimination. The lack of jurisprudence on discrimination cases and thus the lack of experience on how discrimination cases are handled by the judiciary is a deterring factor for a victim of discrimination to bring his/her case to court.[13] The role that associations and organizations can play in this field by bringing cases to court is therefore not to be underestimated.

There are several reasons why the role of these actors in facilitating the enforcement of anti-discrimination legislation is valuable. First, they help to mitigate the psychological stress of a victim of discrimination who has chosen to act against it. They may reduce the financial burden on the victim, which is often a reason for not pursuing legal action. Where a victim of discrimination is unwilling to pursue claims, enforcement of the Directives can be enhanced if organizations can bring such a case to court in their own name.[14] This makes it all the more interesting to note that, so far, there does not appear to be much literature on the interpretation, legal transposition, practical application, and the impact of these articles.

The concepts contained in Article 7(2) RED and Article 9(2) EED that need to be clarified are the following: first, are there any limits to the 'criteria laid down by their national law', by which states can define the organizations and associations that have a 'legitimate interest in ensuring that the provisions of this Directive are complied with'? Second, what exactly is entailed in the possibility for associations and organizations to engage 'on behalf' or 'in support' of a complainant. And finally, what do the articles imply when they require the 'approval' of the complainant for an organization to engage on his/her behalf or in his/her support.

To help clarify these questions, it is interesting first, to look at the drafting history of the articles, and second, whether Article 7(2) RED and/or Article 9(2) EED have been the subject of infringement proceedings started by the Commission. This would shed light on how the Commission is interpreting these concepts and whether it restricts in some way the states' discretion in how to legally transpose the articles in question. Third, it will be helpful to check whether the CJEU has dealt with the articles in its jurisprudence.

'From a 'Common Principle of Equality' to 'European Antidiscrimination Law'', American Behavioral Scientist (2010) 53(12): 1715, 1721, quoting Daniel Kelemen, 'Suing for Europe: Adversarial Legalism and European Governance' (2006) 39(1) Comparative Political Studies 101.

[13] European Commission, 'Report on the application of Council Directive 2000/43/EC implementing the principle of equal treatment between persons irrespective of racial or ethnic origin ("the Racial Equality Directive") and of Council Directive 2000/78/EC establishing a general framework for equal treatment in employment and occupation ("the Employment Equality Directive")' (n 4) 7.

[14] Fundamental Rights Agency, 'The Racial Equality Directive: application and challenges' (2011) <http://fra.europa.eu/sites/default/files/fra_uploads/1916-FRA-RED-synthesis-report_EN.pdf> 14; Fundamental Rights Agency, 'Opinion of the European Union Agency for Fundamental Rights on the situation of equality in the European Union 10 years on from initial implementation of the equality directives' (n 3) 22.

The rules on access to justice for associations (and other collective actors, such as Equality Bodies or trade unions) have resulted mainly from lobbying by civil society.[15] The proposal by the Commission for a Directive implementing the principle of equal treatment between persons irrespective of racial or ethnic origin concerning the rights of associations in discrimination cases read as follows:

> Member States shall ensure that associations, organisations or other legal entities may pursue, on behalf of the complainant with his or her approval, any judicial and/or administrative procedure provided for the enforcement of obligations under this Directive.[16]

It did not refer to the criteria for such organizations to be laid down by national law, and mentioned only the possibility of their engaging on behalf, but not in support, of a complainant. Reference to approval was already contained in this first proposal. Discussions about this provision were quite contentious as some groups, from the European Parliament in particular, favoured the idea of requiring the possibility of some form of collective redress while some Member States strongly opposed this proposal. The possibility for interested organizations to act in their own name on behalf of an identified victim was also not easily accepted by some states.[17] According to an account by a Commission official participating in the final negotiations, 'the precise status of such an organisation before the court is less important than the access to support from a respected organisation'.[18] Actual implementation practice discussed below will show, however, that this position may have been too short-sighted. As the necessity to appear before the court is in many cases connected to psychological stress for the victim and might even deter him/her from bringing a complaint in the first place, the possibility for an organization to act on behalf of a victim would greatly relieve the victim. In any case, the changes incorporated into the final version somewhat weakened the provision, as they first, grant states the option to place restrictions on associations and organizations that want to engage in discrimination cases. Second, the reformulation of 'on behalf of the complainant' into 'either on behalf or in support of the complainant' potentially weakens the position of associations and organizations as a state has correctly transposed the Directives as long as it provides for the much weaker possibility of

[15] Alvaro Oliveira, 'What Difference Does EU Law Make? The Added Value of EU Equality Directives on Access to Justice for Collective Actors' in Elise Muir and others (eds), *How EU Law Shapes Opportunities for Preliminary References on Fundamental Rights: Discrimination, Data Protection and Asylum* (European University Institute, EUI Working Papers 2017) 8–10.

[16] Commission of the European Communities, 'Proposal for a Council Directive implementing the principle of equal treatment between persons irrespective of racial or ethnic origin' (25 November 1999) COM(1999) 566 final, Art 7(2).

[17] Adam Tyson, 'The Negotiation of the European Community Directive on Racial Discrimination' (2001) 3(2) European Journal of Migration and Law 199, 212.

[18] ibid 212.

engaging just in support of a complainant. Altogether, the changes thus give the states more room for manoeuvre in the transposition of this norm.

Comparing the final wording of the Directives with the proposal of the Starting Line Group it becomes evident that the NGO proposal foresaw a stronger role for interested NGOs. The first difference is that the Starting Line proposal did not necessarily require either an identifiable victim or the victim's consent. The two documents also differ in that the Directive leaves it to the Member States and their national law to determine which associations and organizations have a 'legitimate interest' in legal standing while the Starting Line proposal just referred to 'organisations concerned with the defence of human rights and in particular with the combating of racism and xenophobia'.[19] Nevertheless, as underlined by Oliveira, 'this provision was a novelty in EU law at the time of its adoption in 2000 ... [and] constituted undisputable progress in the protection against discrimination'.[20]

In its 2014 Joint Report on the application of the two Directives[21] the Commission notes that infringement proceedings regarding the transposition of the Directives were launched against twenty-five Member States. In the Commission's opinion, the fact that many countries faced initial problems in transposition was linked to the novelty of the Directives at the time. Among the problems typically faced, the Commission also listed the legal standing of interested organizations and initiated infringement proceedings in this regard against Belgium, France, Germany, Ireland, Italy, Spain, and Portugal.

In the cases of Belgium and France, the Commission considered in its letters of formal notice that limiting the possibility to have legal standing to associations which have had legal personality for at least five years is not in compliance with Article 7(2) RED. Whilst acknowledging that it is for the national legislation to establish the criteria for defining which organizations have a legitimate interest to ensure that the provisions of the Directive are respected, the Commission was nevertheless of the view that the criterion regarding the duration of their legal personality seems to limit the very possibility for associations to benefit from the rights that Article 7(2) of the Directive confers on them. In addition, so ran the Commission's argument, it may not respect the principle of proportionality.[22] France responded to this by claiming that the purpose of introducing the criterion of having legal personality for at least five years is to ensure the seriousness and

[19] Isabelle Chopin and Jan Niessen, 'Proposals for Legislative Measures to Combat Racism and to Promote Equal Rights in the European Union' (Starting Line Group, Commission for Racial Equality 1998) Art 4(4)(d).

[20] Oliveira (n 15) 11.

[21] European Commission, 'Joint Report on the application of Council Directive 2000/43/EC of 29 June 2000 implementing the principle of equal treatment between persons irrespective of racial or ethnic origin ("Racial Equality Directive") and of Council Directive 2000/78/EC of 27 November 2000 establishing a general framework for equal treatment in employment and occupation ("Employment Equality Directive")' (Brussels 17 January 2014) COM(2014) 2 final.

[22] Infringement no 2005/2353 (letter of formal notice, Belgium); infringement no 2005/2355 (letter of formal notice, France).

legitimacy of the actions of the association. It further questioned the argument of lack of proportionality of the criterion raised by the Commission and held that in addition to NGOs, the Equality Body had also been given litigation powers. The Commission did not agree with these arguments and underlined the fact that the definition of criteria by national legislation is not supposed to question the protection that the Directive intends to guarantee. In short, the Commission was of the opinion that the requirement of five years' existence undermines the intended effect of the provision. Regarding the lack of proportionality, the Commission was of the opinion that the legitimate aim of ensuring the credibility of the associations concerned does not correspond to the requirement that they be legally registered for at least five years. And finally, the Commission made clear that the right for the Equality Body to have legal standing does not replace the obligation to properly transpose the obligations under Article 7(2). This can be drawn from Article 13 which clearly states that the competences assigned to the Equality Body are 'without prejudice to the right ... of associations ... referred to in Article 7(2)'.[23] Notwithstanding the fact that France insisted on the requirement of duration, the Commission closed the infringement case in June 2009.

In the infringement case against Germany, the Commission also criticized the criteria established by national legislation which define the associations and organizations which can engage in proceedings. The law provides that such associations must have at least seventy-five members. In the view of the Commission this limitation went too far as there is no connection between the size of an organization and its capacity to engage for the enforcement of the provisions of the Directive. Further, the German legislation only allowed non-profit organizations to engage in proceedings. Here the Commission did not accept that for-profit organizations were excluded without further examination of their legitimate interest in ensuring compliance with the provisions of the Directive. And finally, the Commission criticized the fact that associations could only engage in cases where there is no obligation to be represented by a lawyer. This applies to all second and third instance cases and for first instance cases where the amount involved is greater than 5,000 EUR.[24]

In response to the Commission's critique, the German government insisted that, according to the wording of Article 7(2) RED, it is the Member State's right to establish the criteria according to which NGOs have a legitimate interest to engage in proceedings. With regard to the definition of these criteria for the establishment of the legitimate interest, according to the German government, the Directive does not give any specification. It further argued that by providing that the organization had to be a specific size, the government were following the rules already in force in other areas, where organizations have a similar right, and where these criteria

[23] Infringement no 2005/2355 (reasoned opinion, France).
[24] Infringement case 2007/2253 (letter of formal notice, Germany).

have proven their worth. Furthermore, it argued that providing for a certain size of organization ensures that the rights of the persons concerned are protected in a reliable and competent manner. The non-profit orientation of the organizations has been justified by the German government on the basis of the protection of victims. If the organization was profit-oriented, it could be more concerned about its own self-interest rather than the interests of the victim of discrimination. In this context the government referred to some cases in which newly established organizations with only a low number of members and limited resources had tried to profit from the legal uncertainty of some individuals.[25]

Since the point regarding the rights of associations and organizations with a legitimate interest in engaging in discrimination procedures did not reappear in the reasoned opinion without the German government having undertaken any changes to the law implies that the Commission found the argumentation of the German government convincing and the legal situation in line with the requirements under the Directive.

The infringement case against Ireland circulated around the question of the required representation in front of the court by a lawyer. Irish legislation provides the possibility for associations and the Equality Body to represent victims of discrimination cases only before the Equality Tribunal (now the Workplace Relations Commission) and the Labour Courts. Thus, associations could not represent victims before other courts which led the Commission to conclude 'that the Irish legislation seems to contain no provisions which ensure that the *associations* ... can engage in the procedures for the enforcement of all the obligations under the Directive particularly in the non-employment field'.[26] The Irish authorities defended their position by explaining that before other courts, only qualified and recognized lawyers can represent individuals and that in any case offering support does not require representation. The Commission's interpretation of Article 7(2) would therefore be in contradiction with the clear intention

[25] Whether this allegation was well founded has not been verified by the present research. See, however, in this context the account about the generally hostile environment in Germany, created by political and economic actors but also academia, around the adoption of the German Non-Discrimination Act, fearing a flood of litigation, restriction of the principle of private autonomy and contractual freedom, and describing the Equality Body as an 'unconstitutional monster', in Matthias Möschel, 'Litigating Anti-Discrimination Cases in Germany: What Role for Collective Actors?' in Elise Muir and others (eds), *How EU Law Shapes Opportunities for Preliminary References on Fundamental Rights: Discrimination, Data Protection and Asylum* (European University Institute, EUI Working Papers 2017) 68–69, with further references; Sabine Berghahn, Micha Klapp, and Alexander Tischbirek, *Evaluation des Allgemeinen Gleichbehandlungsgesetzes (erstellt im Auftrag der Antidiskriminierungsstelle des Bundes)* (Nomos 2016) 160, with further references; Doris Liebscher, 'Recht als Türöffner für gleiche Freiheit? Eine Zwischenbilanz nach zehn Jahren AGG' (2016) 9 Aus Politik und Zeitgeschichte <http://www.bpb.de/apuz/221577/eine-zwischenbilanz-nach-zehn-jahren-agg?p=all>. For the reaction of the German government see Communication by the Government of the Federal Republic of Germany to the Commission of the European Communities of 12 February 2008, available in German at https://www.bug-ev.org/themen/recht/agg-vertragsverletzungsverfahren/antirassismusrichtlinie.

[26] Infringement case 2005/2357 (letter of formal notice, Ireland). Emphasis in original.

of the Council. The authorities also referred to the Commission's response to the question of an Irish representative on the interpretation of Article 7(2). In that response the Commission had explained that the Directives allow for a broad range of possibilities, given the different legal traditions of Member States, and that there is no particular way recommended by the Directive. In its reasoned opinion, the Commission underlined the fact that Article 7(2) does not say that associations should be able to 'support' victims of discrimination but that they should be able to 'engage' in proceedings.

> If all they can do in practice is to hire a lawyer to personally represent the victim, then there seems little added value in paragraph (2) of Article 7 over and above paragraph (1).[27]

This statement seems to imply an interpretation by the Commission of Article 7(2) which would require states to allow for the representation of victims of discrimination before the courts by associations, potentially departing from an otherwise existing obligation to be represented by a lawyer. This would indeed be an appropriate solution in discrimination cases, where a lot depends on the trust established between the victim of discrimination and the person (from an association) engaging in his/her support. It might be psychologically difficult for a victim to appear in court with a lawyer with whom this level of trust does not exist. However, the Commission went on to acknowledge that it is a matter of national procedure to insist that victims of discrimination can only be represented by a lawyer. At the same time it also underlined that Member States must guarantee that the practical purpose of Article 7(2), which is to 'provide a more effective level of protection' for victims of discrimination—as laid down in recital 19 of the Directive—is correctly and completely ensured.[28] Recital 19, however, also provides that this level of protection shall be achieved 'without prejudice to the national rules of procedures concerning representation and defence before the courts'.

The infringement proceedings against Italy related to the fact that the associations supposed to engage in support or on behalf of victims of discrimination had to be enrolled in a register that had to be approved by a ministerial decree and that this decree had not been adopted more than a year after the entry into force of the legislation transposing the Directive.[29] The decree was finally adopted in 2005 so that the issue was resolved before the Commission sent its reasoned opinion regarding other issues.

In the infringement proceedings commenced against Spain and Portugal, the Commission criticized the fact that in employment matters, only trade unions

[27] Infringement case 2005/2357 (reasoned opinion, Ireland).
[28] ibid.
[29] Infringement case 2005/2358 (letter of formal notice, Italy).

could intervene in judicial procedures in respect of their affiliated workers[30] which left victims of discrimination with no trade union affiliation without the 'more effective level of protection' mentioned by recital 19 of the Directive as the rationale behind the provision of granting associations the right to engage in judicial proceedings.

The case law of the CJEU has made clear that the wording contained in the Directives, according to which an organization or association may engage in judicial and/or administrative proceedings with the approval of the victim, cannot be understood in such a way that it precludes national legislation allowing for the engagement of an association or organization even in the absence of an identifiable victim. The cases in point are *Feryn* and *Asociația Accept* which will be discussed further below as these judgments open up the collective dimension of discrimination complaints in the form of *actio popularis* claims. In the case of *NH* the Court confirmed its approach on the issue.[31]

To come back to the concepts to be clarified, according to the Directives, states have considerable discretion in laying down the conditions under which an organization, association, or other legal entity can engage in support or on behalf of a victim of discrimination. The likelihood of deploying the full potential of the above mentioned advantages is higher, the less restrictions that are placed on organizations which could potentially engage in judicial proceedings. In fact, in order to improve access to justice in discrimination cases and facilitate enforcement, the Fundamental Rights Agency (FRA) recommended that Member States relax the rules on legal standing for NGOs and other civil society organizations.[32] As can be seen from the infringement proceedings, to require the existence as a legal person for at least five years has been considered not proportionate and as limiting the very possibility for associations to benefit from the rights provided under Article 7(2). Requirements for associations to be a particular size were also viewed critically. However, neither of these two national provisions led the Commission to take the case further.

The legal transposition would still be in line with the Directives if states only granted these stakeholders the possibility to intervene in support of a claimant. What exactly is meant by 'engage in support' of a complainant is again left to the discretion of states in the course of implementation and will be discussed in more detail below. According to the interpretation of the Commission it seems that it

[30] Infringement case 2005/2361 (letter of formal notice, Spain); Infringement case 2005/2360 (letter of formal notice, Portugal).

[31] *NH v Associazione Avvocatura per i diritti LGBTI—Rete Lenford* [2020] ECLI:EU:C:2020:289. For a discussion see Alina Tryfonidou, 'Case C-507/18 NH v Associazione Avvocatura per i diritti LGBTI—Rete Lenford: Homophobic Speech and EU Anti-Discrimination Law' (2020) 27(4) Maastricht Journal of European and Comparative Law 513.

[32] Fundamental Rights Agency, 'Opinion of the European Union Agency for Fundamental Rights on the situation of equality in the European Union 10 years on from initial implementation of the equality directives' (n 3) 26.

should include the possibility for associations to represent a victim of discrimination before the court. However this is again limited by the national legislation of some countries providing that victims of discrimination must be represented by a lawyer so that ultimately, national legislation allowing for counselling only is still in line with the requirements of the Directives. However, to engage in judicial proceedings also allows for a transposition that includes an NGO having legal standing in its own name and in the absence of an identifiable victim, thus opening the possibility for an *actio popularis*, an action in the public interest.

In the forefront of the Commission's assessment was one element, which should be kept in mind as guiding criterion in the evaluation of transposition and implementation: National legislation regarding criteria for NGOs and their kind of engagement should be such that it secures the practical purpose of the respective articles in the Directives, namely, to provide a more effective level of protection for victims of discrimination. The following examination of the legal transposition and the practical application of Articles 7(2) RED and 9(2) EED will show whether this expectation is fulfilled. While the above analysis suggests a plethora of different legislative solutions it remains to be seen what impact the different solutions will have on the actual enjoyment of rights.

4.1.2 Legal Transposition

The rules on access of associations to courts in discrimination cases had considerable impact on the legislation in Southern European countries and countries that were still in the accession process. This was because some of these countries still lagged behind in granting associations legal standing, whilst some of them went beyond the strict minimum required by the Directives. In other countries the new rules had just a certain or even no significant impact.[33]

The first issue we are going to look at is the criteria by which EU Member States establish whether associations, organizations, and other legal entities have a legitimate interest in ensuring compliance with the Directives. The second relevant issue is whether national legislation allows such organizations to engage on behalf or only in support of a claimant and what these options imply.

In most countries the criteria for NGOs being able to engage in judicial proceedings are specifically regulated for discrimination cases, while some countries make use of general provisions on legal standing for associations under certain conditions contained in their civil, administrative, or labour law.[34] The following will

[33] Oliveira (n 15) 8–16. Among the countries where the rules had considerable impact, he lists Belgium, Bulgaria, Czech Republic, Greece, Italy, Poland, Portugal, and Romania. The rules had a certain but no radical impact in France, Germany, Hungary, and Spain, and no significant impact in the Netherlands and the UK.

[34] Examples of the first are: Austria, Belgium, Bulgaria, Croatia, Cyprus, the Czech Republic, Estonia, France, Germany, Greece, Hungary, Ireland, Italy, Lithuania, Malta, Portugal, Romania, Slovakia,

give an overview of different groups of criteria foreseen by national legislation and the possibilities for NGOs connected thereto.[35]

As already mentioned above, some laws require organizations who want to engage in support or on behalf of victims of discrimination to exist for a certain number of years. In France, this requirement of at least five years' existence applies to both trade unions and NGOs.[36] Such organizations can act both on behalf and in support of claimants. According to the information provided in the 2020 EELN Country Report on France, NGOs have almost never made use of the possibility to act on behalf of a victim of discrimination. In Luxembourg, in addition to the requirement of legally existing for at least five years and the fight against discrimination being one of their statutory goals, associations need to be recognized by the Ministry of Justice as being nationally representative in the field of anti-discrimination. Such NGOs can, however, only act in support of a claimant, but not on his/her behalf.[37] In Belgium, associations must have recognized legal personality for at least three years and the defence of human rights or the fight against discrimination must be contained in their statutory objectives. The Appeal Court of Brussels clarified that such organizations need not have their head office in Belgium and accepted the standing of the French NGO SOS Racisme.[38] In addition to such organizations, the Equality Body and the workers' and employers' organizations can act both on behalf or in support of a discrimination victim.[39]

Another possible criterion limiting the ability of associations to engage in legal proceedings is related to their size. Germany for instance, notwithstanding the criticism raised by the Commission, continues to require associations to have at least seventy-five members or be the association of seven associations, in addition to working on a non-profit basis, and operating permanently rather than on an ad hoc basis to support one particular claim.[40] Although the initial draft of the General Equal Treatment Act also foresaw the possibility for organizations to act

Slovenia, Spain, and Sweden. Examples of the latter are: Denmark, Latvia, the Netherlands, and Poland. See European network of legal experts in gender equality and non-discrimination, 'A comparative analysis of non-discrimination law in Europe: 2020' (2021) 81.

35 The main sources for this subsection are European network of legal experts in gender equality and non-discrimination, 'A comparative analysis of non-discrimination law in Europe 2017' (2017) 88–95; European network of legal experts in gender equality and non-discrimination, 'A comparative analysis of non-discrimination law in Europe: 2020' (n 34) 81–89; as well as the 2020 Country Reports of the Network.

36 France, Code of Administrative Justice, Art R779-9; New Code of Civil Procedure, Art 3; Code of Penal Procedure, Art 2; Labour Code, Arts L1134-2 and L1134-3; Law No 83-634 of 13 July 1983 in the public sector, Art 8, paras 1 and 2, quoted in European network of legal experts in gender equality and non-discrimination, 'A comparative analysis of non-discrimination law in Europe: 2020' (n 34) 81.

37 Luxembourg, Law of 28 November 2006, Art 7.

38 Appeal Court of Brussels, 10 February 2015, referred to in European network of legal experts in gender equality and non-discrimination, 'A comparative analysis of non-discrimination law in Europe: 2016' (2016) 88.

39 Belgium, Racial Equality Federal Act, Art 32; General Anti-Discrimination Federal Act, Art 30.

40 Germany, General Equal Treatment Act, § 23(1).

on behalf of complainants, this option has been excluded from the final version. Thus, NGOs can only act in support of a complainant[41] in all kinds of proceedings except for criminal ones.[42] Such support is restricted to counselling in the course of proceedings, which implies that, unless the party contradicts, the actions of the counsel are taken as actions of the party.[43] In cases where representation by a barrister is compulsory, organizations can act as counsel in addition to the barrister.[44]

In some countries, organizations that want to engage in judicial proceedings must be entered on a list. This happens, for example, in Italy where, in the case of organizations that want to engage in proceedings regarding discrimination on the ground of racial or ethnic origin, they must appear on a list approved by the Ministries of Labour and Social Policies and that of Equal Opportunities.[45] In order to be included in that list, organizations need to exist for at least one year and the promotion of equal treatment and combatting discrimination must be their only or primary goal. Currently, more than 300 associations are represented therein.[46] The requirement of entry on the list for organizations fulfilling all the above mentioned criteria applies only for cases regarding discrimination on the grounds of racial or ethnic origin. The legislative decree implementing Directive 2000/78 only requires organizations to be nationally representative. No list exists and a court has to decide on an ad hoc basis whether an organization can be regarded as having a legitimate interest.[47] In both cases, organizations can act in support and on behalf of complainants.

In Slovenia the possibility of NGOs to engage in legal action for a victim of discrimination exists only for organizations that have been granted the 'status of an organisation working in the public interest in the field of protection from discrimination or protection of human rights'.[48] That status is granted by the 'competent ministry on the basis of the Associations Act and in line with the implementing act adopted by the competent ministry for this purpose'.[49] A limitation can be seen in the fact that any such registered NGO needs to be represented by an attorney, although under the general civil procedure this is not required for representation in county courts adjudicating disputes worth less than 20,000 EUR.[50] While

41 General Equal Treatment Act, § 23. For criticism on this point see Berghahn, Klapp, and Tischbirek (n 25)159–61.
42 EELN, Country Report Germany, 2020, 76.
43 ibid.
44 ibid.
45 Italy, Legislative Decree 215/2003, Arts 5–6.
46 The list is available from the Equality Body's website at http://www.unar.it/la-nostra-rete/associazioni/.
47 Italy, Legislative Decree 216/2003, Art 5; and EELN, Country Report Italy, 2020, 49. See however, Disability Act 67/2006, Art 4, which provides for a register comparable to that applying in race and ethnicity cases.
48 Slovenia, Protection Against Discrimination Act, Art 41(2).
49 EELN, Country Report Slovenia, 2020, 71.
50 ibid 70.

Bulgarian legislation also provides for the registration of organizations of public interest with the Ministry of Justice, it has been argued that associations which are not registered can still claim this status before the court, by submitting evidence that their activities are of public interest.[51]

Among the more restrictive forms of making use of the discretion provided for in the Directives is to grant the right to engage in judicial proceedings only to one organization. In Ireland, for instance, only the Human Rights and Equality Commission is allowed to represent victims before civil courts. The representation of victims of discrimination by other bodies or associations depends on the discretion of the court. Associations may, however, represent victims in front of the Workplace Relations Commission and the Labour Court.[52] In Austria only the Litigation Association of NGOs against Discrimination and, concerning disability cases, the National Council of Disabled Persons, can act in support of a complainant by intervening as a third party. Although the law does not, in principle, preclude the right of any association with a legitimate interest to act on behalf of a complainant, this possibility is in practice non-existent due the obligation to be represented by an attorney in nearly all judicial proceedings.[53] In Finland, organizations act in support or on behalf of a victim of discrimination only in front of the National Non-Discrimination and Equality Tribunal in cases other than employment. Only the Non-Discrimination Ombudsman must be given the opportunity to be heard before civil or penal courts in issues pertaining to his/her authority.[54] The Finish legislator has thus opted for a very restrictive approach, both in terms of who can engage and also in terms of what can be done. This very restrictive approach can be seen as potentially conflicting with the provisions of the Directives.[55]

On the other hand, a couple of countries have adopted a very open approach and provide no further conditions apart from having the protection of human rights or the fight against discrimination among the *statutory objectives* of the organization. This is the case in Romania for instance. Article 28 of the Romanian Anti-Discrimination Act provides that human rights NGOs can engage in judicial proceedings in cases involving discrimination pertaining to their field of activity. Under the same provision, such organizations can 'appear in court as parties in cases involving discrimination that prejudice a person, if the latter delegates the organisation to that effect'. This is interpreted as allowing both engagement in support and on behalf of a victim of discrimination.[56] The Constitutional Court has rejected a petition regarding the unconstitutionality of this provision.[57] When NGOs

[51] EELN, Country Report Bulgaria, 2020, 66.
[52] EELN, Country Report Ireland, 2020, 80–81.
[53] EELN, Country Report Austria, 2020, 54.
[54] EELN, Country Report Finland, 2020, 46.
[55] ibid 62.
[56] EELN, Country Report Romania, 2020, 69–70.
[57] ibid. See Romania, Constitutional Court, Decision 285, 1 July 2004.

would like to make a particular legal argument, they can ask the court if they may join a case as interested parties also under ordinary civil procedure provisions.[58] In addition to these possibilities, the internal procedures of the National Council for Combating Discrimination foresee the possibility for NGOs with expertise in a particular field to submit *amicus curiae* briefs.[59]

The Hungarian Equal Treatment Act of 2003 provided for a relatively open formulation: Social and interest representation organizations may act as an authorized representative of a victim of discrimination in court. A social and interest representation organization was defined by the law, inter alia, as a 'social organisation or foundation whose objectives set out in its articles of association or statutes include the promotion of the equal social opportunities of disadvantageous groups or the protection of human or personal rights'.[60] Since February 2012, there must be a correlation between the protected characteristic for which legal redress is sought and the objectives as defined in the statute, in the sense that the protected characteristic must be explicitly listed among the objectives of the organization.[61] This potentially limits the range of NGOs allowed to engage on behalf of a victim of discrimination but should not prevent the engagement of an NGO in a case of intersectional discrimination if its statute lists at least one of the protected characteristics which plays a role in the respective case. In the absence of case law, however, it remains to be seen whether such a flexible interpretation will be adopted by the courts.[62] The Hungarian legislation also gives legal standing to the minority self-governments with regard to members of the respective national minority.[63]

The Greek law on the implementation of the principle of equal treatment regardless of racial or ethnic origin, religion or other beliefs, disability, age, or sexual orientation only requires the NGO to have a legitimate interest in ensuring the principle of equal treatment to represent a victim of discrimination in judicial proceedings.[64] However, also in the Greek case the obligation to act before the court through an accredited lawyer considerably restricts this possibility for NGOs. Article 82 of the Greek Code of Civil Procedure provides for the possibility of 'additional intervention' in an already pending court process.

[58] EELN, Country Report Romania, 2020, 70.
[59] ibid.
[60] Hungary, Equal Treatment Act CXXV of 2003, Arts 3 and 18.
[61] European network of legal experts in gender equality and non-discrimination, 'A comparative analysis of non-discrimination law in Europe: 2015' (2016) 83; EELN, Country Report Hungary, 2017, 101–02. The same approach has also been followed by the Croatian Antidiscrimination Act, Art 21. Croatian NGOs can only act in support of a complainant, but not on his/her behalf, unlike trade unions in employment-related cases.
[62] EELN, Country Report Hungary, 2020, 90.
[63] Hungary, Equal Treatment Act CXXV of 2003, Art 3.
[64] Greece, Law 3304/2005, Art 13(3).

The Slovak, Latvian, and Bulgarian[65] legislation also does not introduce any specific requirements for organizations or associations that want to engage in support or on behalf of victims of discrimination. In the Slovak case, however, this right to engage 'on behalf' is limited to ordinary courts and the Supreme Court but excludes the Constitutional Court. The same goes for the Equality Body (Slovak National Centre for Human Rights) and trade unions. According to the Slovak Civil Dispute Act, the court can invite, without any proposal, the Equality Body, an interested NGO, or trade union to engage in a proceeding, if the relevant party agrees. Other forms of possible support include the submission of *amicus curiae* briefs by an NGO or the submission to the court of the expert opinion issued by the Slovak National Centre for Human Rights on the request of a complainant.[66]

The Latvian legislation allows the engagement of NGOs only in lower level courts, but not at the instance of cassation. This rule has been in force since 4 January 2014 and contravenes an earlier judgment of the Constitutional Court in which a similar provision was declared null and void for violating the principle of proportionality and Article 92 of the Latvian Constitution.[67] It thus remains to be seen whether this provision will again be challenged. When it comes to engaging in support of a victim of discrimination, administrative procedural law allows interested organizations to petition the court to submit an opinion. Where the court agrees to this, it determines the questions on which the organization may submit its opinion.[68]

While all the remaining countries do not require from associations or organizations the fulfilment of specific criteria other than having a legitimate interest in the issues at stake, their legislation differs in the scope of action granted to such associations or organizations. Most of them provide for the possibility for NGOs to act in support and on behalf of a complainant.[69] Estonia, Spain, and the UK foresee some restrictions.

In Estonia, a legal or natural person who has a legitimate interest in checking compliance with the requirements for equal treatment can act as a representative in conciliation proceedings for the resolution of discrimination disputes before the Chancellor of Justice. The legislation provides no further criteria or guidance on who is considered to have such an interest. When it comes to civil procedures, an

[65] Bulgarian legislation allows both trade unions and associations to act on behalf and in support of a complainant, in the latter case as an 'interested party'. See Bulgaria, Protection Against Discrimination Act, Art 71(1)–(2).

[66] EELN, Country Report Slovakia, 2020, 81.

[67] Constitution of Latvia, Art 92. Everyone has the right to defend his/her rights and lawful interests in a fair court. Everyone shall be presumed innocent until his/her guilt has been established in accordance with law. Everyone whose rights are violated without basis has a right to commensurate compensation. Everyone has a right to the assistance of counsel. See Latvia, Constitutional Court, Case No 2003-04-01, 27 June 2003.

[68] EELN, Country Report Latvia, 2020, 61.

[69] European network of legal experts in gender equality and non-discrimination, 'A comparative analysis of non-discrimination law in Europe: 2020' (n 34) 85–86.

association's staff member can appear as an adviser, but as such he/she cannot perform procedural acts or file petitions.[70]

In Spain, the peculiarity lies in the fact that organizations and associations may act on behalf of a victim of discrimination only in cases outside employment. Representation in employment cases is reserved to trade unions. To act in support of a complainant is not covered by Spanish legislation.[71] The opposite is the case in the UK. While associations are allowed to do whatever is not explicitly forbidden and on that basis, they are allowed to engage in support of a complainant, they are not entitled to act on behalf of victims of discrimination because this right is granted only to those who are directly affected by the discriminatory act.[72]

To sum up this overview of legal transposition of Articles 7(2) RED and 9(2) EED concerning the role of interested organizations in judicial dispute resolution, the following general statements can be made:

Most countries establish the 'legitimate interest' of entities in engaging in judicial proceedings with a view to their statutory objectives that must include the protection of human rights or the fight against discrimination. While some countries remain at such abstract levels, others require the issue in question in a specific case (for instance, discrimination on the ground of sexual orientation) to match exactly these objectives, which limits the number of NGOs allowed to intervene and might be problematic in cases of intersectional discrimination (see, for instance, the cases of Croatia and Hungary). About one quarter of countries lay down specific criteria related to the size of the organization, the time passed since its establishment, or its inclusion on a specific list. In this latter case, the criteria for being entered can be a combination of the above requirements and/or proof of acting in the public interest. In a few countries, the right to engage in proceedings is granted either only to the Equality Body (such as in Ireland, regarding disputes outside employment) or to one particular NGO (as in Austria).

Most countries allow such entities to act both on behalf and in support of a complainant. Restrictions or obstacles stem from the limitation to certain levels of jurisdiction in some countries (see the examples of Latvia and Slovakia), the obligation to be represented by an attorney (as for instance in Austria, Germany, Greece, Slovenia, and many other countries), the possibility to address only certain bodies (examples are from Austria, Finland, and Ireland), the reservation of the right to act on behalf of a complainant to the Equality Body (as in Ireland) or trade unions in labour disputes, as is the case in Croatia, Denmark, and Spain. To act on behalf of a victim of discrimination is generally understood as representing him/her before the court, while engaging in support of a victim of discrimination implies a variety of possibilities, ranging from the intervention as a third party, the

[70] EELN, Country Report Estonia, 2020, 40–41.
[71] EELN, Country Report Spain, 2020, 69.
[72] EELN, Country Report UK, 2020, 53.

submission of *amicus curiae* briefs, to legal counselling during proceedings or in preparation thereof.

A simple look into legal transposition makes it impossible to form an opinion about whether the chosen rules are appropriate to provide a more effective level of protection for victims of discrimination. A state might have opted for fairly strict rules when laying down the criteria defining the entities that may engage, but such rules do not necessarily result in a low number of associations who, in principle, could engage. The Italian rules, for instance, are relatively comprehensive but still, more than 300 organizations are registered on the list provided in the legislation. Similarly, the fact that only one institution can engage on behalf or in support of a complainant may seem very restrictive, but if this institution is given a strong mandate and the necessary resources, this might be more productive for victims of discrimination than being able to choose from a long list of possible organizations.

For these reasons, it is necessary to study some of the cases in more detail. The cases chosen represent a mix of most promising and apparently most difficult cases as well as the shades in between in order to elaborate on the factors other than legislation that influence the success or failure of a system. The factors that will be looked at, in line with the overall research strategy, are linked to state efforts to facilitate the implementation of the norms and the overall conditions within which NGOs are working. To conclude, an assessment will be made of the effects the combination of legislative commitment and implementation efforts have at the individual and societal levels.

This analysis of practice will be undertaken after a discussion in the following section about collective redress mechanisms, what the Directives say (or rather, do not say) in this respect, and what national legislation provides in this context. Thereafter, the case studies covered by the analysis of practice will deal with both individual and collective litigation.

4.2 Collective Redress

4.2.1 Introduction and Conceptual Clarification

The reasons why collective redress mechanism are important and useful have been discussed elsewhere,[73] however the principal cause should be briefly recalled. It

[73] See, for instance, Lilla Farkas, 'Limited Enforcement Possibilities Under European Anti-Discrimination Legislation—A Case Study of Procedural Novelties: Actio Popularis Action in Hungary' (2010) 3(3) Erasmus Law Review 181, 182, 184, and in particular at 186 and 187; Marie Mercat-Bruns, 'A Comparative Study on Collective Redress in France, Norway and Romania: The Challenges of Strategic Litigation' [2020] European Equality Law Review 19; Mark Bell, Anti-Discrimination Law and the European Union (Oxford University Press 2002), 78; Fundamental Rights Agency, 'The Racial Equality Directive: application and challenges' (2011), 14; Fundamental Rights Agency, 'Access to justice in cases of discrimination in the EU: Steps to further equality' (2012) <http://fra.europa.eu/sites/default/files/

must be acknowledged that a judicial redress approach focusing exclusively on individual complaints is limited by the fact that a judgment in the individual case might resolve the situation for the person involved and compensate him/her for the damages suffered, but it leaves the structural nature of discrimination unaddressed. In contrast to this, collective redress mechanisms are able to fight the systemic background to discrimination and tackle institutional forms of discrimination. As such, collective complaints are able to address practices that result in the discrimination against a large number of individuals. As there is no need for an individual victim to come forward with a discrimination complaint, the risk of victimization is minimized and no individual victim is exposed to the psychological stress connected with bringing a case to court, being personally present, and in some cases even appearing in the media. By raising a complaint above the level of an individual, it is also perceived as receiving more weight. Other advantages connected to this form of redress concern reduced costs, as it is not necessary for an NGO to maintain contact with an individual victim and the fact-finding is less extensive. Furthermore, due to generally greater visibility, collective complaints can be very well used for awareness-raising and lobbying. Due to all these potential advantages, it has been recommended that the European Commission should propose to Member States the adoption of collective anti-discrimination actions (in the sense of actions not referring to a specific victim) as a best practice.[74]

Critics of collective redress mechanisms in Europe warn of excessive enthusiasm towards this kind of legal instrument. They assert that if individual litigation is slow, especially in some Southern European countries, collective litigation will be even slower, due to 'an increased level of complexity … [t]he higher level of social importance and multiplication of the people affected by the judgment [which] could add to the need to take more evidence'. They further claim that an 'endless cycle of remittals' would hamper effective enforcement and that the judicial systems of the 'Mediterranean' model, characterized by formalism and inflexibility would be inappropriate for processing collective claims.[75] These are problems that equally affect individual and group litigation and mainly regard larger problems of the efficiency of justice. But they do not *per se* discredit collective redress mechanisms.

fra-2012-access-to-justice-social.pdf> 41–43 and 47; Slavica Chubrikj and Neda Chalovska-Dimovska, 'Use of actio popularis in Cases of Discrimination' (OSCE Mission to Skopje, Helsinki Committee for Human Rights 2016) 6; Adriána Zimová, 'Strategic Litigation Impacts: Roma School Desegregation' (Open Society Foundations 2016) 17–19.

[74] Constanza Hermanin and Eefje de Kroon, 'The Race Equality Directive: a Shadow Report. Lessons Learnt from the Implementation in Nine EU Member States' (Open Society European Policy Institute 2013) 25.

[75] Alan Uzelaz, 'Why No Class Action in Europe? A View from the Side of Dysfunctional Justice Systems' in Viktoria Harsági and CH van Rhee (eds), *Multi-Party Redress Mechanisms in Europe: Squeaking Mice?* (Intersentia 2014) 61–63.

The European network of legal experts in gender equality and non-discrimination distinguishes between two forms of collective redress mechanism: first, *actio popularis*, which in their definition describes the ability of organizations to act 'in the public interest on their own behalf, without a specific victim to support or represent'.[76] Class action, on the other hand, is defined as 'the ability for an organisation to act in the interest of more than one individual victim for claims arising from the same event'.[77]

The RED and the EED do not impose an obligation on Member States to provide for collective redress mechanism. In fact, the Directives' approach is based on the individual justice model, regardless of several elements contained in the Directives which point towards a shift in the perception of equality 'from an individual to a collective nature'.[78]

The Starting Line Group's proposal had proposed a stronger role for NGOs in fighting discrimination by legal means. Article 4(a)(d) of the proposal contained the following wording: 'organisations concerned with the defence of human rights and in particular with the combating of racism and xenophobia shall be able *to institute or support legal actions* in civil, administrative and criminal courts . . . '. This would have meant that such organizations would have been 'entitled to pursue, regardless of whether this is on behalf of or has the approval of the victims of discrimination, judicial and/or administrative procedure provided for the enforcement of obligations under national law'.[79] Some groups in the European Parliament were also advocating for the inclusion of the possibility of collective redress. However, a number of Member States, unfamiliar with such collective forms of redress, strongly opposed this option.[80]

As a result, the ability for NGOs to act on their own behalf without the existence of an individual victim was not explicitly included in the text of the Directives. On

[76] European network of legal experts in gender equality and non-discrimination, 'A comparative analysis of non-discrimination law in Europe: 2020' (n 34) 88.

[77] ibid 89.

[78] Gabriel N Toggenburg, 'The Race Directive: A New Dimension in the Fight against Ethnic Discrimination in Europe' (2001) 1 European Yearbook of Minority Issues 231, 239. See also Farkas, 'Limited Enforcement Possibilities Under European Anti-Discrimination Legislation—A Case Study of Procedural Novelties: Actio Popularis Action in Hungary' (n 73) 183, quoting Christopher McCrudden, 'International and European Norms Regarding National Legal Remedies for Racial Inequality' in Sandra Fredman (ed), *Discrimination and Human Rights. The Case of Racism* (OUP 2001) 251, 293–97; Bell, *Anti-Discrimination Law and the European Union* (n 73) 78; Nina Althoff, *Die Bekämpfung von Diskriminierung aus Gründen der Rasse und der ethnischen Herkunft in der Europäischen Gemeinschaft ausgehend von Art. 13 EG* (Peter Lang 2005) 252–55.

[79] Isabelle Chopin and Jan Niessen, 'Combating Racism in the European Union with Legal Means: A Comparison of the Starting Line and the EU Commission's Proposal for a Race Directive' (Migration Policy Group 2000) 2 and 7. See also Lilla Farkas, 'Collective Actions Under European Anti-Discrimination Law' [2014] European Anti-Discrimination Law Review 25, 29; Isabelle Chopin and Jan Niessen, 'The Starting Line and the Incorporation of the Racial Equality Directive into the National Laws of the EU Member States and Accession States' (Migration Policy Group, Commission for Racial Equality 2001) 42; Evans Case and Givens 232–33.

[80] Tyson (n 17) 212.

the other hand, it had not been precluded either. This prompted the initiators of the Starting Line proposal to recommend that NGOs seek to ensure in the process of legislative transposition not only that legal standing is provided 'for all relevant organisations' but also that they can 'bring cases both on behalf of complainants and in their own name'.[81]

As the Directives did not explicitly ask Member States to provide for collective redress, this issue has understandably not been raised in any infringement proceedings. However, the CJEU has had the opportunity on several occasions to clarify its standpoint on the issue. In the landmark *Feryn* case the Court said that Member States are not precluded 'from laying down, in their national legislation, the right of associations with a legitimate interest in ensuring compliance with [the Racial Equality Directive], or for the body or bodies designated pursuant to Article 13 thereof, to bring legal or administrative proceedings to enforce the obligations resulting therefrom *without acting in the name of a specific complainant or in the absence of an identifiable complainant*'.[82] What the Court had laid down for the RED with the *Feryn* judgment it did for the EED in the case *Asociatia Accept* case.[83]

In the case of *NH* two questions were asked of the CJEU. The first related to whether Rete Lenford, as an association of lawyers, could be considered as representative organization of collective interests and as such had the right to legal standing. The second question asked whether a violation of the Directive on equal treatment in the field of employment could be considered to exist when the statements do not refer to a recruitment procedure that actually exists, and thus there was no individual victim. The defendant, a lawyer with his own law firm, actually sustained that he made the statement, that he would not assume homosexuals, as a private person and not as an employer and no recruitment procedure was opened nor was one planned.[84]

81 Chopin and Niessen, 'The Starting Line and the Incorporation of the Racial Equality Directive into the National Laws of the EU Member States and Accession States' (n 79) 43.

82 *Centrum voor gelijkheid van kansen en voor racismebestrijding v Firma Feryn NV* [2008] ECLI:EU:C:2008:397, para 27. For a discussion see Kristin Henrard, 'The First Substantive ECJ Judgment on the Racial Equality Directive: A Strong Message in a Conceptually Flawed and Responsively Weak Bottle' [2009] Jean Monnet Working Paper; Rüdiger Krause, 'Case C-54/07, Centrum voor gelijkheid van kansen en voor racismebestrijding v. Firma Feryn NV, [2008] ECR I-5187' (2010) 47(3) Common Market Law Review 917; Mónika Ambrus, Marjolein Busstra, and Kristin Henrard, 'The Racial Equality Directive and Effective Protection Against Discrimination: Mismatches Between the Substantive Law and its Application' (2010) 3(3) Erasmus Law Review 165, 167–68; Farkas, 'Collective Actions Under European Anti-Discrimination Law' (n 79) 35–37.

83 *Asociația Accept v Consiliul Național pentru Combaterea Discriminării* [2013] ECLI:EU:C:2013:275, para 37. For a discussion see Uladzislau Belavusau, 'A Penalty Card for Homophobia from EU Non-Discrimination Law: Comment on Asociatia Accept (C-81/12)' (2015) 21(2) Columbia Journal of European Law 353.

84 *NH v Associazione Avvocatura per i diritti LGBTI—Rete Lenford* (n 31) para 27. See also Rete Lenford—Avvocatura per i diritti LGBTI, 'Discriminazione delle persone omosessuali in ambito lavorativo: la Corte di cassazione richiede una interpretazione pregiudiziale alla Corte di giustizia in un caso avviato da Avvocatura per i Diritti LGBTI—Rete Lenford' (25 July 2018) <http://www.retelenford.it/1030-discriminazione-delle-persone-omosessuali-in-ambito-lavorativo.html>; Giuliana Ubbiali, 'L'avvocato Taormina sui gay, parola alla Corte europea' *Corriere della sera* (6 August 2018).

The facts of the case are slightly different to those in the *Feryn* and *ACCEPT* cases. In *Feryn*, the employer excluded individuals of Moroccan origin from a job advertisement, whereas in *ACCEPT* the statements were made in the context of the potential transfer of a footballer who was rumoured to be gay, even though they were made by someone who did not have the power to bind or represent the employer in recruitment matters. It could therefore be claimed that these cases clearly fell into the sphere of employment whereas in the *NH* case, as there was no existing recruitment procedure, the statements fall outside this sphere. The breadth of the CJEU's statements in *Feryn* (concerning ethnic or racial origin but applicable by analogy to sexual orientation) suggested, however, that the lawyer's statements, being an employer and speaking about his approach to recruitment matters, amounted to discrimination. In *Feryn* the Court stated that

> the fact that an employer states publicly that it will not recruit employees of a certain ethnic or racial origin constitutes direct discrimination in respect of recruitment within the meaning of Article 2(2)(a) of Directive 2000/43, such statements being likely strongly to dissuade certain candidates from submitting their candidature and, accordingly, to hinder their access to the labour market.[85]

The Court started by answering the second question and held indeed that 'the fact that no negotiation with a view to recruitment was under way when the statements concerned were made does not preclude the possibility of such statements falling within the material scope of Directive 2000/78', if 'the link between those statements and the conditions for access to employment and to occupation with that employer' are not 'hypothetical'. In this respect the national court has to take into consideration if the statements come from a person who has or may be perceived as having a decisive influence on an employer's recruitment policy.[86] On the first question, the Court reiterated its approach taken in *Feryn* and *Accept*, that the Directive, while not requiring it, in no way precludes national legislation giving associations the right to bring legal proceedings 'without acting in the name of a specific complainant or in the absence of an identifiable complainant',[87] thus in the public interest. It is furthermore left to national legislation, whether the for-profit status of an association has 'a bearing on the assessment of its standing to bring such proceedings, and to specify . . . the sanctions that may be imposed at the end of

[85] *Centrum voor gelijkheid van kansen en voor racismebestrijding v Firma Feryn NV* (n 82) para 28. In *ACCEPT* it had to decide on the applicability of the Directive to the football club, even if the statements were made by an individual who did not have the legal capacity to bind or represent the club in recruitment matters.

[86] *NH v Associazione Avvocatura per i diritti LGBTI—Rete Lenford* (n 31) paras 42–44.

[87] ibid para 63, referring to *Asociația Accept v Consiliul Național pentru Combaterea Discriminării* (n 83) para 37.

it'.[88] It is therefore not precluded that an association acting in the public interest can also be awarded damages.

The CJEU's interpretation of the Directives as not precluding a national legislator from allowing for legal standing of NGOs in cases with no individual victim is in line with paragraph 25 of the European Commission against Racism and Intolerance's (ECRI) General Policy Recommendation No 7:[89] In this Recommendation, the ECRI recommends that Member States' anti-discrimination law provides 'that organizations such as associations, trade unions and other legal entities which have, according to the criteria laid down by the national law, a legitimate interest in combating racism and racial discrimination, are entitled to bring civil cases, intervene in administrative cases or make criminal complaints, *even if a specific victim is not referred to*'.[90] Without entering into a discussion about details, the HCNM's Recommendations on Access to Justice and National Minorities also include several references to collective redress for persons belonging to national minorities and interested organizations.[91]

In the Commission's proposal for a horizontal directive, the wording regarding the role of non-state actors in judicial dispute resolution is exactly the same as in the Directives from 2000, thus continuing the approach of leaving it to states themselves how to address the issue of collective redress.[92] Interestingly, in the years following the submission of this proposal in 2008, the Commission has initiated a process regarding a 'coherent horizontal approach to collective redress in the European Union without harmonising Member States' systems'.[93] It published a working document in 2011[94] initiating a public consultation on the issue. In 2013 it then adopted 'Recommendations on common principles for injunctive and compensatory collective redress mechanisms in the Member States concerning violations of rights granted under Union Law' aiming at improving access to justice and the level of enforcement of EU law.[95] The Commission emphasized that the

[88] *NH v Associazione Avvocatura per i diritti LGBTI—Rete Lenford* (n 31) para 64.

[89] ECRI, 'General Policy Recommendation No. 7 on National Legislation to Combat Racism and Racial Discrimination' (13 December 2002) CRI(2003)8.

[90] Emphasis added.

[91] HCNM, 'Graz Recommendations on Access to Justice and National Minorities' (November 2017). See, for instance, the explanatory note to Recommendation 1, point v.—Right to an effective remedy, at 15: 'Granting appropriate remedies to persons belonging to minority communities, including in collective redress that can tackle the causes of systemic discrimination, can also serve to signal the State's intent to treat them equally.' See further at 17 and 39.

[92] Commission of the European Communities, 'Proposal for a Council Directive on implementing the principle of equal treatment between persons irrespective of religion or belief, disability, age or sexual orientation' (2 July 2008) COM(2008) 426 final, Art 7(2).

[93] European Commission, 'Press Release: Commission recommends Member States to have collective redress mechanisms in place to ensure effective access to justice' (11 June 2013) IP/13/524, 1.

[94] European Commission, 'Commission Staff Working Document. Public Consultation: Towards a Coherent European Approach to Collective Redress' (4 February 2011) SEC(2011)173 final.

[95] Commission Recommendation of 11 June 2013 on common principles for injunctive and compensatory collective redress mechanisms in the Member States concerning violations of rights granted under Union Law 11 June 2013 (European Commission); European Commission, 'Towards a European Horizontal Framework for Collective Redress: Communication from the Commission to the European Parliament, the Council, the European Economic and Social Committee and the Committee of the Regions' (11 June 2013) COM(2013) 401 final, 7. For a discussion of the Recommendation and the

kind of collective redress it recommends 'needs to be clearly distinguished from so-called "class actions" that are common under the US legal system'.[96] This aloofness towards class actions of the American style arguably comes from the perception of this system as potentially leading to abusive litigation, which would be the case 'when it is intentionally targeted against law-abiding businesses in order to cause reputational damage or to inflict an undue financial burden on them'.[97] The Commission's document thus proposes a number of procedural safeguards to avoid such abusive litigation. They include a prohibition on contingency fees, the requirement for entities representing claimants to be of non-profit character, and a prohibition on punitive damages.[98]

When speaking about the areas to be covered by the Recommendation, the Commission mentions by way of examples consumer protection, competition, environmental protection, and financial services. The intention of the Commission was, however, to establish a horizontal framework for all areas where EU law grants rights to citizens.[99] This clearly includes protection from discrimination.

In summer 2017, the Commission started a consultation calling for evidence on the implementation and operation of its Recommendation in order to be able to evaluate the effectiveness and efficiency of the rules put in place. The Commission's report on the implementation of the Recommendation shows that the availability of collective redress mechanisms is still not consistent across the EU[100] and exists mainly in the area of consumer protection and related fields such as passengers' rights or financial services. The report also mentioned the existence of collective injunctions in anti-discrimination in Hungary, France, and Spain, and of compensatory collective redress regarding discrimination in France, Bulgaria, Denmark, Lithuania,

Communication, see Elisabetta Silvestri, 'Towards a Common Framework of Collective Redress in Europe? An Update on the Latest Initiatives of the European Commission' (2013) 1(1) Russian Law Journal 46.

96 European Commission, 'Press Release: Commission recommends Member States to have collective redress mechanisms in place to ensure effective access to justice' (n 93) 3. In a Memo the Commission puts it even more bluntly by stating that 'the European approach to collective redress clearly rejects the US style system of "class actions"'. European Commission, Memo, Frequently Asked Questions: European Commission recommends collective redress principles to Member States, 11 June 2013, MEMO/13/530, 2.

97 European Commission, 'Towards a European Horizontal Framework for Collective Redress' (n 95) 7.

98 ibid 7–8; European Commission, 'Press Release: Commission recommends Member States to have collective redress mechanisms in place to ensure effective access to justice' (n 93) 2.

99 This is also in line with the European Parliament's Resolution 'Towards a coherent European approach to collective redress' which explicitly asked for a horizontal framework for collective redress. European Parliament, 'Resolution of 2 February 2012 on "Towards a Coherent European Approach to Collective Redress"' 2011/2089(INI).

100 Hodges and Voet have found that while twenty-one countries have established a mechanism of collective complaint, 'no two models are the same, and none correspond to the Commission's model in its 2013 Recommendation'. Christopher Hodges and Stefaan Voet, *Delivering Collective Redress: New Technologies* (Hart Publishing 2018).

the Netherlands, Portugal, and the UK.[101] In addition, the implementation of safeguards against the potential abuse of such mechanisms remains inconsistent. The Commission therefore intends 'to further promote the principles set out in the 2013 Recommendation across all areas, both in terms of ... improving access to justice, and in terms of providing the necessary safeguards against abusive litigation'.[102]

The following looks at the legal approach chosen by EU Member States regarding *actio popularis* and class action. The legal analysis will be followed by a more in-depth study of a selection of countries to find out whether efforts have been undertaken by the state to support the functioning of collective redress mechanism. A look at the national jurisprudence of these countries and an attempt to evaluating the impact such case law has had on reporting behaviour and the level of rights awareness will round off this chapter.

4.2.2 Legal Transposition

A comparative overview of legislation in the EU shows that sixteen out of twenty-seven countries (plus the UK) provide for *actio popularis* (sometimes only with respect to a particular ground or granting that right only to one or few organizations)[103] and ten out of twenty-eight for class action.[104] It leaves seven countries providing for neither one nor the other. These countries are the Czech Republic,[105] Estonia, Finland,[106] Greece, Ireland, Latvia, and Poland.[107] However, these data require some specification.

[101] European Commission, 'Report from the Commission to the European Parliament, the Council and the European Economic and Social Committee on the implementation of the Commission Recommendation of 11 June 2013 on common principles for injunctive and compensatory collective redress mechanisms in the Member States concerning violations of rights granted under Union law (2013/396/EU)' (25 January 2018) COM(2018) 40 final, 3.

[102] ibid 20.

[103] These countries are: Austria, Belgium Bulgaria, Croatia, France, Germany, Hungary, Italy, Luxembourg, Malta (only for the Equality Body), the Netherlands, Portugal, Romania, Slovakia, Spain (only in criminal proceedings), and the UK (requiring, however, judicial interpretation). See European network of legal experts in gender equality and non-discrimination, 'A comparative analysis of non-discrimination law in Europe: 2020' (n 34) 88.

[104] These countries are: Bulgaria, Denmark, France, Germany, Lithuania, the Netherlands, Portugal, Slovakia, Slovenia, and Sweden. ibid 89. For some details on the Swedish case see EELN, Country Report Sweden, 2020, 66–67.

[105] 87 per cent of administrative bodies and 65 per cent of the courts 'would consider it worthwhile if the Ombudsman could file actio popularis. On the other hand, the attitude of public bodies towards the possibility of NGOs bringing actio popularis is rather reserved.' See EELN, Country Report Czech Republic, 2017, 115. In 2019 a bill was tabled that would give NGOs the right to file an *actio popularis*, but there is strong resistance (EELN, Country Report Czech Republic, 2020, 68) and so far it has not been adopted.

[106] Considering that class action is possible in Finland in consumer protection cases, it is conceivable that the Consumer Ombudsman could bring class action claims in cases of discrimination in the provision of goods and services. See EELN, Country Report Finland, 2020, 47.

[107] See European network of legal experts in gender equality and non-discrimination, 'A comparative analysis of non-discrimination law in Europe: 2020' (n 34) 89.

Belgian law, for instance, does not recognize the 'concept of *actio popularis* involving a "representative claimant" acting in court in the name of a collective interest'. However, if there is no identified victim, the Equality Body, NGOs, and trade unions 'may act on their own behalf to challenge a breach of the anti-discrimination legislation'.[108] This made it possible for Unia, the Equality Body, to act in the *Feryn* case, which ended up before the CJEU and led to the clarification that the identification of a complainant who claims to have been a victim of discrimination is no precondition for determining the existence of direct discrimination and that national legislation can also provide for legal standing for NGOs when they are not acting in the name of a specific complainant or in the absence of an identifiable complainant.[109]

Poland introduced the possibility of bringing a class action in 2010 on the premise that parties interested in the case must join it personally, thus choosing the opt-in model (as proposed also by the Commission in the above-discussed Recommendations) which seems to prevail in the countries providing for this possibility.[110] Poland is also exemplary in that class action is mainly restricted to consumer protection claims and torts but not explicitly to discrimination claims. It is, however, not precluded that discrimination cases could also find their way to court on this basis. And finally, Polish legislation only allows attorneys to bring such class action claims and not organizations or associations as such.[111]

With regard to Austria and Germany, it is important to note that collective redress is possible only in cases involving disability. As of 1 January 2018, however, Austrian legislation has improved in this respect. Until then, such legal means was possible only for one organization, the Austrian National Council of Disabled Persons, and only upon recommendation (with a resolution backed by two thirds of the votes) by the Federal Council on Disability. After the amendments, the Litigation Association of NGOs Against Discrimination and the Ombudsperson for People with Disabilities can also bring a collective complaint and an action no longer depends on a recommendation by the Federal Council on Disability. A further improvement is related to the fact that these organizations can not only ask the court to establish that discrimination has actually occurred, but with regard to corporations of a certain size (a limitation criticized by the Litigation Association[112]) they can also bring an action for the prohibition or elimination of discrimination.

[108] EELN, Country Report Belgium, 2020, 90–91.

[109] *Centrum voor gelijkheid van kansen en voor racismebestrijding v Firma Feryn NV* (n 82) paras 25 and 27.

[110] See, for instance, also EELN, Country Report Portugal, 2020, 65.

[111] EELN, Country Report Poland, 2020, 82.

[112] Litigation Association, 'Verbandsklagerecht für den Klagsverband gefordert' (26 September 2017) <https://www.klagsverband.at/archives/12738>.

A limitation that remains in the text of the law concerns the requirement that the discrimination in question adversely affects the general interests of persons with disabilities 'substantially and permanently'.[113] While the option in place until the end of 2017 had never been used, the Litigation Association has already announced that it will make use of this newly created possibility.[114]

Similarly, in Germany the possibility for associations and organizations to file an *actio popularis* is restricted to the field of disability.[115] Organizations that want to address the court in this way need to be registered with the Ministry of Labour and Social Affairs. To be registered, they need to have worked for at least three years to promote the interests of persons with disabilities on the federal level, operate permanently, and provide guarantees of their appropriate handling of the case. Cases can be brought if the duty of public bodies to provide an accessible environment is violated. If an individual victim is harmed, an *actio popularis* can only be filed if the organization shows that the case is of general importance. Before bringing a case to court, the organization must attempt conciliation and only in the event that fails can it file an *actio popularis*.[116]

Croatian legislation is very open in that it allows associations and organizations that have a justified interest in the protection of collective interests of a certain group to bring action against the violation of rights of a larger number of persons belonging to the group whose rights the association defends, without representing or supporting a specific victim, thus a case of *actio popularis*. Besides an action for determining discrimination or for the prohibition or elimination of discrimination, such an organization can also claim to publish in the media the ruling establishing the violation of the right to equal treatment, at the defendant's expense,[117] which adds to the awareness-raising effect collective redress mechanisms are said to have. On the other hand, associations are not able to claim for damages, an approach that is common in other countries too.[118]

[113] Federal Disability Equality Act, § 13(1).

[114] Litigation Association, 'Verbandsklagerecht für Klagsverband im Nationalrat beschlossen' (13 October 2017) <https://www.klagsverband.at/archives/12792>.

[115] Critical in this regard, Berghahn, Klapp, and Tischbirek (n 25) 159–61; Nina Althoff and Sera Choi, 'Verbände aktiv gegen Diskriminierung. Das Project "Diskriminierungsschutz: Handlungskompetenz für Verbände"' (2011) 13.

[116] Germany, Equal Opportunities for Disabled People Act of 2002 (last amended in 2016), § 15. See also the Netherlands, Civil Code, Art 3:305a(2), regarding the inadmissibility of a collective action if it is not preceded by sufficient 'attempts to reach a settlement over its claim through consultations with the defendant'. Similarly, France, Law No 2016-1547 of 18 November 2016 on the modernisation of the justice system in the 21st century, Art 62.

[117] Croatia, Antidiscrimination Act 2008 (last amended in 2012), Art 24.

[118] See, for instance, Hungary and the Netherlands. Italian legislation, on the other hand, allows also the claim for damages.

Denmark allows associations, organizations, and trade unions to bring class actions but not an *actio popularis*. It is interesting to note, however, that the Danish Institute for Human Rights has the competence to take cases of principle to the Board of Equal Treatment which could be considered as a form of *actio popularis*.[119] In France, class action used to be limited to housing cases. In 2016, a specific procedure for class action in discrimination cases more generally was introduced. Employment cases remain reserved to trade unions.[120] In Lithuania, civil and administrative procedural law expressly allows for *actio popularis*. However, in both cases, additional legislation is required to regulate the issue and thus, the possibility has so far remained theoretical.[121] Class action is possible provided a group of at least twenty people is represented by an attorney. An organization or association could thus support such a class action by hiring an attorney that represents the victims before the court.[122] Malta explicitly allows only the Equality Body (the National Commission for the Promotion of Equality—NCPE) to file an *actio popularis*, which does not necessarily, however, have to be interpreted as precluding this possibility for NGOs.[123] In Portugal (as in France) class action in employment cases is reserved to trade unions.[124]

This overview has shown that the two forms of collective redress, *actio popularis* and class action, are legal means that are not yet widely available in European countries beyond the field of consumer protection. Where one or the other form exists for discrimination cases it appears that courts show a certain reluctance in accepting the legal standing of organizations. A deeper look into the case law of a selection of countries is therefore required. As has been seen, some countries restrict these possibilities to the ground of disability only. In other countries, the additional legislation required to bring collective redress mechanisms to life is missing, meaning that these options exist only theoretically. In only one case, *actio popularis* is reserved to the Equality Body alone, while collective redress in labour disputes is sometimes reserved to trade unions. Where class action is provided for, most countries appear to have chosen the opt-in model, requiring interested persons to express the will to join the case. Some countries require that collective actions be preceded by conciliation attempts with the defendant. Claims for damages are normally, but not always, excluded in *actio popularis* cases.

[119] EELN, Country Report Denmark, 2020, 68.
[120] EELN, Country Report France, 2020, 91.
[121] EELN, Country Report Lithuania, 2020, 91.
[122] ibid 92.
[123] EELN, Country Report Malta, 2020, 65.
[124] EELN, Country Report Portugal, 2020, 64.

It appears that Eastern European countries are more open towards collective redress mechanisms and provide less limitations where they do exist. There have been a number of cases brought before the courts on this basis. An examination of the case law will shed light on how such 'generous' legal transposition plays out in practice.

4.3 Practical Implementation

As mentioned above, for the analysis of the practice a mix of—what appear from the legal point of view to be—the most promising and the most difficult cases as well as the shades in between have been chosen in order to highlight the factors that influence success or failure of a system. As an example of permissive legislation, Romania has been chosen. This regards both the criteria provided by law for the legal standing of NGOs as well as the legal avenues open to them. The case of Hungary is similarly open to NGO engagement in litigation, limited by the fact that the issue in question in a specific case must match exactly the objectives for which the NGO is established. NGOs can support individuals but can also make use of collective redress mechanisms. Germany has been chosen for its rather restrictive legislation. As illustrated above, Germany's legislation has introduced a number of limitations in order for NGOs to qualify for supporting victims of discrimination. The possibilities for NGOs to support an individual are fairly limited and collective redress is restricted to the ground of disability.

The case studies first introduce the legal framework for legal standing in detail and then assess whether this framework is perceived as restrictive by the NGOs that engage in litigation or has had an influence on the number of organizations engaging in this field. The aims of NGOs engaging in discrimination cases will also be assessed, as well as the use they have made of the existing possibilities, practical challenges they are facing, and what kind of impact their litigation activities have had, both at the individual and societal levels. This will enable us to identify the good practices and the challenges NGOs are faced with and also to draw some conclusions as to whether state authorities are making sufficient efforts to give the legal provisions a practical effect and whether the purpose of the Directives' provision—to provide a more effective level of protection for victims of discrimination—has been achieved. From these findings, indicators concerning the role of NGOs in judicial dispute resolution will be deduced.

4.3.1 Case Study: Romania

According to the Romanian Ordinance No 137/2000 on Preventing and Sanctioning all Forms of Discrimination, human rights NGOs can appear as parties in court cases involving discrimination pertaining to their field of activity if the discrimination affects an individual (Art 28(2)) or a community or group of persons (Art 28(1)). If the victim is an individual, the written request of the victim is required. The Romanian legislation can thus be described as being among the most permissive legal transpositions of Article 7(2) RED and Article 9(2) EED. There exist no specific requirements for the NGO in terms of length of existence, size, or working for the interest of a particular group. Further, a simple written request by the victim is sufficient for an NGO to be allowed to act on behalf of the person concerned. However, general rules of civil procedure provide that certain tasks before the court can only be performed by lawyers with the power of attorney. Thus while representatives from an NGO can, for instance, present documents to the court, respond to questions from the court, and bring arguments on some preliminary issues, they are not able to file the final pleadings.[125]

The Romanian Constitutional Court ruled on whether this provision granting legal standing to NGOs was in line with the Constitution. It rejected the petition which claimed that the provision led to 'a situation of inequity and discrimination for the parties which did not put themselves under the protection of an NGO of this kind'.[126] The situation was further clarified by Article 37 of the Civil Procedure Code that entered into force on 1 February 2013, which provides that 'in the cases and conditions specifically provided for by the law [such as in Ordinance No 137/2000], complaints can be filed or defences can be submitted by persons, organisations, institutions or authorities which, without justifying a personal interest, act for the defence of rights and legitimate interests of persons who find themselves in special situations or, as necessary, with the purpose of protecting a group or a general interest'.[127]

In addition to the possibility of representing the victim in court in the manner just described, NGOs can also engage through a third party intervention, as provided in civil procedural law, and thereby support victims of discrimination. Such intervention is possible in the interest of the victim, or in the organization's own interest, which has the advantage that the NGO can also appeal the decision independently from the victim if it proves that its interests are affected. Finally, NGOs can submit *amicus curiae* briefs on legal issues. As this form of intervention is not regulated by the rules on civil procedure it is at the judge's discretion whether to admit the *amicus* or not.[128]

As NGOs can also act if the discrimination is directed against a community or a group of persons, they can therefore launch an action in the public interest.

[125] Interview, human rights lawyer II, Romania, EELN legal expert, 25 July 2018.

[126] Romania, Constitutional Court Decision 285, of 1 July 2004, as referred to in EELN, Country Report Romania, 2020, 69.

[127] Quoted from EELN, Country Report Romania, 2020, 70.

[128] EELN, Country Report Romania, 2017, 69–70; interview, human rights lawyer II, Romania, EELN legal expert, 25 July 2018.

This possibility was considered helpful especially in the first years of the non-discrimination legal framework to create jurisprudence and to gain experience on how the law works. More recently, it has been considered more important to support the cases of individual victims. This is partly connected to the limitations of *actio popularis* in the Romanian legal system which, as a legal instrument, has remained rather 'on the surface'.[129] One limitation is related to the fact that procedural law does not provide for the tools that would be required to enforce general measures that require proactive steps. So, for instance, the judge could impose a general measure that requires a local administration to *eliminate* a discriminatory criterion when deciding on the allocation of social housing. However, if the judge ordered that a *proactive measure* be taken, like the adoption of an action plan including the provision of a budget for its implementation, there are no procedural provisions that would allow the judge to make sure this was implemented. Thus while in theory, judges can order, for instance, an employer to adopt a diversity plan for their company or to provide training for employees, they do not make use of this possibility. General measures are not granted in individual cases either because they are not seen to be in the interest of the complainant. *Actio popularis* is further limited by the fact that it is not possible to claim for (punitive) damages that could be paid into a fund for the compensation of future victims.[130]

In cases in the public interest it is considered important for an NGO to have contacts with the group which has suffered the discrimination and to establish a good level of trust with that community. This is of course a more challenging endeavour than in an individual case, considering the divergent views and interests within various communities. However, if a case is built without this community contact, it has less chances of being successful and/or the result might not be accepted by the community.[131]

Furthermore, in order to build a strong case it is necessary to choose it strategically, which requires considerable investment in understanding the problem, documenting developments, and carrying out fact finding. In addition to this experience required, an organization has to factor in that cases could take many years before a decision is final which requires a long-term organizational and financial stability. Against this background and considering the 'funding crisis' Romanian NGOs find themselves in, it is not surprising that there are currently only about five national NGOs that engage in proceedings in support of victims of discrimination. They cover the grounds of disability, sexual orientation, ethnic origin (particularly Roma and Roma women), as well as gender. They are mainly concentrated in Bucharest and Cluj with the rest of the country basically not being covered by national NGOs that engage in discrimination litigation. With regard

[129] Interview, human rights lawyer II, Romania, EELN legal expert, 25 July 2018.
[130] ibid.
[131] ibid.

to discrimination against Roma this is partly remedied by the activities of the European Roma Rights Centre.[132] Also, the existing NGOs try to reach out to, and are contacted by, persons living in peripheral areas. In the absence of local lawyers able to support such court cases, this is also done by the Bucharest or Cluj-based organizations.[133]

One of these organizations is ACCEPT, an NGO working in the field of LGBT rights. They have supported a number of cases, some of which were taken as far as the CJEU and the European Court of Human Rights (ECtHR). They have supported individual complainants but have also brought actions in the public interest. More often, they choose individual cases that have the potential to deploy effects beyond the satisfaction of the interests of the individual. The aim of the association when selecting cases for their strategic litigation is to highlight problematic aspects of the legislation and, by bringing such cases before European level courts, to trigger legislative improvements and improve the accountability of the authorities responsible for implementing legislation. In addition, with their litigation activity, they want to contribute to the development of a human rights culture in their domestic context, shaping the debate beyond the political discourse about certain issues and towards a more nuanced understanding about how to balance certain human rights that appear to be in contradiction.[134]

An example in this context is a case brought before the Romanian tribunal-type Equality Body, the National Council for Combating Discrimination (NCCD), in which they aimed to clarify the concept of instruction to discriminate and to address the relationship between freedom of religion on one hand and the non-discriminatory exercise of the freedoms of expression and assembly. The case regards a gathering organized by high school pupils on women's rights, gender identity, and sexual orientation, which came under pressure by a number of local leaders, including the local archbishop of the Orthodox Church. In the end, the head of the conference venue withdrew permission for the meeting to be held due to the presence of a trans man on the list of speakers. As this was considered a discriminatory measure aiming to restrict the rights to freedom of expression and assembly, ACCEPT decided to file a complaint before the NCCD against those who had exercised pressure to cancel the debate, including the local archbishop, as well as the head of the conference venue. The case was brought because it was felt that there was a need to engage in the debate taking place in Romania since 2015, when a citizens' initiative was started with the aim of rewriting the Romanian Constitution regarding the definition of the term 'family', thereby creating a division in Romanian society. It was felt that the trend was going in the direction of

[132] ibid; Board member of ACCEPT, 6 August 2018; human rights lawyer I, Romania, EELN legal expert, 2 April 2021.
[133] Interview, human rights lawyer I, Romania, EELN legal expert, 2 April 2021.
[134] Interview, Board member of ACCEPT, 6 August 2018.

establishing a hierarchy of rights with the freedom of religion on top, especially when it comes to balancing this with the right not to be discriminated against on the ground of sexual orientation and gender identity. As this was a debate considered to become even more relevant in the future, the association considered it important to engage quasi-judicial and judicial institutions as well. In the particular case, the decision was first to approach the NCCD: a) because it appeared to have limited experience with cases relating to the freedom of religion, considered alone but especially in the context of LGBT rights;[135] and b) it has also been reported that the strategy to approach the NCCD first is sometimes chosen in cases dealing with sensitive issues that have not been addressed before and where the expectation is that the NCCD could have a 'more open' approach. A favourable decision from the NCCD would thus constitute a first step which, even if the decision is appealed, would have a certain impact.[136] In the specific case, the strategy was to support an individual (the speaker invited to the gathering, in relation to the cancelling of the event due to his gender identity and the campaign targeting him after the respondents made his name and private details public) as well as to bring the case in the public interest. The advantage of this double strategy is first, that if the individual decides to withdraw from the case, the NGO can still pursue it further. Second, the association, unlike the individual, can ask for general measures and third, it boosts the visibility of the case.[137] The NCCD decided that the decision to cancel the event amounted to discrimination and sanctioned the head of the venue with a fine of 1,000 RON (approximately 200 EUR). However, it did not find any discrimination with regard to the local authorities and the local archbishop, notwithstanding the pressure they exerted to cancel the event and the hate campaign launched against the trans person. Both the head of the venue and ACCEPT appealed the case.[138]

Another public interest case initiated by ACCEPT, which is widely known as the *ACCEPT* or the *Becali* case,[139] was referred by the national court to the CJEU to clarify, inter alia, the question as to whether the sanctions provided for by the Romanian legal system could be considered adequate under the Directive 2000/

[135] Interview, Board member of ACCEPT, 6 August 2018.

[136] Interview, human rights lawyer II, Romania, EELN legal expert, 25 July 2018. The lawyer also reported that initially more cases were brought by NGOs to the NCCD in order to put the Equality Body to work and to raise awareness of the body's existence. Another reason for choosing to approach the NCCD first was the lack of experience with non-discrimination legislation among judges. Over the years, it was no longer considered necessary to 'feed' the Equality Body with cases and the limitations of the body became apparent (especially regarding decisions involving political figures and more recently, cases involving religious issues), and NGOs started to approach the courts directly. As the Equality Body is asked by the court to offer its opinion on non-discrimination cases, NGOs sometimes also choose to approach the court and at the same time provide information to the NCCD in the hope to get support through its opinion.

[137] Interview, human rights lawyer II, Romania, EELN legal expert, 25 July 2018.

[138] Romanita Iordache, 'Refusal to host conference due to the presence of a trans activist sanctioned by the NCCD' (EELN News Report, 10 July 2020); and interview, human rights lawyer I, Romania, EELN legal expert, 2 April 2021.

[139] *Asociația Accept v Consiliul Național pentru Combaterea Discriminării* (n 83).

78/EC. In this case, Mr Becali, (at that time still) a shareholder of the football club Steaua Bucharest, made homophobic statements in the context of the possible transfer of a professional footballer supposed to be homosexual. Regarding the club, the NCCD found that the circumstances at issue did not fall within the scope of a possible employment relationship, as Mr Becali had no power to make decisions in recruitment matters. However, it issued a warning against Mr Becali as a remedy against his discriminatory remarks which were found to constitute harassment, infringing the dignity of homosexuals. The CJEU found that the facts of the case could lead to a finding of discrimination by the club in recruitment matters and to a shift of the burden of proof to the club, 'even though the statements concerned come from a person presenting himself and being perceived in the media and among the general public as playing a leading role in that club without, however, necessarily having legal capacity to bind it or to represent it in recruitment matters'.[140] Regarding the warning as a sanction the CJEU found that 'a purely symbolic sanction cannot be regarded as being compatible with the correct and effective implementation of Directive 2000/78'.[141] The Romanian courts, however, focused their subsequent decision on the part of the judgment where the CJEU admitted that '[i]t is true that the mere fact that a specific sanction is not pecuniary in nature does not necessarily mean that it is purely symbolic ..., particularly if it is accompanied by a sufficient degree of publicity and if it assists in establishing discrimination within the meaning of that directive in a possible action for damages'.[142]

This case, although it did not achieve the desired outcome in the Romanian context, has nevertheless contributed to a clarification of the meaning of effective, proportionate, and dissuasive sanctions at the European level. It has also had an effect in the Romanian context. In fact, not only have the fines for violations of the prohibition of discrimination before the NCCD been increased but the practice of issuing warnings or recommendations rather than fines also appears to be decreasing.

A more recent CJEU judgment with involvement of ACCEPT is the *Coman* case.[143] Although it does not come within the scope of Directive 2000/43/EC or

[140] ibid para 53.
[141] ibid para 64.
[142] ibid para 68.
[143] *Relu Adrian Coman and Others v Inspectoratul General pentru Imigrări and Ministerul Afacerilor Interne* [2018] ECLI:EU:C:2018:385; commented on in Dimitry Kochenov and Uladzislau Belavusau, 'Same-Sex Spouses in the EU After Coman: More Free Movement, But What About Marriage?' [2019] EUI Working Papers 1; Steve Peers, 'Love wins in the CJEU: Same Sex Marriages and EU free movement law' (EU Law Analysis, 5 June 2018) <http://eulawanalysis.blogspot.com/2018/06/love-wins-in-cjeu-same-sex-marriages.html>; Alina Tryfonidou, 'Free Movement of Same-Sex Spouses within the EU: The ECJ's Coman judgment' (European Law Blog, 19 June 2018) <https://europeanlawblog.eu/2018/06/19/free-movement-of-same-sex-spouses-within-the-eu-the-ecjs-coman-judgment/>; Manon Beury, 'The CJEU's judgment in Coman: a small step for the recognition of same-sex couples underlying European divides over LGBT rights' (Strasbourg Observers, 24 July 2018) <https://strasbourgobservers.com/2018/07/24/the-cjeus-judgment-in-coman-a-small-step-for-the-recognition-of-same-sex-couples-

2000/78/EC it is worthwhile considering it as it shows the impact of litigation supported by NGOs. Mr Coman, a dual Romanian-US citizen and Mr Hamilton were a same-sex couple who married in Belgium. When Mr Hamilton requested a permanent right to residence in Romania as Mr Coman's spouse, the Romanian authorities rejected his request on the basis that the Romanian Civil Code did not recognize same-sex marriages, even if contracted abroad. Supported by ACCEPT, the couple challenged the decision as a case of discrimination based on sexual orientation and the provision of the civil code as being unconstitutional. The Constitutional Court referred the question to the CJEU as to whether the term 'spouse' included in Article 2(2)(a) of the Citizens' Directive[144] and not further defined by the Directive, included the same-sex spouse from a non-EU country who is legally married to an EU-citizen according to the legislation of an EU Member State other than the host country. In its decision of 5 June 2018, the CJEU affirmed that a 'spouse' was 'a person joined to another person by the bonds of marriage'. It further stated 'that the term "spouse" within the meaning of Directive 2004/38 is gender-neutral and may therefore cover the same-sex spouse of the Union citizen concerned'. It thus concluded that 'a Member State cannot rely on its national law as justification for refusing to recognise in its territory, for the sole purpose of granting a derived right of residence to a third-country national, a marriage concluded by that national with a Union citizen of the same sex in another Member State in accordance with the law of that state'.[145]

On 18 July 2018, the Romanian Constitutional Court decided in line with the judgment of the court that same-sex married couples have the right to reside in Romania if one of the spouses is a Romanian citizen.[146] In spite of the decisions of the CJEU and the Constitutional Court, the judge dealing with the case dismissed it on procedural grounds, so that ACCEPT and the individuals concerned decided

underlying-european-divides-over-lgbt-rights/> and Laura Gyeney, 'Sensitive Issues before the European Court of Justice—The Right of Residence of Third Country Spouses Who Became Victims of Domestic Violence, as Well as Same-Sex Spouses in the Scope of Application of the Free Movement Directive (Legal Analysis of the NA and Coman Cases)' [2017] Hungarian Yearbook of International Law and European Law 211. For a more 'conservative' viewpoint on the judgment see Roxana Stanciu, 'A disturbing decision by the EU's Court of Justice redefines the term "spouses"' (European Dignity Watch, 6 June 2018) <http://www.europeandignitywatch.org/disturbing-decision-by-the-eu-court-of-justice-redefines-the-term-spouses/>.

144 Directive 2004/38/EC of the European Parliament and of the Council of 29 April 2004 on the right of citizens of the Union and their family members to move and reside freely within the territory of the Member States.

145 *Relu Adrian Coman and Others v Inspectoratul General pentru Imigrări and Ministerul Afacerilor Interne* (n 143) paras 34–36. For a case still pending before the CJEU, and which builds on *Coman*, in which ACCEPT works together with Bulgarian NGOs, see *V.M.A. v Stolichna Obsthina, Rayon 'Pancharevo' (Sofia municipality, 'Pancharevo' district)* referred to the CJEU on 2 October 2020, opinion of the AG presented on 15 April 2021.

146 Beury (n 143).

to take the case to the ECtHR.[147] What is more, the Romanian authorities continue to deny residence permits to spouses of same-sex couples married abroad. While ACCEPT is thus still fighting for the proper execution of the judgment in Romania, it has had repercussions in other countries. Its findings were, for instance, integrated in a court case before the Administrative Court in Sofia[148] and had an immediate impact in those countries which currently do not provide for legal recognition of same-sex partnerships.[149] This shows the impact created by ACCEPT's strategic litigation case, even if the individual case has still not been satisfactorily resolved. In the view of the ACCEPT representative, the case, in the course of which the association made significant use of mass media, has however contributed to reframe the public debate about the notion of family and the narrative around this term in the sense that an increasing number of Romanians have started to consider the possibility of recognizing the family rights of same-sex couples. He thus noted a slight change of perception and understanding of the question of who can be family in the twenty-first century.[150]

Interesting in this context too is the fact, that already at the level of the Constitutional Court, a number of European and international organizations, amongst them International Lesbian, Gay, Bisexual, Trans and Intersex Association (ILGA)-Europe, intervened by the submission of *amicus curiae* briefs in support of one of the parties. Those interventions pushed the Constitutional Court to refer questions to the CJEU and for some '[i]t is plausible to believe that they indeed weighed in the decision of the Romanian judges to make such referral for the very first time since the country joined the EU'.[151] The Romanian NCCD, together with the government of the Netherlands and the European Commission, intervened before the CJEU, to support the arguments of the applicants 'with observations pointing at the evolution of legal recognition and protection of same-sex couples in the EU'.[152]

ACCEPT has also supported victims of discrimination in cases that reached the ECtHR. The case reported below again does not come within the scope of

[147] ECtHR, App No 2663/21, *Relu-Adrian Coman et al. v Romania*, lodged on 23 December 2020, communicated on 9 February 2021.

[148] See Administrative Court of Sofia, case no 4337, judgment of 26 June 2018. While the Supreme Judicial Council refused to extend support for the judge deciding in line with the *Coman* judgment (she was accused by the media of being part of a 'gay lobby group' (see https://www.mediapool.bg/bulgarian-surge-into-the-eurozone-begins-with-the-banking-union-peevski-amends-the-media-bill-news281495.html)), the Bulgarian Supreme Court upheld the decision on 24 July 2019.

[149] After learning that several Member States are refusing to implement the CJEU's judgment in *Coman*, the ALDE group of the European Parliament has sent a written question to the Commission asking '1. What steps can citizens take if the authorities of a Member State refuse to implement the ruling?' and '2. Will the Commission launch infringement procedures if Member States do not respect case law of the ECJ on free movement of citizens within the EU in the application of national law on civil status?' See https://sophieintveld.eu/written-question-to-the-commission-refusal-by-member-states-to-implement-coman-case/.

[150] Interview, Board member of ACCEPT, 6 August 2018.

[151] Beury (n 143).

[152] ibid.

Directive 2000/78/EC but helps to illustrate the role that can be played by NGOs in litigating cases. In the case of *M.C. and A.C. v. Romania*[153] the two applicants had participated in the Bucharest gay pride march in June 2006. On their way home they were attacked by a group of seven individuals in the metro where they were punched and kicked to their heads and faces so that they sustained injuries, including a minor cranio cerebral trauma, in addition to psychological trauma. The attackers shouted at them: 'You poofs go to the Netherlands!' The two victims immediately filed a criminal complaint, stating that the attack was based on their sexual orientation. Shortly afterwards, they presented the evidence at their disposal, including pictures taken by a photographer who witnessed the assault. The photographer and one of the victims also identified some of the attackers. In 2007, the case was allocated to the Metro Police Station who carried out some investigations. However, in 2011 the police stated that it did not intend to bring a criminal prosecution, a decision endorsed by the prosecuting authorities in 2012. The reasons given related to the impossibility of identifying the culprits and the alleged crimes having become statute-barred in the meantime. For this latter reason, the courts also dismissed the applicants' complaint about the decision not to bring a criminal prosecution.

After the case had thus exhausted the domestic remedies after six years, the two victims approached the ECtHR, complaining that the investigations into their case had been inadequate. The ECtHR employed very clear words in its judgment. In the view of the Court, the authorities

> did not take reasonable steps with the aim of examining the role played by possible homophobic motives behind the attack. The necessity of conducting a meaningful inquiry into the possibility of discrimination motivating the attack was indispensable given the hostility against the LGBTI community in the respondent State ... and in the light of the applicants' submissions that hate speech, that was clearly homophobic, had been uttered by the assailants during the incident.... The Court considers that without such a rigorous approach from the law-enforcement authorities, prejudice-motivated crimes would inevitably be treated on an equal footing with cases involving no such overtones, and the resultant indifference would be tantamount to official acquiescence to, or even connivance with, hate crimes ... Moreover, without a meaningful investigation, it would be difficult for the respondent State to implement measures aimed at improving the policing of similar peaceful demonstrations in the future, thus undermining public confidence in the State's anti-discrimination policy.

[153] ECtHR, *M.C. and A.C. v. Romania*, App No 12060/12, judgment of 12 April 2016.

Thus, the Court concluded 'that the investigations into the allegations of ill-treatment were ineffective as they lasted too long, were marred by serious shortcomings, and failed to take into account possible discriminatory motives.'[154]

For a representative of ACCEPT, this judgment shows that Romanian authorities had no system in place for protecting victims of hate crimes. In the aftermath of this judgment, ACCEPT started collaborating with the prosecutor's office and the Ministry of Justice to identify a clear system for how the police should work in such cases.[155] It resulted in a train the trainers project within the police force, prosecution service, and for judges, funded by an EEA and Norway Grant and the creation of the role of hate crime officers in each police district. It was further planned to develop a common methodology for the investigation by the police and prosecution services of hate crime. As it was not possible to agree on a joint methodology, separate sets of norms on how to deal with hate crime have been developed by police and prosecution services. Another aim of ACCEPT is the collection of disaggregated data on hate crime but it has proved to be difficult to achieve results in this regard. An interesting aspect of ACCEPT's strategic follow-up in this case is that the organization continuously provided the Department for the Execution Judgments of the ECtHR with information about how the Romanian authorities followed up the judgment, which created a greater pressure on them to act.[156]

In general, the fact that ACCEPT managed to win a number of cases, some of which reached the highest European courts, has given hope to those affected by discrimination, especially in the LGBT context, that achieving justice is possible. This is already reflected in the number of requests for information received by ACCEPT which has greatly increased in recent years. Although this is a positive trend, the association is not in a position to handle all requests because of its limited financial and human resources. Due to successful fundraising, ACCEPT has only recently been able to employ one full-time legal consultant and is now doing project and awareness-raising activities as well as its consultation and litigation activities. Under such circumstances, they have to select carefully which cases they can support. They receive requests daily for primary legal aid, and manage to support around ten to fifteen cases, less than half of which they consider to be strategic litigation cases. The lawyers they work with work either pro bono (as do the three psychologists with whom ACCEPT is cooperating in order to be able to provide its

[154] ibid paras 124–25. See the concurring opinion of judge Wojeyczek: 'The judgment links the need to conduct a meaningful inquiry into the possibility of discrimination motiving the attack with the hostility prevailing against the LGBTI community in the respondent State (see paragraph 124). I am not persuaded by this argument. It may give the impression that the Court's approach in discrimination cases can vary from State to State. Whatever the general situation in a specific country, if Article 3 is applicable then the national authorities have a duty to establish all of the circumstances which are relevant for criminal liability, including the motives of the perpetrators.'

[155] Interview, Board member of ACCEPT, 6 August 2018.

[156] Interview, human rights lawyer I, Romania, EELN legal expert, 2 April 2021. See also the information on the HUDOC-EXEC database on the case, at http://hudoc.exec.coe.int/ENG?i=004-13171.

clients with an integrated package of support) or ask only for a much reduced fee, despite the fact that a case often takes years before a final decision is reached. In addition, there is only a small number of lawyers (especially outside Bucharest and Cluj) with experience in the equal treatment legislation or human rights law more generally as this kind of training is often not part of the curriculum at the faculties of law. This has been seen as just one element that requires a strategic approach, which could be introduced by a national non-discrimination strategy. While such a strategy has been discussed for years, it has still not been adopted. To be able to shape the public discourse it is also necessary to invest financial resources into the communication of results to the broader public. This implies the development of a communication strategy, liaising with the media, and so on.[157]

The membership of ILGA-Europe has been considered helpful in that the umbrella organization provides support in strategic litigation cases by monitoring and documenting the situation all over Europe, by submitting *amicus curiae* briefs in national and international court proceedings, and financially supporting training for different stakeholders at national level, including judges, lawyers, prosecutors, and the police. Overall, the support by European level institutions, especially the European Commission and the European Parliament, was considered by the ACCEPT representative to be crucial in times where civil society organizations are coming under threat in various parts of Europe and the value base of the EU is being questioned more than ever before. The initiative taken by the Parliament and the Commission in 2018 to explore the feasibility and possible creation of an 'EU fund for financial support for litigating cases relating to violations of democracy, rule of law and fundamental rights' has thus been appreciated as being timely and necessary, although it has been described as a timid beginning.[158] ACCEPT participated in the call for proposals launched by the Commission in 2019 and was successful with its idea to set up a strategic litigation hub with Hungarian, Lithuanian, and Bulgarian NGOs, and ILGA.[159] While this is a welcome support for its training and capacity-building activities, it is not considered to be a real support for its own strategic litigation activities. To be helpful in this regard, funding would need to be available for the financing of legal and psychological support staff, for the work-intensive follow-up and communication activities and the awareness raising connected with strategic litigation cases.[160]

To conclude, one can summarize that NGOs that took up the opportunities provided by the implementation of EU Directives did it mainly with the aim of

157 Interviews, Board member of ACCEPT, 6 August 2018; human rights lawyer I, Romania, EELN legal expert, e-mail of 6 November 2018.

158 Interview, Board member of ACCEPT, 6 August 2018.

159 For the call and the three projects that won, see Capacity building for litigating cases relating to democracy, rule of law and fundamental rights violations, JUST-PPPA-LITI-AG-2018, at https://ec.europa.eu/info/funding-tenders/opportunities/portal/screen/opportunities/topic-details/just-pppa-liti-ag-2018. ACCEPT will start implementing its project in 2021.

160 Interview, human rights lawyer I, Romania, EELN legal expert, 2 April 2021.

highlighting problematic aspects of legislation and triggering legislative improvements. They also did it to improve the accountability of authorities responsible for implementation and to shape public debate. The example of ACCEPT has shown that NGOs have been quite successful in achieving these goals. Through taking cases as far as the CJEU and the ECtHR, they have managed to clarify the interpretation of non-discrimination legislation and improve legislation. The success of their actions has also given hope to those who have suffered from discrimination that achieving justice is possible. They have also shaped how certain issues are discussed and perceived in the public.

Notwithstanding this individual and societal impact of NGO litigation, it remains the case that state authorities have not contributed to this success. In 2018 legislation was tabled that would have imposed additional financial reporting obligations. The draft was considered to have a further potentially intimidating effect on NGOs and various European institutions called for its reconsideration.[161] This pressure from outside, prompted amongst others by NGO protests, led eventually to an adaptation of the law.[162] Nonetheless, NGOs suffer from severe financial difficulties, non-discrimination legislation is given too little attention in law faculties and in the training of lawyers, and there is currently no Anti-Discrimination Strategy in place that could address these shortcomings. There is only a handful of organizations that provide support to victims of discrimination, operating mainly from the capital (although they are trying to reach out to more peripheral areas as well) and not covering all the fields and discrimination grounds.

This case study was also very instructive in highlighting the limitations of an *actio popularis*. One of them is a national context where there exist no procedural rules that would allow the judge to ensure that general proactive measures are implemented. Furthermore, rules regarding the representation of the group in the interest of whom an NGO acts are often missing. This is related to the challenge in *actio popularis* cases that the NGO needs to work closely with the group in question to build trust and, together with other relevant stakeholders, work on the follow-up to decisions. This requires a huge investment not only in terms of building the case

[161] See, for instance, the European Parliament, 'Resolution of 13 November 2018 on the rule of law in Romania' 2018/2844(RSP), which refers to a resolution of the Parliamentary Assembly of the Council of Europe, a recommendation of the Venice Commission of the Council of Europe and of the Office for Democratic Institutions and Human Rights of the Organisation for Security and Cooperation in Europe (OSCE/ODIHR). The European Parliament resolution '[s]trongly recommends reconsideration of the legislation on the financing, organisation and functioning of NGOs with regard to its potential intimidating effect on civil society and its entry into conflict with the principle of freedom of association and the right to privacy; believes it should be brought fully into line with the EU framework'. See also Civicus—Monitor Tracking Civic Space, 'Parliament to Vote on Alarming NGO Law' (26 July 2018) <https://monitor.civicus.org/newsfeed/2018/07/26/Parliament-to-Vote-on-alarming-NGO-Law/>; and Romanita Iordache, 'The Parliament adopted money laundering provisions which paralyze NGOs, in particular those supporting vulnerable groups' (EELN News Report, 31 October 2018).

[162] European Commission, '2020 Rule of Law Report: Country Chapter on the rule of law situation in Romania' (30 September 2020) SWD(2020) 322 final, 18.

and collecting the necessary documentation but also in following-up on it afterwards. Considering the time all this takes, it is therefore all the more important that the organization has financial and organizational stability.

4.3.2 Case Study: Hungary

According to Article 18 of the Hungarian Equal Treatment Act, 'the NGOs and interest representation organisations, as well as the [Equal Treatment] Authority[[163]] may act as a representative authorised by the party who suffered a violation of law in procedures instigated because of a violation of the principle of equal treatment'. Article 20 further stipulates that an *actio popularis* lawsuit may be instigated by 'NGOs and interest representation organisations, if the violation of the principle of equal treatment or a direct threat of the violation was based on such a characteristic that is an essential feature of the individual, and the violation of law or a direct threat of the violation affects a larger group of persons that cannot be determined accurately'.[164] Until 2020, NGOs could bring a complaint in the public interest also before the Equal Treatment Authority (ETA), the tribunal-type Equality Body. As of January 2021, the Commissioner for Fundamental Rights has taken over the ETA's responsibilities and thus, since then, NGOs can submit an application to the Commissioner for Fundamental Rights.

NGOs and interest representation organizations were initially interpreted by Article 3 of the Act as encompassing organizations 'whose objectives set out in the articles of association or statutes include the promotion of equal social opportunities of disadvantaged groups or the protection of human or civil rights'. In 2011, this provision has been amended and now requires an exact enumeration of the concerned protected ground(s). This has been considered relatively easy to achieve by NGO representatives themselves.[165] Also, this amendment should not prevent organizations from taking action against intersectional discrimination if at least one of the grounds in play is covered by their statute. However, in the absence of any case law, it remains to be seen whether a restrictive or permissive interpretation will be applied by the judges.[166]

Before organizations were able to act as representatives in judicial and administrative proceedings, victims of discrimination were represented in many cases by lawyers employed by interested organizations. The provisions of the Equal

[163] The Equal Treatment Authority was abolished by Act CXXVII of 2020 and, as of 1 January 2021, its responsibilities taken over by the Commissioner for Fundamental Rights. For a critique on this reform see András Kádár, 'Legislation adopted abolishing the Equal Treatment Authority and transferring its tasks to the Ombudsman' (EELN News Report, 10 February 2021).
[164] Act CXXV of 2003 on Equal Treatment and Promotion of Equal Opportunities as amended.
[165] Interview, human rights lawyer, Hungary, 24 July 2018.
[166] EELN, Country Report Hungary, 2020, 89–90.

Treatment Act made it possible for such organizations to represent the victim directly.[167] With the entry into force of the new Civil Procedure Code on 1 January 2018, the obligatory representation by a lawyer of all parties in most court procedures[168] has given rise to legal uncertainty as to whether this obligation applies also in discrimination cases. So far, judges have interpreted the new rules as implying an obligation of representation by a lawyer also in these cases, which theoretically limits the possibilities of interested organizations.[169] In practice, however, all NGOs that are actively engaging in proceedings have lawyers working for them so this restriction should not have a major impact.[170]

A further restriction that has emerged in recent years concerns changes in the Constitution regarding the competences of the Constitutional Court. Originally, anyone could claim that a provision is discriminatory without having to show any interest whatsoever. With the changes that entered into effect in 2012, only natural or legal persons directly concerned with the individual case can approach the Constitutional Court. In a case regarding Roma pupils who were educated in a segregated manner brought before the Constitutional Court by the Chance for Children Foundation (CFCF), the Court declared the complaint inadmissible on exactly this basis. It found that it was not the NGO itself that was concerned with the segregating practice, since the Curia's decision concerned the constitutional rights of the pupils and not of the NGO. The latter therefore had no legal standing before the Constitutional Court. However, two out of the fifteen judges submitted a dissenting opinion. In their view, a public interest claim is possible in the Hungarian legal system, given the difficulties faced by those belonging to the most marginalized groups to act against widespread discriminatory practices. Excluding NGOs that act in the interest of such groups from approaching the Constitutional Court would render the protection against the violation of constitutional rights void. Therefore, the dissenting judges were of the opinion that the term 'concerned' should be interpreted so as to allow such NGOs to file constitutional complaints.[171] Notwithstanding this flexible interpretation of the term 'concerned' by the two dissenters, the decision of the majority of judges deprived NGOs litigating in the public interest by the use of *actio popularis* of the right to approach the Constitutional Court. In the case in question, the Foundation took the case to the ECtHR, complaining about an infringement of its right to access to a court. The ECtHR, however, referring to its own jurisprudence in *Burden v the*

[167] Mónika Ambrus, *Enforcement Mechanisms of the Racial Equality Directive and Minority Protection* (Eleven International Publishing 2011) 216.

[168] László Pribula, 'The New Civil Procedure Code in Hungary' (2017) 62(1) Studia UBB Iurisprudentia 79, 87.

[169] Interview, Director, Háttér Society, 19 July 2018.

[170] Interview, human rights lawyer, Hungary, 24 July 2018.

[171] Hungary, Constitutional Court decision no IV/03311/2012, delivered on 17 June 2013. See also András Kádár, 'Constitutional Court denies legal standing of NGOs in action popularis cases' (EELN News Report, 14 January 2014).

United Kingdom,[172] declared the application inadmissible due to the Foundation's not being directly affected by the measures complained of.[173]

To summarize, the legal limitations on NGOs litigating in cases of discrimination are: 1) the requirement that the ground which forms the basis on which discrimination has taken place is explicitly mentioned in their statute; 2) the legal uncertainty introduced by the new civil procedure code around the question of whether the representation by a lawyer is now mandatory also in discrimination cases; and 3) of the fact that in *actio popularis* cases, associations have no legal standing in front of the Constitutional Court because they are not themselves directly affected by the discrimination complained of. Overall, however, the Hungarian legislation can be considered comparatively permissive when it comes to the provision of criteria for associations and organizations to be considered as having a legitimate interest in ensuring compliance with the provisions of the law and the legal means at the disposal of NGOs.

The courts have also been flexible when it comes to deciding whether NGOs can launch an *actio popularis*.[174] Under the law, an NGO can bring a public interest claim 'if the violation of the principle of equal treatment or a direct threat of the violation was based on such a characteristic that is an essential feature of the individual, and the violation of law or a direct threat of the violation affects a larger group of persons that cannot be determined accurately'.[175] Initially, in the cases regarding the segregation of Roma pupils in the education system, the defendants tried to convince the court that NGOs could not bring such a claim as the group of persons affected could be determined, namely, the pupils of the school in question. However, the courts did not agree, holding that while it might be possible to determine the pupils attending school at a particular moment in time, this was not possible for the whole period during which the alleged discrimination took place. Furthermore, even for a specific moment in time it would be hard to determine accurately the group of people affected by the violation, given that no official data exist as to who belongs to the group of Roma and who does not. Therefore, the court accepted the claim brought by an NGO in the interest of the group of Roma as the persons affected could not be determined accurately.[176]

In practice, there are a handful of NGOs who make or did make use of the litigation possibilities provided for by the Equal Treatment Act, some of them being the local branch of NGOs operating Europe-wide.[177] While some of them started their

[172] ECtHR, App No 13378/05, *Burden v UK*, judgment (Grand Chamber) of 29 April 2008.

[173] ECtHR, App No 786/14, *Esélyt a hátrányos heryzetü gyerekeknek Alapítvány v Hungary*, decision of 25 March 2014.

[174] Interview, human rights lawyer, Hungary, 24 July 2018.

[175] Equal Treatment Act, Art 20. As well as NGOs, such a claim can also be brought by the public prosecutor and the ETA, and since 2021, the Commissioner for Fundamental Rights.

[176] Interview, human rights lawyer, Hungary, 24 July 2018.

[177] These organizations are: the Hungarian Helsinki Committee, the Hungarian Civil Liberties Union, the European Roma Rights Centre, the Chance for Children Foundation (dissolved), NEKI

legal programme before the Equality Directives were transposed into national legislation,[178] other organizations were set up mainly with the aim of making use of these new possibilities for NGOs to engage in judicial proceedings. This is the case, for example, with the Chance for Children Foundation, operating between 2004 and 2016, which aimed at relying on the new legislation in order to fight segregation of Roma pupils through legal means.[179] Given that the grounds on which they litigate have to be mentioned in their statutes, it is primarily sectoral organizations who engage in proceedings. For instance, the Háttér Society, whose legal aid service has been operating since 2000, covers discrimination related to sexual orientation. Discrimination related to disability is also well covered by organizations that are mainly funded by the state, which is not the case for organizations dealing with other discrimination grounds. Discrimination on the ground of ethnic origin, where most cases regard the Roma population, are (were) litigated by the CFCF and the Hungarian Helsinki Committee. However, the former exclusively dealt with cases related to school segregation while the latter has a focus on discrimination by the police and other public bodies. Both the CFCF and NEKI, an organization that used to cover the ground of ethnic belonging more broadly, ceased to exist, mainly because of a lack of funding.[180]

The long-term funding as well as organizational stability have been mentioned by interlocutors as the main factors influencing an organization in deciding whether to engage in judicial proceedings or not.[181] Both the representation of individual victims as well as *actio popularis* cases sometimes last for up to ten years, while NGOs very often run on external funding for phases of a maximum of two years. Also, donors are more inclined to finance activities other than litigation. In the case of the Chance for Children Foundation, for instance, the decision of the Open Society Foundation to limit contributions to 30 per cent of an organization's budget made it impossible for the organization to survive. It tried to raise funds through calls from the European Commission but was unsuccessful.[182]

NGOs engaging in discrimination cases are thus, in the Hungarian case, more limited by financial constraints rather than by restrictive legislation on legal standing of organizations. Furthermore, many NGOs have come under threat if they are connected to one of George Soros' foundations.[183] In such circumstances,

(dissolved), the Háttér Society, as well as some organizations supporting persons with disability, such as the National Federation of Disabled Persons' Associations, and some women's organizations.

178 Interview, Director, Háttér Society, 19 July 2018.

179 Interview, human rights lawyer, Hungary, 24 July 2018.

180 Interviews, Director, Háttér Society, 19 July 2018; human rights lawyer, Hungary, 24 July 2018. For the experience of NEKI (Legal Defence Bureau for National and Ethnic Minorities) see Bea Bodrogi, 'Legal Standing—The Practical Experience of a Hungarian Organisation' [2007] European Anti-Discrimination Law Review 23.

181 Interviews, Director, Háttér Society, 19 July 2018; human rights lawyer, Hungary, 24 July 2018.

182 Interview, human rights lawyer, Hungary, 24 July 2018.

183 The Transparency Act (Act No LXXVI of 2017) has become the subject of an infringement proceeding, with the CJEU deciding in June 2020 that with this law Hungary had introduced

the structural question of what the legal framework on organizational standing in proceedings looks like is less relevant in establishing whether the 'more effective level of protection', as envisaged by the Directives, can be granted in practice. The focus of the evaluation should be on the general environment (regulatory, financial, other) created by the state for organizations to be placed in a position that they can make use of legal possibilities.

Another problem raised by some interlocutors relates to the fact that most of their cases regard discrimination that has taken place in the capital, where they have their headquarters, as they do not have offices in other parts of the country.[184] As well as this limitation regarding their own geographical outreach, there appears to be another missing link when it comes to raising the awareness of victims of discrimination of the possibility of approaching NGOs for support. As was reported by the representative of the Háttér Society in Hungary, the organization was never approached by a victim of discrimination who was referred to them by the legal aid offices or any other public body. These offices and institutions appear to work in a complete vacuum without ever reaching out to NGOs which would be beneficial for victims of discrimination particularly in those cases where they do not fall within the legal aid scheme.[185]

NGOs do profit from cooperating at European level with umbrella organizations. The Háttér Society is, for instance, closely involved in the activities offered and organized by ILGA-Europe. ILGA's litigation officer works with member organizations to develop and implement litigation strategies, conducts comparative and international law research that can be used by member organizations to support their cases, coordinates with organizations that are engaged in litigation for LGBTI rights at European level, and provides capacity development to organizations that engage in or are interested in engaging in strategic litigation at national and European level.[186] ILGA-Europe also maintains an internal database on previously decided cases regarding discrimination on the basis of sexual orientation decided by the ECtHR or the CJEU, as well as on pending cases at national level that might end up before the European courts. Peer-to-peer learning is not systematically encouraged by ILGA-Europe, but bilateral co-operation nevertheless develops naturally and occasionally as a consequence of

'discriminatory, unjustified and unnecessary restrictions on foreign donations to civil society organisations, in breach of its obligations under Article 63 TFEU and Articles 7, 8 and 12 of the Charter'. *Commission v Hungary* [2020] ECLI:EU:C:2020:476. The Commission started a new infringement proceeding in February 2021, noting in its letter of formal notice that Hungary had not complied with the earlier judgment by repealing the Transparency Law. If the case is referred again to the CJEU, it can impose financial sanctions. See https://ec.europa.eu/commission/presscorner/detail/en/inf_21_441.

184 Interview, Director, Háttér Society, 19 July 2018.
185 Interview, Director, Háttér Society, 19 July 2018.
186 See information on ILGA's strategic litigation work at https://www.ilga-europe.org/what-we-do/our-strategic-litigation-work.

the many possibilities provided by the organization for exchange of information and experience.[187]

When it comes to the factors that influence an NGO's decision on whether to engage in a particular case or not, organizations tend to choose those cases that might be harder to win and from which one can expect either a clarification of the law or an impact that potentially goes beyond the individual case. In this context, the representative of the Háttér Society mentioned that cases related to discrimination in employment based on sexual orientation have quite a high chance of settlement and are legally less contested. As a consequence they would rather take up cases in other fields.[188] It is also interesting to note in this context that in Háttér's experience, discrimination based on sexual orientation in employment and occupation happens quite often but it is not the most common area in which discrimination occurs. This indicates of course that the levelling up at European level of the protection from discrimination on grounds other than racial or ethnic origin outside the area of employment would be required in order to grant this protection throughout Europe, and not only in those countries that have deliberately decided to enlarge the scope of application of their anti-discrimination laws.

When it comes to deciding whether to approach the ETA or the courts, Háttér's typical strategy was first, to approach the Equality Body, because of the lower financial risk. Even if the case is lost, the victim does not have to pay the defendant's legal costs. As the ETA can only award fines but no compensation, the case can be brought before the court as a second step in order to claim damages.[189] It remains to be seen how the transfer of responsibilities from the ETA to the Commissioner of Fundamental Rights affects this approach. The strategy of the Chance for Children Foundation, which had a number of *actio popularis* cases regarding school segregation, was to approach the courts if the aim was to achieve a systemic change, since the practice of the ETA was simply to declare whether discrimination has taken place or not, and in the affirmative case to issue a fine that was easily absorbable by the defendant. Although the ETA could have ordered that the situation constituting discrimination be eliminated and prohibited the further continuation of the discrimination,[190] it was either reluctant to clearly spell out the remedies to change the situation or did not follow up on the enforcement of its decision.[191]

In terms of the impact of litigation activities, there are two levels that need to be considered. The first is that of the individual victim and the question whether

[187] Interview, Director, Háttér Society, 19 July 2018.
[188] Interview, Director, Háttér Society, 19 July 2018.
[189] However, in many instances the victims are satisfied with the ETA finding that discrimination has occurred and abstain from claiming for damages. Interview, Director, Háttér Society, 19 July 2018.
[190] Equal Treatment Act, Art 16.
[191] Interview, human rights lawyer, Hungary, 24 July 2018. For a positive example in which enforcement of a decision of ETA was successfully requested by a civil society organization, see András Kádár, 'Successful procedure launched by civil society organisation to enforce equality body decision on providing accessibility' (EELN News Report, 19 July 2019).

the engagement by the interested organization has helped the victim to get redress. The second is the societal level and is related to the question of whether the organization's intervention in proceedings, individual or collective, has helped to raise the general awareness of right holders and duty bearers, the reporting behaviour of victims, and the societal perception of discrimination, and whether it has led to structural changes.

When it comes to the individual level, the Háttér representative reported that many of their clients are satisfied with the finding of discrimination by the ETA and do not seek compensation afterwards before the court.[192] Sanctions awarded however, either in the form of fines imposed by the ETA on the perpetrator or in the form of compensation granted by courts to the victim, are considered to be very low. In one case supported by Hátter, for instance, where a boy raised by a lesbian couple was not admitted to a school for that reason, the ETA imposed a fine of 50,000 HUF (approximately 160 EUR) on the school.[193] More recently, however, in another case supported by Hátter, the ETA imposed a fine of 1 million HUF (approximately 3,250 EUR) on a swimming pool operated by a subsidiary company of one of Budapest's districts for not renting out swimming lanes to a sports club after finding out that it was an LGBTQ club. This is the highest fine ever imposed for discrimination related to sexual orientation and also high when compared to fines imposed for discrimination on other grounds.[194] In terms of moral damages, the amount awarded is normally around approximately 1,000 EUR.

According to the information provided by a lawyer that worked for the Chance for Children Foundation, the capacities of the Foundation did not allow for professional psychological support to victims of discrimination. This would of course be very valuable, considering the stress that victims of discrimination are exposed to and the length of proceedings. The experience of NGOs representing individual victims also shows that it is hard to motivate victims to appeal a decision and take the case to the highest possible level.

The fact that it is not necessary for an individual victim to have suffered discrimination, and to agree to go through the proceedings, exposing him/herself to victimization, has been seen by all interlocutors as a strong advantage of *actio popularis* claims. In addition, such claims can address structural deficiencies that affect the whole community. Furthermore, public interest litigation, at least at first sight, does not require as much effort in terms of client care as individual litigation, where it is sometimes hard to keep a client involved in proceedings for many years.

[192] Inverview, Director, Háttér Society, 19 July 2018.

[193] András Kádár, 'Court confirms that refusal by school to admit pupils raised by a lesbian couple amounts to discrimination and awards damages to one of the parents' (EELN News Report, 10 January 2017). One mother was awarded 350,000 HUF (approx 1,100 EUR) for non-pecuniary damages.

[194] András Kádár, 'Discrimination against an LGBTQ sport club through refusing to rent out two lanes of a swimming pool to the club for a sports event' (EELN News Report, 2 February 2018). The company announced its intention to appeal the decision.

On the other hand, as has already been found in the previous case study and will be further developed below, *actio popularis* cases also need to be supported by information and communication measures targeting the community concerned. In the following a couple of *actio popularis* cases will be presented to analyse what kind of impact they have had in terms of awareness raising, changing policies, practices, and societal perception of discrimination, and the challenges connected with this type of action.

The Háttér Society has managed to win a couple of *actio popularis* cases that led to a change in practices. For instance, a football club offered reduced family tickets for its football games only to families of opposite-sex couples and their children. After a complaint to the ETA, the club changed its practice and now also offers reduced family tickets to same-sex couples. In another case, the information provision practice of a ministry regarding certain social benefits available also to same-sex couples targeted only opposite-sex couples. Again, after a complaint filed by the Háttér Society with the ETA, this information policy changed.

Another instance in which the Háttér Society filed a public interest claim regards the Budapest Gay Pride Marches in 2011 and 2012, which were both been banned by the police, allegedly because the marches would have obstructed the traffic. In both cases the decision by the police was overturned by the court which found the argument unfounded. That the police decision might have had other motives could also be shown by the fact that in the year in between the two marches, a number of other demonstrations on the same route with a significantly larger number of participants were allowed, amongst them a pro-government march with over 100,000 participants, compared to the expected 1,000 people at the pride marches.

Háttér thus decided to launch an *actio popoularis* in the interest of the LGBTQ community and in addition supported an individual complainant in a civil lawsuit, claiming also for moral damages. The first instance court decided in January 2014 that there had been direct discrimination and harassment, since the decision by the Budapest police to ban the Pride March 'contributed to creating and strengthening a degrading, hostile and threatening environment based on sexual orientation [and] it amplified the hostility towards the gay community already present in the society... The court also pointed out that authorities have increased responsibility, as their decisions set examples to the public as to the manner in which legal norms are to be complied with.'[195] While it ordered the police to issue a letter of apology and refrain from future violations it rejected the individual claimant's claim for moral damages. On appeal, the Metropolitan Court of Appeal of Budapest confirmed on 18 September 2014 the decision regarding the finding of discrimination and harassment. Interestingly, however, it rejected not only the individual's claim in relation to the moral damages but it even rejected the individual's legal standing

[195] András Kádár, 'Police ban of LGBTQ demonstration amounts to discrimination and harassment' (EELN News Report, 14 October 2014).

in the case, because his role was very remote to the core of the act. Therefore, in this case, the *actio popularis* was the only way to bring the case.[196]

Háttér litigation also has a societal impact in that the cases raise general awareness of the very existence of discrimination on the ground of sexual orientation. As reported by the Háttér representative, without such cases, the general perception among the population would be that there is no discrimination on this ground and that Hungarian society is very open towards people's sexual orientation. Bringing cases of discrimination on this ground to the media contributes to raising awareness of the persistence of this problem.[197]

The CFCF brought a number of *actio popularis* cases dealing with the school segregation of Roma pupils. Two examples[198] shall be reported about here in detail as they both show the merits but also the limits of *actio popularis.* The first regards the *Nyíregyháza* case, the second is related to the segregation in a school in the municipality of Kaposvár.

The *Nyíregyháza* case started back in 2007, when the CFCF started a court action against the municipality for running a segregated school in a Roma settlement. After extensive negotiations leading to the closure of the school, the CFCF discontinued the case. Children from the school were integrated into mainstream primary schools in the city centre and transportation to these schools was provided free of charge. In 2011, the Greek Catholic Church expressed interest in opening a school in the Roma settlement which was accepted by the municipal authorities so that the school was reopened in September of the same year. Some weeks later the free bus service to the schools in the centre was discontinued and replaced by a 30 per cent discount on tickets. The CFCF initiated again an *actio popularis* against the Church and the municipality claiming that the reopening of the school led to segregation of Roma children. While the municipality did not produce any justification in defence of the measure, the Church declared that it had no official knowledge about the ethnicity of the pupils (although it entered into the agreement with the municipality with a view to providing pastoral care to Roma pupils and their families[199]); that it offered segregated education based on the religion of pupils and not based on their ethnic origin; that the families practised their freedom to choose

[196] Interview, Director, Háttér Society, 19 July 2018.

[197] ibid.

[198] A third case supported by the CFCF, that has interesting repercussions on the debate about effective sanctions, is the *Gyöngyöspata* case, which started in 2011 and ended with a Supreme Court decision in May 2020. The Supreme Court upheld the decisions of the first and second instance courts granting moral damages to over sixty Roma victims of educational segregation. This led to a legislative change, precluding now the award of pecuniary compensation, and mandating instead the award of in-kind compensation for fundamental rights violations in education. See András Kádár, 'Draft Bill on mandatory in-kind compensation for segregation in education submitted' (EELN News Report, 5 August 2020).

[199] ECtHR, App No 53461/15, *Kósa v Hungary*, decision of 21 November 2017, para 12.

religious education for their children; and that children suffered no disadvantage from attending the school in the settlement.[200]

The first instance Court of Nyíregyháza and the Court of second instance in Debrecen took the view that the reopening of the school amounted to racial segregation, which could not be justified by the claim of providing religious education. Besides, the courts pointed out that the parents did not choose the school because of the religious education but because of the proximity to their places of residence and the fact that their children were harassed by teachers and pupils in the mainstream schools.

The Supreme Court, in its decision of 22 April 2015, however, repealed these judgments. While it acknowledged that the CFCF provided prima facie evidence of discrimination through segregation and therefore shifted the burden of proof to the defendant, it came to the conclusion that the Church could provide a justification for the segregation by claiming that it provides religious education and that parents, in exercise of their freedom of religion, had chosen the school by giving their informed consent. The CFCF maintained that most parents had not chosen the school for its religious education but because of its location and the exposure of their children to harassment in mainstream schools. It also made reference to the ECtHR judgment in *DH v Czech Republic* in which it established that '[i]n view of the fundamental importance of the prohibition of racial discrimination ..., the Grand Chamber considers that, even assuming the conditions [informed consent, without constraint] were satisfied, no waiver of the right not to be subjected to racial discrimination can be accepted, as it would be counter to an important public interest'.[201] The Supreme Court, however, negated any relevance of this jurisprudence for the case in question. Notwithstanding these deficiencies of the judgment, it was final as no further appeal or revision was possible in front of the Constitutional Court.[202] However, as a consequence of the infringement proceedings commenced by the European Commission in 2016,[203] Article 28 of the Equal Treatment Act has been amended to prohibit religious education from resulting in unlawful segregation based on race, colour, or ethnicity.[204]

This case, although decided in the end against the desegregation of Roma schools, is interesting from a procedural point of view. The CFCF was well aware of the fact that the ECHR does not provide for the institution of *actio popularis* and thus, that it could not, after the exhaustion of the domestic remedies, approach the

[200] See detailed information about the case on the CFCF website at: http://www.cfcf.hu/en/ny%C3%ADregyh%C3%A1za-resegregation-case.

[201] ECtHR, App No 57325/00, *D.H. v Czech Republic*, judgment (Grand Chamber) of 13 November 2007, para 204.

[202] The CFCF expressed its concern over this judgment also because it feared that further Roma-only schools could 'be handed over to churches under the auspices of Roma pastoral mission'. http://www.cfcf.hu/en/ny%C3%ADregyh%C3%A1za-resegregation-case.

[203] Infringement no 2015/2206 (letter of formal notice of 26 May 2016).

[204] See on this, ECtHR, *Kósa*, para 26.

ECtHR itself. It therefore identified an individual victim of the case, a girl who had attended the segregated school in the Roma settlement, and supported this former pupil in approaching the ECtHR. The strategy was to base the girl's claim to the Court without approaching national courts first on the fact that 'whenever a public interest claim was dismissed by a final judgment, an individual claim based on the same facts could not be successful'.[205] Bringing an individual action domestically would thus be 'futile and unreasonable'.[206] Third-party interventions by the Open Society Justice Initiative as well as the European Roma Rights Centre (ERRC), supported this approach and argued that 'in order not to render the Convention rights theoretical and illusory, the Court should develop its jurisprudence and accept that a victim of discrimination whose situation had been examined and whose interests had been represented in a domestic collective redress procedure had exhausted domestic remedies for the purposes of Article 35 § 1 of the Convention'.[207] The ERRC also pointed in this context, and with the same aim, to the 'specific difficulties which victims of discrimination face in bringing their cases before domestic courts'.[208]

The Court, however, declared the application inadmissible. It did acknowledge that the rule on the exhaustion of domestic remedies needs to be applied 'with some degree of flexibility and without excessive formalism', that it is 'neither absolute nor capable of being applied automatically'. In cases where national law allows civil society organizations to bring proceedings for a larger group of people 'the Court considers that, in principle, it would be conceivable to accept the public interest litigation as a form of exhausting domestic remedies' and that it 'would be especially justified in relation to alleged discrimination against a vulnerable group requiring special protection, such as Roma children'.[209]

The Court, however, found that although the *actio popularis* decided by the Hungarian Supreme Court and the individual case before it were closely related, the former 'did not correspond exactly to the applicant's individual situation'. However, the initial considerations regarding the flexibility required in the interpretation of the rule on the exhaustion of domestic remedies and that potential acceptance of public interest litigation for that purpose in cases regarding discrimination against particularly vulnerable groups give reason to believe that the jurisprudence of the ECtHR might eventually develop in this direction.

While the just described case showed the limitation of *actio popularis* in procedural terms, the next case, related to a segregated school in Kaposvár highlights some substantive aspects of this kind of claim that should not be neglected. The first point relates to the need to keep the dialogue open with the group affected by

205 ibid para 44.
206 ibid.
207 ECtHR, *Kósa*, third party intervention by the Open Society Justice Initiative, para 47.
208 ECtHR, *Kósa*, third party intervention by the European Roma Rights Centre, para 50.
209 ECtHR, *Kósa*, paras 54–57.

the public interest claim. The second concerns the need for a well-designed follow-up to court decisions on desegregation accompanied by appropriate monitoring.

When the CFCF decided in 2013 to bring an *actio popularis* against the ethnically segregated school in Kaposvár this happened against the background of a 2010 Supreme Court decision, which found segregation and a violation of equal treatment by the Municipal Council for not acting against it through, for instance, a re-determination of the local catchment areas of the schools.[210] As the municipality did not take any action to implement the court's decision, the CFCF initiated a lawsuit in 2013. It requested that the court establish the violation and order desegregation by closing the school. It further requested the submission of a preliminary question to the CJEU on the question of whether the sanctions provided by the Hungarian legal system for segregation meet the requirements of being effective, proportionate, and dissuasive.

The Kaposvár Regional Court,[211] as court of first instance, established the violation of the principle of equal treatment and found that the ministry was responsible for it because it did not instruct the centralized state organization responsible for schools to put an end to the segregation. However, the court refrained from submitting the request for a preliminary ruling to the CJEU on the question of whether the sanctions provided in such cases are in line with the requirements under the RED. The court found that nothing in the Hungarian legal framework precluded the possibility to 'provide detailed orders as to how segregation shall be terminated'. It found, however, that 'in the present case ... the desegregation process is such a complex one depending on many factors (such as political will) that it would not be possible to order its implementation with the clarity and unambiguity that is required from a judicial decision in order for it to be executable'.[212] This has been interpreted as reluctance on the part of courts to set out detailed desegregation orders, notwithstanding the fact that it has become obvious that abstract orders attempting to end segregation do not yield the required results. The effectiveness of the remedy available in segregation cases was thus questioned.[213]

The second instance court, the Pécs Appeals Court,[214] confirmed the finding of discrimination through segregation but ordered the desegregation by closing the school in an upgoing system. This meant that starting from the following school year, the school was banned from accepting new first graders so that the school could be phased out over a couple of years. The court also ordered the defendants to adopt a detailed desegregation plan on the placement of those first graders from the school's catchment area who could no longer be admitted. This plan had to be

210 Hungary, Supreme Court decision no Pfv.IV.21.568/2010/5.

211 Hungary, Kaposvár Regional Court, decision no 11.P.21.553/2013/70.

212 András Kádár, 'Ministry of education is also responsible for segregation, but implementation of desegregation plan is not ordered by the court' (EELN News Report, 8 January 2016).

213 ibid.

214 Hungary, Pécs Appeals Court, judgment no Pf.III.20.004/2016/4, 14 October 2016.

published on the defendants' website. While they complied with the order by not admitting new first graders and adopting and publishing the desegregation plan, they also requested a review by the Supreme Court, inter alia on the grounds of the judgment of the Appeals Court not being enforceable and violating the rights of the parents to choose the school for their children.[215]

The Supreme Court, in its judgment of 4 October 2017,[216] upheld the decision and sanctions imposed by the Appeals Court. Importantly, it found that the parents' right to choice of school can be limited and that the earliest possible termination of segregation takes precedence over this right. Given the defendants had already complied with the court order by not admitting new first graders, adopting and publishing the desegregation plan, inter alia by redrawing the school district boundaries, it was further evident that the allegation of the order not being enforceable was erroneous.[217]

This judgment can reasonably be considered as a landmark decision as the highest court upheld the decision of an appeal court that imposed a sanction that can be considered effective: the closing down of a school in which segregation took place and the integration of the children concerned in the mainstream education system. In this sense, the public interest claim launched by the CFCF can be considered successful in contributing to the termination of the structural discrimination suffered by Roma pupils in the field of education.

However, as the lawyer who was litigating the case for the CFCF reported, the problem had now shifted to the level of monitoring the implementation which was hampered by the fact that in the meantime the CFCF, mainly because of a lack of funding, closed down and thus cannot follow up on implementation. As a result, it seems that the defendants are trying to sabotage the desegregation process. For instance, there was no preparation regarding this drastic change in the local educational system either in the schools to which the pupils from the closed school were transferred, in the Roma community, or among the children concerned. No transportation to the new schools was organized. In such circumstances, the whole process might be undermined as it may not be accepted by those who should benefit from it.[218]

The Hungarian expert in the EELN has reported an example in point: A school mostly attended by Roma pupils was closed at the end of the school year 2015–16. No preparations had been made for the smooth transfer of children to other schools, which put the children and their parents in a very difficult situation. The local council of the neighbouring town intervened at the Ministry of Education

[215] András Kádár, 'Curia upholds decision establishing segregation in education and ordering the closing down of segregated school' (EELN News Report, 8 November 2017).
[216] Hungary, Supreme Court judgment no Pfv.IV.20085/2017, 4 October 2017.
[217] Kádár, 'Curia upholds decision establishing segregation in education and ordering the closing down of segregated school' (n 215).
[218] Interview, human rights lawyer, Hungary, 24 July 2018.

against the transfer of the children to their school. This strong political resistance, motivated by anti-Roma sentiments, led to a situation in which only six out of thirty-seven children could be transferred to the school in that town, whilst the others had to be transferred to schools further away. This again caused problems to the parents of these children, who found themselves in a situation where they had children in different neighbouring towns.[219] In such circumstances, where desegregation is not preceded by careful planning and followed by monitoring, and where there is no involvement of, and communication with, all stakeholders concerned throughout the process, the measure thought to produce a long-term benefit for the Roma children might be rejected by parents and children alike. In other words and as Fredman noted,[220] where the participatory dimension of equality is neglected, the transformative dimension, aiming at accommodating diversity, will be hard—if not impossible—to achieve.

A study on the impact of litigation on Roma school segregation also looked into the responses by Roma representatives on the issue of desegregation. Many Roma parents, even if aware of the consequences of separate education of their children, nevertheless deliberately decide to place their children in Roma-only schools for various reasons. These range from financial considerations, related inter alia to transportation or payments to class funds, to concerns about the well-being of their children in mainstream schools, where Roma children are often excluded and bullied by fellow pupils and teachers alike. In such circumstances, parents prefer to place their children in schools that are attended nearly exclusively by Roma, as it can be easier for their children to socialize. Those schools are also, in many cases, closer to home which makes it easier for them to get to school. Desegregation that comes as a result of an *actio popularis* launched by a civil society organization without involving the affected community might thus lead to resentment and rejection of the very desegregation process.[221]

In this context, a recent judgment of the Metropolitan Court can be seen as a ray of hope. In the case, brought by the CFCF back in 2009, the Court decided in April 2018 that the Ministry of Education was in breach of its non-discrimination obligation for not taking action to counter segregation in twenty-eight elementary schools since the school year 2003–04. The court ordered the ministry to arrange for desegregation in the thirteen schools in which segregation still existed in an upgoing system similar to the one described above. This included the preparation, with the assistance of an expert in education equal opportunities, of a

[219] András Kádár, 'Roma pupils face difficulties and uncertainties after segregated school closes in Csobánka' (EELN News Report, 28 September 2016).

[220] Sandra Fredman, 'Emerging from the Shadows: Substantive Equality and Article 14 of the European Convention on Human Rights', Human Rights Law Review (2016), 16(2): 273. She also emphasizes that governments' claims to pursue a transformative strategy (for instance by accommodating special needs of Roma children by placing them in separate classes) often serve to hide a breach of the redistributive dimension (redressing disadvantage). ibid 288.

[221] Zimová (n 73) 17–18, 58–59.

desegregation plan aimed at assisting the integration of Roma pupils in their new schools. Most importantly, this has been coupled with an order to monitor the implementation of these plans over the next five years and the payment of a public interest fine amounting to about 159,000 EUR to finance such civil monitoring of desegregation programmes.[222]

Overall, one can conclude that notwithstanding the permissive legal framework and the positive impact at the individual as well as the societal level of NGOs' litigation activities, it is becoming increasingly difficult for them to support victims of discrimination in getting access to justice. Challenges are related to financial and regulatory constraints which create an overall hostile environment for NGOs and are not conducive for the financial and organizational stability required to embark on litigation that can take years. Furthermore, there are no attempts on the part of state authorities to reach out to NGOs (eg by referring victims to them). Some NGOs were successfully litigating discrimination cases in the past but do not exist any longer. As it stands, the national coverage of NGOs in a position to support victims of discrimination on all the grounds covered by EU Directives is not satisfactory.

The cases chosen to litigate were such that, from their resolution, one could expect a clarification of the law or an impact reaching beyond the individual case. As reported above, some of the *actio popularis* cases managed to bring about a change in practice and also to raise awareness about the very existence of the problem of discrimination. Other cases that reached the ECtHR contributed to the clarification of procedural conditions for approaching the Court. And finally, the *actio popularis* cases regarding segregation of Roma pupils led to a jurisprudence ordering desegregation but highlighted also the importance of follow-up and dialogue with the group concerned. With regard to international cooperation it has been highlighted that the support provided by the umbrella organization ILGA-Europe was very valuable.

4.3.3 Case Study: Germany

Germany has been selected as a case study because at first sight, it is not only the legal criteria that NGOs have to fulfil in order to be considered to have a legitimate interest to engage in proceedings that appear rather restrictive; in addition, the scope of activities that can be set by them is more limited than in the previously discussed cases. This section will analyse how these limitations play out in practice.

[222] András Kádár, 'Education ministry found to be in breach of its nondiscrimination obligations for failing to take effective action against segregation in 28 elementary schools' (EELN News Report, 6 July 2018).

As outlined above, in order for NGOs to be allowed to engage in proceedings they have to have at least seventy-five members or be an umbrella organization of at least seven-member associations. In addition, they cannot be profit-oriented and have to be established on a permanent, and not only ad hoc basis. Finally, their statute has to provide that they are established to defend the interests of persons or groups of persons that are disadvantaged because of their race or ethnic belonging, their gender, their religion or belief, a disability, their age, or their sexual orientation.[223] While the Commission initially had doubts about some of the restrictions, the German government insisted on its position and was apparently able to convince the Commission that it conformed with the Directives.[224] Organizations fulfilling the above criteria are not required to register. It thus rests with the court in the specific case to verify their status.[225]

In the opinion of German NGOs the limitations set by the equal treatment legislation are rather arbitrary. They do not see the alleged connection between the size of the organization in terms of members or member organizations and the competence or reliability of that organization to support victims of discrimination. On the other hand, they do not consider the criteria as overly difficult to fulfil. In fact, one NGO representative, who set up an NGO with the explicit aim of providing support to victims of discrimination in court proceedings said that it was relatively easy to find the required number of members.[226]

The number of NGOs who actually do support victims of discrimination in court proceedings is relatively low. It appears that there are only about three or four NGOs across Germany that in one way or another support claims before courts, in addition to around four to five anti-discrimination offices (at the level or *Länder* or local level, mainly organized by civil society organizations but publicly funded). Only one of these, the NGO *Büro zur Umsetzung von Gleichbehandlung e.V.* (hereafter: BUG) pursues an explicit strategic litigation strategy.[227] As the office is only able to support around three to four cases in parallel,[228] even if it supports complainants throughout Germany, it becomes clear that victims of discrimination have very limited access to NGOs that would support their case in court. However, the reason for this low number of organizations considering the size of Germany is not due to the restrictive legislation but to the fact that only a few organizations have a specialized expertise on the equal treatment legislation and its judicial enforcement. Efforts undertaken by the Equality Body to support a better coverage have so far not been successful.

[223] German Equal Treatment Act, Arts 1 and 23.
[224] For the arguments of the German government see Chapter 4.1.1.
[225] EELN, Country Report Germany, 2020, 75–76.
[226] Interview, Director of BUG, 26 July 2018.
[227] On strategic litigation more generally and its goals see European Roma Rights Centre, Interights and Migration Policy Group, 'Strategic litigation of race discrimination in Europe: from principles to practice' [2004] 35; and Equinet, 'Strategic Litigation. An Equinet Handbook' (2017) 9.
[228] The office receives between twenty-five and thirty requests for support per year.

A search on the webpage of the German Equality Body appears to contradict this finding, considering the big number of 'advice centres' retrievable.[229] The discrepancy between these figures can be explained by the fact that a large majority of NGOs appearing on this list simply provide more or less case specific information concerning the current legislation and the possible redress mechanisms, and, if requested, refers the persons concerned to specialized lawyers, while they are not supporting the victim of discrimination in the actual court procedure. In fact, according to an NGO representative, all over Germany and taking together civil society and public non-discrimination offices, there are some sixty to eighty full-time positions dealing with individuals who feel discriminated, which corresponds to one counsellor for between one and 1.5 million inhabitants. Compared to the number of people who, according to a 2015 study of the Federal Antidiscrimination Agency (FADA), have indicated they have suffered discrimination, this means only 0.05 per cent of them have the chance of seeing a counsellor.[230] The situation has not improved by 2021.[231]

When it comes to support in litigation, what appears to limit German NGOs much more than the legal criteria for engaging in proceedings is what they can actually do to support a complainant before the court. Arguably, this could also be a reason why there is such a limited number of NGOs offering legal support in courts. While an initial draft of the Equal Treatment Act included the possibility for NGOs to represent complainants in court proceedings in their own name (*Prozessstandschaft*), this option was deleted in the final version. This led to a situation in which, if a claim was brought under general labour law, the claimant could be represented by an organization (as, at that time, this was part of labour law courts procedure) but if it was brought under the Equal Treatment Act this possibility did not exist. However, rather than levelling up the standards, the standards

[229] Such a search produces the following results: ninety centres dealing with all discrimination grounds, ninety-six centres dealing with age discrimination, 130 centres dealing with disability and chronical disease, 184 centres dealing with gender discrimination, 151 centres dealing with discrimination related to race and ethnic origin, 134 centres dealing with discrimination related to religion and belief, and 158 centres dealing with discrimination on the ground of sexual orientation. Of these, seventy-six provide 'specialized advice in case of discrimination' and 213 provide general advice and serve as drop-in centres. 217 are non-governmental organizations, fifty-three are public institutions.

[230] Daniel Bartel, 'Keynote: Vom Flickenteppich zur Infrastruktur – Antidiskriminierungsberatung in Deutschland weiterdenken' in Antidiskriminierungsstelle des Bundes (ed), *Mit Rat zur Tat. Perspektiven der Antidiskriminierungsberatung in Deutschland. Dokumentation der Fachtagung im Umweltforum* (2017) 16.

[231] The lack of a country-wide network of consultation and support services has been confirmed by a report of the Working Group on anti-discrimination in the framework of the National Integration Plan, see Antidiskriminierungsstelle des Bundes, 'Bericht des Themenforums Antidiskriminierung im Rahmen des Nationalen Aktionsplans Integration/ Einhellige Forderung nach Ausbau von Beratungsangeboten gegen Diskriminierung' (9 March 2021) <https://www.antidiskriminierungsstelle.de/SharedDocs/Aktuelles/DE/2021/20210309_Integrationsgipfel_NAP_I.html>. See also Antidiskriminierungsstelle des Bundes, 'Gegen Rassismus, für Gleichbehandlung: Vorschläge der Antidiskriminierungsstelle des Bundes zur Stärkung des Schutzes vor Diskriminierung in Deutschland' (August 2020).

were levelled down, so that representation of complainants by organizations in general labour law cases was also abolished.[232] A representative action remains possible, however, in the field of disability law.

As an action in the public interest is not provided for by German equal treatment legislation[233] except in the field of disability law, the only way for NGOs to support complainants in court is thus to counsel them during the court proceedings (*Beistandschaft*).[234] This means that the complainant always needs to be personally present during the proceedings. If the counsel brings something before the court, this is taken as an action of the complainant, unless he/she immediately contradicts the action. A counsel has no access to records, is not allowed to question witnesses, or to hand in written submissions to the court.[235] Considering that the Directives require states to ensure that NGOs fulfilling the required criteria established by law can engage on behalf *or* in support of a victim of discrimination in administrative and judicial proceedings, the opportunity given to NGOs in the German context represents a minimal but faithful transposition of the Directives' requirement. In view of the general reluctance of victims of discrimination to go to court, both academics and NGOs have expressed concern over the effectiveness of the equal treatment legislation and have requested a greater role for NGOs to include also the possibility of representing victims before courts and of bringing public interest complaints.[236]

How have NGOs now made use of this, albeit limited, possibility to engage in administrative and judicial proceedings? The example described here is a case involving BUG which, as mentioned above, pursues a strategic litigation approach. This means a case is supported if it is of strategic relevance in the sense of having the potential to serve as a precedent, thus helping members of the discriminated group beyond the individual case and contributing to the establishment of a court practice and clarification of the law. The aim of strategic litigation is thus to use individual litigation to achieve broader social change. Equally important for the decision whether a case is supported or not is to establish whether the case is well

[232] Möschel, 'Litigating Anti-Discrimination Cases in Germany: What Role for Collective Actors?' (n 25) 69, referring to Wolfgang Däubler and Martin Bertzbach, *Allgemeines Gleichbehandlungsgesetz* (Nomos 2008) 728.

[233] Under Art 55 of the Bavarian State Constitution, everyone can bring an *actio popularis* (*Popularklage*) against state actions considered to be in violation of the Bavarian Constitution. A case regarding upper age limits for certain local representatives made also reference to age discrimination as prohibited by the Equal Treatment Act. The case was rejected by the Bavarian Constitutional Court and also by the Federal Constitutional Court. See Möschel, 'Litigating Anti-Discrimination Cases in Germany: What Role for Collective Actors?' (n 25) 71–72 and 74.

[234] German Equal Treatment Act, Art 23(2).

[235] Büro zur Umsetzung von Gleichbehandlung e.V. 'Dossier zum Thema Klageunterstützung durch Verbände' (2016) 2 and 4.

[236] Berghahn, Klapp, and Tischbirek (n 25) 159–60; Liebscher (n 25); Büro zur Umsetzung von Gleichbehandlung e.V. 'Dossier zum Thema Klageunterstützung durch Verbände' (n 235) 4; Büro zur Umsetzung von Gleichbehandlung e.V. 'Dossier zum Thema Vorschläge zur Stärkung des Antidiskriminierungsrechts' (2017) 29.

enough documented to increase the chances of a positive outcome, which is in the interest of the complainant of course, but also of the organization who wants to achieve a strategic goal.

If the result of this initial evaluation is positive, the NGO seeks close cooperation with a lawyer, even where representation by a lawyer is not required. As it is not always possible to find a lawyer with expertise in the field of equal treatment legislation, the knowledge of the NGO specialized in the field is a useful complement to build the case. An important element in the counselling process is the psychological component. Through regular contact with and moral support of the NGO representative, victims of discrimination often feel strengthened and empowered and are more likely to withstand the psychological stress connected with court proceedings. The NGO also cooperates closely with the relevant community organizations in order to get the necessary background information and expertise required for the case. If a case is won, the NGO informs the press and, in consultation with the complainant, decides on the level of details that are conveyed to the press. The focus of their public relations activity is, however, not so much on getting the news about the proceedings to the press but rather to legal professionals, such as lawyers, judges, and legal academics who potentially discuss the judgments in legal journals. They did note, however, that once they had won one or two cases in the same area, the number of similar cases rose.[237]

An example mentioned in this context was a complaint supported by BUG of a young man, a German citizen with Kurdish roots, who was refused entry to a nightclub. The bouncer quite openly declared that 'foreigners' were not allowed in the club. Although the owner of the club rejected the allegation that persons allowed to enter the club were selected based on their ethnic background, the Court of Hannover found discrimination on the basis of ethnic belonging and ordered the club to pay 1,000 EUR in damages to the young man. In addition, the club was ordered not to refuse entry to the club on unreasonable grounds, and if they did, there would be an additional fine of 250,000 EUR. The complainant called the support by BUG 'very helpful and empowering'. He further underlined that the networking and public relation activities of the NGO have made it clear that there exists a problem in Hannover that needs to be tackled.[238]

Interesting in this context are the networking activities of BUG and the intensive follow-up to the court cases undertaken by the NGO. For instance, in cooperation with the students' council of the University of Hannover and the Antidiscrimination Commissioner of the city, it organized an information event on the topic of discrimination in access to clubs and other recreational facilities.

[237] Interview, Director of BUG, 26 July 2018.

[238] Information available on the BUG webpage, including an assessment by the victim of discrimination, at http://www.bug-ev.org/aktivitaeten/klagen/zugang-zu-waren-und-dienstleistungen/klage-diskothek-hannover.

Together with local actors it analysed the necessary steps to counter this problem which led to training for business owners and security personnel and the distribution of public information leaflets to young people. It further recommended an amendment to the regulation of Lower Saxony's catering industry, which was eventually adopted in 2015. On the basis of this amendment, if a club is found to discriminate, the city authorities can fine the club up to 10,000 EUR. In case of repeated violations of the prohibition on discrimination, the club's operating licence can be withdrawn.

This shows that, notwithstanding the limited possibilities available to NGOs to engage in proceedings, their strategic approach can lead not only to satisfaction in the individual case but also to policy change. To achieve such policy change the sustained follow-up by an interested organization is required. Notwithstanding the positive conclusion in terms of impact on the individual and societal level that can be drawn by this example, the representative of BUG has also relativized the expectations towards policy change. The amendment of the catering industry's regulations appears to be rarely used because the responsible officials are unclear about how to establish discrimination and although checks might take place, a fine may not be imposed in the end.[239]

Another way in which BUG has already succeeded in generating an impact beyond the individual case relates to the fact that it had supported cases in court in cooperation with lawyers, which were then referred to the CJEU for preliminary ruling. One of these cases was brought directly by the founder and manager of BUG who felt discriminated against on the ground of religion, as she was refused by a denominational employer because of her being without confession.[240] Ms Vera Egenberger had applied with the *Evangelisches Werk für Diakonie und Entwicklung* (Protestant Work for Diaconate and Development) for a fixed term contract during which the employee was supposed to draft a parallel report on the application of the United Nations International Convention on the Elimination of All Forms of Racial Discrimination in Germany. According to the job advertisement, the applicants were supposed to be of protestant religion or belong to a church belonging to the Working Group of Christian Churches in Germany. Ms Egenberger was not invited for an interview which she considered to be related to the fact she was non-denominational. She thus sued the *Diakonie* for damages and the Federal Labour Court referred a preliminary question to the Court of Justice.

[239] Interview, Director of BUG, 26 July 2018.

[240] *Vera Egenberger v Evangelisches Werk für Diakonie und Entwicklung e.V.* [2018] ECLI:EU:C:2018:257. For a discussion of the judgment see Peter Stein, 'Diskriminierungsschutz und Kirchenautonomie' [2018] Zeitschrift für europäisches Sozial- und Arbeitsrecht 277; Eleni Frantziou, 'Mangold Recast? The ECJ's Flirtation with Drittwirkung in Egenberger' (European Law Blog, 24 April 2018) <http://europeanlawblog.eu/2018/04/24/mangold-recast-the-ecjs-flirtation-with-drittwirkung-in-egenberger/>.

The German court requested interpretation of Article 4(2) EED which contains a limitation to the principle not to be discriminated against in the field of employment and occupation on the ground of religion. According to this paragraph, 'a difference of treatment based on a person's religion or belief shall not constitute discrimination where, by reason of the nature of these [occupational] activities or of the context in which they are carried out, *a person's religion or belief constitute a genuine, legitimate and justified occupational requirement, having regard to the organisation's ethos*'.[241] This implies that there are activities that are close to the proclamation of the church's message and other that are remote from that and would thus not justify any discrimination on the basis of religion. According to the case law of the German Constitutional Court 'judicial review should be limited to a review of plausibility on the basis of the church's self-perception' in the sense of 'where the church's self-perception itself distinguishes between activities "close to" and activities "remote from" proclamation of the church's message, the courts should not review whether and to what extent that distinction is justified'.[242] The Federal Labour Court thus raised the question with the Court of Justice, whether this interpretation is in line with the Directive.

The CJEU came to the conclusion that where a church asserts 'that by reason of the nature of the activities concerned or the context in which the activities are to be carried out, religion constitutes a genuine, legitimate and justified occupational requirement, having regard to the ethos of the church or organisation, *it must be possible for such an assertion to be the subject*, if need be, *of effective judicial review* by which it can be ensured that the criteria set out in Article 4(2) of that directive are satisfied in the particular case'.[243] It further clarified that the requirement of religious affiliation must be 'necessary and objectively dictated, having regard to the ethos of the church ... by the nature of the occupational activity concerned or the circumstances in which it is carried out ... and must comply with the principle of proportionality'.[244] This case has thus managed to sharpen the understanding of how to balance the right of religious communities to autonomy on the one hand and the effective application of the principle of non-discrimination on the basis of religion on the other. However, the legal dispute is not over. After the Federal Labour Court decided in line with the CJEU judgment, the *Diakonie* lodged a constitutional complaint against this decision. It argued that the CJEU had 'no competence to disregard German constitutional law in the area of the freedom of religious organisations and consequently acted ultra vires. The case may thus have far reaching ramifications for the relation of Union law and the law of Member States'.[245]

[241] Emphasis added.
[242] *Vera Egenberger v Evangelisches Werk für Diakonie und Entwicklung e.V.* (n 240) para 31.
[243] ibid para 59.
[244] ibid para 69.
[245] See Matthias Mahlmann, 'Constitutional complaint in Egenberger case' (EELN News Report, 1 July 2019). The case BVerfG-2 BvR 934/19 is still pending.

Notwithstanding these examples in which litigation supported by an NGO contributed to policy change and clarification of legislation, for a country like Germany it cannot be satisfactory that there is only one such organization doing strategic litigation with another handful of organizations supporting complainants before the courts in one way or another. While non-discrimination associations could thus make better use of the—albeit limited—existing possibilities,[246] another way forward would be to consider increasing the possibilities for all protected grounds to reach the level provided for under disability law.

As mentioned above, for certain violations of the law the Equal Opportunities for People with Disabilities Act allows organizations to bring claims in their own name on behalf of an individual victim.[247] This requires the authorization of the organization by the individual concerned. Further, the organization is required to have a legitimate interest to bring the claim on behalf of the victim, which corresponds with the interests of the victim. Organizations can make use of this possibility only if they are registered by the Ministry for Labour and Social Affairs. For such registration, organizations must, according to their statute, promote the interests of persons with disabilities on a permanent basis; stemming from the composition of its members or member associations, be in a position to promote the interests of persons with disability on a national level (those organizations only operating locally are thus excluded); at the moment of registration, have been in existence for at least three years; ensure the proper fulfilment of their tasks.[248] Such organizations can also bring a complaint in the public interest. In this case they can only request the determination of a violation.

The first, and so far only case in which organizations promoting the interests of persons with disabilities have brought an *actio popularis* has been rejected by the Supreme Administrative Court.[249] As the costs of the claim amounted to 30,000 EUR in addition to the extra-legal costs of the defendant, and these costs had to be borne by the claiming organizations, this case has frightened off other disability organizations from using the instruments at their disposal. As Möschel analysed, 'associations that effectively have the power to bring disability related claims against the state were shocked into a silence by this early decision'.[250]

In the most recent survey carried out by the FRA on the discrimination of migrants and minorities in the EU, the figures for Germany indicate that individuals who feel discriminated against rarely report it or bring a complaint. To the

[246] Möschel, 'Litigating Anti-Discrimination Cases in Germany: What Role for Collective Actors?' (n 25) 74.

[247] German Equal Opportunities for People with Disabilities Act, § 14.

[248] German Equal Opportunities for People with Disabilities Act, § 15(3).

[249] For more details on the case, see Bundesverband für Körper- und Mehrfachbehinderte e.V. 'Bundesverwaltungsgericht weist Klagen wegen eines nicht behindertengerechten Bahnhofs ab: BVerwG, Urteile vom 5.04.2006 – Az. 9 C 1.05 und 9 C 2.05' (April 2006).

[250] Möschel, 'Litigating Anti-Discrimination Cases in Germany: What Role for Collective Actors?' (n 25) 74.

question: 'Did you report or make a complaint about the most recent time you felt discriminated against because of your ethnic or immigrant background in any area?'[251] only 15 per cent of respondents with a Sub-Saharan African background and 11 per cent of respondents with a Turkish background confirmed. In both cases, this is—albeit slightly—below the EU average, which is 16 per cent in the first case and 12 per cent in the second case. Among the group with a Sub-Saharan African background, the level of awareness about any organization that offers support or advice to victims of discrimination is also very low: only 25 per cent as compared to the EU average of 30 per cent in. Among the Turkish community, 27 per cent of the respondents to the survey were aware of any such organization, which is slightly above the EU average of 26 per cent.[252] Overall, however, these figures indicate that the barriers to seeking redress for discrimination continue to be relatively high, and they are linked to lack of awareness about existing support mechanisms on the one hand and partly also to the belief that nothing would change or happen as a result of reporting the discrimination.[253] This shows that more sustained efforts need to be undertaken, first, to inform those being discriminated against about existing support mechanisms and second, to increase the trust of those individuals that their action might not only bring them individual satisfaction but also contribute to a change in policy, practice, and eventually society.

Germany has been taken as an example of a country that has decided to regulate NGOs' engagement in judicial and administrative proceedings rather restrictively. While the criteria laid down by law for an NGO to be in such position are considered arbitrary, they do not appear to be difficult to fulfil so as to limit the possibilities for NGOs. The fact that national coverage is unsatisfactory appears to be more related to the fact that only few NGOs have a specialized expertise on the equal treatment legislation and its judicial enforcement. Furthermore, cooperation and networking amongst themselves when it comes to litigation are apparently not very well developed, notwithstanding an overall intensive cooperation between NGOs, especially within the different sectors (antiracism, disability, etc). While the responsibility to improve this situation rests mainly with the NGOs themselves, the FADA—notwithstanding continued efforts in this direction—has also not managed to serve as a bridge and create a satisfactory coverage of the whole territory with organizations supporting victims of discrimination.[254] The competent ministry did not produce any stimulus in this direction either.

[251] The areas covered by the survey were the following: when looking for work, at work, when looking for housing, when using health care services, when in contact with children's school, in education, when entering a restaurant, nightclub, or hotel, when in contact with public administration, when using public transportation, and when entering a shop.

[252] Fundamental Rights Agency, 'EU-MIDIS II: Main results' (2017) 43 and 51.

[253] ibid 49.

[254] Interview, Director of BUG 26 July 2018 and 2 August 2018 and e-mail on 31 March 2021. She has also reported a loose network of lawyers that have already worked with non-discrimination cases and NGOs. The meetings of this network are dedicated to the discussion of specific issues related to the Equal Treatment Act and its application.

BUG, the one organization explicitly dedicated to strategic litigation in discrimination cases, through supporting well-chosen individual cases aims at contributing to the clarification of legislation, the establishment of court practice, and improving policies and practices. BUG has managed to win all its cases and after successful outcomes in cases, it observed an increase of reported cases based on similar facts. It was also shown that it also managed to trigger changes in policies. However, such an impact beyond the individual case requires sustained follow-up, making use of the results of the legal proceeding to push public authorities towards changes or improvements of existing policies. While in such context public information about litigation outcomes and proposed follow-up are important, BUG focuses more on bringing the outcomes of its cases to the attention of legal practitioners and academics. Thus the German example has shown that it is possible for NGOs to trigger broader change also through individual litigation, even in cases where the legal framework for their engagement is rather restrictive. Nevertheless, improving the legal framework so as to allow a representative action as well as collective action should be seriously considered.

4.4 Good Practices and Challenges

Non-state actors play a prominent role in the EU anti-discrimination regime, which de Búrca qualified as resembling an experimentalist governance regime. In particular she found that 'a range of different social actors are specifically allocated various roles in … raising awareness, providing information, [and] assistance'.[255] However, while the Commission was supportive in building up pan-European networks of NGOs in the various fields, it did not do enough to support the local NGOs active on the ground. State authorities appeared to be even less interested in empowering NGOs to play their role. In reaching these conclusions, the following findings should be highlighted:

The above case studies have shown that a very permissive and open regulation of the criteria for NGOs to be recognized as having a legitimate interest in ensuring the compliance with the Directives, such as in Romania and Hungary, has not led to a situation of satisfactory coverage of all grounds and the whole country. In each of these countries it has been reported that there exists roughly only a handful of organizations who are (or in some cases have been) active in this field. On the other hand, in Germany, where the criteria appear more restrictive, they have—although being considered arbitrary—not been considered as hindering NGOs to engage. However, the geographic outreach is similarly unsatisfactory as in the cases of Romania and Hungary. While this should not suggest that the legal framework

255 de Búrca, 'Stumbling into Experimentalism: The EU Anti-Discrimination Regime' (n 11) 226.

does not matter, it does make clear that open and permissive legislation alone is useful but not sufficient to achieve the objective of providing those who have been subject to discrimination with a more effective level of protection.

What is considered by NGOs as more hindering is national legislation that limits their opportunities to provide counselling. This has been referred to by some as 'holding hands' before the court. Strictly speaking, a country opting for this kind of transposition is still in line with the requirements under the Directives which require simply that NGOs may engage either on behalf or in support of a complainant. The question is, however, whether these measures are also appropriate in securing a more effective level of protection to victims of discrimination. NGOs therefore call for the possibility of representing victims of discrimination directly before the courts and for collective redress mechanisms.

When it comes to the efforts undertaken by Member States to translate the legal framework into results, it is hard to find any good practice. In all three countries the following challenges persist in a more or less pronounced manner. As already mentioned, the number of NGOs engaging in judicial or administrative proceedings in support or on behalf of victims of discrimination is too low (in some cases even decreasing recently) to really be able to provide a more effective level of protection. Furthermore, not all the discrimination grounds are equally well covered and victims of discrimination living in the periphery have hardly any access to such support. Combined with the finding that this is also the case in countries with a very permissive legal framework indicates that the state authorities have so far not done enough to translate these legal provisions into practice. First and foremost this would require providing incentives to NGOs to engage in litigation activities, including the financial support to build up the necessary internal infrastructure to be able to engage in proceedings. Such infrastructure requires either the employment of lawyers with the power of attorney or the necessary financial means to hire external lawyers. Parallel to creating such structures, increasing the awareness of potential victims of the possibility of approaching an NGO for support in proceedings is required and a system of referencing between legal aid services and NGOs established. Not only were no such efforts observed in any of the countries, it appears instead that state authorities are currently attempting by various means to shrink the space for civil society organizations in general.

The increasingly hostile environment civil society organizations are faced with in several European countries expresses itself in over-regulation of the sector (including by problematic registration procedures, disproportionate transparency or lobbying laws), exclusion from effective participation, and being publicly discredited if they promote human rights and non-discrimination by public officials. This comes along with serious funding cuts that affect particularly activities such as advocacy, litigation, and awareness-rasising. Furthermore, possibilities for seeking funding from foreign donors have been restricted or affected by requiring organizations receiving such funds to indicate on all their materials that they are foreign-funded. In such a situation NGOs prefer to opt for activities for which it is easier to raise funds (such as health care and social services)[256] and which in themselves do not carry the financial risk that litigating cases does. While in some countries the funding cuts have been explained by the overall economic situation, this has often been used as a pretext to tame the civil society sector.

One therefore has to conclude that not because of but despite of the legal and practical conditions existing in different countries the litigation activity of the NGOs analysed in the above case studies has managed to have an impact at the individual level but also at societal level. A precondition for that (especially in cases such as Germany, or if there is an obligation to be represented by a lawyer with the power of attorney) is close cooperation with lawyers, who represent the victim before the court, and with whom (or sometimes even for whom) NGOs prepare the whole documentation for the case. Many of these lawyers work *pro bono* or for reduced fees to make this financially feasible. If this was not the case, the opportunities for NGOs to engage in proceedings would be even more limited. The case studies have shown that organizations predominantly have a strategic approach to litigation. The outcome of such cases can also have an effect beyond the individual case. In this context, it is not only the selection of the case is crucial, but all the work around it, including communication with the media thereby raising awareness among the general public, changing public attitudes, and empowering vulnerable groups. The outcomes are further used to push state authorities towards policy reform or for educational purposes of the judiciary and other legal professions. Case results are also used to link up with other stakeholders like Chambers of Commerce to support them in informing their members and devising policies and guidelines for them. Depending on the approach but also on the financial capabilities of the above studied NGOs, such work around the cases has been done more or less intensively, and has shown remarkable results.

A focus on strategic litigation is probably most efficient in a situation where financial resources are scarce, considering that a few cases can have a large impact. However, in order to provide a more effective level of protection for victims of discrimination, it should also be possible for NGOs to engage in cases which are not 'strategic'. In this context it is of course necessary to keep the overall support structure, including Equality Bodies and trade unions, in mind. If low-threshold support of victims of discrimination in bringing their complaints cannot be offered by them, it may be doubted that a strategic litigation approach of NGOs is sufficient to provide the required more effective level of protection for victims of discrimination.

[256] Fundamental Rights Agency, 'Challenges facing civil society organisations working on human rights in the EU' (2018) 7–11. Regarding restrictive legislation see *Commission v Hungary* (n 183) and a new infringement procedure initiated by the Commission against Hungary in February 2021.

The case studies have also shown that where the instrument of *actio popularis* exists, NGOs do make use of it and it has the potential to address institutional discrimination. The most impressive court decision in this context is that of the Hungarian Metropolitan Court in April 2018. The case studies have, however, also shown what is needed for public interest claims to be successful. First, procedural rules should be such as to allow the judge to make sure that general proactive measures can be enforced. Furthermore, rules regarding the representation of the group in the interest of whom an NGO acts should be laid down, amongst others to regulate if compensation can be paid and to whom. Of utmost importance is that NGOs bringing such claims work closely with the group in question in building the case and during the proceedings in order to build trust. In the aftermath of a court decision, it is important that all the relevant stakeholders, in particular the groups concerned, are involved in the implementation of and follow-up to the decision. As shown, such sensitive issues as the desegregation of Roma schools requires careful planning and monitoring.

Overall, the case studies have shown that the litigation activity of NGOs contributes to awareness raising, improving reporting behaviour, change of practices, policies, and attitudes, as well as the clarification of legal standards. This potential should be used in a more systematic way. In fact, if this is not done, one of the core actors in the triangular constellation necessary to make a reflexive governance system work, consisting of Commission, state actors, and civil society actors, would be left out and the success of the overall system would be jeopardized.

In the context of the present research it is relevant to note again the Commission's 2013 guidelines to support civil society in enlargement countries. In this document it announced the achievement of an environment which is conducive to civil society activities as one of its main goals and promised financial and political support to achieve this goal.[257] The working draft of the Guidelines for the period 2021–27 continue to focus on the establishment of an enabling legal, policy, and financial environment for civil society.[258] The European Parliament, referring amongst others to the FRA's report on 'Challenges facing civil society organisations working on human rights in the EU',[259] reminded us that while the EU provides direct funding to CSOs operating in third countries to foster the fundamental values enshrined in Article 2 TEU, such funding within the EU is very limited. It therefore called upon the EU to set up within the Multiannual Financial Framework post-2020 a dedicated funding instrument, with funding corresponding at least to the level of

[257] European Commission, 'Guidelines for EU support to civil society in enlargement countries, 2014–20' (14 October 2013), 1–2.

[258] DG NEAR, 'Guidelines and Strategic Directions for EU Support to Civil Society in the Enlargement Region 2021–2027 – Working Draft' (19 February 2021), 2.

[259] Fundamental Rights Agency, 'Challenges facing civil society organisations working on human rights in the EU' (n 256). See also Fundamental Rights Agency, 'Civil society space: views of organisations—Conference paper' (November 2018).

money spent for CSOs in third countries.[260] Such funding has been proposed by the Commission with its Rights and Values Programme,[261] and agreed upon by the presidency of the Council and the European Parliament in December 2020. The Programme shall dispense an overall budget of 1.55 billion EUR. One of its four objectives will be 'to promote equality and rights, including gender equality, anti-discrimination and the rights of children', by supporting 'civil society organisations and other stakeholders active at local, regional, national and transnational level'.[262]

In 2017, the Parliament has further adopted a preparatory action on an 'EU fund for financial support for litigating cases relating to violations of democracy, rule of law and fundamental rights'.[263] In response, in 2018 the Commission organized a stakeholder exploratory consultation among NGOs that were already active in the field to collect views on gaps and needs in terms of support for litigation. In 2019 it commissioned a feasibility study with the aims of drawing conclusions from this consultation, mapping existing funding possibilities for litigation, and outlining how EU financial support in this area can ensure added value. The study found that 'only a very small number of donors reliably support such litigation to any significant degree'. The vast majority of litigators consulted reported that their litigation budgets are insufficient to carry out all the litigation they think is desirable. The field of non-discrimination was mentioned among those that should be prioritized, in case the Commission should choose to focus on certain areas.[264] While the Commission is aware of the importance of strategic litigation it still remains to be seen what kind of follow-up it gives the results of the feasibility study. For the time being, it seems to prefer the funding of training activities and exchange of knowledge and good practice to develop the litigation capacity among NGOs[265] as

260 European Parliament, 'European Parliament resolution on the need to establish a European Values Instrument to support civil society organisations which promote fundamental values within the European Union at local and national level (2018/2619(RSP))' (19 April 2018).

261 European Commission, 'Proposal for a Regulation of the European Parliament and of the Council establishing the Rights and Values Programme' (7 June 2018) COM(2018) 383 final/2. The Commission's proposal was criticized for overlooking the grassroots organizations in the various states and directing money mainly to pan-European umbrella NGOs György Folk, 'Freedoms Fund: The EU Commission's Half-Hearted Plans to Support Civil Society Groups' (Civil Liberties Union for Europe, 31 May 2018) <https://www.liberties.eu/en/news/ec-commission-evi-proposal-rights-and-values-fund/15107>. For proposals from civil society organizations concerning the overall multiannual financial framework see Civil Society Europe, 'Multiannual Financial Framework Post 2020. Proposals by Civil Society Organisations' (nd), underlining the importance of better access to funding and dialogue with CSOs.

262 The Regulation for the programme is still to be approved. See https://www.consilium.europa.eu/en/press/press-releases/2020/12/17/rights-and-values-programme-council-presidency-and-european-parliament-reach-provisional-agreement/.

263 European Commission, '2017 Annual Report on the Application of the EU Charter of Fundamental Rights' (4 June 2018) COM(2018) 396 final, 5.

264 European Commission, 'Feasibility Study for financial support for litigating cases relating to violations of democracy, rule of law and fundamental rights' (29 June 2020) i–ii.

265 For the first call for proposals launched as a reaction to the Feasibility Study (Capacity building for litigating cases relating to democracy, rule of law, and fundamental rights violations), see https://ec.europa.eu/info/funding-tenders/opportunities/portal/screen/opportunities/topic-details/just-pppa-liti-ag-2018.

less compromising means of support, as compared to providing direct funding for litigation (like financing the legal and psychological support staff, as well as preparation and follow-up activities connected with litigating strategic cases), which might meet with resistance from Member States. It might be telling that in its Application Report on the implementation of the two Directives, the Commission has given relatively little room to the role of NGOs in the defence of rights.[266]

Even if no such explicit fund for litigation should be set up, support for CSOs will be vital, not only in acceding countries but also within the EU. The establishment and support of a Europe-wide network of locally operating NGOs engaged in (strategic) litigation across all discrimination grounds would be very useful. Some sort of exchange among such NGOs took place for a couple of years during the annual NGO platforms organized by the FRA, including through the organization of sessions dedicated to the topic of strategic litigation.[267] There was also an attempt to formalize this cooperation through the setting up of a network of NGOs engaging in strategic litigation. For that purpose a number of proposals were submitted to the European Commission which, however, did not award funding for such a network. With the growing interest and hopefully also support of the Commission for NGO litigation activities it might become also possible to build such a network of organizations undertaking litigation across the various discrimination grounds and across the EU which would certainly stimulate the exchange of experience, in line with reflexive thinking, and thus help improving the access to justice in discrimination cases. While some transnational NGOs, such as ILGA-Europe, already actively engage in supporting litigation, others, like ENAR,[268] could step up their efforts in this context in the future.

4.5 Proposed Indicators

Based on the above comparative assessment of legal transposition and practical implementation in the selected countries, this chapter proposes indicators that could be used by the Commission in pre- and post-accession monitoring of the legal compliance and effective implementation and enforcement. They could equally be used by other bodies engaged in monitoring and evaluation, including

[266] European Commission, 'Report on the application of Council Directive 2000/43/EC implementing the principle of equal treatment between persons irrespective of racial or ethnic origin ('the Racial Equality Directive') and of Council Directive 2000/78/EC establishing a general framework for equal treatment in employment and occupation ('the Employment Equality Directive')' (n 4) 6–8.

[267] In the Fundamental Rights Forum which took place from 25–27 September 2018, one session was dedicated to the topic: 'Current political conditions for NGOs securing fundamental rights through strategic litigation'.

[268] ENAR offers no capacity building activities nor does it offer any other guidance or support to its members in this field. A look into ENAR's theory of change confirms that litigation does not play an important role in its understanding of how such change can be brought about. See ENAR website, Our theory of change, at http://www.enar-eu.org/ENAR-theory-of-change.

civil society organizations, and by policy makers to analyse the situation in view of evidence-based law and policy making. The premise is, as spelled out in recital 19 of RED and recital 29 of EED, that associations and other legal entities should be empowered to engage in proceedings '[t]o provide a more effective level of protection' to persons who have been subject to discrimination based on racial or ethnic origin, religion or belief, disability, age or sexual orientation.

Structural indicators would have to look at how Article 7(2) RED and Article 9(2) EED have been transposed in the respective national legal systems. The minimum required for national legislation to be in line with EU Directives appears to be relatively little, both in terms of criteria laid down for NGOs to be considered as having a legitimate interest in ensuring compliance with the Directives as well as in terms of what they can do. A situation like the Austrian one, where only one NGO is given the explicit right to engage in proceedings is considered to be in line. Also, to support victims of discrimination by counselling, like in Germany, is—even if a minimalistic—correct legal transposition. While the above case studies have shown that NGOs do manage to use this limited space and produce impact, the protection of victims of discrimination would, however, benefit from a larger set of possible legal actions an NGO could choose from, including the possibility of a representative action and of some form of collective redress. The wording of the Commission in the infringement proceedings against Ireland should be recalled, where the Commission found that '[i]f all they [NGOs] can do in practice is to hire a lawyer to personally represent the victim, then there seems little added value in paragraph (2) of Article 7 over and above paragraph (1)'.[269] While the Commission acknowledged that it is a matter of national procedure to insist that victims of discrimination can only be represented by a lawyer, it also underlined that Member States must guarantee that the practical purpose of Article 7(2), which is to 'provide a more effective level of protection' for victims of discrimination—as laid down in recital 19 of the Directive—is correctly and completely ensured.[270] The real test as to whether the legal transposition manages to achieve this objective consists in looking at the practical implementation.

As has been seen above, an evaluation of whether the states have made any effort to translate their legal framework into practice is, therefore, at least equally if not more important than a permissive legal framework. The case studies have shown that the most permissive legal frameworks are not effective if the state authorities do not support implementation—or at the very least, refrain from obstructing it. The *process indicators* that could be used for that purpose would first of all have to look at the number of NGOs engaging in proceedings, whether they manage to cover all discrimination grounds, and the whole territory of the state. In order to understand whether there is sufficient coverage, it would be useful to compare the

269 Infringement case 2005/2357 (reasoned opinion, Ireland).
270 ibid.

number of requests received by the NGOs (but reference could also be made to requests for assistance received by the Equality Body) with the number of cases litigated by such NGOs. If the trend indicates that the number of such NGOs and/or the cases they are litigating are very low as compared to requests or even decreasing over the years, the reasons for such a situation or development would need to be carefully studied. As shown by the case studies, such a trend could be related to a generally hostile environment for NGOs and could thus require intervention by the Commission, either in terms of encouraging the state to provide the necessary framework or, in case this should prove to be impossible, by designing their own strategies on how to support such NGOs (as it currently does). Similarly, if the number of requests for assistance hugely outweighs the number of cases that can actually be supported, this indicates that the support structure at the level of NGOs is insufficiently developed. While it will be difficult and probably even undesirable to set a clear figure for what is enough and what not in each national context, the observation of trends and the opinion of independent institutions (such as NHRI or Equality Bodies) as well as experts from academia and the civil society sector will help in populating and interpreting these indicators.

It has to be emphasized that all interlocutors concur in their assessment that what is essential for NGOs to be able to play their part in the legal fight against discrimination is an appropriate level of funding and also an otherwise conducive environment for their activities. However, what some countries are currently doing is to gradually shrink the space for civil society to even exist, let alone effectively support victims of discrimination over the longer period of time required for litigating a case.

Besides providing for a conducive environment, there are also other measures by which state authorities could support NGOs in their litigation function. One element is the training of the legal profession on the non-discrimination legislation, which would enlarge the pool of lawyers with the specialized knowledge required to litigate discrimination cases. It could further engage in raising awareness of rights holders of the possibility of approaching NGOs for legal support and making sure that a system of referencing exists between legal aid services and NGOs. All these aspects should be part of a national anti-discrimination strategy.

To find out whether the commitment and efforts of state authorities and NGOs have contributed to reaching the practical purpose of Article 7(2) RED and Article 9(2) EED, which is to 'provide a more effective level of protection' for victims of discrimination, *outcome indicators* such as the level of knowledge among right holders about the possibility of addressing an NGO for support and awareness about at least one of them; the level of trust among rights holders in the capacity of NGOs to support them; their experience made with NGO support; and the perception among NGOs about the legal and practical framework for their engagement are proposed. To populate them it will be necessary to carry out surveys into these questions. Table 4.1 summarizes the structural, process and outcome indicators just described, derived from the comparative analysis carried out in this chapter.

Table 4.1 Table of indicators concerning the role of NGOs in judicial dispute resolution

practical purpose of Art 7(2) RED and Art 9(2) EED is to 'provide a more effective level of protection' for victims of discrimination (recital 19 RED, recital 29 EED)	Structural indicators	Details about the transposition in terms of
		• Criteria set up by national legislation determining which NGOs have a legitimate interest in ensuring compliance with the Directives
		• How can they engage in proceedings
		  • Counselling
		  • Representing victims in court
		  • Representing victims before the Equality Body
		  • Some form of collective redress

	Process indicators	• Trend in the number of NGOs engaging in proceedings and explanations for increase/decrease
		• All discrimination grounds covered?
		• The whole territory covered?
		• Number of requests received by NGOs/Equality Body as compared with number of cases actually supported
		• Trend in the number of cases and explanations for increase/decrease
		• State support to NGOs
		  • funding (in general/related to litigation)
		  • conducive regulatory environment for civil society organizations
		• awareness raising about the possibility to approach NGOs
		• system of referencing between legal aid services and NGOs
		• existence of a national anti-discrimination strategy in which NGOs play a role also in terms of providing support to victims of discrimination

	Outcome indicators	Surveys into • Knowledge among right holders about the possibility to address an NGO for support and awareness about at least one of them • Level of trust among rights holders in the capacity of NGOs to support them • Victims' experience made with NGO support • Perception among NGOs about the legal and practical framework for their engagement

5

Reaction to Discrimination by Quasi- and Non-Judicial Mechanisms

The Equality Bodies

Equality Bodies play a central role in the overall EU non-discrimination regime, particularly when it comes to discrimination on the grounds of race and ethnicity as well as gender. The Employment Equality Directive (EED) does not call for the establishment of such bodies. Nevertheless, a large number of countries have established Equality Bodies going beyond the legally required grounds and include age, religion and belief, disability, and/or sexual orientation within the mandate of their bodies.[1] More than half of the Member States even include grounds not covered by the EU Directives.[2] The horizontal directive proposed by the Commission in 2008 replicates Article 13 of the Racial Equality Directive (RED) and would thus extend the obligation to establish such bodies to all grounds contained in EU legislation. Equality Bodies, as one of the social actors that have been formally brought into the governance regime as part (in particular) of the law-application process, can be understood as one of the elements that make the EU anti-discrimination regime an experimentalist one.[3]

Notwithstanding their potential and importance, previous research has found that one of the explanations for the huge gap between the law and the practice is related to these bodies being rather toothless, 'plagued by a lack of visibility, institutional standing and resources'.[4] The lack of visibility was confirmed by a study carried out by the Fundamental Rights Agency (FRA) in 2010, according to which 80 per cent of respondents could not mention a single organization that could provide assistance to victims of discrimination. When interviewees were given the

[1] In all but three Member States, Equality Bodies cover all grounds listed in Art 19 TFEU, in around two thirds of the Member States they are competent for all grounds and all the fields mentioned by RED. See European Commission, 'Equality bodies and the implementation of the Commission Recommendation on Standards for Equality Bodies' (19 March 2021) SWD(2021) 63 final, 4.

[2] European Commission, 'Joint Report on the application of Council Directive 2000/43/EC of 29 June 2000 implementing the principle of equal treatment between persons irrespective of racial or ethnic origin ("Racial Equality Directive") and of Council Directive 2000/78/EC of 27 November 2000 establishing a general framework for equal treatment in employment and occupation ("Employment Equality Directive")' (Brussels 17 January 2014) COM(2014) 2 final, 12.

[3] Gráinne de Búrca, 'Stumbling into Experimentalism: The EU Anti-Discrimination Regime' in Charles F Sabel and Jonathan Zeitlin (eds), Experimentalist Governance in the European Union: Towards a New Architecture (Oxford University Press, 2010), 212–22.

[4] Gerda Falkner and Oliver Treib, 'Three Worlds of Compliance or Four? The EU-15 Compared to New Member States', Journal of Common Market Studies (2008), 46(2): 293.

Reflexive Governance in EU Equality Law. Emma Lantschner, Oxford University Press. © Emma Lantschner 2021.
DOI: 10.1093/oso/9780192843371.003.0006

name of an Equality Body in their respective Member State, 60 per cent said that they had never heard of this body.[5] In the more recent survey carried out by the FRA, 62 per cent of respondents had never heard of the Equality Body.[6] Regarding Roma and Muslims, awareness about Equality Bodies is even lower. 82 per cent of Roma respondents and 72 per cent of Muslim respondents could not indicate one organization that offers support to discrimination victims. When given the name of one such organization, only 29 per cent of Roma and 35 per cent of Muslims indicated that they recognized it.[7] Overall then, the situation has deteriorated in recent years and it is therefore important to look at how Equality Bodies could be strengthened so that they can play the role assigned to them by the Directives.

Article 13(2) RED lays down that the functions of these bodies shall include a) to provide 'independent assistance to victims of discrimination in pursuing their complaints about discrimination'; b) to conduct 'independent surveys concerning discrimination'; and c) to publish 'independent reports and mak[e] recommendations on any issue relating to such discrimination'. Comparing this wording with the proposal of the Commission, it is clear that it has been weakened significantly. First, the proposal called the article 'Independent Bodies', whereas in the adopted version the term 'independence' has been moved from the overall institution to its functioning. Second, the proposal expressly provided that Equality Bodies could receive and pursue complaints from individuals about discrimination on the grounds of race or ethnic origin and commence investigations *suo motu*.[8] Both these points were very much in line with the proposal of the Starting Line Group. Regarding the functions, this proposal laid down clearly that an Equality Body would adjudicate on all complaints and that such conclusions should be public except for, where appropriate, information revealing the identity of the complainant.[9] The proposal of the Commission as well as the Starting Line Group's proposal thus placed greater emphasis on establishing extra-judicial mechanisms for the resolution of disputes.

The changed wording of the final version of the article sheds light on the discussions within the Council, in which the Commission's proposal was met with 'a good deal of concern'.[10] Discussions circulated around the principled question of

[5] Fundamental Rights Agency, 'EU-MIDIS, Data in Focus Report No 3: Rights Awareness and Equality Bodies' (2010) 3, 9–11.

[6] Fundamental Rights Agency, 'EU-MIDIS II: Main Results' (2017) 53.

[7] Fundamental Rights Agency, 'EU-MIDIS II: Roma—Selected Findings' (2016) 40–41; and Fundamental Rights Agency, 'EU-MIDIS II: Muslims—Selected Findings' (2017) 36–38.

[8] Commission of the European Communities, 'Proposal for a Council Directive implementing the principle of equal treatment between persons irrespective of racial or ethnic origin' (25 November 1999) COM(1999) 566 final, Art 12.

[9] Art 4(4)(e) of the Starting Line Group's proposal. For the text and a comment, see Isabelle Chopin, 'Possible Harmonisation of Anti-Discrimination Legislation in the European Union: European and Non-Governmental Proposals' (2000) 2(3/4) European Journal of Migration and Law 413; and Mark Bell, 'Meeting the Challenge? A Comparison between the EU Racial Equality Directive and the Starting Line' in Isabelle Chopin and Jan Niessen (eds), 'The Starting Line and the Incorporation of the Racial Equality Directive into the National Laws of the EU Member States and Accession States' (Migration Policy Group, Commission for Racial Equality 2001) 47–48.

[10] Adam Tyson, 'The Negotiation of the European Community Directive on Racial Discrimination', European Journal of Migration and Law (2001), 3(2): 199, 212.

whether to include such bodies in the Directive at all, to questioning the level of detail by which the Member States were told how to achieve certain objectives (thus including the question on the mandate of the bodies), the meaning of 'independence', and the potential impact of the measure on national budgets.

Resistance from Member States, independently from whether they were familiar with such bodies or not, was strong enough to amend the proposal to its current form. Regarding the issue of independence, Member States could not agree on how to define when a body is independent or not, and they debated whether already existing bodies were to be considered independent or not.[11] In light of these difficulties, the strategy was to shift from calling for 'independent bodies' to prescribing that, however the legal status and financing is regulated, such bodies must be free from interference of outside bodies in organizing their everyday work. For some, 'Member States rejected totally the idea of independence' and the final text of the article constituted the 'biggest loss in the adoption of the directive' as compared to the Commission's proposal.[12]

Regarding the tasks to be granted to the Equality Bodies, the final version of Article 13 has been criticized for its general wording which allowed many states to continue with arrangements they already had in place instead of obliging them to strengthen such bodies.[13] Most of the infringement proceedings were started by the Commission either because the country in question had not yet designated a body which would perform the tasks as listed in Article 13 RED at all,[14] or because the designated body did not grant of all the competences required. With regard to Portugal, for instance, the Commission complained that the designated body was not competent to provide independent assistance to victims of discrimination in pursuing their complaints.[15] In an additional letter of formal notice sent to Malta, the Commission found that the designated body did 'not appear to be empowered to conduct independent surveys nor to publish independent reports and make recommendations, contrary to the minimum competences set out in

[11] Chopin, 'Possible Harmonisation of Anti-Discrimination Legislation in the European Union: European and Non-Governmental Proposals' (n 9) 426.

[12] ibid 428.

[13] Bell, 'Meeting the Challenge? A Comparison between the EU Racial Equality Directive and the Starting Line' (n 9) 48.

[14] Infringement no 2005/2353, Belgium (letter of formal notice of 7 February 2005, reasoned opinion of 23 October 2007) where the Commission criticized that the designated body was responsible only for the federal legislation, but not for the legislation of the communities and regions; infringement no 2005/2361, Spain (letter of formal notice of 1 February 2006, reasoned opinion of 27 June 2007) where the Commission complained that the Equality Body was formally provided for by law but had not been established; infringement no 2005/2363, UK (letter of formal notice of 1 February 2006, reasoned opinion of 27 June 2007) where the Commission complained that no Equality Body had been designated for Gibraltar; infringement no 2006/2258, Malta (letter of formal notice of 28 June 2006); infringement no 2006/2262, Czech Republic (letter of formal notice of 28 June 2006, reasoned opinion of 27 June 2007) where the Commission clarified that it is not enough that de facto some existing bodies carry out some of the functions that should be assigned to a designated body; infringement no 2014/2093, Slovenia (letter of formal notice of 10 July 2014).

[15] Infringement no 2005/2360, Portugal (letter of formal notice of 1 February 2006).

article 13'.[16] Problems with covering the full range of competences in all the fields required by the RED even led to two separate infringement procedures started by the Commission against Finland, and in the second procedure, in which the Commission found that there was no body in place responsible for carrying out the tasks foreseen in Article 13 RED in the field of employment, even to a referral of the case to court. After Finland assigned the required competences to the Non-Discrimination Ombudsman, the Commission withdrew the referral.[17]

Recently, the Commission has increasingly emphasized the effective functioning of Equality Bodies. In its second report to the European Parliament and the Council on the application of the RED (and the EED), the Commission stated that it is 'scrutinizing more widely the Member States' compliance with the requirement of this Directive' including not only the question of whether the Equality Bodies have the required mandate and powers but also whether they are effectively performing all their tasks.[18]

The concern over the bodies' lack of independence and effectiveness led the Commission to launch a public consultation on Equality Bodies in early 2018, followed by the adoption of Recommendations on Standards for Equality Bodies in June 2018.[19] 'To help ensure that equality bodies function properly and in an equivalent way across the Union', the Commission found it 'appropriate to recommend Member States standards for equality bodies'.[20] In March 2021, accompanying the third report to the European Parliament and the Council on the application of the RED (and the EED), the Commission published a Commission Staff Working Document on the implementation of its 2018 Recommendation[21] in which it spelled out some good practice and challenges and reiterated its intention to 'assess whether to propose new legislation to strengthen the role of national equality bodies by 2022'. From an experimentalist governance point of view, this whole process can be seen as closing the feedback loop. On the basis of the information received from various sources and the lessons learned during implementation, the Commission has first taken an interim step with the adoption of the

[16] Infringement no 2006/2258, Malta (additional letter of formal notice of 27 June 2007).

[17] Infringement no 2006/2451, Finland (letter of formal notice of 20 December 2006); infringement no 2013/2084, Finland (letter of formal notice of 20 June 2013, reasoned opinion of 20 November 2013, referral to the Court of 10 July 2014, withdrawal on 29 April 2015).

[18] European Commission, 'Joint Report on the application of Council Directive 2000/43/EC of 29 June 2000 implementing the principle of equal treatment between persons irrespective of racial or ethnic origin ("Racial Equality Directive") and of Council Directive 2000/78/EC of 27 November 2000 establishing a general framework for equal treatment in employment and occupation ("Employment Equality Directive")' (n 2) 12.

[19] European Commission, 'Commission Recommendation on Standards for Equality Bodies' (22 June 2018) C(2018) 3850 final.

[20] ibid recital 25; see also point 1 in Chapter I.

[21] European Commission, 'Equality bodies and the implementation of the Commission Recommendation on Standards for Equality Bodies' (n 1).

Recommendations and may eventually reformulate the framework goal by means of new legislation.

The Recommendations had been intensively lobbied for by Equinet, which published its own vision of such standards in a working paper in 2016.[22] Equinet also influenced the 2017 revision of the General Policy Recommendation (GPR) No 2 regarding Equality Bodies of the European Commission Against Racism and Intolerance (ECRI)[23] and fed into the Commission Staff Working Document of 2021. Equinet has thus become an important transnational network influencing the development of the EU anti-discrimination regime. All the just mentioned documents focus on the issue of independence on one hand and on the effective exercise of the Equality Bodies' functions on the other. Independence and effectiveness can thus be considered as two overarching indicators when it comes to assessing the appropriate implementation of Article 13 RED.[24]

Related to the issues of independence and effectiveness is the question of how Equality Bodies are embedded in the overall institutional structure of institutions set up for the protection of human rights. Therefore, the next section will give an overview of the kind of institutions the Member States have assigned the task of functioning as an Equality Body, the grounds covered, and the level at which they are established (state, sub-state level). Thereafter, the issue of independence will be studied in detail, including how independence is legally entrenched in the different national systems and whether it is possible in practice to just require independent functioning while not insisting also on the independence of the institution as such (5.2). Considering that this research distinguishes between the reaction to discrimination and prevention of discrimination, this will be followed by an analysis of the tribunal-type Equality Bodies (5.3), and those activities of promotion-type Equality Bodies that are related to the assistance provided to victims of discrimination in pursuing their complaints (5.4). These sections look at the legal and practical conditions required for Equality Bodies to be able to carry out this function effectively. The case studies looking into the practical implementation of this function will also cover the question of how far independent functioning is ensured. The three sections will wrap up with the findings on good practices and challenges and propose indicators to assess the independence and effectiveness of Equality Bodies related to the function of assisting victims of discrimination.

[22] Equinet, 'Developing Standards for Equality Bodies. An Equinet Working Paper' (2016).

[23] ECRI, 'General Policy Recommendation No 2: Equality Bodies to Combat Racism and Intolerance at National Level' (7 December 2017) CRI(2018)06.

[24] See in this sense also Council of Europe, Commissioner for Human Rights, 'Opinion of the Commissioner for Human Rights on National Structures for Promoting Equality' (21 March 2011) CommDH(2011)2, 14.

5.1 Overall Institutional Setting

In responding to the requirement of setting up a body or bodies for the promotion of equal treatment of persons irrespective of race or ethnic origin, Member States have taken different routes. Some have established new institutions,[25] others have given existing institutions the functions required by the RED.[26] While most countries have a single body (multi-ground and/or multi-mandate), in some countries the tasks are fulfilled by two institutions. This is the case for instance in Estonia, the Netherlands, and the UK, while in Greece three institutions share the functions outlined in Article 13 RED. In Austria, Denmark, Finland, and Ireland there exist additional institutions to the Equality Body with tribunal-type functions.[27]

As a result of the economic and financial crisis, in recent years there appears to be a trend of merging different institutions into one body, which is given different responsibilities in several areas (multi-mandate bodies). Such mergers often involve National Human Rights Institutions (NHRIs) or Ombudsman Institutions.[28] In fact, Article 13 RED provides that Equality Bodies 'may form part of agencies charged at national level with the defence of human rights'. Some countries have from the outset assigned such institutions the tasks to be carried out by an Equality Body, while others have only later decided to merge different bodies into one.[29] Therefore, in addition to the above-mentioned documents of the Commission, Equinet, and ECRI, the Paris Principles on National Human Rights Institutions[30] are relevant in evaluating the appropriateness of existing Equality Bodies.

Research carried out by the FRA seems to favour a merger of NHRIs with Equality Bodies as 'there is a need for a stronger fundamental rights architecture, that can offer a "one-stop-shop" or at least a portal to a set of institutions and

[25] According to the European network of legal experts in gender equality and non-discrimination, 'A comparative analysis of non-discrimination law in Europe: 2020' (2021), 99, these countries are: France, Germany, Greece, Hungary, Italy, Romania, Slovenia, and Spain.

[26] According to ibid, these countries include Cyprus (Ombudsman), Estonia (Chancellor of Justice and Commissioner for Gender Equality and Equal Treatment), Lithuania (Equal Opportunities Ombudsperson), Malta (National Commission for the Promotion of Equality), Slovakia (National Centre for Human Rights), and Croatia (Ombudsman).

[27] ibid 108.

[28] Fundamental Rights Agency, 'National Human Rights Institutions in the EU Member States. Strengthening the fundamental rights architecture in the EU I' (2010) 26–29. For an update of this study see Fundamental Rights Agency, 'Strong and effective national human rights institutions—challenges, promising practices and opportunities' (2020).

[29] The most recent and controversially discussed example is the abolition of the Hungarian Equal Treatment Authority, and the assignment of its responsibilities to the Commissioner for Fundamental Rights, in force since 1 January 2021. For a discussion see András Kádár, 'Legislation adopted abolishing the Equal Treatment Authority and transferring its tasks to the Ombudsman' (EELN News Report, 10 February 2021).

[30] General Assembly, 'Principles relating to the Status of National Institutions (The Paris Principles)' (20 December 1993) Resolution 48/134; for a commentary on the Paris Principles see Gauthier de Beco and Rachel Murray, *Commentary on the Paris Principles on National Human Rights Institutions* (CUP 2015).

mechanisms, that is sufficiently independent and empowered, and that can make a genuine difference on the ground'.[31] While such an approach certainly has the advantage of creating synergies between the different areas of work, as well as operational advantages, including the saving of costs,[32] there are also a number of risks.[33]

Crowther and O'Cinneide draw attention to the different approaches of NHRIs as compared to Equality Bodies, consisting in a limited focus on supporting individual complaints among NHRIs, their focus on the public sector, and their different way of cooperating with civil society. While for Equality Bodies the partnership with civil society stands in the forefront, NHRIs conceive civil society more as information provider to improve their own monitoring work.[34] An Equinet report on the issue also identifies certain advantages, such as the strengthened voice of the body due to the dual mandate, but emphasizes that symmetry between the human rights-related and equality-related powers and resources is necessary.[35]

Crowley underlines that the two kinds of institutions differ also in the nature of the change they seek. While Equality Bodies are 'institutions for social change', NHRIs are seen as institutions that 'seek corrective change'. This is reflected in the mix of activities each of them pursues which has to be balanced out in any merger process. He finds, however, that '[i]t is not clear that this has been a concern in any of the merger processes to date. As a result, the approach to the equality and human rights mandate pursued by these merged bodies is not integrated and is unlikely to serve both human rights and equality objectives.'[36] Maybe even more importantly he points out that the rationale for mergers is often 'based on the assumption that equality is a human right. However, equality is only a human right where the aspiration is for formal equality. Once the aspiration for equality stretches to substantive

[31] Fundamental Rights Agency, 'National Human Rights Institutions in the EU Member States. Strengthening the fundamental rights architecture in the EU I' (n 28) 8.

[32] European Commission, 'Equality bodies and the implementation of the Commission Recommendation on Standards for Equality Bodies' (n 1) 6; Gay Moon, 'Enforcement Bodies' in Dagmar Schiek, Lisa Waddington, and Mark Bell (eds) *Cases, Materials and Text on National, Supranational and International Non-Discrimination Law* (Hart Publishing 2007) 876.

[33] Tamás Kádár, 'Equality Bodies: A European Phenomenon' [2018] International Journal of Discrimination and the Law 1–19, 8–9.

[34] Neil Crowther and Colm O'Cinneide, 'Bridging the Divide? Integrating the Functions of National Equality Bodies and National Human Rights Institutions in the European Union' (UCL Faculty of Laws, London 2013) vii–xi. Their analysis is based on six country studies on Belgium, Denmark, France, Great Britain, Ireland, and the Netherlands, which are available at https://www.ucl.ac.uk/laws/bridging-the-divide/country-studies.

[35] Equinet, 'Equality Bodies and National Human Rights Institutions: Making the Link to Maximise Impact. An Equinet Perspective' (2011) 12. In this sense, see also European Commission, 'Equality bodies and the implementation of the Commission Recommendation on Standards for Equality Bodies' (n 1) 6.

[36] Niall Crowley, 'Merging Mandates of Equality Bodies and National Human Rights Institutions—A Growing Trend' [2016] European Equality Law Review 34, 38.

equality such a claim is no longer valid.'[37] While some advances in this respect are discernable from the recent case law of the European Court of Human Rights (ECtHR),[38] it remains the case that a merger of bodies might result in the substantive equality side losing out if an integrated approach is not pursued.[39]

In Equinet's Working Paper on 'Developing Standards for Equality Bodies' the institutional structure features as one of the core areas for which standards would be useful. In that context, the issue of merged mandates is dealt with in Section 4.c., requiring, where such bodies exist:

i. A coherent legal basis and powers for all parts of the mandate.
ii. An adequacy of resources to implement all parts of the mandate and to secure an appropriate balancing of resources to ensure parity of focus across all parts of the mandate.
iii. An internal structure capable of ensuring a parity of focus across all parts of the mandate.
iv. A capacity to develop an integrated approach to all parts of the mandate, to the extent that this is possible and appropriate.
v. A multi-disciplinary competence across its staff.[40]

The question about stand-alone bodies or multi-mandate bodies was also discussed in an ECRI seminar with Equality Bodies concerning the revision of ECRI 's General Policy Recommendation No 2, dealing with Specialised Bodies in May 2017. There was no consensus among participants as to which of the options should be preferred. It was acknowledged that Equality Bodies come in different shapes and structures in different countries, there is no one size fits all solution, and that different national traditions need to be respected. Participants agreed, however, that in case of mergers it is essential that the 'equality mandate was not neglected or undermined'.[41] Indeed, in the adopted revision of GPR No 2, ECRI states that if the choice is made to designate a multi-mandate institution with the task of an Equality Body or merge such a body with a multi-mandate institution, the following points apply:

[37] ibid 40.

[38] See Chapter 1.2.

[39] For reflections on such an integrated approach, see Niall Crowley, 'Equality and Human Rights: An Integrated Approach' (Equality and Right Alliance 2015). Setting Standards for the Irish Equality and Human Rights Infrastructure Paper 3.

[40] Equinet, 'Developing Standards for Equality Bodies. An Equinet Working Paper' (n 22) 8.

[41] Michael Farrell, 'ECRI Seminar with National Specialised Bodies to Combat Racism and Intolerance (Equality Bodies): Revision of ECRI General Policy Recommendation No 2 on Specialised Bodies. Report and Conclusions' (ECRI, Strasbourg 23 and 24 May 2017) <https://www.coe.int/t/dghl/monitoring/ecri/activities/61-Seminar_national_specialised_bodies_2017/Conclusions.asp#TopOfPage>.

a. Legislation should explicitly set out the equality mandate of the institution.
b. Appropriate human and financial resources should be allocated to each mandate to ensure an appropriate focus on the equality mandate.
c. Governing, advisory, and management structures should be organised in a manner that provides for clear leadership, promotion and visibility of the equality mandate.
d. Reporting arrangements should give adequate prominence to the concerns arising and work carried out under the equality mandate.[42]

The similarity of the language used by the ECRI in its GPR No 2 and in the Equinet document clearly indicates the influence that the latter had on the former.

According to the European Commission, about half of the Member States have multi-mandate bodies and of these only half actively manage their multiple mandates, whereas in a few Member States, 'the equality mandate has lost priority'. Good practice includes (quite similarly to what is requested by the ECRI) assigning the equality mandate to a separate department with dedicated resources and leadership and an annual report focusing on the equality mandate.[43]

Related to the question of the institutional set-up is that of the discrimination grounds that Equality Bodies are mandated to cover. As a minimum, regarding the Directives focused on in this research, they must cover the ground of race or ethnic origin. Only the Spanish Council for the Elimination of Racial or Ethnic Discrimination is confined to this ground. Austria, Croatia, and Malta have separate bodies for the ground of disability. In Latvia and Poland, the grounds to be covered by the Equality Body are not specified in the relevant legislation, which leads to the assumption that any ground can be covered by these bodies. Overall, in all but three Member States all the grounds listed in Article 19 TFEU are covered.[44] In addition to contributing to cost-effectiveness, advantages connected to having multi-ground bodies involve the possibility of addressing the intersections between discrimination grounds and engaging in strategic litigation. These advantages play out only if the financial resources and staffing of such integrated Equality Bodies are such as to allow them to efficiently fulfil their mandate.

The Commission's Recommendations on Standards for Equality Bodies encourage states to go beyond their obligations under the RED and the various gender-related Directives and to 'consider designating an equality body to cover the

[42] ECRI, 'General Policy Recommendation No 2: Equality Bodies to Combat Racism and Intolerance at National Level' (n 23) para 7.

[43] European Commission, 'Equality bodies and the implementation of the Commission Recommendation on Standards for Equality Bodies' (n 1) 6.

[44] European network of legal experts in gender equality and non-discrimination, 'A comparative analysis of non-discrimination law in Europe: 2020' (n 25) 100–08. See also European Commission, 'Equality bodies and the implementation of the Commission Recommendation on Standards for Equality Bodies' (n 1) 4.

discrimination' for all grounds included in the EED.[45] It thereby tries to remedy the fact that the EED does not ask for the establishment of such bodies. Furthermore, it recommends the provision of a mandate that covers, for all these grounds, the areas of employment and occupation, access to and supply of goods and services, education, social protection, and social advantages,[46] thus anticipating not only the discrimination grounds but also the material scope such bodies would be required to cover if the horizontal directive proposed in 2008 is eventually adopted. The ECRI's GPR No 2 highlight that if an Equality Body has a multi-ground mandate 'it is necessary to ensure a clear and appropriate focus on each of the grounds covered and on the intersections between them'.[47]

Where separate Equality Bodies exist for different grounds, ECRI's GPR No 2 and the Commission's Recommendation concur in their view that regular and effective coordination between them should be enabled by Member States, inter alia, to make sure they develop a common and consistent interpretation of non-discrimination principles and legislation.[48]

Finally, there is the issue of the choices countries with a federal or decentralized state structure have taken when transposing Article 13 RED. In Austria, in addition to the 'federal' Equality Body, nine such bodies to promote equal treatment in the areas of competence of the nine *Länder* have been established. In addition to these sub-state bodies with separate competences, the National Equality Body has four regional offices, thereby reaching out to the more peripheral *Länder*. While Equality Bodies at sub-state level contribute to accessibility for victims of discrimination, there is also the risk of creating an overly complex system which makes it difficult for a victim of discrimination to know which body to approach for help.[49]

Belgium has chosen another approach in this respect. With the signature of a Cooperation Agreement between state, regions, and communities in 2013, the formerly federal Centre for Equal Opportunities and Opposition to Racism and Discrimination (Unia) has been turned into an inter-federal Centre. It has been operational since March 2014 and is competent for anti-discrimination legislation adopted at the regional and federal levels. Unia has its main office in Brussels and thirteen so-called 'local contact points' in Flanders and four in Wallonia.[50] However, in 2019, the Flemish government announced its intention to set up its own Equality Body. Unia fears that this might not only lead to a lack of clarity and confusion for citizens as to the competences of the separate bodies but that it will

[45] European Commission, 'Commission Recommendation on Standards for Equality Bodies' (n 19) point 1 in Chapter II, 1.1.1.

[46] ibid point 2 in Chapter II, 1.1.1.

[47] ECRI, 'General Policy Recommendation No 2: Equality Bodies to Combat Racism and Intolerance at National Level' (n 23) para 6.

[48] European Commission, 'Commission Recommendation on Standards for Equality Bodies' (n 19) point 1 in Chapter II, 1.3.; ECRI, 'General Policy Recommendation No 2: Equality Bodies to Combat Racism and Intolerance at National Level' (n 23) para 9.

[49] See in this sense, EELN, Country Report Austria, 2020, 62.

[50] EELN, Country Report Belgium, 2020, 109.

also negatively affect its financial capacity. The decentralization can be executed in 2023 at the earliest, when the Cooperation Agreement of 2013 terminates.[51]

The situation in Germany, another federal state, is different in that it set up a central Equality Body (the Federal Anti-discrimination Agency) but has not established regional offices in the *Bundesländer*. Several *Länder* have set up their own specialized agencies. This situation has been viewed critically by some, including the ECRI,[52] also in light of the findings of the research carried out on behalf of the European Commission[53] and the ECRI's GPR No 2,[54] who both suggest that the existence of such offices eases the accessibility of the Equality Body for victims of discrimination. The Commission also recommends that Member States, 'where this is necessary for geographical or other reasons', consider enabling Equality Bodies to set up regional offices.[55] Considering that IT literacy and access to digital tools still remains limited for some individuals from vulnerable groups, physical presence remains crucial even in times of digitalization.[56]

In the UK, two commissions exist, one for Great Britain and one for Northern Ireland. The British Equality and Human Rights Commission 'has devolved authorities in Wales and in Scotland and there is a Scottish Human Rights Commission which shares the human rights remit of the EHRC in Scotland'.[57]

Whatever the institutional setting chosen for the Equality Bodies, there is a common understanding within stakeholders involved in such bodies that what matters is that they can effectively fulfil their tasks in an independent manner. This is reflected in Equinet's Working Paper on Developing Standards for Equality Bodies, which emphasizes the need for standards regarding Equality Bodies' mandate, complete independence, and effectiveness, while the points related to the institutional structure often link back to these fields. Similarly, participants in ECRI seminar on the revision of GPR No 2 agreed 'that protecting the core attributes of Equality Bodies and ensuring their independence, the integrity of their mandate, adequate funding and resources, and continued visibility was more important than which structure was adopted'.[58]

51 On the reasons for the split, connected to political attacks on Unia's independence, see EELN, Country Report Belgium, 2020, 102.

52 ECRI, 'Report on Germany (fifth monitoring cycle), adopted on 5 December 2013' CRI(2014)2, paras 20–22; see also Sabine Berghahn, Micha Klapp and Alexander Tischbirek, Evaluation des Allgemeinen Gleichbehandlungsgesetzes (erstellt im Auftrag der Antidiskriminierungsstelle des Bundes) (Nomos 2016), 173–76.

53 Margit Ammer and others, 'Study on Equality Bodies set up under Directives 2000/43/EC, 2004/113/EC and 2006/54/EC. Synthesis Report' (Human European Consultancy in partnership with the Ludwig Boltzmann Institute of Human Rights, October 2010) 8.

54 ECRI, 'General Policy Recommendation No 2: Equality Bodies to Combat Racism and Intolerance at National Level' (n 23) para 40(b).

55 European Commission, 'Commission Recommendation on Standards for Equality Bodies' (n 19) point 5 in Chapter II, 1.2.3.

56 European Commission, 'Equality bodies and the implementation of the Commission Recommendation on Standards for Equality Bodies' (n 1) 22.

57 EELN, Country Report United Kingdom, 2020, 59.

58 Farrell (n 41).

This section does, therefore, not analyse in more detail specific national models, considering that it would be of limited relevance for the main purposes of this part of the book: namely, the pooling of results potentially leading to the identification of good practices others could learn from, and the elaboration of structure, process, and outcome indicators that could inform pre- and post-accession monitoring. Instead, the following sections will look into the independence of Equality Bodies and the effective implementation of their task to provide independent assistance to victims of discrimination in pursuing their complaints.

5.2 Independence of Equality Bodies

5.2.1 Introduction and Conceptual Clarification

As mentioned above, the text of Article 13 RED has been toned down as compared to the initial Commission proposal with regard to the issue of independence. While the Commission proposal, as with the Starting Line Group's proposal, provided for the establishment of 'independent bodies', the requirement of independence now appears only with regard to the execution of their tasks. This change in the text of Directive suggests that there was a shift from requesting an independent status for the overall institution to requiring it only to function independently.[59] If one translates this into thinking in terms of structural, process, and outcome indicators, this means that the Member States are only required to set up a body in whichever way they decide (structural indicator) and to ensure that it performs its tasks in an independent manner (outcome indicator). A structural indicator is, thus, not required to provide information about the independent status of an Equality Body (structural independence). Process indicators are completely lacking. While one can agree that it is legitimate (and perfectly in line with a reflexive and experimentalist governance approach) to leave it to the states to decide on how to secure an outcome (independent performance of tasks), it would be negligent not to assess whether the ways chosen by the states (both in terms of legislation and in terms of practical implementation thereof) really contribute to reaching the required outcome. In practical terms, a state does not necessarily have to directly intervene in the day-to-day work of an Equality Body to unduly influence its behaviour. By establishing the body within a ministerial structure, or cutting funds to Equality Bodies openly criticizing a government, or placing a person in charge of the governing structure of the Equality Body with doubtful dedication to, or expertise in, the issue of discrimination, the independence of such a body must be in doubt, even though a state can still claim to have formally complied with the

[59] Kutsal Yesilkagit and Berend Snijders, *Between Impartiality and Responsiveness: Equality Bodies and Practices of Independence* (Equinet, Brussels 2008) 6.

requirements under the Directive. Therefore, it is claimed that in order to secure the independent execution of the tasks (policy independence), it is important to assess not only whether a state is formally compliant by setting up a body, but also whether the Equality Body is granted independent legal status (structural indicator, giving information on the structural independence), what appointment procedures look like, and whether financial and managerial independence is granted (process indicators).

Along these lines of thinking, Equinet finds that the Directives 'do not guarantee complete independence'.[60] In its Working Paper on Standards for Equality Bodies it nevertheless dedicated a focus to the issue of independence in the broader sense suggested above. The ECRI's revised GPR No 2 also approach the issue of independence in this way. They request, for instance, that Equality Bodies 'should be fully independent at *institutional* and operational level'[61] and dedicate substantial space to independent leadership[62] as well as financial and managerial independence, including the possibility of independently deciding on their internal structure, the management of financial and human resources, the hiring of their own staff while avoiding as much as possible secondments from public sector institutions, and the provision of separate premises.[63]

Apart from looking at the approaches of Equinet and the ECRI to the issue of independence, it is of relevance to see what kind of criteria for independence the Paris Principles lay down for National Human Rights Institutions universally.[64] It is understood that neither the ECRI's recommendations nor the Paris Principles and their interpretation are binding on Member States with regard to their Equality Bodies established under Directive 2000/43/EC. Considering, however, that the criteria for determining 'independence' are not specified in the EU Directives,[65] Equality Bodies do view and define their own concept of independence by borrowing from the ECRI's recommendations and the Paris Principles. Also, it has been assumed 'that the principles of the latter documents are further specifications of the "necessary arrangements" that member states are required to take'[66] for bodies for the promotion of equal treatment, even if the wording of 'make the necessary arrangement' appears only in Article 12 of Directive 2004/113/EC, but not in the RED. It has further been considered that since all EU Member States are also members of the United Nations (UN) and the Council of Europe (CoE) they should be guided by

60 Equinet, 'Developing Standards for Equality Bodies. An Equinet Working Paper' (n 22) 2.

61 ECRI, 'General Policy Recommendation No 2: Equality Bodies to Combat Racism and Intolerance at National Level' (n 23) para 22. Emphasis added.

62 ibid paras 23–26.

63 ibid paras 27–29, and paras 100–03 of the Explanatory Memorandum.

64 General Assembly (n 30).

65 Fundamental Rights Agency, 'National Human Rights Institutions in the EU Member States. Strengthening the fundamental rights architecture in the EU I' (n 28) 11.

66 Yesilkagit and Snijders (n 59) 19 and 41.

these documents when implementing Article 13 RED.[67] The country reports of the European Network of Legal Experts in Gender Equality and Non-Discrimination often refer to ECRI reports and to whether an Equality Body can be considered as independent against the background of ECRI's GPR No 2.

The Commission's Recommendation, limited by the wording of the Directive, restricts itself to requesting that Member States 'should ensure that equality bodies can carry out their functions … in an independent and effective way'.[68] It nevertheless acknowledges that, for instance, 'their place in the overall administrative structure' as well as 'the procedures for appointing and dismissing staff, including persons holding leadership positions' play a role in this context,[69] thus admitting that to achieve independence in carrying out its task it might be necessary to assess whether the Equality Body as such is independent. The Network of Legal Experts even interpreted the Recommendation as calling 'for the "independence" of equality bodies, although the Directive only requires the independent exercise of their functions'.[70] In fact, the Commission dedicated substantial space to the discussion of independence in its report on the implementation of the Recommendation, assessing issues such as the legal status and place in the administrative structure, budgetary independence, rules on leadership and accountability, as well as the political context and public opinion.[71]

It therefore seems that the Commission has come a long way in sharpening its take on the independence of Equality Bodies. In building this understanding, it can be assumed that the Paris Principles and ECRI's GPR No 2 have been key, as they provide in detail how such independence can be achieved. These two documents, together with the Equinet document on standards, are therefore taken as the guidelines to identify the areas that will be covered in the comparative legal and practical sections and for which possible indicators will be proposed.[72]

According to the Paris Principles, there are four factors contributing to the independence of NHRIs: first, NHRIs should be established by law or a constitutional

[67] Rikki Holtmaat, 'Catalysts for Change: Equality Bodies according to Directive 2000/43/EC' (European Network of Legal Experts in the Non-discrimination Field, 2006) 33.

[68] European Commission, 'Commission Recommendation on Standards for Equality Bodies' (n 19) point 2, Chaper I.

[69] ibid point 1, Chaper II, 1.2.1.

[70] European network of legal experts in gender equality and non-discrimination, 'A comparative analysis of non-discrimination law in Europe: 2020' (n 25) 99.

[71] European Commission, 'Equality bodies and the implementation of the Commission Recommendation on Standards for Equality Bodies' (n 1) 16–19.

[72] Recently, Equinet has also published a set of indicators on independence. See Equinet, 'Equinet Project on Standards for Equality Bodies. Independence—Indicators' (nd) <https://equineteurope.org/what-are-equality-bodies/standards-for-equality-bodies/>. Other interesting documents in this context are Venice Commission, 'Compilation of Venice Commission Opinions Concerning the Ombudsman Institutions' (5 February 2016) CDL-PI(2016)001; Venice Commission, 'Opinion No 897/2017—Principles on the Protection and Promotion of the Ombudsman Institution (Venice Principles)' (3 May 2019); Committee of Ministers, 'Recommendation CM/Rec(2019)6 of the Committee of Ministers to member States on the development of the Ombudsman institution' (16 October 2019).

act;[73] second, their composition should be such as to ensure the pluralist representation of society; third, there should be adequate funding by which its own staff and premises can be secured and they should not 'be subject to financial control which might affect its independence'; and finally, the appointment of members should take place by an official act ensuring the duration of the mandate to secure stability of such mandates, 'without which there can be no real independence'.[74] The focus is thus much more on institutional aspects of independence as compared to the approach of the RED that refers more to independent functioning. In the most recent General Observations of the Sub-Committee on Accreditation (SCA) of the Global Alliance of NHRI (GANHRI, formerly known as International Coordinating Committee of NHRIs—ICC) those points were all identified as being 'essential requirements of the Paris Principles' as opposed to proven practices that, from the experience of the SCA, would promote compliance with the Paris Principles.[75]

In terms of pluralist representation, the Paris Principles require the presence of or effective cooperation with representatives of NGOs dealing with human rights and racial discrimination, different trends of philosophical and religious thought, academic and other experts, parliament and governmental departments. With regard to the latter, the 2017 SCA GANHRI General Observations clarify that governmental representatives or members of parliament should not be members or participate in decision making within NHRIs. Where they are represented, they should not exceed the number of other members and legislation should make clear that they participate only in an advisory capacity. This should ensure any interference in the assessment of the human rights situation and decision on strategic priorities will be avoided.[76] Regarding the selection and appointment process, which for the GANHRI SCA is of 'critical importance … in ensuring pluralism and independence', it emphasizes that it must be a transparent process, that it requires broad consultation throughout the whole process, that vacancies must be advertised widely in order to stimulate candidates from a broad range of societal groups, and that members serve in their individual capacity.[77]

Similarly, ECRI's GPR No 2 recommend that the 'leadership, advisory bodies, senior management, and staff of equality bodies should, as far as possible, reflect the diversity of society at large and be gender balanced'.[78] Diversity and gender balance will help, so the Explanatory Memorandum, understanding the situation of

[73] 'Creation by an instrument of the Executive is not adequate to ensure permanency and independence'. ICC SCA, General Observations of March 2009, 1.1.; and in this vein also GANHRI, 'General Observations of the Sub-Committee on Accreditation' adopted by the GANHRI Bureau at its Meeting held in Geneva, Switzerland, 6 March 2017, 7.

[74] General Assembly (n 30) A(2) and B(1–3).

[75] GANHRI (n 73) 3.

[76] ibid 29–30.

[77] ICC SCA, General Observations of March 2009, 2.2.; and ibid 26.

[78] ECRI, 'General Policy Recommendation No 2: Equality Bodies to Combat Racism and Intolerance at National Level' (n 23) para 38.

the groups exposed to discrimination and support the interaction with them.[79] The GPR also place great importance on a transparent, competency-based, and participatory selection process and require that the executive has no decisive influence in any of its stages.[80]

Regarding adequate funding, the GANHRI SCA requires 'as a minimum' that such funding should allow for paying salaries to staff members (comparable to public service salaries) and, where appropriate, remuneration for Commissioners, the establishment of communication systems, and, of course, adequate premises. Such premises should be accessible to the wider community, including persons with disabilities. In terms of accessibility, the General Observations state that this should be, 'where possible, … further enhanced by establishing a permanent regional presence'.[81] In addition to the above, funding should be such as to ensure the fulfilment of the NHRI's mandate. The GANHRI SCA holds that it is the responsibility of the state to adequately finance an NHRI and therefore external funding should not constitute the core funding of such institutions. It recognizes, however, that in particular circumstances, such as post-conflict situations, international community will be needed to secure adequate funding. It further highlights that there should be complete autonomy in deciding how the money is spent while complying with 'financial accountability requirements applicable to other independent agencies of the State'.[82]

While all the above are essential requirements of the Paris Principles, the Observations regarding the recruitment of staff are considered as proven practice to promote compliance with these Principles. In this regard, the GANHRI SCA notes that experience shows that it helps the independence of the NHRI if it is 'legislatively empowered to determine the staffing structure, the skills required to fulfil the NHRI's mandate, set other appropriate criteria (such as diversity), and select their staff … according to an open, transparent and merit-based selection process that ensures pluralism'.[83]

Adequate funding is also a central element in ECRI's GPR No 2. It should be such as to allow the Equality Body to implement its functions and competences with a real impact. Arbitrary or disproportionate reduction of funds should not take place and additional competences should be accompanied by additional funding. Equality Bodies should have the right to raise funds from sources other than the state in and outside the country. They should be able to independently manage their resources, recruit and appoint their own staff, and have their own

[79] ibid para 115 of the Explanatory Memorandum.

[80] ibid para 23. The Commission also places great importance on a transparent and competence-base selection procedure. European Commission, 'Equality bodies and the implementation of the Commission Recommendation on Standards for Equality Bodies' (n 1) 18.

[81] GANHRI (n 73) 32.

[82] ICC SCA, General Observations of March 2009, 2.6.–7.; and ibid 32–34.

[83] ibid 45.

premises. Persons in leadership positions should be remunerated at a suitable level. Equality Bodies should further be subject to the financial accountability rules applicable to public authorities.[84]

To secure a stable mandate and thus add to the independence of an NHRI, GANHRI SCA has a preference for full-time membership in an NHRI. Provisions for dismissals should be laid down in law and 'not be allowed on solely the discretion of appointing authorities'. Both these points are considered a proven practice to promote a stable mandate and thus, independence of the institution.[85] Similarly, ECRI's GPR No 2 provide that 'persons holding leadership positions should benefit from functional immunity, be protected against threats and coercion and have appropriate safeguards against arbitrary dismissal or the arbitrary non-renewal of an appointment where renewal would be the norm'.[86] Adequate remuneration and an appointment for an appropriate time period should further contribute to the stability of the mandate.[87]

The areas covered by both the Paris Principles and ECRI's GPR No 2, are reflected also in the initiative taken by Equinet to define standards for Equality Bodies. Equinet also emphasizes the importance of the mandate being defined in law, in addition to the body having its own legal personality, separate from the government. It also points to the requirement for the governance structure to reflect the diversity and pluralism within society and the necessity of a transparent appointment procedure. In terms of financing, Equinet's proposal emphasized that an Equality Body must be able to deal with its staff and financial resources only on the basis of its own strategic decisions. While the Paris Principles clearly place the primary responsibility for adequate financing on the state, Equinet is also concerned to ensure that Equality Bodies can obtain external funding.[88]

In addition to legal entrenchment, pluralist composition and transparent appointment, and stable mandate, as well as adequate funding and budget autonomy, standards and recommendations include the absence of any external interference with the Equality Body in carrying out its tasks and their capacity to cooperate at the international level, with other organizations, and with groups experiencing discrimination to build trust and confidence.[89] On a similar note, another Equinet publication described independence as meaning that Equality Bodies can, without

[84] ECRI, 'General Policy Recommendation No 2: Equality Bodies to Combat Racism and Intolerance at National Level' (n 23) paras 26–29, 32.

[85] ICC SCA, General Observations of March 2009, 2.8–9.; and GANHRI (n 73) 39–42.

[86] ECRI, 'General Policy Recommendation No 2: Equality Bodies to Combat Racism and Intolerance at National Level' (n 23) para 24.

[87] ibid para 26.

[88] See Equinet, 'Developing Standards for Equality Bodies. An Equinet Working Paper' (n 22) and Equinet, 'Equinet Project on Standards for Equality Bodies. Independence—Indicators' (n 72).

[89] Equinet, 'Developing Standards for Equality Bodies. An Equinet Working Paper' (n 22) 5–6; ECRI, 'General Policy Recommendation No 2: Equality Bodies to Combat Racism and Intolerance at National Level' (n 23) paras 9 and 22; European Commission, 'Commission Recommendation on Standards for Equality Bodies' (n 19) Chapter II, 1.3.

interference from any side, 'identify their own priorities and implement their powers as they deem most appropriate' and thus decide without interference what kind of use they make of their human and financial resources.[90] This aspect of independence is referring to the Equality Bodies' independent functioning (called here 'policy independence') and will be dealt with in sections 5.3 and 5.4.

On the basis of what the documents discussed above have identified as contributing to the independence of an Equality Body as such, the next sub-section 5.2.2 will look into the following issues: what is the legal status of the Equality Body? Does it have its own legal personality in the form of a stand-alone body or as part of a broader structure, or is it attached to a ministry? A second issue to be looked at in more detail relates to the composition and appointment procedures of governing structures and staff. Questions to be dealt with in this context are: Are the appointment procedures transparent and inclusive? How is the stability of the mandate ensured? Where the Equality Body is a collegiate board, does the composition reflect the diversity in society? How is the staff selected and managed? Can the Equality Body decide on the basis of its own strategic choices and priorities where to allocate its staff? A third issue to be discussed relates to adequate financing and spending autonomy, sources of financing, and financing trends. In this context it will also be important to see whether Equality Bodies can allocate their resources according to their own priorities. The sub-section 5.2.2 will look into the formal commitment of states to establish independent bodies but also the efforts they undertake in the above fields to ensure de facto independence. Thereafter, some lessons will be drawn from this comparative overview and indicators to measure the level of independence proposed.

5.2.2 Legal Transposition and Practical Implementation

Some research with regard to the independence of Equality Bodies has already been carried out, most importantly that commissioned by Equinet and the European Commission through the European Network of Legal Experts in the non-discrimination field.[91] The legal analysis in this chapter will draw from the findings of this research and substantiate it with up to date material from the country reports to the Network of Legal Experts in gender equality and non-discrimination.[92] The information regarding practical implementation is in part drawn from the

[90] Equinet, 'Equality Bodies: Current Challenges: An Equinet Perspective' (2012) 13.

[91] See in particular Holtmaat (n 67) 31–45; Yesilkagit and Snijders (n 59); and Ammer and others (n 53) 105–20; Equinet, 'Equality Bodies: Current Challenges' (n 90) 13–15.

[92] The yearly country reports of the Network of Legal Experts contain a specific section on independence and the findings are summarized in the comparative report. For the most recent one, see European network of legal experts in gender equality and non-discrimination, 'A comparative analysis of non-discrimination law in Europe: 2020' (n 25) 112–13.

same sources, in addition to information available from the Equinet webpage on its members.[93] In the case studies contained in sections 5.3 and 5.4, the question of independence is looked at in depth, inter alia, on the basis of interviews with representatives of Equality Bodies and of non-governmental organizations (NGOs). The findings derived from these case studies further inform the conclusions on good practices and challenges as well as the development of the proposed indicators.

The question of the legal status of Equality Bodies has been discussed in detail in section 5.1. This has shown that depending on the different national cultures a variety of approaches exists, ranging from the setting up of either one or more stand-alone institutions with separate legal personality dealing with one or more discrimination grounds, to designating a national human rights institution or ombudsoffice such as the national Equality Body, or merging various bodies into a larger institution dealing with a broader range of issues. Most EU countries have chosen one of these options, and as mentioned above, as long as these bodies can effectively and independently carry out all their tasks, keeping the equality mandate strong and visible, the exact structure is considered less relevant.

One approach chosen by some countries should, however, be looked at more closely. These countries have embedded their Equality Bodies into their ministerial structure. This is the case in Austria, Finland, Germany, Italy, Spain, and Sweden. In practice, this decision has different repercussions on independence. In Germany,[94] for instance, the Federal Anti-discrimination Agency is associated with the Ministry of Family Affairs, Senior Citizens, Women and Youth. Due to the requirement of independence it is, however, considered that this association is of an organizational nature. The director of the Agency is not bound to any directives from the ministry and is not under the supervisory control of the ministry. The director of the Agency is appointed by the Minister of Family Affairs, Senior Citizens, Women and Youth upon proposal by the government. A public call for this position is not provided for by legislation.[95] Notwithstanding all these formal shortcomings, the independence of the Federal Anti-Discrimination Agency has not been questioned, for instance in ECRI reports.[96] Nevertheless, there are also calls for providing it with a separate legal personality with the aim of enhancing its independence.[97]

A similar situation exists in Sweden, where the Equality Ombudsman works under the Minister for Gender Equality (with responsibility for anti-discrimination and anti-segregation), which comes under the Ministry of Employment. It is possible for the government to give instructions to the Equality Ombudsman via

[93] See Equinet's members' page at https://equineteurope.org/what-are-equality-bodies/european-directory-of-equality-bodies/.

[94] For details on this case see the case study at 5.4.3.3.

[95] Berghahn, Klapp, and Tischbirek (n 52) 177–78.

[96] See, for instance, ECRI, 'Report on Germany (fifth monitoring cycle) adopted on 5 December 2013' CRI (2014)2.

[97] Berghahn, Klapp, and Tischbirek (n 52) 176–80.

regulation letter, which have become increasingly detailed. According to the independent expert on Sweden in the EELN, the Ombudsman's 'independence can be questioned', although the institution is established by law, and the legislative materials refer, inter alia, to the Paris Principles.[98]

In Italy, the National Office Against Racial Discrimination (UNAR) is embedded within the Department of Equal Opportunities of the Presidency of the Council of Ministers. The Director of UNAR is appointed by the prime minister or a minister on his behalf. The staff is mostly drawn from government departments and changes of government lead to the exchange of key staff. This situation has been criticized by both CERD and ECRI in their reports on Italy.[99] EELN's independent expert on Italy reports on cases exemplifying the resulting lack of independence. For instance, an awareness-raising campaign on sexual orientation, initiated by UNAR, was stopped by a decision of the government, after it was attacked by catholic organizations and members of parliament. On another occasion the sending of a letter signed by UNAR's director to a member of parliament, addressing her racist comments towards members of the Muslim community and inviting her not to base her messages on stereotypes, had even more serious consequences. The director was dismissed and the contracts of fifteen external independent experts were not renewed.[100]

In Austria, the Equality Body is attached to the Chancellor's Office and although it appears to perform its functions independently, it is not a vibrant and proactive actor in the Austrian non-discrimination scene.

Overall, one can conclude that even if there are examples where embedded Equality Bodies function in an independent way, it is clearly preferable for them to have a separate legal personality, whether as stand-alone body or integrated into a larger institution, such as an NHRI. Indeed, ECRI's GPR No 2 recommend setting up Equality Bodies as 'separate legal entities placed outside the executive and legislature'.[101]

When it comes to the composition and appointment procedures of governing structures a variety of approaches in different countries can be observed. Top positions are in most cases filled by appointment by the government, a minister, or the president, and less often, but becoming increasingly the case, by parliament.[102] Only in rare cases are outside actors such as academic institutions and NGOs

98 EELN, Country Report Sweden, 2020, 82.

99 See CERD, 'Concluding observations on the combined nineteenth and twentieth periodic reports of Italy' (17 February 2017) CERD/C/ITA/CO/19–20, paras 12–13; and ECRI, 'Report on Italy (fifth monitoring cycle) adopted on 18 March 2016' CRI(2016)19, paras 24–29.

100 EELN, Country Report Italy, 2017, 80; EELN, Country Report Italy, 2020, 55–56.

101 ECRI, 'General Policy Recommendation No 2: Equality Bodies to Combat Racism and Intolerance at National Level' (n 23) para 2. See also European Commission, 'Equality bodies and the implementation of the Commission Recommendation on Standards for Equality Bodies' (n 1) 19.

102 See EELN, Country Reports, 2020; see also Equinet, 'Equality Bodies: Current Challenges' (n 90) 15; and European Commission, 'Equality bodies and the implementation of the Commission Recommendation on Standards for Equality Bodies' (n 1) 17.

involved. The Danish Institute of Human Rights (DIHR) operates a very interesting appointment procedure, where board members are appointed by various institutions: four members are appointed by four Danish universities,[103] two by the Danish Conference of Rectors, one by the employees of the DIHR, and six by the Danish Council for Human Rights.[104] Unique to this model is the involvement of the staff from the DIHR. The appointment procedure of the Administrative Board of the Slovak Institute for Human Rights, consisting of nine members, is also quite inclusive. Besides one member each appointed by the President of the Slovak Republic, the Chair of the National Council, and the Minister of Labour, Social Affairs and Family, the Public Defender of Rights also has the right to appoint one member and the deans of the faculties of law of four universities have the right to appoint four members to the Board between them. And finally, the Prime Minister of the Government of the Slovak Republic can appoint another member but he/she has to follow the proposal of NGOs.[105]

NGOs are also involved in the appointment procedure for the Spanish Council for the Elimination of Racial or Ethnic Discrimination, an institution attached to the Ministry of Health, Social Services and Equality through the Institute for Women and Equal Opportunities, but not part of the ministry's hierarchical structure. Ten out of twenty-eight members in the Council are appointed by organizations representing interests related to people's racial or ethnic origins. In addition, four members are appointed by social partners. However, the remaining fourteen positions are filled by members of the public administration upon appointment by ministries with responsibilities in areas referred to by Article 3(1) RED, by autonomous regional and local authorities. Half of the members are thus appointed by government or sub-state institutions and belong to public administration. They have full speaking and voting rights, which is not in line with the Paris Principles. Notwithstanding the relatively good representation of civil society actors, the independence of this body is not secured.[106]

Similarly, the composition of senate members in the Austrian Equal Treatment Commission has been viewed critically, given that they are appointed exclusively by government and social partners from within their employees.[107] Although legally they do their work in the Commission in an individual capacity, the independent expert of the EELN pointed out that 'the image is that the Commission

[103] The University of Copenhagen, the University of Aarhus, the University of Southern Denmark, and the University of Aalborg.

[104] EELN, Country Report Denmark, 2020, 76.

[105] EELN, Country Report Slovakia, 2020, 91. The EELN expert questions the independence of the Slovak Equality Body. EELN, Country Report Slovakia, 2020, 89–92.

[106] See in this sense also, CERD, 'Concluding observations of the Committee on the Elimination of Racial Discrimination' (8 April 2011) CERD/C/ESP/CO/18–20, para 9; ECRI, 'Report on Spain (fifth monitoring cycle) adopted on 5 December 2017' CRI(2018)2, paras 23–27; as well as EELN, Country Report Spain, 2020, 81.

[107] For details on this case see the case study at 5.3.3.3.

consists of persons sent by institutions to represent those institution's attitudes and political opinions'.[108]

Equinet qualified it as good practice if Commissioners, Ombudspersons, or members of collegiate boards are appointed by parliament. Their report considers such a process 'in principle independent of the state administration or any specific political entity'.[109] Parliament appoints the members of the governing structure in Belgium,[110] Croatia, the Czech Republic, Estonia,[111] Greece, Latvia, Lithuania, Poland, Romania, and Slovenia. Parliaments also play a role in the appointment of Equality Body members in France, Ireland, and Luxembourg by way of consultation or nomination. In Bulgaria, five of the nine members are appointed by parliament, and four by the president.[112] That parliamentary appointment is not necessarily a guarantee for independence is shown by the example from Romania, where civil society has expressed concern over nearly every round of appointments.[113] According to Articles 23 and 24 of the Antidiscrimination Act, the nine members of the steering board of the National Council for Combating Discrimination (NCCD) are appointed in a plenary session of the two chambers of parliament upon a joint proposal by six specialized committees following a hearing of all candidates in front of the committees. The main points of concern from civil society organizations regard the lack of professional experience in the field of human rights required by the law, that in most cases the persons backed by political parties are appointed with independent experts having very little chance of even being nominated by the committees. In one case, the committees even organized an additional hearing for a candidate backed by a particular parliamentary group, who had been heard previously but not entered on the shortlist. As a result of the additional hearing, the candidate was included on the list and the only independent expert was not appointed.[114]

Overall it appears that the main recommendation of ECRI in this context, namely that persons holding leadership positions 'should be selected and appointed by transparent, competency-based and participatory procedures' with the executive not playing a decisive role in any stage of the selection process[115] is not

[108] EELN, Country Report Austria, 2020, 65.

[109] Equinet, 'Equality Bodies: Current Challenges' (n 90) 15. See also ECRI, 'General Policy Recommendation No 2: Equality Bodies to Combat Racism and Intolerance at National Level' (n 23) para 95 of the Explanatory Memorandum.

[110] Ten members are appointed by the federal parliament, ten (plus one) by the parliaments of the regions and communities.

[111] Regarding the Chancellor of Justice, upon proposal by the president.

[112] EELN, Country Report Bulgaria, 2020, 73.

[113] For details on this case see the case study at 5.3.3.1.

[114] EELN, Country Report Romania, 2020, 79f. The 2017 report (110) also writes about the initial hearing for the seventeen candidates only taking about half an hour.

[115] ECRI, 'General Policy Recommendation No 2: Equality Bodies to Combat Racism and Intolerance at National Level' (n 23) para 23, and para 95 of the Explanatory Memorandum.

really fulfilled.[116] Problems pertain to the fact that only a few countries, such as, for instance, Ireland and Slovenia, provide for a public call for applications. NGOs are rarely involved in nominations or appointments. Transparency and participation in the appointment procedure could therefore be enhanced in most cases. While competence in the field of non-discrimination is laid down as a prerequisite for appointment by much of the legislation, the fact that in many cases the executive does in the end play a decisive role in the selection process at least allows for political considerations to outweigh competency-based criteria. The recommendation for leadership to reflect the diversity of society at large[117] does not appear to play a central role in the appointment procedures in most countries. It is questionable whether the very cautious wording of the Commission's Recommendations on Standards for Equality Bodies, requesting that states have a 'particular focus on procedures for appointing … staff, including persons holding leadership positions',[118] will manage to change this situation.

A stable mandate has been considered by both the Paris Principles and ECRI's GPR No 2 to be another prerequisite for independence. In terms of length of mandates, ECRI's recommendations suggest a length of four to five years with the possibility of renewal, or a longer term without such possibility.[119] Most statutes provide that members of Equality Bodies hold their position for five to six years. Only in a few cases is the mandate longer, such as in Croatia, where the Ombudsman has a mandate of eight years, renewable once. This provides the body with substantial stability. However, if the body, for whatever reason, does not perform in an independent way, it is blocked for a relatively long period. At the other extreme, members of the National Commission for the Promotion of Equality in Malta hold their mandate for only two years, which, although renewable, might be too short to make an impact and secure independence.[120] Another approach which does not appear to support the independence of the body, is the one chosen by Germany. Here, the mandate of the head of the Federal Anti-Discrimination Agency is connected to the legislative period of the *Bundestag*, which could raise concerns about providing each incoming government with the opportunity to select an agreeable head. Even if it appears that the legal provisions granting the head independence are well respected, such a regulation cannot be regarded as exemplary practice.

[116] The same conclusion is drawn in European Commission, 'Equality bodies and the implementation of the Commission Recommendation on Standards for Equality Bodies' (n 1) 18.

[117] ECRI, 'General Policy Recommendation No 2: Equality Bodies to Combat Racism and Intolerance at National Level' (n 23) para 38, and para 115 of the Explanatory Memorandum.

[118] European Commission, 'Commission Recommendation on Standards for Equality Bodies' (n 19) point 1, Chapter II, 1.2.1.

[119] See ECRI, 'General Policy Recommendation No 2: Equality Bodies to Combat Racism and Intolerance at National Level' (n 23) para 99 of the Explanatory Memorandum.

[120] See ibid para 99 of the Explanatory Memorandum.

Stability of mandate has also been linked by the Paris Principles ECRI Recommendations to the requirement of laying down in law the provisions regarding the dismissal of a Commissioner or Board members. The most common reason for a dismissal from office is if a member of an Equality Body permanently or for a specific period of time loses the ability to perform his/her functions or fails to perform those functions, in most cases for a period of more than six months.[121] Being convicted of a criminal act is in some countries, such as Lithuania, Latvia, Malta, and Slovakia, a reason for dismissing a member of the Equality Body. A serious violation of obligations or breach of official duties justifies dismissal in Germany and Slovakia. Other reasons for dismissal include the persistence of a conflict of interests for more than thirty days and the declaration of false data in the financial statement (Hungary), or a parliamentary vote of no-confidence (Lithuania).

In Poland, one of the reasons that would allow the Sejm to dismiss the Commissioner for Human Rights is if he/she 'defected from the oath made'.[122] In the oath, the Commissioner swears that in performing his/her duties he/she 'keep[s] faith with the Constitution of the Republic of Poland, [and] safeguard[s] the liberties and rights of the human being and the citizen, being guided by the Law and the principles of community life and social justice'.[123] On this basis, politicians, including some from the ruling parties, together with a think tank, started a petition against the Commissioner, signed by 35,000 people. The signed manifesto reads:

> One can not be silent when a constitutional human rights body is opposed to fundamental freedoms and rights guaranteed in the Constitution of the Republic in the name of the particular interests of the LGBT subculture. The events of recent months show that radical social activist Adam Bodnar [the Commissioner for Human Rights] has failed to cope with the difficult mission of impartiality to guard our rights and freedoms.... All these actions demonstrate that the Ombud's biased commitment to the ideology of LGBT leads to violations of constitutional freedoms and the rights of ordinary people. Therefore, we ask for a strong response from the Sejm and the Senate of the Republic of Poland, who are entitled to dismiss the Ombudsman, who has misrepresented the complex vow and dignity of the office. Poles need an Ombudsman who will not be a soldier of radical ideology but a defender of the rights of all citizens.[124]

[121] Examples for this dismissal reason are Cyprus, France, Hungary, Latvia, Lithuania, Malta, Slovakia, and Slovenia.

[122] Poland, Act of 15 July 1987 on the Commissioner for Human Rights, Art 7(2).

[123] ibid Art 4.

[124] Quoted from EELN, Country Report Poland, 2020, 89–90.

For his dismissal a majority of three-fifth is required which the ruling parties do not have.

This is a clear case for how important a robust legal framework concerning the stability of mandate is in order to allow a Commissioner to perform his/her tasks in an independent way. The Polish Commissioner expressed disappointment over how little interest had been shown by EU institutions in the situation of the Polish Equality Body and the overall implementation of the EU Anti-Discrimination Directives and urged them to take a more proactive role in this context.[125] This example highlights the importance of ECRI's recommendation that those holding leadership positions must be protected 'against threats and coercion and [to] have appropriate safeguards against arbitrary dismissal' in place.[126]

The Polish case further shows the importance of leadership for the independence of the Equality Body. An Equinet study points out that strong leadership is not only important in steering the body through a highly unpredictable and at times adverse and hostile political environment. It is also important to counter the politics of framing, which takes place when Equality Bodies are portrayed as supporting a specific group in society to mobilize resistance against the body. A strong leader is able to actively build the body's reputation as being broadly positioned and anchored across a range of policy areas, thus preventing a potential detrimental effect of framing attempts.[127] Liddle formulated the requirements for leaders in the following way: 'They must develop futuristic, imaginative and innovative scenarios, and adapt and harmonise a myriad of processes, structures, institutions, partnerships and agency within turbulent, dynamic, global, national and local regulatory frameworks.'[128]

When discussing the issue of stable mandate, those bodies which are embedded within the government structure require particular attention. In Germany, § 26(3) of the Antidiscrimination Act provides that a dismissal is possible for the same reasons that would justify the dismissal of a judge with lifetime appointment. Notwithstanding the embeddedness in government, this ensures the stability of the mandate. The situation in Italy is drastically different. The government decree on the establishment and organization of UNAR does not contain provisions regarding the dismissal of the civil servant appointed as director of the office. This makes it easy for any government to replace the director where he/she is not performing as the government would like. As the above case has shown, this is not

[125] Farrell (n 41).

[126] ECRI, 'General Policy Recommendation No 2: Equality Bodies to Combat Racism and Intolerance at National Level' (n 23) para 24, and para 96 of the Explanatory Memorandum.

[127] Yesilkagit and Snijders (n 59) 42–43. For a similar case, which threatened not only the position of the leader but the whole institution, see the case study on Romania, at 5.3.3.1.

[128] Joyce Liddle, 'Twenty-First-Century Public Leadership within Complex Governance Systems: Some Reflections' (2010) 38(4) Policy & Politics 657, 660. See also ECRI, 'General Policy Recommendation No 2: Equality Bodies to Combat Racism and Intolerance at National Level' (n 23) para 98 of the Explanatory Memorandum.

just a theoretical possibility; it has actually happened. It can therefore be argued that under such conditions the independent functioning of such an institution can only be a fiction and therefore independent status is a prerequisite for being able to carry out the tasks of an Equality Body independently. When assessing whether an Equality Body can work independently, the Commission cannot but look at the independence of the body itself as any corrective measure targeting only independent functioning is pointless if the problem is not addressed at its root. The recent implementation report on its Recommendation is an encouraging sign in this respect.

Regarding the staff of Equality Bodies, two studies have found that the majority of the bodies act with substantial independence.[129] While thirteen out of forty-one bodies analysed in the later study reported full independence in the appointment and appraisal of personnel, in determining the salaries and the conditions for promotion, as well as in downsizing the organization, only three bodies reported no independence at all in these aspects.[130] The study pointed out, however, that the large degree of independence might also coincide with inadequate staffing,[131] a problem reported by many experts of the EELN in their yearly country reports as well as by ECRI.[132] Another issue analysed by the same study regarded the question of who decides how the staff is allocated to work on different grounds if the body is mandated to work on two or more grounds. Of the twenty-eight bodies to which this applied, eighteen reported that they take this decision themselves. In two cases, the ministry must either be consulted or it sets explicit restrictions for this decision. In four cases, the ministry takes the decision after consultation with the Equality Body.[133] Overall, one can conclude that Equality Bodies enjoy considerable independence with regard to personnel management.

Another important point in this context is the question of financing. Here the salient issues are the adequacy of the available budget and the level of independence in deciding how to spend the money within the institution. Considering the great variety of institutions, mandates, and grounds covered by the Equality Bodies, it is hard to assess whether a specific budget is adequate or not. To simply

[129] Yesilkagit and Snijders (n 59); Ammer and others (n 53).

[130] According to the study, the thirteen bodies were: Belgium—Centre for Equal Opportunities and Opposition against Racism; Bulgaria—Protection Against Discrimination Commission; Denmark—Board of Equal Treatment; Denmark—Danish Institute for Human Rights; Estonia—Chancellor of Justice, Commissioner for Gender Equality and Equal Treatment; France—Equal Opportunities and Anti-discrimination Commission (HALDE); Hungary—Equal Treatment Authority; Latvia—Ombudsman; Lithuania—Equal Opportunities Ombudsperson; Norway—Equality and Anti-discrimination Ombudsperson; Slovakia—Slovak National Centre for Human Rights; Sweden—Equality and Anti-discrimination Ombudsman, UK—Equality Commission for Northern Ireland. The three bodies were: the Finnish Ombudsman for Equality; the Liechtenstein Office of Equal Treatment; and the Spanish Council for the Promotion of Equality. See Ammer and others (n 53) 109–10.

[131] ibid 109.

[132] On the huge variations in terms of staffing, see European Commission, 'Equality bodies and the implementation of the Commission Recommendation on Standards for Equality Bodies' (n 1) 19.

[133] Ammer and others (n 53) 109.

compare budget sizes would, for these reasons, be useless.[134] A combination of quantitative and qualitative indicators might help us to form a clearer picture. On the quantitative side, an important point of reference is the estimation made by the body itself on the amount of money needed to effectively carry out its task.[135] Comparing this figure with the actual budget and looking at the trend over the years provides a first indication of whether the budget is appropriate or not. On the qualitative side it needs to be checked whether the mandate and grounds covered have remained stable or whether additional functions have been assigned to the body and what kind of repercussions this has had on the budget. In cases of budget cuts a qualitative analysis would need to look into the reasons for that. Budget cuts in times of economic crisis that are more or less proportional to the cuts suffered in other sectors should be evaluated differently than disproportional cuts or cuts that might be explained by the fact that the body is performing its mandate in a way that displeases the government.[136]

Some cases in point are Ireland, the UK, Poland, and Romania. Back in 2009, the budget of the Irish Equality Authority was cut by 43 per cent, while in the same year other similar bodies experienced a cut of between only 1 and 9 per cent.[137] According to then chief executive of the Authority, Niall Crowley, who resigned in response to this dramatic cut, the 'only credible explanation' for the measure was that some of its case work, 'particularly in relation to allegations of discrimination in the public sector, has been experienced as a threat by senior civil servants'.[138] Dramatic cuts have also been suffered by the Equality and Human Rights Commission in the UK. While in 2007 it still had a budget of around 97 million EUR it went down to 56 million in 2010 and 18 million in 2020.[139] Similarly dramatic were the cuts in Romania. While the Commission in 2012 had a budget of 4.28 million EUR, in 2016 it was cut to only 1.17 million, rising to 1.75 million EUR in 2020.[140] In the Polish case, the budget discussion in parliament in 2016 was dominated by a negative atmosphere. Members of parliament from the ruling party expressed concern over the Commissioner's general

[134] Yesilkagit and Snijders (n 59) 24.

[135] Holtmaat (n 67) 56.

[136] The Council of Europe Commissioner for Human Rights has identified four factors for assessing whether the funds provided to an Equality Body are sufficient: 'Population size and economic circumstances. The nature and levels of reported and estimated un-reported discrimination. The range and roles of other stakeholders involved in promoting equality and combatting discrimination. The resources required to enable the body to implement all of its functions in a strategic manner and to a scale and standard to make an impact.' Council of Europe, Commissioner for Human Rights (n 24) 15.

[137] Michael Hennigan, 'Niall Crowley—an Irish public official of rare courage resigns in response to act of political revenge' *Finfacts* (12 December 2008) http://www.finfacts.ie/irishfinancenews/article_1015513.shtml.

[138] Quoted from ibid. For further details about this case see the case study at 5.4.3.2.

[139] See information provided on Equinet's members' page at https://equineteurope.org/author/uk_ehrc/.

[140] EELN, Country Report Romania, 2017, 111, and information on Equinet's members' page at https://equineteurope.org/author/romania_nccd/.

policy and criticized him for appointing a gender expert as his deputy. In fact, the Commissioner, who assumed office in September 2015, appointed a deputy responsible for equality issues for the first time. Although he had requested an 18 per cent increase in his budget, the budget approved was even smaller than that of the previous year.[141]

A number of other countries, although not suffering from such sudden budget cuts, nevertheless suffer chronically from being underfinanced. This is the case, for example, in Cyprus and Croatia, a situation criticized by international monitoring bodies such as the HRC in the case of Croatia and ECRI in case of Cyprus.[142] The independent experts of the EELN of Austria, Hungary, and Latvia also report that budgets are too low to fulfil the mandate effectively.[143] The Slovene Equality Body started with a very low budget, which was considerably increased over the last few years. However, according to the EELN expert, it 'still encounters threats to its financial independence and the independence of its work, due to interference by the Ministry of Finance'.[144]

The appropriate funding is one of the few points on which the Commission's Standards for Equality Bodies are quite explicit. It recommends first that Member States ensure 'human, technical and financial resources, premises and infrastructure necessary to perform its [the Equality Body's] tasks and exercise its powers effectively' taking into account the competences and tasks allocated. Most importantly it then spells out that '[r]esources can only be considered adequate if they allow equality bodies to carry out each of their equality functions effectively, within reasonable time and within the deadlines established by national law'.[145] This brief overview has shown that adequate funding is one of Equality Bodies' biggest challenges and it remains to be seen whether the Commission's Recommendations will manage to push states to change their practice. In any case, in its 2021 implementation report, the Commission identified the level of resources as 'a major source of concern'.[146]

As mentioned above, an element of financial independence is the autonomy to dispose of the money available in the way most suitable to the priorities established by the Equality Body. To measure spending autonomy, Yesilkagit proposes

141 EELN, Country Report Poland, 2017, 121; and EELN, Country Report Poland, 2020, 89.

142 HRC, 'Concluding observations on the third periodic report of Croatia' (30 April 2015) CCPR/C/HRV/CO/3, para 5; and ECRI, 'Report on Cyprus (fifth monitoring cycle) adopted on 17 March 2016' CRI(2016)18, paras 96–99.

143 EELN, Country Report Austria, 2020, 64; EELN, Country Report Hungary, 2020, 109; EELN, Country Report Latvia, 2020, 70.

144 EELN, Country Report Slovenia, 2020, 80. See for a similar situation EELN, Country Report Slovakia, 2020, 90.

145 European Commission, 'Commission Recommendation on Standards for Equality Bodies' (n 19) point 1, Chapter II, 1.2.2.

146 European Commission, 'Equality bodies and the implementation of the Commission Recommendation on Standards for Equality Bodies' (n 1) 20.

the following four indicators: possibility for Equality Bodies to shift between personnel and running costs, between budget and investments, to take loans for investments, and to shift budgets over years. Studies carried out have shown that only a few bodies enjoy full spending autonomy on all these aspects, with autonomy being greatest when it comes to shifting between personnel and running costs. Fifteen of the forty-one bodies reported having no independence at all in any of the four aspects.[147] On the other hand, when asked about their level of independence in deciding how to allocate personnel and financial recourses between the different powers of the body, thirty out of thirty-eight bodies responded that the body takes the decision itself.[148] Equinet's working paper on standards dedicates one point to this issue by requesting that financial resources should be managed and deployed 'solely on the basis of decisions made by those in leadership positions' while of course respecting the requirements of sound financial management.[149]

In terms of sources, the EELN country reports suggest that the budget comes nearly exclusively from state sources. Quite a few reports mention the use of EU funds through programmes such as PROGRESS or the European Social Fund.[150] It is not common at all for Equality Bodies to take loans for investments.[151] Self-generated income in the form of payments for services and publications are mentioned only in the case of Portugal. The downside of such external funds is that they are limited in time and purpose.[152]

One of the above-mentioned studies has also tried to establish whether there is a relationship between structural independence (in terms of whether the body is governed by a collegiate body or a single head, and in terms of separate legal personality or being attached to a ministry) and independence related to finances and personnel management. Whereas a higher level of structural independence does not appear to have a decisive impact on the level of financial independence, they found that bodies that were established as separate legal entities had a higher level of personnel management independence. A high level of structural independence also had a positive influence of the bodies' freedom to decide how to weight the different powers and on deciding about the amount of human and financial resources dedicated to them.[153]

[147] See Ammer and others (n 53) 108.
[148] ibid 113.
[149] Equinet, 'Developing Standards for Equality Bodies. An Equinet Working Paper' (n 22) 5 (point 2.e).
[150] See, for instance, the reports on Hungary, Lithuania, and Portugal.
[151] Yesilkagit and Snijders (n 59) 24; Ammer and others (n 53) 107–08.
[152] European Commission, 'Equality bodies and the implementation of the Commission Recommendation on Standards for Equality Bodies' (n 1) 20.
[153] Ammer and others (n 53) 113–17.

5.2.3 Good Practices and Challenges

The above has shown that there exists a great variety of legal structures and appointment procedures for key positions. It has also shown that the issue of adequate financing and spending autonomy is crucial for securing the independence of an Equality Body. There are solutions that, even if at first sight do not appear ideal, such as a body embedded within a ministerial structure, work well in practice as long as the political environment is one that respects the requirement of independence. In order to make a body resilient in more adverse circumstances, the following points appear to be important:

1) The Equality Body should have its own legal personality (either as a standalone body or as part of a broader structure, such as an NHRI) and should not be attached to the government or a ministry.
2) As all the reference documents used in this part (Paris Principle, ECRI's GPR No 2, Equinet Working Paper on Standards for Equality Bodies) recommend, the executive should not have a decisive influence in appointing the person or persons leading the body, as is currently the case in most EU countries. Even in those cases where the parliament makes the appointments, which the above documents consider good practice, additional safeguards might be warranted. The Romanian example has shown that there is always the risk of political appointees being preferred over independent experts, even in the case where the appointment is done by parliament and requirements set out beforehand. Furthermore, such procedures appear to overlook very often the requirement of reflecting the diversity existing within society. If government or parliament are in a position to appoint the person/s in the leadership position/s, it is all the more important that the process is open, transparent, and based on the competence of candidates.
3) The Italian and the Polish examples have shown how important it is to protect those in leadership roles from arbitrary dismissal. The embeddedness in the government structure and the lack of provisions on the circumstances warranting dismissal put the director of the Italian Equality Body in a very vulnerable position and by no means secured the stability of the mandate or the body's independence. In fact, the Polish Ombudsman might have been removed if the law had not provided for a relatively high obstacle in pushing through such an intention.
4) The most powerful means for a government to tame an Equality Body is by not granting it the financial, including human, resources necessary for its independent and effective functioning. In determining this amount, the governing body of the Equality Body should play a role and the reasons for not granting the requested amount should be made transparent. On the amount granted, the governing body ideally has absolute spending autonomy,

including being able to hire its own staff and to assign it to the various competences according to its own strategic decisions.

The requirement of stakeholder participation, an important feature of experimentalist governance, is apparent in most of the just-mentioned points. Both the appointment procedure as well as the resulting composition should be a reflection of such a participatory approach, involving NGOs and organizations representing the interests of persons vulnerable to discrimination. Another stakeholder in this context is of course the Equality Body itself which should have a say in determining the budget necessary for its effective functioning.

This is not to say that only an Equality Body fulfilling all the above criteria can be considered independent. Where one or more of the above criteria are not fulfilled, there should, however, be heightened scrutiny also from the European Commission at least in terms of looking closely at whether these bodies are still able to perform their functions independently. As explained above, this might, however, not be enough to tackle the problem at its roots and thus the Commission might have no choice but to look at the independence of the body per se as well. While the FRA appears to be of the opinion that for this purpose an 'upgrade' of the EU's legal framework would be required,[154] a teleological interpretation of the requirement to carry out the tasks independently would allow for checking the institutional preconditions for that. The Commission will have the opportunity to clarify this debate if it proposes new legislation to strengthen the role of Equality Bodies.

5.2.4 Proposed Indicators

The proposed indicators, summarized below in Table 5.1, are based on the above comparative analysis as well as on the in-depth case studies discussed at 5.3.3 and 5.4.3. As derived from the Paris Principles, ECRI's GPR on Equality Bodies, Equinet's Working Paper on Standards for Equality Bodies, and acknowledged also by the Commission's Recommendations on Standards for Equality Bodies, full independence at institutional level decisively contributes to making it possible for an Equality Body to function without any political interference. A first structural indicator to look at is therefore related to the question of whether the Equality Body is set up as a separate legal entity (either as body dedicated to equality and non-discrimination based on one or more grounds, or integrated into a broader structure) or as part of the government structure. While the former has to be preferred over the latter, it is not excluded that additional safeguards make it possible that the body can work independently also in the latter case.

[154] See Fundamental Rights Agency, 'Access to justice in cases of discrimination in the EU: Steps to further equality' (2012) <http://fra.europa.eu/sites/default/files/fra-2012-access-to-justice-social.pdf>, where the FRA in one opinion states: 'The EU should upgrade its legal framework to secure genuine access to justice by, for instance, ensuring the independence, to a uniform standard, of equality bodies and other institutions involved in the justice system'.

Secondly, all the above-mentioned documents, in varying degrees of detail, pay particular attention to the composition and the appointment procedure for leadership positions in Equality Bodies. In terms of structural indicators, it will be necessary to look at how the respective national laws have been designed this aspect. For instance, are candidates recruited through an open call for applications or can they be nominated, and if the latter is the case, by whom? In this context it is of course relevant to look at whether organizations representing or working with groups exposed to discrimination have a say or not. Furthermore, in terms of structural indicators one needs to look at the selection criteria and whether there is a focus on competence in the area of equality and non-discrimination combined with an effort to make sure that the composition of the governing structure reflects the diversity of society and is gender balanced. Finally, it is crucial to know who makes the final appointment. As all the above quoted documents agree, the executive should play no decisive role in any of these stages.

In terms of process indicators it will then be necessary to look at how the legal framework is put into practice. Is the process transparent in the sense of information being available on the vacancy, the candidates, the procedure? Is it participatory in the sense of involving organizations representing or working with groups exposed to discrimination? And does the final decision reflect the requirement of focusing on the competence of the candidates and the composition of the governing body reflecting as far as possible the diversity in society? In populating these indicators, it will be necessary take into consideration the perception of NGOs as well as the opinion of experts following the process.

The requirement of providing appointees with a stable mandate can be measured by looking at whether the legislation provides for a reasonable length of the mandate (for instance four to five years with possibility of renewal, or longer without such possibility[155]) and for clear rules concerning dismissal and functional immunity of appointees, in order to protect them from arbitrary dismissals (structural indicators). In practice, each dismissal has to be looked at carefully to understand whether it is based in the law or whether it was instead the consequence of a political decision (process indicator).

All standard setting documents agree that adequate funding is decisive for an Equality Body to function independently and effectively. In terms of structural indicators it is relevant to ask whether it is the executive or the parliament who decides on the yearly allocation. Preference should be given to a decision of the parliament and accordingly to the Equality Body being financially accountable to parliament. Ideally, the Equality Body has an advisory role in the process of determining the budget. The law should further allow Equality Bodies to raise additional funds, in and outside the country (without compromising its independence) and dispose of financial resources autonomously, according to their own strategic decisions.

[155] ECRI, 'General Policy Recommendation No 2: Equality Bodies to Combat Racism and Intolerance at National Level' (n 23) para 99 of the Explanatory Memorandum.

Process indicators will help to determine whether the amount of money actually placed at the disposal of the Equality Body can be considered adequate. To measure that, account should be taken of the amount of money calculated by the Equality Body as being required in order for it to fulfil all its competences effectively, compared to the amount granted. The criteria for calculating these amounts should be transparent. In particular they should take into consideration the 'nature and levels of reported and estimated un-reported discrimination' as well as the 'range and roles of other stakeholders involved in promoting equality and combating discrimination'.[156] ECRI further proposes peer-to-peer reviews with other states to assist the determination of the appropriate level of funding.[157] The amount must in any case be such that it allows the Equality Body to carry out all its functions effectively.[158] A state would not be compliant with its obligations under Article 13 RED if, from the yearly reports of the Equality Body or the information provided by representatives of the Equality Body or informed observers, it is clear, that for instance the Equality Body does not conduct surveys or produce reports or does so to a very limited extent because of a lack of available resources.[159]

By observing the trend over time, it will be possible to discern whether there have been significant cuts which have to be looked at closely. If they cannot be explained by objective factors (such as general austerity measures in times of economic crises) and if they are not proportionate when compared to cuts suffered by other sectors, the motivation of the cuts might be legitimately questioned. Furthermore, any additional function attributed to the Equality Body has to be accompanied by adequate additional funding.

The result of all these commitments and efforts to secure institutional independence should be that the Equality Body is vested also with policy and operational independence. This means that it has a qualified and diverse membership with strong leadership that functions without interference from government or political parties, that it employs qualified staff in adequate numbers, and is provided with the funding required to enable the body to implement all of its functions in a strategic manner and to a scale and standard to make an impact. Institutional independence thus ultimately leads to what appears to be the primary intent of Article 13 RED: the independent carrying out of tasks.

This leads us to the next sections in which the effective functioning of Equality Bodies will be discussed. One of the three tasks an Equality Body has to be charged

156 Council of Europe, Commissioner for Human Rights (n 24) 15; taken over also by ECRI, 'General Policy Recommendation No 2: Equality Bodies to Combat Racism and Intolerance at National Level' (n 23) para 101 of the Explanatory Memorandum.

157 ECRI, 'General Policy Recommendation No 2: Equality Bodies to Combat Racism and Intolerance at National Level' (n 23) para 101 of the Explanatory Memorandum.

158 European Commission, 'Commission Recommendation on Standards for Equality Bodies' (n 19) Chapter II, 1.2.2. point 1.

159 See on this European Commission, 'Equality bodies and the implementation of the Commission Recommendation on Standards for Equality Bodies' (n 1) 10–16.

Table 5.1 Table of indicators concerning the independence of Equality Bodies

Independence of Equality Bodies	Structural indicators	• Equality Body embedded in the governmental structure or separate legal personality
		• Legal design of appointment procedure and composition
		  • Open call? If not, candidates proposed by whom?
		  • Role of NGOs, organizations working on protected grounds
		  • Criteria for selection (competence, diversity)
		  • Appointment by whom?
		• Stable mandate
		  • Rules on length of term
		  • Safeguards against arbitrary dismissal in place?
		  • Functional immunity granted?
		• Funding
		  • Yearly assigned by whom, accountable to whom?
		  • Possibility of raising additional funds, in and outside the country?
		  • Autonomy in managing resources granted?

	Process indicators	• Practical implementation of appointment procedure
		  • Transparent: is information available on the vacancy, the candidates, the procedure?
		  • Participatory: are organizations representing or working with groups exposed to discrimination involved?
		  • Competency-based: does the decision take the expertise and experience of candidates into due account?
		  • Does the composition reflect the diversity in society?
		• Stable mandate
		  • Can dismissals be justified on the basis of existing legislation?
		• Adequate funding
		  • Amount requested compared to amount granted and trend over time
		  • Does the budget allow the Equality Body to work effectively on all its competences?
		  • Are cuts proportionate and capable of being explained by objective factors?
		  • Are additional competences accompanied by additional funding?

	Outcome indicators	• Qualified and diverse membership with strong leadership functioning without interference from government or political parties • Qualified staff in adequate numbers • Provided with the funding required to enable the body to implement all of its functions in a strategic manner and to a scale and standard to make an impact

with, is to provide independent assistance to victims of discrimination in pursuing their complaints about discrimination. The following sections will discuss how states have chosen to translate this into their national legislation and how these choices play out in practice. While some states have set up Equality Bodies for this purpose that predominantly deal with complaints brought before them and can issue recommendations or binding decisions and can therefore be seen to have a tribunal-type function, predominantly promotion-type bodies offer a greater range of ways in which they can support victims of discrimination. How the different types of Equality Bodies implement the preventive part of their mandate will be discussed in section 6.2.

5.3 Effectiveness of Predominantly 'Tribunal-Type' Equality Bodies

5.3.1 Introduction and Conceptual Clarification

Equinet, most studies on Equality Bodies carried out on behalf of Equinet, and the EELN, as well as academic literature, all distinguish between two types of bodies. For the purposes of this research, we refer to the classification provided by Ammer et al:

> Predominantly tribunal-type equality bodies ... are impartial institutions which spend the bulk of their time and resources hearing, investigating and deciding on individual instances of discrimination brought before them.
>
> Predominantly promotion-type equality bodies ... spend the bulk of their time and resources on a broader mix of activities that include supporting good practice in organisations, raising awareness of rights, developing a knowledge base on equality and nondiscrimination, and providing legal advice and assistance to individual victims of discrimination.[160]

Equinet adds to this a third category, made up of bodies that are a combination of the two types: 'They hear, investigate and decide on cases of discrimination, but also implement a range of activities to raise awareness, support good practice and conduct research.'[161]

160 Ammer and others (n 53) 43–44.
161 See Equinet webpage, at https://equineteurope.org/comparative-data/functions/.

Since the requirement of 'providing independent assistance to victims of discrimination' (Art 13(2) RED) could be satisfied by simply providing victims of discrimination with information about the anti-discrimination laws in force and the possible legal avenues that can be pursued, no Member State is legally required to set up an Equality Body with a quasi-judicial function. The FRA has recognized the advantages of quasi-judicial Equality Bodies, namely that procedures before them, as compared to court procedures, are 'less costly, simpler and more specialized in cases of discrimination'.[162] The downside of such bodies is that they prevent mainstream courts from developing expertise in non-discrimination cases and creating a body of jurisprudence. In addition, Equality Bodies might have limited powers in terms of imposing sanctions or awarding compensation.[163]

For the Paris Principles, the focus of the NHRI's work is on the promotional side and they lay down only 'Additional principles' regarding those commissions having a quasi-judicial function. The General Observations of the SCA of GANHRI list the powers that such a complaints-handling mandate 'might include'. Among others, these are the ability to start a complaint *suo motu*, to investigate complaints and compel the production of evidence, to protect an individual from victimization for having filed a complaint or for having provided evidence, to settle complaints through a binding decision, to seek enforcement of its decisions through the court system, and to follow up and monitor the implementation of its decisions. NHRI that have been assigned this function should ensure that their complaints handling is fair, transparent, efficient, speedy and consistent.[164]

Similarly, ECRI's GPR No 2 set out that Equality Bodies 'should be assigned' promotion and prevention functions as well as support and litigation functions, and that they 'may also be assigned ... the function to take decisions on complaints (decision-making function)'.[165] *If* such a function is assigned to Equality Bodies, it should include the competences to '[r]eceive, examine, hear and conciliate individual and collective complaints ..., [d]ecide whether there has been a breach of civil or administrative anti-discrimination legislation ..., [i]ssue legally binding decisions ... and impose effective, proportionate and dissuasive sanctions'

[162] Fundamental Rights Agency, 'Access to justice in cases of discrimination in the EU: Steps to further equality' (n 154) 21.
[163] ibid.
[164] GANHRI (n 73) G.O. 2.10, 57–58.
[165] ECRI, 'General Policy Recommendation No 2: Equality Bodies to Combat Racism and Intolerance at National Level' (n 23) para 10.

including compensation, fines, and the publication of the decision and to '[e]nsure the execution and implementation of their decisions'.[166] Such decisions should be appealable before the courts.[167] Where they are not given the power to take legally binding decisions and issue sanctions, they should have the competence to issue non-binding recommendations, ensure their implementation, and, as appropriate, publish their decisions and recommendations.[168] Paragraph 21 further regulates in detail what the powers to obtain evidence and information in the context of deciding on complaints should include.

In the Explanatory Memorandum, ECRI makes clear that where Equality Bodies have a decision-making competence it has a preference for allowing them to take legally binding decisions including issuing effective, proportionate, and dissuasive sanctions. It further underlines the importance of explicitly setting out in law that the rules on the shared burden of proof are applicable and of laying down additional provisions on the procedure before such bodies, including basic procedural guarantees.[169]

Considering the wording of Article 13(2) RED it is not surprising that the Commission's Recommendation on Standards for Equality Bodies also states that the decision-making function is a possibility but not a must. Unlike ECRI's Recommendations, however, it does not express a preference for legally binding decisions. However, if such competence is given under national law, Equality Bodies should also have the capacity to issue 'adequate, effective and proportionate sanctions'. It is interesting to note that the third element required for sanctions under the Directive, that is, dissuasiveness, is not mentioned in the Commission's Recommendation. Like ECRI's Recommendation, the Commission recommends that it should be possible to appeal such legally binding decisions before the courts.[170]

An aspect that decisively contributes to effectiveness is accessibility. Both ECRI's GPR No 2 as well as the Commission's Recommendation on Standards for Equality Bodies place considerable importance on this aspect. For ECRI, accessibility requires, inter alia, easily accessible premises; flexible contact hours; online, e-mail, and telephone services; geographic outreach through local initiatives and regional offices; the opportunity to contact and engage with the Equality Body in a confidential way and in a language in which

[166] ibid para 17.
[167] ibid para 19.
[168] ibid para 18.
[169] ibid paras 86–87 of the Explanatory Memorandum.
[170] European Commission, 'Commission Recommendation on Standards for Equality Bodies' (n 19) points 3–6, Chapter II, 1.1.2.

persons exposed to discrimination are proficient; a minimum of admissibility conditions when submitting complaints and face-to-face contact when dealing with them; adjustments in premises and services for persons with disability; and provision of services free of charge.[171] Also the Commission recommends offering the procedure to submit complaints free of charge, ensuring that complaints may be submitted in various ways and in a language of the complainant's choice but still common in the respective Member State. Similarly to ECRI, the Commission recommends that physical and digital access to its services be adapted to meet the needs of persons with disability and, where necessary for geographical or other reasons, to consider enabling Equality Bodies to establish regional offices.[172]

As the RED imposes no legal obligation, in the next sub-section we cannot speak about legal transposition but we will look at the legal solutions used by the states that have nevertheless opted to install a quasi-judicial body and into the practice of some selected bodies. In doing so, we will look at how proceedings can be brought before the tribunal-type Equality Bodies, their investigation powers, whether their decisions are binding or not, and what kind of sanctions can be awarded. Finally, we will examine the follow-up to decisions. Before looking at these issues, all case studies will analyse the level of overall independence of the Equality Body as well as assessing its outreach.

5.3.2 Legal Solutions

The maps in Figure 5.1 and Figure 5.2 gives an overview of the states that have decided to establish or, in some cases, already set up quasi-judicial body dealing with issues of equality and non-discrimination. Predominantly tribunal-type or combined bodies (Figure 5.2) prevail in new Member States and acceding countries (except for Poland, Czech Republic, and Slovakia[173]), Austria, and the northern countries Belgium, the Netherlands, Denmark, Finland, and the Baltic states.

[171] ECRI, 'General Policy Recommendation No 2: Equality Bodies to Combat Racism and Intolerance at National Level' (n 23) para 40.

[172] European Commission, 'Commission Recommendation on Standards for Equality Bodies' (n 19) Chapter II, 1.2.3.

[173] Although their bodies can also be categorized as combined tribunal-type and promotion-type bodies since, like the other bodies in this category, they formally decide on complaints or address recommendations to the parties, even if these decisions or recommendations are not legally binding (which is also the case for some other combined types).

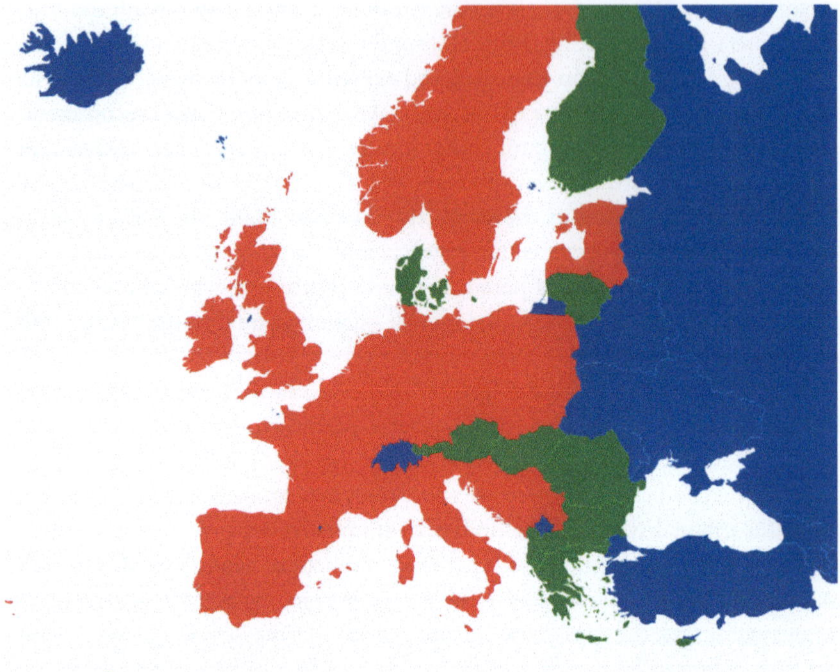

Predominantly tribunal-type bodies (source: Equinet, adapted by the author based on EELN reports)

GREEN: matches in this country
RED: no match in this country
BLUE: doesn't apply to this country

ALBANIA: Commissioner for the Protection from Discrimination
AUSTRIA: Equal Treatment Commission [not mentioned in the Equinet list]
AUSTRIA: Disability Ombudsman
BULGARIA: Commission for Protection against Discrimination
CYPRUS: Office of the Commissioner for Administration and Human Rights
DENMARK: Board of Equal Treatment [The Board is not the officially designated Equality Body]
FINLAND: Ombudsman for Equality [not a quasi-judicial body according to EELN Country Report 2020, 54]
GREECE: Greek Ombudsman [not a quasi-judicial body according to EELN country report 2020, 77]
HUNGARY: Equal Treatment Authority [since 1 January 2021 replaced by the Commissioner for Fundamental Rights, to be considered a combined tribunal-type and promotion-type body]
LITHUANIA: Office of the Equal Opportunities Ombudsperson
MACEDONIA: Commission for Protection against Discrimination
ROMANIA: National Council for Combating Discrimination

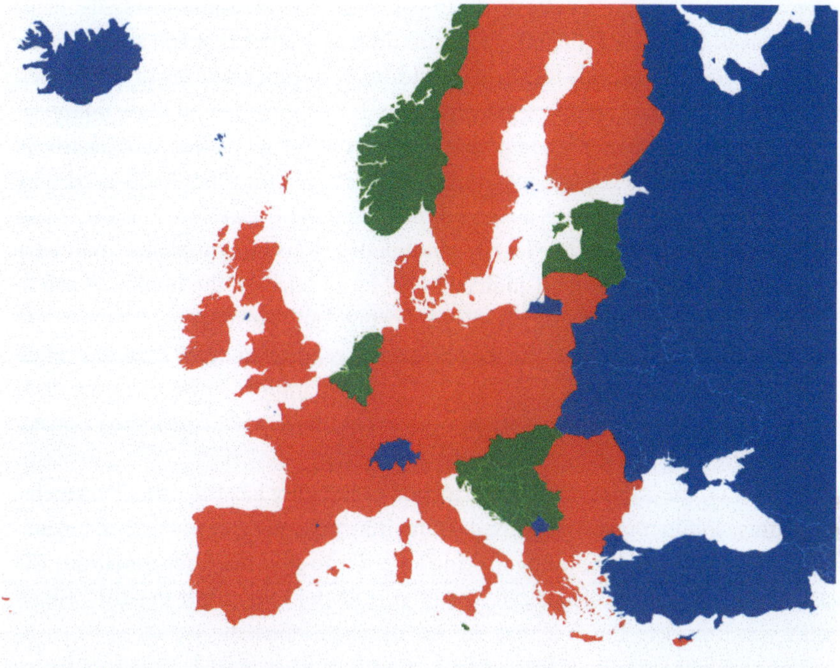

Combined tribunal-type and promotion-type bodies (source: Equinet, adapted by the author based on EELN reports)

GREEN: matches in this country
RED: no match in this country
BLUE: doesn't apply to this country

BELGIUM: Unia (Interfederal Centre for Equal Opportunities)
BIH: Institution of Human Rights Ombudsman of Bosnia and Herzegovina
CROATIA: Ombudsperson for Gender Equality
ESTONIA: Gender Equality and Equal Treatment Commissioner
HUNGARY: Commissioner for Fundamental Rights
LATVIA: Office of the Ombudsman
MALTA: Commission for the Rights of Persons with Disability
MALTA: National Commission for the Promotion of Equality
MONTENEGRO: Protector of Human Rights and Freedoms of Montenegro (Ombudsman)
NETHERLANDS: Netherlands Institute for Human Rights
NORWAY: Equality and Anti-discrimination Ombud
SERBIA: Commissioner for the Protection of Equality
SLOVENIA: The Advocate of the Principle of Equality

According to the Equinet site on the litigation powers of its members,[174] it turns out, however, that a large majority of states do have bodies that can receive complaints and formally decide on them or address recommendations to the parties, even if their decisions are not legally binding. If one included all these countries under the category of combined bodies, the picture would be different: nearly all states could be considered to have combined bodies. On the other hand, according to the information provided by Equality Bodies themselves to Equinet, more bodies have the power to take legally binding decisions on complaints than have indicated that they are a quasi-judicial body. In addition to the bodies shown in Figure 5.1, these are the Equality Bodies of Portugal and Slovenia.

With regard to Portugal, the EELN expert reports in 2020 that the High Commission for Migrations does have the power to impose fines, that such decisions are legally binding and may be appealed, but that it is not considered a quasi-judicial institution due to its lack of independence.[175]

In Slovenia, the Advocate of the Principle of Equality has the power to receive complaints, conduct investigations, demand information from the defendant, and take binding decisions including making an order to stop the discrimination. The reason why it was not categorized as a quasi-judicial body until the 2017 EELN report was linked to the fact that the Advocate cannot issue penalties when its decisions are not complied with, nor can it issue fines or award compensation in the first place. Although this has not changed, it has been categorized as a quasi-judicial body since the 2018 report.

This shows that depending on how the terms are interpreted, a larger or more restricted number of countries have predominantly tribunal-type Equality Bodies. The present analysis will focus on the bodies of EU Member States contained in the Figure 5.1 above, as they are the ones who self-defined them as predominantly tribunal-type bodies. All of these bodies, except for the Equal Treatment Commission in Austria and the Netherlands Institute for Human Rights, have the power to take legally binding decisions after having investigated the complaints brought before them. According to the Commissioner for Human Rights of the CoE, not to be empowered to take binding decisions considerably limits the effectiveness of the Equality Body.[176] On the other hand, ECRI points out that even if decisions are not binding or sanctions cannot be imposed, in practice they can still have a considerable impact.[177]

In most cases, the bodies can start investigations on their own initiative. This is precluded for the Danish Board of Equal Treatment and for the Estonian Chancellor of Justice. When a complaint is brought before them by an individual, bodies have different approaches to dealing with the complaints. While in the Danish case, oral

[174] See https://equineteurope.org/comparative-data/functions/.
[175] EELN, Country Report Portugal, 2020, 74 and 76.
[176] Council of Europe, Commissioner for Human Rights (n 24) 16.
[177] ECRI, 'General Policy Recommendation No 2: Equality Bodies to Combat Racism and Intolerance at National Level' (n 23) para 84 of the Explanatory Memorandum.

proceedings are excluded, the Bulgarian and Romanian bodies foresee hearings with both parties. Most bodies, such as the ones from Austria and Romania, can, in addition, make use of witnesses, documents, and expert opinions. Some of them, such as the Bulgarian CPAD or the Romanian NCCD, can conduct on-site visits.[178]

The kind of sanctions that can be imposed by the Equality Bodies vary from body to body. The Lithuanian Equal Opportunities Ombudsperson, in addition to being able to impose administrative sanctions, can also refer relevant material to the public prosecutor, admonish a perpetrator, and address a recommendation (which is essentially non-binding) to discontinue discriminatory actions, halt advertising activities temporarily if a campaign can incite hatred against a group or an individual based on sex, sexual orientation, race or ethnicity, age, disability, religion or belief or nationality, or stop discriminatory advertisement campaigns. The decision cannot include compensation for damage,[179] an option open to the Danish Board of Equal Treatment as well as the Estonian Chancellor of Justice as a result of a conciliation procedure. The Hungarian Equal Treatment Authority may order the termination or prohibit the continuation of a discriminatory situation or conduct, order the publication of its decision, and impose a fine (between about 167 EUR and 20,000 EUR). These sanctions can be applied jointly. The Bulgarian Protection Against Discrimination Commission can impose fines or soft penalties, such as a public apology or the publication of its decision or information about it.[180] The Cypriot Equality Body can order the perpetrator to discontinue the discriminatory practice or impose small fines. In practice, however, it prefers to resort to mediation, as fines are considered too low to be dissuasive.[181]

In line with the requirement of due process, all binding decisions can be appealed, in some cases in front of civil courts, in other cases a specific court has the exclusive competence for appeals against decisions of Equality Bodies. This is the case, for example, in Hungary, where the Metropolitan Administrative and Labour Court is responsible for appeals, whereas in Cyprus appeals have to be directed to the Supreme Court.

The effectiveness of decisions and sanctions might be limited where the body does not have the powers or sufficient resources to engage in follow-up to ensure the implementation of its decisions.[182] The Bulgarian, Hungarian, Estonian, and Cypriot bodies can enforce their decisions if they are not respected. The Cypriot Equality Body can, for instance, impose fines if the perpetrator does not comply with the decision within a prescribed period.[183] Other bodies rarely dispose of information as to whether their decisions are respected. An exception to this is the

[178] See EELN Country Reports 2020; and Ammer and others (n 53) 88–89.
[179] EELN, Country Report Lithuania, 2020, 110.
[180] EELN, Country Report Bulgaria, 2020, 79.
[181] EELN, Country Report Cyprus, 2020, 111.
[182] Council of Europe, Commissioner for Human Rights (n 24) 16; see also Ammer and others (n 53) 185.
[183] EELN, Country Report Cyprus, 2020, 111.

Netherlands Institute for Human Rights, which gives precise yearly figures on compliance with its non-binding decisions to take either an individual or structural measure, or a combination of both measures. Despite of the fact that its recommendations lack binding force, the overall compliance rate is relatively high: it rose from 73 per cent in 2016 to 87 per cent in 2017 but fell again to 77 per cent in 2018.[184] Since 2016, the Lithuanian Equal Opportunities Ombudsperson, following the creation of an administrative follow-up system, is providing information about the implementation of its recommendations. In fact, although it can impose administrative fines, appealable to the court, the Ombudsperson usually admonishes the perpetrator and issues a non-binding recommendation. Of the fifteen recommendations to various institutions in 2019, nine were implemented and six were in the process of implementation.[185]

In the case of the two institutions producing exclusively non-binding decisions (the Austrian Equal Treatment Commission and the Netherlands Institute for Human Rights) complainants need to approach a court to get a binding decision. Although in Austria courts have to provide reasons if they come to a different conclusion than the Equal Treatment Commission in their opinions, their value is reportedly 'quite low, mainly due to the fact that the procedure before the Equal Treatment Commission does not even meet most of the basic procedural standards of courts'.[186] This shows the relevance of the above-mentioned ECRI recommendation to lay down basic procedural guarantees that could be drawn from the codes of civil and administrative procedure.[187] Contrary to the NIHR, the Austrian Equal Treatment Commission has no statistics concerning the level of compliance with its decisions and does not collect information on how many cases are continued in the courts.

Comparative studies on the competences of Equality Bodies generally recommend the strengthening of alternative dispute resolution mechanisms, including the establishment of quasi-judicial Equality Bodies with investigative and sanctioning powers.[188] It is thus useful to study bodies with such functions in detail to see how they can contribute to improving the access to justice for victims of discrimination. When looking at predominantly tribunal-type bodies from the perspective of bindingness of decisions, the kind of sanctions they can award, the investigative powers they are accorded, and the kind of follow-up provided, one can conclude that the Equality Bodies of Romania and Bulgaria start from a

[184] EELN, Country Report The Netherlands, 2020, 78, and Netherlands Institute for Human Rights, 'Annual Report 2018', 19.

[185] EELN, Country Report Lithuania, 2020, 112.

[186] EELN, Country Report Austria, 2017, 84.

[187] ECRI, 'General Policy Recommendation No 2: Equality Bodies to Combat Racism and Intolerance at National Level' (n 23) para 86 of the Explanatory Memorandum.

[188] Nina Althoff and Sera Choi, 'Verbände aktiv gegen Diskriminierung. Das Project "Diskriminierungsschutz: Handlungskompetenz für Verbände"' (2011), 13; Martina Benecke, 'Rechtsvergleich der europäischen Systeme zum Antidiskriminierungsrecht' (Expertise im Auftrag der Antidiskriminierungsstelle des Bundes, 2010) 72.

relatively favourable legislative framework whereas the Austrian Body is vested with considerably less powers. These three cases will be studied in depth to investigate whether these different points of departure have an impact on the effectiveness of the bodies in carrying out their tasks, in their visibility, and overall impact on the situation of rights holders. On this basis good practice and challenges will be identified and possible indicators derived, in particular at the level of process and outcome. However, before going into the details with regard to their powers to decide on discrimination complaints, each of the case studies will also look into the level of institutional independence against the background of recommendations from ECRI, Equinet, and the European Commission. It has been decided to cover independence jointly with the effectiveness of the respective Equality Body, rather than placing the case studies on independence separately under the above section 5.2 on independence, in order to give the overall picture about one particular body and to show the impact of the two overarching indicators on each other. The case studies are based on interviews with representatives from the respective Equality Bodies and from NGOs, on documents produced by the Equality Bodies, and research carried out on their functioning.

5.3.3 Practical Implementation

5.3.3.1 Case Study: Romania—The National Council for Combating Discrimination

The Romanian National Council for Combating Discrimination (NCCD) has its legal basis in Ordinance No 135/2000 on Preventing and Sanctioning all Forms of Discrimination. According to Article 16, it is autonomous and has legal entity status under parliamentary control.[189] Article 17 states that the NCCD 'performs its duties independently, without any restraint or influence from other public institutions or authorities'. In two judgments of 2008 and 2009 the Constitutional Court clarified the legal status of the NCCD and confirmed the constitutionality of its quasi-judicial nature: the NCCD is an administrative authority with a jurisdictional mandate, which enjoys the required independence to carry out administrative-jurisdictional activities. The Constitutional Court further found no incompatibility with the constitutional provisions prohibiting the establishment of extraordinary courts of law.[190]

The steering board is the governing body of the NCCD and the body responsible for deciding on complaints. It is composed of nine members who have the rank of

[189] Before the amendments to the Antidiscrimination Law, the NCCD had been criticized for its hierarchical subordination to the government. See ECRI, 'Report on Romania (fourth monitoring cycle) adopted on 19 March 2014' CRI(2014)19, para 22.

[190] Romania, Constitutional Court Decision 1096 of 15 October 2008; Constitutional Court Decision 444 of 31 March 2009; EELN, Country Report Romania, 2020, 67 and 77–78.

secretary of state. Any Romanian citizen with a higher education degree and recognized experience in the protection of human rights and combating discrimination can apply to become a member of the steering board. Further preconditions are that the applicant has no criminal record and has not collaborated with the Communist political police or the secret service. Candidacies are published on the website of the Standing Bureau of the parliament and within fifteen days 'well-substantiated objections against candidates can be filed in writing'. Candidates are then interviewed in a joint session of specialized committees of both chambers who draft a joint report and a shortlist of candidates. When members are appointed during a plenary session of both chambers of the parliament by the majority of votes of the deputies and senators present, at least six of them should have a law degree.[191]

While the legal framework is thus perfectly in line with the above-mentioned recommendations, appointments of new members to the NCCD have been regularly accompanied by criticism from international monitoring bodies[192] as well as civil society organizations. The EELN expert describes the appointment procedure as 'usually follow[ing] a political algorithm of distribution of the positions of members of the NCCD steering board, based on political support'.[193] Already back in 2007, when the first appointments under the amended legislations were made, a coalition of twenty NGOs proposed and requested to apply professional standards for assessing the candidates.[194] In 2009, six positions became vacant and the procedure for filling the vacancies took several months. NGOs filed objections against some of the candidates complaining that they did not have the required expertise in the field of human rights and protection against discrimination. The objections were dismissed and the candidates backed by the political parties present in parliament were appointed while the independent candidates were not. In 2012, three appointments were made. In one case an outgoing steering board member with significant experience in the anti-discrimination field was confirmed in spite of lack of political support. The two other members appeared to be political appointees. In 2015, six new appointments had to be made. This procedure was particularly contested because of a lack of transparency and irregularities during the procedure. In fact, a candidate who was already heard by the specialized parliamentarian committees was heard a second time because after the first hearing the candidate was not included in the shortlist of six candidates proposed by the committees to the parliament. After the second hearing, the candidate was included in the list proposed to the parliament and the only candidate who had no backing from any political party, a former steering board member, was taken off the list. Apart from

191 Ordinance 137/2000, Arts 23–24; EELN, Country Report Romania, 2017, 110.

192 See, for instance, ECRI, 'Report on Romania (fourth monitoring cycle) adopted on 19 March 2014' (n 189) paras 55–56.

193 EELN, Country Report Romania, 2017, 109; and Country Report Romania, 2020, 78.

194 EELN, Country Report Romania, 2017, 109; and Country Report Romania, 2020, 81.

these procedural irregularities, the appointments were criticized for not respecting the required ratio of two thirds of the members being law graduates.[195]

This ratio was again not respected with regard to appointments made in 2017 and 2018 and a group of parliamentarians challenged these appointments before the Constitutional Court. In addition to the flouting of this requirement, it was submitted that some of the members of the steering board did not have the required expertise in the field. The complaint was supported by an *amicus curiae* brief by the NGO Anti-discrimination Coalition based on the same arguments and asserting 'that the failure to observe the legal requirements lead to the politicization and de-professionalization of the national equality body'.[196] In June 2018, the Constitutional Court found a violation of the law in the appointments of 2018 for not complying with the requirement of two-thirds of the steering boards member having a law degree. Thus the decision of the parliament on the appointment was annulled. While the wording of the Ordinance in this respect left some doubt about whether the 2/3 ratio was a legal obligation or a mere recommendation, this judgment makes clear that is has to be understood as an obligation.[197]

The Court, therefore, only dealt with the issue regarding the 2/3 ratio of lawyers on the steering board but not with the alleged lack of expertise in the field of human rights and combating discrimination. As confirmed by all interlocutors, including a current member of the Steering Committee, this is, however, also a problematic issue and an example of the fact that even if the legal framework is sound, its application in practice may not be satisfactory.[198] Combined with the huge influence of political parties in the appointment of steering board members this leads to a situation in which the functioning of the body also cannot be considered as independent. Indeed, several interlocutors agreed that when political figures are at play or political interests are involved in a discrimination case, the NCCD has, at times, come to absurd conclusions in such cases.[199] More recently, the NCCD has also taken some controversial decisions with regard to cases involving the Orthodox Church and religious issues.[200] And yet, the NCCD is perceived as the last functioning human rights institution in Romania which needs to be professionalized

[195] EELN, Country Report Romania, 2017, 109–10; see also Country Report, 2020, 80.

[196] Romanita Iordache, 'Constitutional Court revokes the mandate of one of the members of the Steering Board of the NCCD' (EELN News Report, 21 June 2018).

[197] ibid.

[198] Interviews, human rights lawyer I, Romania, EELN legal expert, 2 July 2018; steering board member of NCCD, 10 July 2018.

[199] Interviews, human rights lawyer II, Romania, EELN legal expert, 25 July 2018; Forin Buhuceanu, 6 August 2018; steering board member of NCCD, 10 July 2018. For a recent decision that was widely criticized for being political, involving Prime Minister Viorica Dancila, seeRomanita Iordache, 'The Prime Minister calling political critics pejoratively as "autistic" does not amount to discrimination finds the national equality body' (EELN News Report, 6 March 2018).

[200] Interview, human rights lawyer I, Romania, EELN legal expert, 2 April 2021. In the 2020 appointment procedure for steering board members, one candidate was nominated by the Orthodox Church but was not appointed.

and at the same time defended against the attacks by some political groups who would like to see a more decorative institution instead of one that is an effectively sanctioning institution.[201] One interlocutor put it quite dramatically when he said there were attempts to 'legally, institutionally and financially castrate' the NCCD.

One way to defend it against such attacks, is to provide for strong protection for steering board members against arbitrary dismissal during their five-year term. Under the law, a member can be dismissed only if he/she is unable to fulfil their duties (without specifying for how long), in case of a criminal conviction, or if it transpires that a condition for being appointed in the first place is not met. Another possibility is where two thirds of the steering board members propose the dismissal.[202] Except for the above-described case, in which the appointment decision of the parliament was annulled by the Constitutional Court for not complying with the requirement of appointing six members with a legal background, there have been no dismissals so far. However, there appear to be attempts not only at 'castrating' the institution but at 'killing' it altogether.

A bill initiated by a politician who was previously fined by the Equality Body for discriminatory statements against the Romanian LGBT community, sought to abolish the Anti-Discrimination Law and through this to remove the Equality Body. The explanatory memorandum to the bill invoked the 'alleged anti-Romanian character of the national equality body, its alleged control by the Hungarian Democratic Union, the allegation that it supports terrorism and presented the [NCCD] as working to nullify "Romanian values, traditional Christian values and the rights of Romanians in their own country"'.[203] The bill was repealed by a large majority in the Senate[204] after having been tacitly accepted in the Chamber of Deputies, which had given rise to protests from civil society organizations and the NCCD. In the Senate, the main reason for rejecting the bill was that this would amount to a breach of EU obligations. However, it did not make any statements against the allegation of the anti-Romanian character of the NCCD. As the issue was widely reported in the media, it has been perceived as negative publicity for the NCCD and placed the institutions in a very uncomfortable situation.[205]

Calls to abolish the NCCD did not end in 2018. The NCCD's aligning itself with the LGBT association ACCEPT in the *Coman* case before the CJEU and the Constitutional Court, the signing of a partnership agreement with the same association for the purpose of the development and holding of training for judges,

201 Interview, Board member of ACCEPT, 6 August 2018.

202 Ordinance 137/2000, Art 23(5).

203 Romanita Iordache, 'Draft bill aiming to abrogate Anti-discrimination Law is adopted by the Chamber of Deputies tacitly' (EELN News Report, 1 March 2017).

204 Romanita Iordache, 'The Senate rejects draft bill aiming to abrogate Antidiscrimination Law' (EELN News Report, 15 March 2017); and Equinet, 'Romania: Senate rejects Draft Bill aiming to repeal Anti-Discrimination Law and disable the Equality Body' (27 March 2017) <https://www.archive.equineteurope.org/Romania-Senate-rejects-Draft-Bill-aiming-to-repeal-Anti-Discrimination-Law-and>.

205 Interview, steering board member of NCCD, 10 July 2018.

prosecutors, lawyers, teachers, medical doctors, and social workers, its public support for a draft bill on civil partnership as well as the summoning of the (former) Romanian president, of a Liberal Senator, and of the spokesperson of the Orthodox Church when complaints were filed against these persons have all given rise to a fierce reaction by some political leaders. The vice-president of the Liberal Party and other politicians called for the institution to be closed down. They argued that 'the NCCD is a Gestapo type institution which does nothing else but try to oppress any form of freedom of expression as well as belief and religious freedom' and that 'the abolition of this institution is absolutely necessary and vital to the health of public opinion, so that people can express themselves publicly'. The proactive position of the president of the NCCD is described by these voices as 'a threat against social peace'.[206]

While the attacks on the very existence of the institution have—so far—not brought about the desired result, another way to curtail the scope of action and effectiveness of the NCCD is of course through its budget. While the Commission in 2012 had a budget of 4.28 million EUR, in 2016 it amounted to only 1.17 million and to 1.2 million in 2018.[207] It rose to 1.75 million EUR in 2020.[208] While there has been a slight increase in recent years, the NCCD is reportedly barely able to cover the costs with regard to its adjudicatory function, and there is hardly any budget available for activities to prevent discrimination and promote equality.[209] Between 2015 and 2018 the NCCD was not in a position to publish the yearly survey on the perceptions and attitudes regarding discrimination in Romania. Such surveys are carried out as part of the projects with external funding.[210] One of these projects aimed at the elaboration of a national strategy to prevent and combat discrimination for the period 2014–20 based on relevant European standards. The resulting document was, however, not taken up by the government.[211]

In terms of staff it has been observed that for many years the approved number of ninety-six staff positions has not been filled. Currently sixty-four positions are occupied.[212] It has also been observed that the salary for staff members is very low

[206] Romanita Iordache, 'Attacks against the Romanian equality body (NCCD)' (EELN News Report, 31 October 2018).

[207] EELN, Country Report Romania, 2017, 111; and Country Report Romania, 2020, 81; Romanita Iordache, 'National equality body publishes annual activity report for 2017' (EELN News Report, 28 May 2018).

[208] Information on Equinet's members' page, at https://equineteurope.org/author/romania_nccd/.

[209] Interview, steering board member of NCCD, 10 July 2018. See also ACFC, 'Fourth Opinion on Romania adopted on 22 June 2017' ACFC/OP/IV(2017)005, para 34; and ECRI, 'Report on Romania (fifth monitoring cycle) adopted on 3 April 2019' CRI(2019)20, paras 20–21.

[210] Romanita Iordache, 'Report on attitudes and perceptions regarding discrimination in Romania released by the national equality body' (EELN News Report, 21 September 2015); Romanita Iordache, 'National survey on attitudes and perceptions of discrimination in Romania' (EELN News Report, 5 March 2019).

[211] Part of the project was also an evaluation of the former national strategy, undertaken by external experts. The documentation to the project is available at http://nediscriminare.ro/proiect_en.

[212] NCCD, Activity Report 2019, 59.

which leads to constant staff turnover. Regarding the NCCD's premises, ECRI had critically observed in 2014 that they 'were not clearly indicated or easy to find; furthermore, they did not appear to be suitable for such an important institution'.[213] The situation does not appear to have improved since then. The NCCD has had to move several times already and its current premises are still not considered to be appropriate.[214]

According to Article 29(2) of the law, the NCCD is required to set up 'territorial structures'. Outside of Bucharest, the NCCD is running two offices, one in Buzau and one in Tirgu Mures. The staff in these offices do not provide support to victims of discrimination but focus instead on monitoring the media in these cities and reporting back to the office in Bucharest. It is only rarely that these outreach offices have sent cases to be analysed by the steering board. Persons who feel discriminated against need to address their complaint to the NCCD in Bucharest and have to travel there for the hearings. Conversely, if an investigation into an individual complaint is needed in one of these cities, the staff from the regional offices would not carry this out, staff from Bucharest would be sent to do so. So the outreach offices should be strengthened considerably and more efficiently functioning offices should be established throughout the country.[215]

When comparing this situation with ECRI's revised GPR No 2 on Equality Bodies, it becomes quite clear that the NCCD is facing challenges in many respects. Not only is the appointment procedure of its governing board far from being transparent, competency-based, and participatory, even if the executive has no influence in the selection process. The independence of its members can be questioned when looking at decisions taken that involve political figures or interests. The body is even exposed to the threat of being abolished altogether and, as this has proven unsuccessful so far, it is hampered in its functioning by a very limited budget, insufficient staffing, and inadequate premises. Geographic outreach is insufficient. As one interlocutor put it in a nutshell: 'The state is doing really nothing to support NCCD'. In such circumstances it would be reasonable to expect the European Commission at least to engage in a dialogue with Romanian authorities to make it clear that it is not sufficient to set up a structure but then not provide it with the necessary support in order for it to fulfil its mandate. It appears, however, that the Commission has other priorities in Romania (as someone said 'for good reasons'), with the Cooperation and Verification Mechanism still in place, corruption continuing to be a widespread phenomenon, and political turbulence calling for its attention. Against this background it seems that the way the NCCD manages to deploy its adjudicatory functions, notwithstanding all the above-mentioned

[213] ECRI, 'Report on Romania (fourth monitoring cycle) adopted on 19 March 2014' (n 189) paras 57 and 59.
[214] Interview, steering board member of NCCD, 10 July 2018.
[215] Interview, steering board member of NCCD, 10 July 2018.

difficulties and the recent controversial decisions involving religious issues, is still considered to be satisfactory.[216]

As already mentioned, the handling of complaints as well as ex officio started cases as a quasi-judicial body is the task that absorbs most of the NCCD's resources.[217] Yet, according to the law, it is supposed to carry out other functions, such as preventing and combating discrimination through awareness-raising campaigns and the proposal of special measures for persons affected by discrimination, mediating between the parties, monitoring discrimination cases, proposing legislation with a view to harmonizing the legal framework with the principle of non-discrimination, as well as the preparation of surveys and undertaking research on issues related to discrimination.[218]

In its 2014 report, ECRI took note of the fact that according to information provided by NGOs who deal with Roma issues many Roma do not know of the existence of the body or do not trust it. It also noted that the NCCD highlighted that additional funds would be needed for the proper fulfilment of their awareness-raising obligations. With regard to its mediating activities, ECRI 'recommended that the law establish a clear mediation procedure to preclude NCCD from acting both as mediator and judge'. And finally, it recommended that the NCCD's competences be extended to allow it to comment on draft legislation and that it should make more extensive use of its power to bring issues of non-compliance with the equal treatment legislation which it encounters in the context of its case-work to the attention of the parliament.[219]

When it comes to the 'core business' of the NCCD, namely, the handling of complaints, in 2019, NCCD received 904 petitions. The most recurrent discrimination ground was the one related to belonging to a social category (386 complaints), followed by discrimination on grounds of disability (eighty-seven complaints), nationality (eighty complaints), ethnicity (forty-eight complaints), age (thirty-five complaints), gender (twenty-nine complaints), language (twenty complaints), religion and belief (seventeen and fifteen complaints respectively), and sexual orientation (thirteen complaints). Nearly half of the cases regarded discrimination in the field of employment (432 complaints), followed by discrimination in the access to public services (181 complaints), in education (forty-three complaints), in the access to public facilities (twenty-one complaints) and housing (four complaints). 163 cases concerned a violation of the personal dignity. The NCCD found discrimination in 192 cases.[220] About ten to fifteen cases per year are initiated by the

[216] Interview, Board member of ACCEPT, 6 August 2018.
[217] Ordinance 137/2000, Art 19(1c) and (2).
[218] Ordinance 137/2000, Art 18 and 19(1). Government Decision 1194 from 27 November 2001 sets out the details of NCCD's mandate.
[219] ECRI, 'Report on Romania (fourth monitoring cycle) adopted on 19 March 2014' (n 189) paras 54, 61–67.
[220] NCCD, Activity Report 2019.

NCCD ex officio. These cases mostly go back to reports in the mass media or to observations the NCCD makes on Romanian society.[221]

The NCCD has at its disposal an array of investigation tools.[222] If the steering board member responsible for a case file finds that an investigation is necessary, two lawyers visit the place where the alleged discrimination took place, take declarations from witnesses, obtain documentation and make copies of relevant material, and subsequently draft a report about their findings which is then part of the evidence for the decision of the case.[223] Where an alleged perpetrator does not cooperate during the investigations, the NCCD can impose a fine. Given that a failure to cooperate automatically means in most cases, that the alleged perpetrator will not be in a position to prove that no discrimination has taken place, this leads to an additional fine related to the finding of discrimination. Therefore, in the experience of the NCCD, alleged perpetrators normally cooperate during investigations.[224] With a view to ensuring impartiality and the adversarial principle of the proceedings, the internal regulations provide that it can summon the accused perpetrator during the hearings.[225]

If the NCCD finds discrimination it can impose a fine or issue a recommendation or warning. In its initial practice, the NCCD preferred warnings to fines, which became an issue in the *ACCEPT* case involving George Becali that reached the CJEU. In essence, the Court found that the fact that a sanction is of a non-pecuniary nature alone does not mean that the requirement of sanctions being effective, proportionate, and dissuasive is not fulfilled, especially if accompanied by a sufficient degree of publicity. However, it also made clear that if warnings are normally used only for very minor offences, such a sanction would not be commensurate to the seriousness of a breach of the principle of equal treatment.[226] The NCCD is increasingly imposing fines instead of just issuing a warning. In 2011 it imposed a fine only in 23 per cent of the cases in which it found discrimination. In 2012, this figure slightly rose to 31 per cent.[227] While in 2016 it imposed a fine in 111 cases out of the 112 cases in which it found discrimination, thus reaching nearly 100 per cent, this figure dropped again in the following years.[228] In the 192 cases in which the NCCD found a discrimination in 2019, it issued 111 fines, 104

221 Interview, steering board member of NCCD, 10 July 2018.

222 Ordinance 137/2000 Art 26(3).

223 In 2019, NCCD undertook forty investigations, twenty-two of which were in the Bucharest-Ilfov region. NCCD, Activity Report 2019, 12.

224 Interview, steering board member of NCCD, 10 July 2018.

225 Iordache, 'Attacks against the Romanian equality body (NCCD)' (n 206).

226 *Asociația Accept v Consiliul Național pentru Combaterea Discriminării*, [2013] ECLI:EU:C:2013:275, paras 68 and 70.

227 Figures calculated on the basis of the information available in ECRI, 'Report on Romania (fourth monitoring cycle) adopted on 19 March 2014' (n 189) fn to para 58.

228 Romanita Iordache, 'National equality body publishes annual activity report for 2016' (EELN News Report, 7 June 2017); Iordache, 'National equality body publishes annual activity report for 2017' (n 207).

warnings, eighty recommendations, and in nineteen cases it ordered that a summary of its decision be published in the media, the ratio of fines thus falling to 58 per cent.[229]

As a consequence of the *ACCEPT* case, in 2013 the range of fines that can be imposed by the NCCD has been considerably increased. While for individual victims the range used to be between 400 and 4,000 RON (approximately 85 and 850 EUR), it has been increased to 1,000 to 30,000 RON (approximately 215 to 6,500 EUR). Where the victim is a group or community, the range was increased from 600 to 8,000 RON (approximately 130 to 1,700 EUR) before the amendments to 2,000 to 100,000 RON (approximately 430 to 21,500 EUR) after the amendments.[230] In 2017, the highest fine applied in one case was of 50,000 RON (approximately 10,700 EUR).[231] The usual amount of a fine is however close to the lower limit that can be imposed.[232] The amount of the fine is considered to be less important than the sign that is sent to the population at large, if important public figures are fined, even if with low amounts. The example of the Romanian president who was subject to a fine of about 130 EUR for anti-Roma statements was given in this context.[233] The decision of the NCCD in this case was upheld on appeal and led to wide discussion in the media and Romanian society, thereby contributing to a better understanding of discrimination and its harmful effects on society.[234] It was however suggested that guidelines for applying fines should be developed that would take into consideration different degrees of seriousness of violations and make the application of fines more transparent.[235]

NCCD decisions can be appealed within fifteen days before the administrative courts. If they are not appealed within the time limit, they represent a writ of execution.[236] The success rate of NCCD decisions passing the scrutiny of administrative courts is approximately 82 per cent.[237] While this is a respectable percentage, it is interesting to note that it has gone down from 95 per cent in 2007 and 86 per cent in 2016.[238] A possible explanation for this is that in the early years judges were themselves not very familiar with the equal treatment legislation and thus relied more often on the assessment of the body established with an explicit mandate to oversee

[229] NCCD, Activity Report 2019, 22; sanctions can be cumulated.

[230] EELN, Country Report Romania, 2020, 73. Also the ACFC took note of this increase in its opinion. See ACFC, 'Fourth Opinion on Romania adopted on 22 June 2017' (n 209) para 32.

[231] Iordache, 'National equality body publishes annual activity report for 2017' (n 207).

[232] In fact, according to the NCCD, Activity Report 2019, 25, eighty of the 111 fines amounted to 1,000 or 2,000 RON.

[233] Interview, steering board member of NCCD, 10 July 2018.

[234] ACFC, 'Fourth Opinion on Romania adopted on 22 June 2017' (n 209) para 63.

[235] Interview, steering board member of NCCD, 10 July 2018; human rights lawyer I, Romania, EELN legal expert, 2 April 2021.

[236] Ordinance 137/2000, Art 20(9–10).

[237] NCCD, Activity Report 2019, 29.

[238] Interview, Istavan Haller, 11 July 2018; and Iordache, 'National equality body publishes annual activity report for 2016' (n 228).

the proper observance of this legislation. With the increasing experience of judges, inter alia due to training provided by the NCCD, they have started overturning NCCD decisions. The increasing number of successfully appealed decisions could also be related to the fact that the quality of legal reasoning provided by the NCCD is reportedly getting lower recently.[239] However, since some of the NCCD's current decisions are influenced by political interests or pressure from the Orthodox Church, some interlocutors even expressed their hope that the courts *will* overturn the NCCD's decisions.

When it comes to following up on decisions taken by the NCCD, until recently there was no structured and consistent monitoring mechanism in place to deal with compliance with NCCD decisions. Initiatives depended on the interest taken by the steering board member responsible for the file.[240] Recently, however, the body has assigned the task to one staff member from the legal department to verify whether fines are paid or not, and if necessary inform the financial authorities so that their decision may be enforced.[241] Furthermore, it is worth mentioning that in one case the NCCD undertook a monitoring exercise, following up on two previous decisions related to the failure of local authorities to ensure the necessary conditions for persons with mobility disabilities to be able to use local transportation.[242] Finding that the local authorities had still failed to provide the necessary conditions as recommended by the NCCD, it started another ex officio case and imposed a cumulative fine of 314,000 RON (approximately 67,400 EUR) on the Ministry of Labour, the National Agency for Payments and Social Inspection, and thirty-four city mayors.[243] While all these decisions were confirmed by courts when challenged on appeal, the most recent decision in a case involving the issue of accessibility of public transportation for persons with disabilities departs from the established NCCD jurisprudence.[244] In the view of the NCCD the individual complainant did not provide enough evidence of the facts required to substantiate the misdemeanour. The decision has been criticized for departing from an adequate application of the principle on the sharing of the burden of proof and even members of the NCCD publicly distanced themselves from this decision as being politically motivated. They alleged that the majority of steering board members

[239] This has been noted by ECRI in its 'Report on Romania (fourth monitoring cycle) adopted on 19 March 2014' (n 189) para 58, and confirmed by interlocutors, for instance, in the interview with human rights lawyer II, Romania, EELN legal expert, 25 July 2018 and human rights lawyer I, Romania, EELN legal expert, 2 April 2021.

[240] EELN, Country Report Romania, 2017, 106–07; and interview, steering board member of NCCD, 10 July 2018.

[241] Interview, steering board member of NCCD, 11 July 2018.

[242] NCCD, Decision 251 of 30 April 2014, imposing a cumulative fine on thirty-nine mayors and the National Agency for Payments and Social Inspection of 75,000 RON (approximately 16,100 EUR). This case involved an ex officio investigation in the capital cities of all Romanian counties. See also NCCD, Decision 271 of 10 June 2015.

[243] NCCD, Decision 357 of 11 May 2016.

[244] NCCD, Decision 170 of 9 May 2018.

appointed with the backing of political parties in the then governing coalition did not want to take a decision which would have sanctioned the mayor of Bucharest, a key political figure in the ruling Social Democratic Party.[245] It thus appears to be one of those cases where hope remains that the decision will be overturned by the courts in appeal.

The NCCD's decisions often receive significant media coverage, especially if they involve political figures. These cases, as well as cases on sensitive issues, also contributed to enhancing the visibility and prestige of the NCCD[246] and caused the increasing number of complaints submitted to it.[247] However the NCCD's ability to order the perpetrator to publish a summary of its decision on its website or the media does not appear to be so strong. Even if this order is followed, it does not appear that this is leading to an increase in complaints. The body itself does not appear to pursue a very active media strategy. It informs the media mainly about its decisions in those cases that have already been covered by the media. This cautiousness is also related to the experience in one case where a bank that had been found to discriminate against persons with disabilities sued the NCCD for damages as it had publicized its decision in the media and this had allegedly destroyed the image of the bank.[248] The perception of NGO representatives is that the NCCD is doing a good job in informing the media about cases before it, however the focus of this information appears to be on 'mainstream topics' such as discrimination of pregnant women or mothers or discrimination based on disability. The perception is that the NCCD is more reluctant to bring to the media's attention cases that relate to discrimination of Roma,[249] even though there have been important decisions involving Roma.

In a decision taken in 2016, for instance, the NCCD decided that criteria for social housing indirectly discriminate against Roma in that they disproportionately factored in the level of education: the higher the level of education the higher the chances of getting access to social housing. Taking into consideration statistical data, according to which a much higher percentage of Roma did not graduate as compared to non-Roma, the NCCD (and on appeal, the Targu Mures Court of Appeal) found that this criterion negatively affected especially persons of Roma origin and could not be justified.[250] In another case it found for the first time

[245] Romanita Iordache, 'NCCD jurisprudence on ensuring accessibility of public transportation reversed' (EELN News Report, 17 May 2018).

[246] EELN, Country Report Romania, 2020, 79.

[247] Interview, steering board member of NCCD, 11 July 2018. For the trend in the number of petitions since 2002 see NCCD, Activity Report 2019, 8.

[248] Interview, steering board member of NCCD, 11 July 2018.

[249] Interview with human rights lawyer II, Romania, EELN legal expert, 25 July 2018.

[250] NCCD decision 511 of 20 July 2016, confirmed by Targu Mures Court of Appeal decision 30/2017 of 17 March 2017. See Romanita Iordache, 'Court of Appeal maintains NCCD decision on social housing criteria leading to discrimination' (EELN News Report, 31 January 2018). In a similar case, the NCCD found direct discrimination on the ground of disability, as the criteria for the allocation of social housing in Bucharest assigned four points for persons with disability, while it assigned ten points for persons with higher education and fifteen points for veterans and war widows, revolutionaries, and

intersectional discrimination against Romani women, a case that passed completely unnoticed by the media.[251] On the other hand, LGBT issues, although definitely considered a 'hot topic', have been addressed by the NCCD through the media and it even brought an *amicus curiae* to the Constitutional Court in the *Coman* case.[252] As mentioned above, its positioning on LGBT issues has also contributed to its being exposed to attacks from various sides, including political leaders.

A problematic aspect of the legislation could be that the procedure before the NCCD has no suspensive effect as to time limits for complaining before courts. According to Article 27(2) of Ordinance 137/2000 this time limit is three years from the commission of the discriminatory act. The law states that the NCCD should deliver its decision within ninety days from receiving the complaint.[253] In practice, the NCCD is able to decide complaints within six to nine months. The lack of suspensive effect should therefore not constitute a problem in practice.

Victims of discrimination can of course decide to approach the courts right away instead of filing a complaint with the NCCD first. Or they could address the courts after getting a decision from the NCCD in order to ask for compensation, as the NCCD is not allowed to compensate for damages. In both options, the court has to summon the NCCD as an expert institution.[254] The body regularly participates in more than 700 civil cases per year which is a further strain on its already limited resources.[255] In principle, this legal provision should be welcomed as it provides the Equality Body with an opportunity to support the judiciary with its expertise in the equal treatment legislation and can thus contribute to well-informed and legally sound decisions. However, considering the huge number of cases in which the NCCD is required to participate, this can be reasonably done only if the necessary human and financial resources are made available—a precondition which does not appear to be met in the case of the NCCD.

Comparing the situation with regard to the effective functioning of the NCCD with ECRI's revised GPR No 2 the following conclusions can be drawn: When dealing with complaints before it, it uses the investigative powers as recommended by ECRI, it can issue legally binding decisions and is comparatively quick in reaching decisions, although not within the time limit provided by law. While it increasingly imposes fines, it still continues the practice of issuing a warning only

former political detainees. See Romanita Iordache, 'National equality body decision on social housing criteria in Bucharest' (EELN News Report, 12 August 2016).

[251] Iustina Ionescu, 'First case of multiple discrimination against Romani women sanctioned by the Romanian national equality body' (EELN News Report, 23 January 2018); interview, Istavan Haller, 11 July 2018.

[252] Interview with human rights lawyer II, Romania, EELN legal expert, 25 July 2018.

[253] Ordinance 137/2000, Art 20(7).

[254] Ordinance 137/2000, Art 27(3).

[255] EELN, Country Report Romania, 2020, 83–84; confirmed by the interview with steering board member of NCCD, 10 July 2018.

which cannot be considered an effective, proportionate, and dissuasive sanction. More recently, its decisions do not appear to be independent from political influence in all instances and pressure from the Orthodox Church in particular is noticeable. The legal reasoning is not always well developed. Follow-up to its decisions and recommendations has so far been sporadic and is just starting to be developed. In the past, the NCCD has found discrimination in cases involving important political figures and has thereby sent out an important message to the public that discrimination is unacceptable. These cases have received a lot of media attention and have contributed to increasing the visibility of and trust in the Equality Body. This shows how important it is that the body is absolutely immune from outside (political or other) influence. As well as deciding cases brought before it, the NCCD also intervenes as *amicus curiae* in important and sensitive cases. By law the NCCD has to be involved in all civil cases relating to discrimination. While this is, in principle, to be welcomed, the resources for this task do not appear to be sufficient. Overall, the Equality Body is dedicating most of its resources to complaints handling so that promotional and preventive activities are very limited. Nearly all of the just-described deficiencies are not related to the legislation on which the NCCD is founded but to the way it is implemented. Most importantly, they are related to a lack of independence and qualification of some of the steering board members as well as to insufficient human and financial resources.

In order to properly comply with the requirements under the RED the appointment procedure for Steering Board members urgently needs to be depoliticized and the selection process be made transparent and competency-based. The budget would need to be increased so as to allow the Equality Body 'to carry out each of [its] equality functions effectively'.[256] For the same purpose, additional staff is needed, especially to establish more regional offices with a mandate going beyond the mere monitoring of the media. All these challenges could be addressed systematically with the adoption of a national strategy for combating discrimination. All these issues remain within the remit of the state authorities and the lack of acting on them could be considered an infringement of the obligations under the RED or at least to require that the Commission enter into a dialogue with state authorities on how to remedy the shortcomings.

5.3.3.2 Case Study: Bulgaria—The Commission for Protection Against Discrimination

The Bulgarian Commission for Protection Against Discrimination (CPAD) has also been selected as a case study because from a legal point of view it is a quasi-judicial Equality Body with strong competences. Among Equinet members it has

[256] European Commission, 'Commission Recommendation on Standards for Equality Bodies' (n 19) 8.

'one of the most formal quasi-judicial procedures'.[257] In the following, the legal aspects related to its independence and functioning will briefly be recalled before discussing its practical functioning to assess the good practices and the challenges of the body in improving access to justice for victims of discrimination.

According to Article 40 of the Protection Against Discrimination Act (PADA) the Commission is an 'independent specialized state body for prevention of discrimination, protection against discrimination and ensuring equal opportunities'. The wording of the law thus goes beyond the strict requirement under the RED, which does not require the institution as such to be independent but just that its functioning is independent. Article 41 PADA regulates the appointment procedure for the Commission: it shall be composed of nine members, five of whom are elected by the National Assembly (among them the Chairperson and the Deputy Chairperson), and four are appointed by the President of the Republic. They shall serve for a five-year term and the composition should be balanced in terms of participation of women and men as well as persons belonging to national minorities. According to Article 42 PADA, Bulgarian citizens who have graduated from a university (at least four members need to have a law degree), have knowledge and experience in the field of human rights, and have not been convicted of an intentional public law offence can become members of the Commission. Any other professional activity, except for engaging in scientific activities, as well as membership of a governing body of a political party, is incompatible with becoming a member of the Commission. A Commissioner can be dismissed upon the member's own request, if he/she is not capable of performing his/her duties for more than six months or if a conflict of interest arises as regulated under the Conflict of Interest Prevention and Ascertainment Act (Art 44 PADA). The remuneration is coupled with the remuneration of the Chairperson of the National Assembly.[258] The budget is approved by the parliament to which the Commission is accountable. It reports to the parliament annually.[259] The law lays down explicitly that the 'Commission shall have its own regional representatives'.[260]

Albeit the provisions regarding the independence of the Commission and the competency-based appointment procedure as well as (at least to some extent) the pluralist representation of society appear promising, various international monitoring bodies have raised concern over the practical implementation of these provisions. The Committee on the Elimination of Racial Discrimination, for instance, has identified the limited independence of the Commission as one of the reasons

[257] Equinet, 'Learning More About Functions of Quasi-Judicial Equality Bodies: Commission for the Protection from Discrimination, Bulgaria in Focus' (7 June 2017) <https://www.archive.equineteurope.org/Learning-more-about-quasi-judicial-functions-of-equality-bodies>.

[258] The Chairperson of the CPAD receives 90 per cent of the Chairperson of the National Assembly's monthly remuneration, the Deputy Chairperson receives 80 per cent, and a member 75 per cent. See Art 45 PADA.

[259] Art 40(3) and (5) PADA.

[260] Art 40(4) PADA.

explaining 'persistent shortcomings in the function of the ... bod[y]' and thus recommends that the state 'take immediate measures to strengthen the ... independence' of the CPAD.[261] The Advisory Committee under the Framework Convention for the Protection of National Minorities also noted 'that concerns have been voiced about the lack of a sufficiently clear, transparent and participatory selection process for Commission members that would promote the independence of the Commission and public confidence therein.'[262] In this context, it referred to the review of status carried out by the International Coordinating Committee of National Institutions for the Promotion and Protection of Human Rights' Sub-Committee on Accreditation in which concerns about independence were amongst the reasons for recommending that the Commission be accredited with B status.[263] The Advisory Committee thus called on the Bulgarian authorities 'to strengthen the recruitment procedures for the members of the Commission for Protection against Discrimination ... in order inter alia to increase the transparency of these procedures at all stages and widen the circle of potential candidates.'[264] While rules on the nomination of candidates have been introduced by parliament and the president in 2017, they do not fully address the criticism raised by international monitoring bodies.[265] ECRI was of the view that the legal framework could also be strengthened by including a provision expressly stating that members of the CPAD may not receive instructions.[266]

With regard to the appointments of CPAD members in 2012, the Bulgarian expert in the EELN reported that two former members were re-elected but the others 'demonstrate no expertise at all in anti-discrimination law. One is a member of the openly racist Ataka party.' The expert also reported that the procedure for the appointment of the president of the CPAD lasting for one year, arguably linked

[261] CERD, 'Concluding observations on the combined twentieth to twenty-second periodic reports of Bulgaria' (31 May 2017) CERD/C/BGR/CO/20–22, paras 9–10; see also Bulgarian Helsinki Committee, 'Human Rights in Bulgaria in 2017' (2018) 90.

[262] ACFC, 'Third opinion on Bulgaria adopted on 11 February 2014' ACFC/OP/III(2014)001, para 40. See also the recommendation of CERD in para 10(b) which call for 'effective measures to reinforce public confidence in existing institutions and mechanisms.'

[263] ibid, referring to ICC Sub-Committee on Accreditation Report—October 2011, item 2.3, pp 8–9: 'The existing legislation does not provide a clear, transparent and participatory selection process that promotes the independence of, and public confidence in, the CPD. The SCA encourages the CPD to advocate for legislative amendments to: – publicise vacancies; – maximise the number of potential candidates from a wide range of societal groups; – promote broad consultation and/or participation in the application, screening and selection process; and – ensure pluralism in the composition of the Commission.' Further reasons for granting B status were the fact that the mandate covered equality and non-discrimination but not all human rights, and that PADA did not provide for immunity for actions undertaken by Commissioners in their official capacity. See on this also Tamás Kádár, 'The Standing of National Equality Bodies before the European Union Court of Justice: the Implications of the Belov Judgment' (2013) 11 The Equal Rights Review 13, 14.

[264] ACFC, 'Third opinion on Bulgaria adopted on 11 February 2014' (n 262) para 45.

[265] EELN, Country Report Bulgaria, 2020, 73–74; ACFC, 'Fourth opinion on Bulgaria adopted on 26 May 2020' ACFC/OP/IV(2020)001Final, para 39.

[266] ECRI, 'Report on Bulgaria (fifth monitoring cycle) adopted on 19 June 2014' CRI(2014)36, paras 28–29.

to political intervention.[267] Further, she notes in the EELN report the continuing attacks on the CPAD by certain political parties, also in the context of nomination of new members, calling for the body to be closed down or the budget cut. The reason for these attacks are considered to be less about the fact that the CPAD deals with issues of sexual orientation, but rather about racism against Roma and Turks. She further observed that the parliament and the president influence the body's performance by choosing CPAD members. This has resulted in a situation in which some proceedings against political leaders or high-ranking public officials 'have been unreasonably lengthy' and/or the CPAD's decisions 'have been marked by a tendency to exonerate the public figures involved'.[268]

A common concern of both the Committee on the Elimination of Discrimination (CERD) and ECRI appears to be the extent to which the CPAD raises awareness and reaches out to groups particularly vulnerable to discrimination. The CERD more generally recommends that Bulgarian authorities 'embark on awareness-raising campaigns … on the mechanisms available to submit complaints' addressing both the general public and particularly vulnerable groups, and to 'ensure that complaint procedures are simple, widely known and accessible to all'.[269]

ECRI's comments focus more specifically on the issues of awareness raising and accessibility in terms of different languages used in the country and the regional representation. In its report in the fifth monitoring cycle, ECRI noted that information about PADA and the procedures before the CPAD were available only in Bulgarian and partly in English. It further noted that Bulgarian was the only language in which complaints could be submitted to the Commission. This raised ECRI's concern over the appropriate access to justice for some of the most vulnerable groups in the country.[270] Presently, the CPAD's website 'contains a built-in translation tool which converts the information into an extensive list of world languages. ECRI considers this simple innovation most ingenious; even if the automatic translations are far from perfect, they still manage to convey the essential information.'[271] However, complaints submitted in a language other than Bulgarian need to be accompanied by a Bulgarian translation which limits the ability of individuals belonging to certain vulnerable groups to submit a complaint.

[267] Quoted from Lilla Farkas, 'NGO and Equality Body Enforcement of EU Anti-Discrimination Law: Bulgarian Roma and the Electricity Sector' in Elise Muir and others (eds), *How EU Law Shapes Opportunities for Preliminary References on Fundamental Rights: Discrimination, Data Protection and Asylum* (European University Institute, EUI Working Papers 2017) 41.

[268] EELN, Country Report Bulgaria, 2018, 79–80 and 82–83. See also EELN, Country Report Bulgaria, 2020, 74.

[269] CERD, 'Concluding observations on the combined twentieth to twenty-second periodic reports of Bulgaria' (n 261) paras 9–10(c–d).

[270] ECRI, 'Report on Bulgaria (fifth monitoring cycle) adopted on 19 June 2014' (n 266) paras 10 and 91–92.

[271] ECRI, 'Conclusions on the Implementation of the Recommendations in Respect of Bulgaria Subject to Interim Follow-Up' (23 March 2017) CRI(2017)22, para 2.

Thus, as far as the ECRI is concerned, its recommendation has been implemented only partially.[272]

Since its fourth report adopted in 2009,[273] ECRI is also observing carefully the developments regarding the opening of regional CPAD offices. While in 2011, eighteen local branches were set up, the number increased to twenty in 2014, with however only eighteen being fully operational. ECRI therefore found no improvement, underlining the importance of these regional offices as they provide advice to victims of discrimination, assist them with filing complaints to the Commission, and refer cases to the Commission. However, in the view of ECRI, the offices do not have the necessary equipment and human resource to operate effectively. In fact, a single staff member with no additional support runs an office. ECRI therefore repeated its recommendation to invest more effort in setting up regional representatives in all twenty-eight administrative districts and to equip them with adequate human and financial resources to work effectively.[274] By 2020, twenty-four offices were set up, of which three had to be discontinued due to lack of funds needed to staff them.[275]

ECRI's focus on accessibility is also reflected in its revised GPR No 2 where it underlines that this requires, amongst other things, the establishment of local and regional offices and the possibility for those exposed to discrimination to contact and engage with the Equality Body in a language in which they are proficient.[276] While the Commission's Recommendations also require that it is possible to submit a complaint 'in the language of the complainant's choosing' it somewhat dilutes this recommendation by requiring that such a language 'is common in the Member State where the equality body is located'.[277] The language regarding regional offices appears to be a bit less demanding, as it recommends that states consider, where necessary for geographical or other reasons, enabling Equality Bodies to establish regional offices.[278] Compared to the situation in Romania, where only two regional offices exist, the situation is Bulgaria already appears more advanced. However, as ECRI pointed out in its report, they also need to be equipped with the adequate human and financial resources to work effectively. Furthermore, the EELN expert questioned the existence of preconditions for the independent operation of regional representatives, in particular when it comes to complaints against the regional or municipal government, considering that they are located

[272] ibid.

[273] ECRI, 'Report on Bulgaria (fourth monitoring cycle) adopted on 20 June 2008' CRI(2009)2, paras 35 and 37 and p 41.

[274] ECRI, 'Report on Bulgaria (fifth monitoring cycle) adopted on 19 June 2014' (n 266) 88–90.

[275] EELN, Country Report Bulgaria, 2020, 72.

[276] ECRI, 'General Policy Recommendation No 2: Equality Bodies to Combat Racism and Intolerance at National Level' (n 23) para 40.

[277] European Commission, 'Commission Recommendation on Standards for Equality Bodies' (n 19) Chapter II, 1.2.3., point 1.

[278] ibid Chapter II, 1.2.3., point 5.

in regional government buildings and rely on municipal employees during on-site consultations.[279]

The funding of the Commission is another issue of concern to various monitoring bodies. In 2017, the CERD thus recommended that Bulgarian authorities '[t]ake immediate measures to strengthen the … financial resources' of the CPAD.[280] The Commission suffered a serious budget cut in 2012. Since then, the budget steadily increased to reach an amount slightly higher in 2017 than in 2012 and the budget has continued to increase slightly until 2020.[281] As in the Romanian case, the biggest part of the budget is spent on the Commission's adjudicating activities, while it needs to raise funds from external donors to carry out the rest of its functions.[282] The financial resources are therefore not adequate to fulfil all its tasks and the Recommendation of the Commission on Standards for Equality Bodies has not been implemented. This Recommendation indeed says that '[r]esources can only be considered adequate if they allow equality bodies to carry out each of their equality functions effectively'.[283] ECRI 's revised GPR No 2 in addition lay down that if functions are expanded, 'this should be … accompanied by appropriate additional funding',[284] while the opposite happened in the Bulgarian case, when the assignment of an additional task coincided with a budget cut.[285]

This brings us to the analysis of the tasks assigned to the CPAD. While the whole range of functions assigned to the CPAD by the law will be briefly outlined, the analysis of the practical use will focus on its decision-making function.

Article 47 PADA is the central article laying down the tasks of the CPAD. The listing of tasks is clearly inspired by the attempt to have a faithful legal transposition into national legislation of the tasks required for Equality Bodies under the RED. Points 9 to 11 repeat the tasks as set out in the RED nearly word for word. Points 1 to 5 in a way may be seen as a specification of the task to support victims of discrimination. The first four points lay down how the Commission can do that in proceedings before itself: it shall establish violations of equal treatment legislation; order the prevention and termination of the violation and the restoration of the original situation; and impose sanctions and issue mandatory directions for

279 EELN, Country Report Bulgaria, 2020, 74–75.

280 CERD, 'Concluding observations on the combined twentieth to twenty-second periodic reports of Bulgaria' (n 261) para 10(a).

281 See the information about the Commission on Equinet's members' page, at https://equineteurope.org/author/bulgaria_cpd/, as well as Commission for Protection Against Discrimination, 'Annual Report for 2017' (2018) 158. According to the same sources, the number of staff increased from forty-six in 2012 to seventy-seven in 2017, although the plan since 2013 is to reach a number of eighty-nine staff members. See also ACFC, 'Fourth opinion on Bulgaria adopted on 26 May 2020' (n 265) para 42.

282 Interview, Head of unit Analysis, Prevention and International Cooperation, CPAD, 31 July 2018.

283 European Commission, 'Commission Recommendation on Standards for Equality Bodies' (n 19); para 1 in chapter 1.2.2., at 8.

284 ECRI, 'General Policy Recommendation No 2: Equality Bodies to Combat Racism and Intolerance at National Level' (n 23) para 28.

285 In 2012, the CPAD was assigned the task of informing the public about non-discrimination standards through the mass media. Art 47(12) PADA.

compliance with equal treatment legislation. Point 5 regulates how the CPAD may approach the courts: the Commission can appeal against administrative acts that it considers in violation of equal treatment legislation, bring actions to court on its own motion, and join as a concerned party in proceedings instituted under equal treatment legislation.

Points 6 and 8 can be seen as specification of the task to make recommendations on issues relating to discrimination: the CPAD has the authority to recommend to 'state and municipal authorities to discontinue discriminatory practices and revoke their acts issued in violation of' equal treatment legislation. It can further issue opinions on the conformity of draft laws with equal treatment legislation as well as recommendations for the 'adoption, revocation, amendment and supplementing of' legislation. Point 12, which was only introduced in 2012, contains the obligation to 'inform the public via the mass media of the provisions applicable in the area of protection against discrimination'.

Article 4 PADA list seventeen grounds on the basis of which discrimination is prohibited, as well as containing the phrase that 'any other grounds established by law or by an international treaty to which the Republic of Bulgaria is a party' is covered by it. It thus goes far beyond the grounds protected by EU equal treatment legislation. The material scope of PADA covers all areas of life as formulated in the RED. It thus has broad horizontal effect and the CPAD a large mandate to cover.

Proceedings before the Commission can be initiated either by the aggrieved person, on the initiative of the Commission, or by a so-called 'signal' from natural or legal persons, state and municipal authorities.[286] Ex officio cases are relatively rare and amount to five to six cases per year. They are mostly related to cases reported in the media, such as instances of hate speech. The number of cases initiated through signals roughly constitute between 5 and 10 per cent of complaints. Thus, the overwhelming majority of complaints are brought by the aggrieved person themselves. The Commission receives around 6,000 inquiries per year,[287] as compared to between around 600 and nearly 1,000 complaints. On that basis, it initiates an average of 443 cases and decides an average of 405 cases per year.[288] It has considerably improved on the number of decisions taken per year, which was necessary in order to complete work on the backlog of cases it had accumulated in earlier years.

As already mentioned, complaints written in a language other than Bulgarian must be accompanied by a translation to Bulgarian.[289] This potentially limits

[286] Art 50 PADA.

[287] It is interesting to note that there was a quite considerable drop in inquiries in recent years: while there were still 8,218 inquiries in 2013, this number went slightly down to 8,210 in 2014 and dropped further to 6,126 in 2015. See the information about the Commission on Equinet's members' page, at https://equineteurope.org/author/bulgaria_cpd/.

[288] EELN, Country Report Bulgaria, 2018, 92; Country Report Bulgaria, 2020, 81. Calculated based on the figures from 2012–18.

[289] Art 51(1) PADA.

the ability of particularly vulnerable groups to bring a complaint. ECRI's revised GPR No 2 recommend that individuals who have been exposed to discrimination should be able to engage with the Equality Body in a language in which the person concerned is proficient. The Commission should thus consider admitting complaints written in a minority language without translation.[290]

Signals are mostly made by NGOs.[291] However, the right to appeal a decision of the CPAD for NGOs who have launched a complaint in the interest of a particular group, appears to be restricted by the jurisprudence of administrative courts, including the Supreme Administrative Court. According to this line of jurisprudence, organizations initiating a procedure before the CPAD through a signal lack the legal interest required under the Administrative Procedure Code to legitimize an appeal. An example is the case in which a Roma NGO had appealed against a CPAD decision concerning a brochure with the title *Gypsy Crime—Danger to the State* and anti-Roma statements by the chairman of the nationalist party, Ataka. When the case reached the Supreme Administrative Court, it ruled that while under Article 50 point 3 PADA natural and legal persons are entitled to bring proceedings before the Commission, this right is 'limited only to reference to the competent administrative body [the Commission], but does not justify the existence of legal interest for those persons and organisations to challenge the judgments relevant to their signal'.[292] For some[293] even the reference to Article 50 point 3 PADA was erroneous in this context. In fact Article 3(2) PADA provides that '[a]ssociations of natural persons, as well as legal persons, shall benefit from the rights under this Act when they are discriminated against on the grounds referred to in Article 4 (1) regarding their members or the persons employed by them'. A Roma NGO, being an association of Roma citizens, so the argument goes, can thus be considered an aggrieved person under Article 50 point 1 PADA and not as a legal person that provides a signal as laid down in Article 50 point 3 PADA. In addition, the right to appeal decisions of the CPAD is ensured with no limitations by Article 68(1) PADA. While the same provision indeed lays down that appeals are to take place according to the procedure established by the Administrative Procedure Code, this cannot be interpreted to mean that, if the legislator has decided that organizations can bring proceedings under PADA in the public interest, such interest is insufficient for them to appeal against the decision of the Commission.

In another case, members of parliament from the Movement for Rights and Freedoms party, which holds the biggest share of Romani voters, started

[290] See on this, ACFC, 'Fourth opinion on Bulgaria adopted on 26 May 2020' (n 265) para 41.

[291] Although the Commission has signed a Memorandum of Understanding with the largest trade unions in Bulgaria, hardly any signals come through them. Interview, Head of unit Analysis, Prevention and International Cooperation, CPAD, 31 July 2018.

[292] Supreme Administrative Court, Ruling No 1582 of 7 February 2017 on administrative case No 693/2017, 5th Panel, as quoted in Bulgarian Helsinki Committee, 'Human Rights in Bulgaria in 2017' (n 261) 92.

[293] ibid.

proceedings before the CPAD against the former Minister of Health. Following an incident in which an emergency medical care team was attacked in a Roma neighbourhood, the minister publicly threatened to use his ministerial powers to stop—as collective punishment on these neighbourhoods—emergency care services from responding to calls coming from addresses in these areas. The CPAD found no discrimination and the appeal of the MPs against the decision was declared inadmissible. The Supreme Court upheld the decision of inadmissibility and stated, with reference to a previous decision of the Constitutional Court, that '[t]he possibility of introducing *actio popularis* [in cases for protection against discrimination] would be in conflict with the ... understanding of legal certainty' as enshrined in Article 120(2) of the Bulgarian Constitution. Reference to the Constitutional Court is, however, misleading in this case as the case before the Constitutional Court regarded the 'rights to defence in court on the part of citizens and legal entities against acts of the executive' but the CPAD is not part of the executive but is an independent body.[294] Thus, a decision on whether an *actio popularis* in front of the CPAD is per se unconstitutional remains with the Constitutional Court and not the Supreme Administrative Court. Apart from that, the Supreme Administrative Court provided no explanation as to how legal certainty would be threatened by an *actio popularis* in discrimination cases. In fact, the opposite might be true if courts are deprived of the opportunity to verify the decisions taken by the independent Equality Body.[295] For this reason, the recommendations of ECRI and the Commission also lay down that there should be a right to appeal legally binding decisions of Equality Bodies before the courts, without making a distinction between cases brought before the Equality Body by an individual and cases initiated by NGOs in the public interest.

The case law of the Supreme Administrative Court appears to have led to another limitation to *actio popularis* complaints before the CPAD. In some cases the court required an individual victim to be identified in order for the CPAD to establish a sanctionable breach of PADA.[296] There are, however, also judgments in which the Supreme Administrative Court revokes the judgments of lower courts decided in this way.[297]

The investigative powers of the CPAD are very broad and include the obligation of all persons as well as state and local authorities to provide the required information, documents, and explanations. The Commission can thus also question witnesses. No secret protected by law can constitute a reason to refuse the requested information. If information or access to premises or any other kind of assistance

[294] ibid 93.
[295] ibid 94. See also EELN, Country Report Bulgaria, 2020, 66.
[296] EELN, Country Report Bulgaria, 2017, 72.
[297] One such case is reported in Bulgarian Helsinki Committee, 'Human Rights in Bulgaria in 2017' (n 261) 97–98.

is refused, the culprits are liable under PADA.[298] Furthermore, when 'there is a danger that evidence may be lost or concealed or where the collection of evidence is particularly difficult, compulsory collection of evidence may be effected'. This can be requested by the complainant, requires the permission of the Sofia City Court, and is carried out in cooperation with the police. In carrying out its investigations, external experts can be used.[299] Depending on the requirements of the case and within the limitations in terms of staff, the Commission makes use of all these powers.[300] The legal provisions are therefore perfectly in line with paragraph 21 of ECRI's revised GPR No 2. An increase in the number of staff members would make the use of all the given powers more effective.

Once the investigations are closed and the parties have had the opportunity to familiarize themselves with the collected information, the hearings take place. The hearings are open as a rule, but can take place behind closed doors in the circumstances laid down in Article 136 of the Code of Civil Procedure. An interesting aspect of the procedure is that during the first hearing, the parties are called to conciliation. Such conciliation takes place in a separate room in the absence of any Commission member. If parties reach an agreement, they communicate the details to the Commission who 'shall approve it by a decision'.[301] A settlement thereby approved by the CPAD is enforceable with the Commission having control over its implementation.[302] In case no settlement is reached, the Commission decides by simple majority with the possibility for panel members who do not agree to submit a dissenting opinion.[303]

Where discrimination is found, the Commission awards a fine ranging between around 125 and 1,000 EUR[304] (in practice fines are closer to the lower end of this scale[305]) and/or imposes a compulsory administrative measure.[306] The purpose of these measures is not only to terminate a violation but also to prevent future violations, as well as to prevent or eliminate harmful consequences of such violations. This is a positive approach, as it includes a forward-looking dimension into the possible sanctions that can be awarded. The range of possibilities for the CPAD in this context is laid down by law in the following way: 'issue mandatory directions to employers and officials to eliminate violations of the legislation for prevention of discrimination; [and] stay the execution of unlawful decisions or orders of employers or officials which lead or may lead to discrimination'.[307]

298 See Arts 78–81 PADA which lays down different fines for different failures to assist the CPAD in its investigations.
299 Arts 55–57 PADA.
300 Interview, Head of unit Analysis, Prevention and International Cooperation, CPAD, 31 July 2018.
301 Art 62 PADA.
302 Interview, Head of unit Analysis, Prevention and International Cooperation, CPAD, 31 July 2018.
303 Art 64 PADA.
304 Arts 65 and 78 PADA.
305 Interview, Head of unit Analysis, Prevention and International Cooperation, CPAD, 31 July 2018.
306 Arts 65 and 76–77 PADA.
307 Art 76 PADA.

The interpretation of these two options in practice does not appear to be clear. An illustrative case in point relates to the responsibility of online media to ban hate speech in the comments section of their website. A man of Turkish origin brought a complaint before the CPAD about comments on the *Mediapool* website, which contained insults on racial, ethnic, and religious grounds, and calls for ethnic intolerance. As the media did not remove the content, the CPAD found harassment and incitement to discrimination on the basis of Article 8 PADA, which provides that anyone who 'consciously assisted in the commitment of acts of discrimination' shall be liable under the Act. It thus imposed a sanction of 500 BGN (around 250 EUR) and a compulsory administrative measure that ordered the company 'to undertake the necessary measures of contractual, technical and organizational nature in order to prevent violations'.[308] While this would have been an adequate forward-looking and preventive sanction, it was quashed by the Supreme Administrative Court because 'the measure imposed is not among the exhaustively listed measures in PADA'.[309]

The CPAD is responsible for controlling the implementation of its decisions and sanctions. This is reportedly very difficult in practice, given the budget and staff restrictions, and it is not done in a systematic manner.[310] Under Article 82 PADA, for instance, a person who fails to implement a decision of the Commission is punished with a fine of between 2,000 and 10,000 BGN (approximately 1,000 and 5,00 EUR). If the violation persists three months after the decision, a fine between 5,000 and 20,000 BGN (approximately 2,500 and 10,000 EUR) shall be imposed.

Paragraph 17 of ECRI's revised GPR No 2 is met to the extent that the decisions of the CPAD are legally binding. However, given that the fines imposed are situated at the lower end of the possible range and the limited possibilities that exist when it comes to the imposition of compulsory administrative measures, the conclusion may be drawn that they are not effective when it comes to achieving full equality and preventing future discrimination, and are probably also not dissuasive. A further problem exists in the limited capacities of the CPAD to oversee the enforcement of the sanctions awarded.

It is also interesting to note that the CPAD requested a preliminary ruling to the CJEU which was rejected because the Equality Body could not be regarded as a court or tribunal within the meaning of Article 267 TFEU.[311] To establish whether this is the case or not, the Court referred to its established case law according to which a number of factors have to be taken into consideration, 'such as whether

[308] Bulgarian Helsinki Committee, 'Human Rights in Bulgaria in 2017' (n 261) 105.

[309] ibid 105–06.

[310] EELN, Country Report Bulgaria, 2020, 79–81.

[311] *Valeri Hariev Belov v CHEZ Elektro Balgaria AD and Others* [2013] ECLI:EU:C:2013:48. For a comment on the judgment see Kádár, 'The Standing of National Equality Bodies before the European Union Court of Justice: the Implications of the Belov Judgment' (n 263); and Matthias Möschel, 'Race Discrimination and Access to the European Court of Justice: Belov' (2013) 50(5) Common Market Law Review 1433.

the body is established by law, whether it is permanent, whether its jurisdiction is compulsory, whether its procedure is *inter partes*, whether it applies rules of law . . . whether it is independent', and whether its decisions are of judicial nature.[312]

The CJEU came to the conclusion that the CPAD cannot be considered a court or tribunal for the following reasons: first, the proceedings that give rise to the request for a preliminary ruling can be brought by a person concerned but also by the CPAD acting on its own motion, and the same procedural rules apply and the results of proceedings are the same regardless of how they were initiated. Secondly, the CJEU established that the CPAD can, on its own motion, join persons other than those appointed by the applicant to the proceedings. Thirdly, where its decisions are appealed in front of an administrative court, the CPAD has standing in such proceedings to defend its decisions and can appeal a decision of the administrative court in front of the Supreme Administrative Court. And finally, the Commission can revoke its decision where it is appealed, 'if the party to whom the decision is addressed is favourable'.[313] All these factors led the CJEU to conclude that the decisions of the CPAD are 'similar in substance to an administrative decision and do not have a judicial nature' within the meaning of Article 267 TFEU.[314] Furthermore, the Court considered that the possibilities for appeal against CPAD decisions 'ensure the effectiveness of the mechanism of the request for a preliminary ruling ... and the uniform interpretation of European Union law'.[315] The Court, having found that the decisions taken by the CPAD are not of a judicial nature, did not further assess the existence of other disputed factors required for an institution to be considered a court or tribunal, namely its independence and the compulsory character of its jurisdiction.[316]

This is all the more surprising considering that in the *Österreichischer Rundfunk* case,[317] as well as in the *Westbahn Management* case,[318] it found the references admissible without even examining whether the requesting bodies' decisions were of a judicial nature. In the *Abrahamsson and Anderson* case it found that the Swedish Universities' Appeals Board was established by law, permanent, independent, having *inter partes* procedures and applying the rules of law, and that 'although an administrative authority, is vested with judicial functions'.[319]

[312] *Valeri Hariev Belov v CHEZ Elektro Balgaria AD and Others* (n 311) paras 38–39.

[313] ibid paras 47–50.

[314] ibid para 51.

[315] ibid para 52.

[316] ibid para 54. The requirement to be established by law, to be permanent, that its procedures are *inter partes* and that it applies rules of law would have been clearly fulfilled.

[317] *Kommunikationsbehörde Austria (KommAustria) v Österreichischer Rundfunk (ORF)* [2007] ECLI:EU:C:2007:613.

[318] *Westbahn Management GmbH v ÖBB-Infrastruktur AG* [2012] ECLI:EU:C:2012:740.

[319] *Katarina Abrahamsson and Leif Anderson v Elisabet Fogelqvist* [2000] ECLI:EU:C:2000:367, para 35. See on these and other cases, Kádár, 'The Standing of National Equality Bodies before the European Union Court of Justice: the Implications of the Belov Judgment' (n 263) 18–19.

Advocate General Kokott addressed all three questions and came to the conclusion that the CPAD could be considered a court or tribunal in the case at issue. Regarding the judicial nature of the CPAD's decisions and the points addressed in the later judgment of the Court, she found it to be irrelevant that CPAD can, in theory, initiate proceedings before it also *suo motu*. While the Court had taken this abstract possibility for the CPAD as the relevant basis for reaching its conclusion, for Kokott, to determine whether an institution can be considered a court or tribunal, only the case that has led to the request for preliminary ruling in question needs to be taken into consideration. As this case in question had been brought by a presumed victim of discrimination, for Kokott, the CPAD's involvement was of a judicial nature. In her view, the fact that the CPAD could also join other parties to the complaint procedure was no obstacle as this is 'perfectly common in proceedings before conventional administrative courts'. The point that the CPAD can revoke its decision in case it is appealed, if the parties agree, was construed by Kokott as an expression of a broad understanding of the dispositive principle[320] in judicial proceedings. In this context she acknowledged however, that the fact that the CPAD's 'decisions may apparently be altered under facilitated conditions may be regarded as an expression of the status of [CPAD] as a kind of "hybrid" of a conventional administrative authority and a conventional court'.[321]

Regarding the question of whether the CPAD can be considered to be independent, Kokott found that both the external as well as the internal aspects of independence were met. As regards the external aspect, which entails protection against external influence and pressures that could jeopardize the CPAD's independent judgement, Kokott found that 'there are no doubts' about its presence. She did not, however, provide much detail for her finding. In particular, she did not look into issues such as the selection process and appointment procedures. It would have been interesting to see whether she would have limited herself to an assessment of the legal framework for appointing members to the CPAD or whether she would have taken into consideration also the practice, including observations raised by civil society organizations as to the actual independence of CPAD members. However, she limited herself to establishing that the 'rules on the independence of the judiciary in the Bulgarian Code of Civil Procedure apply to them *mutatis mutandis*', referring to Article 61(3) PADA, which in turn refers to Articles 22–24 of the Code of Civil Procedure.[322] These provisions of the code, however, do not address the external aspect of independence, but the internal, which is linked to impartiality of

[320] *Valeri Hariev Belov v CHEZ Elektro Balgaria AD and Others—opinion of the AG* [2012] ECLI:EU:C:2012:585, fn 39: 'The dispositive principle, according to which it is for the parties to initiate, terminate and organise proceedings, applies in the (civil) procedural orders of many Member States and enables the parties, for example, to terminate legal proceedings without a judgment being delivered, by means of a settlement. The possibility of the parties jointly dispensing with a judgment even after it has been delivered is ultimately based on the same idea.'

[321] ibid paras 37–45.

[322] ibid paras 29–30.

the judge vis-à-vis the parties involved in the case before him/her. The existence of external independence was thus not convincingly shown by the Advocate General.

In terms of internal independence, the defendants alleged that considering the structure and functions of the CPAD this was not ensured. They found there was a link between the decision-making body within the CPAD and the administrative body subordinate to it. Considering that this administrative body was providing legal assistance to presumed victims of discrimination the defendants found that this does not provide the necessary equidistance to both parties involved. However, in this respect Kokott rightly pointed out that such legal advice is given only by the administrative body and not by the members of the Commission themselves and only outside the context of pending procedures. Furthermore, the task of the Commission is to monitor compliance with the legal provisions of PADA in an objective way, which implies that it can find the existence, but also the non-existence, of discrimination during proceedings before it.[323]

The last issue addressed by Kokott was the question of compulsory jurisdiction. The defendants claimed that, under Article 71 PADA, persons concerned can also address a civil court and therefore the jurisdiction of the CPAD is not compulsory. Kokott referred to the CJEU's judgment in *Dorsch Consult*, where the Court distinguished 'compulsory' in the sense of the only option for obtaining legal protection, and 'compulsory' in the sense of its decisions being binding and mandatory. While in *Dorsch Consult* the Court did not have to express any preference for one or the other option as both were present, Kokott (similarly to the European Commission in *Dorsch Consult* and in the case under consideration) favoured the second interpretation. In her view, if it was interpreted as meaning the only option, strictly speaking not even the civil courts could submit a request for a preliminary ruling as there existed another option for getting legal protection, namely the procedure before the CPAD. Considering, therefore, that the decisions of the CPAD become final, are binding, and infringements of the decisions can be punished by a fine, she considered the criterion of 'compulsory jurisdiction' to be fulfilled.[324]

The decision of the court to just undertake a 'simplified test'[325] on whether the CPAD could be considered a court or tribunal and on this basis reject the referral as inadmissible was criticized in the literature because it did not take into consideration the interdependent and interconnected nature of some of the factors to be analysed.[326] The fact that cases of discrimination on the grounds of racial or ethnic

323 ibid paras 31–35.

324 ibid paras 46–49.

325 Kádár, 'The Standing of National Equality Bodies before the European Union Court of Justice: the Implications of the Belov Judgment' (n 263) 18–20 and 22.

326 Kádár argues that 'it could arguably prove very difficult or impossible in certain cases to determine the judicial character of the procedure before a body without conducting a careful analysis of its independence (including an analysis of the links between the decision-making body and the administrative body) and compulsory jurisdiction'. See ibid 19. See also Gráinne de Búrca, 'The Decline of the EU Anti-Discrimination Law?' (Note for the Colloquium on Comparative and Global Public Law, 19

origin outnumber cases on all other grounds and, nevertheless, so far only a few cases have been referred to the CJEU for a preliminary ruling, suggests that courts are reluctant to bring such cases to the CJEU and that Equality Bodies play a significant role in adjudicating racial and ethnic discrimination.[327] It has thus been suggested that the European Commission consider proposals for amending the Equal Treatment Directives to ensure detailed standards for quasi-judicial bodies to fulfil the criteria required by the CJEU for being considered a court or tribunal. At the same time, Member States which have such bodies in place should consider revising their legal basis for the same purpose.[328]

While in the above-described *Belov* case, the Court did not assess the case in its merits,[329] it had the chance to do so in another case which was based on similar facts, again involving the CPAD. In the case of *CHEZ Razpredelenie Bulgaria AD v CPAD*,[330] Ms Nikolova, a non-Roma operating a business in a Roma neighbourhood, approached the CPAD complaining about discrimination because the state-owned electricity company CHEZ had placed electricity meters at a level of 7 metres whereas outside Roma districts they were placed at a height of up to 1.70 metres, usually in the consumer's own home. The reason for placing them at such a high level was allegedly to prevent fraud. The practice of the CPAD in this and similar cases brought before it was to find indirect discrimination. However, when its decisions were appealed and finally reached the Supreme Administrative Court, that Court regularly found that being unable to access the electricity meters did

October 2016) <http://www.law.nyu.edu/sites/default/files/upload_documents/The%20Decline%20of%20the%20EU%20Anti-Discrimination%20Law.pdf>.

[327] Kádár, 'The Standing of National Equality Bodies before the European Union Court of Justice: the Implications of the Belov Judgment' (n 263) 22–23. Regarding Bulgaria, see, however, ACFC, 'Third opinion on Bulgaria adopted on 11 February 2014' (n 262) paras 11 and 40 as well as CERD, 'Concluding observations on the combined twentieth to twenty-second periodic reports of Bulgaria' (n 261) para 9, which are both concerned about the 'low number of discrimination-related complaints on grounds of race or ethnicity submitted to the [Bulgarian] Commission [for Protection against Discrimination]' and that '[issues faced by persons belonging to national minorities do not appear to be high on its [the Commission's] agenda ... and the Commission does not appear to be closely attuned to the need to take adequate measures to promote their full and effective equality'.

[328] Kádár, 'The Standing of National Equality Bodies before the European Union Court of Justice: the Implications of the Belov Judgment' (n 263) 23.

[329] For a discussion on the way the Advocate General Kokott addressed the merits see Simon Cox, 'Case Watch: Strengthening Europe's Non-Discrimination Law' (Open Society Foundations—Voices, 2 October 2002); and Kádár, 'The Standing of National Equality Bodies before the European Union Court of Justice: the Implications of the Belov Judgment' (n 263) 21–22.

[330] *'CHEZ Razpredelenie Bulgaria' AD v Komisia za zashtita ot diskriminatsia* [2015] ECLI:EU:C:2015:480. For a discussion of the case see Zsuzsanna Nyitray and Simon Cox, 'Case Watch: Roma Ruling Advances Antidiscrimination Protections in the European Union' (Open Society Foundations—Voices, 16 July 2015); Simon Cox, 'When all the people in a district are victims of race discrimination: CJEU ruling in CHEZ v Nikolova' (EU Law Analysis, 24 July 2015) <http://eulawanalysis.blogspot.com/2015/07/when-all-people-in-district-are-victims.html>; Rossen Grozev, 'A Landmark Judgment of the Court of Justice of the EU—New Conceptual Contributions to the Legal Combat against Ethnic Discrimination' (2015) 15 The Equal Rights Review 168; Christopher McCrudden, 'The new architecture of EU equality law after CHEZ: Did the Court of Justice Reconceptualise direct and indirect discrimination' [2016] European Equality Law Review 1; and Farkas, 'NGO and Equality Body Enforcement of EU Anti-Discrimination Law: Bulgarian Roma and the Electricity Sector' (n 267).

not result in adverse effects, that there is a lack of ethnic homogeneity in the Roma districts, and that explicit racial motives for the measures could not be established. Discrimination could not therefore be established.[331] To counterbalance this interpretation, the CPAD tried to refer the *Belov* case to the CJEU. Faced with the rejection by the Court of Justice, it had to rely on the Sofia Administrative Court to refer the case involving Ms Nikolova.[332] The cases were supported by a number of NGOs and in the particular case of Ms Nikolova, the Open Society Justice Initiative took over her legal representation to intervene on the side of the CPAD in the case before the CJEU.[333] The case was successful and clarified a number of issues.

First, the Court clarified that 'discrimination on the grounds of ethnic origin ... must be interpreted as being intended to apply in circumstances such as those at issue in the main proceedings irrespective of whether the measure at issue in those proceedings affects persons who have a certain ethnic origin or persons who, without possessing that origin, suffer, together with the former, the less favourable treatment or particular disadvantage resulting from that measure'.[334] In the present case this meant that Ms Nikolova, although not herself Roma, suffered the same less favourable treatment as Roma and was thus discriminated on the grounds of ethnic origin. Or, as Cox put it, 'if a measure against a district is based on grounds of the Roma origin of the district's majority, then the minority in that district are also victims of that discriminatory measure'.[335]

Second, the Court had to deal with the question of whether the term 'apparently neutral practice' contained in the definition of indirect discrimination was to be understood as 'obviously neutral' or that it 'only seems neutral, at first glance' and thus 'ostensibly neutral'. The Court, following the Opinion of the Advocate General, found that the 'concept must be understood in the second sense'. Not only does this correspond 'to the most natural meaning of the term used', it is also in line with the Court's previous case law 'according to which, unlike direct discrimination, indirect discrimination may stem from a measure which, albeit formulated in neutral terms, that is to say, by reference to other criteria not related to the protected characteristic, leads, however, to the result that particularly persons possessing that characteristic are put at a disadvantage'. It further clarified that 'a national provision under which, in order for there to be indirect discrimination on the grounds of racial or ethnic origin, the measure in question is required to have been adopted for reasons of racial or ethnic origin' is not in line with the concept

[331] For an in-depth overview on the topic, including the CPAD's decisions and the courts' jurisprudence, see Daniela Mihaylova and Momtchil Iordanov, 'Access to Electricity in Roma Settlements in Bulgaria' (Equal Opportunities Initiative Association 2015).

[332] See Farkas, 'NGO and Equality Body Enforcement of EU Anti-Discrimination Law: Bulgarian Roma and the Electricity Sector' (n 267) 41.

[333] ibid 39–40.

[334] *'CHEZ Razpredelenie Bulgaria' AD v Komisia za zashtita ot diskriminatsia* (n 330) para 50.

[335] Cox, 'When all the people in a district are victims of race discrimination: CJEU ruling in CHEZ v Nikolova' (n 330).

of indirect discrimination under Directive 2000/43. If it is, in fact, 'apparent that a measure which gives rise to a difference in treatment has been introduced for reasons relating to racial or ethnic origin, that measure must be classified as "direct discrimination" '.[336]

Third, the Court considered the previously relatively unexplored question of whether the different terminology used by the Directive in the definitions of direct and indirect discrimination to describe the effects of the discrimination ('treated less favourably' in the first case, 'particular disadvantage' in the second) implied that only a ' "serious, obvious and particularly significant case" is capable of resulting in a "particular" disadvantage' required to find indirect discrimination. Such an interpretation could be justified by the fact that indeed the measure in the case of indirect discrimination was 'adopted for some other reason, and not explicitly on the grounds of the protected characteristic'.[337] However, the Court, perhaps also influenced by the majority of submissions and the opinion of the Advocate General, found that there is no substantial difference between the concepts used so that an interpretation that would require a serious, obvious, and particularly significant case of inequality in order to find indirect discrimination had to be rejected. 'Particular disadvantage' must be understood 'as meaning that it is *particularly* persons of a given ethnic origin who are at a disadvantage because of the measure at issue'.[338] In this sense, indirect discrimination arises when a measure, even if formulated neutrally, 'works to the disadvantage of *far more* persons possessing the protected characteristic than persons not possessing it'. Furthermore, the Court found that such an interpretation is 'the one that is most consistent with the objectives pursued by the EU legislature'.[339] From this the Court found that there was no lack of compliance with the Directive if the Bulgarian legislation did not 'make a distinction according to the degree of seriousness of the unfavourable treatment concerned'.[340]

The final important point in the judgment then related to the question of whether the practice in the case concerned constituted direct or indirect discrimination. While the Court left it for the referring court to answer this question, it provided guidance on how to reach a conclusion. To find direct discrimination, three cumulative conditions have to be met: first, the measure was taken on the basis of ethnic origin, second, it leads to a less favourable treatment as, third, compared to others in a comparable situation.

Regarding the first point the following factors need to be taken into account: the finding that CHEZ had introduced or maintained the practice of placing meters

[336] *'CHEZ Razpredelenie Bulgaria' AD v Komisia za zashtita ot diskriminatsia* (n 330) paras 37, 93–95, 97.

[337] Grozev (n 330) 175.

[338] Emphasis added.

[339] *'CHEZ Razpredelenie Bulgaria' AD v Komisia za zashtita ot diskriminatsia* (n 330) paras 98–102.

[340] ibid paras 37 and 103.

at up to 7 metres high only in districts known to be inhabited mainly by people of Roma origin; that CHEZ itself asserted in similar cases before the CPAD that in its view the illegal connections to the electricity network were mainly carried out by Roma without, however, being able to produce evidence of this allegation; and the widespread nature of the practice.[341]

Regarding the second point, the Court found that 'it cannot be denied that the treatment resulting from that practice is unfavourable for the inhabitants—for the most part of Roma origin—of the urban district concerned, having regard both to the fact that it is extremely difficult, or even impossible, for them to check their electricity meters for the purpose of monitoring their consumption and to that practice's offensive and stigmatizing nature'.[342] Finally, regarding the comparator to be used in the present case, for the Court 'all final consumers of electricity who are supplied by the same distributor within an urban area must ... be regarded as being, in relation to that distributor, in a comparable situation'.[343] All these points clearly hint at the preference of the Court to find direct discrimination in the case in question.

Nevertheless, it also provided its view in case the referring court should come to the conclusion that the practice constituted indirect discrimination and in that context, whether the measure could be objectively justified through a legitimate aim and the means to achieve that aim could be considered appropriate and necessary.[344] The Court accepted that the alleged aim to prevent unauthorized connections to the distribution network, resulting in 'non-technical losses of electricity' as well as the protection of consumers' health, were legitimate. However, while it left it to the national court to determine whether these were the real aims of the measure it 'provided strong indications that it did not believe these were the facts'.[345] The Court again left it to the referring court to ascertain whether the remaining criteria for objectively justifying the indirectly discriminatory measure exist. It concluded however, that 'it seems ... that the practice at issue cannot be justified within the meaning of Article 2(2)(b) of Directive 2000/43 since the disadvantages caused by the practice appear disproportionate to the objectives pursued'.[346]

Did the cases of *Belov* and *CHEZ* have only a legal-conceptual effect or did they have an impact also in practice?[347] It is definitely true that the cases contributed to the further development of the CJEU's case law in the field of discrimination

[341] ibid paras 82–84; see also Grozev (n 330) 177–78.

[342] *'CHEZ Razpredelenie Bulgaria' AD v Komisia za zashtita ot diskriminatsia* (n 330) para 87. Fredman's recognition dimension resonates in this part of the judgment. See Sandra Fredman, 'Emerging from the Shadows: Substantive Equality and Article 14 of the European Convention on Human Rights' (2016) 16(2) Human Rights Law Review 273.

[343] *'CHEZ Razpredelenie Bulgaria' AD v Komisia za zashtita ot diskriminatsia* (n 330) para 90.

[344] ibid paras 110–28.

[345] Grozev (n 330) 181.

[346] *'CHEZ Razpredelenie Bulgaria' AD v Komisia za zashtita ot diskriminatsia* (n 330) para 127.

[347] Farkas, 'NGO and Equality Body Enforcement of EU Anti-Discrimination Law: Bulgarian Roma and the Electricity Sector' (n 267) 40.

based on racial or ethnic origin and thus to conceptual clarifications. *Belov* has further highlighted in which directions Equality Bodies with a tribunal-type function would need to be developed in order for them to be able to refer cases to the CJEU. It is equally true that, in the wake of the *CHEZ* judgment, the Bulgarian government introduced legislative amendments to PADA to clarify the concepts of indirect discrimination and the understanding of less favourable treatment, thus leading to improved legislation beyond the ground of racial and ethnic origin.[348]

The case also had some practical repercussions. As mentioned above, Ms Nikolova intervened in the procedure before the CJEU with the support of the Open Society Justice Initiative. When the case returned to the court in Bulgaria, the Justice Initiative cooperated with a Bulgarian NGO active in the field of Roma rights, the Equal Opportunities Initiative Association, to ensure implementation of the decision.[349] In December 2015, five months after the CJEU judgment, the electricity company met with representatives from the NGOs. In February 2016, after adopting a plan to pilot alternative metering in the Roma communities concerned, CHEZ started replacing the contested meters with accessible 'smart meters' for more than 900 households. Ms Nikolova's meter was exchanged in this process as well. In two other Roma communities, the company planned to pilot secure boxes, each with twenty-five smart meters inside. The two NGOs accepted this plan at a hearing in January 2016 at the Sofia Administrative Court. The Equal Opportunities Initiative Association has continued to meet with CHEZ to ensure consultation with the communities concerned and to monitor the proper implementation of the plan.[350] What the litigation did not manage to address are the regulatory shortcomings of pricing for the economically destitute, which includes many people of Roma origin. Nevertheless, it showed the potential that can be deployed if an Equality Body strategically engages with the groups protected by legislation and NGOs.[351]

[348] Margarita Ilieva, 'ADL draft amendments of definitions of "indirect discrimination" and "unfavourable treatment"' (EELN News Report, 15 July 2016).

[349] On the difficult environment for human rights NGOs to work in the Bulgarian context, see Bulgarian Helsinki Committee, 'Human Rights in Bulgaria in 2019' (2020) 7–8.

[350] See information provided at Open Society Foundations, Nikolova v. CEZ Electricity, at https://www.opensocietyfoundations.org/litigation/nikolova-v-cez-electricity.

[351] Farkas, 'NGO and Equality Body Enforcement of EU Anti-Discrimination Law: Bulgarian Roma and the Electricity Sector' (n 267) 42. In another area, namely, housing, the success and impact of the CPAD appears to be more limited. In fact, PADA does not explicitly provide that it applies in the area of housing. For that reason, the CPAD has no practice on the cases of demolition of houses inhabited by persons of Roma origin and it has no power to suspend or quash the execution of demolition orders. This shortcoming in terms of legislation and the devastating practice of forced demolitions of Roma homes and their residents' forced eviction without providing alternative accommodation has prompted the Equal Opportunities Initiative Association, in cooperation with the Open Society European Policy Institute, to send a memorandum to the European Commission requesting that it commence infringement proceedings against the Bulgarian government. Equal Opportunities Initiative Association and Open Society European Policy Institute, 'Memorandum to the European Commission: Violations of EU Law and Fundamental Rights by Bulgaria's Discriminatory Treatment of Roma in the Area of Housing' (February 2017).

The development of the *CHEZ* case on returning to the national level after the CJEU decision is, however, a source of concern with regard to the independence of the CPAD as well as its capacity to implement decisions of the Court of Justice. In fact, a renewed decision was quashed by the Sofia City Administrative Court for failure to implement the CJEU's decision. In the subsequent CPAD decision taken in 2019, it not only failed to comply with the judicial instruction of the Sofia City Administrative Court but even concluded that there was no discrimination at all. This time the case reached the Supreme Administrative Court which confirmed the decision of the Sofia Court.[352] Such decisions by the CPAD confirm the worrying assessment by the EELN expert that the 'anti-minority stances' of 'Parliament-elected individuals belonging to extreme nationalist parties' to the CPAD affects its case law accordingly.[353]

While the CPAD can therefore receive individual and collective complaints, deploy extensive investigation powers, issue legally binding decisions, and has the mandate to follow up on its decisions, it is faced with a number of challenges. Although figures show some improvement, it continues to struggle with a backlog of cases which risks cases being dealt with only superficially in order that they can be closed within an acceptable time, and making limited use of the different powers to obtain evidence and information. The fines it imposes are reportedly low and the circumstances in which compulsory administrative measures may be imposed relatively limited. It is therefore questionable whether the sanctions can be considered as effective, proportionate, and dissuasive. Furthermore, it has only limited capacities to follow up on its decisions. Its outreach, while covering twenty-one of the twenty-eight administrative districts, would also need to be extended and strengthened. These challenges could be addressed by additional funding, which would also remedy the situation that, for the fulfilment of its functions other than decision making, it has to rely on external sources. Furthermore, it is crucial to keep the quality of its decisions at a high level. For that purpose the overall independence of the body and a merit-based appointment of CPAD members needs to be ensured.

5.3.3.3 Case Study: Austria—The Equal Treatment Commission

To compare Equality Bodies with the competence to take legally binding decisions with Equality Bodies that can take only non-legally binding decisions, the case of the Equal Treatment Commission (or ETC) in Austria has been chosen. The Austrian landscape of institutions dealing with issues of equality and non-discrimination is highly complex. This situation is related to historic developments as well as to the federal structure of the country. At federal level there exist

[352] Margarita Ilieva, 'Supreme Administrative Court follow-up in Nikolova/ CHEZ Case (C-83/ 2014)' (EELN News Report, 10 February 2021).

[353] EELN, Country Report Bulgaria, 2020, 74.

- the Equal Treatment Commission, responsible for all discrimination grounds and areas of life covered by EU legislation—except for disability—in relation to the private sector (tribunal-type body);
- the Federal Equal Treatment Commission responsible for all discrimination grounds covered by EU legislation—except for disability—with regard to federal employees (tribunal-type body);
- the Ombud for Equal Treatment, responsible for all grounds and areas of life covered by EU legislation—except for disability (promotion-type body);
- the Ombudsperson for Persons with Disabilities (qualified as predominantly tribunal-type body by Equinet, not mentioned as such in the EELN reports).

Before bringing cases involving the ground of disability to court there is an obligation to attempt an out-of-court settlement before the Service of the Ministry of Social Affairs. This list does not include the Federal Equal Treatment Commissioners or the Women's Commissioners working within the different Ministries.

In addition to these national bodies, each of the nine *Länder* has established its own institutions to deal with discrimination issues in their own fields of competence. They are not regional branches of the national bodies but constitute separate structures with no shared responsibilities with the national ones. The only national body that does have regional offices is the Ombud for Equal Treatmen, which has offices in four of the nine *Länder.*[354] Until 2017 these offices were, however, only responsible for discrimination issues related to women and men in the area of employment and occupation. Since then their mandate has been enlarged to include also other discrimination grounds (except for disability) and other areas of life, without, however, increasing the budget or human resources accordingly.

This complex institutional structure makes it rather difficult for persons concerned to understand to whom they can turn for assistance and there is a danger they will give up pursuing their cause if they continue to be redirected from institution to institution. In the public perception, the Equal Treatment Commission and the Ombud for Equal Treatment in particular are often mixed up and more information should be available to the general public about their respective responsibilities.[355] The situation is also regularly criticized by international monitoring bodies, like ECRI , who in its 2015 report even spoke of 'about 50 institutions' and makes a series of proposals on how the situation could be improved.[356] The

[354] The regional office in Graz is responsible for Styria, the regional office in Klagenfurt is responsible for Carinthia, the regional office in Linz is responsible for Upper Austria, and the one in Innsbruck is responsible for Tyrol, Salzburg, and Vorarlberg. Lower Austria and Burgenland are covered by the head office in Vienna.

[355] Ministerium für Frauen und Gesundheit and Sozialministerium, 'Evaluierung der Instrumente des Gleichbehandlungsrechts. Weiterentwicklung des Gleichbehandlungsrechts und der Gleichbehandlungsinstrumente—Expert/inn/enbericht' (2016) 56.

[356] ECRI, 'Report on Austria (fifth monitoring cycle) adopted on 16 June 2015' CRI(2015)34, paras 12–14.

recommendation in this context was urgent enough to be included in the list of interim follow-up recommendations, which were reviewed in 2017. In its conclusions, ECRI, while it had to ascertain that no simplification of the institutional landscape was initiated, welcomed the fact that the mandate of the regional offices of the Ombud for Equal Treatment had been extended in 2017 as just described above. It also took note of the cooperation between the Ombud for Equal Treatment, the Federal Chancellery, and the FRA for setting up a tool to provide assistance to victims of discrimination in finding the right institution to which it could turn for advice.[357] As a number of the proposals for simplifying the system were however not taken into consideration, ECRI concluded there was room for further improvement and that the recommendation has been only partly implemented.[358] It therefore repeated its recommendation in its 2020 report.[359]

The ACFC also criticized the situation and, similar to ECRI, welcomed the plans to produce guidelines for inclusion in the first National Action Plan for Human Rights, offering an overview of the various bodies that can be approached in cases of discrimination.[360] However, neither the guidelines nor the National Action Plan for Human Rights have since been adopted.

For the present case study, the focus will be on the Equal Treatment Commission (or ETC) as the tribunal-type body responsible for the private sector. The ETC has its origin in a Commission that was established by law already in 1979 for equal treatment between men and women in the employment field. With the obligation to transpose the RED and EED, the mandate was extended in 2004. This has been done by establishing three different so-called senates. Senate I continued to be responsible for equal treatment between men and women in the employment field. The newly created senate II is now responsible for discrimination in employment and occupation covering all other grounds mentioned in Article 19 TFEU, except for disability, while the newly created senate III deals with discrimination on the grounds of gender and ethnic origin in the access to goods and services and, on the ground of ethnic origin only, also in relation to social protection, social advantages, and education.

Under the law, the ETC is established within the Federal Chancellery[361] (currently it comes under the responsibility of the Ministry for Women, Families and Youths, established under the Federal Chancellery). The senates are composed of

[357] The tool can now be found at https://beta.e-justice.europa.eu/459/EN/fundamental_rights_interactive_tool, where it is described as tool that 'allows you to find the right organisation to help you with your fundamental rights problem'.

[358] ECRI, 'Conclusions on the Implementation of the Recommendations in Respect of Austria Subject to Interim Follow-Up' (23 May 2018) CRI(2018)21.

[359] ECRI, 'Report on Austria (sixth monitoring cycle) adopted on 7 April 2020', paras 7 and 97–98.

[360] ACFC, 'Fourth opinion on Austria adopted on 14 October 2016' ACFC/OP/IV(2016)007, paras 13 and 15.

[361] Law on the Equal Treatment Commission and the Ombud for Equal Treatment, BGBl. No 108/1979, § 1.

the president, who is a civil servant nominated by the Federal Chancellor, and an additional six members. Of these, in senates I and II (those dealing with discrimination in employment), one member each is sent by the Economic Chamber, the Chamber of Labour, and the Chamber of Industries, as well as the Austrian Union Federation. One member each is nominated by the Federal Chancellor and the Ministry of Social Affairs. Among the six members, a parity between interest representation for employers, workers, and the state is thereby achieved. In senate III (that dealing with discrimination outside employment), one member each is sent by the Economic Chamber and the Chamber of Labour, while four members are nominated by the executive: one by the Federal Chancellor, one by the Minister for Digital and Economic Affairs, one by the Ministry of Justice, and one by the Ministry of Social Affairs.[362] Under the law, members of the senates work on a honorary basis, while the presidents of the senates are exempted from duty while still being paid their salaries for the time needed for the deployment of their tasks.[363] None of the members is therefore working on a full-time basis, which has repercussions on the frequency of their meetings and thus the speed at which cases are decided by the Commission. At least 50 per cent of the members shall be women.[364] They are nominated for a period of four years with the possibility of extension. Their mandate can be terminated by the Federal Chancellor where the dispatch or nomination is withdrawn, if they seriously violate their obligations or are permanently negligent in fulfilling them, or if they are permanently unable to fulfil their mandate for health-related reasons.[365] In practice, nominations or dispatch have never been withdrawn and mandates are usually renewed if the person in question is still interested in continuing working in the Commission.

Before members begin work, they have to vow to the president of their respective senate to carry out their tasks diligently and impartially.[366] Furthermore, the law provides that president and members of the senate are free from any obligations to receive instructions and act independently.[367] The ETC thus falls under Article 20(2) of the Austrian Constitution according to which it is possible to create by law institutions that are exempted from the obligation to receive instructions from the authority to which they are attached. Although these provisions

[362] Law on the Equal Treatment Commission and the Ombud for Equal Treatment, § 2(1)–(6).

[363] Law on the Equal Treatment Commission and the Ombud for Equal Treatment, § 10(1)–(1a). In practice, it has been reported that meetings are held during the working time of the members as well. E-mail communication with one of the presidents of the ETC, 21 November 2018.

[364] Law on the Equal Treatment Commission and the Ombud for Equal Treatment, § 2(9). Since the wording of the law provides that 50 per cent applies to members and substitutes, who have to be dispatched and nominated for each member, in theory all members could be men and all substitutes could be women.

[365] Law on the Equal Treatment Commission and the Ombud for Equal Treatment, §§ 2(7) and 10(1c).

[366] Law on the Equal Treatment Commission and the Ombud for Equal Treatment, § 2(8).

[367] Law on the Equal Treatment Commission and the Ombud for Equal Treatment, § 10(1a).

give the ETC an independent status when it comes to the exercise of its functions, the attachment to the Federal Chancellery as well as the composition dominated by persons dispatched by the interest representations or nominated by Ministries has been criticized. Regarding the latter it has been said that the 'image is that the Commission consists of persons sent by institutions to represent those institutions' attitudes and political opinions'.[368] In an expert evaluation of the instruments of the equal treatment legislation, the participation of social partners in the work of the Commission was also discussed. It was, however, considered useful for the Commission's case work to draw on the expertise of the members working with social partners and at the same time these members can bring back their experience from the work in the Commission in the interest-policy work of their organization. It has been considered a way to raise awareness among important stakeholders such as employers or workers councils.[369] Interestingly, the overall independence of the Commission and its embeddedness within the governmental structure has not been a matter of discussion in this evaluation.

Apart from issues related to independence, the fact that the senates are composed of persons having their main occupation in ministries or interest representations has the downside that meetings take place about twice a month in senate I or even only once a month in senates II and III. This leads to lengthy procedures which will be discussed further below. A way of improving the situation would be to establish at least the position of president of a senate as a full-time position. This would be especially useful for the president of senate I who is also responsible for the overall coordination of the Commission.[370] This would, however, require to increase the budget of the Commission.[371]

In terms of geographic outreach, the fact that the Commission is a centralized body with its seat in Vienna and no branches anywhere else in Austria has been seen as an obstacle for those faced with discrimination to have access to the Commission. Knowledge of the ETC is more limited outside Vienna and having to travel to Vienna for oral hearings might be a further deterrent for victims of discrimination, especially those from the western parts of the country. Increased awareness raising about the possibility of approaching the Commission would however need to be matched by improved procedures and additional funds in order for the Commission to be able to absorb additional cases.[372] The situation has

368 EELN, Country Report Austria, 2020, 65.

369 Ministerium für Frauen und Gesundheit and Sozialministerium (n 355) 42. The report, which contains a number of proposals and recommendations on how to improve and strengthen the equal treatment legislation, as well as the access to justice and appropriate remedies, has been rejected by both the Economic Chamber and the Chamber of Industries. For their statements see https://www.frauen-familien-jugend.bka.gv.at/frauen/gleichbehandlung/gleichbehandlungsberichte/evaluierung-der-instrumente-des-gleichbehandlungsrechts.html.

370 Ministerium für Frauen und Gesundheit and Sozialministerium (n 355) 44.

371 See also the budget for the Ombud for Equal Treatment: 50,000 EUR from 2010–13, 61,000 EUR from 2014–16, and 65,000 EUR in 2017 and 2018. Source: Equinet, page no longer retrievable.

372 Ministerium für Frauen und Gesundheit and Sozialministerium (n 355) 41.

been partly remedied by the fact that the Ombud for Equal Treatment has regional offices in four cities and the mandate of these offices was extended in 2017 to cover the whole Equal Treatment Act. For the organization of hearings in cities other than Vienna, cooperation with higher regional courts has been suggested, with individuals being invited to these premises to be heard, or to be heard via video conference.[373] While there have been some isolated attempts in this direction, this has by no means become an established practice.

The accessibility of information about the Commission via their website is also very limited, with such information only available in German. On the old webpage, the information was accessible for the visually impaired by clicking on a reading device. However, since the page was moved to the new website of the Ministry of Women, Family and Youths, this option is no longer available.

When comparing this legal and practical situation with ECRI's revised GPR No 2 the following conclusion can be drawn: The recommendations clearly propose that Equality Bodies should be 'separate legal entities placed outside the executive' and 'the executive should not have a decisive influence in any stage of the selection process'[374] which is clearly not the case in Austria. The Commission is attached to the Federal Chancellery and the Ministry for Women, Family and Youths operates under it. Some of the members in the senates are civil servants, employed by the ministries that nominate them, and work most of their time within these ministries. The law does not explicitly require expertise in issues related to equality and non-discrimination in order to be nominated to the senates. A transparent, competency-based, and participatory procedure is not at all provided for in the Austrian legislation. All these shortcomings are somewhat mitigated by the fact that senate members are exempted from the obligation to receive instructions when carrying out their function within the Commission.

ECRI recommends that members should 'have appropriate safeguards against arbitrary dismissal or arbitrary non-renewal of appointment where renewal would be the norm'.[375] However, Austrian legislation provides that the nomination by the ministry or dispatch by the interest organization can simply be withdrawn. In fact, § 2(7) provides this possibility without connecting it to any violation of obligations or negligence in the fulfilment of functions. Even if this has not happened so far, the legislation would need to be changed to strengthen the stability of the mandate of Commission members. The legal provision that members, except for the presidents, of the senates have to carry out their activities on a honorary basis is not in line with ECRI's recommendation that those holding leadership positions should be remunerated at a suitable level.[376]

[373] ibid.
[374] ECRI, 'General Policy Recommendation No 2: Equality Bodies to Combat Racism and Intolerance at National Level' (n 23) paras 2 and 23.
[375] ibid para 24.
[376] ibid para 26.

Furthermore, Equality Bodies should have the power to recruit their own staff and operate from their own premises.[377] Through the attachment to the Federal Chancellery, none of these conditions is met since the staff, as well as the Commission members, are civil servants of the Chancellery on the selection of whom the Commission has no influence.[378] Also, the premises are within the Chancellery.

In terms of reflecting the diversity of society at large and being gender-balanced,[379] the law only provides for the above-mentioned quota of at least 50 per cent women among members and their substitutes. But this provision could lead to having all men as members and all substitutes as women. The law does not provide for other segments of society to be represented in the Commission.

All these issues seem secondary, as long as the independence of the Commission in the exercise of its functions is guaranteed and it exercises its functions effectively. While this might be the case, within the budgetary restrictions and the shortcomings in terms of effective functioning discussed below, it is for the law to regulate these issues in a clear and precise manner, rather than leaving it to the good will of the responsible institutions to take decisions that contribute to promote equality and non-discrimination.[380] Furthermore, several of ECRI's recommendations regarding accessibility, including the establishment of regional offices, the adjustment of their information and services to take account of all forms of disabilities, as well as the provision of easy-to-read or translated information and publications,[381] cannot be considered as being properly implemented in the Austrian context.

The tasks of the Commission can essentially be divided in three parts: first, it can draft expert opinions on issues relating to the violation of the right to equal treatment upon the request of an interest group represented in the respective senate, the Ombud for Equal Treatment, or on its own motion.[382] Second, the ETC deals with individual complaints submitted to it by an employee, a workers council, an employer, an interest group, a person concerned by discrimination outside the field of employment, the Ombud for Equal Treatment, or on its own motion.[383] And third, the Commission can request a report from an employer or another person or institution responsible for an alleged discrimination. Such a request is based on the information provided by one of the just-mentioned persons or institutions.[384]

[377] ibid para 27.

[378] The management of the ETC and support for its work is carried out by a department within the Federal Chancellery.

[379] ECRI, 'General Policy Recommendation No 2: Equality Bodies to Combat Racism and Intolerance at National Level' (n 23) para 38.

[380] In the 2018 EELN report on Austria the expert noted that 'it is too early to even speculate about any possible impact of the new right-wing populist coalition forming the government since the end of 2017'. EELN, Country Report Austria, 2018, 80.

[381] ECRI, 'General Policy Recommendation No 2: Equality Bodies to Combat Racism and Intolerance at National Level' (n 23) para 40(b, d–f).

[382] Law on the Equal Treatment Commission and the Ombud for Equal Treatment, § 11.

[383] Law on the Equal Treatment Commission and the Ombud for Equal Treatment, § 12.

[384] Law on the Equal Treatment Commission and the Ombud for Equal Treatment, § 13.

Expert opinions allow the Equal Treatment Commission to deal with a legal question that requires clarification. The Commission can make use of this instrument to take a position on issues that continue to appear before it in its case-work or for which it finds that they constitute a widespread phenomenon and would thus benefit from an in-depth analysis by the Commission, also beyond the individual context. Expert opinions can thus be seen as means of awareness raising about structural discrimination and of legal clarification. So far, only five such expert opinions have been adopted, one by the senate dealing with equality between men and women in the employment field,[385] and four by senate III, dealing with discrimination based on gender or ethnic origin outside employment.[386] Two have been requested by the Ombud for Equal Treatment and two have been written by the Commission on its own motion. Regarding the fifth it is not clear who requested the opinion. In the expert evaluation of the instruments of the equal treatment legislation there was agreement about the potential positive role such opinions could play. However, due to constraints in terms of financial and human resources, the instrument has not been used more extensively.[387]

The number of individual complaints before the Equal Treatment Commission is relatively low when compared to the number of inquiries received by the Ombud for Equal Treatment. While in the period 2018–19, for instance, the latter received 4,017 requests for information, advice, or support,[388] only 242 complaints were submitted to the three senates (135 to senate I, seventy-three to senate II, thirty-four to senate III).[389] In senate III, discrimination on the ground of ethnic origin in the access to goods and service ranks highest among the areas in which discrimination is brought to the attention of the Commission. It is interesting to note that in this senate, in the period 2018–19, seventeen cases were brought by men, while only seven were brought by women.[390]

As mentioned above, the examination of individual cases can be initiated by a request from the person concerned, an interest organization represented in the respective senate, the Ombud for Equal Treatment, or the Equal Treatment Commission on its own motion. The majority of cases in senate I are brought to the

[385] Opinion on sexist advertising materials.

[386] Opinion on gender pricing; Opinion on the prohibition of discrimination on ethnic grounds in the context of education; Opinion on sex-based hairdressing rates; Opinion on equal treatment for women and men—tariff reductions, leisure facilities.

[387] Ministerium für Frauen und Gesundheit and Sozialministerium (n 355) 41–42. In these circumstances, reducing the backlog of cases is the highest priority. E-mail communication with one of the presidents of the ETC, 21 November 2018.

[388] Gleichbehandlungsanwaltschaft, 'Gleichbehandlungs bericht für die Privatwirtschaft 2018 und 2019. Teil II—Anwaltschaft für Gleichbehandlung' (2020) 13.

[389] Bundeskanzleramt, 'Gleichbehandlungsbericht für die Privatwirtschaft 2018 und 2019. Teil I—Gleichbehandlungskommission, Bundesministerium für Arbeit, Familie und Jugend und Beiträge der Interessenvertretungen' (2020) 8, 37, and 63. For a comparison with figures from previous years see Ministerium für Frauen und Gesundheit and Sozialministerium (n 355) 39.

[390] Bundeskanzleramt (n 389) 64; see also Ministerium für Frauen und Gesundheit and Sozialministerium (n 355) 39–40.

attention of the Commission by the Ombud for Equal Treatment, which is likely to explain why this senate has to deal with nearly twice or four times as many complaints as compared to senates II and III respectively. In those senates, complaints are mainly brought by the person concerned, in senate III partly also by the NGO ZARA, based in Vienna.[391]

According to § 12(2) of the Law on the ETC, the person concerned in a discrimination case can be represented by an NGO or any other person of trust. The proceedings are free of charge and travel expenses are reimbursed by the Commission. The formal requirements for a submission to the Commission are limited so that overall access to the Commission is considered to be fairly open. A major challenge appears to be the length of the proceedings which is directly correlated with the number of cases before the different senates of the Commission. According to the information provided by the Commission itself, proceedings in front of senate I and II last on average for sixteen and a half and thirteen months respectively, in front of senate III on average for seven months.[392] When not factoring in rejections and withdrawals (eg due to an out-of-court settlement) the duration in senate I is reportedly more than two years, with isolated cases, in which a case was only decided after four years.[393]

The Ombud for Equal Treatment informs persons concerned who approach the Ombud for initial advice about the length of time procedures can take and has found that some are so discouraged by this information that they do not file a complaint at all. However, some interest representations grant legal aid to their members in court cases only if they have first attempted to bring proceedings before the Equal Treatment Commission. The lengthy procedures, however, make the preservation of evidence for a possible future court case difficult and thus heightens the risk in such procedures. Furthermore, given the pressure on the senates to speed up decision making on cases, they have no resources to invest in the drafting of expert opinions or in establishing and maintaining regular exchanges with the judiciary. The Commission's Recommendation on Standards for Equality Bodies, although relatively vague in many other parts, is quite explicit in establishing that resources (human, technical, financial) 'can only be considered adequate if they allow equality bodies to carry out each of their equality functions effectively [and] within reasonable time'.[394] In the Austrian context it would appear that, at the minimum, the establishment of the position of president of a senate (especially senate I, who also coordinates the whole commission) as a full-time position would be

[391] E-mail communication with one of the presidents of the ETC, 21 November 2018.
[392] Bundeskanzleramt (n 389) 10, 39, and 64.
[393] Director of the Regional Representation Styria, Ombud for Equal Treatment, Austria, 20 July 2018.
[394] European Commission, 'Commission Recommendation on Standards for Equality Bodies' (n 19) 8.

required.[395] A more radical and probably more effective approach in terms of allowing the Commission to deal with the current (and possibly also bigger) caseload would be to reconsider the overall composition of the Commission by establishing at least part-time or (for the sake of independence even better) full-time positions for all its members.

During the first hearing in front of the Commission, the parties concerned are asked if they are ready to reach a friendly settlement. In practice, such settlement is achieved in about half of all cases.[396] In carrying out its investigations, the Commission hears in all cases the parties concerned and witnesses. The president of a senate can, or—following a request by the Ombud for Equal Treatment or more than one third of the senate's members—must, invite experts to the hearings.[397] Further, the Ombud for Equal Treatment is allowed to participate at the hearings of the Commission and at his/her request has to be given the right to speak.[398] The Commission can also decide to charge the Ombud to carry out investigations in a particular case.[399] In practice, this possibility is used often and has been considered useful. In most such cases, the Ombud requests written information and statements but does not make use of the possibility to undertake an on-the-spot visit and inspect documentation in this context.[400] The employer and all other employees are under the obligation to provide all requested information to the Commission necessary to fulfil its task.[401] The Commission thus has a wide range of investigation possibilities at its disposal, as recommended in ECRI 's revised GPR No 2.

If the Equal Treatment Commission finds that discrimination has taken place it asks the perpetrator to end the discrimination and makes a proposal on how the principle of equality could be fully achieved. Such recommendations are non-binding. The decisions of the Commission are published in anonymized form on

[395] For further suggestions on how the length of proceedings could be reduced, see Bundeskanzleramt, Bundesministerium für Arbeit, Soziales und Konsumentenschutz and Bundesministerin für Frauen und Gesundheit, 'Gleichbehandlungsbericht für die Privatwirtschaft 2014 und 2015. Teil II—Anwaltschaft für Gleichbehandlung' (2016) 102; and Ministerium für Frauen und Gesundheit and Sozialministerium (n 355) 40–46.

[396] Bundeskanzleramt and Bundesministerium für Arbeit, Soziales, Gesundheit und Konsumentenschutz, 'Gleichbehandlungsbericht für die Privatwirtschaft 2016 und 2017. Teil I—Gleichbehandlungskommission und Bundesministerium für Arbeit, Soziales, Gesundheit und Konsumentenschutz' (2018) 7, 83, and 131.

[397] Law on the Equal Treatment Commission and the Ombud for Equal Treatment, § 14(4a).

[398] Law on the Equal Treatment Commission and the Ombud for Equal Treatment, § 5(3). Since the entry into force of amendments to the law in 2013, only one representative from the Ombud for Equal Treatment can participate at the hearings of a senate, which has created difficulties in practice in cases of multiple discrimination. As the Ombud for Equal Treatment is divided in the same way as the Commission, in such cases the representative of the Ombud had to overstep his/her legally circumscribed field of action. It has been resolved so that two are allowed to be present with only one having the right to engage in the discussion. See Bundeskanzleramt, Bundesministerium für Arbeit, Soziales und Konsumentenschutz and Bundesministerin für Frauen und Gesundheit (n 396) 100.

[399] Law on the Equal Treatment Commission and the Ombud for Equal Treatment, § 5(7).

[400] Ministerium für Frauen und Gesundheit and Sozialministerium (n 355) 54.

[401] Law on the Equal Treatment Commission and the Ombud for Equal Treatment, § 10(2).

its webpage.[402] These provisions have been seen by the ACFC as limiting the effectiveness of the Equal Treatment Commission.[403] ECRI's revised GPR No 2 acknowledge that states may establish Equality Bodies with the competence to either take legally binding or non-binding decisions.[404] However, the explanatory memorandum makes it clear that there is a preference for Equality Bodies to be able to take binding decisions and, in addition, to be able to impose effective, proportionate, and dissuasive sanctions, including the payment of compensation, the imposition of fines, and the publication of the decision with the name of the perpetrator.[405] In the Austrian context however, these possibilities are not available and even the publication of the decision finding a violation is done anonymously so that there is not even a naming and shaming effect. Only in cases where an employer or a person otherwise responsible for an alleged discrimination does not submit a report requested by the Commission under § 13 of the law, does the Commission publish this fact on its webpage, including the name of the person or institution requested to submit a report. However, the Commission reportedly makes little use of this option under § 13. It has been recommended that it could be used more often and more efficiently not only in the context of investigations but also in the context of following up on its recommendations.[406]

The law provides in fact, that the perpetrator shall be given a deadline of two months to implement the Commission's recommendation. If it is not implemented within that time frame, which could be verified by requesting a report under § 13, the Ombud for Equal Treatment (with the consent of the complainant) and the interest groups represented in the senate have the right to submit to the court an action for the declaration that discrimination has occurred.[407] In practice, this measure is not used to its full extent. While the Commission does request information regarding the fulfilment of its recommendations, it simply takes note of it without producing any statistics on the number of cases in which the recommendations have been followed. Follow-up actions by the Ombud for Equal Treatment do not appear to be taken.

Furthermore, it has been suggested that the recommendations of the Commission should be formulated in a more concrete manner.[408] Where the senates find discrimination they mainly recommend that the perpetrator intensively engage with equal treatment legislation and pay appropriate compensation for damages. Only in a few cases does the Commission recommend an exact

402 Law on the Equal Treatment Commission and the Ombud for Equal Treatment, § 12(3)(7).

403 ACFC, 'Fourth opinion on Austria adopted on 14 October 2016' (n 360) para 14.

404 ECRI, 'General Policy Recommendation No 2: Equality Bodies to Combat Racism and Intolerance at National Level' (n 23) paras 17 and 18.

405 While the complainant's name should only be published with his/her consent. See ibid para 87 of the explanatory memorandum.

406 Ministerium für Frauen und Gesundheit and Sozialministerium (n 355) 41.

407 Law on the Equal Treatment Commission and the Ombud for Equal Treatment, § 12(4)(5).

408 Ministerium für Frauen und Gesundheit and Sozialministerium (n 355) 41, 55.

amount that would be considered appropriate. In some cases it recommends the organization of training and workshops on the equal treatment legislation within a company or the setting up of structures to prevent future discrimination. Sometimes it recommends the inclusion of information on the perpetrator's website about the equal treatment legislation and on the opportunities for support and advice available from the Ombud for Equal Treatment or an NGO. Although the ETC requests information as to compliance with its recommendations, there is no information available about whether compensation is paid, training is held, and even less so whether the perpetrators have engaged with equal treatment legislation.[409]

A forward-looking sanction included in the law can be seen in the provisions of the Equal Treatment Act that provide guidelines for the disbursement of financial support by the federal authorities only to those companies that respect the provisions of the Equal Treatment Act.[410] However, these provision are not made use of in practice as it is, for instance, not clear who should establish disrespect for the Equal Treatment Act and how the authorities deciding on the support should receive the required information.[411] In addition to the creation of the required legal framework, cooperation between the judiciary and the Equal Treatment Commission, coordinated by the Ministry of Justice, would most likely be required in order to bring together the required data.

As the decisions of the Equal Treatment Commission are not binding, no formal appeal against its decisions is possible. The only exception in this context is that the Ombuds for Equal Treatment can request from the court a declaration establishing whether discrimination has taken place in cases where the decision of the Equal Treatment Commission does not correspond with the request submitted by the Ombud for Equal Treatment.[412] In the past, such requests to the courts have often ended with a settlement and have been considered an effective tool. However, since the costs for such proceedings are no longer covered by the Federal Chancellery but need to be covered by the budget for public relations of the Ombud for Equal Treatment, such requests have become hardly feasible. The experts evaluating the instruments of equal treatment thus recommended the establishment of a litigation fund, which was however rejected by the Economic Chamber.[413] The Ombud for Equal Treatment further would like to see this competence extended to all cases, not only those in which it has itself submitted the request to the ETC.[414]

409 Information provided by the president of one of the senates of ETC, 4 December 2018.

410 Equal Treatment Act, §§ 14, 28, and 40.

411 Ministerium für Frauen und Gesundheit and Sozialministerium (n 355) 42.

412 Law on the Equal Treatment Commission and the Ombud for Equal Treatment, § 5(6) in conjunction with § 12(5).

413 Ministerium für Frauen und Gesundheit and Sozialministerium (n 355) 54–55.

414 Bundeskanzleramt, Bundesministerium für Arbeit, Soziales und Konsumentenschutz and Bundesministerin für Frauen und Gesundheit (n 396) 126.

To obtain a legally enforceable decision, for instance on compensation, a victim of discrimination needs to approach a court. Courts have to take the decision of the ETC into consideration and where they come to a different conclusion about the existence or non-existence of discrimination, this has to be provided with reasons.[415] However, this is only the case if the judge comes to the same conclusion as regards the facts of the case. It has thus been recommended that the ETC follows similar procedures as the courts when it comes to the establishment of facts and further, to structure the decision clearly in sections dealing with the complaint, the facts of the case, the evaluation of evidence, and the legal assessment.[416] The ETC does not collect any data on the way in which their opinions are treated by judges[417] but reportedly, the value of the ETC's decisions in a court case is 'quite low, mainly due to the fact that the procedure before the Equal Treatment Commission does not even meet most of the basic procedural standards of courts'.[418] In order to promote the uniform interpretation of equal treatment legislation and to further develop proceedings before the Equal Treatment Commission it has been recommended that cooperation between ETC members, judges, and the Ombuds for Equal Treatment be enhanced. For this purpose, judgments coming under equal treatment legislation should be designated as such and be transmitted to both the ETC as well as the Ombud for Equal Treatment.[419]

Summing up, the following conclusions can be drawn: the members of the different senates in the Commission have certainly made great efforts to engage with equal treatment legislation and to improve its procedures. It also seems that the low-threshold service, that is, the informal procedure without risking any costs is generally appreciated. However, the effectiveness of the ETC appears to be hampered by the following challenges: the current composition and set-up of the Commission makes it vulnerable to political influence and it appears to make it difficult to cope with the caseload in a reasonable time. If a reorganization of the overall body, detaching it from the governmental structure, is not seen as an option to remedy this challenge, there is an urgent need to find other ways by which the procedures could be made speedier. Its decisions could be formulated more precisely so as to allow for better follow-up. Change could also be made to the legislation regarding the anonymized publication of decisions. In fact, ECRI's Recommendations state, at least for the publication of the decision as a form of sanction, that the name of the perpetrator should be published, while that of the complainant should be published only with his/her consent.[420] It would be more

[415] Equal Treatment Act, § 61.

[416] Ministerium für Frauen und Gesundheit and Sozialministerium (n 355) 51, 53.

[417] E-mail communication with one of the presidents of the ETC, 21 November 2018.

[418] EELN, Country Report Austria, 2017, 84.

[419] Ministerium für Frauen und Gesundheit and Sozialministerium (n 355) 51–53; see also ibid 104, according to which there exists an obligation to designate judgments related to equal treatment as such but that this obligation is not respected.

[420] ECRI, 'General Policy Recommendation No 2: Equality Bodies to Combat Racism and Intolerance at National Level' (n 23) para 17; and para 87 of the Explanatory Memorandum.

dissuasive for a perpetrator if it became public knowledge that discrimination had occurred. More generally, the sanctions imposed cannot be considered dissuasive. A related and fundamental problem is that if a perpetrator does not follow the recommendation of the Commission there are no real consequences. In such circumstances it is easy for perpetrators simply to disregard the recommendation.

The Commission can thus be considered rather toothless. Additionally, the Commission currently does not appear to be exercising all its functions, since very few opinions have been adopted and it rarely makes use of its right to request a report from an alleged (or confirmed, where there is already a Commission decision) perpetrator.

Overall, the task under the RED to provide independent assistance to victims of discrimination is also part of the mandate of the Ombud for Equal Treatment and therefore an evaluation of whether this obligation is complied with in Austria needs to consider them together. Without entering into any detail as to the competences of Ombud for Equal Treatment in this respect, it should be mentioned that while it is quite successful in supporting individuals by means of conciliation, it has practically no way of bringing a case before a court. It can, and does, bring cases before the ETC, which however, as just discussed, has limited impact.[421]

5.3.4 Good Practices and Challenges

Even if independence is interpreted in the strict sense as requiring 'only' the independent carrying out of an Equality Body's functions, these three case studies have shown that in order to achieve this aim it is necessary to look at the level of independence granted to the Equality Body as such. The case study of Romania has been particularly instructive. In this case, the executive has no role in the appointment of those leading the Equality Body and the appointments are instead made by parliament, which, according to ECRI, is to be considered good practice. More important than who makes the final appointment, however, is the question of how the whole selection process is implemented. The focus of any monitoring should thus be on the above-mentioned (Table 5.1) process indicators, looking at whether the procedure is inclusive, transparent, and competency-based, another requirement spelled out by ECRI in its recommendations. The Romanian example has also shown that it is not only necessary to legally provide for protection of members appointed to Equality Bodies against arbitrary dismissals, but that safeguards need to be in place to protect the existence of the body as such from politically motivated attacks. In this context it might even be necessary to entrench the Equality Body in the Constitution, which makes it more difficult to abolish the body altogether.

[421] EELN, Country Report Austria, 2020, 67.

The experience from Bulgaria leads to quite similar conclusions. While the independence of members of the Equal Treatment Commission in Austria (so far) does not appear to be an issue, especially given the fact that they are exempted from receiving instructions, the vulnerability to political influence of such a body, embedded in the executive and appointed in large parts by the executive, is definitely higher. Such influence does not necessarily have to come around in the form of instruction but can happen in much more subtle ways. The Romanian and Bulgarian examples have shown clearly that proximity to political parties can have a negative influence on the quality of the body's decisions. Furthermore, the composition of the Austrian body appears to hamper its functioning because sessions are rare, meaning that it takes a long time to decide cases. For these reasons it appears preferable, as recommended by ECRI, to set up the body as a separate legal entity placed outside the executive.

Funding has turned out to be a challenge for all the bodies looked at above. None of them has sufficient funds to carry out all their functions effectively. Suggestions made in the Austrian context regarding how to speed up decision making have been rejected on the basis that additional funds are not available. The Romanian and Bulgarian bodies manage to (partly) implement some of their functions not related to decision making only through external funding. The ability to raise additional funds thus appears vital. It was also clear that additional competences have not been matched with additional money. The inability to carry out all the functions was partly also connected to insufficient staffing. And finally, in terms of outreach, the Romanian and Austrian bodies in particular have a huge need to catch up, while in the context of the Bulgarian regional representatives their ability to operate independently has been questioned. All these issues have been covered by the indicators proposed at 5.2.4 (Table 5.1).

When it comes to the carrying out of their decision-making function it can be concluded that all the Equality Bodies under consideration here can be approached by a variety of actors, that the formal barriers for approaching the body are relatively low (with the exception of the Bulgarian CPAD, which should make it possible to submit complaints in the language in which the complainant is proficient without needing to provide also a translation to Bulgarian), and that proceedings being free of charge is a factor which positively influences the decision of whether to raise a complaint or not. On the other hand, the length of time proceedings can take, in the case of the Austrian Equal Treatment Commission, has been perceived as a deterrent. The Bulgarian Commission is also dealing with a backlog of cases.

When it comes to the investigatory competences, all bodies appear to be formally well equipped. Whether all the competences can be made use of depends, however, on sufficient staffing which is not always given. Common to all bodies is the fact that the sanctions in most cases appear not to be dissuasive. Although the requirement of dissuasiveness has not been included as a standard in the

Commission's Recommendations,[422] the lack of a deterrent effect has been addressed by the Commission in its implementation report.[423] While it might well be that a complainant is satisfied with the finding of discrimination, the sanction should also have an impact on the perpetrator. The practice, for instance, of the Romanian NCCD to just issue a warning cannot be considered as an effective and dissuasive sanction. It should be noted however, that the Commission is increasingly imposing fines.

While fines imposed by the Romanian and Bulgarian Equality Bodies can be enforced due to their binding nature, these bodies do not have the necessary capacity to follow up on their decisions. This is a shortcoming which they have in common with the Austrian Equal Treatment Commission, which, in this latter case, is exacerbated by the fact that its decisions are not legally binding. In such cases it is even more important to dedicate enough resources to a follow-up and monitoring of decisions. While the legal framework for such follow-up is in place, it is not made use of systematically.[424]

Notwithstanding all these challenges, the Romanian and Bulgarian bodies in particular have managed to have an impact not only on the legal development of the respective national anti-discrimination frameworks (eg the increase of sanctions in Romania, or the sharpening of definitions of direct and indirect discrimination in Bulgaria), but also on the interpretation of core concepts at the European level by playing a role in cases that reach the CJEU. Furthermore, by its clear positioning, for instance on such a sensitive issue as LGBT rights, the Romanian NCCD has also contributed to shaping the national debate around this issue, even if it thereby exposed itself to harsh criticism and attacks from various political and other actors. Similarly, the Bulgarian CPAD, through its strategic cooperation with NGOs and the group concerned, managed to address one of the many ways by which the Roma community is exposed to discrimination, while its more recent decisions on the issue are a source of concern.

The cases dealt with by the Austrian Equal Treatment Commission have more of an impact on the individual level. Its cases do not impact public perception which contributes to a lack of visibility of the body. In fact, the most recent FRA survey among minorities has revealed that 90 per cent of the respondents have never heard of the Equal Treatment Commission. This is the fourth-worst result

[422] Lack of dissuasiveness has been identified as limiting the effectiveness of quasi-judicial Equality Bodies already in Council of Europe, Commissioner for Human Rights (n 24) 16.

[423] European Commission, 'Equality bodies and the implementation of the Commission Recommendation on Standards for Equality Bodies' (n 1) 10.

[424] Insufficient 'resources or powers to engage in follow-up to ensure implementation of the decisions and recommendations' as well as situations where Equality Bodies can only take non-legally binding decisions have been identified as limiting the effectiveness of quasi-judicial Equality Bodies also in Council of Europe, Commissioner for Human Rights (n 24) 16. See also European Commission, 'Equality bodies and the implementation of the Commission Recommendation on Standards for Equality Bodies' (n 1) 10.

after the Equality Bodies of Spain, Northern Ireland and the Austrian Ombud for Equal Treatment. That both Equality Bodies in Austria have such bad results might be connected to the complexity of the Austrian non-discrimination system and should definitely be a cause for concern for the Austrian authorities. While the results of Romania and Bulgaria are somewhat better, where 77 per cent of respondents in Bulgaria and 75 per cent of respondents in Romania have never heard of the Equality Body,[425] these results too show that there is still much room for improvement.

5.3.5 Proposed Indicators

While the above conclusions regarding independence of Equality Bodies have been taken into consideration in the development of the proposed indicators at 5.2.4 (Table 5.1), the focus here is on indicators to measure the effectiveness of the decision-making function, where this has been assigned to an Equality Body by national legislation (for a summary see Table 5.2).

The aspects to be taken into consideration in this context at the level of structural indicators are: who can approach the Equality Body with a complaint; what powers does it have to obtain evidence and information and what are the consequences if cooperation during investigations is refused; can the Equality Body issue legally binding decisions or not; are the sanctions that can be awarded effective, proportionate, and dissuasive; can its decisions be enforced; and is accessibility ensured?

Process indicators would then need to look into all these aspects from the perspective of actual practice: are possibilities granted by legislation used and if not, how can this be explained? What is the level of sanctions imposed? Can they be considered effective, proportionate, and dissuasive? Is there any follow-up to decisions and if not, why not? Are there enough regional offices? Can Equality Bodies be approached in minority languages and have measures been taken to make sure their services are accessible to persons with disability? Allocating adequate financial and human resources will be key to enable the Equality Body to carry out all its functions in a way that makes an impact.[426] In terms of efforts by the state in implementing the legal provisions on the decision-making function of Equality Bodies it would further be necessary to evaluate if awareness among rights holders about the existence of the Equality Body and the possibility of approaching it with a discrimination complaint is raised.

In principle, the benchmarks for all these indicators are given by ECRI's revised GPR No 2 and the Commission's Recommendation on Standards for Equality Bodies. While the former are, however, much more detailed and clearer in terms of expressing preferences for one or the other option, based on more than twenty

[425] Fundamental Rights Agency, 'EU-MIDIS II: Main results' (n 64) 123–24.
[426] Kádár, 'Equality Bodies: A European Phenomenon' (n 797) 11.

years' monitoring experience, the Commission's recommendations in many instances just list the various options that states should take into consideration, thereby leaving the states probably too much leeway in making choices which might have a negative impact on the overall effectiveness of the decision-making function of the body. In its implementation report is has already become clearer what the Commission considers to be good practice and what causes concern.

If both commitment and efforts of states bear fruit, the outcome would be an increased awareness of the Equality Body and its decision-making function which most likely will go hand in hand with an increase in the number of complaints brought before it. The ultimate goal, however, is not an increase in the number of complaints—as ideally the discriminatory situations should become less over time—but improved reporting behaviour. Such a development also depends of course on the level of trust in the Equality Body, which should be surveyed regularly. At the same time, the impact on the outcome could also be measured by looking into the level of compliance with the recommendations coming from the Equality Body, which is particularly important to measure where the Equality Body can issue only non-binding decisions.

Table 5.2 Table of indicators concerning the effectiveness of predominantly tribunal-type Equality Bodies

Effective functioning	Structural indicators	• Who can approach the Equality Body with a complaint? • What powers does the Equality Body have to obtain evidence and information and what are the consequences if cooperation during investigations is refused? • Can the Equality Body issue legally binding decisions or not? • Are the sanctions that can be imposed effective, proportionate, and dissuasive? • Can its decisions be enforced? • Is accessibility ensured by law?
	Process indicators	• Are possibilities granted by legislation used and if not, how can this be explained? • What is the level of sanctions imposed? Can they be considered effective, proportionate, and dissuasive? • Is there any follow-up to decisions and if not, why not? • Are there enough regional offices, can Equality Bodies be approached in minority languages, and have measures been taken to make sure their services are accessible to persons with disability? • Is awareness of the existence and kind of service provided by the Equality Body given?
	Outcome indicators	• Levels of awareness about the Equality Body increasing • Level of trust in the Equality Body increasing • Reporting behaviour improving • Compliance with the Equality Body's recommendations

5.4 Effectiveness of Predominantly 'Promotion Type' Equality Bodies

5.4.1 Introduction and Conceptual Clarification

As mentioned above, predominantly promotion-type Equality Bodies 'spend the bulk of their time and resources on a broader mix of activities that include supporting good practice in organisations, raising awareness of rights, developing a knowledge base on equality and nondiscrimination, and providing legal advice and assistance to individual victims of discrimination'.[427] As the focus in this chapter is on access to complaints mechanisms as a reaction to a violation that has already taken place, it will only deal with the activity concerning the provision of legal advice and assistance to victims of discrimination.[428] The other activities will be dealt with in Chapter 6.2.

The legal basis for the activity regarding advising and assisting victims can be found in Article 13(2) RED, which, inter alia, provides that Equality Bodies are to be vested with the competence to provide 'independent assistance to victims of discrimination in pursuing their complaints about discrimination'. As the Directive does not provide any further guidance on the exact meaning of this obligation, it has been implemented by Member States in a variety of ways. These can be grouped in the following way:

- Legal advice and information about anti-discrimination provisions in force and about the available redress mechanisms;
- Alternative dispute resolution by supporting amicable settlements between persons who feel discriminated and the alleged perpetrators through mediation or conciliation;
- Assistance in the courts by:
  - o providing legal advice to victims of discrimination and representing them in the courts;
  - o bringing legal action in the Equality Body's own name;
  - o intervening before the court as a third party or *amicus curiae*;
- Investigating and hearing discrimination complaints and deciding on the merits of the case, in the case of predominantly promotion-type bodies normally with a legally non-binding decision.[429]

It is submitted that for an Equality Body to fulfil the requirements under the RED it is not necessary to have all the above-mentioned competences. Indeed, the

[427] Ammer and others (n 53) 43–44. More or less the same wording is used by the definition of the two types of bodies on the Equinet webpage: https://equineteurope.org/comparative-data/functions/.

[428] For a detailed analysis of this aspect in the Scandinavian context see Bjørn Dilou Jacobsen, *Assistance to Victims of Discrimination by Equality Bodies of the EU Member States: A Scandinavian Perspective* (DJOF Publishing 2010).

[429] Based on Equinet, https://equineteurope.org/comparative-data/functions/. A similar grouping is provided in Equinet, 'Strategic Plan 2015–2018' (2015) 7.

preparatory works to the Directive suggest that the intention was to leave it to the discretion of the Member States to decide on the way in which their Equality Body provides assistance to victims of discrimination. This can be drawn from the fact that the UN Model Legislation for the Guidance of Governments in the Enactment of Further Legislation against Racial Discrimination[430] as well as ECRI's GPR No 2 in its original version of 1997[431] formed the basis for the requirements formulated under Article 13 RED. Both documents list numerous ways in which assistance to victims of discrimination can be provided, without however indicating which of these functions 'should be assigned' to Equality Bodies and which 'may also be assigned'.[432] An indicator that a right for Equality Bodies to participate in legal proceedings cannot be inferred directly from the RED stems from the fact that Equality Bodies are not mentioned in the provisions on remedies and enforcement. In particular, Article 7(2) only mentions 'associations, organisations and other legal entities' that may engage in support or on behalf of the complainant in judicial or administrative procedures. This again leaves it to the states to decide whether Equality Bodies should be granted this right or not.[433]

The assumption is, however, that the more of these competences an Equality Body has at its disposal, the more likely it is that the body can develop visibility and standing as an important player in the fight against discrimination. Whether more competences will also lead to a stronger Equality Body will of course very much depend also on other factors, such as the possibility to carry out its activities independently and effectively, which—as has been seen above—includes also being provided with adequate human and financial resources.

For the Paris Principles the provision of assistance to individual victims of a violation of a human right is not at the centre of the NHRI's activities. The GANHRI's General Observations explain that '"[p]rotection" functions may be understood as those that address . . . actual human rights violations. Such functions include monitoring, inquiring, investigating and reporting on human rights violations, *and may include individual complaint handling*.'[434] All bodies provided with a mandate to handle complaints qualify, according to GANHRI, as quasi-judicial bodies. If they are provided with such a mandate, their functions 'might' include receiving complaints against public and private bodies, initiating a complaint *suo motu*, carrying

430 United Nations, 'Model National Legislation for the Guidance of Governments in the Enactment of Further Legislation Against Racial Discrimination: developed in the context of the Third Decade to Combat Racism and Racial Discrimination (1993–2003)'.

431 ECRI, 'General Policy Recommendation No 2 on Specialised bodies to combat racism, xenophobia, anti-Semitism and intolerance at national level' (ECRI, 13 June 1997) CRI(97)36. This original version stated that, '[s]ubject to national circumstances, law and practice, specialised bodies should possess as many as possible of the following functions and responsibilities' and then listed thirteen possible functions.

432 Such a distinction is made by the ECRI's revised GPR No 2, as will be further discussed below.

433 Equinet, 'Influencing the law through legal proceedings: the powers and practices of equality bodies' (2010) 9–11; Jacobsen (n 428) 89.

434 GANHRI (n 73) 9. Emphasis added.

out its own investigations, seeking amicable settlement of the dispute, deciding on the complaint through a binding decision, following up and monitoring the implementation of the decision, and most importantly, reporting its findings to the government where the case 'provides evidence of a widespread or systematic violation of human rights'.[435] The NHRI given this function should ensure that their complaints handling is fair, transparent, efficient, speedy, and consistent.[436] So while the NHRI, under the Paris Principles, might be given a mandate to handle complaints and either seek amicable settlement and/or decide on them, the Principles are silent on the role such bodies can play in court proceedings.

While the original version of ECRI's GPR No 2 did not distinguish between functions that 'should be assigned' to Equality Bodies and functions that 'may be assigned' to them, such a differentiation is made by the revised version. In paragraph 10(b) it lays down that '[t]he function to support people exposed to discrimination and intolerance *and* to pursue litigation on their behalf (support and litigation function)'[437] should be assigned to Equality Bodies. While an active litigation function is therefore included in ECRI's text, the RED does not explicitly call for such an active role before courts. ECRI's recommendation goes beyond Article 7(2) RED, by which Equality Bodies can be among the legal entities to which certain procedural rights are given. Article 7(2) however offers the alternative 'on behalf or in support of the complainant', whereas ECRI seems to require that Equality Bodies are permitted not only to act in support but also on behalf of a complainant.

Paragraph 14 sets out in more detail which competences the support and litigation function 'should include':

a. Receive complaints and provide personal support and legal advice and assistance to people exposed to discrimination or intolerance, in order to secure their rights before institutions, adjudicatory bodies and the courts.
b. Have recourse to conciliation procedures when appropriate.
c. Represent, with their consent, people exposed to discrimination or intolerance before institutions, adjudicatory bodies, and the courts.
d. Bring cases of individual and structural discrimination or intolerance in the equality body's own name before institutions, adjudicatory bodies and the courts.
e. Intervene as amicus curiae, third party or expert before institutions, adjudicatory bodies, and the courts.
f. Monitor the execution of decisions of institutions, adjudicatory bodies, and the courts dealing with equality, discrimination and intolerance.[438]

[435] ibid 57.
[436] ibid 57.
[437] Emphasis added.
[438] ECRI, 'General Policy Recommendation No 2: Equality Bodies to Combat Racism and Intolerance at National Level' (n 23) para 14; and paras 71–79 of the Explanatory Memorandum.

Furthermore, it lays down in paragraph 15 that Equality Bodies should publish criteria on the basis of which they choose 'the cases they take up for representation and strategic litigation and the venues in which they seek to secure the rights of people exposed to individual and structural discrimination'.[439]

While ECRI's recommendations are explicit in prompting states to include all these competences in the support *and* litigation function, the Commission's recommendations do include all these possibilities as well but use less demanding wording in that they state that Member States 'should take [these possibilities] into consideration'.[440] In particular, when it comes to addressing 'structural and systematic discrimination', the Commission mentions that assistance '*can* include granting equality bodies the possibility to engage or assist in ligitation ... either in the body's own name or in the name of the victims or organisations representing the victims, in accordance with national procedural law'.[441] Although the wording chosen by the Commission, for understandable reasons, remains quite vague, it is still valuable as it has given the states some guidance as to how the requirement of providing assistance to victims of discrimination could be translated into practice. Indeed, in its implementation report, the Commission states that 'good practice in line with the Recommendation involve entrusting the equality bodies with a broad set of powers and appropriate legal standing to enable them to offer effective assistance to victims'.[442] The CoE Commissioner for Human Rights also pointed out that if Equality Bodies are not given the power to investigate a case or to bring cases to court in their own name, this limits their effectiveness.[443]

The following sub-sections look at which of the above options have been chosen by those Member States that have decided to transpose Article 13 RED by setting up a predominantly promotion-type body, and how independently and effectively the Equality Bodies are able to exercise their function in practice. The aim is to identify good practices and challenges at the level of transposition and implementation on the basis of which indicators can be proposed by which the effectiveness of predominantly tribunal-type Equality Bodies in providing independent assistance to victims of discrimination can be measured.

[439] ECRI, 'General Policy Recommendation No 2: Equality Bodies to Combat Racism and Intolerance at National Level' (n 23) para 14. In para 80 of the Explanatory Memorandum it spells out the aims of strategic litigation: 'to (i) generate case law that clarifies the interpretation of the equal treatment legislation, (ii) ensure a critical mass of casework on the different grounds covered, (iii) develop case law on issues of structural discrimination, (iv) generate publicity and use this publicity to sensitise individuals and institutions about their obligations under the equal rights legislation and (v) motivate individuals and institutions to respect these obligations and to bring about societal change'.

[440] European Commission, 'Commission Recommendation on Standards for Equality Bodies' (n 19) Chapter II, 1.1.2, point 1.

[441] ibid Chapter II, 1.1.2, point 2.

[442] European Commission, 'Equality bodies and the implementation of the Commission Recommendation on Standards for Equality Bodies' (n 1) 10.

[443] Council of Europe, Commissioner for Human Rights (n 24) 16. See in this context also Venice Commission, 'Opinion No 897/2017—Principles on the Protection and Promotion of the Ombudsman Institution (Venice Principles)' (n 72); and Committee of Ministers (n 72).

5.4.2 Legal Transposition

Table 5.3 gives an overview of the prevalence of individual functions in the different countries. The table does not include the provision of legal counsel and advice as in one way or another all national Equality Bodies carry out this function to assist victims of discrimination.[444] The focus of the table and also the main focus of the subsequent analysis is thus on their engagement in alternative dispute resolution through mediation or conciliation, on the assistance provided by Equality Bodies to victims of discrimination in the courts, and on the possibility to decide on individual complaints, which in the case of predominantly promotion-type bodies is normally done in legally non-binding form.

Before entering into an analysis and discussion of these three fields of activity, however, it is important to highlight some of the practices of Equality Bodies in providing *legal advice and information* to individuals who feel they have been discriminated against. The two overarching indicators for the advice and information being provided effectively and efficiently are accessibility to this service as well as the high quality of the advice given.[445] Both these requirements are well reflected in the Recommendations of ECRI and the Commission.[446]

Accessibility to the service can be provided by various means: To start with it is useful if an Equality Body's webpage has a dedicated area for discrimination victims, containing information material on the legislation in force and step-by-step assistance on the possible avenues, such as on how to lodge a court case or how to address the Equality Body for help.[447] Another important element in ensuring accessibility to the legal advice service of the Equality Body is the availability of different channels by which the Equality Body can be contacted. In most cases, people can address the body in person, by phone, regular post or e-mail, and, increasingly, also via social media. Telephone hotlines are generally available, however with variations in terms of the number of hours and days on which the body can be reached and their availability free of charge. Some Equality Bodies have established special open consultation hours while in other bodies victims of discrimination can turn up at any time during opening hours.

Accessibility is greatly enhanced by the establishment of regional offices[448] or the conclusion of cooperation agreements with regional authorities or local NGOs[449]

[444] Equinet, 'Providing independent assistance to victims of discrimination: An Equinet report' (Equinet: European Network of Equality Bodies, Brussels 2011) 15.

[445] Information contained in the following paragraphs is partly drawn from Equinet, 'Providing independent assistance to victims of discrimination: An Equinet report' (n 444) 15–18.

[446] ECRI, 'General Policy Recommendation No 2: Equality Bodies to Combat Racism and Intolerance at National Level' (n 23) para 40(a–b, d–g); European Commission, 'Commission Recommendation on Standards for Equality Bodies' (n 19) Chapter II, 1.2.3.

[447] An example of this is the webpage of the Equality Commission for Northern Ireland: http://www.equalityni.org/Individuals.

[448] Such offices exist for instance in Croatia, Belgium, and Bulgaria.

[449] Such cooperation exists for instance in Croatia, Greece (Ombudsman), and Northern Ireland.

Table 5.3 Functions of Equality Bodies (source: Equinet, with adaptations by the author based on EELN reports 2020)[a]

	Alternative dispute resolution by mediation or conciliation	Representing victims before courts	Bringing proceedings in the EB's own name	Intervening before the court	Deciding on complaints (not legally binding)	Deciding on complaints (legally binding)
Austria						
Disability Ombudsman	x	x*[1]	x		x	
Ombud for Equal Treatment			x*[2]			
Equal Treatment Commission					x tribunal type	
Belgium						
Unia (Interfederal Centre for Equal Opportunities)	x	x	x	x	x	
Bulgaria						
Commission for Protection against Discrimination			x	x		x tribunal type
Croatia						
Office of the Ombudsman	x		x	x	x	
Cyprus						
Office of the Commissioner for Administration and Human Rights						x tribunal type

Continued

Table 5.3 *Continued*

	Alternative dispute resolution by mediation or conciliation	Representing victims before courts	Bringing proceedings in the EB's own name	Intervening before the court	Deciding on complaints (not legally binding)	Deciding on complaints (legally binding)
Czech Republic						
Public Defender of Rights	x				x	
Denmark						
Danish Institute for Human Rights		x**1	x**1	x		
Board of Equal Treatment			x**2			x tribunal type
Estonia						
Chancellor of Justice					x	
Commissioner for Gender Equality and Equal Treatment	x legally binding		x		x	
Finland						
Non-Discrimination Ombudsman		x	x	x	x	
France						
Defender of Rights	x		x***	x	x	
Germany						
Federal Antidiscrimination Agency	x				x	
Greece						
Greek Ombudsman					x	

Hungary						
Equal Treatment Authority (no longer in place)			*x*	*x*		x tribunal type
Commissioner for Fundamental Rights					x	
Ireland						
Irish Human Rights and Equality Commission	x	x	x	x		
Italy						
National Office against Racial Discrimination					x	
Latvia						
Office of the Ombudsman	x	x	x	x****	x	
Lithuania						
Equal Opportunities Ombudsperson					x	x tribunal type
Luxembourg						
Centre for Equal Treatment					x	
Malta						
National Commission for the Promotion of Equality	x				x	
Netherlands						
Netherlands Institute for Human Rights			x		x	

Continued

Table 5.3 *Continued*

	Alternative dispute resolution by mediation or conciliation	Representing victims before courts	Bringing proceedings in the EB's own name	Intervening before the court	Deciding on complaints (not legally binding)	Deciding on complaints (legally binding)
Poland Commissioner for Human Rights		x	x	x	x	
Portugal High Commission for Migration	x					x
Romania National Council for Combating Discrimination	x			x		x tribunal type
Slovakia National Centre for Human Rights		x	x	x	x	
Slovenia Advocate of the Principle of Equality		x	x	x	x	x
Spain Council for the Elimination of Racial or Ethnic Discrimination						
Sweden Equality Ombudsman		x	x		x	

United Kingdom						
Equality and Human Rights Commission	x	x	x	x	x	
Equality Commission for Northern Ireland		x	x	x	x	
33 EQUALITY BODIES	**13**	**12**	**20**	**15**	**24**	**8**

*[1] only before the Austrian Equal Treatment Commission, which can issue non-binding decisions

*[2] only an action for a declaratory judgment if in a case brought before the Equal Treatment Commission by the Ombud for Equal Treatment the respondent does not comply with the ETC's recommendation

**[1] only before the Board of Equal Treatment

**[2] if its decision is not respected, at the request of the complainant

*** only before criminal courts, if a perpetrator rejects the proposed negotiated *criminal* sanction or fails to comply with it

**** only in administrative cases

[a] For the figures collected by the Commission for its implementation report see European Commission, 'Equality bodies and the implementation of the Commission Recommendation on Standards for Equality Bodies' (n 1) 8. Detailed research about Equality Bodies' functions and their effectiveness can also be found in Niall Crowley, 'Equality bodies making a difference' (European network of legal experts in gender equality and non-discrimination, 2018).

to reach out to remote areas or particularly vulnerable groups. Establishing a network with NGOs also helps to build their capacity so that they can engage in assisting victims in court (where possible) and other awareness-raising and advocacy activities. A peculiar case in this regard is Spain. Providing independent assistance to victims of racial or ethnic discrimination is the core function of its Council for the Elimination of Racial or Ethnic Discrimination. While other bodies, as just described, have entered into cooperation agreements with NGOs to secure the provision of this service also in peripheral regions, in Spain this task is completely contracted to a network of NGOs under the umbrella of the Assistance and Orientation Service to Victims of Discrimination on Grounds of Racial or Ethnic Origin.[450] The network has a coordination office in Madrid and offices distributed all over Spain thereby allowing regional coverage. While the service ultimately provided to victims of discrimination might be of high quality and thus the ultimate goal reached, such a solution also has several downsides. First, it does not contribute to the visibility of the Equality Body and the developing of the body into an authoritative player in the fight against discrimination. Secondly, the body is deprived of the possibility of learning about the levels and forms of discrimination existing in the country, which is an important element in strategically planning its future activities[451] and efficiently carrying out the rest of its competences as provided by Article 13 RED. In light of the above finding that the independence of the Spanish Equality Body could be questioned, one could be inclined to conclude, that in such circumstances the provision of 'independent assistance to victims of discrimination' is better ensured by NGOs. On the other hand it raises doubts about whether, overall, Spain can be considered to be complying with Article 13 RED.

Another way to enhance accessibility is by providing information in different languages, including minority languages, preparing written answers in such languages, or having them translated and recruiting multilingual staff. Special consideration in all these contexts must be given to people with disabilities.

A precondition for high-quality advice is the availability of a sufficient number of well-trained, possibly multilingual staff members, who are able to deal with the number of requests within a reasonable time.

5.4.2.1 Alternative Dispute Resolution Mechanisms

Once an individual's request turns into a real case the mandates of Equality Bodies might provide for the possibility for a national Equality Body to resort to *alternative dispute resolution mechanisms*, including mediation and conciliation/negotiation.

Mediation can be defined as 'multi-stage structured process of conflict resolution' in which parties to the conflict communicate and negotiate over the issues in

[450] For the website of this Service see http://asistenciavictimasdiscriminacion.org.

[451] On this beneficial effect of offering legal advice, see Equinet, 'Providing independent assistance to victims of discrimination: An Equinet report' (n 444) 15.

dispute with the aim of reaching an agreement acceptable to both parties. They are assisted in this attempt by a neutral third party.[452] Common to various definitions found in national legislation[453] are the following criteria: first, the mediator must be neutral and impartial and perceived as such by both parties involved. This requirement could in fact be difficult to ensure by an Equality Body, whose mandate is to assist the victim of a discrimination. The alleged perpetrator might thus find it difficult to accept the Equality Body as being impartial and neutral.[454] Second, the parties to the dispute participate in the mediation on a voluntary basis[455] and the outcome of the mediation is, in principle, non-binding. However, parties can agree to conclude a civil contract including the mediation result which would therefore be enforceable in the courts.[456] Third, the process is, in principle, confidential but in practice, and depending on the respective national legislation, Equality Bodies approach this issue differently. Strict confidentiality could be seen as hampering the Equality Body's ability to raise awareness in society. Some Equality Bodies thus reject demands for confidentiality from perpetrators, while others agree to keep the identity confidential but not the substance of the discrimination case.[457] And finally, the solution is up to the parties. This gives the parties ownership of the process and contributes to low rates of breaching mediation outcomes even in cases where they are not binding.[458] Mediation can be seen as a formal intervention by a third party, which in many countries is the subject of a dedicated law, regulating in particular the required qualifications of persons carrying out mediation.[459]

Conciliation and negotiation, on the other hand, as defined for instance by the Belgian Equality Body, is an 'informal intervention where a third party tries to convince all the parties, but especially the source of the presumed discrimination, to reach a solution, [or] to obtain compensation or reparation for a victim of discrimination'.[460] As in the UK, the difference between mediation and conciliation/

[452] On various definitions see eg Ulrike Salinger, 'Mediation as a Tool for Specialised Equality Bodies' (Equinet, 2007) 1; Equinet, 'Providing independent assistance to victims of discrimination: An Equinet report' (n 444) 19; Ingrid Aendenboom and Nathalie Denies, 'What Place for Mediation and Conciliation/Negotiation in Discrimination Cases?' [2012] European Anti-Discrimination Law Review 21, 23; in which they draw from Council of Europe Recommendation Rec (2002)10 of the Committee of Ministers to Member States on mediation in civil matters and on Rec (1999)19 of the Committee of Ministers to Member States on mediation in penal matters.

[453] See Salinger (n 453) 1–2.

[454] Equinet, 'Providing independent assistance to victims of discrimination: An Equinet report' (n 444) 20; ECRI, 'Report on Seminar with national specialised bodies to combat racism and racial discrimination on mediation and other forms of dispute resolution in cases of racism and racial discrimination' (Strasbourg, 16–17 February 2006) 3–4.

[455] In Belgium, in addition to voluntary mediation, court-ordered mediation is also available.

[456] ECRI, 'Report on Seminar with national specialised bodies to combat racism and racial discrimination on mediation and other forms of dispute resolution in cases of racism and racial discrimination' (n 455) 4.

[457] Equinet, 'Providing independent assistance to victims of discrimination: An Equinet report' (n 444) 21.

[458] Aendenboom and Denies (n 452) 25.

[459] Special training for mediators is required, for instance, in Austria, Belgium, and France.

[460] Equinet, 'Providing independent assistance to victims of discrimination: An Equinet report' (n 444) 19.

negotiations lies primarily in the level of involvement of the third party: while in the case of mediation the role is more facilitative, in the case of conciliation it is more interventionist.[461]

There are a number of advantages offered by resolving a discrimination case through one of these methods. It is not only cheaper and faster but it allows also for a greater variety of solutions, which might satisfy the need of the victim in a much better way than a court judgment would do. Such solutions include an apology or a public declaration, reintegration or financial compensation, or an engagement for the future, such as the introduction of a diversity policy or charter in a company or reasonable accommodation.[462] Because the parties are empowered, within the limits of the law, to negotiate directly and find their own solution to the problem, their agreements are more likely to be sustainable than solutions imposed by a third party or a court.[463] Furthermore, a mediation or conciliation/negotiation process, in which parties work towards mutual understanding, can play a transformative role in which the parties involved become aware of prejudices and stereotypes.[464] Also, if a case is resolved by resorting to mediation or conciliation, it is much more likely that a non-conflicting relationship between the parties can be kept or restored. These methods can also be a good solution in cases where evidence is lacking and litigation would thus be difficult.[465]

On the other hand, mediation or conciliation should not be used in very severe cases of discrimination, which are best adjudicated by courts. It has further been argued that such alternative forms of dispute resolution are not appropriate to tackle cases of structural discrimination, where they could prevent 'issues from being addressed as part of a more general problem'.[466] An alleged perpetrator could also use a mediation procedure to buy time without a real intention to engage in finding a commonly agreed solution. Also, if confidentiality is granted, there is no 'naming and shaming' which in some cases can add to the awareness-raising effect of a case. Even if results can be made public, it is likely that it has less power of example than if it is found by a court. However, this will depend very much on the general standing and authority of the Equality Body. As already mentioned, the outcomes of a mediation are generally non-binding, enforcement might thus be difficult. But regarding this, it has been suggested that this could be resolved by the

[461] Aendenboom and Denies (n 452) 27.

[462] Equinet, 'Providing independent assistance to victims of discrimination: An Equinet report' (n 444) 19 and 22.

[463] Salinger (n 453) 8.

[464] ibid 3; ECRI, 'Report on Seminar with national specialised bodies to combat racism and racial discrimination on mediation and other forms of dispute resolution in cases of racism and racial discrimination' (n 455) 3.

[465] Equinet, 'Providing independent assistance to victims of discrimination: An Equinet report' (n 444) 22.

[466] ECRI, 'Report on Seminar with national specialised bodies to combat racism and racial discrimination on mediation and other forms of dispute resolution in cases of racism and racial discrimination' (n 455) 3.

inclusion of the mediation outcome in a civil contract. Also, experience has shown that strong ownership generally leads to low breaching rates.[467]

It is evident from Table 5.3 that not all Equality Bodies are (explicitly or implicitly) equipped with mediation powers. Some Equality Bodies, even if the mandate would allow for mediation, prefer not to engage in it due to the above-mentioned difficulty of being perceived as neutral by both parties. Other Equality Bodies, in response to this problem, cooperate with external mediators.[468] The UK Equality and Human Rights Commission used to fund an independent Equalities Mediation Service for mediation and conciliation in cases not related to employment and engages with the Advisory Conciliation and Arbitration Service in employment cases.[469] If mediation is carried out by the staff of the Equality Body, other ways need to be found to ensure the maximum possible neutrality, for instance by assigning the case for mediation to a person who has not initially dealt with the victim of discrimination. Either way it requires adequate funding.[470] ECRI recommends that '[c]onciliation should be entrusted to an impartial person or unit in or outside the equality body'.[471]

For a deeper analysis of the functioning of and outcomes produced by alternative dispute resolution, in the sub-section on practical implementation (5.4.3) the Belgian Equality Body, Unia has been chosen as an example. In fact, the way in which Unia deals with complaints brought before it is first, to seek a negotiated solution and if this fails, to consider supporting the victim of discrimination in bringing a complaint before the court.

This leads to some general considerations on what the support offered to victims whose cases come before the courts can look like and which of these competences have been legally granted to Equality Bodies in the various EU Member States.

5.4.2.2 Assistance Before the Courts

The kind of assistance that can be offered by Equality Bodies to victims of discrimination whose cases come before the courts can take various forms. In Table 5.3, we have divided them up into representing them in legal proceedings, bringing cases in the Equality Body's own name, and intervening in legal proceedings. The overview shows that there is quite some variation among the powers attributed to Equality Bodies in different Member States. Only a few

[467] Equinet, 'Providing independent assistance to victims of discrimination: An Equinet report' (n 444) 22.

[468] This was for instance the case of the predecessor of the French Defender of Rights, the *Haute autorité de lutte contre les discriminations et pour l'égalité* (HALDE, the Equal Opportunities and Anti-Discrimination Commission. See Aendenboom and Denies (n 452) 26.

[469] See ibid 27; and EELN, Country Report United Kingdom, 2020, 63.

[470] ECRI, 'Report on Seminar with national specialised bodies to combat racism and racial discrimination on mediation and other forms of dispute resolution in cases of racism and racial discrimination' (n 455) 4.

[471] ECRI, 'General Policy Recommendation No 2: Equality Bodies to Combat Racism and Intolerance at National Level' (n 23) para 74 of the Explanatory Memorandum.

countries provide their bodies with all possibilities (nine, although some with restrictions) while slightly more countries (ten) provide their Equality Bodies with no litigation power at all. An Equinet study published in 2010[472] sheds light not only on how much use Equality Bodies make of their powers but also on the barriers for making use of them more often or in a more effective way. Although the data are nearly ten years old, a reading of the EELN's country reports from 2020 and of the report published by the Commission in 2021[473] suggests that the situation has not dramatically changed. Back in 2010 about half of the bodies that were vested with the competence to represent victims of discrimination in court actually made use of this power. This ratio went down to about one third regarding bodies that legally could have brought an action in their own name and about one quarter of the bodies that, under the law, could have intervened in a discrimination procedure. Also a comparison of the numbers of individuals assisted through representation by an Equality Body, where cases were brought by Equality Bodies in their own name or in which the Equality Body intervened, confirms that the power to represent victims before courts is the one used most. Relying again on the figures provided by the Equinet survey, Equality Bodies represent victims of discrimination ten times more often than they bring cases in their own name. Interventions take place in even less cases than cases filed in the Equality Body's own name.[474]

Currently, twelve out of thirty-three Equality Bodies have the power to represent individuals in either courts, tribunals, or in front of quasi-judicial bodies. Among the main barriers for not using this possibility more consistently, back in 2010 as well as today, Equality Bodies mentioned the lack of state funding or staff resources, as well as the risk of costs being awarded against the Equality Body.[475] Considering the limited resources, Equality Bodies select strategically the cases in which they represent the victim. The decision to do so will depend, inter alia, on whether the case raises an important matter of principle; whether there exists any significant case law or precedents on the matter in the absence of which the decision of the case would contribute to the clarification of the law or allow a possible breach of EU law (through a referral of specific questions to the CJEU) to be established; whether the proceedings are likely to have a beneficial impact for others in similar conditions; for change to be effected in the practice of employers or service providers; for the development of equality policies; or positive changes to be made to the standing and perception of the Equality

[472] Equinet, 'Influencing the law through legal proceedings: The powers and practices of equality bodies' (n 433).

[473] European Commission, 'Equality bodies and the implementation of the Commission Recommendation on Standards for Equality Bodies' (n 1) 8.

[474] In 2009, 411 individuals were represented in court, while Equality Bodies only brought forty cases in its own name and intervened in thirty-five cases. Equinet, 'Influencing the law through legal proceedings: The powers and practices of equality bodies' (n 433) 13, 16, and 19.

[475] ibid 13–14; European Commission, 'Equality bodies and the implementation of the Commission Recommendation on Standards for Equality Bodies' (n 1) 9.

Body.[476] While Equality Bodies in about half of the Member States reportedly engage in such strategic litigation, the Commission also reports that the risks of litigation may lead to Equality Bodies choosing cases that are not too complex or where the risk of losing the case is low. This could 'limit trust and the effectiveness of offering victim assistance'.[477]

Examples of court cases in which the victims of discrimination were represented by Equality Bodies and made their way to the CJEU, and thus contributed to the clarification of how the RED and EED are to be interpreted, are the cases of *Coleman*, where the victim was represented by the British Equality and Human Rights Commission,[478] and *Braathens Regional Aviation*, where the victim was represented by the Swedish Equality Ombudsman.[479] The Irish Equality Body, initially established as a stand-alone body (Equality Authority), also used the power to represent victims in court proceedings extensively before its merger with the Irish Human Rights Commission. How this merger affected its case work will be discussed below in the case study of the Irish Human Rights and Equality Commission.

Bringing cases in the Equality Body's name is particularly relevant where there is no identifiable victim or where a victim can be identified but he/she is reluctant to file a complaint.[480] Currently twenty out of thirty-three Equality Bodies have the power to bring cases in their own name, but EELN reports suggest that only a few bodies make use of this possibility.[481] The main reasons for such a limited use are again, at least in part, related to the limited financial and human resources. Another barrier can be found in national legislation limiting the use of this tool to only specific situations, such as where the victim gives his/her consent (which clearly excludes cases where there is no identifiable victim), where national legislation is considered to be unconstitutional, or where a settlement reached by the Equality Body is rejected or not met. Some bodies have never made use of this power because they consider it to be in conflict with their impartial decision-making role.[482]

Already in their 2013 report to the European Commission to feed into the Commission's report on the implementation of the RED and the EED, Equality

[476] For the criteria established by the Belgian and Irish Equality Bodies see the case studies below (5.4.3.1 and 5.4.3.2).

[477] European Commission, 'Equality bodies and the implementation of the Commission Recommendation on Standards for Equality Bodies' (n 1) 8–9. See also Emma Lantschner, 'Strategic Litigation: Equality Bodies' Strategic Use of Powers to Enforce EU Non-Discrimination Law' [2020] European Equality Law Review 1.

[478] *S. Coleman v Attridge Law and Steve Law* [2008] ECLI:EU:C:2008:415.

[479] *Diskrimineringsombudsmannen v Braathens Regional Aviation AB* [2021] ECLI:EU:C:2021:269.

[480] ECRI, 'General Policy Recommendation No 2: Equality Bodies to Combat Racism and Intolerance at National Level' (n 23) para 77 of the Explanatory Memorandum.

[481] See for instance the reports from Bulgaria, Croatia, Hungary, Latvia, the Netherlands, and Slovakia.

[482] Equinet, 'Influencing the law through legal proceedings: The powers and practices of equality bodies' (n 433) 17.

Bodies suggested that the Commission consider expanding the competences of Equality Bodies to include, inter alia, the competence to bring cases to court in their own name.[483] This suggests that where this power has been given to Equality Bodies, it has had a positive impact. An example is the *Feryn* case,[484] where the Belgian Equality Body brought an *actio popularis* against a company because of a discriminatory job posting about which no one had filed a complaint. The case eventually reached the CJEU and gave it the opportunity to clarify that direct discrimination can be established also in cases where there is no identifiable victim. The Belgian Unia thus serves also as a good example of why a closer look should be taken at litigation activity which consists of bringing cases in the Equality Body's own name.

The last way in which Equality Bodies can assist victims of discrimination before the courts is by intervening in a case that the victim has started alone or supported by an NGO or trade union. To be accurate, not all interventions can be understood as assistance to the victim. *Amicus curiae* briefs are typically understood as providing information to the court to help the court in making the right decision without being a party to the case. For *amicus curiae* interventions there is no tradition in a number of EU countries and it appears that there is greater resonance for this form of intervention in Member States with a common law background.[485] On the other hand, an intervention where the intervener takes the side of one of the parties is quite common in EU countries. An important case where the Belgian Equality Body intervened on the side of the victim and that even reached the CJEU, is *Achbita*.[486] This case will be discussed in depth in the case study below on Unia.

About half of the Equality Bodies have the power to intervene at their disposal, either because it is provided explicitly in the mandate of the Equality Body or because of general provisions to be found in civil law. However, only a few Equality Bodies make use of this power. The British Equality and Human Rights Commission appears to have the most experience with this instrument.[487] More recently, the Romanian NCCD has also intervened in a case not only before the Constitutional Court but also before the CJEU.[488] The British Equality Body explained the application of this mechanism with 'an increased need to use the [Commission's] legal budget more effectively and a realisation that an intervention

[483] Equinet, 'Equality Law in Practice: Report on the Implementation of the Race and General Framework Directives' (2013) 10.

[484] *Centrum voor gelijkheid van kansen en voor racismebestrijding v Firma Feryn NV* [2008] ECLI:EU:C:2008:397.

[485] Eilís Barry, 'Interventions and Amicus Curiae Applications' in Soraya Obura and Fiona Palmer (eds), *Strategic Enforcement: Powers and Competences of Equality Bodies* (Equinet 2006) 39.

[486] *Samira Achbita and Centrum voor gelijkheid van kansen en voor racismebestrijding v G4S Secure Solutions NV* [2017] ECLI:EU:C:2017:203.

[487] Equinet, 'Influencing the law through legal proceedings: The powers and practices of equality bodies' (n 433) 19.

[488] In the case *Relu Adrian Coman and Others v Inspectoratul General pentru Imigrări and Ministerul Afacerilor Interne* [2018] ECLI:EU:C:2018:385.

can achieve a court decision without the same degree of financial and resource commitment as full assistance to an individual entails.'[489]

The use of interventions thus appears to combine effectiveness in terms of impact with moderate use of financial and human resources. Furthermore, as long as judges continue to be under-exposed to discrimination cases due to a persistent underreporting, it appears particularly useful for judges to receive objective factual and legal submissions by an experienced body which will help them to reach a well-reasoned decision.

The downside of interventions is related to the fact that an intervener has little control over the development of the case. Furthermore, there is a perception that it adds to costs and delays the hearing, and—an issue widely discussed—that the intervention, even if in the form of an *amicus curiae*, is not neutral and objective. It is submitted that an *amicus curiae* has to provide well-founded and legally sound factual and legal information. This does not, however, preclude that the *amicus* has an interest in a particular outcome of the litigation. As the Chief Justice of the Irish Supreme Court put it: 'While it is still the case that an amicus curiae is allowed to appear because the court would be thereby assisted in coming to a correct resolution of an issue in dispute by being informed of all the relevant cases, statutes and other materials relevant to its determination, the amicus is no longer expected to be wholly disinterested in the outcome of the litigation.'[490] Equinet too found that there is no contradiction between providing objective information on the one hand while also having a mandate to assist victims of discrimination in their discrimination complaints.[491]

Another issue discussed in this context concerns the question of whether the power to intervene has to be expressly provided in either the legal framework established for the Equality Body or in general procedural law provisions. It has been suggested that a combined reading of the required competences of Equality Bodies under the RED would permit an assumption that the power to intervene in relevant cases can be considered as incidental to these competences.[492] Given that, particularly in those countries where no tradition of interventions exists, courts might be reluctant to accept the power to intervene in discrimination cases as being inherent to the mandate of Equality Bodies, it seems advisable to regulate this power explicitly by law.

In addition to the reluctance of courts to accept the intervention even in cases where there is an explicit mandate for it, the Equality Bodies who have the power

[489] Quoted from Barry (n 485) 40.

[490] ibid 37.

[491] Equinet, 'Providing independent assistance to victims of discrimination: An Equinet report' (n 444). Equinet, 'Influencing the law through legal proceedings: The powers and practices of equality bodies' (n 433) 21.

[492] Barry (n 485) 38–39 and 41; Equinet, 'Influencing the law through legal proceedings: The powers and practices of equality bodies' (n 433) 20–21.

to intervene also mention limited human and financial resources as a barrier. Where interventions are admitted, they are sometimes accepted only in written form, which constitutes a barrier to providing submissions concerning issues that only arise in the course of the proceeding.[493] Below, the Irish Human Rights and Equality Commission will be discussed as an example of an Equality Body submitting *amicus curiae* briefs to courts.

The financial and human resource argument has been mentioned throughout as a reason for not making use of litigation competences more often,[494] and it appears essential for Equality Bodies to develop strong cooperation networks with NGOs and social partners. First, this cooperation will help to identify cases these stakeholders are involved in and where an intervention by the Equality Body would be possible. Second, it allows for strategic selection of cases that could have an impact beyond the individual concerned.[495]

To conclude, the following points should be highlighted:

First, the Directive does not require Member States to grant Equality Bodies litigation competences. The Commission recommends that Member States should consider granting Equality Bodies the right to represent complainants in court, to act in their own name, and to act as *amicus curiae*. Entrusting them with 'a broad set of powers and appropriate legal standing' has been called 'good practice in line with the Recommendation'.[496] ECRI's recommendation also calls for the assignment of a broad range of litigation functions.[497] Different types of cases require different tools and it is thus advisable to equip Equality Bodies with a variety of options from which they can choose according to the situation. Even if some of the powers might be implicit to the overall mandate of the Equality Body it is advisable to set those powers down by law.

While in this regard we are at the level of commitment of the state, it appears from the above that, secondly, a state's effort to put the legal framework into action is equally decisive. Many Equality Bodies have stated that even if they are vested with certain competences they are not in a position to make use of them due to constraints in terms of human and financial resources. While in such circumstances Equality Bodies have to strategically decide how to allocate the limited resources, any monitoring would need to verify whether the state adequately funds the Equality Body so that it can fulfil all its competences provided for by law.

493 Equinet, 'Providing independent assistance to victims of discrimination: An Equinet report' (n 444) 28; Equinet, 'Influencing the law through legal proceedings: The powers and practices of equality bodies' (n 433) 20.

494 See in this sense also Crowley, 'Equality bodies making a difference' (n 445) 110.

495 Equinet, 'Providing independent assistance to victims of discrimination: An Equinet report' (n 444) 29 and 38–39.

496 European Commission, 'Equality bodies and the implementation of the Commission Recommendation on Standards for Equality Bodies' (n 1) 10.

497 ECRI, 'General Policy Recommendation No 2: Equality Bodies to Combat Racism and Intolerance at National Level' (n 23) paras 10(b) and 14.

Third, the responsibility does not only lay with the state. It is within the control of the Equality Body to develop a litigation strategy to maximize the impact of its support with the limited resources available. If victims realize that the support from the Equality Body increases their chances of winning their case, applications for such support will rise. The number of supported cases should not be too low, as this would limit the use of litigation as a means to raise awareness and might undermine trust in the institution. Interventions seem to be underused so far. A strategic approach is also necessary in this case.[498]

And last, but not least, close links, exchanges of information, and cooperation with NGOs and social partners are necessary in order for Equality Bodies to be aware of ongoing or upcoming litigation and to decide where their assistance might be required or well invested.

5.4.2.3 Receiving, Investigating, and Deciding on Complaints

Finally, Table 5.3 makes clear that Equality Bodies in nearly all countries can *receive complaints* and in the large majority of cases decide them through a non-legally binding decision. Exceptions are those countries which have a predominantly tribunal-type body or have more than one body, one of which is tribunal-type.

Figures on the number of complaints and the number of decisions are not indicative of the effectiveness of the Equality Body regarding this function if they are not interpreted together with a consideration of the conditions in which the Equality Body works and the policy decisions it has taken on that basis. In this context, it is of course relevant to consider the exact mandate of the body, its human and financial resources, as well as the level of awareness among potential victims of discrimination. Equality Bodies covering several discrimination grounds will have different numbers of complaints as compared to bodies dealing with only one or two such grounds. In cases in which Equality Bodies are integrated into a larger human rights institution, figures on the number of discrimination-related cases are not always available, although this should be the case. Whether a complaint leads also to a decision depends very much on the investigative powers the Equality Body is vested with. And finally, some Equality Bodies have chosen not to invest a lot of resources in handling individual complaints which they leave to courts.[499]

Equality Bodies usually accept complaints either orally or in writing. While some bodies can start an investigation only on the basis of an individual complaint (like in the case of the Belgian Unia), most bodies can also start investigations

[498] Equinet, 'Providing independent assistance to victims of discrimination: An Equinet report' (n 444) 23 and 29–30; Barry (n 485) 41–42; Bjørn Dilou Jacobsen and Eddie Omar Rosenberg Khawaja, 'Legal Assistance to Individual: Powers and Procedures of Effective and Strategic Individual Enforcement' in Soraya Obura and Fiona Palmer (eds), *Strategic Enforcement: Powers and Competences of Equality Bodies* (Equinet, 2006) 16; Moon (n 32) 892–97; European Roma Rights Centre, Interights and Migration Policy Group, 'Strategic litigation of race discrimination in Europe: from prinicples to practice' [2004], 35.

[499] Holtmaat (n 67) 53–54.

ex officio. In terms of investigative powers, solutions range from the conduct of on-site visits, the obligation for parties to produce documentation, the hearing of witnesses, or a combination of these.[500] In Austria and France, all involved are obliged to cooperate with the Equality Body. In Germany and Greece this obligation is restricted to other public agencies.[501] In case of non-cooperation, the French Defender of Rights can request a court order and pursue the respondent for contempt. The Defender can further ask any state service to carry out the necessary investigations.[502] While some bodies mainly or exclusively decide their complaints on the basis of written submissions, for other bodies the oral hearing of complainant and alleged perpetrator is very important.

If the violation of an equality provision is likely, the Austrian Ombud for Equal Treatment can establish a case before the Equal Treatment Commission, who can ask the Ombud for further enquiry (the ability to enter premises and inspect documents) to then take a legally non-binding decision. Similarly, the Irish Human Rights and Equality Commission can refer cases to the Workplace Relations Commission which has the power to issue binding decisions.[503] In Latvia, where, upon termination of its own investigation, a violation is found, the Ombudsman can issue an opinion and recommendations, but can also apply to a civil court.[504]

The Belgian Equality Body tries to reach a negotiated settlement between the two parties. Only cases where no such settlement can be reached, and which are highly relevant to establish a precedent or to clarify a point of law or are particularly serious, are brought to court.[505] The German Federal Antidiscrimination Agency tries to reach an amicable settlement between the parties and can give recommendations. It appears, however, that '[t]here is no larger scale conflict resolution practice in place'.[506] Data on the number of complaints and decisions are collected by the body but are not readily available to the public. Given that the Agency has no legal standing before the courts and does not intervene in proceedings, it can be seen as an example of an Equality Body with relatively weak powers when it comes to assisting victims of discrimination.

The French Defender of Rights ends his investigations with conclusions and recommendations that can be addressed to the parties, the government, public bodies, or interest groups. He can propose legislative reforms. Addressees are given a time period within which they have to comply. In cases involving a criminal

500 Ammer and others (n 53) 81.

501 EELN, Country Report Germany, 2020, 84; German Equal Treatment Act, § 28(2). EELN, Country Report Greece, 2020, 77–78.

502 EELN, Country Report France, 2020, 102–03.

503 EELN, Country Report Ireland, 2020, 96.

504 EELN, Country Report Latvia, 2020, 74 and 77.

505 In 2018, out of 7,498 complaints, UNIA opened a file in 2,192 cases and took thirty-three cases to court. This suggests first, an intensive out of court settlement approach and second, a strategic litigation approach. Belgium, EELN, Country Report Belgium, 2020, 109–10.

506 EELN, Country Report Germany, 2020, 84.

offence the Defender of Rights can suggest a specific criminal sanction to the perpetrator, which could be a fine, a publication of the result of the Defender's investigation, and/or compensation to the victim.[507]

Only a few bodies have the competence to issue binding decisions. These are the Equality Bodies of Portugal and Slovenia, but in the Slovene case the body cannot impose fines.[508]

Differences also exist in the ways in which Equality Bodies follow up on their decisions, if they do that at all. This can include an obligation by parties to notify the Equality Body of the measures taken to fulfil its recommendations, or the collection of data on how many cases are brought to court afterwards to reach a binding settlement. In case of non-compliance, the French Defender of Rights can issue injunctions, failing which it can draw public attention to the failure to comply with its recommendations.[509] In several countries there are no data on the extent to which the recommendations of the Equality Body are implemented.[510]

In the next section looking into practical implementation, two cases for in-depth study have been chosen that dispose of a wide range of possible functions. The first is Unia, the Belgian Equality Body, which on one hand tries to settle complaints brought before it through negotiating solutions (thus a form of conciliation) and on the other hand also has strong litigation competences of which it makes extensive and successful use. The second example studied in depth is the Irish Human Rights and Equality Commission, a body only recently created via the merger of the Irish Equality Authority and the Irish Human Rights Commission, of which the Irish Equality Authority used to have a strong record of providing assistance to victims of discrimination before the courts. The third example chosen is the German Federal Antidiscrimination Agency as an example of an Equality Body equipped with only very limited competences in the field of assisting victims of discrimination. As in 5.3.3 the analysis of effectiveness is preceded by a discussion of overall institutional independence.

5.4.3 Practical Implementation

5.4.3.1 Case Study: Belgium—The Interfederal Centre for Equal Opportunities—Unia

The Belgian Equality Body has one of the longest histories amongst Equality Bodies in Europe as it dates back to 1993 when it was established as the federal Centre for Equal Opportunities and Opposition to Racism. Because it was created long before

507 EELN, Country Report France, 2020, 103.
508 EELN, Country Report Slovenia, 2020, 85.
509 EELN, Country Report France, 2020, 103.
510 European Commission, 'Equality bodies and the implementation of the Commission Recommendation on Standards for Equality Bodies' (n 1) 10.

EU equal treatment legislation required the establishment of such bodies, it has been considered a model for EU Equality Bodies.[511] On 12 June 2013 the federal state, the regions, and communities signed a Cooperation Agreement[512] which made the Centre competent not only regarding the federal Antidiscrimination Acts but also for such Acts adopted at the level of the regions and communities. The Centre thus became a centralized interfederal centre. This change from a federal into an interfederal centre was the (albeit delayed) response of the Belgian government to the letter of formal notice and reasoned opinion of the European Commission that its transposition of Article 13 RED was incomplete, since it was only responsible for the federal legislation.[513] The Cooperation Agreement quoted from the Commission documents, stating that '[c]onsidering that the complete transposition of this directive requires the organization promoting equal treatment, as mentioned in article 13 of the directive, to be competent not only in federal matters but also in community and regional matters'.[514] The several references to Directive 2000/43/EC both in the Cooperation Agreement as well as in the Decree of 2014 approving it are in contrast to the previous practice of Belgian equal treatment legislation not to refer to the relevant EU sources thus hiding the fact that this legislation is adopted in transposition of EU Directives.[515] On 15 March 2014, the Cooperation Agreement entered into force and has since regulated the details regarding organization, competences, and functioning of the Centre.[516] Finally, on 22 February 2016 the Centre was renamed 'Unia'.[517] The Flemish government has decided to establish its own Equality Body and withdraw from Unia as soon as the Cooperation Agreement expires in March 2023.[518]

A deeper study of the Centre/Unia in this chapter dealing with its approach to discrimination is particularly relevant considering the number of high-profile cases brought by it, in particular the cases reaching the CJEU through the preliminary ruling procedure. Before looking at its competences in terms of providing assistance to victims of discrimination, however, we will look at how independence and accessibility is secured.

[511] Elise Muir and Sarah Kolf, 'Belgian Equality Bodies Reaching out to the CJEU: EU Procedural Law as a Catalyst' in Elise Muir and others (eds), *How EU Law Shapes Opportunities for Preliminary References on Fundamental Rights: Discrimination, Data Protection and Asylum* (European University Institute, EUI Working Papers 2017) 22.

[512] Cooperation Agreement, 'between the federal authority, the Regions and the Communities aimed at creating an Interfederal Centre for Equal Opportunities and Opposition to Racism and Discrimination in the form of a joint institution, in the sense of article 92bis of the Special Act of 8 August 1980 on the Reform of the Institutions' (12 June 2013).

[513] Infringement no 2005/2353, Belgium (letter of formal notice of 7 February 2005, reasoned opinion of 23 October 2007).

[514] Cooperation Agreement (n 512).

[515] Muir and Kolf (n 511) 28.

[516] EELN, Country Report Belgium 2020, 104.

[517] Information from the Unia website, at https://www.unia.be/fr/a-propos-dunia.

[518] EELN, Country Report Belgium 2020, 102. See also Unia, 'Rapport annuel 2019. Contribuer à une société plus égale pour tous' (2020) 14–15.

Article 2 § 1 of the Cooperation Agreement provides that the purpose of the agreement is to create 'an *independent* Interfederal Centre for Equal Opportunities and Opposition to Racism and Discrimination'.[519] Article 3 § 3 further stipulates that '[t]he Centre *exercises its missions independently*, in accordance with the Principles of Paris'.[520] Thus, the Cooperation Agreement—unlike Article 13 RED—explicitly lays down both the independence of the institution as well as its independent functioning. In terms of composition of the managing body, the Cooperation Agreement provides for an interfederal board composed of twenty members plus one member from the German-speaking Community for matters relating to this community.[521] Ten members are appointed by the federal chamber of representatives and ten by the regional and community parliaments whereby parity between the Flemish and French side is secured. In addition, parity between men and women is obligatory. Furthermore, the board (as well as its chambers) 'must be composed in the most pluralist manner possible'.[522] Members are appointed 'on the basis of their competence, their experience, their independence and their moral authority'. They are representatives of the academic or legal world, civil society, and social partners.[523] They are appointed for a period of six years, which is renewable twice.[524] The Cooperation Agreement further lays down rules on incompatibility, essentially related to a mandate in the European Parliament or the federal, regional, or community parliament, the position of minister or state/regional secretary at one of these levels, member of a ministerial cabinet, or any role as a staff member of the Centre.[525] The Cooperation Agreement does not, however, contain rules on the conditions under which a board member can be dismissed which could be potentially detrimental to the stability of the mandate of board members.

Interestingly, both the Committee on the Rights of Persons with Disabilities (CRPD) and the Committee on the Elimination of Racial Discrimination, in 2014, thus after the Cooperation Agreement had entered into force, expressed concern that the Centre lacked the required independence.[526] While the CRPD Committee did not explain what exactly raised its concern, simply recommending that the authorities 'complete the process to ensure the Centre's compliance with the Paris Principles',[527] CERD related its concern to the assumption 'that the board of the new Centre will be appointed by the Executive, which may compromise

[519] Emphasis added.
[520] Emphasis added.
[521] Cooperation Agreement (n 512) Art 8 § 1.
[522] ibid Art 8 § 2.
[523] ibid.
[524] ibid Art 8 § 5.
[525] ibid Art 8 § 7.
[526] See on this also EELN, Country Report Belgium, 2020, 104.
[527] Committee on the Rights of Persons with Disabilities, 'Concluding Observations on the initial report of Belgium adopted by the Committee at its twelfth session' (15 September 2014) paras 48–49.

its independence'.[528] Although from the wording it is not entirely clear whether CERD meant the Centre or the Federal Centre for the Analysis of Migratory Flows[529] the assessment appears to be unfounded, since the members of the board of both centres are appointed by parliment(s). Indeed, ECRI, in its report adopted in December 2013 and published in February 2014, recommended that Belgian authorities, as part of its interim follow-up recommendations, 'conclude as soon as possible the legislative process to turn the Centre for Equal Opportunities and Opposition to Racism into a fully independent inter-federal institution dedicated to helping all victims of discrimination on the grounds within its competence'.[530] By reference to the rules contained in the Cooperation Agreement on the composition of the board, the criteria regarding incompatibility, and the fact that the board was elected in February 2015, in its conclusions on the implementation of this interim recommendation, ECRI found that the recommendation had been implemented.[531]

The national expert for Belgium in the EELN however also reported on the controversial appointment of a lawyer and law professor to the board who is well-known as fierce opponent of both equal treatment legislation as well as the Centre/Unia. He started actions for annulment of many of the provisions of the Federal Antidiscrimination Acts of 2007, which were, however, rejected by the Constitutional Court in 2009. Furthermore, he publicly stated that equal treatment legislation was a '"blunder and an attack against democracy" [and] that "to discriminate is a fundamental freedom"'. According to the co-director of Unia it is nevertheless possible for the board to work in a satisfactory manner.[532] However, there have been instances in which the board's decision not to bring a case to court has reportedly been influenced by the political preferences of board members.[533] Worrying too are the verbal attacks by the Belgian Federal Secretary of State for Equal Opportunities and the Flemish Minister for Equal Opportunities in 2017 on Unia. The latter, for instance, expressed doubts about the neutrality and objectivity of Unia's work as it allegedly 'protects "allochtonous" people more than Belgian citizens'.[534]

The budget of the Centre/Unia steadily increased over the years. With the entry into force of the Cooperation Agreement the contributions of the federal state and

528 CERD, 'Concluding observations on the sixteenth to nineteenth periodic reports of Belgium' (14 March 2014) CERD/C/BEL/CO/16–19, para 7.

529 MYRIA, see http://www.myria.be/fr.

530 ECRI, 'Report on Belgium (fifth monitoring cycle) adopted on 4 December 2013' CRI(2014)1, 41.

531 ECRI, 'Conclusions on the implementation of the Recommendations in respect of Belgium subject to interim follow-up, adopted on 8 December 2016' CRI(2017)5.

532 EELN, Country Report Belgium, 2020, 104–05.

533 Confidential information provided to the author.

534 EELN, Country Report Belgium 2020, 101. See also the Foreword in Unia, 'Rapport annuel 2017—Refuser l'inertie' (2018) 4, where the co-directors write: 'Especially in Flanders some voices in certain political environments have raised doubts about our [Unia's] role and certain of our positions. Our status, independent and interfederal, is disturbing.' Translation from French by the author.

the federated entities are laid down in that document and are updated annually, linked to the health index.[535] This meant a budget in 2019 of 8,479.316 EUR with the state contributing 6,653,310 EUR thereto.[536] In addition to this, Unia is allowed to accept donations, business proceeds, take part in calls for subsidized projects, and acquire and dispose of movable and immovable property.[537] Additional tasks may be entrusted to Unia 'on condition that the party making the request assumes financial responsibility for them'.[538] It has been generally considered that the budget allocation is sufficient to implement Unia's mandate and the fact that it is included in the Cooperation Agreement gives it greater stability.[539] However, there have been parliamentary questions about the costs of the *Achbita* case and in 2018 and 2019 Unia suffered a slight budget deficit.[540]

The number of staff, which is currently at 106.7 full-time equivalents, is reportedly at a satisfactory level.[541] In 2010, an additional twelve people were employed as a late reaction to the extension of the Centre's mandate in 2003. Similarly, when the Centre was assigned the task of being the independent mechanism in charge of promoting, protecting, and monitoring the implementation of the Convention of the Rights of Persons with Disabilities, a department of seven employees was especially set up to carry out this task.[542] In 2017, Unia was given the mandate to deal with the Citizens' Rights Directive[543] but has not been given additional staff for that purpose. It has thus not undertaken any effort to raise awareness of this new competence as it would not be able to deal with such cases.[544] According to the Cooperation Agreement it is the responsibility of the interfederal board to decide on the hiring procedure and to hire staff. Except for the positions of co-directors (managing Unia) and coordinators it can, however, delegate the power to hire staff to the co-directors,[545] which is what happens in practice.[546] The selection procedure is anonymized in the written phase and only at the stage of the oral exam does the identity of the applicant become known to the selection committee. Although this allows for a selection based on the qualification of the applicants it

[535] Cooperation Agreement (n 512) Art 16 § 2. The contribution of the federated entities is divided as follows: Flanders: 48 per cent; Walloon Region: 36 per cent; French-speaking Community: 12 per cent; Brussels Region: 3 per cent; German-speaking Community: 1 per cent.

[536] Unia, 'Rapport annuel 2019. Contribuer à une société plus égale pour tous' (n 519) 99.

[537] Cooperation Agreement (n 512) Art 16 § 1.

[538] ibid Art 16 § 4.

[539] Interview, legal adviser at Unia, 31 May 2018; and EELN, Country Report Belgium, 2020, 104.

[540] EELN, Country Report Belgium, 2020, 106; Unia, 'Rapport annuel 2019. Contribuer à une société plus égale pour tous' (n 518) 100.

[541] Unia, 'Rapport annuel 2019. Contribuer à une société plus égale pour tous' (n 518) 95.

[542] EELN, Country Report Belgium 2020, 103 and 105.

[543] Directive 2004/58/EC of the European Parliament and of the Council of 29 April 2004 on the right of citizens of the Union and their family members to move and reside freely within the territory of the Member States.

[544] Interview, legal adviser at Unia, 31 May 2018.

[545] Cooperation Agreement (n 512) Art 10 § 2.

[546] Interview, legal adviser at Unia, 31 May 2018.

has led to a situation in which diversity of staff is not very high. Most of the recently employed staff members are young, white women, even though the job advertisements explicitly encouraged people from underrepresented groups to apply.[547] It remains within the interfederal board's responsibility, supported by the two co-directors, to draw up the organization chart and staff plan, while the co-directors, assisted by coordinators, are responsible for the staff management.[548] Finally, the Cooperation Agreement lays down that the 'staff members fulfil their jobs with loyalty, awareness and integrity, under the authority of the co-directors'.[549] It can thus be said that Unia has full managerial independence in staff-related issues.

A final important point regards the accessibility and outreach of Unia. In terms of accessibility of its offices for disabled people, Article 2 of the Cooperation Agreement in general terms provides that the 'Centre will be housed in an accessible place'. In Article 6 it specifies that the Centre 'ensures the accessibility of its services, including persons with reduced mobility'. As another aspect of physical accessibility, understood in terms of geographic outreach, the same article provides that the Centre 'organizes local points of contact' in cooperation with the federated entities and communities, which 'must be sufficiently spread out on the geographic level in order to guarantee citizens easy access'. In practice, such contact points are in place throughout the country.[550] All contacts are registered in Unia's central database and are first also considered by the staff in the central office in Brussels. It is then decided whether it is more appropriate to have the case handled by the local office or to keep it at the Brussels office.[551]

When comparing the legal framework and practical implementation of Unia's independence and accessibility with ECRI's[552] and the European Commission's Recommendations,[553] the following conclusions can be drawn:

Unia appears to be fully independent at the institutional and operational level, even though attempts by government representatives and political parties at discrediting or interfering in the work of Unia are not unknown. The executive has no role to play in the appointment of the members of the interfederal board, the governing body of Unia, or the two co-directors. The appointment by parliaments

[547] ibid.

[548] Cooperation Agreement (n 512) Art 10 § 2 and Art 12 §§ 3 and 4.

[549] ibid Art 13 § 2, which further provides that '[o]utside of work, they must abstain from any behavior that might undermine the public's trust in their service'.

[550] In Flanders there used to be thirteen such local contact points, currently only five are indicated on its website. There are four such offices in Walonia (in addition to the collaboration with ten Wallonia Spaces [Espaces Wallonie]) and one for the German-speaking Community. See EELN, Country Report Belgium 2020, 109; and Unia, 'Rapport annuel 2019. Contribuer à une société plus égale pour tous' (n 518) 77–80.

[551] Interview, legal adviser at Unia, 31 May 2018.

[552] In particular ECRI, 'General Policy Recommendation No 2: Equality Bodies to Combat Racism and Intolerance at National Level' (n 23) paras 22–40.

[553] In particular section 1.2. of European Commission, 'Commission Recommendation on Standards for Equality Bodies' (n 19).

seems to work well in general, albeit there has been a case where an appointed member to the interfederal board openly opposed the antidiscrimination legislation as well as Unia. While the Cooperation Agreement contains provisions about activities that are incompatible with holding a mandate in the interfederal board, it does not provide for a board member's protection against threats and coercion or for appropriate safeguards against the arbitrary dismissal of board members or co-directors. The adequate representation of linguistic communities and regions as well as of both men and women is guaranteed on a parity basis in law and practice. Pluralist representation beyond these criteria is ensured in law and, to some extent, in practice. Unia has, as required by ECRI's Recommendations, the power to manage its resources, and to recruit its own staff and adequate premises. The staff and funds appear to be sufficient to implement all their functions and competences, although recently it has had to deal with slight annual deficits, due to the rising number of complaints it has had to deal with. It is therefore necessary for Unia to raise additional funds. Because the budget is laid down in the Cooperation Agreement, it is protected against arbitrary or disproportionate reductions. Selection procedures for Unia's staff ensure adequate qualification but could be modified to better reflect the diversity in society, an issue which is acknowledged by its leadership who have tried to identify solutions. Unia is accountable to the parliaments, prepares annual reports for them, and holds presentations of the report in all of them. The reports are not subject to the parliaments' approval. Through local contact points throughout the Belgian territory it has a good geographic outreach and ensures accessibility of all its services for people with reduced mobility.

Against this background, Unia has to fulfil its overall mission 'to promote equal opportunities taking into account the diversity of our [the Belgian] society and to fight any form of discrimination, distinction, exclusion, restriction, exploitation or preference based on race, colour, descent, nationality, national or ethnic origin, sexual orientation, civil status, social origin, birth, wealth, age, religious or philosophical conviction, state of health, political conviction or trade union conviction, disability, or a physical or genetic characteristic'.[554] For discrimination on the grounds of gender, a separate body exists in Belgium, the Institute for the Equality of Women and Men.[555] Discrimination on the grounds of language, an issue of high sensitivity in the Belgian context, is not covered by any of the Equality Bodies.[556]

For the purpose of fulfilling its mandate, Unia is given the competence to carry out studies and research, collect, and publish statistical data and case law, provide independent advice and recommendations to authorities, private organizations,

[554] Cooperation Agreement (n 512) Art 3 § 1a. Art 3 § 1b lays down the mission to function as the body designated to promote, protect and monitor the implementation of the Convention on the Rights of Persons with Disabilities.

[555] See the Institute's website, at https://igvm-iefh.belgium.be/en.

[556] EELN, Country Report Belgium, 2020, 105.

and private persons, provide support and guidance for institutions and organizations, organize awareness-raising actions, and last, but not least, assist any person requesting professional advice on the extent of their rights and obligations. When it receives reports about discrimination it is authorized to carry out conciliation or mediation missions or bring cases to court. If the victim is known, his/her authorization is required. If there is no known victim, Unia can bring the case in its own name.[557] Article 6 of the Cooperation Agreement lists all federal and sub-federal laws, decrees, and orders on the basis of which Unia can take a legal action. This means that the competences cover all tasks required by Article 13(2) RED and the Belgian legislation goes beyond EU requirements in that Unia is responsible for many more grounds than those provided by EU legislation.

When looking at the number of staff dedicated to the different fields of activity it becomes clear that the biggest department is the one providing independent assistance to victims of discrimination.[558] This is partly due to the increase in reports of discrimination reaching Unia. Between 2013 and 2018, the number of reports and cases opened doubled.[559] This could be linked to the fact that people have become more aware of their rights and the existence and work of Unia, inter alia, because of discussion in the media of some of the high-profile cases that Unia has brought to court. Another factor that may have increased the number of reports of discrimination is related to the terrorist attacks in March 2016 which had an impact on Unia's cases involving people belonging to the Muslim community.[560]

Of the 2,655 cases handled in 2019, Unia found in 44.2 per cent of the cases that the presumption of discrimination was founded. Of these, around 53 per cent ended in an extrajudicial solution or with an opinion or recommendation, whereas only 6.2 per cent of cases are brought to court, with or without Unia's assistance.[561]

The Belgian expert in the EELN noted that 'UNIA has been particularly efficient in providing advice and legal assistance to victims of discrimination', that it is particularly known for its practice of seeking an amicable settlement between the victim and the alleged perpetrator, and that it 'has developed significant expertise in this discreet way to proceed'.[562] In fact, the approach of Unia is to seek a dialogue if possible and to go to court only if it is necessary.[563] Its handling of

[557] Cooperation Agreement (n 512) Arts 4–6.

[558] Of the 106.7 full-time equivalents working at Unia in 2017, twenty-nine were employed in the department dealing with individual support, while seventeen full-time equivalents are working in the area of training and communication, eleven in the public policies service, seven on the mandate regarding the UN CRPD, 17.2 in the local contact points and 27.5 in the transversal central service. See Unia, 'Rapport annuel 2017—Refuser l'inertie' (n 534) 120.

[559] EELN, Country Report Belgium, 2020, 106.

[560] Interview, legal adviser at Unia, 31 May 2018.

[561] Unia, 'Rapport chiffre 2019' (2020) 20–21. The remaining cases were either forwarded to another organization or were abandoned for various reasons, such as interruption of the contact or withdrawal of the case by the complainant.

[562] EELN, Country Report Belgium 2020, 109.

[563] See the information on Unia's website, at https://www.unia.be/fr/jurisprudence-alternatives.

individual complaints is hampered by its lack of investigative powers. In fact, there is no obligation to respond to inquiries by Unia nor can it request the submission of documentation, which would allow facts to be established from which it may be presumed that discrimination has taken place. While it can approach public authorities asking them to obtain the required information and report back to Unia about their findings, Unia has found that there is often a lack of transparency and flow of information.[564]

Unia has the authority, as already mentioned above, to 'accomplish any conciliation or mediation missions it considers necessary'.[565] It does not consider its activities in reaching an amicable settlement as mediation but classifies them rather as negotiated solutions or conciliation.[566] This has been considered to be connected, as is the case with many other Equality Bodies as well, to the idea that mediation requires neutrality which might not be perceived to exist by all parties involved.[567] In the course of reaching a negotiated solution for a case in which it finds that discrimination has taken place, Unia seeks to achieve agreement and guarantees on the following points: First, the perpetrator recognizes that she/he has discriminated. Second, some form of reparation or satisfaction for the victim is agreed upon, such as paying compensation, issuing an apology, or giving the victim a second chance in a job selection procedure from which he/she had been excluded for discriminatory reasons. Third, the perpetrator commits not to discriminate in the future and accepts structural and/or preventive measures, such as the adaptation of company policies, or the participation in or organization of anti-discrimination training. Finally, Unia publishes the result (mostly in anonymized form) in order to raise their awareness for the issue of discrimination.[568]

An example of such a negotiated solution is the case in which a handicapped person complained about his insurance contract which did not provide him with an adapted replacement car in case his own adapted car was not available. After the intervention of Unia, the individual contract was adapted to include the

[564] Unia, 'Evaluation: Loi du 10 mai 2007 modifiant la loi du 30 juillet 1981 tendant à réprimer certains actes inspirés par le racisme ou la xénophobie (MB 30 mai 2007) (loi antiracisme) Loi du 10 mai 2007 tendant à lutter contre certaines formes de discrimination (MB 30 mai 2007) (loi antidiscrimination)' (2017) 97, 22.

[565] Cooperation Agreement (n 512) Art 6 § 2.

[566] Unia, 'Evaluation: Loi du 10 mai 2007 modifiant la loi du 30 juillet 1981 tendant à réprimer certains actes inspirés par le racisme ou la xénophobie (MB 30 mai 2007) (loi antiracisme) Loi du 10 mai 2007 tendant à lutter contre certaines formes de discrimination (MB 30 mai 2007) (loi antidiscrimination)' (n 565) 23.

[567] Interview, legal adviser at Unia, 31 May 2018.

[568] Unia, 'Evaluation: Loi du 10 mai 2007 modifiant la loi du 30 juillet 1981 tendant à réprimer certains actes inspirés par le racisme ou la xénophobie (MB 30 mai 2007) (loi antiracisme) Loi du 10 mai 2007 tendant à lutter contre certaines formes de discrimination (MB 30 mai 2007) (loi antidiscrimination)' (n 565) 18; and interview, legal adviser at Unia, 31 May 2018. For summaries of cases closed through a negotiated solution see https://www.unia.be/fr/jurisprudence-alternatives/solutions-negociees.

contribution of the insurance to an adapted replacement car and the insurance is considering the inclusion of such a clause in its standard contract.[569] Although this practice of reaching a negotiated solution with the parties involved appears to be successful, it could be strengthened by the introduction of stronger investigative powers and of a follow-up procedure. The lack of the latter has, indeed, been recognized as being problematic and ideas of doing follow-up by situation tests are being developed, but these would require an increase in human resources.[570]

Outside these attempts of reaching a negotiated solution, Unia also participates in court-ordered mediations or cases of restorative justice by suggesting and being involved in alternative measures in cases where legal action has been initiated. The idea is that through their educational/pedagogical leaning such measures help both the victim and the perpetrator.[571] An example is the case of a sixteen-year-old who, acting with some friends, attacked a passerby who they identified as homosexual. In addition to the blows that led to the victim being incapacitated for work for several months, the aggressor also shouted homophobic words at the victim. The interrogation of the aggressor revealed that the attack had been motivated by hatred and hostility towards the victim because of his alleged homosexuality, thus constituting a hate crime. Unia was informed by the police of the incident[572] and the local contact point in Gand, where the event took place, suggested educational alternative measures. After a session in which the perpetrator, the victim, and Unia all participated, the judge decided that the perpetrator had to follow an individualized educational project. The project was organized by Unia in collaboration with local organizations.[573]

Only where a negotiated solution seems unsatisfactory, for instance because of the non-cooperation of the defendant,[574] Unia takes a case to court, with the consent of the victim.[575] As already mentioned, compared to the number of case files, few of Unia's cases reach court. In 2019, it launched eighteen court cases. Five of these were related to discrimination in employment or access to goods and services, six to hate speech, and seven to hate crime.[576] The cases are well chosen and

[569] See Unia, Une voiture de remplacement aussi pour les personnes handicapées, 29 August 2018, at https://www.unia.be/fr/jurisprudence-alternatives/solutions-negociees/une-voiture-de-remplacement-aussi-pour-les-personnes-handicapees.

[570] Interview, legal adviser at Unia, 31 May 2018.

[571] See information on alternative measures on Unia's webpage at https://www.unia.be/en/jurisprudence-alternatives/alternative-measures.

[572] In conformity with a circular COL 13/2013.

[573] See Unia, De la violence homophobe au projet éducatif individualisé, 13 October 2015, at https://www.unia.be/fr/jurisprudence-alternatives/mesures-alternatives/de-la-violence-homophobe-au-projet-educatif-individualise.

[574] EELN, Country Report Belgium 2020, 109.

[575] Cooperation Agreement (n 511) Art 6 § 4.

[576] Unia, 'Rapport annuel 2019. Contribuer à une société plus égale pour tous' (n 518) 41–42.

some of them have reached the highest European courts. The criteria for bringing a case before a court are the following:

1) if the case relates to one of the areas or criteria prioritized by Unia;
2) if the case has the potential to contribute to the clarification of legislation (eg by leading to a preliminary ruling by the CJEU);
3) if the case is an illustration of a social debate (some of the cases brought in this context relate to discrimination on the ground of disability in the context of employment[577]);
4) if there is a link with jurisprudence of the Court of Justice or the ECtHR, that allows Unia to apply this jurisprudence at national level;
5) if the case regards an area, phenomenon, or criterion for which there exists only limited jurisprudence;
6) if it appears to be a returning issue for which extrajudicial solutions have proven not to be sufficient;
7) if the case regards question on which the expectations of NGOs and other partners of Unia are high.

In cases of hate speech, Unia decides to go to court if it is an organized hate speech phenomenon, if it is invited by the public prosecutor to join, and if the law on negationism and denialism is applicable. The decision to go to court in these cases also depends on the person behind the hate speech (persons with responsibilities, teachers, politicians, etc). In cases of hate crime, Unia almost always goes to court.[578]

One of the most prominent cases in which Unia supported a victim of discrimination in court (the case had actually already been initiated by the victim and Unia joined her in support only later[579]) is the case of *Samira Achbita v G4S Secure Solutions*.[580] The case was referred to the European Court of Justice for a preliminary ruling which has been widely commented on.[581]

[577] For an example of discrimination by association see Unia, 'Licencié en raison du handicap de sa fille' (12 December 2013) <https://www.unia.be/fr/articles/licencie-en-raison-du-handicap-de-sa-fille>.The facts were indeed similar to those in *S. Coleman v Attridge Law and Steve Law* (n 478). See in particular para 56.

[578] Information provided by e-mail by legal adviser at Unia, 6 June 2018.

[579] Muir and Kolf (n 511) 25.

[580] *Samira Achbita and Centrum voor gelijkheid van kansen en voor racismebestrijding v G4S Secure Solutions NV* (n 486).

[581] See, for instance, Ronan McCrea, 'Faith at Work: The CJEU's Headscarf Rulings' (EU Law Analysis, 17 March 2017) <http://eulawanalysis.blogspot.com/2017/03/faith-at-work-cjeus-headscarf-rulings.html>; Eva Brems, 'European Court of Justice Allows Bans on Religious Dress in the Workplace' (IACL-AIDC Blog, 25 March 2017) <https://blog-iacl-aidc.org/test-3/2018/5/26/analysis-european-court-of-justice-allows-bans-on-religious-dress-in-the-workplace>; Gareth Davies, 'Achbita v G4S: Religious Equality Squeezed between Profit and Prejudice' (European Law Blog, 6 April 2017) <http://europeanlawblog.eu/2017/04/06/achbita-v-g4s-religious-equality-squeezed-between-profit-and-prejudice/>; Erica Howard, 'Islamic Headscarves and the CJEU: Achbita and

Samira Achbita is a woman of Muslim faith who worked as a receptionist for G4S, an agency offering, inter alia, reception services. After she had worked for G4S for three years, she informed the employer that she intended to start wearing the Islamic headscarf. The employer told her that this would not be tolerated as it was against the unwritten rule for employees not to wear 'visible signs of their political, philosophical and religious beliefs', in line with its 'position of neutrality'.[582] As she refused to work without a headscarf she was dismissed. Ms Achbita started proceedings in the first instance Labour Court in Antwerp. Unia joined this procedure in support of Ms Achbita. As the first instance court and the court of appeal rejected the claim, the applicant approached the Court of Cassation who referred the case to the CJEU for a preliminary ruling.

Unia's support for Ms Achbita was crucial for this case, as without it she could not have afforded to pay a lawyer to litigate her case up until the CJEU. Unia proposed the list of questions to be submitted to the CJEU for preliminary ruling to the Court of Cassation, which rephrased them into a single question. Also, in the course of the proceedings before the Court, she did not submit observations herself but allowed Unia to do so.[583] As this was the first case in which the Court of Justice had to consider the question of discrimination on the ground of religion, Unia thus managed to contribute to an important clarification of equality law in a so far untouched sector,[584] although it can be presumed that it had hoped for a stronger

Bougnaoui' (2017) 24(3) Maastricht Journal of European and Comparative Law 348; Joseph H H Weiler, 'Je Suis Achbita!' (2017) 28(4) European Journal of International Law 989; Muir and Kolf (n 512); Joseph Marko, 'Einleitende Bemerkungen zur interdisziplinären Perspektive von Politik und Recht in der Rechtsprechung' in Stephan Hinghofer-Szalkay and Herbert Kalb (eds), *Islam, Recht und Diversität* (Verlag Österreich 2018) 518–21; Dagmar Schiek, 'On Uses, Mis-Uses and Non-Uses of Intersectionality before the European Court of Justice (ECJ). The ECJ Rulings Parris (C-433/15) Achbita (C-157/15) and Bougnaoui (C-188/15) as a Bermuda Triangle?' (2018) 7(3) CETLS online paper series 1; Elke Cloots, 'Safe Harbour or Open Sea for Corporate Headscarf Bans? Achbita and Bougnaoui' (2018) 55(2) Common Market Law Review 589; Andrew Hambler, 'Neutrality and Workplace Restrictions on Headscarves and Religious Dress: Lessons from Achbita and Bougnaoui' (2018) 47(1) Industrial Law Journal 149; Aiste Mickonyte, 'Bougnaoui (Rs C-188/15) and G4S Secure Solutions (Rs C-157/15) in European Legal Scholarship' in Stephan Hinghofer-Szalkay and Herbert Kalb (eds), *Islam, Recht und Diversität* (Verlag Österreich 2018); José R Marín Aís, 'Freedom of Religion in the Workplace v. Freedom to Conduct a Business, the Islamic Veil Before the Court of Justice: Ms. Samira Achbita Case' (2018) 3(1) European Papers 409; Zoe Adams and John Olusegun Adenitire, 'Ideological Neutrality in the Workplace' (2018) 81(2) Modern Law Review 348; Eugenia Relaño Pastor, 'Religious Discrimination in the Workplace: Achbita and Bougnaoui' in Uladzislau Belavusau and Kristin Henrard (eds), *EU Anti-Discrimination Law beyond Gender* (Hart Publishing 2018).

[582] *Samira Achbita and Centrum voor gelijkheid van kansen en voor racismebestrijding v G4S Secure Solutions NV* (n 486) paras 11–13.

[583] Muir and Kolf (n 511) 26, 29.

[584] On the same day, the court took a decision in another religion-related case: *Asma Bougnaoui and Association de défense des droits de l'homme (ADDH) v Micropole SA* [2017] ECLI:EU:C:2017:204. Ms Bougnaoui was supported by an NGO in litigating her case as far as the CJEU. Thereafter, the following cases involved questions related to discrimination on the ground of religion: *Vera Egenberger v Evangelisches Werk für Diakonie und Entwicklung e.V.* [2018] ECLI:EU:C:2018:257 (discussed in subsection 4.3.3, Ms Egenberger is herself the director of an NGO in Germany offering strategic litigation support to victims of discrimination); *IR v JQ* [2018] ECLI:EU:C:2018:696, discussed in Ronan

stance by the CJEU. In fact, the judgment has been commented on as not coming 'even close to what one may expect from a supreme judicial voice of justice of our Union in a case of this nature'.[585] Weiler further found that while the threshold for the justification of policies betraying 'common decency and humanity . . . should be high . . . in *Achbita* there seemed to be hardly any threshold at all'.[586]

What did the judgment say? In essence, it qualified the policy of G4S as not constituting direct discrimination as 'the internal rule at issue in the main proceedings refers to the wearing of visible signs of political, philosophical or religious beliefs and therefore covers any manifestation of such beliefs without distinction'. It further found that such a rule treated all workers in the same way and that 'it is not evident . . . that the internal rule at issue in the main proceedings was applied differently to Ms Achbita as compared to any other worker'.[587] This conclusion has, quite rightly from this author's point of view, been disputed by a number of authors. Weiler asks for instance: 'Does it make a difference that "all" religions and beliefs are targeted? I am not sure.'[588] Similarly, Brems finds it 'astonishing that, in the eyes of the European Court, direct discrimination on grounds of religion or belief exists only when a measure targets a single religion or a selection of religions, but not when a measure targets all religions and beliefs. Generalized hostility toward religions is apparently a manifestation of neutrality.' She further argues that 'it seems unthinkable that the ECJ would rule that a measure excluding without distinction persons with all kinds of disabilities would not constitute direct discrimination. What is different about religion? Has anti-religious sentiment become so normalized in Europe, that it has become invisible—the new normal?'[589] There are thus good reasons to believe that the Court could reasonably have reached the conclusion that such a policy constitutes direct discrimination.[590]

While the question of the referring court only asked whether the policy constituted direct discrimination, the Court decided to give guidance also to the question of whether the policy could be seen as being indirectly discriminatory. In doing so, it had to consider whether the policy is objectively justified by a legitimate aim and if the means of achieving that aim are appropriate and necessary, thus proportionate, in which case the policy would not amount to indirect discrimination.[591] The Centre/Unia, siding also with the French and the Belgian governments, was of

McCrea, 'Religious Discrimination at Work: Can Employees be Fired for Getting Divorced?' (EU Law Analysis, 12 September 2018).

585 Weiler (n 581) 989.
586 ibid 1008.
587 *Samira Achbita and Centrum voor gelijkheid van kansen en voor racismebestrijding v G4S Secure Solutions NV* (n 486) paras 30–31.
588 Weiler (n 582) 1006.
589 Brems, 'European Court of Justice Allows Bans on Religious Dress in the Workplace' (n 582).
590 In this sense also Howard (n 581).
591 EED, Art 2(2)(b).

the opinion that G4S's policy could not be objectively justified by a legitimate aim and even if the aim was considered legitimate the means used would not pass the proportionality test.[592]

On the first point (legitimate aim) the Court found that 'the desire to display, in relations with both public and private sector customers, a policy of political, philosophical or religious neutrality must be considered legitimate'.[593] It backed this finding by referring to Article 16 of the Charter of Fundamental Rights (CFR) on the freedom to conduct business, in the context of which the wish to project an image of neutrality is legitimate, 'notably where the employer involves in its pursuit of that aim only those workers who are required to come into contact with the employer's customers'.[594] The Court did not however make reference to Article 31(1) CFR, which requires that 'every worker has the right to working conditions which respect his or her … dignity'. Commentators further criticized the extension of the duty of neutrality of the state, finding expression in the principle of secularism, to private parties. For Brem, such an extension is a 'big leap' and '[n]eutrality can be an easy cover-up for prejudice'.[595]

The Court then assessed whether the means used to achieve the aim of a policy of neutrality are appropriate and necessary. For the Court the ban on visible political, philosophical, or religious signs was appropriate 'provided that the policy is genuinely pursued in a consistent and systematic manner'.[596] Regarding the necessity of the measures, the Court held 'that it must be determined whether the prohibition is limited to what is strictly necessary' which it considered to be the case if the rule 'covers only G4S workers who interact with customers'. In that context, the Court left it for the referring court to ascertain whether G4S, 'without … being required to take on an additional burden' could have offered Ms Achbita a workplace 'not involving visual contact with the customers, instead of dismissing her'.[597]

[592] *Samira Achbita and Centrum voor gelijkheid van kansen en voor racismebestrijding v G4S Secure Solutions NV—opinion of the AG* [2016] ECLI:EU:C:2016:382, para 63.

[593] *Samira Achbita and Centrum voor gelijkheid van kansen en voor racismebestrijding v G4S Secure Solutions NV* (n 486) para 37.

[594] ibid para 38.

[595] Brems, 'European Court of Justice Allows Bans on Religious Dress in the Workplace' (n 582). See also Marko, 'Einleitende Bemerkungen zur interdisziplinären Perspektive von Politik und Recht in der Rechtsprechung' (n 581) 519.

[596] *Samira Achbita and Centrum voor gelijkheid van kansen en voor racismebestrijding v G4S Secure Solutions NV* (n 486) para 40.

[597] ibid paras 42–43. Weiler (n 582) 1006, invented a very illustrative hypothetical conversation between a lawyer and his client:

'CLIENT: I really don't like all those religious guys with their crosses and yarmulkes and hijabs serving my clients. Can I just prohibit that?

LAWYER: No, that would be direct discrimination specifically prohibited by the EU law.

CLIENT: So?

LAWYER: I'll tell you what. Let's add philosophical conviction too, which incidentally is also prohibited and call it a "policy of neutrality". At worst it will be defined as "indirect discrimination", for which the tests are weaker; at best, since neutrality is legitimate purpose, all you might need is to prove you have no back office jobs available. And thus you can get rid of them altogether.'

The Court thus applied a very loose justification test and did not sufficiently, if at all, include in its considerations the right to freedom of religion of Ms Achbita that includes the manifestation of her religion also in public. In *Eweida and others v the UK*,[598] in which a British Airways employee was prohibited from wearing a small silver cross with her uniform, also for reasons of corporate neutrality, the ECtHR held 'that a fair balance was not struck. On one side of the scales was Ms Eweida's desire to manifest her religious belief. As previously noted, this is a fundamental right: because *a healthy democratic society needs to tolerate and sustain pluralism and diversity*; but also because of the value to an *individual who has made religion a central tenet of his or her life* to be able to communicate that belief to others. On the other side of the scales was the employer's wish to project a certain corporate image. The Court considers that, while this aim was undoubtedly legitimate, the domestic courts accorded it too much weight.'[599]

This stands squarely opposite to AG Kokott's opinion in which she found that '[w]hile an employee, cannot "leave" his sex, skin colour, ethnicity, sexual orientation, age or disability "at the door" upon entering his employer's premises, he may be expected to moderate the exercise of his religion in the workplace, be this in relation to religious practice, religiously motivated behavior or (as in the present case) his clothing'.[600]

When the CJEU handed down its judgment, Unia underlined in its reaction the fact that the judgment made it clear that a general ban on wearing headscarves was not permitted and showed satisfaction that the Court had clarified 'how an employer can handle religious diversity'.[601] There was, however, also disappointment about the fact that the Court weighted the economic interests (freedom to conduct business) higher than the human rights issues (freedom to manifest one's religion) and that it found no fault in suggesting as a solution that people wearing religious signs should be hidden from visual contact with customers.[602]

The Belgian Court of Cassation annulled the decision of the Labour Court. The new decision of the Labour Court of Ghent of October 2020, quite surprisingly,

[598] ECtHR, *Eweida and others v. the UK*, judgment of 15 January 2013.

[599] ECtHR, *Eweida*, para 94. Emphasis added.

[600] *Samira Achbita and Centrum voor gelijkheid van kansen en voor racismebestrijding v G4S Secure Solutions NV—opinion of the AG* (n 592) para 116. See, for a different approach to this question, the opinion of AG Sharpson in the parallel case of *Bougnaoui* (n 584) para 118: 'Here, I emphasise that, to someone who is an observant member of a faith, *religious identity is an integral part of that person's very being*. The requirements of one's faith ... are not elements that are to be applied when outside work ... but that can politely be discarded during working hours. Of course, depending on the particular rules of the religion in question and the particular individual's level of observance, this or that element may be non-compulsory for that individual and therefore negotiable. But it would be *entirely wrong to suppose that, whereas one's sex and skin colour accompany one everywhere, somehow one's religion does not*.' Emphasis added.

[601] Unia, 'The Achbita case: clarity about the headscarf ban in the workplace' (15 March 2017) <https://www.unia.be/en/articles/the-achbita-case-clarity-about-the-headscarf-ban-in-the-workplace>.

[602] Interview, legal adviser at Unia, 31 May 2018.

found that there was no discrimination as Muslim women were not more disadvantaged than others by a policy of neutrality. It further found that G4S did not have to assess alternatives to dismissal, such as placing the employee in a back-office function with no visual contact with customers. Unia's director found that this ruling ignored the delicate balancing act that the European Court of Justice had already carried out in this case.[603] While Unia thus contributed to the clarification of EU legislation, it did not achieve the desired result at the national level.

Unia can also bring a complaint in its own name if there is no known victim. A very prominent case in this context is the *Feryn* case.[604] The director of Feryn, a company which specialized in the sale and installation of up-and-over and sectional doors, publicly stated 'that his undertaking was looking to recruit fitters, but that it could not employ "immigrants" because its customers were reluctant to give them access to their private residences'.[605] From such statements the Centre drew the conclusion that the company applied a discriminatory recruitment policy. Since there was no known person who was discriminated on the basis of his/her ethnic origin, the Centre brought the case to the court in its own name. The appeal court referred the case to the CJEU for a preliminary ruling, asking for clarifications on the scope of the concept of direct discrimination, on the conditions in which the rule on the reversal of the burden of proof can be applied, and on the interpretation of an 'effective, proportionate and dissuasive' sanction.[606]

The first question was answered by the Court in a substantive and procedural way. The governments of Ireland and the UK contended that the facts in the main proceedings could not amount to direct discrimination since there was 'no identifiable complainant contending that he has been the victim of that discrimination'.[607] The Court, however, was of the opinion that the objective 'to foster conditions for a socially inclusive labour market' referred to in recital 8 of RED's preamble, would be difficult to achieve if the Directive's scope were to be limited to cases in which an unsuccessful applicant for a job considered themselves to have been discriminated against and brought an action against the employer. In this context, the Court also referred to Article 3(1) RED which included in the scope of the Directive the selection criteria and recruitment conditions. It thus concluded that the finding of direct discrimination does not depend on the identification of a complainant and that the public statements of the employer amounted to such as they are 'clearly likely to strongly dissuade certain candidates from submitting their candidature and, accordingly, to hinder their access to the labour market'.[608]

[603] More details are provided at https://www.unia.be/en/articles/what-is-the-achbita-case.
[604] *Centrum voor gelijkheid van kansen en voor racismebestrijding v Firma Feryn NV* (n 484).
[605] ibid paras 15–16.
[606] ibid paras 18.
[607] ibid paras 21.
[608] ibid paras 21–25 and 28. See also Gulara Guliyeva, 'Joining Forces or Reinventing the Wheel? The EU and the Protection of National Minorities' (2010) 17(2) International Journal on Minority and Group Rights 287, 299.

From the procedural point of view, the Court clarified that the legal procedures provided for under Article 7 RED are to be considered only as minimum requirements (as stated in Art 6 RED) and that consequently Member States are not precluded 'from laying down, in their national legislation, the right of associations with a legitimate interest in ensuring compliance with that [the Racial Equality] directive, or for the body or bodies designated pursuant to Article 13 thereof, to bring legal or administrative proceedings to enforce the obligations resulting therefrom *without acting in the name of a specific complainant or in the absence of an identifiable complainant*'.[609]

The Court has thus made it clear that national legislation allowing NGOs or the Equality Body to bring legal actions on their own behalf, without a specific victim to support or represent, thus an *actio popularis*, is to be considered legislation that is 'more favourable to the protection of the principle of equal treatment'[610] than that which is strictly required under Articles 7 and 13 of the Directive. Considering the widespread incidence of situations similar to that described in the facts at issue in the *Feryn* case, as well as the finding that the existence of direct discrimination does not depend on the identification of a victim, it appears reasonable to conclude that in order to meet the objective of the Directive as described in recital 8 of the preamble it is necessary to allow NGOs and Equality Bodies to bring such unlawful situations to the attention of the judiciary.

Regarding the application of the rule on the reversal of the burden of proof, the Court states that the precondition for the rule to be applied 'is a simple finding that a presumption of discrimination has arisen on the basis of established facts'. To verify whether the facts that lead to this finding are established is the task of the national court. In the view of the Court, the statements of *Feryn's* director 'are sufficient for a presumption of the existence of a recruitment policy which is directly discriminatory'.[611]

Regarding the last question, the Court stated that sanctions must be effective, proportionate, and dissuasive, 'even where there is no identifiable victim'. While the Court acknowledges that Article 15 RED leaves it to the Member States to choose between different solutions, it finds that sanctions in cases like the one at issue 'may … include a finding of discrimination … in conjunction with an adequate level of publicity, the cost of which is to be borne by the defendant', they 'may also take the form of a prohibitory injunction' ordering to cease the discriminatory practice, and 'may, moreover, take the form of the award of damages to the body bringing the proceedings'.[612] Especially the last possibility suggested by the

609 *Centrum voor gelijkheid van kansen en voor racismebestrijding v Firma Feryn NV* (n 484) para 27.
610 ibid para 26.
611 ibid paras 29–34. See also Zaneta Poposka, 'Shift in the Burden of Proof—Mechanism to Ensure Enforcement of Anti-Discrimination Legislation' (2013) 2 Balkans Social Science Review 133, 140
612 *Centrum voor gelijkheid van kansen en voor racismebestrijding v Firma Feryn NV* (n 484) paras 35–40.

Court would be an important contribution to NGOs and Equality Bodies that support individual victims but also bring cases in the public interest. Cases brought in the public interest constitute, however, the big exception in Unia's litigation strategy. While their usefulness is acknowledged, its focus is clearly on dealing with the individual complaints it receives.

As described above, a final possibility for Equality Bodies to engage in judicial proceedings is by intervening as *amicus curiae*. Unia has done so mainly in international proceedings. One example is the *amicus curiae* submitted to the Council of Europe Committee of Social Rights (ECSR) in the context of a collective complaint submitted to the Committee by the Mental Disability Advocacy Center (MDAC) against Belgium.[613] The Centre alleged that the Flemish Community 'denies access to mainstream education to disabled children, in particular to children with intellectual disabilities and fails to provide the necessary accommodation to ensure such inclusion'.[614] Unia was invited explicitly by the president of the ECSR to submit written observations in its capacity as an independent mechanism charged with monitoring compliance with CRPD and 'in its capacity as an independent interfederal public service specialising in equality and non-discrimination policy'.[615] In its decision, finding in fact that the accessibility criterion was not fulfilled and that 'children with intellectual disabilities do not have an effective right to an inclusive education in the Flemish Community',[616] the ECSR followed the opinion of Unia.[617] In addition to this intervention in an international case, Unia submitted a written submission to the Committee of the CRPD on the implementation of inclusive education in Belgium. Furthermore, Unia can give advice on cases before the CJEU and the ECtHR that fall within its competence. The Ministry of External Affairs informs Unia about such pending cases. Advice of this kind was given by Unia in the *Jette Ring* case, for instance.[618]

The Cooperation Agreement does not appear to include a rule that would allow Unia to submit an *amicus curiae* in national court procedures. Unia would rather

[613] ECSR, *Mental Disability Advocacy Center (MDAC) v. Belgium*, complaint no 109/2014, decision of 16 October 2017.

[614] ECSR, *MDAC v Belgium*, para 2.

[615] ibid para 10.

[616] ibid paras 106–07.

[617] Unia, 'La réclamation collective MDAC contre la Belgique devant le CEDS: observations du Centre' (11 March 2015) <https://www.unia.be/fr/legislation-et-recommandations/recommandations-dunia/la-reclamation-collective-mdac-contre-la-belgique-devant-le-ceds-observations-du-centre>, and Unia, 'Le Comité européen suit l'avis d'Unia sur le droit à l'éducation inclusive en Flandres' (29 March 2018) <https://www.unia.be/fr/articles/le-comite-europeen-suit-lavis-dunia-sur-le-droit-a-leducation-inclusive-en-flandres>. For a similar case regarding the Wallonia-Brussels Federation (French Community) in which Unia again submitted an *amicus curiae*, see Emmanuelle Bribosia and Isabelle Rorive, 'Belgium fails to guarantee the right to inclusive education for children with intellectual disabilities within the French Community' (EELN News Report, 25 February 2021).

[618] *Joined cases HK Danmark, acting on behalf of Jette Ring v Dansk almennyttigt Boligselskab and HK Danmark, acting on behalf of Lone Skouboe Werge v Dansk Arbejdsgiverforening, acting on behalf of Pro Display A/S* [2013] ECLI:EU:C:2013:222. Information provided by legal adviser at Unia in the interview of 31 May 2018 and an e-mail of 5 June 2018.

join a victim of discrimination in the victim's support. In one case, Unia had been asked by the court of first instance for an expert opinion (which is different from *amicus curiae*), which, according to Belgian legislation, is, however, reserved to natural persons. The judge at the appellate court thus rejected the request.[619]

Overall, Unia has a plethora of ways in which it can act in support of victims of discrimination and it actively uses all of them. The use of its litigation competence in particular appears important in the Belgian context, given that proceedings started or supported by NGOs are not very common.[620] Although Unia resolves far more cases by managing to reach a negotiated solution, the possibility of bringing cases to court is likely to contribute to the willingness of the respondent to co-operate. It thereby strengthens Unia's role in a double sense: first, by making a negotiated solution more likely and second, by having in its hands another way of supporting a victim of discrimination if the conciliation attempt fails.

ECRI's revised GPR No 2 deals with the support and litigation competences of Equality Bodies in paragraph 14 and Unia holds nearly all of them. It does not appear to have the competence to 'monitor the execution of decisions of institutions, adjudicatory bodies, and the courts dealing with equality, discrimination and intolerance'. The Minister of Justice is obliged to send Unia the legal statistics relating to the application of the anti-discrimination legislation as well as court decisions taken in application of this legislation.[621] While this is certainly useful for data collection reasons, it does not appear to include a competence of monitoring the execution of the decisions. On the basis of this information, Unia does, however, undertake an evaluation of the anti-discrimination legislation.[622]

In line with the recommendation in paragraph 15 of ECRI 's revised GPR No 2, Unia has established its own criteria on the basis of which it chooses the cases that it takes on for representation and strategic litigation. Paragraph 18 of ECRI's GPR is also respected as the elements present in any negotiated solution 'require action to put an end to discrimination, achieve full equality, and avert future discrimination'. It makes public the results of the negotiated solutions but could do a better follow-up on the actual implementation of the solution. The lack of powers to obtain evidence and information as requested by paragraph 21 of ECRI's GPR No 2 appears to be hampering its handling of cases.

Unia's litigation activity is considered to have had an impact on the level of trust in the institution, in terms of reporting behaviour as well as awareness of rights and obligations. This trust is shown, inter alia, by the fact that NGOs only rarely engage

[619] Information provided by legal adviser at Unia in the interview of 31 May 2018 and an e-mail of 5 June 2018.

[620] Muir and Kolf (n 511) 30.

[621] Cooperation Agreement (n 513) Art 4 § 3. No comparable obligation exists for instance in Austria.

[622] Unia, 'Evaluation: Loi du 10 mai 2007 modifiant la loi du 30 juillet 1981 tendant à réprimer certains actes inspirés par le racisme ou la xénophobie (MB 30 mai 2007) (loi antiracisme) Loi du 10 mai 2007 tendant à lutter contre certaines formes de discrimination (MB 30 mai 2007) (loi antidiscrimination)' (n 564) 27–51.

in court proceedings themselves, preferring to refer the case to Unia,[623] and by the steadily increasing reports addressed to it by persons who feel discriminated. An increasing awareness of the existence of the body and its services can be related to the fact that Unia chooses well the cases which it brings to the media, something it does especially in cases where the outcome of the litigation is relevant not only for the party concerned but for many others in similar situations. Thus bringing cases to court and spreading information about the outcome in the media is seen as important tool to counter underreporting and increasing visibility.[624] This is helped of course by the fact that some of Unia's cases have reached the CJEU and have thus been widely discussed not only in the media but also academically. It appears, however, that this success is not solely down to the legal possibilities created through the implementation of EU law. As Miur and Kolf state, for instance, 'EU law acted as a catalyst in a legal landscape that was already broadly favourable to public interest litigation.'[625] Quite unsurprisingly, they further conclude that 'solid financial resources' and independence are *conditio sine qua non* for the efficient use of enforcement competences of Equality Bodies.[626]

5.4.3.2 Case Study: Ireland—The Irish Human Rights and Equality Commission

The Irish Human Rights and Equality Commission is an example of the recent trend towards merging Equality Bodies with national human rights institutions.[627] The merger concerned the Irish Equality Authority (EA) as well as the Irish Human Rights Commission (IHRC). The former was launched in 1999 on the basis of the Employment Equality Act of 1998, then replacing the Employment Equality Agency. The establishment of the EA was thus not connected to a requirement flowing from the transposition of EU legislation considering that the respective Directives were adopted only later.[628] The IHRC was launched in July 2001 on the basis of the Human Rights Commission Act of 2000 and was partly a result of the Good Friday Agreement which stipulated that human rights protection should apply equally on both sides of the Irish border. Its establishment could also be seen partly in response to the encouragement of the then UN High Commissioner for Human Rights Mary Robinson, a former president of Ireland.[629]

623 Muir and Kolf (n 511) 30.

624 Interview, legal adviser at Unia, 31 May 2018.

625 Muir and Kolf (n 511) 22.

626 ibid 31–32.

627 Other such cases are from Great Britain, the Netherlands, Denmark, Poland, France, and most recently, Hungary. For a comprehensive study on the issue of merging these two kinds of institutions see Crowther and O'Cinneide; see further Crowley, 'Merging Mandates of Equality Bodies and National Human Rights Institutions—A Growing Trend' (n 36); Equinet, 'Equality Bodies and National Human Rights Institutions: Making the Link to Maximise Impact. An Equinet Perspective' (n 35).

628 Sarah Spencer and Colin Harvey, 'Context, Institution or Accountability? Exploring the Factors that Shape the Performance of National Human Rights And Equality Bodies' (2014) 42(1) Policy & Politics 89, 95.

629 Crowther and O'Cinneide (n 34) 23.

Plans to review the Irish human rights infrastructure were announced in 2011 and were preceded by large-scale budget cuts for both institutions in 2008. The EA's and IHRC's budgets were reduced by 43 per cent and 32 per cent respectively.[630] The government justified the cuts with reference to the financial crisis. The argument, however, was at odds with an overall increase of the national budget of 2 billion EUR from 2008 to 2009.[631] It was thus 'widely acknowledged that motives really lie in political choices to reconfigure institutions of the state to reduce the values of equality, rights and solidarity rather than solely economic imperatives and value for money'.[632]

The impact of these budget cuts was assessed in 2009.[633] In doing so, the study first assessed the impact of the bodies prior to the cuts. Regarding the EA, the study found that it 'has been commended for its casework and negotiation for change' while its powers of enquiry were underdeveloped and the *amicus curiae* function had only started to be developed. Structured engagement with NGOs could have been strengthened. When assessing the impact of the cuts, the study referred to ECRI's comments in its 2007 report in which it already questioned whether either body was sufficiently resourced. It then concluded that '[b]oth bodies continue to exist and remain "open", but at a lower level of activity'. Precise conclusions as to the impact of the cuts on the EA were hampered by the fact that the Authority provided limited information and did not enter into a dialogue. One obvious impact was the reduction of staff numbers from fifty-one to thirty-eight (down to fifteen in 2013[634]), compounded by the relocation of most of the remaining staff members to a provincial location. The authors concluded that '(t)he perceptions of those observing the work of the two bodies is one of a greater awareness of a diminished capacity on the part of the Equality Authority than the Irish Human Rights Commission. This is seen to be evident in four areas in particular: a decline in media coverage; fewer significant case outcomes; a much reduced engagement with the NGO community; and a sharp falling off of the equality agenda in the business and enterprise community'.[635] The casework considerably suffered from the budget cuts. While in 2008, out of the seventy-one applications for assistance in court, sixty-eight were granted, in 2012, twenty-six applications were considered and fifteen were granted.[636]

The authors of the study highlighted another important point: while the focus of the debate was on the financial cutbacks, these came along with increasing attempts

[630] ibid.
[631] Brian M Harvey and Kathy Walsh, 'Downgrading Equality and Human Rights: Assessing the Impact' (Equality and Right Alliance, 2009) <http://www.eracampaign.org/uploads/Downgrading Equality & Human Right Assessing the Impact.pdf> 81.
[632] ibid 3.
[633] ibid summary in EELN, Country Report Ireland, 2014, 126.
[634] See EELN, Country Report Ireland, 2014, 125.
[635] Harvey and Walsh (n 631) 77–80.
[636] EELN, Country Report Ireland, 2014, 126.

at limiting the independence of both institutions, with the former possibly having 'obscured the importance of the latter'.[637] Comparing the independence of the EA with ECRI's GPR No 2, the study raised concern over the fact that all appointments of board members were made by the competent minister, that one of the board members was a ministerial representative, and that there was no clarity and transparency in the appointment procedure which appeared 'to be open to political favouritism'.[638] All staffing decisions had to be negotiated with the Department of Justice, Equality and Law Reform and staff members were drawn from civil service with limited scope for external appointments. The reporting obligation, instead of to the parliament, was to the same government department. In addition to these disturbing facts, the authors found that the legislation was amended to give the responsible minister new powers to appoint additional members to the boards and that there was evidence showing attempts by the ministry to influence the work of the EA. While, for instance, it is the court's responsibility to decide on whether an *amicus curiae* will be admitted, the Department contested any such right of the EA. Regarding the budget, the authors criticized the lack of insulation or protection from ministerial intervention such as existed for other state agencies with sensitive functions.[639]

The increasing attempts at taking control of the EA have been described as a 'very quiet coup'[640] that culminated in the budget cuts of 2008. The then CEO of the EA, Niall Crowley, resigned from his position as a consequence of these cuts. He argued that the cuts were connected to the fact that the casework pursued by the EA, in particular against public authorities, was seen as a threat by high-level civil servants and that the EA had been 'silenced for being an awkward witness to the inequality and discrimination in our society'.[641]

In its 2012 report, ECRI regretted the budget cuts and took note of the fact that the budget was further reduced in 2010 and 2011. It further took note of the plans to merge the EA and the IHRC with the objective 'to set up a streamlined body able

[637] Harvey and Walsh (n 631) 83.

[638] ibid 89–90. On a positive note, however, it has been reported that board members had to include nominations from social partnerships as well as the National Women's Council which ensured a degree of representation and diversity on the board. Interview, human rights and equality expert from Ireland, 21 November 2018.

[639] Harvey and Walsh (n 632) 83–85, 89–90.

[640] Ivana Bakic, 'The story of a very quiet coup' *The Irish Times* (22 May 2010) https://www.irishtimes.com/culture/books/the-story-of-a-very-quiet-coup-1.668763.

[641] ibid. In 2010, Crowley published a book entitled 'Empty Promises: Bringing the Equality Authority to Heel' (A&A Farmar). In one statement, Crowley said that the motivation to write the book did not stem from taking revenge or as a form of therapy. He wrote it because of the 'extraordinary vulnerability of the Equality Authority to attack and to denigration. What struck me was how could a strong, a necessary and an effective institution be taken down so quickly. And I felt there was a need to document that.' See Lise Hand, 'Former Equality Authority chief praised as a 'pioneer'' *Independentie* (14 May 2010) <https://www.independent.ie/irish-news/former-equality-authority-chief-praised-as-a-pioneer-26654982.html>.

to champion human rights and equality effectively, efficiently and cohesively'.[642] It recommended that authorities made sure the merger would result in a body set up in line with the Paris Principles and ECRI's GPR No 2 and 7, and with a comprehensive monitoring function in the field of discrimination on various grounds. It further recommended they 'ensure that sufficient financial and human resources are available to the new body to allow it to fulfil its terms of reference'.[643]

Considering the EA was the designated Equality Body under the requirements of Article 13 RED, the fact that an independent, let alone effective, functioning of the body was not guaranteed under the circumstances at the time could have raised the attention of the European Commission. The Commission did in fact receive a complaint from an Irish NGO coalition supported by the General Secretary of the Irish Congress of Trade Unions in September 2009. They asked the Commission to examine whether the Irish government was failing to comply with its obligations under the Equality Directives considering the sweeping budget cuts. While the Commission regretted the budget cuts it stated 'that due to the minimal-standard nature of EU Directives, they were unable to instigate infringement proceedings against the Irish Government'.[644] Thus, for the Commission, the mere existence of an Equality Body was sufficient for Ireland to be compliant with the requirement under Article 13 RED, not at all taking into consideration the clear and well-documented attack on the independent functioning of the institution, let alone the independence of the institution per se. The Commission was thus placing the bar for initiating infringement proceedings very high. If it was not even willing to intervene in the case of such a sweeping budget cut, it is quite unlikely that it would intervene in other Member States in which the Equality Bodies suffer from a chronical underfinancing.[645]

The NGO coalition submitted the same information to the European Parliament's Petition Committee,[646] in this case supported by all opposition Irish Members of the European Parliament. The Committee considered the petition in May 2010 and decided to request information from the Irish government 'on the nature of the cuts to the Equality Authority and how it is continuing to discharge on its functions under EU equality directives'.[647]

[642] ECRI, 'Report on Ireland (fourth monitoring cycle) adopted on 5 December 2012' CRI(2013)1, paras 44–45 and 53.

[643] ibid paras 55–56.

[644] Equality and Rights Alliance, 'Shadow report to UNCERD in response to the Irish Government's combined second and third progress report under ICERD' (October 2010), 12.

[645] A possible explanation for the reluctance of the Commission to take a stronger stance on the issue has been seen in the fact that around that time there were still a number of countries that had not yet established an Equality Body at all or had not vested it with the minimum competences required under the Directives. The Commission might therefore have found it inappropriate to 'go after Ireland', which after all had had a well-established structure in place for a number of years. Interview, human rights and equality expert from Ireland, 21 November 2018. No information is available to the author on whether the Commission, if not bringing infringement proceedings, at least sought an explanation from the government.

[646] Equality and Rights Alliance, 'Petition to the European Parliament' (nd).

[647] Equality and Rights Alliance, 'Shadow report to UNCERD in response to the Irish Government's combined second and third progress report under ICERD' (n 1409) 12; see also Alison Healy, 'EU to ask about cuts to Equality Authority' *The Irish Times* (1 June 2010) <https://www.irishtimes.com/news/

The merger process was announced in July 2011 with the stated aims of making efficient use of resources and enhancing the role of the newly created body. There was suspicion, however, that the financial motive was overriding and that the merger could be 'the final act in a series of attempts by the Irish government to increase its influence over' the two bodies.[648] The process started with the establishment by the Ministry for Justice, Equality and Defence of a Working Group in October 2011. Although the lack of civil society representatives in the Working Group was criticized, the presence of some renowned human rights and equality experts, well known for their independence, gave some confidence in the results produced by the Working Group. Furthermore, the Working Group instigated a large consultative process to enhance the legitimacy of the process. This resulted in sixty-nine submissions that have been well coordinated amongst the different NGOs.[649]

The Working Group published its report in April 2012. The response of various stakeholders was generally positive. However, there was a sense that 'the tension between developmental or promotional work (strongly underpinned in the Paris Principles) and enforcement actions (a core function under the Race Equality Directive 2000/43/EC) has been left unresolved'.[650] Too much focus on strategic litigation cases which are 'precedent-setting', in the view of some, risked undermining the broader legal duty under the RED to provide independent assistance to victims of discrimination.[651]

On the basis of the Working Group's report the government elaborated Heads of Bill which were published in June 2012 and submitted to the Parliamentary Committee on Justice, Defence and Equality for review, combined with an invitation to conduct a further consultation process.[652] The Irish Human Rights and Equality Commission Act (IHRECA) was finally adopted on 27 July 2014 and the new Commission established on 1 November 2014. The following analysis will focus exclusively on the IHREC's independence and effective functioning with regard to its task to provide independent assistance to victims of discrimination in pursuing their complaints.

Compared to the appointment procedure in place for the EA, where leadership was subject to ministerial discretion, the one for the IHREC is an improvement as

eu-to-ask-about-cuts-to-equality-authority-1.672420>. For a summary of other international bodies' reaction to the budget cuts see Equality and Rights Alliance, 'International concern regarding the erosion of the Irish statutory equality and human rights infrastructure' (nd).

[648] Thomas Pegram, 'Bridging the Divide: The Merger of the Irish Equality Authority and Human Rights Commission' (2013) 29 Studies in Public Policy 5–6.

[649] ibid 37–40.

[650] ibid 41.

[651] ibid 41–42.

[652] ibid 43–45, where it is reported that the Committee, by July 2012 received '17 submissions on the HOB, including robust interventions from the ICCL, IHRC, EA and the Scottish Human Rights Commission as the Chair of the European Group of NHRIs at the ICC'.

the power of the competent minister to influence the process has been reduced, although not completely eliminated.[653] Members of the Commission are appointed by the Irish president, on the advice of the government and following a resolution of the parliament. The Minister of Justice and the Public Appointments Service agree on selection criteria and the process to be implemented to fill the vacancy. The Service then publicly advertises the vacancy and appoints an independent selection panel.[654] One of the panel members is nominated by the director of the FRA. The panel recommends people for appointment and subsequently the Public Appointment Service makes recommendations for appointment to the government. The government shall accept the recommendation, unless it is unable to do so for substantial and stated reasons. The Service can disagree with such reasons and make representations to the government on that basis. In making recommendations for appointment, both the Service and the government have to take into consideration that the composition of the Commission should 'broadly reflect the nature of Irish society' and that the persons recommended have experience in human rights matters and matters connected with discrimination on the grounds covered by the Act.[655] Furthermore, women and men shall be equally represented.[656] The recommendation by government is followed by a resolution of parliament and the appointment by the president. The government's/minister's power to influence the selection process is thus rather limited, considering that the initial selection is made by the independent selection panel and the government has to act upon the recommendation by the Public Appointment Service which it can reject only in exceptional circumstances.[657] The Minister of Justice still has an influence on determining the selection criteria which is, however, limited by the provisions of the law.

The Commission shall consist of between twelve and fifteen members. With the aim of securing continuity and an institutional memory, for the initial composition a three-year term is laid down in the Act for seven members, while eight members, including the Chief Commissioner, shall be appointed for five years. Mandates are renewable once. As the Commission started its work in November 2014, by the end of 2017, seven new members had to be appointed. The government nominated seven candidates in February 2018 and the motion recommending their appointment to the IHREC was discussed in the lower house of the parliament on 29 March 2018. On that occasion, the responsible minister underlined the fact that the

[653] The appointment of members of Commission is regulated by the Irish Human Rights and Equality Commission Act (IHRECA) of 27 July 2014, s 13.

[654] The selection panel for the initial composition of the Commission was unilaterally appointed by the minister in summer 2012, thus when the IHREC Act was still pending. After the UN OHCHR raised concerns over this fact, the panel stepped down after just four days in post. See Pegram (n 648) 15. However, while pressure came from the UN, there was no reaction from the EU.

[655] IHRECA, s 13(13).

[656] IHRECA, s 12(2).

[657] See, in this sense, also EELN, Country Report Ireland, 2020, 87.

selection process, from 149 applications, was carried out totally independently by the Public Appointments Service, with no governmental representative involved in the shortlisting panel or interviewing board. The Service also made the final selection of the seven persons to be recommended for the position of Commissioner.[658] While all members of the house who took the floor praised the expertise and qualification of the proposed candidates, there were also voices that were concerned about the process having left out an outgoing Commissioner (probably because of her position on issues related to refugees and abortion[659]) and the selection criteria established by the minister in agreement with the Public Appointments Service. For those critics, these criteria placed too much emphasis on skills in finance and corporate governance and therefore excluded a range of individuals with an impeccable record in human rights and equality issues. It was thus criticized that the minister had a say in the definition of the selection criteria.[660] Another point of concern raised by an independent expert consisted in the fact that the chair of the IHREC was also the chair of the interviewing board.[661]

The stability of the mandate of Commissioner is secured by the provision in the Act which allows the government to dismiss a member from office only if both houses of parliament have passed a resolution calling for the member's removal. This is possible only if the member, without reasonable justification, has failed to discharge the functions for more than three months, if he/she, for health reasons, is incapable of performing the functions of Commissioner, or is guilty of stated misbehaviour. If a member becomes an undischarged bankrupt or is convicted of a criminal offence that vote of the parliament is not required.[662] The exhaustive list of reasons for which a Commissioner can be dismissed and the required vote of both houses of parliament secures the Commissioners a reasonably stable mandate.

When it comes to the power to recruit and manage its own staff, the situation has not changed as compared to the previously existing EA. The staff is still part of the civil service, for appointments of staff members, as well as for the terms and conditions of service of staff members, the Commission needs the consent of the competent minister and the approval of the Minister for Public Expenditure and Reform.[663]

658 See the debate at the Dáil Éireann, at https://www.oireachtas.ie/en/debates/debate/dail/2018-03-29/25/.

659 See Justine McCarthy, 'Rights watchdog "in the wrong"' *The Times* (14 January 2018) <https://www.thetimes.co.uk/article/rights-watchdog-in-the-wrong-wx8mxwfg7>.

660 See the debate at the Dáil Éireann, the interventions of deputies Donnchadh Ó Laoghaire and Richard Boyd Barrett at https://www.oireachtas.ie/en/debates/debate/dail/2018-03-29/25/. As one of the outgoing Commissioners who was not reappointed (unsuccessfully) challenged the selection process, the new Commissioners were appointed by the president only on 1 June 2018.

661 Interview, human rights and equality expert from Ireland, 21 November 2018. The legal expert in EELN proposed that greater transparency in the selection process 'could perhaps be ensured by according the Oireachtas an oversight role in the appointment of the selection panel'. EELN, Country Report Ireland, 2018, 96.

662 IHRECA, s 14.

663 IHRECA, s 24.

Quite understandably, considering the experience of its predecessors, the regulation of the budget for the future merged body was of central importance. From the Heads of Bill it appeared that the intention was to retain the discretionary control of the minister over the budget of the merged body with financial safeguards lacking. Section 26 of IHRECA in the end provides that '[i]n each financial year, the Minister may, after consultation with the Commission, advance to the Commission out of moneys provided by the Oireachtas such sums as appear to the Minister, with the consent of the Minister for Public Expenditure and Reform, to be reasonably sufficient for the purposes of expenditure by the Commission in the performance of its functions'. This has prompted the UN SCA, in the context of the re-accreditation procedure of the IHREC in 2015, to be 'concerned that the Minister for Justice and Equality has significant discretion over the allocation of funds to the IHREC, and that this has the potential to impact on its effectiveness and independence'.[664] So, although there is a need for consultation with the Commission, the competent minister is still in a position to decide over the budget and no insulation of the budget has taken place. In practice, it has been reported that the IHREC currently has sufficient funds as well as a sufficient amount of highly qualified staff,[665] although its budget is still lower than the combined budgets of the EA and IHRC were prior to the cuts.[666]

In terms of geographic outreach there is room for improvement, since the IHREC only has an office in Dublin and no local branches.[667] Considering the size of Ireland this situation has not, however, been considered as hampering the work of the Commission.[668]

Section 10 IHRECA lays down the functions of the Commission. The focus of the list in section 10(1) is clearly on promotion and awareness raising, rather than on enforcement and such a focus in the Heads of Bill has already raised concerns that the merger of the EA and the IHRC could lead to a 'de-prioritization of legal action'.[669] In fact, the Heads of Bill did not contain provisions regarding legal assistance

664 ICC Sub-Committee on Accreditation, 'Report and Recommendations of the Session of the Sub-Committee on Accreditation (SCA)' (16 November 2015) 10.

665 Interview, human rights and equality expert from Ireland, 21 November 2018.

666 EELN, Country Report Ireland, 2020, 86

667 The Equality Authority had been moved from Dublin to Roscrea in 2006 as part of a government decentralization drive. The ECRI had raised concerns over this relocation as it could negatively affect access to the EA's services to the most vulnerable as well as staff retention and the Authorities cooperation with partners such as NGOs, trade unions, government bodies, and businesses. See ECRI, 'Third report on Ireland' (15 December 2006) CRI(2007)24, para 40. In para 42 the ECRI recommended 'that the Irish authorities ensure that the decision to relocate the Equality Authority outside Dublin does not result in members of minority groups having difficulties in accessing this body and in the loss of valuable institutional knowledge. The ECRI further recommends that the authorities consider opening local offices in order to enable as many members of minority groups as possible to have access to the Equality Authority.'

668 Interview, human rights and equality expert from Ireland, 21 November 2018.

669 Crowley, 'Merging Mandates of Equality Bodies and National Human Rights Institutions—A Growing Trend' (n 36) 42.

to be provided by the Commission to individual victims of discrimination during proceedings or the possibility for the Commission to institute legal proceedings in its own name. These two powers have, however, been included in detail in the final version of IHRECA in sections 40 and 41.[670] In addition, section 10(2)(e) explicitly allows the Commission to apply to the High Court or the Supreme Court for the liberty to appear as *amicus curiae* and makes clear that it is in the absolute discretion of the said courts to decide whether or not to grant this liberty.

In addition to being able to provide assistance to victims before the courts, the IHREC is mandated to 'review the adequacy and effectiveness of law and practice', to give its opinion on legislative proposals and make recommendations on measures to be taken to strengthen human rights and equality.[671] It can undertake or commission research and conduct inquiries and prepare and publish reports on the outcomes.[672] It can provide education and training on human rights and equality issues and consult with national, EU, and international bodies having knowledge or expertise in the field of human rights and equality.[673] The competences thus cover all the requirements under the RED. The focus in the following analysis will be on the different possibilities to provide independent assistance to victims of discrimination.

The IHREC lacks the competence to formally decide on complaints brought before it by addressing its decision or recommendation to the parties. Furthermore, it has no competence to mediate or conciliate in discrimination cases. The IHREC has the competence to start inquiries on its own motion where there is evidence of a serious violation of equality of treatment obligations in respect of a person or a class of persons, or of a systemic failure to comply with such obligations and the matter is of grave public concern.[674] The threshold has been considered as relatively high and in fact, the IHREC has not made use of this competence so far. The twenty-three requests to conduct an inquiry received in 2015 and 2016 were rejected, as the 'majority of requests did not meet the threshold for intervention' as set out by IHRECA.[675] According to section 32, IHREC has the competence to invite organizations to undertake an equality review or to conduct such reviews itself. So far, it has rarely made use of this power. In one instance, it invited local government bodies to conduct a review of compliance with equality law obligations in the field of traveller accommodation.[676]

[670] These powers are listed in more general terms in Art 10(2)(f–g) of the Act, which lays out in more detail how the functions mentioned in Art 10(1) can be furthered.

[671] IHRECA, s 10(2)(b)–(d). The latter two activities can be undertaken *suo motu* or if requested by the government or a minister.

[672] IHRECA, s 10(2)(j), (o), (p).

[673] IHRECA, s 10(2)(h), (k).

[674] IHRECA, s 35.

[675] Irish Human Rights and Equality Commission, 'Annual Report 2016' (2017) 16; and interview, human rights and equality expert from Ireland, 21 November 2018.

[676] Judy Walsh, 'National equality body instigates equality reviews of Traveller accommodation provision' (EELN News Report, 9 July 2019).

Although the IHREC has the power to 'institute proceedings in any court of competent jurisdiction for the purpose of obtaining relief of a declaratory or other nature, in respect of any matter concerning the human rights of any person or class of persons',[677] it has so far not yet made use of this possibility. It therefore remains unclear whether the formulation 'class of persons' allows the IHREC to file an *actio popularis* or whether identifiable victims will be required by a court. While the Heads of Bill included a formulation according to which identifiable victims were not required, this clarification was omitted in the adopted legislation. In line with section 29 IHRECA, 'human rights' has to be interpreted as those guaranteed under the Irish Constitution, the European Convention on Human Rights Act 2003 or under any such agreement, treaty, or convention which has been given the force of law in the state. It has been considered that this definition 'should be broad enough to enable IHREC to litigate on compliance with EU equality provisions'.[678]

The IHREC's work thus focuses on the provision of initial information, and—from among the possibilities of becoming active in front of courts—on the granting of legal assistance, which may take the form of legal advice or legal representation,[679] and the application to appear as *amicus curiae.*

Drawing on the figures published in the annual reports, it appears that the activity of the IHREC in terms of granting legal assistance has gained momentum in its first years of functioning and in most cases concerns equality-related issues. While, as reported above, the requests for legal assistance submitted to the EA have dropped from seventy-one in 2008 (sixty-eight granted) to twenty-six in 2012 (fifteen granted) and still amounted to only thirty-nine such requests to IHREC in 2015 (on human rights and equality related issues combined), this number has risen to 112 in 2017 (seventy-two granted) but dropped again to eighty in 2019.[680] In sixteen of these latter requests, legal advice was granted, in twenty-six cases the IHREC granted legal representation. The number of cases in which the IHREC grants legal assistance to victims of discrimination or human rights violations has thus not yet managed to stablilize at the level of cases to which the EA granted legal assistance in discrimination cases. In 2019, about two thirds of the completed cases in which assistance was granted regarded equal treatment legislation.[681] The number of queries has ranged from 2,173 in 2015 (987 of which were related to equality legislation, 398 to human rights, and 788 were referred to other

[677] IHRECA, s 41(1).

[678] EELN, Country Report Ireland, 2020, 96.

[679] IHRECA, s 40(10)(c) provides in addition to these two, the power to provide 'such other assistance to the applicant as the Commission deems appropriate in the circumstances'.

[680] Irish Human Rights and Equality Commission, 'Annual Report 2017' (2018) 38; and Irish Human Rights and Equality Commission, 'Annual Report 2019' (2020) 16.

[681] Of the twenty-five client files closed in which advice was given, ten were about a discrimination issue; of the twenty-one cases closed in which the IHREC represented the victim, twenty-eight concerned cases of discrimination. Irish Human Rights and Equality Commission, 'Annual Report 2019' (n 681) 17–21.

institutions) to 1,890 in 2017 (909 of which were related to equality legislation, 231 to human rights, and 750 were referred to other institutions) and 2,165 in 2017 (1,175 of which were related to equality legislation, 316 to human rights, and 622 were referred to other institutions, while fifty-two cases concerned equality issues but were not covered by legislation).

Disability is the ground that appears most prominently in the queries related both to the Equal Status Acts (29 per cent) and the Employment Equality Acts (36 per cent). From among the grounds protected by EU directives, race follows in second place with 12 per cent for both Acts. While these figures are similar since the first Annual Report, it is interesting to note that when it comes to the prevailing discrimination grounds in cases in which the Commission has granted legal assistance, the ground of religion came first by a long way in cases assisted under the Equal Status Acts, whereas in cases assisted under the Employment Equality Acts the ground of age appeared most.[682] This appears to have changed by 2019 as disability and race are the two grounds most often represented among the closed assistance cases.[683]

It is thus interesting to see how the Commission selects the cases to which it grants legal assistance. First of all, it needs to take into consideration the criteria as prescribed by section 40(3)–(4) IHRECA. Subsection 3 provides that the Commission must first of all consider whether the applicant could be assisted under the civil or criminal justice legal aid acts by any other means. Having decided on this question in the negative, subsection 4 requires the Commission to then consider whether the matters at issue in the related proceedings raise a question of principle and whether it would be unreasonable to expect a person to deal with the matter without assistance because of its complexity. The Commission can take into consideration other special circumstances which make it appropriate to grant legal assistance.

In 2017, the Commission has further adopted 'Guidelines on applications for legal assistance'.[684] The purpose of the guidelines is to outline the legislative criteria applied and the procedures adopted by the IHREC in assessing applications for assistance.[685] They do so by further specifying non-exhaustively which factors it may take into consideration when deciding whether the matter at issue in the proceedings raises a 'question of principle'. In this context, the Commission may consider whether the question raised is one of significant public importance; whether it concerns an area of law or practice that requires development and/or clarification; or whether it raises an issue of compatibility of national law or practice

[682] Irish Human Rights and Equality Commission, 'Annual Report 2015' (2016) 30.
[683] Irish Human Rights and Equality Commission, 'Annual Report 2019' (n 681) 17–21.
[684] Irish Human Rights and Equality Commission, 'Guidelines on applications for legal assistance' (2017) https://www.ihrec.ie/app/uploads/2017/06/Guidelines-on-applications-for-legal-assistance-April-2017-3.pdf.
[685] ibid para 6.

with the applicant's human rights as guaranteed by the Constitution, the ECHR, or any other international agreement which has been given force within Ireland. Furthermore, it may consider if the facts of the case are strong enough to make it likely that the applicant would succeed in the proceedings and if in such a case persons other than the applicant would benefit from the outcome or the laws and practice relating to human rights and/or equality would be strengthened.[686]

Among the reasons which would make it unreasonable to expect the applicant to deal with the matter without assistance, the Commission lists—again non-exhaustively—the complexity or legal novelty of the issues raised, the forum in which the proceedings would need to be brought (which would presumably include also the prospect of a referral of questions to the CJEU), or a disability of the applicant which impairs the capacity of the applicant to represent himself/herself without assistance.[687] Other special circumstances that the Commission may take into consideration when deciding on a request for granting legal assistance relate, for example, to the gravity of the issues raised or the 'severity of any discrimination, injury, loss or damage suffered' by the applicant.[688]

Even where a case fulfils the statutory criteria, the Commission may refuse to grant assistance if it considers that it 'would not represent the most appropriate and/or proportionate use of the Commission's functions'.[689] This is, for instance, the case when the anticipated costs of the proceedings outweigh the potential benefit.[690]

The first person responsible for taking the decision on whether or not to grant legal assistance is the Head of Legal, who will inform the applicant in writing. If the decision is negative, the reasons are to be set out. Within twenty-eight days, the applicant can appeal the decision to the Director of the Commission whose decision is final. If the decision is positive, a solicitor will be assigned to the applicant to provide the appropriate assistance.[691]

While individual applicants for legal assistance receive an explanation for the rejection in writing, nothing is publicly known about the overarching patterns leading to an acceptance or decline of an application. What informs the strategic approach of the Commission thus remains unclear. This could include, for instance, that the Commission is basing its decision on research findings that suggest the endemic or persistent nature of discrimination in a certain area which warrants the engagement of the Commission.[692]

For the purpose of illustration, two cases in which the Commission granted legal assistance are briefly reported. The first case concerned a group of individuals

[686] ibid para 14.
[687] ibid para 15.
[688] ibid para 16.
[689] ibid para 19.
[690] ibid para 20.
[691] ibid paras 26–34.
[692] EELN, Country Report Ireland, 2020, 90–91.

belonging to the traveller community who had been denied service in a licensed premises. The individuals were granted legal representation by the Commission to bring their complaints before the District Court. The case was settled before hearing. The legal settlement included the payment by the owner of the licensed premises of 6,000 EUR in compensation to each of the complainants, and a further 500 EUR to each of them, to be donated to a charity of their choice. Furthermore, the staff involved in the incident had to attend an equality training. In the Commission's release on the settlement, the Chief Commissioner welcomed the settlement 'and the clear message it sends that discrimination in private services, including licensed premises is not acceptable and can be challenged'.[693]

In the second case the IHREC represented two men before the Workplace Relations Commission (WRC, then Equality Tribunal), who complained about having been discriminated on the grounds of age. They were excluded from the recruitment procedure for new police officers to the Irish national police force (An Garda Síochána) on the ground that they were above the maximum age for recruitment laid down by the Admissions and Appointments Regulations. The question thus rose whether the Workplace Relations Commission has the power to disapply national law that conflicts with EU law. The Minister for Justice and Equality challenged the authority of the WRC to do so in the High Court, as under the Constitution this power is given to the High Court alone. While the High Court ruled in favour of the minister, the WRC appealed the decision to the Supreme Court, which submitted the question to the CJEU.[694] Before the Court, the IHREC continued representing the men concerned and appeared before the Grand Chamber.[695] The Court considered that if a body such as the WRC 'were unable to find that a national provision is contrary to that directive and, consequently, were unable to decide to disapply that provision, the EU rules in the area of equality in employment and occupation would be rendered less effective'. It further stated that not even constitutional provisions can 'be allowed to undermine the unity and effectiveness of EU law'. Therefore, '[i]t follows from the principle of primacy of EU law . . . , that bodies called upon, within the exercise of their respective powers, to apply EU law are obliged to adopt all the measures necessary to ensure that EU law is fully effective, disapplying if need be any national provisions or national case-law that are contrary to EU law'.[696]

693 Irish Human Rights and Equality Commission, 'Travellers Denied Service Secure Settlement and Redress' (18 December 2017) <https://www.ihrec.ie/travellers-denied-service-secure-settlement-redress/>.

694 *The Minister for Justice and Equality and The Commissioner of the Garda Síochána v Workplace Relations Commission* [2018] ECLI:EU:C:2018:979; discussed in Sara Drake, 'The Principle of Primacy and the Duty of National Bodies Appointed to Enforce EU Law to Disapply Conflicting National Law: An Garda Síochána' (2020) 57(2) Common Market Law Review 557.

695 Irish Human Rights and Equality Commission, 'EU Court of Justice Issues Landmark Equality Law Ruling' (4 December 2018) <https://www.ihrec.ie/eu-court-of-justice-issues-landmark-equality-law-ruling/>.

696 CJEU, The Minister for Justice and Equality and The Commissioner of the Garda Síochána, paras 48–50.

Notwithstanding this important casework generating an impact beyond the individual case and the positive trend in terms of engagement in legal proceedings shown by the figures drawn from annual reports, it is not yet clear whether the IHREC supports a 'critical mass of cases'.[697] The perception is rather, also compared to the intensive casework carried out by the EA involving defendants from the private and public sector, that the IHREC is not yet active enough in this field. It was therefore not yet able to remove 'concerns that its approach to legal assistance is more restrictive or less well resourced than that of the Equality Authority'.[698] The fact that queries are fluctuating has been explained by the fact that the IHREC is not a very high-profile institution, that procedures are bureaucratic, and the perception that it is difficult to get assistance, so that even lawyers specialized in human rights and equality would be slow to recommend people to approach the Commission for assistance.[699] Such assistance is, however, very much needed, since only very limited legal aid is available and NGOs are not allowed to represent victims of discrimination in the courts.

As well as being able to provide legal assistance, it is a statutory competence of the IHREC to apply to the High Court, the Court of Appeal, or the Supreme Court for liberty to appear before these courts as *amicus curiae* in proceedings relating to human rights or equality.[700] This competence has been widely used by one of its predecessors, the IHRC,[701] while the Equality Authority, which did not have an explicit competence to apply for liberty to appear as *amicus curiae*, supported victims rather by granting legal representation. By adding this possibility to the competences of the IHREC, it increases the repertoire of legal means at the disposal of the Commission also in equality cases, which it can make use of depending on its priorities. The competence is, however, limited by the fact that it is restricted to the Superior Courts, whereas the bulk of discrimination cases is litigated before the Labour Court and the Workplace Relations Commission, with several significant cases also before lower civil courts. The competence could thus be extended to include these fora.[702]

In 2016, the IHREC published Amicus Curiae Guidelines.[703] The Guidelines emphasize at several points that the Commission carries out this function in an

[697] Council of Europe, Commissioner for Human Rights (n 24) 21.

[698] EELN, Country Report Ireland, 2020, 91.

[699] Interview, human rights and equality expert from Ireland, 21 November 2018.

[700] IHRECA, ss 10(2)(e) and 44(1) which transferred all the 'functions that, immediately before the establishment day, were vested in a dissolved body' to the Commission. The power to apply to the Court of Appeal for liberty to appear as *amicus curiae* was contained in the Human Rights Commission Act, s 8(h).

[701] The IHRC regularly had between two and four cases per year in the period between 2007 and 2011. In 2012 it had nine such cases and in the last two years of its existence one each. Information can be found at https://www.ihrec.ie/publications/.

[702] EELN, Country Report Ireland, 2020, 97.

[703] Irish Human Rights and Equality Commission, 'Amicus Curiae Guidelines' (2016) https://www.ihrec.ie/app/uploads/2016/12/IHREC-Amicus-Curiae-Guidelines.pdf.

independent and impartial way. It therefore also underlines, that IHRECA does not confer on any party a right to request the Commission to apply for liberty to appear as *amicus curiae* and that it exercises this function on its own volition.[704] A decision on whether or not to apply for liberty to appear as *amicus curiae* is taken by the Commission, and is made on the basis of a recommendation by the casework committee, which in turn can request the Head of Legal to prepare an assessment as to how to decide.[705] The Guidelines lay down the factors—in a non-exhaustive way—that the Commission may take into consideration when making a decision. These include, inter alia, the importance of the human rights and/or equality rights raised, whether they concern priority areas as defined by the Commission in its strategic statement, whether the determination of the issues in question may deploy a significant effect also on the human and/or equality rights of persons not involved in the proceedings, whether the relevant court is likely to accept the application of the Commission, as well as any resource implications for the Commission.[706] The Guidelines acknowledge that the decision as to whether the application to appear as *amicus curiae* is accepted, remains within the absolute discretion of the court.[707]

Most of the IHREC's applications for liberty to appear as *amicus curiae* relate to its human rights mandate.[708] Furthermore, it has been generally questioned whether such interventions have a meaningful impact on a case. There appears to be a perception that the IHREC is favouring *amicus curiae* over legal representation, which has been seen critically. This criticism is related to the fact that an *amicus* 'doesn't upset anyone', since it is supposed to provide objective information to the court to assist it in finding a solution, while the IHREC should take on a more promotional role for equality and position itself more outspokenly for that cause.[709]

Overall, it can be concluded that, while missing some of the competences recommended by ECRI, such as receiving, investigating, and deciding on complaints or mediating them, the merged IHREC is vested with strong powers but it appears to be relatively soft in the use made of them. This has not been seen to be related

[704] See ibid paras 13–14, 16, 27(a).
[705] ibid paras 17, 19–22.
[706] ibid paras 23–24.
[707] ibid para 25.
[708] EELN, Country Report Ireland, 2020, 97. An example of an *amicus curiae* intervention in a discrimination related case is *Culkin v Sligo County Council*, in which the Commission's argumentation heavily relied on the interpretation of national law in line with EU law. Irish Human Rights and Equality Commission, 'Outline Submission on Behalf of the Irish Human Rights and Equality Commission in the case Ciaran Culkin v. Sligo County Council' (Record no 2015/103, 12 January 2016) paras 12–18. IHREC intervened as *amicus curiae* also in *Daly v Nano Nagle*, a case before the Supreme Court relating to the interpretation of reasonable accommodation. See on this case Irish Human Rights and Equality Commission, 'Annual Report 2019' (n 681) 26–27; and Niall Crowley, 'Taking Stock. A Perspective from the Work of Equality Bodies on: European Equality Strategies, Equal Treatment Directives, and Standards for Equality Bodies' (Equinet, 2020) 20.
[709] Interview, human rights and equality expert from Ireland, 21 November 2018.

to limited resources or lack of qualified Commission or staff members. It may instead be related to negative learning from the experience of the predecessors, the Equality Authority, and the IHRC: it seems that the Commission does not want to be too outspoken in order not to run the risk of meeting the same fate as its predecessors. It has been considered that it could do much more case work, start engaging also in inquiries on its own motion thereby also strengthening its visibility, and at least raise a critical voice and take a position when faced with events that raise a serious equality or human rights concern. When it comes to an assessment as to whether the merger has been a success, it is perceived that human rights dominate over equality issues and that equality has slid off the agenda.[710]

5.4.3.3 Case Study: Germany—The Federal Anti-Discrimination Agency

As mentioned above, the German Anti-Discrimination Agency has been chosen as a case study to assess the extent to which an Equality Body vested with very limited competences to provide assistance to victims of discrimination in pursuing their complaints manages in practice to live up to this obligation. Like in the other case studies, before looking at the legal and practical implementation of this function, the question of independence is addressed.

§§ 25–30 of the General Equal Treatment Act (GETA) regulate the organizational structure and the tasks of the Federal Agency for the Protection against Discrimination (Federal Anti-Discrimination Agency or FADA). According to § 25, the Agency is established within the Federal Ministry for Family Affairs, Senior Citizens, Women and Youth. It is thus one of the examples of an embedded institution. The head of FADA is appointed by the minister, based on a suggestion by the government, for the duration of a legislative period. Thus, every incoming government and minister has the opportunity to appoint a new head of FADA. The law further provides that the head of FADA is in an official public law relationship with the Federal Administration but is independent in the execution of its duties and only subject to the law. The minister can discharge the head of FADA upon his/her own request or 'when grounds arise which, in the case of a judge appointed for life, would give rise to discharge from duty'.[711] The necessary human and financial resources required for the fulfilment of its tasks shall be identified as a separate chapter within the ministry's overall budget plan.[712]

From a comparative point of view, the independence of the FADA could potentially be affected by multiple factors: the nomination and appointment of its head are both in the hands of the executive; the duration of the mandate is limited by the duration of the parliament and thus the head can be exchanged by new incoming governments/ministers; and the body is embedded within a ministry. Due to the

[710] ibid.
[711] German Equal Treatment Act, § 26.
[712] German Equal Treatment Act, § 25(2).

legally provided independence in the execution of his/her duties and the fact that the FADA is neither bound to directives from the ministry nor subject to supervision from the ministry (it remains, however, subject to control of legality), it has been considered that the head of the FADA nevertheless enjoys independence in the execution of their daily business.[713] Furthermore, as provided by § 26(4) GETA, the relationship between the head of the FADA and federal authorities is regulated by a contract and is thus a public law relationship of a specific kind, which has been seen as further contributing to the independence of the head.[714] Another positive factor is the provision regarding the situations in which the head of the institution can be discharged. The fact that this can happen only in the cases of judges appointed for life gives the mandate considerable stability.

The nomination of candidates by the government with subsequent appointment by the minister has led some to conclude that the position is very much politically entrenched and would profit from, at least, the organization of a public call for applications.[715] This could ensure that the nomination would be made from a pool of pre-selected qualified persons. In the past, the current legal framework has led to contested nominations. The decision on the appointment to this position in 2018 was challenged by one of the appointee's competitors in the Berlin Administrative Court. The Court decided that the selection decision by the ministry 'was not compatible with the "best selection principle" enshrined in the Basic Law' and that the application process showed serious shortcomings.[716] As the legal dispute is still ongoing and parliamentary elections are coming up soon, the position for the full period has been filled by an acting head.

As mentioned above, the budget comes under a separate heading in the ministry's budget but is administered independently by the Agency. There is some degree of flexibility to move resources between the different headings of the overall budget. In recent years, the budget has steadily increased, from 2.6 million EUR in 2011 up to 4.3 million EUR in 2017 and 5.4 million EUR in 2019.[717]

In terms of geographic outreach, it is important to note that the German Equality Body is a centralized one with no regional offices outside Berlin. This is partly mediated by the fact that some *Länder* and municipalities have established non-discrimination offices at regional and/or local level. There are also a number of non-discrimination offices run by civil society organizations. However, many of them work under precarious conditions,[718] and—as with the publicly run offices—offer advice only on selected grounds. With the initiative *Offensive*

[713] Berghahn, Klapp, and Tischbirek (n 52) 177. See also EELN, Country Report Germany, 2020, 82.
[714] Berghahn, Klapp, and Tischbirek (n 52) 178.
[715] ibid 179.
[716] Country Report Germany, 2020, 82.
[717] See the member information on the website of Equinet, at https://equineteurope.org/author/germany_fada/.
[718] Consider, for instance that BUG, one of the few NGOs offering strategic litigation, is wholly run by persons working in honorary capacity. Interview, Director of BUG, 31 March 2021.

diskriminierungsfreie Gesellschaft (discrimination-free society) the FADA has financially supported the establishment of ten 'Networks against Discrimination' and has provided them also with capacity building. As a follow-up, in the period 2015–17 it has supported eleven counselling offices in ten different *Länder* with the aim of 'closing gaps' in the network of offices both in terms of coverage of protected grounds and geography.[719] After receiving initial start-up financing by the FADA, they are expected to secure their funds by themselves later on.[720] On its website, the FADA provides a tool to search for anti-discrimination offices. Notwithstanding these efforts, there appears to persist a lack of offices providing counselling services across all discrimination grounds,[721] which could potentially be ensured by if the FADA—which works horizontally—had regional offices. An NGO representative spoke of a 'massive structural shortage' which is all too often overlooked (seemingly including by the FADA[722]) and it is the existence of any counselling service that is the exception, rather than the gap.[723] How this affects the evaluation of whether Germany has properly implemented the obligation to establish an Equality Body that provides independent assistance to victims of discrimination will be further discussed below.

In terms of independence and accessibility, it can be concluded that the FADA appears to fall short of ECRI's recommendations. Not only is the institution embedded in the executive, the executive is also exclusively responsible for the appointment of the head of the Equality Body and the procedure for the appointment is far from being transparent and inclusive. Although some legal safeguards still make it possible for the body to function independently, the procedure leading to the appointment of the head of the FADA at least should be reviewed. While the budgetary allocations appear to be increasing, there have been no attempts at establishing regional offices. Notwithstanding the initiatives taken by the FADA to create a network of organizations providing information and assistance to victims of discrimination throughout the country, it remains that this offer continues to

719 See the respective information on both initiatives on the FADA webpage at http://www.antidiskriminierungsstelle.de/DE/ThemenUndForschung/Projekte/Foerderung_von_Antidiskriminierungsarbeit/netzwerk_node.html.

720 Interview, staff member, Research and General Affairs Department of FADA, 26 July 2018.

721 Berghahn, Klapp, and Tischbirek (n 52) 174–76.

722 In an interview with a representative from the FADA, the representative held the view that the offer is out there and it remains within the responsibility of the persons who feel discriminated against to make use of it. At another point in the interview he said he is not sure whether the offer is sufficient, but in any case it is extensive. Interview, staff member, Research and General Affairs Department of FADA, 26 July 2018.

723 Daniel Bartel, 'Keynote: Vom Flickenteppich zur Infrastruktur – Antidiskriminierungsberatung in Deutschland weiterdenken' in Antidiskriminierungsstelle des Bundes (ed), 'Mit Rat zur Tat. Perspektiven der Antidiskriminierungsberatung in Deutschland. Dokumentation der Fachtagung im Umweltforum' (2017), 16. See also Antidiskriminierungsstelle des Bundes, 'Bericht des Themenforums Antidiskriminierung im Rahmen des Nationalen Aktionsplans Integration/ Einhellige Forderung nach Ausbau von Beratungsangeboten gegen Diskriminierung' (9 March 2021) <https://www.antidiskriminierungsstelle.de/SharedDocs/pressemitteilungen/DE/2021/20210309_Integrationsgipfel_NAP_I.html>.

be underdeveloped, which limits its accessibility and is already a first point of concern when it comes to evaluating the effective carrying out of tasks assigned to the Equality Body.

These tasks are regulated by § 27 of the Equal Treatment Act. Any person who believes that he/she has been discriminated against on the grounds of race or ethnic origin, gender, religion or belief, disability, age or sexual orientation can address the FADA which shall give independent assistance which may, in particular, involve 1) providing information on legal provisions and possible legal actions concerning their case, 2) referring to other authorities for advice, and/or 3) trying to achieve an out-of-court settlement between the parties. The Equality Body is thus not in a position to represent a complainant in court, or to bring cases in its own name, or to intervene as third party or *amicus curiae* in court proceedings. Furthermore, trying to achieve an out-of-court settlement cannot be considered as having the power to decide on complaints in a non-binding way.[724] The German government has therefore, like in the case of engagement of civil society organizations in administrative and judicial proceedings, opted for the minimal variant among possible options of transposition.

In addition to providing independent advice to victims of discrimination, the FADA is tasked with carrying out public relations activities, taking measures to prevent discrimination on any of the grounds referred to in § 1, and undertaking research into such discrimination.[725] Such research regularly contains recommendations to various stakeholders, so that—although not explicitly mentioned in the law—the activities mentioned cover the requirements of the RED. In the following, the focus will be on its assistance to victims of discrimination.

When it comes to providing independent assistance to victims of discrimination, the wording of § 27 referred to above ('in particular') could be interpreted as implying that the practice of the FADA can go beyond the listed activities. This could in theory include supporting victims of discrimination in court cases, at least in the limited way it is done by NGOs. However, such an extension has so far not been developed in practice.[726] With regard to the activities enumerated in the Act, it can be deduced from the materials of GETA that the intention of the first element (providing information on legal provisions and possible legal actions concerning their case) was only to provide general information, whereas a more targeted consultation related to the individual case is supposed to be offered by the 'authority' mentioned by the second element listed in § 27 (referring to other authorities for advice). This situation has led some to see the consultation activity of the FADA rather critically and to conclude that real consultation does actually not

[724] According to the information provided on the Equinet members' page, the FADA does have this competence.
[725] German Equal Treatment Act, § 27(3).
[726] Berghahn, Klapp, and Tischbirek (n 52) 185.

take place.[727] Considering the above described lack of coverage of the whole territory with organizations to which the FADA could refer for the provision of focused advise on the individual case, it is all the more problematic that the FADA has only the competence to give general advice. In this context it remains in doubt whether the practical implementation of the Equal Treatment Act achieves the intended effect of the legislator and thus complies with the requirements of the Directive. It is the prerogative of the legislator to make an initial assessment as to how the goal can be achieved. If it turns out, however, as seems to be the case, that the measures adopted do not suffice to reach the goal, the legislator would be required to make the necessary adaptations.[728]

§ 27(2) GETA provides in the last sentence for a specific kind of referral. It stipulates that '[w]here responsibility lies either with a Parliamentary Commissioner of the German *Bundestag* or a Federal Government Commissioner, the Federal Anti-Discrimination Agency shall immediately pass on the matters of the person referred to in Subsection (1), with their prior approval'. This applies for instance to the Federal Government Commissioner for Matters relating to Persons with Disabilities. However, providing advice to individuals is not within the mandate of the Commissioner.[729]

The last element provided by law when providing independent assistance to victims of discrimination consists in the Equality Body trying to achieve an out-of-court settlement between the parties. While, for some, this task is potentially conflicting with the requirement of independence, most commentators understand the role of the FADA in this context as one of a neutral moderator. Furthermore, whether such out-of-court settlement takes place does not depend on the FADA's decision but rather on the will and interest of the parties concerned.[730] It has been questioned however, to what extent such a role of the Equality Body can be seen as effective support to victims of discrimination, especially against the background that the FADA has no mandate to carry out targeted consultation relating to the individual case but only to provide general information. Furthermore, the competence to achieve out-of-court settlements is hampered by the fact that the FADA, under § 28(1) GETA, can ask the respondent for a statement, but if the respondent is a private actor he/she is under no obligation to reply to the request (as will be seen below, there is such an obligation if the respondent is a federal authority or public office). Furthermore, the FADA is not equipped with a competence to take the case a step further, in case no out-of-court settlement can be reached. It cannot, for

[727] ibid 185–86.

[728] ibid 186–87.

[729] According to the information provided on the website of the Commissioner, he/she is not in the position to evaluate individual cases or to offer legal advice. This is reserved for lawyers and advisory organizations. https://www.behindertenbeauftragter.de/DE/DerBeauftragte/DieAufgabe/Aufgabe_node.html.

[730] Berghahn, Klapp, and Tischbirek (n 52) 187, with further references.

instance, approach a tribunal-type Equality Body (as is possible in Austria, for instance, where the Ombud for Equal Treatment can approach the Equal Treatment Commission) or the court (as can be done by Unia in the Belgian case). In such circumstances it is even possible that victims of discrimination may see no other option but to agree to an out-of-court settlement.[731]

In 2019, the Antidiscrimination Agency received 3,580 requests for advice.[732] Reportedly only a handful of such requests for advice ended in an out-of-court settlement. However, the exact number is not known because the parties do not necessarily inform the FADA about the developments of the case.[733] This shows first, that there does not appear to be systematic data collection about such cases and even more importantly, that, even in the absence of precise data in this respect, the number of out-of-court settlements appears to be extremely low.[734] As already mentioned, the investigatory powers of the FADA are very restricted as it can only request a statement from the alleged perpetrator, who has no legal obligation to submit such a statement to the Agency. This is different for federal authorities and public offices which are obliged, under § 28(2) GETA, to assist the FADA in carrying out its tasks, 'in particular to supply the necessary information' while respecting provisions concerning data protection. It is not clear whether this implies the right to access records.[735]

Overall, the conclusion must be drawn that the mandate of providing independent assistance to victims of discrimination in pursuing their complaints of discrimination has been weakly transposed into national legislation and practice shows that its effects are very limited, also considering the fact that the limited support provided by the Agency is not absorbed by a country-wide network of support organizations set up either by the *Länder* or municipalities, or by civil society organizations. As one judge put it, the work of the FADA in terms of law enforcement is not noticeable.[736] Therefore, it might be legitimately questioned whether this part of Article 15 RED, albeit its legally correct (even if minimal) transposition, is in practice in line with the Directive.

Against this background and notwithstanding the legal compliance with the requirements from the RED, the following proposals for strengthening the

[731] ibid 187–88.

[732] Antidiskriminierungsstelle des Bundes, 'Jahresbericht 2019' (2020) 43. Comparing this figure, coming from a country with a population of more than 80 million, with the more than 8,400 reports received by Unia in a country with a population of just over 11 million is striking. Even taking into account that Unia, in addition to the grounds covered by EU legislation—except for gender, also covers the grounds of political orientation, social status, health condition, wealth, and civil status, cannot explain this discrepancy.

[733] Interview, staff member, Research and General Affairs Department of FADA, 26 July 2018.

[734] Again as a comparison: Unia manages to achieve an extra-judicial solution in about 400 cases yearly.

[735] Berghahn, Klapp, and Tischbirek (n 52) 191.

[736] ibid 195.

independence and the effectiveness of the task to provide assistance to victims of discrimination can be made:

To strengthen the independence and democratic legitimation of the FADA, the Agency should be transformed into an independent federal agency, detached from any ministry. For the same reasons, the head of the Agency should be appointed after a public call for applications. A pre-selection should be based on the qualification of candidates and their professional achievements in the field of promotion of equality and prevention of discrimination. The final appointment should be made by the parliament.[737]

The task of providing independent assistance to victims of discrimination should be strengthened to include at least the provision of in-depth individual assistance in concrete individual cases, beyond the currently given general information about the legal situation and possible redress. Such targeted consultation should ideally be offered and carried out locally, while the central office in Berlin could keep the role of providing general information and coordination. Competences should further be enlarged to include the ability to support victims in court proceedings, at least by acting as counsel, but preferably by bringing claims on behalf of the victims, submitting *amicus curiae* briefs, or bringing an action in its own name.[738] A right to support victims in the courts has been claimed by the FADA itself, making reference to the Commission's Recommendations on Standards for Equality Bodies which, in the FADA's interpretation, 'have made it clear, that an institution like the Antidiscrimination Agency requires more effective tools, in order to efficiently act against systematic and structural discrimination'.[739] In the same statement, the FADA suggested that it could be provided with the power to take binding decisions in individual or collective complaint cases combined with the power to impose sanctions. Whatever the substantive offer provided by the FADA is, it is of utmost importance to strengthen the regional and local presence of counselling offices, either in the form of regional branches or an enhanced and appropriately funded network of offices run by the *Länder*, municipalities and/or civil society organizations.[740]

5.4.4 Good Practices and Challenges

Although these case studies are obviously only a fraction of the variety of solutions present in the different EU countries, nevertheless they highlight some important

[737] ibid 176–77 and 184; Büro zur Umsetzung von Gleichbehandlung e.V. 'Dossier zum Thema Vorschläge zur Stärkung des Antidiskriminierungsrechts' (2017), 30.

[738] Berghahn, Klapp, and Tischbirek (n 52) 191; Büro zur Umsetzung von Gleichbehandlung e.V. 'Dossier zum Thema Vorschläge zur Stärkung des Antidiskriminierungsrechts' (n 738) 31.

[739] FADA, Bundesregierung sollte EU-Empfehlung zu Gleichbehandlungsstellen rasch umsetzen, statement of 3 July 2018, at https://www.antidiskriminierungsstelle.de/SharedDocs/Aktuelles/DE/2018/20180703_EU-Standard_Gleichbehandlungsstellen.html (own translation). See also Antidiskriminier ungsstelle des Bundes, 'Gegen Rassismus, für Gleichbehandlung: Vorschläge der Antidiskriminier ungsstelle des Bundes zur Stärkung des Schutzes vor Diskriminierung in Deutschland' (August 2020).

[740] Berghahn, Klapp, and Tischbirek (n 52) 184 and 198.

findings. The first is related to the observation that a minimalist transposition like the one chosen by Germany is not able to achieve the objective of providing effective (in addition to independent) assistance to victims of discrimination in pursuing their complaints. This is particularly so because the chosen legal framework did not provide for the conditions which would have made it possible to set up, over the years, a country-wide network of institutions covering all the protected grounds, contributing to what appears to be one of the objectives of the Directive: a more effective level of protection for victims of discrimination. While this objective is explicitly laid down in the recital of the RED referring to support by NGOs, it has to be taken into consideration also in the evaluation of the effectiveness of services provided by the Equality Body in a situation in which the two systems (support by NGOs on one hand and support by the Equality Body on the other) are so much intertwined as is the case in Germany, which vests the Equality Body only with general advisory competence, with the provision of more targeted advice being referred to NGOs. The German solution is further unsatisfactory as the Equality Body is given no rights at all to engage in court proceedings. The only way by which the Equality Body can thus assist 'victims of discrimination in pursuing their complaints' is by referring them to the patchy network of NGOs or a lawyer.

A second finding from the case studies is that even in cases where the Equality Body is equipped with more competences and appears to be also sufficiently funded and staffed, as is the case of the IHREC, it can still not be taken for granted that the body forcefully makes use of its competences. It appears that in such a case it remains fully within the responsibility of the Equality Body to develop into a dynamic body confidently carrying out its task to assist victims of discrimination. In the Irish case there remain doubts, however, whether the cautious use of competences could be ascribed to what has been called 'negative learning' from the past, where a very outspoken body has been tamed by sweeping budget cuts. Although this might just be speculation, it nevertheless highlights, once more, the importance of stable financing of the Equality Body.

A third finding can be derived from the Belgian case study. It first of all confirmed that stable financing, adequate staffing, and independence of the Equality Body are *conditio sine qua non* for effective functioning. It also showed the impact an Equality Body can have if it is vested with a broad range of competences which can be used depending on what it finds to be the most appropriate in the particular circumstance. The ability for the Equality Body to escalate the case from trying to achieve a negotiated solution (including forward-looking recommendations, trying to address the root cause of the discrimination) to initiatng a court case has proven to be a successful tool in the assistance of victims of discrimination. By litigating cases or supporting victims in the courts, sometimes even as far as the CJEU, Unia has shown that Equality Bodies have great potential not only in providing assistance to individual victims but also in addressing structural discrimination and contributing to the clarification of law.

The importance of an Equality Body having strong competences has also been highlighted in a recent study looking into what makes National Human Rights Institutions effective. The study found that bodies with a strong complaints-handling mandate gained considerable publicity and visibility which increased the number of complaints and eventually led also to an increase in budget. Government attempts to capture the body were met with street protests. On the other hand, institutions with narrow powers in this field received only few complaints and were perceived as inefficient which was then used as an argument by the government to cut funds.[741] ECRI's approach when it comes to the support and litigation function appears to be to vest Equality Bodies with all the above-mentioned possibilities, ranging from complaints-handling, to mediation and legal standing in court procedures. The Commission's approach, on the other hand, is simply to invite countries to take all these possibilities into consideration, leaving it to the state to pick and choose. While this is understandable from the point of view of the need to remain within the wording of the Directive, it could have based its recommendations on the experience collected in fifteen years' implementation of the Directives and the finding that a very limited legal transposition does not lead to the desired objective: effective assistance to victims of discrimination. While the Commission has highlighted the importance of litigation undertaken or supported by Equality Bodies in its implementation report,[742] it remains to be seen whether and how this translates into new legislation strengthening the role of Equality Bodies in providing independent assistance to victims of discrimination.

5.4.5 Proposed Indicators

A study on Equality Bodies carried out as early as 2006 concluded that 'it would seem most desirable to have more specific guidelines on the issue of effectiveness … [and] that a common format for the evaluation of the actual carrying out of the core competencies of the Directives be agreed within the European Community'.[743] While the Commission has partly responded to this desideratum more than ten years later with its Recommendation on Standards for Equality Bodies, this document cannot be considered as providing a 'common format for evaluation'. Rather, it enumerates possibilities for how the core competences can be transposed. In the following, therefore, a proposal will be offered on what evaluation, making use of indicators, could look like.

[741] Katerina Linos and Tom Pegram, 'What Works in Human Rights Institutions?' (2017) 112(3) American Journal of International Law 1, 55–56.

[742] European Commission, 'Equality bodies and the implementation of the Commission Recommendation on Standards for Equality Bodies' (n 1) 7–10.

[743] Holtmaat (n 67) 57.

From the above it is clear that in the case of assistance provided by predominantly promotion-type Equality Bodies to victims of discrimination in pursuing their complaints, the *structural indicator* providing information about the legally foreseen competences in this field is of course crucial. As mentioned above, the competences ideally include all possible measures, ranging from complaints handling, to mediation or conciliation and rights in front of courts, so that the body itself can choose the most appropriate way to address a particular problem. It is clear that such a mandate requires sufficient human and financial resources to be workable. A state may therefore decide to grant just some of these competences. If an evaluation of the impact of these competences on the objective to provide effective assistance to victims of discrimination shows that this objective cannot be reached, a state would be required to amend the legislative provisions concerning the competences of the Equality Body in this field. Such evaluation would need to be carried out in cooperation with the Equality Body including all relevant stakeholders and duly respect the independence of the Equality Body (*process indicator*). As independent assistance needs to be provided to victims of discrimination throughout the country, another structural indicator would need to look into how this national coverage is secured.

At the level of *process indicators*, the monitoring of state compliance would need to differentiate between an evaluation of the efforts that can be expected to be undertaken by the state in order for the Equality Body to be able to work effectively and efforts of the body itself to fulfil its mandate, and would need to focus on the former. This requires first of all, as just mentioned above, the evaluation of the appropriateness of the competences granted by legislation. It further requires asking whether the Equality Body makes use of all its competences, including its litigation competences, and if not, whether the reasons for lack of use are attributable to the state or the Equality Body itself. Reasons attributable to the state would include of course lack of funding or insufficient staffing, but also more or less open pressure exerted by public authorities or political parties to disengage in a particular form of support. Reasons attributable to the Equality Body could be related to a decision that it is not appropriate for the Equality Body to carry out mediation considering the risk of a perceived lack of neutrality. A particular focus on one competence could be explained by the finding that the exercise of this competence has been shown to have the greatest impact in the past. Explanations for a lack of use of particular competences which at first sight appear to be attributable to the body itself, need to be interpreted also in light of the overall importance and significance given to the issue of equality and non-discrimination in the public discourse and in the context of the history of the institution. While it would be impossible to construe an infringement case in such circumstances, it should nevertheless be taken note of in the monitoring and addressed to the state concerned.

Similarly, consideration should be given to whether all protected grounds are adequately covered by the assistance provided by the Equality Body. Here again, the reason to litigate more cases related to one particular ground might be a decision of the Equality Body well founded in the objective criteria according to which it decides which cases to support. It could, however, also be grounded in the fact that a particular ground is perceived to be more sensitive than another and in order not to displease the government such cases are not taken up for representation in courts. While it might be difficult to get a clear-cut reply to a question addressing this issue from Equality Body, let alone, state representatives, it would be necessary to compare the figures about the prevalence of a the various discrimination grounds among the requests addressed to the Equality Body with the figures on the numbers of cases in which the Equality Bodies provided assistance to victims of discrimination on these grounds. Ideally there should also be data about the perceived levels of discrimination on various grounds, that could be taken as a basis for deciding which cases to take to court. While the FRA does, at intervals, survey discrimination related to race and ethnic origin and sexual orientation, more efforts from states, including their Equality Bodies need to be invested in this field. Such data are required not only to design a litigation strategy for Equality Bodies (and possibly also NGOs) but also, more generally for the design of promotional and preventive measures.

The existence of a litigation strategy and the level at which the Equality Body engages with NGOs and other stakeholders in this context are indicators that could be taken into consideration when evaluating whether an Equality Body is making efficient use of its competences. A complaints-handling body should also follow up on its recommendations. This latter point, however, appeared to be very much related to the question of human and financial resources and is thus, again a factor that is attributable to the state.

Two other areas where the state authorities and the Equality Body share responsibility concern the level of accessibility and awareness. Regarding the former, questions to be addressed are whether there are enough regional offices, whether the Equality Body can be approached in minority languages, and whether measures are taken to make sure their services are accessible to persons with a disability. While the Equality Body has the responsibility to take all these aspects into account, it will be in a position to do so only to the extent it is provided with the required human and financial resources. Finally, it is a shared responsibility of the Equality Body and the state to make sure that the information of the existence and kind of assistance offered by the Equality Body is provided to rights holders.

This brings us to the proposed *outcome indicators*. An indicator of the effective carrying out of the function of providing independent assistance to victims of discrimination is the perception among those concerned that this assistance is available throughout the country, is accessible, and if a high percentage of those concerned express satisfaction at how the Equality Body displays this function.[744] Related to

[744] ibid 50–51.

this, increasing levels of awareness about the Equality Body and levels of trust in the body, that might also find expression in an improved reporting behaviour, indicate that the body is providing effective assistance to victims of discrimination.

A further indicator is related to the level of satisfaction within the Equality Body itself with regard to the number of victims approaching it and the number of victims that it could assist. If this level of satisfaction is low, it would need to be asked why the body believes that this is so. This can be related to the appropriateness of competences or of the funding provided. Other explanations might contribute to reconsidering the design chosen for this field of activity. All these indicators are summarized in Table 5.4.

Table 5.4 Table of indicators concerning the effectiveness of predominantly promotion-type Equality Bodies in carrying out the function of providing independent assistance to victims of discrimination in pursuing their complaints

Effective functioning	Structural indicators	• Which powers does Equality Body have to support victims of discrimination (complaints handling, mediation/conciliation, litigation)? • Some form of territorial coverage provided for?
	Process indicators	• Has appropriateness of powers been evaluated and, if necessary, have they been adapted accordingly? • Are powers granted by legislation used and if not, how can this be explained? (reasons to be attributed to state or Equality Body?) • Are all the protected grounds adequately covered and if not, what are the reasons? • Is there any follow-up to decisions of the Equality Body? • Are there enough regional offices, can Equality Bodies be approached in minority languages, and have measures been taken to make sure their services are accessible to persons with disability? • Do rights holders know that there is an Equality Body and that they can turn to it for assistance?
	Outcome indicators	• Adequate territorial coverage of support and support perceived as accessible • Level of satisfaction among victims of discrimination • Level of awareness about the Equality Body increasing • Level of trust in the Equality Body increasing • Reporting behaviour improving • Level of satisfaction within the Equality Body with regard to the number of victims approaching it and the number of victims that it could assist. What are the reasons if it is low? • Compliance with the Equality Body's recommendations

6
Promotion of Equality and Prevention of Discrimination

While litigating discrimination cases definitely has its merits and, if pursued strategically, has the potential to generate an impact beyond the individual case, it also has its limitations. Sometimes it is felt that the attempt to influence prejudicial attitudes by imposing sanctions on discriminatory behaviour is less effective than taking measures that would challenge these attitudes, for instance awareness raising, dialogue, or education and training. In part this is because sanctions are not considered to be dissuasive enough, they would not be able to change discriminatory attitudes and because, depending on the kind of sanction, they would simply address an individual incident but 'could not redress discrimination against entire groups'.[1]

It is therefore not enough to focus only on dispute settlement procedures (either before ordinary courts or before Equality Bodies) but any attempt to address discrimination must be combined with efforts to prevent discrimination from happening in the first place and promoting equality. The Fundamental Rights Agency (FRA) underlined in this context that '[w]here the difficulties faced by particular minorities relate to a number of interlocking social and economic factors, litigation alone may not provide an adequate solution'.[2] The FRA's analysis particularly emphasized that the lower levels of enjoyment of equality for instance, in the fields of employment, education, or housing are often not caused by direct discrimination. For instance, the fact that minority candidates lack adequate qualifications may constitute a legitimate reason to prefer a majority candidate over the minority candidate, but this may result in the effective exclusion of certain groups who show a lower level of education from certain areas of employment. In such cases, structural disadvantages prevent individuals from attaining adequate qualifications which in turn has an impact on their employment situation which affects their wages, access to housing, and health care. The FRA thus concludes that the 'interlocking nature of discrimination in the area of health, education, housing and employment reveals the need for holistic policies to improve the socio-economic position facing many members of minorities'.[3]

[1] Fundamental Rights Agency, 'The Racial Equality Directive: application and challenges' (2011), 21–22. <http://fra.europa.eu/sites/default/files/fra_uploads/1916-FRA-RED-synthesis-report_EN.pdf>
[2] ibid 22.
[3] ibid 22–23.

Reflexive Governance in EU Equality Law. Emma Lantschner, Oxford University Press. © Emma Lantschner 2021.
DOI: 10.1093/oso/9780192843371.003.0007

This is where positive action comes in. Both Directives allow, but do not oblige,[4] Member States to maintain or adopt 'specific measures to prevent or compensate for disadvantages linked to' any of the grounds referred to in the Directives.[5] Marko, by reference to Council recommendation of 13 December 1984 on the promotion of positive action for women (Recommendation 84/635/EEC) and to the *Oršuš* judgment of the European Court of Human Rights (ECtHR), has identified three different stages of positive action: first, information and awareness raising; second, group-specific training and education as well as other supportive measures; and third, quota, favouring the underrepresented group.[6] For reasons of space, the second and third kind of positive action measures are not dealt with in the present research, although they are understood to be of utmost importance for the promotion of equality and the prevention of discrimination.[7] It should be added that the FRA has concluded that positive action measures could have several advantages, namely to address disadvantages experienced by a group as a whole and, due to their preventive power, to supersede the need for litigation, even though 'these initiatives require long-term commitment for their results to have an impact on the ground'.[8] It also found that while good practice examples of adopting holistic policies exist, a major obstacle for such proactive policies is the lack of disaggregated data.[9] An Equinet-sponsored paper identified 'a lack of understanding

[4] Bruno de Witte, 'From a 'Common Principle of Equality' to 'European Antidiscrimination Law'' (2010) 53(12) American Behavioral Scientist 1715.

[5] Art 5 RED, Art 7 EED.

[6] Joseph Marko, 'Against discrimination: The right to equality and the dilemma of difference' in Joseph Marko (ed), Human and Minority Rights Protection by Multiple Diversity Governance: History, Law, Ideology and Politics in European Perspective (Routledge, 2019), 323, 327–30. For a different typology see Dagmar Schiek, Lisa Waddington, and Mark Bell (eds), *Cases, Materials and Text on National, Supranational and International Non-Discrimination Law* (Hart Publishing 2007) 762.

[7] For discussions of the concept of positive action and its application, partly with a focus on women where the debate about such measures started first, see for instance Anne Peters, 'The Many Meanings of Equality and Positive Action in Favour of Women under European Community Law—A Conceptual Analysis' (1996) 2(2) European Law Journal 177; Catherine Barnard and Tamara Hervey, 'Softening the Approach to Quotas: Positive Action After Marschall' (1998) 20(3) Journal of Social Welfare and Family Law 333; Daniela Caruso, 'Limits of the Classic Method: Positive Action in the European Union After the New Equality Directives' (2002) Jean Monnet Working Paper 10/02; Noreen Burrows and Muriel Robison, 'Positive Action for Women in Employment: Time to Align with Europe?' (2006) 33(1) Journal of Law and Society 24; Marc de Vos, 'Beyond Formal Equality: Positive Action under Directives 2000/43/EC and 2000/78/EC' (European Network of Legal Experts in the Non-discrimination Field, 2007); Kristin Henrard, 'Equal Rights versus Special Rights? Minority Protection and the Prohibition of Discrimination' (European Network of Legal Experts in the Non-discrimination Field, 2007); European Commission, 'International Perspectives on Positive Action Measures: A Comparative Analysis in the European Union, Canada, the United States and South Africa' (2009); Lizzie Barmes, 'Equality Law and Experimentation: The Positive Action Challenge' (2009) 68(3) Cambridge Law Journal 623; Equinet, 'Positive Action Measures. The Experience of Equality Bodies' (2014); Niall Crowley, 'Making Europe More Equal: A Legal Duty?' (Equinet 2016).

[8] Fundamental Rights Agency, 'The Racial Equality Directive: application and challenges' (n 1) 24.

[9] In July 2017, the European Commission presented a series of studies analysing 'why and what kind of data should be collected in relation to equality and discrimination'. See http://ec.europa.eu/newsroom/just/item-detail.cfm?item_id=112035. They complement the previous study by Timo Makkonen, *European Handbook on Equality Data. 2016 Revision* (European Commission 2016). A subgroup of the EU High Level Group on Non-Discrimination, Diversity and Equality has developed 'Guidelines on improving the collection and use of equality data', a 'Compendium of Practices on Equality Data' as well as a 'Diagnostic mapping tool'; see https://fra.europa.eu/en/themes/equality-non-discrimination-and-racism/about-compendium.

of the range of positive action among key institutions in the public and private sectors' and called for 'European level guidance and promotion'.[10]

This chapter's main focus is on the role played by the state authorities, national Equality Bodies, as well as social partners and non-governmental organizations (NGOs), regarding the dissemination of information and awareness raising on national legislation adopted in pursuance of the Directives or already in place. From a legal point of view, the main burden in this context is on the state (see Art 10 RED and Art 12 EED), while Equality Bodies and NGOs only play a complementary role. As will be shown below, in practice the opposite is the case. It is understood, that awareness raising (including training) does not only have a preventive and promotional function but is also a precondition in order to appropriately react to instances of discrimination once they have occurred. This aspect can thus be described as cutting across reaction on one hand and prevention of discrimination and promotion of equality on the other.

More clearly of a preventive and promotional nature is the advisory role of Equality Bodies that is assigned to them on the basis of Article 13 RED in addition to their function to independently assist victims of discrimination in pursuing their complaints. This aspect is discussed at 6.2, in addition to the awareness raising carried out by Equality Bodies. Finally, including the encouragement to the state and NGOs with a legitimate interest in combatting discrimination (Art 11 RED, Art 13 EED) to enter into a dialogue was motivated by the expectation that this would not only contribute to awareness raising but also have positive effects on the effectiveness of national polities[11] and thus also on the prevention of discrimination. Their involvement in law and policy making will be discussed at 6.3.

Before looking at each of the three actors separately and their preventive and promotional functions, the chapter starts by expanding a little on the reactive and preventive function of awareness raising and introducing some data which give a picture on the current state of affairs regarding both these aspects.

Being aware of existing rights and mechanisms on how to invoke them in case of violation is essential in terms of reacting to discrimination. If a victim of discrimination is unaware that a certain behaviour constitutes discrimination or of organizations offering support or advice, perpetrators cannot be brought to justice and their behaviour becomes more easily socially accepted. Rights awareness is thus intimately linked to the reporting behaviour of victims of discrimination and both have been identified as being among the factors hampering more effective application and enforcement of the Directives.

In its most recent Minorities and Discrimination Survey (EU-MIDIS) the FRA found that 88 per cent of respondents who have experienced discrimination in the

[10] Niall Crowley, 'Taking Stock. A perspective from the work of equality bodies on: European equality strategies, equal treatment directives, and standards for equality bodies' (Equinet, 2020), 21.

[11] Adam Tyson, 'The Negotiation of the European Community Directive on Racial Discrimination' (2001) 3(2) European Journal of Migration and Law 199, 216.

past twelve months have not reported about it. Compared to the 82 per cent in the 2009 survey, this shows that efforts to increase reporting rates have so far not been successful at all and need to be improved.[12] FRA's 2020 LGBTI survey revealed that even 89 per cent of respondents (90 per cent in 2014) did not report about the most recent incident.[13] Of these, 15 per cent indicated that they did not know how and where to report such incidents, which is quite an improvement compared to the 30 per cent who indicated this reason in 2014.[14] The EU-MIDIS survey asked separately whether respondents were aware of a law that forbids discrimination based on skin colour, ethnic origin, or religion. Although an average of 67 per cent of all respondents responded that there is such a law[15] there were great variations among groups and countries. The lowest level of awareness was found amongst Roma (36 per cent), with only 13 per cent of Roma respondents in Portugal compared to over 50 per cent of Roma respondents in the Czech Republic, Slovakia, and Croatia.[16] Eurobarometer data are less positive as they suggest that 45 per cent of respondents 'would know their rights should they fall victim to discrimination or harassment'.[17] According to the 2014 LGBT survey carried out by the FRA, 56 per cent of respondents are aware of a law that prohibits discrimination on the basis of sexual orientation when applying for a job.[18]

While the average figure regarding awareness of anti-discrimination legislation, especially of the EU-MIDIS survey, might appear relatively high, the picture looks different when looking at the level of awareness of organizations supporting or advising victims of discrimination, or about the designated Equality Body. According to EU-MIDIS data, 38 per cent of all respondents are aware of an Equality Body, with the lowest level of awareness in Spain with only 6 per cent and the highest level of awareness in Ireland with 67 per cent of all respondents stating that they had heard of the Equality Body when given its name.[19] Only an average of 27 per cent of respondents indicated that they knew about an organization that offers support or advice to victims of discrimination. In this case, recent immigrants from

[12] Fundamental Rights Agency, 'EU-MIDIS II: Main results' (2017) 15 and 42.

[13] Fundamental Rights Agency, 'EU-LGBTI II. A long way to go for LGBTI equality' (2020), 35–36; Fundamental Rights Agency, 'EU LGBT survey. European Union lesbian, gay, bisexual and transgender survey: Main results' (2014), 47.

[14] Fundamental Rights Agency, 'EU-LGBTI II. A long way to go for LGBTI equality' (n 13) 37; Fundamental Rights Agency, 'EU LGBT survey. European Union lesbian, gay, bisexual and transgender survey: Main results' (n 13) 49.

[15] Knowing that there exists a law prohibiting discrimination does not necessarily mean, however, that a person is knowledgeable about the details of the law, the situations in which discrimination is prohibited, and the possible means of redress.

[16] Fundamental Rights Agency, 'EU-MIDIS II: Main results' (n 12) 55.

[17] European Commission, 'Special Eurobarometer 437. Discrimination in the EU in 2015' (2015) 72.

[18] Fundamental Rights Agency, 'EU LGBT survey. European Union lesbian, gay, bisexual and transgender survey: Main results' (n 13) 42.

[19] Fundamental Rights Agency, 'EU-MIDIS II: Main results' (n 12) 52–54. 61 per cent of all respondents to the 2020 LGBTI survey have heard of at least one Equality Body in their country. Fundamental Rights Agency, 'EU-LGBTI II. A long way to go for LGBTI equality' (n 13) 35.

non-EU countries showed a lower level of awareness (12 per cent) than Roma (15 per cent).[20] If persons who have experienced discrimination do not know where to turn for advice and assistance, it is unlikely that an incident will be reported, even if they know there is a law that prohibits discrimination.

Apart from the rights holders, the wording of the dissemination provision in Article 10 RED and Article 12 EED of the Directives, in addressing the 'persons concerned', includes also the duty bearers, including employers, service providers, and civil servants, as well as those responsible for providing access to justice to victims of discrimination. This involves judges, prosecutors, lawyers, and the police. Including police in awareness-raising activities is particularly important considering that according to Eurobarometer data, 35 per cent of respondents stated that 'if they were the victim of discrimination or harassment, ... they would prefer to report their case to the police'.[21] Awareness of existing non-discrimination legislation among duty bearers is essential in order to be able to devise a company's diversity plan, for instance, to adequately train human resources and other personnel, and to make service providers and persons working in an educational environment or healthcare sensitive to potential instances of discrimination. Information, awareness raising, and training therefore have an eminently preventive function.

Whose task is it then to provide both rights holders and duty bearers with information about the relevant provisions contained in national legislation regarding the right to equality and the protection from discrimination? The Directives assign this responsibility in the first place to the Member States. In the second place it also assigns some responsibility to the designated Equality Bodies in the framework of their promotion of equal treatment. However, it needs to be kept in mind that as long as the horizontal Directive is not passed, Member States are obliged to establish such bodies only under the RED but not under the EED. The fact that most countries have established Equality Bodies which also cover the grounds under the EED (or going even beyond those grounds) is fortunate, but highlights that the primary responsibility to disseminate information and raise awareness remains with the state authorities. With a view to promoting the principle of equal treatment, Member States are encouraged to further keep a dialogue with social partners and NGOs which can lead to a situation of cooperation between state and NGOs or social partners when it comes to awareness-raising activities.

In the following sections these three actors will be looked at separately so that we may understand how the provisions of the Directives regarding awareness raising have been legally transposed and how they play out in practice. In addition to the awareness-raising activities, the section 6.2 dealing with Equality Bodies will look at

[20] Fundamental Rights Agency, 'EU-MIDIS II: Main results' (n 12) 50–51. Compare: 66 per cent of the LGBTI survey are aware of such an organization.

[21] European Commission, 'Special Eurobarometer 493. Discrimination in the European Union' (2019) 158.

the other preventive and promotional functions of these bodies, which can essentially be summarized as an advisory function. The section 6.3 dealing with NGOs (and social partners) will in addition focus on the extent to which they are involved in law and policy making with a view to promoting the principle of equal treatment.

6.1 The States' Responsibility to Disseminate Information and Raise Awareness

6.1.1 Introduction and Conceptual Clarification

According to Article 10 RED and Article 12 EED, Member States are expected to disseminate information about provisions adopted pursuant to the Directives or already existing relevant provisions to 'persons concerned by all appropriate means throughout their territory'. However, in its 2014 evaluation report on the application of RED and EED, the Commission clearly acknowledged a lack of awareness.[22] In this report, it reiterated the recommendation of the FRA to design targeted awareness-raising campaigns to persons who are most at risk, and focus also on 'those who are in a position to commit breaches', thereby addressing both rights holders and duty bearers.[23] The FRA more explicitly recommended that '[n]ational and local authorities should … substantially intensify awareness-raising activities', including Equality Bodies and NGOs which can operate as multipliers.[24] The Agency thus clearly indicated that the responsibility lies with the Member States, with Equality Bodies and NGOs playing only a complementary role. Again, in 2016, the FRA concluded that 'EU Member States should fully implement Article 10 of Directive 2000/43/EC'.[25] Based on the above survey results, the FRA repeated this recommendation in its 2017 final report on the EU-MIDIS study in several instances.[26] It thereby underlines on one hand the fact that a continued lack of awareness is considerably hindering an efficient implementation of the Directives and on the other hand that Member States are still not live up to their legal

[22] European Commission, 'Joint Report on the application of Council Directive 2000/43/EC of 29 June 2000 implementing the principle of equal treatment between persons irrespective of racial or ethnic origin ("Racial Equality Directive") and of Council Directive 2000/78/EC of 27 November 2000 establishing a general framework for equal treatment in employment and occupation ("Employment Equality Directive")' (Brussels 17 January 2014) COM(2014) 2 final, 4–5.

[23] ibid 5; and Fundamental Rights Agency, 'Opinion of the European Union Agency for Fundamental Rights on the situation of equality in the European Union 10 years on from initial implementation of the equality directives' (2013) 1/2013, 3.

[24] Fundamental Rights Agency, 'Opinion of the European Union Agency for Fundamental Rights on the situation of equality in the European Union 10 years on from initial implementation of the equality directives' (n 23) 3.

[25] Fundamental Rights Agency, 'EU-MIDIS II: Roma—selected findings' (2016), 11.

[26] Fundamental Rights Agency, 'EU-MIDIS II: Main results' (n 12) 13–16, see in particular opinions 1, 3, and 4.

obligation as contained in Article 10 RED and Article 12 EED. In the 2021 report on the application of the two Directives the Commission found that awareness about legislation and Equality Bodies remains low. It then listed its own activities and campaigns to counter this problem but did not review in detail Member States' activities in this context. It concluded that continuing efforts at both national and EU levels are needed 'to raise awareness among the public at large and among those particularly at risk of discrimination, in particular about their rights and existing support mechanisms'.[27]

When looking at the drafting history of Article 10 RED it is clear that the Commission, in addition to the relevance of rights awareness for the reaction to discrimination, also had the preventive potential of dissemination in mind. In its commentary on individual articles, the Commission stated: 'The more effective the system of public information and prevention, the less need for individual remedies'.[28] Its initial proposal was more elaborate in that it added to the general requirement of ensuring adequate information, stating that this was particularly relevant 'in vocational training and educational bodies and in the workplace'. It further included a second paragraph according to which 'Member States shall ensure that competent public authorities are informed by appropriate means as regards all national measures taken pursuant to this Directive'.[29] During negotiations, some Member States felt that the level of detail infringed the principle of subsidiarity in that it prescribed how to achieve the objective of the Directive. They successfully called for the deletion of the second paragraph[30] and in the final version of RED, the reference to information on provisions transposing the Directive in vocational training and educational bodies and in the workplace was also dropped, while reference to the workplace was kept in Article 12 EED.

The motivation of Member States to have as much freedom as possible in implementing these provisions was presumably also the reason why amendments proposed by the European Parliament were not taken into consideration. The Committee on Employment and Social Affairs proposed to include a provision that the information provided to the persons concerned should be 'in understandable language, free from jargon, initials and abbreviations'.[31] It further proposed to add to the later deleted paragraph 2 'that training is provided on the provisions of the directive in all

[27] European Commission, 'Report on the application of Council Directive 2000/43/EC implementing the principle of equal treatment between persons irrespective of racial or ethnic origin ("the Racial Equality Directive") and of Council Directive 2000/78/EC establishing a general framework for equal treatment in employment and occupation ("the Employment Equality Directive")' (Brussels 19 March 2021) COM(2021) 139 final, 11–12 and 25.

[28] Commission of the European Communities, 'Proposal for a Council Directive implementing the principle of equal treatment between persons irrespective of racial or ethnic origin' (25 November 1999) COM(1999) 566 final, 9.

[29] ibid 18.

[30] Tyson (n 11) 214.

[31] European Parliament, 'Report on the proposal for a Council directive on implementing the principle of equal treatment between persons irrespective of racial or ethnic origin (COM(1999) 566—C5-0067/2000—1999/0253(CNS))' (16 May 2000) A5-0136/2000, 62.

public bodies, including those responsible for social protection and social security'.[32] The issue of providing training to all public authorities was also part of the proposal of the Starting Line Group[33] and would have highlighted the importance of bringing the provisions adopted pursuant to the Directives to the attention of those who could be in a position either to breach these provisions or to make sure that justice is brought to victims of discrimination. Not mentioning training in the provision explicitly is down to the effort of states to keep maximum leeway in implementation but does not take away the fact that a good faith implementation of these articles requires training activities. The part of the provisions requiring dissemination of information 'throughout their territory' has not raised further debate in the negotiations.

None of the infringement proceedings started by the Commission with regard to the implementation of the RED or EED concerned the Member States' obligation to disseminate information about the measures adopted pursuant to the Directives or already in place, or the lack of legislative entrenchment of this obligation. Considering the ever increasing relevance given to the lack of awareness by the FRA, the Commission should exert more pressure on the Member States regarding this point.

6.1.2 Legal Transposition and Practical Implementation

The provisions on disseminating information about the legal framework and mechanism in place pursuant to the Directives have hardly seen any formal implementation. Based on EELN Reports, this chapter will thus focus on the practice, for which the picture is equally discouraging.

Many country reports submitted to the European Equality Law Network (EELN) in 2020 describe the situation regarding the information provided to persons concerned as superficial, insufficient, and as not receiving high priority by the state.[34] This is the case, for instance, in Austria, Bulgaria, Latvia, Poland, and Spain.[35] In the context of Spain, the term 'hidden transposition' was coined, as there was no dissemination of information about the Directives or the resulting national legislation before, during, or after transposition. Although this changed between 2004 and 2011[36] with some publicity campaigns being organized, they did not have significant effects on awareness, with the exception of awareness in areas of gender, disability, and sexual orientation.[37]

[32] ibid 63.

[33] Isabelle Chopin and Jan Niessen, 'Combating Racism in the European Union with Legal Means: A comparison of the Starting Line and the EU Commission's proposal for a Race Directive' (Migration Policy Group, 2000), 8.

[34] For an overview see also European network of legal experts in gender equality and non-discrimination, 'A comparative analysis of non-discrimination law in Europe: 2020' (2021), 114–15.

[35] EELN, Country Report Austria, 2020, 72; EELN, Country Report Bulgaria, 2020, 83; EELN, Country Report Latvia, 2020, 83; EELN, Country Report Poland, 2020, 102–04.

[36] In this period the Spanish Socialist Workers' Party was in power.

[37] EELN, Country Report Spain, 2017, 100; and Country Report Spain, 2020, 86.

In other countries, some awareness-raising and training activities seem to have taken place in the two to four years following the adoption of the respective anti-discrimination legislation. In Belgium, for instance, from 2007 to 2009 the Federal Ministry in charge of equal opportunities funded an inter-university chair on law and discrimination, involving scholars from three universities, offering training that was part of the continuing education of lawyers and judges.[38] In recent years, however, some experts from the EELN have reported that there have been no notable dissemination activities organized by the government.[39] In Portugal, the Labour Code places a duty on employers 'to display in their premises information on the rights and duties of workers in relation to equality and non-discrimination'. Dissemination efforts of this kind have, however, not been very visible so far. Also, there is no obligation to display the information in a form that is accessible to those with disabilities.[40]

Positive examples of dissemination activities come from Finland, France, and the Netherlands. In Finland, the Unit for Democracy, Language Affairs and Fundamental Rights within the Ministry of Justice maintains a website for interested persons, authorities, and organizations containing information on legislation, equality planning, good practices, research, ongoing campaigns, and discrimination data.[41] In France, the inter-ministerial delegate for the fight against racism and homophobia has set up a training programme for 50,000 civil servants in contact with the public on how to offer adequate support to victims of racism and how 'to respond to situations of overt racism'.[42] In the Netherlands, several ministries engage in activities in their respective fields of competence to inform the general public as well as social partners about the non-discrimination legislation in place and promote studies and surveys in this field.[43]

Unfortunately, the yearly reports of the country experts of the EELN only provide scattered information about whether training and education on anti-discrimination legislation is provided to professions related to the access to justice, such as the judiciary and law enforcement bodies. It is of utmost importance to offer such training to future and practising judges and prosecutors, lawyers as well as the police. It can be concluded from the case studies looked at in the framework of this research that training on non-discrimination legislation is not a compulsory part of the curriculum for judges and prosecutors and that the subject is not given enough attention in law faculties.

[38] EELN, Country Report Belgium, 2020, 113.

[39] See, for instance, EELN, Country Report Cyprus, 2020, 114; EELN, Country Report Czech Republic, 2017, 126; EELN, Country Report Italy, 2020, 61, which reports, however, of occasional dissemination actions promoted by regional or local authorities.

[40] EELN, Country Report Portugal, 2020, 78.

[41] See the website at https://yhdenvertaisuus.fi/en/frontpage and EELN, Country Report Finland, 2020, 57.

[42] EELN, Country Report France, 2020, 111.

[43] EELN, Country Report the Netherlands, 2020, 81.

In many countries, as will be seen below, the obligation to undertake dissemination and awareness-raising activities is understood to be the responsibility of the Equality Body. If provided with the required human and financial resources to carry out such activities it can still be seen as being in compliance with EU requirements. Whether this is always the case, however, will be discussed below. Ideally, the Equality Body and responsible state institutions should collaborate in their efforts to disseminate information about the non-discrimination legislation in place and to organize training for relevant stakeholders. An example of such collaboration comes from Sweden, where the Equality Ombudsman is part of the training programme organized by the National Courts Administration for all public prosecutors and judges, thereby jointly reaching important actors involved when it is necessary to react to a discrimination that has already occurred. The Equality Ombudsman's cooperation with the Swedish National Agency for Education and the Swedish School Inspectorate on issues such as discrimination, harassment, and other degrading treatment of children in school, is of a more promotional and preventive nature.[44]

In some other countries the awareness raising is left to NGOs, which is problematic if they are not adequately funded for such activities. In Slovenia for instance it is reported that until 2013 most awareness-raising activities were carried out by NGOs supported by foreign funds.[45] The UK, on the other hand, made available considerable funds for awareness-raising projects implemented by NGOs. However, this funding took place primarily in the years following the entry into force of the implementing legislation (between 2003 and 2007) and the projects appear to have had a focus on discrimination based on sexual orientation.[46] Regarding France it is reported that '[m]ost NGOs ... are subsidized by the State and pursue information dissemination activities'.[47] Also the Slovak Ministry of Justice launched a call for proposals to financially support NGOs in promoting human rights including the elimination of discrimination.[48] In the context of low awareness among Roma of their rights, the FRA called on 'EU Member States and the European Commission [to] strengthen support for civil society efforts to raise rights awareness among Roma'.[49]

Finally, in many countries the European Commission's campaigns and funding have played an important role in raising awareness.[50] Currently, the Commission

[44] EELN, Country Report Sweden, 2017, 95.
[45] EELN, Country Report Slovenia, 2017, 104.
[46] EELN, Country Report United Kingdom, 2017, 82.
[47] EELN, Country Report France, 2020, 111.
[48] EELN, Country Report Slovakia, 2020, 98.
[49] Fundamental Rights Agency, 'EU-MIDIS II: Roma—selected findings' (n 25) 11.
[50] See on this European Commission, 'Report on the application of Council Directive 2000/43/EC implementing the principle of equal treatment between persons irrespective of racial or ethnic origin ("the Racial Equality Directive") and of Council Directive 2000/78/EC establishing a general framework for equal treatment in employment and occupation ("the Employment Equality Directive")' 11–12.

is raising awareness on discrimination by supporting NGOs, social partners, and Equality Bodies, by supporting equality policies at a national level, by establishing anti-discrimination training activities, and by pushing for diversity management in companies.[51] Through the Rights, Equality and Citizens programme, the Commission funds, for instance, training for judges, prosecutors, and other members of the judiciary on 'Applying EU Antidiscrimination Law', offered on a regular basis by the Academy of European Law (ERA).[52]

6.1.3 Good Practices and Challenges

Disseminating information about the measures adopted pursuant to the Non-Discrimination Directives or already existing in a country is not a one-off exercise but requires continuous efforts, which should be coordinated with other actors in the field, such as Equality Bodies and NGOs, and which requires careful addressing of different target groups. As can be seen from the above, however, Member States were more active right after the entry into force of the Directives or the respective national legislation while recently, in the majority of countries, awareness-raising activities are superficial, insufficient, and are not considered to be high priority by the Member States. This is an unacceptable situation in light of the low level of awareness in particular of support structures in place in the different countries. In some countries there appears to be a prioritization of issues where information about the legal framework and existing policies regarding some discrimination grounds that are understood to be less controversial (such as age or disability) receive higher attention than discrimination grounds which run counter to the ideological orientation of the governing elite. This is very much an issue regarding discrimination based on sexual orientation and often also regarding discrimination on the ground of ethnic or racial origin. In these cases, it often remains with the NGOs and/or the Equality Bodies to raise awareness about rights and existing redress mechanisms and sometimes even to counter-frame the negative and stereotypical narrative of state authorities about particular groups. In countries in which governing parties create a climate in which homosexuality is considered as abnormal or which generates the feeling of mistrust and even rejection of parts of the population not belonging to the majority population, it is of course all the more

[51] See the information provided at the Commission's website at https://ec.europa.eu/info/policies/justice-and-fundamental-rights/combatting-discrimination/tackling-discrimination/raising-awareness-discrimination_en#legallyprotected.

[52] Previously this training was financed through the PROGRESS 2007-13 programme. See European Commission, 'Joint Report on the application of Council Directive 2000/43/EC of 29 June 2000 implementing the principle of equal treatment between persons irrespective of racial or ethnic origin ("Racial Equality Directive") and of Council Directive 2000/78/EC of 27 November 2000 establishing a general framework for equal treatment in employment and occupation ("Employment Equality Directive")' (n 22) 4.

important that Equality Bodies do have a strong mandate, have sufficient means to deploy all their competences, and maintain the necessary independence and courage to inform rights holders and duty bearers about existing rights and legal obligations.

In sum, there are rare examples of good practice when it comes to the states' dissemination activities which consists in either continued attention being given to this topic by state authorities or at least the provision of adequate funding to Equality Bodies or NGOs to carry out awareness-raising and training activities.

6.1.4 Proposed Indicators

Considering the low (and actually decreasing) levels of awareness as documented by the EU-MIDIS studies, it would be negligent to consider the monitoring of Article 10 RED and Article 12 EED as a secondary or marginal issue. In its 2014 report on the application of the two Directives, the Commission concluded that '[t]he main challenge now is to increase awareness of the already existing protection and to ensure better practical implementation and application of the Directives'. It further stated that the awareness-raising and training activities need 'to be further strengthened by the Commission in cooperation with Member States to ensure tangible improvements in the awareness of rights throughout the EU'.[53] The Commission thus does not appear to be taking the issue lightly, although its wording in the 2021 wording seems less demanding.[54]

In terms of *structural indicators* (for a summary of all proposed indicators see Table 6.1 below), the above analysis has shown that the obligation incumbent on Member States under Article 10 RED and Article 12 EED has seen hardly any legal transposition. Structural indicators used to evaluate the level of compliance in this context would indeed need to reveal the extent to which this obligation has been entered in either national legislation or action plans taking due account of all the stakeholders to be considered. The lack of an explicit norm on the obligation to disseminate information is an indicator for the understanding that these provisions of the Directives are more of a programmatic nature, do not require transposition into law, but rather some steps must to be taken to achieve their objectives.[55] Many countries, however, do not deliver in this sphere either. If separate, the act establishing the Equality Body needs to be taken into consideration, as the state

[53] ibid 16.

[54] European Commission, 'Report on the application of Council Directive 2000/43/EC implementing the principle of equal treatment between persons irrespective of racial or ethnic origin ("the Racial Equality Directive") and of Council Directive 2000/78/EC establishing a general framework for equal treatment in employment and occupation ("the Employment Equality Directive")' (n 27) 25.

[55] European network of legal experts in gender equality and non-discrimination, 'A comparative analysis of non-discrimination law in Europe 2017' (2017), 121.

could have transferred the task to this specialized body by including an explicit competence in this regard. Furthermore, some labour codes oblige the employer to display information about the non-discrimination legislation within their premises. As well as these most pertinent pieces of legislation, the state would ideally carry out non-discrimination mainstreaming which would allow for the inclusion of a reference to the right to equality and non-discrimination in legislation in all relevant areas (such as education, social protection, housing, etc) as this would help to increase awareness among both right holders and duty bearers.

A structural indicator that is relevant across the board is the adoption of a non-discrimination strategy and action plan which duly take into consideration the need to organize awareness-raising and training activities in a coordinated manner.

In terms of *process indicators*, it would be necessary to evaluate if and how national and local authorities are addressing the different target groups with information and training, and observe the trend over time. As mentioned above, awareness raising is not a one-off exercise as the stakeholders are in a continuous state of flux. One important target group consists of 'those who are in a position to commit breaches'.[56] This can be employers and service providers but also leaders of educational institutions, public authorities, and law enforcement bodies. Coordinated efforts with trade unions and social partners as well as cooperation with the Equality Body will be required in this context.

Another target group consists of those bodies involved in access to justice, namely judges and prosecutors and again, law enforcement bodies. It needs to be seen, whether the national, European, and international legal framework and case law relating to non-discrimination is included in the compulsory curriculum of the Judicial and Police Academies, for future and already practising judges, prosecutors, and persons employed in the law enforcement bodies. An indicator for the efforts undertaken to comply with the awareness-raising obligation is also whether a state, with due regard to the autonomy of universities, promotes the inclusion of the topic of non-discrimination in the curriculum of law faculties.

[56] European Commission, 'Joint Report on the application of Council Directive 2000/43/EC of 29 June 2000 implementing the principle of equal treatment between persons irrespective of racial or ethnic origin ("Racial Equality Directive") and of Council Directive 2000/78/EC of 27 November 2000 establishing a general framework for equal treatment in employment and occupation ("Employment Equality Directive")' (n 22) 5; Fundamental Rights Agency, 'Opinion of the European Union Agency for Fundamental Rights on the situation of equality in the European Union 10 years on from initial implementation of the equality directives' (2013) FRA Opinion—1/2013 [EU Equality Directives], 3, where the FRA states: 'Evidence collected by FRA indicates that the legal obligation and the resulting political efforts to bring EU anti-discrimination legislation to the public's attention have not raised sufficient awareness to render anti-discrimination legislation an efficient and sufficiently invoked instrument. National and local authorities should therefore substantially intensify awareness-raising activities, including among bodies that can help to disseminate information such as equality bodies, non-governmental organisations (NGOs), trade unions and employers. Targeting persons who belong to groups most at risk of discrimination, as well as those in a position to commit breaches, such as employers and service providers, may allow for a more effective use of resources.'

A third target group is composed of the rights holders. In principle, awareness-raising activities should target all persons who could potentially become victims of discrimination on any of the grounds covered by legislation. Prioritizing specific groups on the basis that members of this group are particularly vulnerable to discrimination would of course be legitimate and could make sense in a context of limited resources. Not reaching out to members of a particular group for ideological reasons is, however, unacceptable.

Awareness-raising measures should also reach out to the general public in order to create a climate of respect for diversity, tolerance, and understanding.

An indicator for the efforts of the state to raise awareness would also be its choice of means. In addition to training activities, awareness-raising campaigns via a diversity of channels (print, media, social media, etc) should be implemented. While the number of such training activities, the number of individuals they have reached, and the number of awareness-raising campaigns will give a first indication as to whether the measures are appropriate to really make an impact, it will always be necessary to include expert opinions in the population of these indicators. In particular, it will be necessary to observe over time if there is continuity in raising awareness.

If the population of the above indicators leads to the conclusion that the state is not or not sufficiently making efforts to raise awareness and offer training to relevant stakeholders, it will be necessary to examine more closely the competences assigned to the Equality Body to see whether the state's approach to fulfil this obligation was to give the Equality Body the mandate to set activities in this field. Apart from giving it that mandate, the state also needs to equip the Equality Body with the necessary financial resources to enable it to deliver on all the above-mentioned points (ie to cover all target groups with appropriate means the impact of which is evaluated).

As part of its dialogue with NGOs, the state could also entrust them with the task (at least partly) to raise the awareness about non-discrimination legislation and policies. Cooperation with NGOs might be particularly useful to reach out to particular groups in whose interest they are working, and also for reaching out to areas outside the capital cities in order to meet the obligation to disseminate information throughout the country. Again, the crucial point will be whether the state is providing sufficient financial support to NGOs for them to meaningfully engage in awareness-raising activities.

One *outcome indicator* would clearly be an increasing level of awareness of rights, obligations, and existing support mechanisms (especially of the Equality Body) among all target groups, shown through regular surveys. Ultimately, increased awareness should lead to less discrimination and if discrimination happens, reporting should steadily increase. The FRA has tried to pin down these two issues by asking persons belonging to the groups at risk about the instances of discrimination in the past twelve months and whether they have reported it. While such large-scale surveys carried out by the FRA are very useful, it should also be a regular state exercise (in cooperation with, or via the Equality Body) to monitor

Table 6.1 Table of indicators concerning the states' responsibility to disseminate information and raise awareness

• Persons concerned (rights holders and duty bearers) • All appropriate means • Throughout the territory	Structural indicators	Dissemination and awareness-raising obligation contained in • relevant pieces of legislation (non-discrimination law, law establishing the Equality Body, labour law, and other pertinent laws) • national Non-Discrimination Strategy and Action Plan
	Process indicators	All target groups addressed? • Duty bearers (employers, service providers, professions involved in education and health care, civil servants) • Bodies involved in access to justice (judges, prosecutors, lawyers, police, Judicial Academies, law faculties) • Right holders (with focus on persons most at risk) • General public Means • Non-discrimination issues/legislation included in training for all relevant professions • Campaigns via different channels • Cooperation with Equality Body and NGOs or provision of sufficient funds to them • Continued efforts Whole territory covered?
	Outcome indicators	• Increasing level of awareness of rights and obligations as well as existing support mechanisms (especially Equality Body) among all target groups and throughout the country • Fewer instances of discrimination • Ratio of reported instances of discrimination increasing

and evaluate whether the efforts undertaken have brought about the desired result. In such surveys, particular attention should be paid to the levels of awareness in the more remote areas in order to ensure that the measures really do reach the target groups throughout the country.

6.2 The Role of Equality Bodies: Awareness Raising and Advising

6.2.1 Introduction and Conceptual Clarification

As mentioned earlier, '[p]redominantly promotion-type equality bodies ... spend the bulk of their time and resources on a broader mix of activities that include supporting good practice in organisations, raising awareness of rights, developing a knowledge base on equality and nondiscrimination, and providing legal advice and assistance to individual victims of discrimination'.[57] Apart from this latter type of activity, which comes under the reactive function of Equality Bodies, the rest of the activities proactively try to shape the social environment such as to reduce the amount of discrimination taking place. As such, Equality Bodies can be considered to be institutions for social, policy, and institutional change.[58] From a reflexive governance point of view, Equality Bodies thus clearly belong to the stakeholders to be involved in the lawmaking process, and to the actors supporting exchange of good practice at national level and contributing to national and transnational monitoring and evaluation.

These activities have been set out by Article 13 RED as 'conducting independent surveys concerning discrimination, [as well as] publishing independent reports and making recommendations on any issue relating to such discrimination'. It is understood that in countries where it has been decided to transpose Article 13 RED by the sole establishment of an Equality Body with predominantly tribunal-type functions, these promotional and preventive activities have to be fulfilled by that body too, in order for the state to be compliant with the requirements under the Directive.

It is interesting to note that the proposal of the Starting Line Group placed a lot of emphasis on the reactive side of the Equality Bodies' function but did not include any wording concerning tasks oriented towards promotion and prevention.[59]

[57] Margit Ammer and others, 'Study on Equality Bodies set up under Directives 2000/43/EC, 2004/113/EC and 2006/54/EC. Synthesis Report' (Human European Consultancy in partnership with the Ludwig Boltzmann Institute of Human Rights, October 2010), 44. More or less the same wording is used by the definition of the types of bodies on the Equinet webpage: https://equineteurope.org/comparative-data/functions/.

[58] ibid 12 and 128. See also Equinet, 'Advancing Equality by Making Policy Recommendations. An Equinet Good Practice Guide' (2014) 6; and Council of Europe, Commissioner for Human Rights, 'Opinion of the Commissioner for Human Rights on National Structures for Promoting Equality' (21 March 2011) CommDH(2011)2.

[59] See Art 4 of the Starting Line proposal, to be found, for instance, in Isabelle Chopin, 'Possible Harmonisation of Anti-Discrimination Legislation in the European Union: European and Non-Governmental Proposals' (2000) 2(3/4) European Journal of Migration and Law 413.

The Commission's initial proposal already included the conducting of surveys concerning discrimination, the publication of reports, and the making of recommendations on issues related to discrimination based on racial or ethnic origin among the functions to be assigned to Equality Bodies.[60] In the final version of the Directive it was added that these functions had to be carried out independently. This was, as mentioned above, the concession made to those countries which were reluctant to accept that the bodies per se had to be independent.[61]

There have been quite a number of infringement proceedings initiated by the Commission dealing with the transposition of Article 13 RED. In most cases the criticism was related to the fact that the respective country had taken no steps towards transposing this provision at all or that the Equality Body had been formally provided for but not yet established in practice.[62] Only a small number of infringements revolved around the issue that the designated body did not have the required promotional and preventive functions at its disposal. In 2006, for instance, the Commission criticized Finland because none of the existing bodies appeared to be responsible for conducting surveys.[63] In the infringement proceedings commenced in 2013 against Finland, the Commission found fault with the fact that no body was responsible for the adoption of recommendations and the conduct of surveys in the field of employment.[64]

The minimum competences foreseen by the RED roughly correspond to the Paris Principles which, however, lay out these competences in much more detail. A National Human Rights Institution (NHRI) shall, for instance, be responsible for submitting advisory opinions, recommendations, proposals, and reports to the government, parliament, and any other competent body 'on any matters concerning the promotion and protection of human rights'.[65] In this context, the NHRI shall be able to examine legislation in force as well as proposals and, if necessary, recommend the adoption of new legislation or the amendment of existing legislation. It shall also draft reports on the human rights situation in general or on specific matters, or draw the attention of the government to situations where human rights are violated and make proposals on how such violations could be ended.[66] Apart from these advisory activities, the NHRI shall have the competence to encourage the ratification of international human rights instruments and to promote harmonization of national law with these instruments, to contribute to the reporting to international

60 Commission of the European Communities, 'Proposal for a Council Directive implementing the principle of equal treatment between persons irrespective of racial or ethnic origin' (n 28) Art 12.

61 Tyson (n 11) 216–17.

62 Infringement no 2005/2361 (letter of formal notice, Spain); infringement no 2005/2363 (letter of formal notice, UK, in relation to Gibraltar); infringement no 2006/2258 (letter of formal notice, Malta); infringement no 2262 (letter of formal notice, Czech Republic).

63 Infringement no 2006/2451 (letter of formal notice, Finland).

64 Infringement no 2013/2084.

65 Paris Principles A(3)(a).

66 Paris Principles A(3)(a)(i)–(iv).

monitoring bodies, to increase public awareness on human rights, to contribute to teaching of and researching human rights issues, and, finally, to cooperate with international organizations and their homologues in other countries.[67]

Broadly speaking, all these activities can be distinguished as having two main functions: first, an advisory function and second an awareness-raising function, although it is understood that the two in many instances are intertwined. The *advisory function* presupposes the carrying out of surveys and other research (in addition to providing assistance to victims, which also allows for a better understanding of the general state of affairs, of structural problems, or specific situations calling for the intervention of the state or other actors) resulting in reports and recommendations to the competent authorities or private actors. In carrying out this function, Equality Bodies try to influence and shape the content of government policies and legislation, the practices and procedures of public and private institutions, and the wider institutional infrastructure, including NGOs.[68]

In line with the Paris Principles, the ECRI's revised GPR No 2 recommend that Equality Bodies should have, in the framework of their promotion and prevention function, the competence to '[t]ake part in the consultation procedures for new policy, legislation and executive acts, monitor existing policy, legislation and executive acts and make recommendations for the modification or introduction of policy, legislation or executive acts'.[69] Recommendations of the Equality Body can also result from inquiries conducted on its own initiative addressing individual and structural discrimination, or from research conducted or commissioned.[70]

The addressees of the advice, as well as decision makers for legislation and policies, can also be the duty bearers in the public and private sector, including employers, service providers, and their representative organizations.[71] Equality Bodies can, as the ECRI's GPR No 2 suggest, advise and support them in developing good practices in organizations,[72] or '[p]romote and support the use of positive action to remedy inequalities' in the public and in the private sector.[73]

The wording of the RED limits the competence of the Equality Bodies to the *making* of recommendations. In order for them to be effective, an Equality Body should also be able to provide *guidance and support to implement* these recommendations.[74] Furthermore, they should also be in the position to *monitor* the

[67] Paris Principles A(3)(b)–(g).

[68] Niall Crowley, 'National Specialised Bodies: Effective Implementation of their Advisory Function' (ECRI 2016) 7.

[69] ECRI, 'General Policy Recommendation No. 2: Equality Bodies to Combat Racism and Intolerance at National Level' (7 December 2017) CRI(2018)06, para 13(j).

[70] ibid para 13(c)–(d).

[71] Equinet, 'Joint Responsibility for Equal Treatment: How Equality Bodies Work With Duty Bearers. An Equinet Strategy Development Report' (2013) in particular 41 ff.

[72] See ECRI, 'General Policy Recommendation No. 2: Equality Bodies to Combat Racism and Intolerance at National Level' (n 69) para 13(g).

[73] See ibid para 13(h).

[74] Crowley, 'National Specialised Bodies: Effective Implementation of their Advisory Function' (n 68) 9–10.

follow-up given to their recommendations.[75] The General Observations of the Sub-Committee on Accreditation of the Global Alliance of National Human Rights Institutions (SCA of GANHRI) put a lot of emphasis on 'rigorous and systematic follow-up' to recommendations by NHRIs. They state, for instance, that '[p]ublic authorities are encouraged to respond to recommendations from NHRIs in a timely manner, and to provide detailed information on practical and systematic follow-up action, as appropriate, to the NHRI's recommendations'. Furthermore, NHRIs 'should publicize detailed information on the measures taken or not taken by public authorities in implementing specific recommendations'.[76]

The ECRI's revised GPR No 2 also emphasize the need to follow up on recommendations and monitor their implementation.[77] The Explanatory Memorandum to GPR No 2 further notes that in this context it might be helpful to engage in a dialogue with the addressees of the recommendations in order to explain them, discuss ways of implementing them, and motivate persons responsible to take the necessary steps. Similar to the SCA of GANHRI, the ECRI also recommends that Equality Bodies 'track the progress in implementation of their recommendations and regularly publish an overview of their implementation status'.[78]

In implementing their advisory function, Crowley has identified three challenges for Equality Bodies. First, they have to establish what kind of change they seek. They can either choose to aim for formal or for full and effective equality, with the latter allowing of course for a greater impact. The second challenge is related to the establishment of sufficient leverage for their recommendations and advice to have an impact. For that purpose they can think of ways other powers can support their advisory function, for instance, by using their work on discrimination complaints to back up their recommendations. Furthermore they can add to their leverage by participating in public debates, developing institutional relationships, disseminating their expertise and arguments for change, and by engaging international support. Related to this is the third challenge, namely, to identify strategies for change. One viable option, as suggested by Crowley, consists in the establishment of an ongoing dialogue with relevant stakeholders. In addition, or where such partnerships are not an option, an Equality Body, based on networking with NGOs, can rely on exerting pressure on other statutory bodies dealing with issues of equality and non-discrimination or based on public support or peer pressure. A third strategy proposed is related to the triggering of values related to equality, non-discrimination, and diversity among decision makers.[79]

[75] Both providing guidance on the implementation of recommendations as well as following up as part of the 'life cycle of a recommendation' have been included in Equinet's Good Practice Guide: Equinet, 'Advancing Equality by Making Policy Recommendations. An Equinet Good Practice Guide' (n 58).

[76] GANHRI, 'General Observations of the Sub-Committee on Accreditation' adopted by the GANHRI Bureau at its Meeting held in Geneva, Switzerland, 6 March 2017.

[77] See ECRI, 'General Policy Recommendation No. 2: Equality Bodies to Combat Racism and Intolerance at National Level' (n 69) para 13(l).

[78] ibid Explanatory Memorandum, para 65.

[79] Crowley, 'National Specialised Bodies: Effective Implementation of their Advisory Function' (n 68) 13–22. For an example of an organization trying to achieve this, see http://www.values-lab.ie/.

Barriers to the advisory function can be related to the making of recommendations at all or to their effectiveness. In the first case, there can be impediments related to the mandate, for instance restricting the addressees of any recommendations. Equality Bodies might also have to work on limited human and financial resources and choose to give their enforcement activities higher priority than their advisory function. Even if Equality Bodies do make recommendations they encounter difficulties as they might not be informed about a legislative process early enough to have the opportunity to influence the decision-making process. Successful implementation of the advisory function can also be hampered by a lack of interest among legislators, policy makers, employers, or service providers who might also question the expertise and authority of the Equality Body. If there is also no public interest in the issue it might be difficult for Equality Bodies to build up pressure. A further barrier is related to the resistance of stakeholders to implement a recommendation if it entails additional costs. Another difficulty is that Equality Bodies are not given feedback on the effectiveness of the recommendations and monitoring their implementation can be difficult.[80] To counter some of these difficulties it would be useful to have clear standards, possibly linked with sanctions for their violation, combined with international support.[81]

It remains to be seen to what extent these barriers can be addressed by following the Recommendations of the Commission on standards for Equality Bodies. They recommend that Member States 'ensure that their public authorities take into account, to the extent possible, recommendations from equality bodies on legislation, policy, procedure, programmes and practice', inform the Equality Body 'of how the recommendations have been taken into account and make this information public'.[82] Furthermore, Member States should enable their Equality Bodies to contribute to the prevention of discrimination by, inter alia, 'providing information, advice, guidance and support to duty bearers'.[83] While the Commission's recommendations thus address the same target groups as the ECRI, they are less detailed when it comes to the kind of advice that can be given (in particular when taking into consideration the detailed Explanatory Memorandum of the ECRI's recommendations) as well as the role of the Equality Body during implementation. On the other hand, they emphasize the need to follow up on recommendations and

[80] Crowley, 'National Specialised Bodies: Effective Implementation of their Advisory Function' (n 68) 10–11, Equinet, 'Advancing Equality by Making Policy Recommendations. An Equinet Good Practice Guide' (n 58) 8; ECRI, 'ECRI's seminar with national Specialised Bodies: The role of national Specialised Bodies in advising legislative and executive authorities and other stakeholders. Background note' (26 May 2016).

[81] Crowley, 'National Specialised Bodies: Effective Implementation of their Advisory Function' (n 68) 10–11.

[82] European Commission, 'Commission Recommendation on standards for equality bodies' (22 June 2018) C(2018) 3850 final, Chapter II, 1.1.2., point 10.

[83] ibid Chapter II, 1.1.2., point 11.

in this context expect public authorities to explain how they have been taken into account.

It is also worth mentioning the comparatively strong wording chosen by the Commission in its recommendation dealing with independent surveys, which can be at the basis of recommendations. Equality Bodies should be enabled to carry out such surveys 'regularly' and they should be designed in such a way to allow the 'gathering of a sufficient amount of sound quantitative and qualitative data on discrimination' which in turn allow for the drawing of 'evidence-based conclusions on where the main challenges lie and how to address them'.[84]

The Commission was quite critical about the application of these recommendations. It found that '[i]n a number of countries . . . their lack of resources and independence or the unfriendly political climate in which they operate' hampers the fulfilment of the advisory role of Equality Bodies and that they 'regret the absence of response from the relevant public authorities or the fact that they are not engaged early enough in the policy-making or legislative process'.[85] Lack of resources and independence also prevent two thirds of the Equality Bodies from regularly conducting surveys and producing reports.[86]

To carry out independent surveys and publish independent reports can, as well as building the basis for advice, *raise awareness* of rights and obligations among decision makers, duty bearers, the general public, and especially among potential victims, and develop a knowledge base on equality and non-discrimination.[87] Awareness raising and giving advice are of course often intertwined and the former leads to the latter.

While the dissemination of information to persons concerned throughout the territory of a country is an obligation of the state under Article 10 RED, it has been found in 6.1.2 that it has become established practice that the Equality Bodies play an important role in this context. Cases where a state does not itself set awareness-raising activities and the Equality Body is not explicitly equipped with such a competence would amount to a violation of this obligation. Even where such a competence is provided for, it might be questioned whether the state can completely withdraw form dissemination activities and leave this task to the Equality Body. This has to be evaluated on a case-by-case basis against the background that many Equality Bodies appear to be understaffed and underfinanced and the danger that when resources are short, Equality Bodies tend to dedicate more resources to their reactive activities (assisting victims of discrimination) rather than

[84] ibid Chapter II, 1.1.2., point 7.

[85] European Commission, 'Equality bodies and the implementation of the Commission Recommendation on standards for equality bodies' (19 March 2021) SWD(2021) 63 final, 13–14, 16, and 25–26.

[86] ibid 11–13 and 15, where the reports says that good practice includes 'carrying out very regular surveys'.

[87] Ammer and others (n 57) 44.

to their preventive and proactive activities.[88] However, considering that lack of awareness is one of the main obstacles for a more efficient operation of the non-discrimination regime it is essential that all stakeholders join efforts in order to both prevent discrimination from happening but also be able to react to instances of discrimination.

As mentioned above, the FRA has underlined the necessity for stronger efforts by states in this sphere and highlights the potential role of Equality Bodies in this context. It is of the opinion that Member States should provide these bodies 'with the necessary staff and human resources, as required by the Racial Equality Directive and called for by FRA in its Opinion on the implementation of the equality directives (FRA Opinion 1/2013). This would enable them to [inter alia] collect data through independent surveys, which provides the evidence base for monitoring levels of discrimination and awareness of the existence of equality bodies among the populations they were set up to serve.'[89]

The ECRI's revised GPR No 2 are again very helpful in defining the target groups to be addressed by awareness-raising activities. Just as described for the awareness-raising activities of the state, they include the groups experiencing discrimination, individuals and institutions in the public and the private sector (decision makers and duty bearers), as well as the population at large.

Regarding the first group, Equality Bodies should build 'knowledge about the rights and remedies established under the equal treatment legislation, capacity to exercise these rights and trust in the equality bodies'.[90] The focus is thus on empowering rights holders by building their capacity to react to instances of discrimination. In doing so, the perception that the discriminatory behaviour is normal and that nothing can be done against it should be dispelled.[91] Equality Bodies have developed a number of ways to get the relevant information to potential victims of discrimination. These include the production of printed materials introducing the legislation and the role of the Equality Body in getting redress; the provision of comprehensive information on the Equality Body's webpage,[92] and the implementation of a media strategy (TV and radio spots, media campaigns, appearance on printed media, social media).[93] Considering the wide reach of social media, Equinet has elaborated a guide for Equality Bodies on communicating

[88] European Commission, 'Equality bodies and the implementation of the Commission Recommendation on standards for equality bodies' (n 85) 13.

[89] Fundamental Rights Agency, 'EU-MIDIS II: Main results' (n 12) Opinion 4, 16.

[90] ECRI, 'General Policy Recommendation No. 2: Equality Bodies to Combat Racism and Intolerance at National Level' (n 69) para 13(f).

[91] 41 per cent of respondents of the FRA's 2020 LGBTI survey said they do not report discrimination as nothing would happen or change. This reason ranked highest in nearly all areas (between 27 per cent and 42 per cent) also in the EU-MIDIS II survey.

[92] It is good practice to publish printed materials and provide information on webpages in different languages. Equinet, 'Providing Independent Assistance to Victims of Discrimination: An Equinet Report' (Equinet: European Network of Equality Bodies, Brussels 2011), 9–10.

[93] ibid.

equality through social media.[94] Furthermore, it has published a guide to strategic communication in which it introduces and uses the concept of framing and explains how this concept can be used to communicate with different interlocutors with the aim of creating sustainable social change.[95] According to the ECRI, this competence would also include the analysis, in cooperation with the police, the prosecution services, as well as educational and labour inspectorates, the reasons for underreporting of discrimination and the taking of the necessary steps to ensure that persons who feel discriminated against do not shy away from systematically reporting such cases to the competent bodies.[96]

The Recommendations thereby address already the second target group for awareness-raising activities: individuals and institutions in the public and the private sector.[97] Relevant actors in this group include politicians, senior officials and other decision makers, educationalists, persons working in the judiciary, other legal professions, or the police, employers and service providers, trade unions and human resource professionals, religious communities, civil society organizations, and media professionals.[98] With regard to these actors, Equality Bodies should sharpen their understanding of equality issues and thereby 'bring an equality perspective into policy-making and the legislative process and to implement internal equality and diversity systems and safeguards'.[99] This should contribute to the development, exchange, and implementation of good practices, some examples of which the ECRI gives in its Explanatory Memorandum.[100] The ECRI further recommends that Equality Bodies have the competence to 'promote and contribute to the training of key groups in relation to equality and non-discrimination', referring to all the above-mentioned groups of actors.[101]

And finally, Equality Bodies should build awareness and knowledge about equal treatment legislation and non-discrimination 'across society'.[102]

The Commission's recommendation deals with the awareness-raising function of Equality Bodies only in a limited way. To promote equality and diversity, and prevent discrimination, states should enable Equality Bodies to provide training and information to duty bearers and raise awareness of the general public of the bodies' existence, the content of non-discrimination legislation, and on how to seek redress.[103] It is therefore rather vague when it comes to the target groups. The

[94] Equinet, 'Communicating Equality through Social Media: A Guide for Equality Bodies' (2017).

[95] Equinet & PIRC, 'Framing Equality: Communication Toolkit for Equality Bodies' (2017).

[96] ECRI, 'General Policy Recommendation No. 2: Equality Bodies to Combat Racism and Intolerance at National Level' (n 69) Explanatory Memorandum, para 58.

[97] ibid para 13(g)–(e).

[98] ibid Explanatory Memorandum, para 57.

[99] ibid Explanatory Memorandum, para 59.

[100] ibid Explanatory Memorandum, paras 59–60.

[101] ibid para 13(k) and Explanatory Memorandum, para 64.

[102] ibid para 13(e).

[103] European Commission, 'Commission Recommendation on standards for equality bodies' (n 82) Chapter II, 1.1.2., point 11.

recommendation of the Commission that Member States should provide sufficient budget and resources to allow Equality Bodies to carry 'effective awareness-raising' is important.[104]

For both functions, the advisory and the awareness-raising function, cooperation with another important actor in the field, NGOs, is important. The SCA of GANHRI recommends that 'NHRIs should develop, formalize and maintain regular, constructive and systematic working relationships with other domestic institutions and actors established for the promotion and protection of human rights'. Among those actors, the SCA mentions civil society and non-governmental organizations. 'Interaction may include the sharing of knowledge, such as research studies, best practices, training programmes, statistical information and data, and general information on its activities.'[105] The ECRI also recommends a regular dialogue with a wide range of societal groups to improve the Equality Body's understanding of the concerns, needs, and priorities of individuals and groups experiencing discrimination. All this is required in order to plan and successfully implement the promotion and prevention function of an Equality Body. Such dialogue further contributes to mutual education and the building of trust.[106] Cooperation in the broader framework of institutions concerned with non-discrimination helps to coordinate and increase the impact of their activities.[107] This also includes cooperation with Equality Bodies in other countries as a source for peer learning and improvement of Equality Bodies. The 'valuable role' of Equinet has been mentioned explicitly by the ECRI's recommendation[108] and acknowledged by the Commission.[109]

In implementing their preventive and promotional mandate, Equality Bodies are thus required to reach out to a range of different stakeholders, including NGOs, trade unions, employer bodies, and public authorities. They are therefore well placed to act as a hub around which these stakeholders constituting part of the wider institutional architecture can cooperate and coordinate their efforts with a view to enhancing the overall impact of activities carried out by different actors.[110]

[104] ibid Chapter II, 1.2.3., point 6. The Commission dealt with the issue of awareness raising and training carried out by Equality Bodies in European Commission, 'Equality bodies and the implementation of the Commission Recommendation on standards for equality bodies' (n 85) 14–15.

[105] GANHRI (n 76) G.O. 1.5, 17.

[106] See Equinet, 'Providing Independent Assistance to Victims of Discrimination: An Equinet Report' (n 92) 11, where it is stated that '[d]ialogue with civil society allows equality bodies to reach unidentified victims and specific groups due to a trust-building relationship and exchange of contacts'.

[107] See in this context Equinet, 'Effective Strategies to Empower Civil Society' (2010).

[108] ECRI, 'General Policy Recommendation No. 2: Equality Bodies to Combat Racism and Intolerance at National Level' (n 69) para 13(b) and (o) and Explanatory Memorandum, paras 50–52 and 69–70. On Equality Bodies' networking with NGOs and among themselves, see also Ammer and others (n 57) 148–50; and Equinet, 'Equality Bodies: Current Challenges' (2012), 19–20.

[109] European Commission, 'Equality bodies and the implementation of the Commission Recommendation on standards for equality bodies' (n 85) 25.

[110] Equinet, 'The Bigger Picture: Equality Bodies as part of the National Institutional Architecture for Equality' (2014) 22–25; Council of Europe, Commissioner for Human Rights (n 58) 18.

6.2.2 Legal Transposition

Most Equality Bodies in Europe qualify themselves as predominantly promotion-type bodies (twenty-two Equinet members). If one further considers the bodies that declare themselves to be a combination of promotion- and tribunal-type body, another sixteen bodies must be added.[111] A few countries have established more than one body, of which one has a tribunal-type function while the other has predominantly promotion-type functions or a combination thereof. These countries include: Austria, Denmark, Estonia, Finland, and Ireland.[112] And finally, in Bulgaria, Cyprus, Lithuania, and Romania only predominantly tribunal-type bodies are established,[113] without assigning the promotion functions to a separate body. This means that these bodies, in order to be in compliance with EU law, need to fulfil the promotion-type tasks as described above as well as their predominantly tribunal-type functions.

Looking at the enumeration of tasks assigned to Equality Bodies by national law, it appears that at the level of commitment, all bodies, except for the Estonian Chancellor of Justice that has no competence to conduct surveys or publish reports, are equipped with the competences strictly required by the RED.[114] In Estonia, the Commissioner for Gender Equality and Equal Treatment can compensate for this lack of competence as it is able conduct surveys and publish reports. All Equality Bodies do have the competence to make recommendations on discrimination-related issues.[115]

While from the legal point of view, the requirements of Article 13 RED are thus fulfilled, the Commission found that Equality Bodies in only one third of Member States conduct surveys on a regular basis without being limited by a lack of resources. As a result, only in around one third of Member States are Equality Bodies also able to produce not only annual reports but also reports on specific topics related to discrimination.[116] In Austria, for instance, reports of the Ombud for Equal

[111] See the information provided on Equinet's webpage, at https://equineteurope.org/comparative-data/functions/.

[112] Austria: the Equal Treatment Commission (quasi-judicial body) and the Ombud for Equal Treatment; Denmark: the Board of Equal Treatment (quasi-judicial body) and the Institute for Human Rights; Estonia: the Chancellor of Justice (can be qualified as quasi-judicial body in conciliation procedures) and the Commissioner for Gender Equality and Equal Treatment; Finland: the National Non-discrimination and Equality Tribunal (quasi-judicial body) and the Non-Discrimination Ombudsman; Ireland: the Workplace Relations Commission (quasi-judicial body) and the Irish Human Rights and Equality Commission.

[113] Bulgaria: the Commission for Protection Against Discrimination; Cyprus: the Office of the Commissioner for Administration and the Protection of Human Rights; Lithuania: Equal Opportunities Ombudsperson; Romania: National Council for Combatting Discrimination.

[114] In Slovenia, the tasks of conducting research and issuing reports have been added to the mandate of the Equality Body only with the establishment of the Advocate of the Principle of Equality in 2016. See EELN, Country Report Slovenia, 2020, 83.

[115] European network of legal experts in gender equality and non-discrimination, 'A comparative analysis of non-discrimination law in Europe: 2020' (n 34) 110.

[116] European Commission, 'Equality bodies and the implementation of the Commission Recommendation on standards for equality bodies' (n 85) 11 and 13.

Treatment 'are scarce and few surveys have been conducted so far'.[117] The 2017 report of the EELN expert on the UK reported that the Equality and Human Rights Commission does 'have the competence (if not necessarily the resources)' to conduct independent surveys and to publish independent reports. Limitations on its overall functioning due to 'ongoing constraints in funding' have been qualified as 'increasing and significant'. In 2020, the level of resources remains reportedly 'insufficient … to fulfil their general mandate in an optimal manner' and affects in particular the recommendation function of the Equality Body.[118] In other countries, the legal experts report on the respective Equality Bodies producing surveys, reports, and recommendations but they question their independence.[119] This is, for instance, the case in Portugal, Slovakia, and Spain.[120]

The practice of Equality Bodies working on their advisory and awareness-raising role will be discussed in the next sub-section 6.2.3, dividing the analysis into cases in which Equality Bodies exercise predominantly tribunal-type functions, cases in which Equality Bodies have a mandate for equality and non-discrimination alone, and cases in which they are part of a larger human rights institution. The purpose of this division is to figure out if the assumption that predominantly tribunal-type Equality Bodies find it harder to put promotional and preventive measures into practice is correct and whether any difference in performance can be observed when comparing dedicated Equality Bodies with cases where this task has been integrated into a broader human rights institution. Considering the limited number of cases where there exist only predominantly tribunal-type institutions, the respective sub-section (6.2.3.1) will cover all of them. In the other two sub-sections (6.2.3.2 and 6.2.3.3) the focus will be on one particular body.

6.2.3 Practical Implementation

6.2.3.1 Predominantly Tribunal-Type Equality Bodies

According to the definition of *predominantly tribunal-type Equality Bodies* given on Equinet's webpage, these are bodies who 'spend the bulk of their time and resources on hearing, investigating and deciding on individual instances of discrimination brought before them. Some can and do take on certain promotional functions alongside these activities.'[121] As mentioned above, there are a couple of countries which, in transposing Article 13 RED, have only set up a tribunal-type

[117] EELN, Country Report Austria, 2020, 67.

[118] EELN, Country Report United Kingdom, 2017, 80; Country Report United Kingdom, 2020, 61–62.

[119] European network of legal experts in gender equality and non-discrimination, 'A comparative analysis of non-discrimination law in Europe: 2020' (n 34) 110.

[120] EELN, Country Report Portugal, 2020, 74; Report on Slovakia, 2020, 89–90; Report on Spain, 2020, 81–82.

[121] See Equinet's website at https://equineteurope.org/comparative-data/functions/.

Equality Body. In these cases, assigning them also promotional functions is not a possibility but a must. These countries are Bulgaria, Cyprus, Lithuania, and Romania.

The Lithuanian Equal Opportunities Ombudsperson was formally given awareness-raising competences only in 2017. In practice, it had been active in this field from the beginning. The Office was given an important role in the implementation of a number of Action Plans and Programmes and in these contexts carried out educational, awareness-raising, and research activities targeting, amongst others, vulnerable groups, employers, and the general public.[122] The Lithuanian legal expert thus concludes that 'the Government considers the Ombudsperson as the key institution for awareness raising and promoting equal opportunities, despite the fact, that the law provides for a . . . , mainly quasi-judicial mandate'.[123] Some of the awareness raising and promotional measures foreseen by the Action Plan for the Promotion of Non-discrimination 2015–20 that required substantial financing were, however, not implemented for bureaucratic or financial reasons. While the power to carry out research and publish reports had remained relatively unused until 2014, ever since, it has also become more active in this field. It should be underlined, however, that this activity has been mainly (co)financed through EU-funded projects and has reportedly 'limited ability to plan its promotional functions several years ahead'.[124]

When it comes to the Body's advisory function, the EELN report states that the Ombudsperson has the power to make proposals to state and municipal institutions and agencies concerning the improvement of legal acts and to include recommendations in its annual reports to the parliament. As far as stakeholders are concerned, the Ombudsperson could be more active in carrying out its advisory function but also pointed out that this would require an increase in human resources.[125] The report is silent on whether there is any follow-up to the recommendations[126] and as to whether the Equality Body is also engaging with the private sector in the context of providing advice and guidance in non-discrimination-related matters.

One can therefore conclude that, although the Lithuanian Equality Body is a predominantly tribunal-type body, it legally has an awareness-raising mandate and in practice, performs relatively well on it. Financing of activities, however, appears to be challenging, as seems to be the case also with regard to reaching out to duty bearers when it comes to advising them on equality issues. Furthermore, the

[122] EELN, Country Report Lithuania, 2020, 107–08.
[123] ibid 108.
[124] ibid 102.
[125] ibid 106–07.
[126] Since 2017, however, there has been a follow-up system in place regarding the recommendations taken by the Ombudsperson in the framework of deciding on complaints. A table of recommendations and the status of their implementation has since become accessible online. ibid 86–87.

advisory function could be carried out more actively and there is no information regarding the follow-up on recommendations addressed to governmental and municipal institutions.

When the new Commissioner for Administration and the Protection of Human Rights (Ombudsperson) of Cyprus took office in 2017, the two departments dealing with the non-discrimination mandate (the Equality Authority and Antidiscrimination Authority) ceased functioning. The nomination was widely perceived as political and the result of nepotism.[127] The ECRI noted with concern two years later, that under the new Ombudsperson the Office had 'not carried out any activities aimed at supporting vulnerable groups or communication activities, and has not issued any publications or reports, including annual reports, or recommendations on discrimination issues'.[128] This is also confirmed by the EELN expert, who further reports that even where the Ombudsperson is involved in legislative consultation processes to bring in a more general human rights angle, her proposals are not necessarily complied with.[129] In terms of awareness-raising, no activities are set, either by state authorities or the Ombudsperson.[130]

The overall situation is clearly not compatible with the requirements under the Directives. Neither the advisory nor the awareness-raising function is fulfilled by the Cypriot Equality Body.

In Bulgaria, the awareness-raising activities of both the state and the Equality Body have been qualified as 'superficial and insufficient'.[131] The Commission for Protection Against Discrimination (CPAD) was only given the duty to inform the public via mass media about non-discrimination standards in 2012.[132] This provision appears restrictive in that it seems to limit the choice of means as well as the target group to be addressed by the information. In the same year when this competence was assigned to the CPAD, its budget was significantly cut.[133] Nevertheless, the CPAD made a considerable effort to increase its media appearances in 2012 but reduced this activity again in subsequent years.[134] Currently, funding for awareness raising is lacking, in particular for campaigns directed at the public at large or at vulnerable communities. Through PROGRESS funds, the CPAD implemented a project that ended in May 2014, which aimed at the dissemination of information on EU and national non-discrimination

[127] EELN, Country Report Cyprus, 2020, 105–06.

[128] ECRI, 'Conclusions on the implementation of the Recommendations in respect of Cyprus subject to interim follow-up, adopted on 3 April 2019' CRI(2019)23, 5.

[129] EELN, Country Report Cyprus, 2020, 109.

[130] ibid 114.

[131] ibid 83.

[132] Article 47(12) PADA.

[133] Interview, Head of unit Analysis, Prevention and International Cooperation, CPAD, 31 July 2018.

[134] According to information provided on Equinet's members' page the media appearances increased from seventy in 2011 to 129 in 2012, but dropped to fifty, fifty-four, and sixty-seven in the years to follow. See https://equineteurope.org/author/bulgaria_cpd/.

legislation to legal practitioners, Ministry of Interior Officials, educators, and journalists.[135] Furthermore, it tries to raise awareness through its regional offices.[136]

In terms of advising different target groups on non-discrimination and equality, the CPAD does have at its disposal the competence to carry out research and surveys, draft reports, and make recommendations to state and municipal authorities relating to discriminatory practices and legislation. Outside of its quasi-judicial function, in the framework of which it also makes recommendations to state and municipal authorities, it does, however, not appear to be very active in these fields. It has reportedly published only five studies since its establishment and 'demonstrated a distinct lack of independence' with regard to one of them. Its reporting activity is limited to producing its annual report to parliament, in which it appear to avoid any political, social, or legal analysis related to discrimination. This appears to be connected to the fact that approval of the report is conditional for the parliamentary approval of the CPAD's annual budget.[137]

It can therefore be concluded, that the promotional and preventive activities of the CPAD, understood as advising and raising awareness of a range of stakeholders on non-discrimination and equality-related issues needs to be strengthened in practice. Problems appear to be related to the structural level (legislation does not include all the relevant stakeholders and appears to limit the means for awareness raising, lack of independence, approval of annual report condition for approval of budget) as well as the financial means and capacities of the CPAD.

According to the national transposition legislation, the Romanian National Council for Combating Discrimination (NCCD) is responsible for the 'harmonization' of provisions in national legislation and administrative acts infringing the principle of non-discrimination and for 'preparing and enforcing public policies in matters of non-discrimination'. To fulfil this obligation it 'will hold advisory meetings with the public authorities, NGOs, trade unions and other legal entities' with an interest to combat discrimination.[138] Further details of its functions are given in the Government Decision regarding the organization and functioning of the NCCD. In addition to spelling out this clearly advisory function, the Government Decision also assigns the Council an awareness-raising role and requests it to cooperate with NGOs, other Equality Bodies, and international organizations.[139]

With money provided by EEA Grants,[140] the NCCD has implemented a project from 2014–16 which aimed at contributing to the development of the national anti-discrimination strategy based on wide-ranging consultations with all relevant

[135] Interview, Head of unit Analysis, Prevention and International Cooperation, CPAD, 31 July 2018. EELN, Country Report Bulgaria, 2017, 77.

[136] Commission for Protection Against Discrimination, 'Annual Report for 2017' (2018), 6.

[137] EELN, Country Report Bulgaria, 2020, 77–78.

[138] Ordinance 137/2000, Art 18(1)–(2).

[139] Government Decision 1194/2001 regarding the organisation and functioning of the National Council for Combating Discrimination, as amended, 17 November 2003, Art 2(1)(b), (c), (d).

[140] EEA Grants are jointly financed by Iceland, Liechtenstein, and Norway. See https://eeagrants.org/.

actors and at raising awareness of discrimination in Romanian society, both at national and local level. In the framework of this project, surveys on the perception of and attitudes towards discrimination in the population were carried out, courses for school inspectors, teachers, judges, and policemen were held and an information campaign was implemented. For the drafting of the strategy, an external assessment of the previous strategy was commissioned, a Working Group was established, roundtables at regional level with the involvement of NGOs,[141] local authorities, legal professionals, and social partners were organized to identify the needs and possible solutions. Consultations took place with institutions supposed to implement the strategy, including ministries, other central and local authorities, as well as with representatives of vulnerable groups, NGOs active in the field, and professional categories addressed by the strategy. The resulting draft strategy was not, however, taken up by the government.

After the end of the project, only one further survey was conducted[142] and awareness raising is mainly limited to informing the media about the outcome of the complaints that are decided by the NCCD as quasi-judicial body.[143] The fact that the NCCD does not have the required funds to carry out a sufficient number of awareness-raising campaigns has been noted by the ECRI's reports.[144] In cooperation with the NGO ACCEPT and financed by external funds, the Council still offers some training on LGBT issues to judges, prosecutors, police, and teachers. The activities in the area of prevention and promotion are, however, considered to be limited for financial reasons as the focus of the work is on dealing with complaints.[145]

The challenges of the Romanian Equality Body when it comes to the practical implementation of its preventive and promotional mandate appear to be related first of all to the lack of sufficient funding for these kinds of activities. The budget appears to cover only the minimum needed in order to deal with complaints but does not allow for adequate activities in other fields. Additional tasks assigned to the NCCD have not come with additional funding. This leads to a situation in which one observer found that the NCCD is on the verge of being paralyzed,[146] notwithstanding the fact that the Council has been successful in securing external funds

[141] The most active NGOs in the process of drafting the strategy were ACCEPT, working for the interests of the LGBTI community, as well as NGOs promoting gender equality issues. According to the information provided by one interviewee, other NGOs have been relatively weak in giving their input to the drafting process. Interview, Steering Board member of NCCD, 10 July 2018. On the other hand, the EELN Report states that NGOs have criticized the NCCD for not sufficiently reaching out to them in the context of assessing the 2007–13 National Strategy and the drafting of the new strategy. EELN, Country Report Romania, 2020, 88.

[142] Romanita Iordache, 'National survey on attitudes and perceptions of discrimination in Romania' (EELN News Report, 5 March 2019).

[143] Interview, Steering Board member of NCCD, 10 July 2018.

[144] ECRI, 'Report on Romania (fourth monitoring cycle) adopted on 19 March 2014' CRI(2014)19, para 64; ECRI, 'Report on Romania (fifth monitoring cycle) adopted on 3 April 2019' CRI(2019)20, paras 20–21.

[145] Interview, Steering Board member of NCCD, 10 July 2018.

[146] Interview, human rights lawyer I, Romania, EELN legal expert, 2 July 2018.

for promotional or preventive activities. The second challenge appears to be the lack of responsiveness by state authorities to the advisory function of the NCCD. This is exemplified by the fact that the draft National Strategy for Prevention and Combating Discrimination 'Equality, Inclusion, Diversity' for the period 2018–22 has not been taken up by the government.

The functions to promote equality and prevent discrimination of all assessed predominantly tribunal-type Equality Bodies thus appear to be mainly limited by a lack of funding, and in the case of Cyprus also by a political nomination process and the related inactivity of the Equality Body. Notwithstanding the formal commitment of states in terms of legally assigning these functions to the Equality Bodies, they fail to show sufficient efforts to translate this commitment in practice. This goes against the ECRI's recommendation that '[a]ppropriate human and financial resources should be allocated to all functions',[147] as well as against the Commission's recommendation that the state should ensure that the Equality Body is provided with adequate financial resources to perform 'each of their equality functions effectively'.[148] This failure can be considered a breach of Article 13 RED.

It further appears that legislation (and practice) sometimes focuses too much on public authorities to the detriment of the private sector and is restricting the choice of means by which the Equality Body is expected to raise awareness. Unequivocal inclusion of all relevant stakeholders as well as the liberty of the Equality Body to choose the means considered to be the most appropriate should be guaranteed. One target group that is particularly badly covered by predominantly tribunal-type Equality Bodies appear to be duty bearers (employers, service providers) both in terms of awareness raising and in terms of advising them on how to approach issues of equality and discrimination. Finally, effectiveness of the advisory role of tribunal-type Equality Bodies appears to be limited by the lack of responsiveness of the addressees of the advice.

6.2.3.2 Predominantly Promotion-Type Bodies: The Belgian Unia as an Example

The Belgian Equality Body's overall mission is to promote equal opportunities and to fight discrimination in a spirit of dialogue and collaboration with NGOs and other bodies having the same mission. For that purpose it has been assigned the competence to carry out studies and research, to collect and publish statistical data, and on this basis 'give independent advice and recommendations to any authority or private organization or private person'. It can give such advice and recommendations also to 'any authority with a view to improving the regulations and legislation'.

[147] ECRI, 'General Policy Recommendation No. 2: Equality Bodies to Combat Racism and Intolerance at National Level' (n 69) para 11.

[148] European Commission, 'Commission Recommendation on standards for equality bodies' (n 82) para 1 of Part 1.2.2. Resources, 8.

The legal framework thus covers all the relevant stakeholders that can be potential addressees of advice and guidance by Unia, including public and private actors, but limits it to the making of recommendations without mentioning what a follow-up to recommendations should look like. In addition to this advisory function, Unia is also mandated to 'organize awareness-raising actions'.[149] This open formulation allows Unia to address all the relevant target groups by the means it finds most appropriate.

In implementing its advisory function, Unia makes recommendations to all levels of government (federal, regional, and community level). The focus of this activity is 'on improving legislation and developing action plans or seeking a better understanding by the political leaders of specific new phenomena'.[150] Since 2014, the Centre has had a separate department for public policies, including representatives from regions and communities 'to ensure the link between federal and regional policies'.[151] An example of a set of recommendations is the one directed to Wallonian municipalities concerning accessibility of public buildings, services, and events for handicapped people. The recommendations were preceded by a survey on the accessibility of Wallonian municipalities resulting in a report, as well as monitoring of the accessibility of the municipalities' websites.[152] Another set of recommendations, preceded by a survey, regarded the participation of traveller children in education in Belgium.[153] In 2017, Unia published a report evaluating the Belgian non-discrimination legislation and has given twenty-seven recommendations on how to improve it.[154] In recent years, since Unia has been functioning as an interfederal centre, it has been very active in preparing recommendations and opinions to various actors and is recently experiencing an increasing interest from local authorities in receiving guidance on specific topics.[155]

[149] Cooperation Agreement, 'between the federal authority, the Regions and the Communities aimed at creating an Interfederal Centre for Equal Opportunities and Opposition to Racism and Discrimination in the form of a joint institution, in the sense of article 92bis of the Special Act of 8 August 1980 on the Reform of the Institutions' (12 June 2013), Arts 3–5.

[150] EELN, Country Report Belgium, 2020, 107.

[151] ibid. According to its 2017 Annual Report, 11 (out of 106.7) full time equivalents are employed in this service. See Unia, 'Rapport annuel 2017—Refuser l'inertie' (2018), 120. The most recent annual report does not provide the exact staff numbers for the different services.

[152] Unia, Recommendation of 24 September 2018. For further information see https://www.unia.be/fr/legislation-et-recommandations/recommandations-dunia/laccessibilite-des-communes-wallonnes-aux-personnes-handicapees.

[153] Unia, Recommendation of 17 December 2017. For further information see https://www.unia.be/fr/legislation-et-recommandations/recommandations-dunia/participation-a-lenseignement-des-enfants-des-gens-du-voyage-en-belgique.

[154] Unia, 'Evaluation: Loi du 10 mai 2007 modifiant la loi du 30 juillet 1981 tendant à réprimer certains actes inspirés par le racisme ou la xénophobie (MB 30 mai 2007) (loi antiracisme) Loi du 10 mai 2007 tendant à lutter contre certaines formes de discrimination (MB 30 mai 2007) (loi anidiscrimination)' (2017). Such evaluation is necessary every five years under Belgian legislation. On the basis of such evaluation reports the legislator is expected to adopt changes to the existing laws. It has been found that the state could be more responsive when it comes to proposed legislative changes. Interview, legal adviser at Unia, 31 May 2018.

[155] For a list of recommendations, see Unia's webpage at https://www.unia.be/fr/legislation-et-recommandations/recommandations-dunia.

Advice and recommendations to duty bearers in the private and public sectors are given through the Support and Training department.[156] If a company or public service is interested in developing non-discrimination and diversity-related initiatives, Unia provides tailor-made solutions in the form of training, support for diversity Working Groups, and advice in terms of internal and external communication or the development of action plans. In 2017 it addressed 3,932 participants in interventions of less than four hours and 500 participants from police, public institutions, and the fields of education and employment in training sessions lasting ten days or more.[157] For 2019, it reported that 14,698 people had experienced its awareness and training activities, with police and the employment sector ranking highest when it comes to training of long duration, and the education sector and public institutions when it comes to shorter trainings.[158] Where the amount of assistance required goes beyond Unia's capacities, it follows a 'train the trainers' approach. The findings of training courses are translated into recommendations to the respective group. In support activities, Unia pays attention to the ownership of the solutions found by the institutions which it supports. It does so by understanding its role as providing complementary expertise to the already existing expertise in the institution and facilitating a co-creative process.[159] In addition to individualized support measures, Unia has developed the 'EDiv' initiative which provides a 'free online training tool on anti-discrimination law, aimed at fostering diversity in companies by providing employers with practical situations and solutions'.[160]

In its outreach activities, Unia also profits from the regional offices in Flanders and Wallonia, some of which work primarily on preventive actions. Furthermore, Unia cooperates with NGOs active in the field of discrimination, national trade unions, and European universities and foundations. Such joint activities also have the purpose of exchanging information and practical experience.[161] Finally, Unia is actively involved in Equinet activities and Working Groups.

In conclusion, Unia can be seen as an example of an Equality Body that quite successfully fulfils all the requirements under Article 13 RED. It can be said to be vested with a strong advisory and awareness-raising function and, by combining

[156] This department was composed of ten (out of 106.7) full-time equivalents in 2017. Unia, 'Rapport annuel 2017—Refuser l'inertie' (n 151) 120. The most recent annual report does not provide the exact staff numbers for the different services.

[157] ibid 92.

[158] Unia, 'Rapport chiffre 2019' (2020), 77–78.

[159] Unia, 'Rapport annuel 2017—Refuser l'inertie' (n 151) 90–92.

[160] EELN, Country Report Belgium, 2020, 108. See https://www.ediv.be/. In 2017, Unia won an e-gov award with the module on handicap on the eDiv platform. This course makes companies aware of the anti-discrimination legislation and answers questions about diversity with practical examples. See https://www.archive.equineteurope.org/Belgium-Unia-wins-the-e-Gov-Award-for-Innovation.

[161] EELN, Country Report Belgium, 2020, 106. Unia has an agreement with some NGOs that they can forward cases for consideration to Unia. Unia meets with representatives of these organizations at regular intervals to discuss the cases and to report back on the steps it has taken. Interview, legal adviser at Unia, 31 July 2018.

its regular funding with other public resources, has the necessary financial means and human resources to put these functions into practice. Its advice is partly actively sought by public and private actors, and partly Unia comes up with monitoring, research, and recommendations on its own initiative. Its awareness-raising and advisory activities target all relevant stakeholders by a variety of means. It appears to have a country-wide network, either through its own local offices and/or NGOs, and to fulfil its mandate in an independent way.[162] At the level of outcomes, more information would be required on the follow-up given by private and in particular public authorities to recommendations as well as on the impact they have had on rights holders. And even more awareness-raising efforts appear to be necessary, considering that 'only' 32 per cent of respondents of the 2017 EU-MIDIS study stated they knew of Unia. Compared to the situation in Austria, where only 9 per cent knew of the respective Equality Body, this is still a lot but does not yet come close to the 42 per cent of respondents who knew the Swedish Equality Ombudsman, or the 52 per cent of respondents in the UK who knew the Equality and Human Rights Commission (EHRC).[163]

6.2.3.3 Equality Bodies Merged with a Larger Human Rights Institution: The Irish HREC as an Example

The main functions of the Irish Human Rights and Equality Commission (IHREC) as laid down in section 10 of the Irish Human Rights and Equality Commission Act (IHRECA) are primarily promotional and preventive in nature. The IHREC shall for instance 'promote understanding and awareness of the importance of human rights and equality in the State … [and] promote tolerance and acceptance of diversity'. For that purpose, the Commission shall 'provide information to the public in relation to human rights and equality generally' and in particular relating to the major acts transposing obligations from EU Directives.[164] Details of this function are spelled out in section 30 IHRECA. It shall also 'provide or assist in the provision of education and training on human rights and equality issues'.[165] Furthermore, it shall monitor the adequacy and effectiveness of existing laws and practices and provide its views on the implications of legislative proposals for human rights and equality. It should further make recommendations to the government on measures that it deems necessary to strengthen human rights and equality.[166] It shall provide guidance to public bodies to perform their functions in full respect of human rights and the principle of non-discrimination[167] and 'carry out equality

[162] EELN, Country Report Belgium, 2020, 105–08.

[163] See Fundamental Rights Agency, 'EU-MIDIS II: Main results' (n 12) 123–24. The high level of awareness of the British EHRC might also be connected to the fact that it is not only responsible for discrimination but for human rights issues overall.

[164] IHRECA, s 10(2)(a). These are the Employment Equality Acts 1998–2015, the Equal Status Acts 2000–15 and the Intoxicating Liquor Act 2003, s 19 on discrimination in licensed premises.

[165] IHRECA, s 10(2)(k).

[166] IHRECA, s 10(2)(b)–(d).

[167] IHRECA, s 10(2)(n) and Art 42.

reviews and prepare equality action plans' in businesses or invite them to do so.[168] It can conduct research and inquiries and publish reports about the respective outcomes.[169] The legal framework thus covers all relevant target groups for advisory and awareness-raising activities and can be considered an exemplary transposition of the requirements under the RED.

In the first year of its existence as a merged body, the IHREC carried out a 'survey to measure awareness and attitudes towards human rights and equality in the general population as a baseline to inform its work'.[170] Other surveys and research have also been carried out by the IHREC or commissioned to external independent actors, which have all been found to be of excellent quality.[171] It has further organized awareness-raising campaigns, financed project aiming at awareness raising and training, and sought to increase equality issues in schools.[172] It launched a re-designed webpage that aimed at providing easily accessible information and resources as well as guidance material for a range of stakeholders who are interested in embedding human rights and equality in their organization or business. The page provides detailed information for employers and service providers on the legal framework, the benefits of promoting equality and diversity for employers and employees, and examples of good practice.[173] In 2018, the Commission started using its power to conduct equality reviews which may be followed by a request to prepare and implement an equality action plan.[174] It does not appear to be vocal in calling the attention of employers to codes of practice developed by the IHREC or its predecessors on particular issues, such as for instance on sexual harassment.[175]

Since the merger, the IHREC yearly submits some two to three observations on legislative drafts, about half of which are related to legislation relevant for the field of non-discrimination and equality. It also prepares an increasing number of policy statements and submissions, however only a few of them fall within the area of non-discrimination and equality.[176] It has been noted that many of these

[168] IHRECA, s 10(2)(m) and Art 32.

[169] IHRECA, s 10(2)(j), (o) ,(p).

[170] IHREC, Annual Report 2015, 34. The results of the survey are available at https://www.ihrec.ie/documents/ihrec-awareness-and-attitudes-research-2015/. A further research paper on 'Attitudes to Diversity in Ireland' was published by the IHREC in 2018. See https://www.ihrec.ie/documents/attitudes-to-diversity-in-ireland/.

[171] EELN, Country Report Ireland, 2018, 102; and Country Report Ireland, 2020, 91.

[172] EELN, Country Report Ireland, 2020, 94.

[173] IHREC, Annual Report 2016, 30. See the IHREC website at https://www.ihrec.ie/guides-and-tools/.

[174] EELN, Country Report Ireland, 2020, 93; Irish Human Rights and Equality Commission, 'Annual Report 2019' (2020), 44–45.

[175] It has been reported that the Commission remained silent in a case in which sexual harassment was complained about at a theatre. In such circumstances, the IHREC could have carried out an equality review or started an inquiry, or at least called attention to the code of practice. Interview, human rights and equality expert from Ireland, 21 November 2018.

[176] EELN, Country Report Ireland, 2020, 92. One area in which the IHREC's involvement was important concerned its position on abortion. In the Annual Report 2017 it noted in this regard: In a

positions have been openly critical of government, which has been taken as a sign of the independent exercise of the IHREC's functions. Overall, it has been found that the IHREC has so far exercised its power to make independent recommendations largely in a reactive manner[177] and could thus be intensified, especially when it comes to the field of equality and non-discrimination.

In 2017, it established a so-called events space for its own, but also external training courses, workshops, conferences, etc and which facilitates the interaction between the IHREC and partners from civil society. The first strategic plan launched in 2016 was extensively discussed and consulted on with the general public and NGOs and a public consultation was organized for the Strategy Statement 2019–21.[178] There are, however, also critical voices, which find that the IHREC, unlike the Equality Authority, is not engaging in a regular exchange and cooperation with NGOs which would make it possible to reach out to the groups affected by discrimination and be aware of their needs as well as to coordinate efforts in the promotion of equality.[179]

On the international plane, the IHREC has been very active from the beginning in reporting to the United Nations (UN) and Council of Europe (CoE) treaty monitoring bodies. It further actively participates in Equinet's activities and Working Groups.

Overall, it can be concluded that the IHREC has not yet made use of all of its statutory competences or has started doing so only recently. Its role in advising decision makers in legislative and policy drafting has reportedly been used in a rather reactive manner and could be pursued more proactively. An area that needs to be strengthened is its engagement with private employers and service providers beyond the provision of general information and examples of good practice on its website. The IHREC has to constantly make sure that it appropriately balances its activities in the human rights and equality fields.

6.2.4 Good Practices and Challenges

This look into the legal transposition and practical implementation of promotional and preventive functions of Equality Bodies has shown that whatever the structure of the Equality Body, the required functions are provided for in the respective legislation. When it comes to the commitment of states expressed how

policy document published in October 2017, it 'recommended that the state hold a referendum to put to the people the deletion of Article 40.3.3 of the Constitution in order to permit the development framework governing access to abortion in Ireland that has a basis in primary legislation and regulation'. IHREC, Annual Report 2017, 2018, 4, 24.

177 EELN, Country Report Ireland, 2020, 92.
178 ibid 98.
179 Interview, human rights and equality expert from Ireland, 21 November 2018.

they regulate this function of their Equality Body it is important to ensure that all the target groups (right holders, duty bearers, decision makers, general public) are covered and that the legislation does not restrict the means by which the Equality Body can engage in advising or awareness raising. While a narrow understanding of the wording of the RED would imply that states only have to make sure that Equality Bodies have, for instance, the ability to 'make' recommendations, a teleological interpretation of this provision leads to the conclusion that the full life cycle of a recommendation needs to be taken into consideration. In fact, what would be the point of a recommendation from a specialized body if the provision were not understood as implying also some sort of obligation by the addressee of the recommendation to at least take the recommendation into consideration and to provide a reasonable justification if the advised measures are not taken. From the above evaluated legal frameworks, none is considering this part of the life cycle of a recommendation.

Apart from this shortcoming, the main challenges, however, relate to the level of effort made by the state to translate commitment into results. Here the Commission would have some ground to intervene as, in some cases, the Equality Bodies are not performing according to the requirements of the RED. Although the above examples might suggest that this is particularly problematic with regard to predominantly tribunal-type bodies, the same challenges can be encountered also by predominantly promotion-type bodies. Attention should be paid in particular that equality is not slipping off the agenda in merged bodies.

A major challenge appears to be the adequate financing of the Equality Body so that it can effectively implement all its legally assigned functions. It is true that tribunal-type bodies are particularly prone (and understandably so) to dedicate the bulk of their financial resources to their quasi-judicial function to the detriment of the preventive and promotional functions. Many of these bodies are not in a position to engage in awareness raising beyond informing the media about the outcome of their cases. If they are active in this field, in many cases this is often possible only through external funds, including EU funds, which do not, however, guarantee the sustainability of the work of the Equality Body.

Another challenge of predominantly tribunal-type bodies appears to be the appropriate coverage of private sector employers and service providers, both in terms of awareness raising and in terms of advising them on how to approach issues of equality and discrimination. The advisory function in particular would require, in order to safeguard the impartiality and independence of the tribunal-type body, to have a sufficient number of staff, separate from those dealing with complaints, who can engage with duty bearers and other stakeholders.

Unia has been taken as a good practice example of a predominantly promotion-type Equality Body. Its organizational structure well reflects its different functions, it includes regional representatives to ensure the link between the national and regional level, and it has a network of local contact points. While this might be particularly useful and needed in the context of a federal state like Belgium, outreach to regions outside the capital in order to inform them of developments, needs, and priorities is of utmost importance for every Equality Body. Another good practice is Unia's intensive engagement with duty bearers as described above. While the IHREC, just a couple of years into the merger of the IHRC and the Equality Authority, appears to be increasingly using its competences under its preventive and promotional mandate, one of the additional challenges here is to give equality issues appropriate weight within the overall work of the institution.

At the level of outcome and for all types of Equality Bodies, effectiveness of the advisory role of tribunal-type Equality Bodies appears to be limited by the lack of responsiveness of the addressees of the advice. More information would be required (and probably need to be collected) on the follow-up given by private and in particular public authorities to recommendations as well as on the impact they have had on the rights holders. This is of course also an issue related to financing. If an Equality Body already has limited resources to engage in awareness raising and giving advice, it will be even more difficult to monitor the implementation of its recommendations. In particular public bodies should therefore be obliged to respond to recommendations coming from the Equality Body. This would add to the transparency of a public body's position towards certain issues and could potentially contribute also to promoting a public debate about them, thus raising the overall awareness of issues related to discrimination.

6.2.5 Proposed Indicators

Tables 6.2 and 6.3 summarize in the first column the interpretation given to the advisory and the awareness-raising function of Equality Bodies and proposes structural process and outcome indicators that could be used to measure whether an Equality Body is given the required functions and the required support by the state to comply with the requirements under the RED and achieve impact.

Any monitoring of these functions has to consider in particular whether all target groups are covered. Of particular relevance are those professions that play a particular role in the implementation of the non-discrimination legislation. They include, as well as politicians, senior officials and other decision makers, employers, and service providers (and within these categories persons in leadership positions, those employed in the human resource departments, those engaged in

Table 6.2 Table of indicators concerning the awareness-raising function of Equality Bodies

TARGET GROUPS • right holders • decision makers (government/parliament) • duty bearers (employers, service providers, educationalists, etc.)	Structural Indicators	Awareness-raising function • foreseen in legal mandate • existence of a strategy/action plan assigning awareness-raising role to Equality Body • including all target groups and means (or at least not excluding any)
• general public MEANS • printed materials, webpage, events, campaigns, media, social media, etc.	Process indicators	• Equality Body sufficiently funded • to address all target groups • by means considered most effective by Equality Body • on a regular basis (numbers over time) • throughout the country
• training and education for target groups • (cooperation with state/ NGOs)	Outcome indicators	• increased awareness/knowledge (of legislation, Equality Body/ies and other supportive organizations; of means of redress or how to address discrimination) among all target groups

Table 6.3 Table of indicators concerning the advisory function of Equality Bodies

Advisory function ('make recommendations') understood as including the full life cycle of a recommendation MAKING RECOMMENDATIONS AT ALL • Recommendation to government/parliament	Structural indicators	Making recommendations at all and follow-up • provided in mandate • existence of a strategy/action plan assigning advisory role to Equality Body • existence of institutionalized dialogue between state and Equality Body
• on draft/existing/ legislation/ policies • resulting from inquiries, surveys, research • Recommendation to public/ private sector • on good practices • on possible positive action measures EFFECTIVENESS – FOLLOW-UP • obligation to respond to recommendation	Process indicators	Making recommendations at all • sufficiently funded • recommendations and dialogue with Equality Body actively sought by public actors • on a regular basis (numbers over time) • required information provided on time • Equality Body addressing all stakeholders • throughout the country
• dialogue on how to implement recommendation • Equality Body monitoring/ tracking progress of implementation • Equality Body publish status	Outcome indicators	Effectiveness – follow-up • success rate of recommendations (number of recommendations given/number of recommendations followed) • impact of recommendations on right holders

work councils) media professionals, persons employed in educational or health care institutions, law enforcement bodies, as well as in the judiciary and other legal professions. Different target groups need to be addressed by different means and it should remain within the competence of the Equality Body to decide which means is most effective.

Some of the indicators might appear to be too vague to be able to give a clear idea on the performance. One example of this is the indicator: 'sufficient funding'. Such an indicator might imply that if the amount x is provided to the Equality Body, it is sufficient, while if the amount y is provided it is not. Of course it will not be possible to make such a clear determination. Attention should rather be paid to evaluating whether, for instance, awareness-raising activities can only be implemented by the use of external funds or whether a good stock of activities can be carried out with the body's own resources while external funds are a surplus for a determined period of time. An evaluation of the sufficiency of funds should also factor in the activity of the state in awareness raising, which (according to the Directives) has the primary responsibility for disseminating information on non-discrimination legislation. Further, 'sufficient funding' needs to be interpreted in connection with another indicator that probably appears to be equally vague: 'on a regular basis'. Awareness raising is not a one-off exercise and it will definitely not be enough if the state or the Equality Body organizes an information campaign only when legislation transposing EU law is enacted. It needs constant engagement. Therefore, a state in which no meaningful awareness raising (either by the state or by the Equality Body) has taken place for a number of years, probably combined with a survey showing low, or even decreasing levels of awareness, would be in breach of its obligation flowing from Article 10 RED. Indicators therefore need to be interpreted in conjunction with each other.

There are similar considerations regarding the advisory function of the Equality Bodies. In this context, the existence and the use in good faith of a structured dialogue between the state and the Equality Body (as well as civil society actors) is central. At the level of process, this implies that the information required for the Equality Body to give recommendations in particular on draft legislation is shared in a timely manner, its recommendations are actively sought by decision makers, and they engage in a dialogue with the Equality Body on the implementation of the recommendations. There should be a focus on monitoring the follow-up and on the success rate of recommendations, in particular when it comes to public authorities.

While state authorities have less influence on whether private sector actors are seeking the advice of the Equality Body, such engagement is more likely in circumstances in which the Equality Body is taken seriously and equality and non-discrimination advocated also by state actors. The state is however under the obligation to provide the Equality Body with the human and financial resources enabling the body to actively engage with the private sector as well.

6.3 The Role of Social Partners and Non-Governmental Organizations: Involvement in Law and Policy Making and Awareness Raising

6.3.1 Introduction and Conceptual Clarification

The involvement of non-state actors in the law- and policy-making process is a central element of an experimentalist governance approach and a distinctive feature of the EU anti-discrimination regime established since the year 2000.[180] As mentioned in Chapter 2, experimentalist thinking opens agenda setting and problem solving to a wide range of actors, particularly from civil society. '[T]he broadest possible degree of stakeholder participation compatible with effective decision-making' has been identified as one of the most important factors for an experimentalist governance system to succeed.[181] In an experimentalist governance setting, civil society organizations play an important role also in monitoring and evaluation.[182] It is thus interesting to look into the genesis of those articles in the EU Non-Discrimination Directives that clearly bring in this dimension into the Directives (in addition to the role of NGOs in supporting victims of discrimination) and what Member States and different stakeholders have made out of this opportunity.

Article 11 RED (and the parallel provision in Art 13 EED) reads as follows (with the parts that have been added in negotiations to the initial proposal of the Commission in italics):

Article 11
Social dialogue

1. Member States shall, *in accordance with national traditions and practice,* take adequate measures to promote the social dialogue between the two sides of industry with a view to fostering equal treatment, including through the monitoring of workplace practices, collective agreements, codes of conduct, research or exchange of experiences and good practices.
2. *Where consistent with national traditions and practice,* Member States shall encourage the two sides of the industry *without prejudice to their autonomy* to conclude, at the appropriate level, agreements laying down anti-discrimination rules in the fields referred to in Article 3 which fall within the scope of collective bargaining. These agreements shall respect the minimum requirements laid down by this Directive and the relevant national implementing measures.

[180] Gráinne de Búrca, 'Stumbling into Experimentalism: The EU Anti-Discrimination Regime' in Charles F Sabel and Jonathan Zeitlin (eds), Experimentalist Governance in the European Union: Towards a New Architecture (Oxford University Press, 2010), 221–22.

[181] Gráinne de Búrca, 'New Governance and Experimentalism: An Introduction' [2010] Wisconsin Law Review 227, 235; the second being 'effective and informed monitoring'.

[182] Gráinne de Búrca, 'Human Rights Experimentalism' (2017) 111(2) American Journal of International Law 277.

Tyson points out that the initial proposal of the Commission was problematic for some Member States for three reasons.[183] First, the provision did not formulate as clearly as in previous Directives in the social field the possibility for Member States to entrust the social partners with the implementation of the Directive through collective agreements. This is common practice as long as those agreements are legally enforceable and cover the entire target group, but such a provision is usually found in the final provisions regarding implementation. The Commission wanted to give the potential role of social partners more prominence and thus proposed the inclusion of this article in the main text. The proposed text also implied 'a more promotional role for the Member States to encourage the social partners to become involved in fighting discrimination'.[184] For the sake of clarity, in the end the usual text, in addition to the slightly amended version of Article 11, was included in the final provisions.[185]

The second difficulty for some Member States related to the perception that the provision 'require[d] Government interference in the affairs of the social partners'.[186] This was resolved by including in the text a provision that any engagement of the state is not supposed to prejudice the autonomy of the social partners.

Finally, some Member States found the proposal problematic in that 'it appeared to require Member States which were not used to social dialogue arrangements to introduce them'.[187] These fears were dissipated by adding text to the second paragraph to the effect that encouraging social partners to conclude agreements laying down anti-discrimination rules applies only where this is consistent with national traditions and practices.[188]

The Starting Line Group's proposal did not include a comparable provision. Some of the leading figures of the Group, however, when commenting on the Commission's initial proposal, suggested amending Article 11 'to the effect that other organisations than the two sides of industry are involved in the social dialogue'.[189]

None of the initial proposals contained a provision on encouraging dialogue with NGOs. This was particularly surprising with regard to the Starting Line Group's proposal, which came from a coalition of civil society organizations. While the Group did not include a provision on the cooperation between state and

[183] Tyson (n 11) 215.

[184] ibid. In the explanatory memorandum to its initial proposal the Commission underlined its commitment to strengthen the role of social partners in the implementation of the Directive and the monitoring of equal treatment in the workplace. Commission of the European Communities, 'Proposal for a Council Directive implementing the principle of equal treatment between persons irrespective of racial or ethnic origin' (n 28) 10.

[185] See Art 16(1) RED and Art 18(1) EED.

[186] Tyson (n 11) 215.

[187] ibid.

[188] ibid.

[189] Chopin and Niessen, 'Combating Racism in the European Union with Legal Means: A comparison of the Starting Line and the EU Commission's proposal for a Race Directive' (n 33) 9.

non-state actors in the legislative and policy-making sphere, it did foresee a role for NGOs in the reporting process from the Member States to the Commission. The proposal provided that the Commission, after receiving reports from Member States, due every two years after an initial one year from the date of the implementation deadline, could request further information from NGOs. On the basis of all the information gathered, the Commission would draft a report for submission to the European Parliament and the Council and, most importantly, could issue recommendations to states. Furthermore, the Starting Line Group's proposal saw a role of the then European Monitoring Centre on Racism and Xenophobia. The Monitoring Centre was to specify 'standard criteria for monitoring the annual performance of Member States in fulfilling their obligations under the directive'.[190] The reporting provisions of the final versions of the Directives provide for a five-year interval for Member States to submit reports to the Commission, and the viewpoints of NGOs, social partners, and the FRA(which succeeded the European Monitoring Centre on Racism and Xenophobia) shall be taken into account 'as appropriate'. The report shall also include, 'if necessary, proposals to revise and update' the Directives.[191] This was an improvement compared to the proposal of the Commission,[192] made possible due to the intervention by the European Parliament,[193] but did not reach the level of the Starting Line Group's proposal, in particular when it comes to the issuing of recommendations to states.

In its reports to the European Parliament and the Council, the Commission increasingly requests information from social partners and civil society organizations, in addition to Equality Bodies, Equinet, the FRA, and the European Equality Law Network.[194] Although the involvement of different actors in the preparation

[190] Chopin, 'The Starting Line Group: A Harmonised Approach to Fight Racism and to Promote Equal Treatment' (n 31) 127. The European Parliament also supported the involvement of the Monitoring Centre in continued monitoring of the effectiveness of measures taken by states in implementing the Directives: 'The European Monitoring Centre for Racism and Xenophobia in Vienna should play a complementary role in monitoring the way the directive is implemented. While the Commission monitors compliance with the directive, the Monitoring Centre should monitor the effectiveness of the measures taken by the Member states. This is important because compliance and effectiveness are not necessarily the same thing.' European Parliament, 'Report on the proposal for a Council directive on implementing the principle of equal treatment between persons irrespective of racial or ethnic origin (COM(1999) 566—C5-0067/2000—1999/0253(CNS))' (n 31) 39.

[191] Art 17 RED, Art 19 EED.

[192] The Commission's proposal provided: 'Member States shall communicate to the Commission, within two years of the date mentioned in Article 15, all the information necessary for the Commission to draw up a report to the European Parliament and the Council on the application of this Directive.'

[193] European Parliament, 'Report on the proposal for a Council directive on implementing the principle of equal treatment between persons irrespective of racial or ethnic origin (COM(1999) 566—C5-0067/2000—1999/0253(CNS))' (n 31).

[194] See European Commission, 'Report on the application of Council Directive 2000/43/EC implementing the principle of equal treatment between persons irrespective of racial or ethnic origin ("the Racial Equality Directive") and of Council Directive 2000/78/EC establishing a general framework for equal treatment in employment and occupation ("the Employment Equality Directive")' (n 27) 3; European Commission, 'Joint Report on the application of Council Directive 2000/43/EC of 29 June 2000 implementing the principle of equal treatment between persons irrespective of racial or ethnic origin ("Racial Equality Directive") and of Council Directive 2000/78/EC of 27 November 2000

of the Commission's reports is to be welcomed, the overall reporting mechanism is considerably weaker compared to the one proposed by the Starting Line Group and supported also by the European Parliament.

The European Parliament was also the driving-force behind the article concerning dialogue with NGOs (Art 12 RED and Art 14 EED). In its report on the Commission's proposal it highlighted the importance of 'mention[ing] specifically the civil dialogue with NGOs alongside the social dialogue between social partners'.[195] The Commission amended its proposal accordingly and the Council accepted it without major discussions. The Commission believed that the engagement with NGOs would have positive effects on the effectiveness of national policies and awareness raising.[196]

The provisions on social and civil dialogue have been described as 'exhortatory' and 'declaratory' and Tyson found it 'difficult to imagine that there will be many challenges to Member States' implementation'.[197] In fact, none of the infringement proceedings brought against a Member State regarded these two articles. In its initial reports to the European Parliament and the Council, the Commission touched on them only in passing as one of the aspects common to both Directives without entering into any detail.[198] Its most recent report gave it a bit more space, observing that some Member States have established regular dialogue with civil society organizations by law, while in others it found that such dialogue was limited or even lacking. In some countries it noted the existence of restrictive legislation, difficult financial situations of NGOs, and even harassment.[199]

As will be discussed below, NGOs have shown great motivation to engage with other stakeholders to promote the principle of equal treatment. They have done so,

establishing a general framework for equal treatment in employment and occupation ("Employment Equality Directive")' (n 22) 3; Commission of the European Communities, 'The application of Directive 2000/43/EC of 29 June 2000 implementing the principle of equal treatment between persons irrespective of racial or ethnic origin' (30 October 2006) COM(2006) 643 final, 3; Commission of the European Communities, 'The application of Directive 2000/78/EC of 27 November 2000 establishing a general framework for equal treatment in employment and occupation' (8 July 2008) COM(2008) 225 final/2.

195 European Parliament, 'Report on the proposal for a Council directive on implementing the principle of equal treatment between persons irrespective of racial or ethnic origin (COM(1999) 566—C5-0067/2000—1999/0253(CNS))' (n 31) 27 and 64.

196 Tyson (n 11) 216.

197 ibid 215–16.

198 See eg European Commission, 'Joint Report on the application of Council Directive 2000/43/EC of 29 June 2000 implementing the principle of equal treatment between persons irrespective of racial or ethnic origin ("Racial Equality Directive") and of Council Directive 2000/78/EC of 27 November 2000 establishing a general framework for equal treatment in employment and occupation ("Employment Equality Directive")' (n 22) 5 and 8.

199 European Commission, 'Report on the application of Council Directive 2000/43/EC implementing the principle of equal treatment between persons irrespective of racial or ethnic origin ("the Racial Equality Directive") and of Council Directive 2000/78/EC establishing a general framework for equal treatment in employment and occupation ("the Employment Equality Directive")' (n 27) 12.

inter alia, by trying to influence law and policy making and by raising awareness. Social partners, in particular on the employers' side, have not played an important role so far. De Búrca explains this by the fact that 'employers and service providers often have—or understand themselves to have—little independent interest in developing equality norms.'[200] Research carried out by the FRA found that besides those employers' organizations that felt the RED had a positive impact, or little or no impact, there were also some organizations that had a negative view of the Directive. This view related to the cost of compliance and in particular the provision on the burden of proof. Some 'did not believe that the directive was capable of influencing behavior' while others opposed any interference with employer prerogatives. Among employer organizations of new Member States the view prevailed that non-discrimination legislation did not concern their organization or denied the existence of ethnic discrimination in employment in their countries. Some even saw non-discrimination legislation as an '"exotic" issue ... forced upon them from the outside.'[201] While greater awareness of the RED could be observed among trade unions, and many reported about active policy changes that could be directly or indirectly connected to the Directive, some believed that the RED 'was not the right instrument to fight discrimination' and similar to the employers' unions, denied the existence of discrimination.[202] Social dialogue as encouraged by RED has led, according to the findings of the same research, to many joint initiatives but there is still considerable room for improvement.[203] The focus in the following sub-sections 6.3.2 and 6.3.3 will be on the civil rather than on the social dialogue.

6.3.2 Legal Transposition and Practical Implementation

The provisions on encouraging dialogue with NGOs with a view to promoting the principle of equal treatment and encouraging dialogue between social partners 'have seen the least formal implementation by Member States and candidate countries and probably the most varied response. To some extent, this is due to the vagueness of these articles and the interpretation by some Governments that they are not bound to transpose these provisions into law but simply to take some steps towards achieving their objectives.'[204] This sub-section 6.3.2 will therefore

[200] de Búrca, 'Stumbling into Experimentalism: The EU Anti-Discrimination Regime' (n 180) 222.

[201] Fundamental Rights Agency, 'The impact of the racial equality directive: Views of trade unions and employers in the European Union' (2010) 9–10.

[202] ibid 10–11.

[203] ibid 12. For two more recent studies, also showing some improvement, see Eurofound, 'Role of social partners in tackling discrimination at work' (2020) <https://www.eurofound.europa.eu/publications/customised-report/2020/role-of-social-partners-in-tackling-discrimination-at-work>; and European Commission, 'Trade union practices on non-discrimination and diversity 2019' (2019).

[204] European network of legal experts in gender equality and non-discrimination, 'A comparative analysis of non-discrimination law in Europe 2017' (n 55) 121. This finding appears in all comparative analyses between 2012 and 2018, but the situation has not changed thereafter.

deal with both aspects—legal transposition to the extent it exists, and practical implementation—at the same time. The focus will be on the existence of such dialogue in general, whether these actors have been/are included in law and policy making and the role they play in awareness raising.

Formal, more or less permanent structures to foster dialogue with NGOs or between social partners are in place only in a few countries and the situation has not improved over the years.[205] In Finland, an Advisory Board on Non-Discrimination was set up in 2016 for the period until October 2019 and this was renewed in 2020. The Board is chaired by the Non-Discrimination Ombudsman and is composed of another thirty-seven members 'representing significant expertise in combatting discrimination' (key ministries, social partners, NGOs). The Board has no decision-making role but serves as a communication network between the Ombudsman, civil society organizations CSOs, and authorities.[206] France has established commissions at state and sub-state level. At national level, the National Consultative Commission on Human Rights serves as an advisory body to the prime minister and the government and is consulted on all human right-related legislative reforms. It is composed of representatives of all major human rights and anti-racism NGOs, trade unions, and branches of the public sector. One of its six sub-commissions is dealing with racism and anti-semitism. At the level of *départements*, commissions for the promotion of equality and citizenship are established. They bring together all local actors under the authority of the prefect. There are also national and local commissions concerning disability that involve NGOs representing disabled and social partners.[207]

In Slovakia, the Government Council for Human Rights, National Minorities and Gender Equality is established as a permanent advisory body to the government. It is composed of forty members coming from government, regional and local bodies, NGOs, and academia. Seven Committees of the Council cover all discrimination grounds except for religion and belief. Due to the fact that no clear mechanism exists for the Council on how to feed into legislative processes and that there is no monitoring of compliance with its recommendation, which appear not to be taken seriously by the government, the Council is 'often a forum for formal discussion only'.[208] In Belgium, a specific taskforce has been established within the Ministry of Employment with the active cooperation of Unia 'to establish more systematic links with the social partners'.[209]

[205] European network of legal experts in gender equality and non-discrimination, 'A comparative analysis of non-discrimination law in Europe: 2020' (n 34) 115.

[206] EELN, Country Report Finland, 2020, 57; and https://syrjinta.fi/en/advisory-board-for-non-discrimination.

[207] EELN, Country Report France, 2020, 112. Similarly, structured dialogue with NGOs acting in the interests of the disabled exists in Latvia (Latvian National Council for the Affairs of Disabled Persons) and Spain (National Disability Council). European network of legal experts in gender equality and non-discrimination, 'A comparative analysis of non-discrimination law in Europe: 2020' (n 34) 115.

[208] EELN, Country Report Slovakia, 2020, 98–99.

[209] EELN, Country Report Belgium, 2020, 115.

In Germany, institutionalized dialogue and cooperation with NGOs takes place, for instance, through the Alliance for Democracy and Tolerance.[210] The Alliance bundles initiatives of a wide range of civil society actors, supports networking and problem solving, and raises awareness about the engagement of civil society for democracy and tolerance. Board members come from various NGOs in addition to members of parliament from different political parties. In Austria, the minister responsible for the field of discrimination holds a yearly meeting with NGOs. Although this can hardly be considered a proper dialogue, it can be mitigated by the fact that it is common practice to invite interested NGOs to comment on draft legislation and they regularly make use of this possibility.[211] However, in 2018 Austria's civic space rating was downgraded from open to narrowed. Among the reasons given for this was that 'the new administration has steadfastly refused to engage in structured dialogue with civil society in a range of sectors. Instead, leaders have made a number of derogatory remarks about non-governmental organisations.' Furthermore, '[f]unding to NGOs in many sectors has … been drastically reduced'.[212] With the change of government, Austria's rating has been upgraded again to 'open' in 2020.[213]

Some countries, such as Belgium, France, Finland, Greece, and Spain, have established specific structures addressing the situation of Roma. The Austrian Federal Chancellery has also set up a National Contact Point for Roma Integration including a dialogue platform through which contacts with NGOs are maintained. The Hungarian government established a Consultation Council for Roma Affairs, which is co-chaired by the president of the National Roma Self-Government.[214]

On the other hand, there are countries in which dialogue with NGOs takes place on an ad hoc basis rather than within formal structures. One example for this is the UK where government departments, when controversial issues arise, often establish ad hoc groups to consult with NGOs on these issues. It is considered a positive duty of public authorities 'to consult on the equality impact of their policies and practices, which has encouraged greater engagement with civil society and local communities'.[215] Similarly, as just described with regard to Austria, there are countries which generally involve different social actors in a consultation process regarding draft legislation. This is also the case in Germany, for instance. The Slovene Protection against Discrimination Act requires the government to cooperate

[210] EELN, Country Report Germany, 2020, 87.
[211] EELN, Country Report Austria, 2020, 72.
[212] Civicus—Monitor Tracking Civic Space, 'Austria's Civic Space Rating Downgraded from Open to Narrowed' (19 November 2018) <https://monitor.civicus.org/newsfeed/2018/11/19/austrias-civic-space-rating-downgraded-open-narrowed/>.
[213] Civicus—Monitor Tracking Civic Space, 'Austria Civic Space Rating Upgraded to Open' (15 September 2020) <https://monitor.civicus.org/updates/2020/09/15/austria-civic-space-rating-upgraded-open/>.
[214] European network of legal experts in gender equality and non-discrimination, 'A comparative analysis of non-discrimination law in Europe: 2020' (n 34) 116.
[215] EELN, Country Report United Kingdom, 2020, 64.

with NGOs when working on proposals aimed at reaching the goals of the Non-Discrimination Act.[216]

In quite a number of countries, the responsibility to engage in a dialogue with CSO is either by law or in practice delegated or left (mainly) to the Equality Body. Intensive collaboration and dialogue between Equality Bodies and CSOs is of course of great relevance for enhancing the effectiveness and the impact of their activities.[217] However, considering that the Directives require the Member States to encourage dialogue with NGOs, it needs to be asked whether a delegation of this task to the Equality Body can be considered to be compliant with the Directives. While it is true that in some cases the Equality Bodies (such as in Italy or Austria) are embedded within the governmental structure and thus their activity can be considered as 'state' activity, the above discussion of the issue of independence has shown that the compliance of such a construction with the requirements of the Directive is itself questionable. In other cases, where civil dialogue is legally provided for exclusively with regard to the Equality Body (as in Croatia), it is reasonable to consider this as transposition non-compatible with the requirements of the Directives. Among the purposes of including such a provision encouraging the state to seek the dialogue with civil society organizations was, as described above, to increase the effectiveness of national policies. This is more likely to happen if a regular and meaningful dialogue between the relevant state institutions and these organizations takes place, rather than in a situation in which the Equality Body functions as an intermediary body. And finally, if national legislation obliges the state to engage in dialogue with CSOs but in practice this dialogue is left to the Equality Body, there might be correct legal transposition but the application is lacking which equally represents a compliance problem.

Croatia is an example where the legislation explicitly provides that the Equality Body has an obligation to consult civil society organizations when fulfilling some of its tasks,[218] while a provision regarding state–CSO dialogue does not exist. The Ombudsperson keeps in regular contact with NGOs and after a public call it has concluded a Cooperation Agreement with eleven of them, making them the Ombudsperson's contact points at regional and local level.[219] The Greek Ombudsman established an anti-discrimination network of CSOs in 2013, thereby establishing a partnership between various stakeholders with the purpose of sharing information and knowledge and collectively promoting equality.[220] In Romania, the NCCD engages with NGOs, for instance by carrying out joint projects and training activities. It also consults with major NGOs on the development of its programmes. More recently, the NCCD has been criticized by NGOs

216 EELN, Country Report Slovenia, 2020, 87.

217 Examples for how Equality Bodies in particular can empower CSOs are collected and analysed in Equinet, 'Effective Strategies to Empower Civil Society' (n 107).

218 Croatia, ADA, Art 15.

219 EELN, Country Report Croatia, 2020, 98.

220 EELN, Country Report Greece, 2020, 84.

for not adequately involving them in a dialogue on the amendments to the anti-discrimination legislation and the evaluation of the old and subsequent drafting of the new anti-discrimination strategy.[221] In Italy, the establishment of a dialogue with NGOs is supposed to be one of UNAR's priorities. Its most relevant activity in this context is reportedly the establishment of a consultative committee on LGBT issues involving NGOs working on such issues.[222]

In some countries NGOs play a rather weak role (such as in Lithuania and Sweden[223]) or EELN experts report no major efforts either from the state or the Equality Body to engage in a dialogue. This is the case in Bulgaria for instance, where, according to the Bulgarian EELN expert, the CPAD 'has not involved NGOs in cooperation or dialogue in any inclusive or meaningful way. In the past, it engaged in selective contacts with some NGOs on a non-transparent basis.'[224] The report is silent about any kind of dialogue between state authorities and NGOs. The Cypriot expert reports that '[c]onsultation with NGOs in Cyprus is a rather new practice that is not significantly developed.... The views of NGOs are very rarely taken into account.... The new Ombudsman, who took office in 2017, halted all interaction with NGOs.'[225] In the Czech Republic '[t]here has been no notable action in recent years to encourage dialogue with NGOs', except for the engagement of the Ombudsman.[226] The same is reported from Denmark.[227]

This gives an overall picture of many governments not taking NGOs seriously as partners, even though they could play a positive role in a number of fields, especially during the development of legislation, policies, and strategies, their evaluation and monitoring, as well as in awareness raising, training, and outreach to vulnerable groups.

According to the information provided by the European Equality Law Network only some countries consulted with civil and social partners in the transposition process of the Directives. In some cases, such actors were included in the Working Group elaborating the draft anti-discrimination law or amendments to such law. This was the case in Croatia, Denmark, and Slovakia, for example. In other cases conceptual papers and/or draft laws were sent to NGOs and/or social partners (as well as Equality Bodies) for their comments or put on the Ministry of Justice's website with a public call for comments. This kind of consultation was undertaken by Hungary, Ireland, the Netherlands, and the UK.[228] In the UK, however (and

221 EELN, Country Report Romania, 2020, 88. In the interview with the Steering Board member of NCCD on 10 July 2018 he expressed the opinion that the state authorities leave it to the Equality Body to keep the dialogue with NGOs.

222 EELN, Country Report Italy, 2020, 61.

223 EELN, Country Report Lithuania, 2020, 115–16; Country Report on Sweden, 2020, 91.

224 EELN, Country Report Bulgaria, 2020, 83.

225 EELN, Country Report Cyprus, 2020, 114.

226 EELN, Country Report Czech Republic, 2020, 9 and 80.

227 EELN, Country Report Denmark, 2020, 84.

228 European network of legal experts in gender equality and non-discrimination, 'A comparative analysis of non-discrimination law in Europe 2017' (n 55) 123.

probably in some other countries as well) it appears that this consultation was not undertaken with the purpose of meeting the Directives' requirement of engaging in civil dialogue but to 'inform Government and to seek to secure wider acceptance of its policies'.[229] In Romania, the Ordinance 137/2000 cannot formally be seen as transposition of the EU Equality Directives because it was adopted before them. However, in this context it is important to note that the Working Group drafting the ordinance was mainly composed of human rights activists convened by the Romanian Soros foundation and supported by the Ministry of National Minorities. In subsequent amendments to the legislation, the Antidiscrimination Coalition offered support as well,[230] but felt excluded from the dialogue about these amendments with the NCCD.[231]

In other countries, NGOs or social partners reportedly played no role in the transposition phase or during amendments to anti-discrimination acts. Regarding Spain, for instance, reference was made to 'hidden transposition', considering that not only did no consultation with stakeholders take place but also there was no dedicated law transposing the Directives and the act containing provisions about their transposition did not refer to either 'equal treatment' or 'discrimination' in its title. There was no parliamentary debate and no member of government made any statement about the transposition.[232] In Bulgaria, amendments to the Anti-Discrimination Act were not at all consulted on with NGOs.[233]

Dialogue with NGOs and social partners should of course not be confined to the transposition of Anti-Discrimination Directives but inform all legislative processes potentially having an impact in the field of equal treatment and non-discrimination. As described above, inclusive consultation processes have become a routine in some countries but do not constitute general practice in all Member States. From some countries it is reported that the situation has deteriorated in the last couple of years. In Croatia, for instance, there existed a code of good practice in counselling regarding the adoption of legal and strategic documents. NGO representatives were involved in Working Groups and the acceptance rate of NGO comments on drafts was higher than it is today. A couple of years ago, when comments were not accepted, the explanation for it was more forthcoming whereas today it is very scarce. Also, where NGO representatives are involved in Working Groups today, they are often 'there to be there' but have no real opportunity to influence the process.[234]

Beyond legislation, dialogue with NGOs is important in drafting relevant strategies and action plans as well as in the monitoring and evaluation of

[229] EELN, Country Report United Kingdom, 2020, 64.
[230] Interview, Board member of ACCEPT, 6 August 2018.
[231] EELN, Country Report Romania, 2020, 88.
[232] EELN, Country Report Spain, 2017, 100.
[233] EELN, Country Report Bulgaria, 2020, 83.
[234] Interview, Executive Board Member of Centre for Peace Studies, Zagreb, 1 August 2018.

anti-discrimination legislation and policies. The EELN reports reveal very little information about the extent to which NGOs are involved such kind of activities. An interesting initiative has been implemented in Belgium, where a national debate lasting over two years on multiculturalism and diversity was initiated by the government with large stakeholder involvement, including the Equality Body and numerous NGOs. The final report included sixty-seven recommendations, most of which were, however, not given any follow-up.[235] In Croatia, a network of NGOs evaluated the National Anti-discrimination Strategy and came up with recommendations on how to improve the subsequent one. The outcome of this evaluation was taken as a basis for the drafting of the new strategy. However, with a new incoming government that version was re-drafted and some NGOs, who had previously played an important role, were not accepted into the Working Group any more. The pressure they exerted from outside, together with the efforts by the Ombudsperson, managed to avoid the watering down of many of the innovative elements of the draft.[236] In Romania, the NCCD took the lead in first evaluating the expiring strategy then drafting a new one. It organized a number of roundtables and consultations throughout Romania, including NGOs, which nevertheless had the feeling that consultation could have been more intensive. The resulting draft strategy has so far not been taken into consideration by the authorities.

These examples give evidence of the generally lamented shrinking space for NGOs. Civic space ratings in the European Union consider it open in fourteen countries,[237] narrowed in thirteen countries,[238] and obstructed in one country (Hungary).[239] This makes it all the more important that the European Union puts pressure on Member States to retain a meaningful dialogue with NGOs especially in those cases where it is explicitly provided by EU law. For that purpose it is first of all required to build NGOs capacities to enable them to play their role in law and policy making as well as in monitoring and evaluating legislation and policies. Secondly, the structures need to be put in place that will allow them to raise their voice. And most importantly, their voice must also be heard. The funding and support activities of the European Commission in the past are to be welcomed in this context and it is to be hoped that programmes launched within the current Multiannual Financial Framework take these needs into due consideration.

235 EELN, Country Report Belgium, 2020, 114. On the process, see Julie Ringelheim, 'Du Dialogue aux Assises: heurts et malheurs de l'interculturalité en Belgique' in Emmanuelle Bribosia and Isabelle Rorive (eds), *L'accommodement de la diversité religieuse. Regards croisés—Canada, Europe, Belgique* (Peter Lang 2015).

236 Interview, Executive Board Member of Centre for Peace Studies, Zagreb, 1 August 2018; staff member at the Office of the Ombudsperson, 26 October 2018.

237 Austria, Belgium, Czech Republic, Cyprus, Denmark, Estonia, Finland, Germany, Ireland, Lithuania, Luxembourg, the Netherlands, Portugal, and Sweden.

238 Bulgaria, Croatia, France, Greece, Italy, Latvia, Malta, Poland, Romania, Slovakia, Slovenia, Spain, UK.

239 Civic space in all Western Balkan countries is narrowed, except for Serbia, where it is obstructed, while in Turkey it is repressed. Information taken from https://monitor.civicus.org/.

Last but not least, NGOs have an important role to play when it comes to awareness raising and training in general and in particular when it comes to reaching out to potential victims of discrimination in whose interests they are working.[240] This does not of course take away the fact that it is the states' responsibility to disseminate information about the equality and non-discrimination legislation in place throughout their territories (Art 10 RED and Art 12 EED). In many countries, such dissemination is mainly carried out by either NGOs or the Equality Body or those two together. In France, for instance, most NGOs receive state subsidies and pursue dissemination activities through their websites, by presenting case law and legal tools, and by holding seminars and events.[241] In Latvia, the Latvian Centre for Human Rights organized a number of training events for NGOs, trade unions, police officers, judges, health and social workers, civil servants, and journalism students, it published brochures and reports, created an anti-discrimination database, collecting legislative and policy documents, court cases, surveys, and reports. The public Society Integration Fund in cooperation with NGOs and funded by the EU PROGRESS programme implemented various awareness-raising and dissemination projects, including training for judges, a Roma survey, a poster campaign, and video spots.[242] In Poland, CSOs received funding through EU programmes allowing them to disseminate information about the anti-discrimination legal framework and policies to various stakeholders. According to the EELN report it is thanks to this external funding that 'CSOs have become a good source of information for victims of discrimination, and several lawyers have been trained by them on legal protection against discrimination'.[243] The report, however, also notes that awareness raising and training should not be the sole responsibility of NGOs and that 'appropriate activities by state bodies and the equality body are needed'.[244] The UK government made available considerable sums to fund NGOs' awareness-raising projects particularly in relation to the implementation of the prohibition of discrimination based on sexual orientation. Most NGOs that have an interest in combatting discrimination depend, however, on non-government funding.[245] NGOs also engage in awareness raising in Lithuania and Malta.[246]

The above has shown that formal structures for dialogue with relevant NGOs are rare and only in a few cases entrenched in law. Considering that the Commission has not raised this as a problematic issue in either infringement proceedings or its

[240] See, in this sense, for instance Fundamental Rights Agency, 'EU-MIDIS II: Roma—selected findings' (n 25) 11; and Equinet, 'Providing Independent Assistance to Victims of Discrimination: An Equinet Report' (n 92) 11.

[241] EELN, Country Report France, 2020, 111.

[242] EELN, Country Report Latvia, 2020, 83.

[243] EELN, Country Report Poland, 2017, 136.

[244] ibid.

[245] EELN, Country Report United Kingdom, 2020, 64.

[246] EELN, Country Report Lithuania, 2020, 115 (in cooperation with Ombudsman); Country Report Malta, 2020, 78.

first two evaluations on the state of implementation of the Directives, this indicates that the Commission shares the view of some Member States that the respective provisions of the Directives do not require legal transposition but 'simply to take some steps towards achieving their objectives'.[247] However, the above overview allows us to conclude that a number of states have not taken any or sufficient steps towards maintaining a dialogue with NGOs, which should, at best, be regular, informed and meaningful, 'with a view to promoting the principle of equal treatment' as required by the Directives. To maintain dialogue with NGOs cannot be fully delegated to the Equality Bodies. NGOs themselves, quite conveniently for the state, most easily assume the role of disseminating information and raising awareness, thus taking over yet another obligation of the state, without however being involved by the state in other important phases of the policy cycle: drafting legislation, policy making, and evaluation and monitoring thereof. From this perspective one can conclude that one central element of experimentalist governance, namely the 'broadest possible degree of stakeholder participation compatible with effective decision-making'[248] is so far largely neglected and its potential remains untapped.

6.3.3 Good Practices and Challenges

Examples from various countries, such as Croatia, Hungary, and Romania have shown that the opportunities for NGOs to engage in a constructive dialogue with state authorities and to be meaningfully involved in law and policy making are shrinking. Such developments usually affect not only the field of equality and non-discrimination but the general state of democracy in a country. The challenges NGOs are exposed to in such circumstances are many. The most existential one is related to developments in some countries that could lead to the actual closing down of the organizations. An example in point is Romania, where legislation was tabled in 2018 that would have imposed very restrictive financial and reporting obligations on NGOs, including the publication of the names of all their donors and a publication of reports of their revenues and expenses in the Official Gazette twice a year, with non-observance leading to closure. Furthermore, in order for organizations to attain the 'public utility status', required to get public funds, they may not have engaged in 'any political activities' in the previous two years. What was meant by 'political activities' was not defined in the draft law, which would have risked a broad interpretation of the term, eventually excluding all NGOs taking a critical

[247] European network of legal experts in gender equality and non-discrimination, 'A comparative analysis of non-discrimination law in Europe 2017' (n 55) 121.
[248] de Búrca, 'New Governance and Experimentalism: An Introduction' (n 181) 235.

stance towards government from public funding.[249] Due to international pressure (including from the European Commission (EC) but also from Parliamentary Assembly of the Council of Europe (PACE)) following the protests from civil society organizations, the proposed language was amended and the law adopted in a more acceptable form.[250]

Even if not faced with the threat of being closed down, many NGOs suffer from a lack of funding. All this adds to an environment which is not conducive for NGOs to thrive and makes it difficult for them to contribute to the promotion of the principle of equal treatment. In addition to these unfavourable factors, further shortcomings relate to the fact that non-discrimination laws usually do not provide for the legal framework, within which a dialogue between state and NGOs could unfold. If they do touch on the issue, it is to delegate this obligation to the Equality Body. While Equality Bodies do engage with CSOs to inform their work, the purpose of Article 12 RED and Article 14 EED was to increase the effectiveness of national policies. This can only be achieved if there is a direct dialogue between decision makers and CSOs. Furthermore, even if in some cases consultation practices between the state and NGOs have been in place, they have either been curbed or taken less seriously. Taking into consideration the requirement deriving from the Directives to engage in a dialogue with appropriate NGOs, the Commission mentioned in its last report that such dialogue is sometimes limited or even missing but it did not derive from that any recommendations for the countries concerned.[251]

When it comes to good practice, it should be mentioned that some countries have established formal, permanent dialogue structures between the state authorities and NGOs dealing with issues relating to equality and non-discrimination. While in some countries specific advisory bodies have been set up for specific discrimination grounds or particular groups, such as disability or Roma, it should be ensured that there are channels of communication between the state and NGOs regarding all grounds. These are fora where the needs and priorities of different interest organizations can be discussed and legislative shortcomings or gaps identified. When drafting legislation, it is good practice to include NGO representatives in the Working Groups

[249] Civicus—Monitor Tracking Civic Space, 'Parliament to Vote on Alarming NGO Law' (26 July 2018) https://monitor.civicus.org/updates/2018/07/26/Parliament-to-Vote-on-alarming-NGO-Law/ . Attacks on civil society actors are also increasingly reported from Croatia. See, for instance, Lovorka Šošić, 'Croatian Government Called on to stop Attacking Civil Society' (Civil Liberties Union for Europe, 8 November 2018) <https://www.liberties.eu/en/news/criminalization-of-solidarity-croatia/16115>.

[250] European Commission, '2020 Rule of Law Report: Country Chapter on the rule of law situation in Romania' (30 September 2020) SWD(2020) 322 final, 18. For more on a similarly difficult legal environment for NGOs in Hungary, see Chapter 4.3.2 and the infringement case, decided by the CJEU, *Commission v Hungary* [2020] ECLI:EU:C:2020:476. New infringement proceedings on a similar issue were started by the Commission against Hungary in February 2021.

[251] European Commission, 'Report on the application of Council Directive 2000/43/EC implementing the principle of equal treatment between persons irrespective of racial or ethnic origin ("the Racial Equality Directive") and of Council Directive 2000/78/EC establishing a general framework for equal treatment in employment and occupation ("the Employment Equality Directive")' (n 50) 12.

developing the legislation. The adoption of codes of good practice in counselling as well as the practice of submitting every legal draft to public consultation for a reasonable amount of time are also positive examples of how the dialogue with CSOs can be brought into the decision-making process.

When it comes to awareness raising, the analysis has shown that in many countries NGOs play an important role, either alone or in cooperation with the Equality Body. Funding for such activities, however, very often comes either from the European Commission or other external funds, but not from the states concerned.

Considering this overall very difficult situation for NGOs, the Commission's proposal of June 2018 for a new Rights and Values programme[252] aiming, inter alia, 'to support NGOs protecting European values in response to widespread attacks against civil society organizations',[253] was therefore good news, although it was also criticized for not providing enough money, for making funds available only 'for helping to implement EU law and policy, rather than to defend rights and democracy more broadly', and for focusing on the financing of pan-European network or umbrella NGOs, while 'it is hard to see how the fund will make a real impact if it does not also provide similar grants for organisations working at national level that are short of resources'.[254] In October 2018, the European Parliament's Civil Liberties Committee (LIBE) presented its draft report on the Commission's proposal.[255] The rapporteur highlighted the European Parliament's resolution of April 2018[256] in which it urged the Commission to propose an instrument focusing on the provision of 'financial support for civil society on local and national level to counter the backlash against democracy, rule of law and fundamental rights in the EU'.[257] It also noted the FRA's recommendation of early 2018 addressed to EU institutions and Member States 'to ensure that funding is made available for CSOs working on the protection and promotion of the EU's foundational values of fundamental rights, democracy and the rule of law; including for small grassroots organisations. Such funding should cover, as appropriate, the variety of activities of CSOs, such as service provision, watchdog activities, advocacy, litigation, campaigning, human rights and civic education and awareness raising.'[258] The rapporteur therefore proposed

[252] European Commission, 'Proposal for a Regulation of the European Parliament and of the Council establishing the Rights and Values Programme' (7 June 2018) COM(2018) 383 final/2.

[253] See the news on Civil Liberties Union, at https://www.liberties.eu/en/short-news/22125/22125.

[254] György Folk, 'Freedoms Fund: The EU Commission's Half-Hearted Plans to Support Civil Society Groups' (Civil Liberties Union for Europe, 31 May 2018) https://www.liberties.eu/en/stories/ec-commission-evi-proposal-rights-and-values-fund/14988.

[255] European Parliament, Committee on Civil Liberties, Justice and Home Affairs, 'Draft Report on the proposal for a regulation of the European Parliament and of the Council establishing the Rights and Values programme (COM(2018)0383—C8-0234/2018—2018/0207(COD))' (Rapporteur: Bodil Valero, 2 October 2018) 2018/0207(COD).

[256] European Parliament, 'European Parliament resolution on the need to establish a European Values Instrument to support civil society organisations which promote fundamental values within the European Union at local and national level (2018/2619(RSP))'(19 April 2018).

[257] European Parliament, Committee on Civil Liberties, Justice and Home Affairs 49.

[258] Fundamental Rights Agency, 'Challenges facing civil society organisations working on human rights in the EU' (2018)9, opinion 3.

amendments to the Commission's proposal to the effect that more funding would be given to grassroots projects and to CSOs active at local, regional, and national levels. While acknowledging that 'actions on transnational level plays an important role, many challenges to European values have local origins and needs to be addressed both at local and European level'. In addition to the simplification of procedures and easier access to funding, she further proposed an augmentation of the funds from 642 million EUR for seven years as proposed by the Commission, to nearly 2 billion EUR, with 1 billion reserved for the values strand of the programme. Such a substantial increase as compared to the Commission's proposal was, in the view of the rapporteur, 'both crucial and necessary in order to respond effectively to today's challenges to European values.'[259] According to the proposal of the rapporteur, 40 per cent of funding shall be earmarked for NGOs.

During negotiations the programme value has been raised to 1.55 billion EUR. One strand will deal with equality, rights, and gender equality, which together with the strand focusing on the fight against violence, including gender-based violence (Daphne) will be assigned 24.5 per cent of the budget. The values strand has been described as 'one of the big innovations of the programme' and has been assigned 44.4 per cent of the overall budget. 'At a time where European societies are confronted with extremism, radicalism and divisions and a shrinking space for independent civil society, this strand will place civil society organisations at the heart of its priorities by funding projects which promote and raise awareness on EU values and EU fundamental rights and by providing financial support to local, regional and transnational civil society organisations.'[260] The respective regulation is expected to be adopted in April 2021, and will hopefully contribute to strengthening the capacities of, and mutual learning among, civil society organizations as well as to securing a more conducive environment for them to operate effectively within EU Member States.

6.3.4 Proposed Indicators

A dialogue with CSOs is not possible if the general approach towards CSOs is hostile. This becomes visible if a state is regulating these organizations in a way which make it hardly possible for them to survive. A first structural indicator, although not deriving directly from the Equality Directives, needs to look into whether there exists a generally conducive environment for NGOs to work. Apart from an enabling legal environment (including transparent and non-discriminatory

[259] European Parliament, Committee on Civil Liberties, Justice and Home Affairs (n 257) 51.

[260] For details see https://ec.europa.eu/info/funding-tenders/opportunities/portal/screen/programmes/cerv and https://ec.europa.eu/newsroom/just/item-detail.cfm?item_id=704241& newsletter_id=1148&utm_source=just_newsletter&utm_medium=email&utm_campaign=Funding+opportunities&utm_content=The+new++billion+CERV+programme+is+coming+learn+more+and+get+ready+to+&lang=en.

registration procedures, no undue financial reporting obligations, or other legal limitations) this also requires an enabling financial environment (including a transparent state-funding policy and ways of accessing funds from different sources in and outside the country). The above-quoted Commission Guidelines for EU support to civil society organizations in enlargement countries could be taken as reference on how to monitor the existence of a conducive environment.[261]

Directly flowing from the Directives, other structural indicators would look into whether a state provides for the legal framework within which NGOs can make their contribution. This means that the state–CSO dialogue should be entrenched in the legislation transposing the Directives and followed by the establishment of a stable, albeit open and flexible, structure within which such dialogue can take place. This allows state authorities to be aware of the situation on the ground, the needs, and priorities, so that it can direct its policy accordingly. Dialogue within such structures would need to be regular and continuous. Meetings once a year, like in the case of Austria, cannot be considered sufficient. Furthermore, it is necessary to evaluate whether mechanisms are in place that allow NGOs to participate meaningfully in law- and policy-making processes. NGO representatives should be regularly included in Working Groups and drafts sent out for comments either to a targeted audience or for general public consultation. For that purpose codes of good practice in counselling are a useful tool. In order to give these mechanisms a greater chance of having an impact, such codes should also state that authorities are obliged to explain the reasons for rejecting proposals.

In terms of *process indicators* it is necessary to look at how the existing structures are implemented and used in practice. A possible indicator is the percentage of legislation, policy documents, and strategies effectively consulted with CSOs. 'Effectiveness' has been described in this context to include 'adequate access to information, sufficient time to comment, selection and representativeness/diversity of working groups, … degree to which input is taken into account, [as well as] feedback/publication of consultation results'.[262] For the purpose of the division of indicators into structural, process, and outcome indicators, these last two points can be categorized as *outcome indicators*. Another outcome indicator measures the quality of structures and mechanisms in place for dialogue and cooperation between CSOs and public institutions. This can be done by evaluating CSO representation in those structures in general, the representation of smaller/weaker CSOs, and their visibility.[263] For that purpose, the government perception as well as CSOs' perception should be surveyed. In the area of awareness raising, the most important way by which state authorities can support NGO activities in this field

[261] European Commission, 'Guidelines for EU support to civil society in enlargement countries, 2014–2020' (14 October 2013).

[262] ibid.

[263] ibid.

is by providing adequate funding and by coordinating awareness raising efforts with its own as well as the Equality Body's activities, ultimately leading to increased awareness of rights, remedies, and obligations among rights holder, duty bearers, and the general public (for a summary of indicators see Table 6.4).

Table 6.4 Table of indicators concerning the role of NGOs in law and policy making and awareness raising

Effective participation in law and policy making and awareness raising	Structural indicators	• Conducive legal and financial environment • State–NGO dialogue on equality issues laid down in law • Stable structure for regular and continuous dialogue in place • Codes of good practice in counselling in place
	Process indicators	• percentage of legislation, policy documents, and strategies effectively consulted on with CSOs • Level of coordination of awareness-raising activities between state–Equality Body–CSOs
	Outcome indicators	• Percentage of recommendations taken into account • Quality of structures and mechanisms in place for dialogue and cooperation between CSOs and public institutions • Increased awareness of rights, remedies, and obligations among rights holders, duty bearers, and general public

Conclusions

This research has set out to investigate how compliance with EU Equality Directives and practical implementation of norms and policies adopted in this context in the course of EU enlargement could be improved, and the likelihood of sustainability (or continuation) of reforms after accession and resilience to circumstances adverse to the issue of equality and non-discrimination being enhanced.

The principle of conditionality, following the logic of consequences and focusing on a strategy of reinforcement by reward, has been widely accepted as the model which probably best explains why norms are adopted.[1] However, the adoption of norms, that is, legal transposition, comes at a relatively early stage in the life cycle of an international norm.[2] According to Finnemore and Sikkink, this life cycle starts with the norm emergence (in our case: norm entrepreneurs persuade others about the necessity of a new norm which converges in a piece of secondary legislation at EU level, for instance the Racial Equality Directive (RED) and the Employment Equality Directive (EED)) and goes on in a second phase with norm acceptance, which they call a 'norm cascade'. In the context of EU Directives, this second phase is composed not only of legal transposition but also of effective implementation. In this phase, there is certainly a considerable amount of pressure for conformity, which leads EU Member States to legally transpose the norm to avoid infringement proceedings and ensuring acceding countries conform with the EU norm in order to get the reward of membership. There is, however, also considerable room for argumentative persuasion, participation, and mutual learning. What is 'appropriate' might be perceived differently by various actors involved in this phase. The governance mode applied in the first two phases of a norm's life cycle is decisive for the question of whether the norm passes the tipping point to enter the third stage, which comes at the very end of the norm cascade. It is the phase where norm internalization occurs and the understanding of appropriateness has shifted for all actors involved. Norm compliance is no longer dependent on individual belief systems but has become 'depersonalized' through institutionalization and

[1] Frank Schimmelfennig and Ulrich Sedelmeier, 'Governance by conditionality: EU rule transfer to the candidate countries of Central and Eastern Europe' (2004) 11(4) Journal of European Public Policy 661; Frank Schimmelfennig and Ulrich Sedelmeier (eds), *The Europeanization of Central and Eastern Europe* (Cornell University Press 2005).

[2] Martha Finnemore and Kathryn Sikkink, 'International Norm Dynamics and Political Change', International Organization (1998), 52(4): 887.

Reflexive Governance in EU Equality Law. Emma Lantschner, Oxford University Press. © Emma Lantschner 2021.
DOI: 10.1093/oso/9780192843371.003.0008

habitualization.[3] Because the norms have acquired a 'taken-for-granted quality',[4] they are less likely to be reversed.

The principle of conditionality, which primarily focuses on legal transposition, has shown its limits when it comes to producing such sustainable change and preventing backsliding. One of the problems in the practical implementation of the equality-related acquis is related to the access to justice. This includes low reporting rates, fear of victimization, a lack of support by civil society actors, and relatively weak Equality Bodies. Furthermore, a continued lack of awareness has been identified as hampering a more effective enforcement of the Directives. The central hypothesis, which has been tested by this research, is that a stronger emphasis of reflexive governance in the pre-accession phase (but not only then) has the potential to address these shortcomings in practical implementation and sustained compliance, even in the face of changing governmental preferences. In other words, it is submitted that reflexive governance contributes to passing the tipping point towards internalization and thus helps to prevent backsliding.

The reflexive governance approach has been found to be particularly well suited to capturing the triangle of actors involved in transposition *and* implementation of the two Equality Directives in focus. As well as EU institutions (in particular the Commission, but also the European Parliament and the European Court of Justice) and state authorities, this triangle involves various social actors (such as non-governmental organizations (NGOs) and Equality Bodies and their transnational networks), which can turn into important veto players after accession, contributing to a lock-in of the institutional change that has taken place in the pre-accession phase.[5] Applying reflexive governance to the field of equality and non-discrimination in the enlargement context, but also in the context of current EU Member States, is thus a test case for the theory of multilevel governance, with its emphasis on shared authority and policy-making influences across various actors at subnational, national, and supranational levels.

Before drawing the conclusions from this research as to the validity of the hypothesis, the basic tenets of reflexive governance should be recalled: Reflexive governance is concerned with creating the conditions required in order for a learning operation to be successful. This requires in its experimentalist expression the co-design of a framework rule, regulating in a flexible terms a commonly identified problem. This leaves discretion to the states and other actors involved regarding the mode of implementation. This is all present in the case of the EU non-discrimination regime. The experimentalist approach to reflexive

3 Thomas Risse and Kathryn Sikkink, 'The Socialization of International Human Rights Norms into Domestic Practices: Introduction' in Thomas Risse, Stephen Ropp, and Kathryn Sikkink (eds), *The Power of Human Rights: International Norms and Domestic Change* (CUP 1999) 16–17.

4 Finnemore and Sikkink (n 2) 895.

5 Ulrich Sedelmeier, 'Is Europeanisation through Conditionality Sustainable? Lock-in of Institutional Change after EU Accession' (2012) 35(1) West European Politics 20.

governance further requires benchmarking and monitoring. Monitoring in the reflexive sense is understood as the gathering of information as to the different forms of transposition and implementation chosen by the local actors (states) and an evaluation of their successes and failures in order to make it possible on one hand to adapt, if necessary, the framework rule and on the other hand to allow the actors involved to mutually learn from each other. To determine whether a form of transposition and implementation is successful or not, it has been suggested that indicators should be used. Monitoring understood in this sense is part of a collective search for solutions that could be replicated elsewhere. While the system thereby autonomously improves, it remains the case that if local actors experiment in a way which creates negative outcomes, this could lead to the imposition of standards from above.[6] In this case, the learning derives from failures and is a built-in part of the iterative process, in which the feedback to the 'centre' from the relevant stakeholders can lead to a revision of the original framework rule. Furthermore, local actors can be incentivized to cooperate by what de Búrca, in the context of experimentalist governance regimes, has called a 'penalty default'. This is a background system or a threatened sanction which can be activated in case local actors fail to cooperate.[7] While in the context of enlargement this could consist of a delay in obtaining membership, the commencement of infringement proceedings would be such a sanction vis-à-vis a Member State. This makes clear that conditionality and reflexive governance are not mutually exclusive but are interwoven, so that one could speak of 'reflexive conditionality'. The advantage of linking the two is that it broadens the picture by looking at the full life cycle of a norm and allows the focus to be on all the actors that are crucial for making change sustainable.

This relates to the next essential element of reflexive governance, which is the involvement of stakeholders in rule adoption, implementation, evaluation, and the provision of feedback. In the context of the acquis related to the right to equality and non-discrimination, stakeholder involvement appears to be particularly important, considering the central role assigned to them, in particular to NGOs and Equality Bodies, through the Directives. The participatory dimension of Fredman's typology of substantive equality[8] is thus perfectly reflected in the reflexive governance approach. A further element of reflexive governance consists in the creation of conditions in which the actors involved are triggered to reconsider their representation of the problem, to question their own positioning and to give up what

[6] Olivier de Schutter, 'The Role of Evaluation in Experimentalist Governance: Learning by Monitoring in the Establishment of the Area of Freedom, Security and Justice' in Charles F Sabel and Jonathan Zeitlin (eds), *Experimentalist Governance in the European Union: Towards a New Architecture* (OUP 2010) 261.

[7] Gráinne de Búrca, 'Human Rights Experimentalism' (2017) 111(2) American Journal of International Law 277.

[8] Sandra Fredman, 'Emerging from the Shadows: Substantive Equality and Article 14 of the European Convention on Human Rights' (2016) 16(2) Human Rights Law Review 273.

has been called 'institutional fetishism'.[9] In other words, by supporting them in thinking out of the box it should be made possible to discover new solutions to a problem that has so far not been satisfactorily addressed. Exposing them to the experiences that others have had when dealing with the same problem, is one of the ways by which such reframing could be triggered.

Let us now turn to the findings of this research:

Modifying the title of de Búrca's 2010 contribution to the volume, *Experimentalist Governance in the European Union*, in which she discussed the EU anti-discrimination regime,[10] *it can be concluded that this regime, both in the EU internal as well as in the external realm, is 'stumbling into reflexivity'*. But can it therefore be concluded that reflexive governance as an application of the multilevel governance theory has failed to explain processes and outcomes of integration in the non-discrimination field? And can it therefore be concluded that reflexive governance is not able to enhance sustainability of reforms and their resilience to changing governmental preferences?

In order to be able to answer these questions, each level (supranational, national, and subnational/non-state) and the interplay between them, has to be looked at separately. Let us start with the weakest side of the triangle. It is the one linking the state with the national stakeholders. The most important of these stakeholders in the context of the implementation of the non-discrimination acquis are the NGOs and the Equality Bodies, which have been given different important roles by the EU Equality Directives, ranging from supporting victims of discrimination to raising awareness, advising on law and policy making, as well as monitoring and evaluation. Various examples throughout this research have shown that NGOs are ready to reconsider their role and also take up functions that may not so far have been part of their repertoire, such as litigating discrimination cases. It has, however, also shown that a number of EU Member States show limited commitment and have made even less effort to create the conditions necessary for NGOs to fully take up these roles. The lack of commitment is shown, for instance, by the fact that legislation in some countries is rather restrictive when it comes to the opportunities granted to NGOs to engage in judicial proceedings. The case studies have further shown that not only do states offer minimal support to NGOs to play their role in providing a more effective level of protection to victims of discrimination (as required by recital 19 RED and recital 29 EED) by supporting them in engaging in judicial proceedings; but in a number of countries, the very existence of NGOs

[9] Olivier de Schutter and Jacques Lenoble, 'Introduction: Institutions Equipped to Learn' in Olivier de Schutter and Jacques Lenoble (eds), Reflexive Governance: Redefining the Public Interest in a Pluralistic World (Hart Publishing, 2010), xix–xxi; Olivier de Schutter, 'The New Architecture of Fundamental Rights Policy in the EU' [2011] European Yearbook on Human Rights 107; Jacques Lenoble and Marc Maesschalck, *Democracy, Law and Governance* (Ashgate 2010).

[10] Gráinne de Búrca, 'Stumbling into Experimentalism: The EU Anti-Discrimination Regime' in Charles F Sabel and Jonathan Zeitlin (eds), Experimentalist Governance in the European Union: Towards a New Architecture (Oxford University Press, 2010.

is threatened. In none of the countries analysed in detail in this research is there a satisfactory coverage of the whole territory and all the grounds protected under the Directives with NGOs engaging for victims of discrimination. The positive results of NGO litigation that were nevertheless shown in section 4.3 exist therefore not because of, but in spite of, the role played by states in this context. It remains the case that overall, the number of discrimination cases litigated in the courts, perhaps even reaching the Court of Justice of the European Union (CJEU) is still limited and could be increased if states were more active in supporting NGOs in this area.

The lack of commitment and effort undertaken by states can further be seen by the fact that the Directives' provisions on dialogue with NGOs have seen hardly any legal transposition and in practice, only a few structured and regular dialogues between state authorities and NGOs exist. The task of maintaining a dialogue with NGOs is instead delegated to the Equality Bodies. The advisory role of both NGOs but also of Equality Bodies in law and policy making needs to be strengthened to meet the objective of the relevant provision in the Directives: to have a positive effect on the effectiveness of national policies and awareness raising.

Regarding Equality Bodies, this research has shown that more substantial commitment and efforts are needed from state authorities in order to ensure their independence and effective functioning. Political influence on appointment procedures is an issue in many countries and even more so is the chronic underfunding of Equality Bodies which makes it difficult, if not impossible, for them to gain visibility (which continues to be dramatically low throughout EU Member States), authority, and legitimacy. While Equality Bodies might be charged with the allegation of institutional overkill, they should instead be perceived as a hub around which a range of different stakeholders, including NGOs, trade unions, employer bodies, and public authorities, which all make up part of the wider institutional structure can cooperate and coordinate their efforts with a view to enhancing the overall impact of activities carried out by different actors.[11]

The overall conclusion that can be drawn from this is that *liberal intergovernmentalism continues to govern the approach of state authorities* that remain stuck in the idea that national governments are the key actors of integration and whose decisions depend mainly on economic, but also ideological interests. In order to make the EU's equality regime work, *it is necessary first, however, to empower the local stakeholders* (in particular NGOs and Equality Bodies) that play an important role in this regime and *second, to strengthen the participatory dimension in the relation between state authorities and these local stakeholders.*

While this conclusion derives from the comparative analysis of the transposition and implementation of the Equality Directives in the EU Member States, it also has

[11] Equinet, 'The Bigger Picture: Equality Bodies as Part of the National Institutional Architecture for Equality' (2014), 22–25; Council of Europe, Commissioner for Human Rights, 'Opinion of the Commissioner for Human Rights on National Structures for Promoting Equality' (21 March 2011) CommDH(2011)2, 18.

a bearing in the enlargement context, in view of creating sustainable change and resilience against adverse political changes after accession. In fact, based on a case study of gender equality institutions in five new Member States, Sedelmeier found that 'pre-accession institutional change appears to matter for post-accession compliance and sustained diffusion'.[12] He further found that even if government preferences change, 'the presence of veto players can lock in conditionality-induced institutional change'.[13] While he was referring to veto players in the narrow sense (parties within a government coalition or second chambers, having effectively the power to block a decision by their veto), the concept can be extended to other actors involved in the law- and policy-making process and in its implementation, such as NGOs and the Equality Bodies. As an example in point one could mention the role played by Croatian NGOs and the Equality Body in preventing the watering down of the Croatian National Plan to Combat Discrimination (see Chapter 2.6.3.2). In other words, empowered domestic veto players, such as NGOs and Equality Bodies, can prevent the dismantling of institutional change after accession even if government preferences shift away from supporting the field of equality and non-discrimination. This backs the next conclusion that can be drawn from the present research:

In order to secure the potential role of stakeholders (especially of NGOs and Equality Bodies) as veto players preventing backsliding, they need to be empowered and their involvement institutionalized before accession. If states are reluctant in securing this, the Commission has an important role to play, before and after accession.

This leads us to the second side of the triangle, the one linking the subnational actors discussed above with the European institutions (mainly the Commission but also the European Parliament) and the interplay between them. Is the participatory dimension between local stakeholders and their transnational networks on the one hand, and European institutions on the other, better developed than the just-described relation between local stakeholders and state authorities? To what extent does monitoring in the reflexive sense described above take place and what have different actors learned from that?

When it comes to the Commission's learning, it relies heavily on the information and feedback provided by the transnational networks created and financed by the Commission as part of the EU non-discrimination regime. The Network of Legal Experts in Gender Equality and Non-Discrimination and Equinet play the most important role in this context, thereby contributing to the feedback loop and a potential revision of the framework rule. Through the yearly reports submitted by the legal experts as well as their ad hoc reports about new legislation, policies, and case law, the Commission has an overview of where the problems in implementation lie. Combined with the input it receives from Equinet, it became aware of the above-mentioned deficiencies regarding the independence and

[12] Sedelmeier, 'Is Europeanisation through Conditionality Sustainable? Lock-in of Institutional Change after EU Accession' (n 5) 35.

[13] ibid 35–36.

effectiveness of Equality Bodies. This information, together with quite intensive lobbying of Equinet for standards for Equality Bodies, led the Commission to open a consultation process among Equality Bodies, which eventually led to the adoption of the Recommendations on Standards for Equality Bodies. As a consequence of this process, the independence and effectiveness of Equality Bodies in carrying out their tasks has received much more attention by the Commission. The present research has laid out how these two broad notions could be honed further by more detailed indicators. It is interesting to note further in this context that EELN experts have reported for a number of years already not only of the level of independence of Equality Bodies in carrying out their functions, but also of their general independence.

The Commission itself understands the Recommendations on Standards for Equality Bodies primarily as an instrument which offers guidance for Member States on how the provisions of Equality Bodies could and should be transposed, and therefore mainly as an instrument for learning, rather than an instrument of monitoring. Nevertheless, it published a report on the implementation of the Recommendations as a document accompanying the report on the application of the RED and EED in 2021. Furthermore, it announced it would assess by 2022 if new legislation to strengthen the role of Equality Bodies was needed. The adoption of the Recommendations and the implementation report, and the consideration of new legislation are clearly examples of the iterative process characterizing an experimentalist regime[14] and underlines, once more, the role of stakeholders. Information about successes and (as in this case) failures or challenges in the transposition and implementation of the framework rule provided by these stakeholders have led, if not to a revision of the rule, at least to its clarification through the Recommendation. Since a revision of the Directives, along the lines of the procedure foreseen by the last sentences of Articles 17(2) RED and 19(2) EED,[15] appeared unlikely to receive the necessary support by Member States in the Council, the adoption of Recommendations was the only way in which the Commission could react. However, if local experiments should lead to outcomes not reflected by the Recommendations (already documented in the implementation report) this should be taken as a basis to intensify the bilateral dialogue with the respective Member State and could eventually lead to new legislation, thus closing the feedback loop.

Another area where EU institutions have learned from the input of various networks (including the network of legal experts, various umbrella organizations of NGOs, and the Fundamental Rights Agency (FRA)) regards the above-mentioned

[14] de Búrca, 'Human Rights Experimentalism' (n 7) 293–96.

[15] They both say: 'In light of the information received [by the Member States, the FRA, social partners, and NGOs], this report [of the Commission to be drawn up every five years] shall include, if necessary, proposals to revise and update this Directive'.

precarious situation in which civil society finds itself in many European countries. The way in which the Commission is trying to address this situation in the candidate countries is by the Guidelines for EU support to civil society in enlargement countries, which aim to achieve an environment which is conducive to civil society activities and it has promised financial and political support to achieve this goal. For the current Member States the driving force is the European Parliament: first, it adopted a preparatory action on an 'EU fund for financial support for litigating cases relating to violations of democracy, rule of law and fundamental rights', of which NGOs supporting or pursuing litigation in discrimination cases could take advantage. Considering the low number of discrimination cases pursued in the courts and the reluctance of some NGOs to engage more intensively in litigation due to financial constraints, this could be a valuable support to the access to justice for victims of discrimination. In order to achieve that goal, the funding would need to move beyond the current focus on capacity building and include all activities relevant in the context of litigation. Second, the European Parliament pushed the Commission to increase considerably the budget allotted to be spent within the multiannual financial framework post-2020 for the Citizens, Equality, Rights and Values programme. A considerable part of this programme is dedicated to supporting civil society organizations, at transnational level and, as urgently called for by the European Parliament, at regional and local levels.

A positive development is furthermore, as part of the EU Action Plan against Racism, the planned appointment of the first ever EU Anti-Racism Coordinator who will 'interact with Member States, the European Parliament, civil society, academia and the Commission to strengthen policy responses in the field of antiracism'.[16]

It can be concluded that the relationship between national and transnational stakeholders and the European institutions is well developed, in particular when it comes to the gathering of comparative information and feeding this back to the 'centre', where the policies are then adapted in order to best reach the commonly agreed framework goal. While the Commission is mostly, although not exclusively, relying on and targeting transnational networks, the European Parliament is putting emphasis on the need to empower grassroots civil society organizations at the national and local levels.

Of the networks supported by the Commission, Equinet is the one that appears to be the most vibrant when it comes to supporting collective learning processes, be these of its own members, the Commission, or other actors involved. According to its strategic plan 2019–22 it pursues, inter alia, the objective to build capacity and provide peer-to-peer support among Equality Bodies, to contribute

[16] European Commission, 'Press release: State of the Union: A new Action Plan to turn the tide in the fight against racism' (18 September 2020) <https://ec.europa.eu/commission/presscorner/detail/en/ip_20_1654>.

to the European equality agenda by sharing Equality Bodies' expertise, experience, and recommendations with European policy makers and partners, and to serve as a knowledge and communication hub on equality issues.[17] It facilitates capacity building of and interaction between different members by organizing visits, seminars, Working Groups, and clusters on different topics. Bilateral cooperation between different Equality Bodies often emerges naturally from the contacts established within the network through its various activities. Equinet has an impressive output in terms of comparative publications on various aspects of the work of Equality Bodies. It engages intensively with different players at the European level, ranging from the Commission and the FRA to the European Commission against Racism and Intolerance (ECRI) at the Council of Europe. From the point of view of membership it has a very broad coverage as it includes all candidate and potential candidate countries and countries of the Eastern Partnership, such as Moldova and Georgia. In its activities the focus is on topics rather than on regions so that there have been no special attempts to bring together, for instance, Equality Bodies from the Westers Balkans in order to support the exchange of experience at this more regional level.[18] However, in 2016 the Equality Bodies from Serbia, Albania, Bosnia and Herzegovina, Croatia, Macedonia, and Montenegro launched the regional Forum of South-East European Equality Bodies with yearly meetings in different countries to work together on better visibility of Equality Bodies, and on further strengthening their capacities through dialogue and exchange of experience.[19]

Equinet can be seen as exemplary in the context of the reflexive governance approach. It pursues a strategy that focuses on the pooling of results from local experiments in setting up such bodies and making them effective, thereby stimulating the collective search for solutions, feeding back the experience collected also to the national governmental and supranational levels. *It thus constitutes an effective link between the locally based Equality Bodies, the national, and the supranational levels.*

The last side of the triangle to be looked at concerns the interplay between state authorities and the European institutions, first and foremost the Commission. A promising forum for mutual learning in this context is the High Level Group on Non-Discrimination, Equality and Diversity. The High Level Group has been established by the Commission to 'deepen cooperation between Member States' relevant authorities and the Commission on questions relating to achieving diversity and full equality in practice … in particular through the exchange of experience and good practices'.[20] It remains to be seen if the seminars on best practices in different areas will bear some fruit. Noteworthy in any case is the establishment of a

[17] Equinet, 'Strategic Plan 2019–2022' (2019), 5.
[18] Interview, representative from Equinet, 1 June 2018.
[19] Ivana Krstic, 'Regional conference of equality bodies in South-East Europe' (EELN News Report, 2 December 2016).
[20] European Commission—Directorate-General Justice and Consumers, 'High Level Group on Non-discrimination, Equality and Diversity. Mandate' (2015).

subgroup on equality data, started in January 2018 together with the Commission and the FRA, which has developed 'Guidelines on improving the collection and use of equality data', a 'Compendium of Practices on Equality Data', as well as a 'Diagnostic mapping tool'.[21] The group discusses challenges and ways forward regarding data collection related to LGBTI persons, non-discrimination, and civil society, the impact of awareness-raising activities, the Commission Recommendation on standards for Equality Bodies, and the impact of the Covid pandemic on equality.[22] This is encouraging as the present research has revealed shortcomings in all these fields. Its work should continue to be supported by both the Commission and the FRA. In particular it should be ensured that representation in the Group is ensured at a high political level, to increase its potential impact on decisions taken at national level and to expose decision makers to the variety of possible approaches to the issues of equality and non-discrimination.[23] Furthermore, while there appears to be good cooperation between the Group and Equinet, it should also systematically reach out to NGOs, especially when it comes to discussing good practices. Finally, the mandate should be amended to systematically include members from candidate and potential candidate countries, as currently participants from countries outside the EU and the European Economic Area may be invited by the Commission to participate in the Group only if it is found relevant. *This forum offers excellent opportunities for learning from the successes and failures of others*, in line with the reflexive governance approach.

But according to this approach there is another source for learning, namely, monitoring and evaluation. *The first conclusion that can be drawn from the present research in this context is that pre-accession monitoring needs to be strengthened by the use of indicators.* This would not only address Kochenov's still valid critique about the lack of clarity and consistency regarding the standards that candidate countries are expected to comply with, which makes an assessment of pre-accession compliance with the EU non-discrimination regime extremely difficult, if possible at all.[24] Monitoring strengthened by the use of indicators would also increase the transparency of the Commission's evaluation and would allow civil society organizations to contribute to the process, for instance, by shadow reporting to the Commission and empowering them to hold their governments to account. This also fits into the idea of learning by monitoring because the benchmarks and indicators make it possible to arrive at a conclusion as to whether a chosen approach can be considered a success or a failure and thereby inform the learning within the system.

21 See https://fra.europa.eu/en/themes/equality-non-discrimination-and-racism/about-compendium.

22 Information available from the FRA website.

23 Interview, representative from Equinet, 1 June 2018.

24 Dimitry Kochenov, EU enlargement and the failure of conditionality: Pre-accession conditionality in the fields of democracy and the rule of law (Kluwer Law International 2008), ; Dimitry Kochenov, 'The Aquis and Its Principles: The Enforcement of the 'Law' versus the Enforcement of 'Values' in the EU' in András Jakab and Dimitry Kochenov (eds), The Enforcement of EU Law and Values: Ensuring Member States' Compliance (Oxford University Press, 2017), 15.

The second conclusion to be drawn from this research in the context of monitoring is that some form of post-accession monitoring of the two Directives, targeting all Member States, is needed, thereby creating the recursive process as envisaged by experimentalist governance. In fact this recursive process would require that the lessons learned from the local experimentation are collected and fed back into the centre, potentially leading to a re-evaluation or reformulation of the framework rule. Such monitoring/evaluation should go beyond the above-discussed exchange of experience in the framework of the High Level Group. It should also go beyond the current approach of the Commission to prepare a report for the European Parliament and the Council every five years on the basis of reports submitted to it by Member States and further information received by the FRA, Equinet, and NGOs.[25] This kind of monitoring includes neither a bilateral (state–Commission) nor a multilateral follow-up[26] and therefore lacks the learning component which monitoring in a reflexive system is supposed to have. The kind of monitoring proposed here is triangular (involving domestic civil society) and multilateral.

While bilateral dialogue between the Commission and a state about the implementation of the Equality Directives does take place, this seems to be crisis-driven and ad hoc.[27] The bilateral dialogue should be regular and extended into a triangular constellation, involving the Commission, the state authorities, and the relevant stakeholders, most importantly independent Equality Bodies and NGOs. This should lead to a structured implementation trilogue with transparency and wide stakeholder involvement being an essential part. Such a trilogue should take place at shorter intervals than the current five-year monitoring cycles and contribute to a reflection on how to address the challenges and needs of the respective country. It should result in country-specific recommendations that can be followed up by local stakeholders. Such an approach could be considered as a hegemonic imposition from above not fitting the reflexive governance approach proposed by the current research. In the context of the UN human rights treaty system, however, de Búrca has underlined 'that the open-endedness of the human rights standards and the existence and involvement of domestic civil society within the treaty systems examined[28] has the effect of facilitating genuinely two-way interaction and engagement between locally situated actors and institutions and internationally situated actors and institutions'.[29] The specific role of civil society organizations consists in what de Búrca calls a 'two way cultural translation' which means on one hand to provide contextualized knowledge and information to the international

[25] As provided by Art 17 RED and Art 19 EED.

[26] The multilateral follow-up would be provided for in the Directives which, as mentioned above, provide in Art 17 RED and Art 19 EED that the report of the Commission 'shall include, if necessary, proposals to revise and update this Directive'.

[27] Interview, representative from DG Justice, 1 June 2018.

[28] She examined the monitoring in the framework of the Convention on the Elimination of all Forms of Discrimination against Women (CEDAW), the Convention on the Rights of the Child (CRC), and the Convention on the Rights of Persons with Disabilities (CRPD).

[29] de Búrca, 'Human Rights Experimentalism' (n 7) 280.

actors and, on the other, to adapt or vernacularize the norms and recommendations within domestic and local contexts.[30] This assessment can also be applied by analogy to the proposed monitoring of EU Equality Directives.

As a layer in between the bilateral-triangular and the multilateral monitoring, a peer-to-peer evaluation between experts of different countries could further improve mutual learning. Such cooperative and mutual learning should be explicitly declared as one of the objectives of the peer evaluation. Finally, at multilateral level, the existing monitoring could be enriched with the findings of the trilogue and the peer-to-peer evaluations and could include country-specific recommendations that serve as guidance for states on how to target their future actions. Furthermore, the results of the report should be discussed in the High Level Group, with the involvement of other stakeholders, in order to strategically discuss the way forward,[31] which could include the adoption of Recommendations similar to those on Standards for Equality Bodies in other areas, the revision of the Directives, or the adoption of new legislation (as is currently being considered for Equality Bodies).

In such a framework, and as with the pre-accession process, indicators could play a constructive role. For both contexts domestic ownership and a participatory approach in construction and use should be secured so that indicators are perceived as technology of reform rather than as technology of control. The indicators proposed in the present research could be used as a starting point, while national specificities could be taken into account. Monitoring construed in such a way would thus be part of a cooperative and reflexive process.

The conclusions drawn with regard to each side of the triangle of actors have served to explain the initial statement that one can observe a 'stumbling into reflexivity'. Different actors have internalized to different degrees the various elements of reflexivity. Some of these elements could not unfold their full potential as their use has only been half-hearted (like the use of benchmarks without the simultaneous use of indicators in monitoring) or processes have been interrupted halfway (like not pursuing monitoring after accession). The conclusions have also shown that the implementation of the EU non-discrimination regime can only be effective, and backsliding after accession can only be prevented, if the necessity to effectively involve stakeholders in the rule-making and rule-application process is taken seriously by all actors involved. For the time being state actors are reluctant to accept this which suggests that liberal intergovernmentalism prevails. If this remains the case, stagnation will continue. In its 2021 report, the Commission found indeed

[30] ibid 280 and 291.

[31] The EU Environmental Implementation Review is more or less following such a proposed structure. See European Commission, 'Communication from the Commission to the European Parliament, the Council and the Economic and Social Committee and the Committee of the Regions. The EU Environmental Implementation Review: Common challenges and how to combine efforts to deliver better results' (3 February 2017) COM(2017) 63 final.

that '[t]here seems to be a general sentiment that little progress has been made in the fight against discrimination since 2014'.[32]

To sum it up, this research has come to the following major results, from which a set of recommendations can be drawn that will help to improve the effective implementation of the existing EU equality and non-discrimination legal framework and develop it further:

1) The field is still dominated by the intergovernmental approach, thinking in a top-down vs bottom-up dichotomy. The related focus on conditionality does not, however, lead to effective implementation and the non-discrimination regime stagnates. It is therefore necessary to shift the focus to a triangular constellation of equal partnership involving state authorities, EU institutions, and transnational/national societal actors. This triangulation is important throughout the life cycle of the respective norms, starting from their emergence at EU level, their transposition and implementation at national level, as well as in the phase of monitoring and evaluation. Some initiatives in this direction have been recently taken by the Commission and need to be forcefully pursued.
2) In reference to Fredman's four dimensions of equality (namely, the distributive, recognition, participative, and transformative dimensions)[33] and applying these dimensions also to the governance approach, this research has shown that the focus has so far been mainly on redistribution and the provision of incentives. To reach the last stage (transformation, where difference can be accommodated, including through structural change), it is, however, necessary to shift the focus on the recognition and, most importantly, on the participative dimensions, through the empowerment and equal participation of local stakeholders. This enhances mutual social learning in the processes of socialization and internalization, and thereby contributes to the prevention of backsliding.
3) Monitoring has so far been understood as a hegemonic interference, imposing standards and, if necessary, sanctions from above. Monitoring should, however, be understood as a dynamic norm contestation in which the three actors involved critically engage with the norms under consideration. As such, it helps to deconstruct own-preference formations and is yet another opportunity to learn from successes and failures in a cooperative

[32] European Commission, 'Report on the application of Council Directive 2000/43/EC implementing the principle of equal treatment between persons irrespective of racial or ethnic origin ("the Racial Equality Directive") and of Council Directive 2000/78/EC establishing a general framework for equal treatment in employment and occupation ("the Employment Equality Directive")' (Brussels 19 March 2021) COM(2021) 139 final, 2.

[33] Fredman, 'Emerging from the Shadows: Substantive Equality and Article 14 of the European Convention on Human Rights' (n 8).

and recursive process. As access to regular contestation has been seen 'as a key condition to enhance legitimacy in global governance',[34] monitoring understood in this way needs to be permanent. This means that monitoring should not only take place in the pre-accession phase but should include all Member States and be carried out on the basis of clear and transparent benchmarks and indicators. The indicators developed in this research can serve as a starting point.

Reflexive governance is an approach which well reflects all the above proposed shifts of focus and understanding. It is thus seen to be the governance mode which suits well to get norms over the tipping point leading to norm internalization and to prevent backsliding in old and new/future Member States. This research thus makes the case for multilevel governance.

[34] Antje Wiener, 'A Theory of Contestation—A Concise Summary of Its Argument and Concepts' (2017) 49(1) Polity 109, 114–15.

References

ACFC, 'Fourth opinion on Austria adopted on 14 October 2016' ACFC/OP/IV(2016)007.

ACFC, 'Fourth opinion on Bulgaria adopted on 26 May 2020' ACFC/OP/IV(2020)001Final.

ACFC, 'Fourth Opinion on Romania adopted on 22 June 2017' ACFC/OP/IV(2017)005.

ACFC, 'Third opinion on Bulgaria adopted on 11 February 2014' ACFC/OP/III(2014)001.

ACFC, 'Thematic Commentary No. 3: The Language Rights of Persons Belonging to National Minorities under the Framework Convention' (24 May 2012) ACFC/44DOC(2012)001 rev.

ACFC, 'Thematic Commentary No. 4: The Framework Convention: a key tool to managing diversity through minority rights' (2016) ACFC/56DOC(2016)001.

Adams Z and Adenitire JO, 'Ideological Neutrality in the Workplace' (2018) 81(2) Modern Law Review 348.

Aendenboom I and Denies N, 'What Place for Mediation and Conciliation/Negotiation in Discrimination Cases?' [2012] European Anti-Discrimination Law Review 21.

Althoff N, *Die Bekämpfung von Diskriminierung aus Gründen der Rasse und der ethnischen Herkunft in der Europäischen Gemeinschaft ausgehend von Art. 13 EG* (Peter Lang 2005).

Althoff N and Choi S, 'Verbände aktiv gegen Diskriminierung. Das Project "Diskriminierungsschutz: Handlungskompetenz für Verbände"' (2011) .

Ambrus M, *Enforcement Mechanisms of the Racial Equality Directive and Minority Protection* (Eleven International Publishing 2011).

Ambrus M, Busstra M, and Henrard K, 'The Racial Equality Directive and Effective Protection Against Discrimination: Mismatches Between the Substantive Law and its Application' (2010) 3(3) Erasmus Law Review 165.

Amiraux V and Guiraudon V, 'Discrimination in Comparative Perspective: Policies and Practices' (2010) 53(12) American Behavioral Scientist 1691.

Ammer M and others, 'Study on Equality Bodies set up under Directives 2000/43/EC, 2004/113/EC and 2006/54/EC. Synthesis Report' (Human European Consultancy in partnership with the Ludwig Boltzmann Institute of Human Rights, October 2010).

Antidiskriminierungsstelle des Bundes, 'Jahresbericht 2019' (2020).

Antidiskriminierungsstelle des Bundes, 'Gegen Rassismus, für Gleichbehandlung: Vorschläge der Antidiskriminierungsstelle des Bundes zur Stärkung des Schutzes vor Diskriminierung in Deutschland' (August 2020).

Antidiskriminierungsstelle des Bundes, 'Bericht des Themenforums Antidiskriminierung im Rahmen des Nationalen Aktionsplans Integration/ Einhellige Forderung nach Ausbau von Beratungsangeboten gegen Diskriminierung' (9 March 2021) <https://www.antidiskriminierungsstelle.de/SharedDocs/Aktuelles/DE/2021/20210309_Integrationsgipfel_NAP_I.html>.

Argyris C, *Knowledge for Action. A Guide to Overcoming Barriers to Organizational Change* (Jossey Bass 1993).

Argyris C and Schön D, *Theory in Practice: Increasing Professional Effectiveness* (Jossey Bass 1974).

Argyris C and Schön D, *Organisational Learning: A Theory of Action Perspective* (Addison Wesley 1978).

Arnull A, 'Sex Discrimination in Occupational Pension Schemes' [1986] European Law Review 365.

Bakic I, 'The story of a very quiet coup' *The Irish Times* (22 May 2010) <https://www.irishtimes.com/culture/books/the-story-of-a-very-quiet-coup-1.668763>.

Bárd P and others, 'An EU mechanism on Democracy, the Rule of Law and Fundamental Rights' (CEPS Paper in Liberty and Security in Europe, April 2016).

Barmes L, 'Equality Law and Experimentation: The Positive Action Challenge' (2009) 68(3) Cambridge Law Journal 623.

Barnard C, 'The Contribution of Anti-discrimination Law to European Integration: The Added Value of the EU Level' in Olivier de Schutter and Violeta Moreno Lax (eds), *Human Rights in the Web of Governance: A Learning-Based Fundamental Rights Policy for the EU* (Bruylant 2010).

Barnard C and Hervey T, 'Softening the Approach to Quotas: Positive Action After Marschall' (1998) 20(3) Journal of Social Welfare and Family Law 333.

Barrett J, 'Part-time Workers and Equal Pay: The Case of Jenkins v. Kingsgate' [1981] The Human Rights Review 174.

Barry E, 'Interventions and Amicus Curiae Applications' in Soraya Obura and Fiona Palmer (eds), *Strategic Enforcement: Powers and Competences of Equality Bodies* (Equinet 2006).

Bartel D, 'Keynote: Vom Flickenteppich zur Infrastruktur—Antidiskriminierungsberatung in Deutschland weiterdenken' in Antidiskriminierungsstelle des Bundes (ed), *Mit Rat zur Tat. Perspektiven der Antidiskriminierungsberatung in Deutschland. Dokumentation der Fachtagung im Umweltforum* (2017) Antidiskriminierungsstelle des Bundes .

Belavusau U, 'A Penalty Card for Homophobia from EU Non-discrimination Law: Comment on Asociatia Accept (C-81/12)' (2015) 21(2) Columbia Journal of European Law 353.

Bell M, 'Meeting the Challenge? A Comparison between the EU Racial Equality Directive and the Starting Line' in Isabelle Chopin and Jan Niessen (eds), *The Starting Line and the Incorporation of the Racial Equality Directive into the National Laws of the EU Member States and Accession States* (Migration Policy Group, Commission for Racial Equality 2001).

Bell M, *Anti-Discrimination Law and the European Union* (OUP 2002).

Bell M, *Racism and Equality in the European Union* (OUP 2008).

Bell M, 'The Principle of Equal Treatment: Widening and Deepening' in Paul Craig and Gráinne de Búrca (eds), *The Evolution of EU Law* (OUP 2011).

Benecke M, 'Rechtsvergleich der europäischen Systeme zum Antidiskriminierungsrecht' (Expertise im Auftrag der Antidiskriminierungsstelle des Bundes 2010).

Benedek W and others, 'Mainstreaming human and minority rights in the EU enlargement with the Western Balkans' (European Parliament, Directorate-General for External Policies, Policy Department 2012).

Bennett A and Checkel JT (eds), *Process Tracing: From Methaphor to Analytical Tool* (Cambridge University Press 2015).

Benson D and Jordan A, 'What Have We Learned from Policy Transfer Research? Dolowitz and Marsh Revisited' (2011) 9(3) Political Studies Review 366.

Berghahn S, Klapp M, and Tischbirek A, *Evaluation des Allgemeinen Gleichbehandlungsgesetzes (erstellt im Auftrag der Antidiskriminierungsstelle des Bundes)* (Nomos 2016).

Beury M, 'The CJEU's judgment in Coman: a small step for the recognition of same-sex couples underlying European divides over LGBT rights' (Strasbourg Observers, 24 July 2018) <https://strasbourgobservers.com/2018/07/24/the-cjeus-judgment-in-coman-a-small-step-for-the-recognition-of-same-sex-couples-underlying-european-divides-over-lgbt-rights/>.

Bieber F, 'Conclusion: Rethinking Europeanisation' in Jelena Dzankic, Keil Soeren, and Marko Kmezić (eds), *The Europeanisation of the Western Balkans: A Failure of EU Conditionality?* (Palgrave Macmillan 2019).

Bodiroga-Vukobrat N, Vinković M, and Petričušić A, 'Legal Protection Against Discrimination in Croatia' in Barbara Liegl (ed), 'Legal Protection Against Discrimination in South East Europe: Synthesis Report' (Centre for South East European law school network (SEELS) 2016).

Bodrogi B, 'Legal Standing—The Practical Experience of a Hungarian Organisation' [2007] European Anti-Discrimination Law Review 23.

Boduszyński MP, *Regime Change in the Yugoslav Successor States: Divergent Paths toward a New Europe* (Johns Hopkins University Press 2010).

Böhmelt T and Freyburg T, 'Diffusion of Compliance in the 'Race towards Brussels?' A Spatial Approach to EU Accession Conditionality' (2015) 38(3) West European Politics 601.

Börzel T and others, 'Obstinate and Inefficient: Why Member States Do Not Comply with European Law' (2010) 43(11) Comparative Political Studies 1363.

Börzel T and Risse T, 'From Europeanisation to Diffusion: Introduction' (2012) 35(1) West European Politics 1.

Božić Krstanović L and Lalić S, 'How Much Equality? Monitoring the Implementation of the Legal Aid Act and of the Anti-discrimination Act' (Centre for Peace, Nonviolence and Human Rights—Osijek, Centre for Peace, Legal Advice and Psychosocial Assistance—Vukovar, Serbian Democratic Forum, in cooperation with Centre for Peace Studies—Zagreb 2013).

Brems E, 'European Court of Justice, case C-450/93, Eckhard Kalanke v. Freie Hansestadt Bremen, 17 October 1995' [1995] Columbia Journal of European Law 172.

Brems E, 'European Court of Justice Allows Bans on Religious Dress in the Workplace' (IACL-AIDC Blog, 25 March 2017) <https://blog-iacl-aidc.org/test-3/2018/5/26/analysis-european-court-of-justice-allows-bans-on-religious-dress-in-the-workplace>.

Bribosia E and Rorive I, 'Belgium fails to guarantee the right to inclusive education for children with intellectual disabilities within the French Community' (EELN News Report, 25 February 2021).

Brosig M, 'No Space for Constructivism? A Critical Appraisal of European Compliance Research' (2012) 13(4) Perspectives on European Politics and Society 390.

Bröstl A, 'Positive Action and the Principle of Equality: Discussing a Decision of the Constitutional Court of the Slovak Republic' (2007) 5 European Yearbook of Minority Issues 377.

Bulgarian Helsinki Committee, 'Human Rights in Bulgaria in 2017' (2018).

Bulgarian Helsinki Committee, 'Human Rights in Bulgaria in 2019' (2020).

Bundeskanzleramt, 'Gleichbehandlungsbericht für die Privatwirtschaft 2018 und 2019. Teil I—Gleichbehandlungskommission, Bundesministerium für Arbeit, Familie und Jugend und Beiträge der Interessenvertretungen' (2020).

Bundeskanzleramt, Bundesministerium für Arbeit, Soziales und Konsumentenschutz and Bundesministerin für Frauen und Gesundheit, 'Gleichbehandlungsbericht für die Privatwirtschaft 2014 und 2015. Teil II—Anwaltschaft für Gleichbehandlung' (2016).

Bundeskanzleramt and Bundesministerium für Arbeit, Soziales, Gesundheit und Konsumentenschutz, 'Gleichbehandlungsbericht für die Privatwirtschaft 2016 und 2017. Teil I—Gleichbehandlungskommission und Bundesministerium für Arbeit, Soziales, Gesundheit und Konsumentenschutz' (2018).

Bundesverband für Körper- und Mehrfachbehinderte e.V. 'Bundesverwaltungsgericht weist Klagen wegen eines nicht behindertengerechten Bahnhofs ab: BVerwG, Urteile vom 5.04.2006—Az. 9 C 1.05 und 9 C 2.05' (April 2006).

Büro zur Umsetzung von Gleichbehandlung e.V., 'Dossier zum Thema Klageunterstützung durch Verbände' (2016).

Büro zur Umsetzung von Gleichbehandlung e.V., 'Dossier zum Thema Vorschläge zur Stärkung des Antidiskriminierungsrechts' (2017).

Burrows N and Robison M, 'Positive Action for Women in Employment: Time to Align with Europe?' (2006) 33(1) Journal of Law and Society 24.

Carrera S, Guild E, and Hernanz N, 'The Triangular Relationship between Fundamental Rights, Democracy and Rule of Law in the EU—Towards an EU Copenhagen Mechanism. Study prepared for the European Parliament' (CEPS Commentary 2013).

Caruso D, 'Limits of the Classic Method: Positive Action in the European Union After the New Equality Directives' (2002) Jean Monnet Working Paper 10/02.

Cattaneo LB and Chapman AR, 'The Process of Empowerment: A Model for Use in Research and Practice' (2010) 65(7) American Psychologist 646.

CERD, 'Concluding observations of the Committee on the Elimination of Racial Discrimination' (8 April 2011) CERD/C/ESP/CO/18-20.

CERD, 'Concluding observations on the sixteenth to nineteenth periodic reports of Belgium' (14 March 2014) CERD/C/BEL/CO/16-19.

CERD, 'Concluding observations on the combined nineteenth and twentieth periodic reports of Italy' (17 February 2017) CERD/C/ITA/CO/19-20.

CERD, 'Concluding observations on the combined twentieth to twenty-second periodic reports of Bulgaria' (31 May 2017) CERD/C/BGR/CO/20-22.

Checkel JT, 'Why Comply? Social Learning and European Identity Change' (2001) 55(3) International Organization 553.

Checkel JT, 'It's the Process Stupid! Process Tracing in the Study of European and International Politics' [2005] ARENA Working Paper.

Chhotray V and Stoker G, *Governance Theory and Practice: A Cross-Disciplinary Approach* (Palgrave Macmillan 2010).

Chopin I, 'The Starting Line Group: A Harmonised Approach to Fight Racism and to Promote Equal Treatment' (1999) 1(1) European Journal of Migration and Law 111.

Chopin I, 'Possible Harmonisation of Anti-Discrimination Legislation in the European Union: European and Non-Governmental Proposals' (2000) 2(3/4) European Journal of Migration and Law 413.

Chopin I and Niessen J, 'Proposals for Legislative Measures to Combat Racism and to Promote Equal Rights in the European Union' (Starting Line Group, Commission for Racial Equality 1998).

Chopin I and Niessen J, 'Combating Racism in the European Union with Legal Means: A Comparison of the Starting Line and the EU Commission's Proposal for a Race Directive' (Migration Policy Group 2000).

Chopin I and Niessen J, 'The Starting Line and the Incorporation of the Racial Equality Directive into the National Laws of the EU Member States and Accession States' (Migration Policy Group, Commission for Racial Equality 2001).

Chubrikj S and Chalovska-Dimovska N, 'Use of actio popularis in Cases of Discrimination' (OSCE Mission to Skopje, Helsinki Committee for Human Rights 2016).

Civicus—Monitor Tracking Civic Space, 'Parliament to Vote on Alarming NGO Law' (26 July 2018) <https://monitor.civicus.org/newsfeed/2018/07/26/Parliament-to-Vote-on-alarming-NGO-Law/>.

Civicus—Monitor Tracking Civic Space, 'Austria's Civic Space Rating Downgraded from Open to Narrowed' (19 November 2018) <https://monitor.civicus.org/newsfeed/2018/11/19/austrias-civic-space-rating-downgraded-open-narrowed/>.

Civicus—Monitor Tracking Civic Space, 'Austria Civic Space Rating Upgraded to Open' (15 September 2020) <https://monitor.civicus.org/updates/2020/09/15/austria-civic-space-rating-upgraded-open/>.

Civil Society Europe, 'Multiannual Financial Framework Post 2020. Proposals by Civil Society Organisations' (nd).

Cloots E, 'Safe Harbour or Open Sea for Corporate Headscarf Bans? Achbita and Bougnaoui' (2018) 55(2) Common Market Law Review 589.

Collier P, 'Understanding Process Tracing' (2011) 44(4) Political Science and Politics 823.

Commission for Protection Against Discrimination, 'Annual Report for 2017' (2018).

Commission of the European Communities, 'Communication on racism, xenophobia and anti-semitism and proposal for a Council Decision designating 1997 as European year against racism' (13 December 1995) COM(95) 653 final.

Commission of the European Communities, 'Communication from the Commission to the European Parliament and the Council on the interpretation of the judgment of the Court of Justice on 17 October 1995 in Case C-450/93, Kalanke v Freie Hansestadt Bremen' (27 March 1996) COM(96) 88 final.

Commission of the European Communities, 'Proposal for a Council Directive establishing a general framework for equal treatment in employment and occupation' (25 November 1999) COM(1999) 565 final.

Commission of the European Communities, 'Proposal for a Council Directive implementing the principle of equal treatment between persons irrespective of racial or ethnic origin' (25 November 1999) COM(1999) 566 final.

Commission of the European Communities, 'The application of Directive 2000/43/EC of 29 June 2000 implementing the principle of equal treatment between persons irrespective of racial or ethnic origin' (30 October 2006) COM(2006) 643 final.

Commission of the European Communities, 'Communication from the Commission to the European Parliament, the Council, the European Economic and Social Committee and the Committee of Regions: Non-discrimination and equal opportunities: A renewed commitment' (2 July 2008) COM(2008) 420 final.

Commission of the European Communities, 'Decision setting up a non-discrimination governmental expert group' (2 July 2008) C(2008)3261 final.

Commission of the European Communities, 'Proposal for a Council Directive on implementing the principle of equal treatment between persons irrespective of religion or belief, disability, age or sexual orientation' (2 July 2008) COM(2008) 426 final.

Commission of the European Communities, 'The application of Directive 2000/78/EC of 27 November 2000 establishing a general framework for equal treatment in employment and occupation' (8 July 2008) COM(2008) 225 final/2.

Commission Recommendation of 11 June 2013 on common principles for injunctive and compensatory collective redress mechanisms in the Member States concerning violations of rights granted under Union Law 11 June 2013 (European Commission).

Committee of Ministers, 'Recommendation CM/Rec(2019)6 of the Committee of Ministers to member States on the development of the Ombudsman institution' (16 October 2019).

Committee on the Rights of Persons with Disabilities, 'Concluding Observations on the initial report of Belgium adopted by the Committee at its twelfth session' (15 September 2014).

Consultative Commission on Racism and Xenophobia, 'Final Report' (23 May 1995) Ref 6906/1/95.

Cooperation Agreement, 'between the federal authority, the Regions and the Communities aimed at creating an Interfederal Centre for Equal Opportunities and Opposition to Racism and Discrimination in the form of a joint institution, in the sense of article 92bis of the Special Act of 8 August 1980 on the Reform of the Institutions' (12 June 2013).

Council of Europe, Commissioner for Human Rights, 'Opinion of the Commissioner for Human Rights on National Structures for Promoting Equality' (21 March 2011) CommDH(2011)2.

Council of Europe, Congress of Local and Regional Authorities, Monitoring Committee, 'Developing indicators to raise awareness of human rights at local and regional level' (6 October 2011) CG(21)10.

Council Regulation (EC) No 168/2007 of 15 February 2007 establishing a European Union Agency for Fundamental Rights.

Cox S, 'Case Watch: Strengthening Europe's Non-Discrimination Law' (Open Society Foundations—Voices, 2 October 2002).

Cox S, 'When all the people in a district are victims of race discrimination: CJEU ruling in CHEZ v Nikolova' (EU Law Analysis, 24 July 2015) <http://eulawanalysis.blogspot.com/2015/07/when-all-people-in-district-are-victims.html>.

Crowley N, 'Equality and Human Rights: An Integrated Approach' (Equality and Right Alliance 2015). Setting Standards for the Irish Equality and Human Rights Infrastructure Paper 3.

Crowley N, 'Making Europe More Equal: A Legal Duty?' (Equinet 2016).

Crowley N, 'Merging Mandates of Equality Bodies and National Human Rights Institutions—A Growing Trend' [2016] European Equality Law Review 34.

Crowley N, 'National Specialised Bodies: Effective Implementation of their Advisory Function' (ECRI 2016).

Crowley N, 'Equality Bodies Making a Difference' (European network of legal experts in gender equality and non-discrimination 2018).

Crowley N, 'Taking Stock. A perspective from the work of equality bodies on: European equality strategies, equal treatment directives, and standards for equality bodies' (Equinet 2020).

Crowther N and O'Cinneide C, 'Bridging the Divide? Integrating the Functions of National Equality Bodies and National Human Rights Institutions in the European Union' (UCL Faculty of Laws, London 2013).

Däubler W and Bertzbach M, *Allgemeines Gleichbehandlungsgesetz* (Nomos 2008).

Davies G, 'Achbita v G4S: Religious Equality Squeezed between Profit and Prejudice' (European Law Blog, 6 April 2017) <http://europeanlawblog.eu/2017/04/06/achbita-v-g4s-religious-equality-squeezed-between-profit-and-prejudice/>.

de Beco G, 'Human Rights Indicators for Assessing State Compliance with International Human Rights' (2008) 77(1–2) Nordic Journal of International Law 23.

de Beco G and Murray R, *Commentary on the Paris Principles on National Human Rights Institutions* (CUP 2015).

de Búrca G, 'EU Race Discrimination Law: A Hybrid Model?' in Gráinne de Búrca and Joanne Scott (eds), *Law and New Governance in the EU and the US* (Hart Publishing 2006).

de Búrca G, 'New Governance and Experimentalism: An Introduction' [2010] Wisconsin Law Review 227 <http://wisconsinlawreview.org/wp-content/files/De-Burca-Final.pdf>.

de Búrca G, 'Stumbling into Experimentalism: The EU Anti-Discrimination Regime' in Charles F Sabel and Jonathan Zeitlin (eds), *Experimentalist Governance in the European Union: Towards a New Architecture* (OUP 2010).
de Búrca G, 'The Decline of the EU Anti-Discrimination Law?' (Note for the Colloquium on Comparative and Global Public Law, 19 October 2016) <http://www.law.nyu.edu/sites/default/files/upload_documents/The%20Decline%20of%20the%20EU%20Anti-Discrimination%20Law.pdf>.
de Búrca G, 'Human Rights Experimentalism' (2017) 111(2) American Journal of International Law 277.
de Búrca G, Keohane RO, and Sabel CF, 'Global Experimentalist Governance' (2014) 44(3) British Journal of Political Science 477.
de Schutter O, 'Three Models of Equality and European Anti-Discrimination Law' (2006) 57(1) Northern Ireland Legal Quarterly 1.
de Schutter O, 'A New Direction for the Fundamental Rights Policy of the EU' (2010) Working paper series: REFGOV-FR-33.
de Schutter O, 'The Role of Evaluation in Experimentalist Governance: Learning by Monitoring in the Establishment of the Area of Freedom, Security and Justice' in Charles F Sabel and Jonathan Zeitlin (eds), *Experimentalist Governance in the European Union: Towards a New Architecture* (OUP 2010).
de Schutter O, 'The New Architecture of Fundamental Rights Policy in the EU' [2011] European Yearbook on Human Rights 107.
de Schutter O, 'The Prohibition of Discrimination under European Human Rights Law. Relevance for the EU Non-discrimination Directives—An Update' (European Network of Legal Experts in the Non-discrimination Field 2011).
de Schutter O, 'Follow-up to the European Parliament's Resolution of 8 September 2015 on "The situation of fundamental rights in the European Union (2013–2014)"' (European Parliament, Policy Department for Citizens' Rights and Constitutional Affairs, Brussels 2016).
de Schutter O and Lenoble J, 'Introduction: Institutions Equipped to Learn' in Olivier de Schutter and Jacques Lenoble (eds), *Reflexive Governance: Redefining the Public Interest in a Pluralistic World* (Hart Publishing 2010).
de Schutter O and Lenoble J (eds), *Reflexive Governance: Redefining the Public Interest in a Pluralistic World* (Hart Publishing 2010).
de Vos M, 'Beyond Formal Equality: Positive Action under Directives 2000/43/EC and 2000/78/EC' (European Network of Legal Experts in the Non-discrimination Field 2007).
de Witte B, 'From a "Common Principle of Equality" to "European Antidiscrimination Law"' (2010) 53(12) American Behavioral Scientist 1715.
Del Sarto R, Schumacher T, and Lannon E, 'Benchmarking Democratic Development in the Euro-Mediterranean Area: Conceptualising Ends, Means, and Strategies' (EuroMeSCo Report October 2006).
Della Porta D and Keating M (eds), *Approaches and Methodologies in the Social Sciences* (CUP 2008).
DG NEAR, 'Guidelines and Strategic Directions for EU Support to Civil Society in the Enlargement Region 2021–2027—Working Draft' (19 February 2021).
Dimitrova A and Buzogany A, 'Post-Accession Policy-Making in Bulgaria and Romania: Can Non-State Actors Use EU Rules to Promote Better Governance?' (2014) 52(1) Journal of Common Market Studies 139.
Diz Conde L, 'The Impact of EU-funded Projects on Minority Protection in the Republic of Serbia' (Master thesis, University of Graz 2018).

Đokić I and Sumpor M, 'The Role of Croatian Civil Society Organisations in the European Union Accession Process' (Technical Assistance for Civil Society Organisations Croatia Office, International Swedish Institute for Public Administration, Zagreb June 2013).

Dolowitz DP and Marsh D, 'Who Learns What from Whom? A Review of the Policy Transfer Literature' (1996) 44(2) Political Studies 343.

Dolowitz DP and Marsh D, 'Learning from Abroad: The Role of Policy Transfer in Contemporary Policy-Making' (2000) 13(1) Governance 5.

Dorf MC and Sabel CF, 'A Constitution of Democratic Experimentalism' (1998) 98(2) Columbia Law Review 267.

Drake S, 'The Principle of Primacy and the Duty of National Bodies Appointed to Enforce EU Law to Disapply Conflicting National Law: An Garda Síochána' (2020) 57(2) Common Market Law Review 557.

ECRI, 'Conclusions on the implementation of the Recommendations in respect of Belgium subject to interim follow-up, adopted on 8 December 2016' CRI(2017)5.

ECRI, 'Conclusions on the implementation of the Recommendations in respect of Cyprus subject to interim follow-up, adopted on 3 April 2019' CRI(2019)23.

ECRI, 'Report on Austria (fifth monitoring cycle) adopted on 16 June 2015' CRI(2015)34.

ECRI, 'Report on Austria (sixth monitoring cycle) adopted on 7 April 2020'.

ECRI, 'Report on Belgium (fifth monitoring cycle) adopted on 4 December 2013' CRI(2014)1.

ECRI, 'Report on Bulgaria (fifth monitoring cycle) adopted on 19 June 2014' CRI(2014)36.

ECRI, 'Report on Bulgaria (fourth monitoring cycle) adopted on 20 June 2008' CRI(2009)2.

ECRI, 'Report on Cyprus (fifth monitoring cycle) adopted on 17 March 2016' CRI(2016)18.

ECRI, 'Report on Germany (fifth monitoring cycle), adopted on 5 December 2013' CRI(2014)2.

ECRI, 'Report on Ireland (fourth monitoring cycle) adopted on 5 December 2012' CRI(2013)1.

ECRI, 'Report on Italy (fifth monitoring cycle) adopted on 18 March 2016' CRI(2016)19.

ECRI, 'Report on Romania (fifth monitoring cycle) adopted on 3 April 2019' CRI(2019)20.

ECRI, 'Report on Romania (fourth monitoring cycle) adopted on 19 March 2014' CRI(2014)19.

ECRI, 'Report on Slovakia (fourth monitoring cycle) adopted on 19 December 2008' CRI(2009)20.

ECRI, 'Report on Spain (fifth monitoring cycle) adopted on 5 December 2017' CRI(2018)2.

ECRI, 'General Policy Recommendation No. 2 on Specialised bodies to combat racism, xenophobia, anti-Semitism and intolerance at national level' (ECRI, 13 June 1997) CRI(97)36.

ECRI, 'General Policy Recommendation No. 7 on National Legislation to Combat Racism and Racial Discrimination' (13 December 2002) CRI(2003)8.

ECRI, 'Report on Seminar with national specialised bodies to combat racism and racial discrimination on mediation and other forms of dispute resolution in cases of racism and racial discrimination' (Strasbourg, 16–17 February 2006).

ECRI, 'Third report on Ireland' (15 December 2006) CRI(2007)24.

ECRI, 'ECRI's seminar with national Specialised Bodies: The role of national Specialised Bodies in advising legislative and executive authorities and other stakeholders. Background note' (26 May 2016).

ECRI, 'Conclusions on the Implementation of the Recommendations in Respect of Bulgaria Subject to Interim Follow-Up' (23 March 2017) CRI(2017)22.

ECRI, 'General Policy Recommendation No. 2: Equality Bodies to Combat Racism and Intolerance at National Level' (7 December 2017) CRI(2018)06.

ECRI, 'Conclusions on the Implementation of the Recommendations in Respect of Austria Subject to Interim Follow-Up' (23 May 2018) CRI(2018)21.

Engle Merry S, *The Seductions of Quantification: Measuring Human Rights, Gender Violence, and Sex Trafficking* (University of Chicago Press 2016).

Equal Opportunities Initiative Association and Open Society European Policy Institute, 'Memorandum to the European Commission: Violations of EU Law and Fundamental Rights by Bulgaria's Discriminatory Treatment of Roma in the Area of Housing' (February 2017).

Equality and Rights Alliance, 'International concern regarding the erosion of the Irish statutory equality and human rights infrastructure' (nd).

Equality and Rights Alliance, 'Petition to the European Parliament' (nd).

Equality and Rights Alliance, 'Shadow report to UNCERD in response to the Irish Government's combined second and third progress report under ICERD' (October 2010).

Equinet, 'Equinet Project on Standards for Equality Bodies. Independence—Indicators' (nd) <https://equineteurope.org/what-are-equality-bodies/standards-for-equality-bodies/>.

Equinet, 'Strategic Plan 2019–2022' (2019).

Equinet, 'Effective Strategies to Empower Civil Society' (2010).

Equinet, 'Influencing the law through legal proceedings: The powers and practices of equality bodies' (2010).

Equinet, 'Equality Bodies and National Human Rights Institutions: Making the Link to Maximise Impact. An Equinet Perspective' (2011).

Equinet, 'Providing independent assistance to victims of discrimination: An Equinet report' (Equinet: European Network of Equality Bodies, Brussels 2011).

Equinet, 'Equality Bodies: Current Challenges: An Equinet Perspective' (2012).

Equinet, 'Equality Law in Practice: Report on the Implementation of the Race and General Framework Directives' (2013).

Equinet, 'Joint Responsibility for Equal Treatment: How Equality Bodies Work With Duty Bearers. An Equinet Strategy Development Report' (2013).

Equinet, 'Advancing Equality by Making Policy Recommendations. An Equinet Good Practice Guide' (2014).

Equinet, 'Positive Action Measures. The Experience of Equality Bodies' (2014).

Equinet, 'The Bigger Picture: Equality Bodies as part of the National Institutional Architecture for Equality' (2014).

Equinet, 'Strategic Plan 2015–2018' (2015).

Equinet, 'Developing Standards for Equality Bodies. An Equinet Working Paper' (2016).

Equinet, 'Communicating Equality through Social Media: A Guide for Equality Bodies' (2017).

Equinet, 'Strategic Litigation. An Equinet Handbook' (2017).

Equinet, 'Romania: Senate rejects Draft Bill aiming to repeal Anti-Discrimination Law and disable the Equality Body' (27 March 2017) <https://www.archive.equineteurope.org/Romania-Senate-rejects-Draft-Bill-aiming-to-repeal-Anti-Discrimination-Law-and>.

Equinet, 'Learning More About Functions of Quasi-Judicial Equality Bodies: Commission for the Protection from Discrimination, Bulgaria in Focus' (7 June 2017) <https://www.archive.equineteurope.org/Learning-more-about-quasi-judicial-functions-of-equality-bodies>.

Equinet and PIRC, 'Framing Equality: Communication Toolkit for Equality Bodies' (2017).

Eurofound, 'Role of social partners in tackling discrimination at work' (2020) <https://www.eurofound.europa.eu/publications/customised-report/2020/role-of-social-partners-in-tackling-discrimination-at-work>.

European Commission, '2005 Enlargement Strategy Paper' (9 November 2005) COM(2005) 561 final.

European Commission, 'Enlargement Strategy and Main Challenges 2006–2007' (8 November 2006) COM(2006) 649.

European Commission, 'Enlargement Strategy and Main Challenges 2007–2008' (6 November 2007) COM(2007) 663 final.

European Commission, 'Enlargement Strategy and Main Challenges 2008–2009' (5 November 2008) COM(2008) 674 final.

European Commission, 'International perspectives on positive action measures: A comparative analysis in the European Union, Canada, the United States and South Africa' (2009).

European Commission, 'Commission Staff Working Document. Public Consultation: Towards a Coherent European Approach to Collective Redress' (4 February 2011) SEC(2011)173 final.

European Commission, 'Comprehensive Monitoring Report on Croatia's state of preparedness for EU membership' (10 October 2012) COM(2012) 601 final.

European Commission, 'Monitoring Report on Croatia's accession preparations' (26 March 2013) COM(2013) 171 final.

European Commission, 'Press Release: Commission recommends Member States to have collective redress mechanisms in place to ensure effective access to justice' (11 June 2013) IP/13/524.

European Commission, 'Towards a European Horizontal Framework for Collective Redress: Communication from the Commission to the European Parliament, the Council, the European Economic and Social Committee and the Committee of the Regions' (11 June 2013) COM(2013) 401 final.

European Commission, 'Guidelines for EU support to civil society in enlargement countries, 2014–2020' (14 October 2013).

European Commission, 'Joint Report on the application of Council Directive 2000/43/EC of 29 June 2000 implementing the principle of equal treatment between persons irrespective of racial or ethnic origin ("Racial Equality Directive") and of Council Directive 2000/78/EC of 27 November 2000 establishing a general framework for equal treatment in employment and occupation ("Employment Equality Directive")' (Brussels 17 January 2014) COM(2014) 2 final.

European Commission, 'EU Anti-Corruption Report' (3 February 2014) COM(2014) 38 final.

European Commission, 'Instrument for Pre-accession Assistance (IPA II). Indicative Strategy Paper for Serbia (2014–2020)' (19 August 2014).

European Commission, 'Special Eurobarometer 437. Discrimination in the EU in 2015' (2015).

European Commission, 'Twinning Review Mission Report' (January 2015).

European Commission, 'Guidelines for EU support to civil society in enlargement countries, 2014–2020' (June 2015).

European Commission, 'EU Enlargement Strategy' (10 November 2015) COM(2015) 611 final.

European Commission, 'Communication from the Commission to the European Parliament, the Council and the Economic and Social Committee and the Committee of the Regions. The EU Environmental Implementation Review: Common challenges and how to combine efforts to deliver better results' (3 February 2017) COM(2017) 63 final.

European Commission, 'Follow up to the European Parliament resolution with recommendations to the Commission on the establishment of an EU mechanism on democracy, the rule of law and fundamental rights, adopted by the Commission on 17 January 2017' (17 February 2017) SP(2017)16.

European Commission, 'Report from the Commission to the European Parliament, the Council and the European Economic and Social Committee on the implementation of the Commission Recommendation of 11 June 2013 on common principles for injunctive and compensatory collective redress mechanisms in the Member States concerning violations of rights granted under Union law (2013/396/EU)' (25 January 2018) COM(2018) 40 final.

European Commission, 'A Credible Enlargement Perspective for and Enhanced EU Engagement with the Western Balkans' (6 February 2018) COM(2018) 65 final.

European Commission, '2017 Annual Report on the Application of the EU Charter of Fundamental Rights' (4 June 2018) COM(2018) 396 final.

European Commission, 'Proposal for a Regulation of the European Parliament and of the Council establishing the Rights and Values Programme' (7 June 2018) COM(2018) 383 final/2.

European Commission, 'Commission Recommendation on standards for equality bodies' (22 June 2018) C(2018) 3850 final.

European Commission, 'Annex to the Commission Implementing Decision amending Commission Decision C(2014)5872 of 19.8.2014 adopting the Indicative Strategy Paper for Serbia for the period 2014-2020' (10 August 2018) C(2018) 5064 final.

European Commission, 'Special Eurobarometer 493. Discrimination in the European Union' (2019).

European Commission, 'Trade union practices on non-discrimination and diversity 2019' (2019).

European Commission, 'Enhancing the accession process—A credible EU perspective for the Western Balkans' (5 February 2020) COM(2020) 57 final.

European Commission, 'A Union of Equality: Gender Equality Strategy 2020–2025' (5 March 2020) COM(2020) 152 final.

European Commission, 'Feasibility Study for financial support for litigating cases relating to violations of democracy, rule of law and fundamental rights' (29 June 2020).

European Commission, 'A Union of Equality: EU Anti-Racism Action Plan 2020–2025' (18 September 2020) COM(2020) 565 final.

European Commission, 'Press release: State of the Union: A new Action Plan to turn the tide in the fight against racism' (18 September 2020) <https://ec.europa.eu/commission/presscorner/detail/en/ip_20_1654>.

European Commission, '2020 Rule of Law Report: Country Chapter on the rule of law situation in Romania' (30 September 2020) SWD(2020) 322 final.

European Commission, 'A Union of Equality: EU Roma strategic framework for equality, inclusion and participation for 2020–2030' (7 October 2020) COM(2020) 620 final.

European Commission, 'Union of Equality: LGBTIQ Equality Strategy 2020–2025' (12 November 2020) COM(2020) 698 final.

European Commission, 'Union of Equality: Strategy for the Rights of Persons with Disabilities 2021–2030' (3 March 2021) COM(2021) 101 final.

European Commission, 'Equality bodies and the implementation of the Commission Recommendation on standards for equality bodies' (19 March 2021) SWD(2021) 63 final.

European Commission, 'Report on the application of Council Directive 2000/43/EC implementing the principle of equal treatment between persons irrespective of racial or ethnic origin ("the Racial Equality Directive") and of Council Directive 2000/78/EC establishing a general framework for equal treatment in employment and occupation ("the Employment Equality Directive")' (Brussels 19 March 2021) COM(2021) 139 final.

European Commission—Directorate-General Justice and Consumers, 'High Level Group on Non-discrimination, Equality and Diversity. Mandate' (2015).

European network of legal experts in gender equality and non-discrimination, 'A comparative analysis of non-discrimination law in Europe: 2015' (2016).

European network of legal experts in gender equality and non-discrimination, 'A comparative analysis of non-discrimination law in Europe: 2016' (2016).

European network of legal experts in gender equality and non-discrimination, 'A comparative analysis of non-discrimination law in Europe 2017' (2017).

European network of legal experts in gender equality and non-discrimination, 'A comparative analysis of non-discrimination law in Europe: 2020' (2021).

European Parliament, 'Resolution of 13 November 2018 on the rule of law in Romania' 2018/2844(RSP).

European Parliament, 'Resolution of 2 February 2012 on "Towards a Coherent European Approach to Collective Redress"' 2011/2089(INI).

European Parliament, 'Committee of Inquiry into the Rise of Fascism and Racism in Europe: Report on the findings of the inquiry' (December 1985).

European Parliament, 'Report for the Committee on Internal Affairs and Citizens Rights on Equal Rights for Homosexuals and Lesbians in the European Community' (1994) A3-28/94.

European Parliament, 'Resolution on equal rights for homosexuals and lesbians in the EC' (8 February 1994).

European Parliament, 'Report on the proposal for a Council directive on implementing the principle of equal treatment between persons irrespective of racial or ethnic origin (COM(1999) 566—C5-0067/2000—1999/0253(CNS))' (16 May 2000) A5-0136/2000.

European Parliament, 'Report with recommendations to the Commission on the establishment of an EU mechanism on democracy, the rule of law and fundamental rights (2015/2254(INL))' (10 October 2016) A8-0283/2016.

European Parliament, 'European Parliament resolution on the need to establish a European Values Instrument to support civil society organisations which promote fundamental values within the European Union at local and national level (2018/2619(RSP))' (19 April 2018).

European Parliament, Committee on Civil Liberties, Justice and Home Affairs, 'Draft Report on the proposal for a regulation of the European Parliament and of the Council establishing the Rights and Values programme (COM(2018)0383—C8-0234/2018—2018/0207(COD))' (Rapporteur: Bodil Valero, 2 October 2018) 2018/0207(COD).

European Roma Rights Centre, Interights and Migration Policy Group, 'Strategic litigation of race discrimination in Europe: from principles to practice' (2004).

Evans Case R and Givens TE, 'Re-engineering Legal Opportunity Structures in the European Union? The Starting Line Group and the Politics of the Racial Equality Directive' (2010) 48(2) Journal of Common Market Studies 221.

Fagan A and Wunsch N, 'Fostering Institutionalisation? The Impact of the EU Accession Process on State–Civil Society Relations in Serbia' [2018] Acta Politica 1.

Falkner G and Treib O, 'Three Worlds of Compliance or Four? The EU-15 Compared to New Member States' (2008) 46(2) Journal of Common Market Studies 293.

Falkner G, Treib O, and Holzleithner E (eds), *Compliance in the Enlarged European Union: Living Rights or Dead Letters?* (Ashgate 2008).

Fariss CJ, 'The Changing Standard of Accountability and the Positive Relationship between Human Rights Treaty Ratification and Compliance' (2018) 48(01) British Journal of Political Science 239.

Farkas L, 'Limited Enforcement Possibilities Under European Anti-Discrimination Legislation—A Case Study of Procedural Novelties: Actio Popularis Action in Hungary' (2010) 3(3) Erasmus Law Review 181.

Farkas L, 'Collective Actions under European Anti-Discrimination Law' [2014] European Anti-Discrimination Law Review 25.

Farkas L, 'NGO and Equality Body Enforcement of EU Anti-Discrimination Law: Bulgarian Roma and the Electricity Sector' in Elise Muir and others (eds), *How EU Law Shapes Opportunities for Preliminary References on Fundamental Rights: Discrimination, Data Protection and Asylum* (European University Institute, EUI Working Papers 2017).

Farrell M, 'ECRI Seminar with National Specialised Bodies to Combat Racism and Intolerance (Equality Bodies): Revision of ECRI General Policy Recommendation No. 2 on Specialised Bodies. Report and Conclusions' (ECRI, Strasbourg 23 and 24 May 2017) <https://www.coe.int/t/dghl/monitoring/ecri/activities/61-Seminar_national_specialised_bodies_2017/Conclusions.asp#TopOfPage>.

Finnemore M and Sikkink K, 'International Norm Dynamics and Political Change' (1998) 52(4) International Organization 887.

Folk G, 'Freedoms Fund: The EU Commission's Half-Hearted Plans to Support Civil Society Groups' (Civil Liberties Union for Europe 31 May 2018) <https://www.liberties.eu/en/news/ec-commission-evi-proposal-rights-and-values-fund/15107>.

Frantziou E, 'Mangold Recast? The ECJ's Flirtation with Drittwirkung in Egenberger' (European Law Blog 24 April 2018) <http://europeanlawblog.eu/2018/04/24/mangold-recast-the-ecjs-flirtation-with-drittwirkung-in-egenberger/>.

Fredman S, 'Emerging from the Shadows: Substantive Equality and Article 14 of the European Convention on Human Rights' (2016) 16(2) Human Rights Law Review 273.

Fredman S, 'Substantive Equality Revisited' (2016) 14(3) International Journal of Constitutional Law 712.

Fredman S, 'Substantive Equality Revisited: A Rejoinder to Catharine MacKinnon' (2016) 14(3) International Journal of Constitutional Law 747.

Fundamental Rights Agency, 'Developing indicators for the protection, respect and promotion of the rights of the child in the European Union. Summary Report' (2009).

Fundamental Rights Agency, 'EU-MIDIS Data in Focus Report No. 1: The Roma' (2009).

Fundamental Rights Agency, 'EU-MIDIS Data in Focus Report No. 2: Muslims' (2009).

Fundamental Rights Agency, 'EU-MIDIS Main Results Report' (2009).

Fundamental Rights Agency, 'EU-MIDIS, Data in Focus Report No. 3: Rights Awareness and Equality Bodies' (2010).

Fundamental Rights Agency, 'National Human Rights Institutions in the EU Member States. Strengthening the fundamental rights architecture in the EU I' (2010).

Fundamental Rights Agency, 'The impact of the racial equality directive: Views of trade unions and employers in the European Union' (2010).

Fundamental Rights Agency, 'Developing indicators for the protection, respect and promotion of the rights of the child in the European Union' (November 2010).

Fundamental Rights Agency, 'The Racial Equality Directive: application and challenges' (2011) <http://fra.europa.eu/sites/default/files/fra_uploads/1916-FRA-RED-synthesis-report_EN.pdf>.

Fundamental Rights Agency, 'Access to justice in cases of discrimination in the EU: Steps to further equality' (2012) <http://fra.europa.eu/sites/default/files/fra-2012-access-to-justice-social.pdf>.

Fundamental Rights Agency, 'Opinion of the European Union Agency for Fundamental Rights on the situation of equality in the European Union 10 years on from initial implementation of the equality directives' (2013) 1/2013.

Fundamental Rights Agency, 'Opinion of the European Union Agency for Fundamental Rights on the situation of equality in the European Union 10 years on from initial implementation of the equality directives' (2013) FRA Opinion—1/2013 [EU equality directives].

Fundamental Rights Agency, 'EU LGBT survey. European Union lesbian, gay, bisexual and transgender survey: Main results' (2014).

Fundamental Rights Agency, 'The right to political participation for persons with disabilities: human rights indicators' (2014).

Fundamental Rights Agency, 'The right to political participation of persons with disabilities: human rights indicators' (2014).

Fundamental Rights Agency, 'Annual Report 2014. Fundamental rights: challenges and achievements in 2014' (2015).

Fundamental Rights Agency, 'EU-MIDIS II: Roma—selected findings' (2016).

Fundamental Rights Agency, 'EU-MIDIS II: Main results' (2017).

Fundamental Rights Agency, 'EU-MIDIS II: Muslims—Selected findings' (2017).

Fundamental Rights Agency, 'Challenges facing civil society organisations working on human rights in the EU' (2018).

Fundamental Rights Agency, 'Experiences and perceptions of antisemitism. Second survey on discrimination and hate crime against Jews in the EU' (2018).

Fundamental Rights Agency, 'Civil society space: views of organisations—Conference paper' (November 2018).

Fundamental Rights Agency, 'EU-MIDIS II. Migrant women—Selected findings' (2019).

Fundamental Rights Agency, 'Young Jewish Europeans: perceptions and experiences of antisemitism' (2019).

Fundamental Rights Agency, 'EU-LGBTI II. A long way to go for LGBTI equality' (2020).

Fundamental Rights Agency, 'Strong and effective national human rights institutions—challenges, promising practices and opportunities' (2020).

Fundamental Rights Agency and ECtHR, *Handbook on European Non-Discrimination Law* (2018) .

Fuszara M, 'The OMC, Gender Policy and the Experience of Poland as a New Member State' in Fiona Beveridge and Samantha Velluti (eds), *Gender and the Open Method of Coordination. Perspectives on Law, Governance and Equality in the EU* (Ashgate 2008).

GANHRI, 'General Observations of the Sub-Committee on Accreditation' adopted by the GANHRI Bureau at its Meeting held in Geneva, Switzerland, 6 March 2017.

General Assembly, 'Principles relating to the Status of National Institutions (The Paris Principles)' (20 December 1993) Resolution 48/134.

Givens TE and Evans Case R, *Legislating Equality: The Politics of Antidiscrimination Policy in Europe* (OUP 2014).

Gleichbehandlungsanwaltschaft, 'Gleichbehandlungs bericht für die Privatwirtschaft 2018 und 2019. Teil II—Anwaltschaft für Gleichbehandlung' (2020).

Green M, 'What We Talk About When We Talk About Indicators: Current Approaches to Human Rights Measurement' (2001) 23(4) Human Rights Quarterly 1062.

Grgić A, 'Recognizing Formal and Substantive Equality in the Oršuš Case' (2012) 9 European Yearbook of Minority Issues 327.

Grozev R, 'A Landmark Judgment of the Court of Justice of the EU—New Conceptual Contributions to the Legal Combat against Ethnic Discrimination' (2015) 15 The Equal Rights Review 168.

Guild E, 'The EC Directive on Race Discrimination: Surprises, Possibilities and Limitations' (2000) 29(4) Industrial Law Journal 416.

Guliyeva G, 'Joining Forces or Reinventing the Wheel? The EU and the Protection of National Minorities' (2010) 17(2) International Journal on Minority and Group Rights 287.

Gyeney L, 'Sensitive Issues before the European Court of Justice—The Right of Residence of Third Country Spouses Who Became Victims of Domestic Violence, as Well as Same-Sex Spouses in the Scope of Application of the Free Movement Directive (Legal Analysis of the NA and Coman Cases)' [2017] Hungarian Yearbook of International Law and European Law 211.

Habermas J, *Theorie des kommunikativen Handelns* (Suhrkamp 1982).

Hambler A, 'Neutrality and Workplace Restrictions on Headscarves and Religious Dress: Lessons from Achbita and Bougnaoui' (2018) 47(1) Industrial Law Journal 149.

Hand L, 'Former Equality Authority chief praised as a "pioneer"' *Independentie* (14 May 2010) <https://www.independent.ie/irish-news/former-equality-authority-chief-praised-as-a-pioneer-26654982.html>.

Harvey BM and Walsh K, 'Downgrading Equality and Human Rights: Assessing the Impact' (Equality and Right Alliance 2009) <http://www.eracampaign.org/uploads/Downgrading Equality & Human Right Assessing the Impact.pdf>.

Havelková B, 'Resistance to Anti-Discrimination Law in Central and Eastern Europe—A Post-Communist Legacy?' (2016) 17(4) German Law Journal 627–56.

HCNM, 'Graz Recommendations on Access to Justice and National Minorities' (November 2017).

Healy A, 'EU to ask about cuts to Equality Authority' *The Irish Times* (1 June 2010) <https://www.irishtimes.com/news/eu-to-ask-about-cuts-to-equality-authority-1.672420>.

Hennigan M, 'Niall Crowley—an Irish public official of rare courage resigns in response to act of political revenge' *Finfacts* (12 December 2008) <http://www.finfacts.ie/irishfinancenews/article_1015513.shtml>.

Henrard K, 'Equal Rights versus Special Rights? Minority Protection and the Prohibition of Discrimination' (European Network of Legal Experts in the Non-discrimination Field 2007).

Henrard K, 'The First Substantive ECJ Judgment on the Racial Equality Directive: A Strong Message in a Conceptually Flawed and Responsively Weak Bottle' [2009] Jean Monnet Working Paper.

Hermanin C and de Kroon E, 'The Race Equality Directive: A Shadow Report. Lessons learnt from the implementation in nine EU member states' (Open Society European Policy Institute 2013).

Hirschl R, *Comparative Matters: The Renaissance of Comparative Constitutional Law* (OUP 2014).

Hodasz M, Köhler K, and Liegl B, 'Indicators and Monitoring Systems as Preventive Tools in the Area of Ethnic and Religious Discrimination' in Julia Kozma, Manfred Nowak, and Roland Schmidt (eds), *Indicators and Monitoring Systems as Preventive Tools for Ensuring Peace and Security and Respect for Human Rights in External Policy-Making of the EU: Proceedings of the COST workshop "Human Rights, Peace and Security in EU Foreign Policy"* (NWV, Neuer Wissenschaftlicher Verlag 2009).

Hodges C and Voet S, *Delivering Collective Redress: New Technologies* (Hart Publishing 2018).

Holtmaat R, 'Catalysts for change: Equality bodies according to Directive 2000/43/EC' (European Network of Legal Experts in the Non-discrimination Field 2006).

Hooghe L and Marks G, *Multi-level Governance and European Integration* (Rowman & Littlefield Publishers 2001).

Howard E, 'Islamic Headscarves and the CJEU: Achbita and Bougnaoui' (2017) 24(3) Maastricht Journal of European and Comparative Law 348.

HRC, 'Concluding observations on the third periodic report of Croatia' (30 April 2015) CCPR/C/HRV/CO/3.

Hunt P, 'Interim report of the Special Rapporteur of the Commission on Human Rights on the right of everyone to enjoy the highest attainable standard of physical and mental health, Mr. Paul Hunt' (UN General Assembly, 2003) A/58/427.

ICC Sub-Committee on Accreditation, 'Report and Recommendations of the Session of the Sub-Committee on Accreditation (SCA)' (16 November 2015).

Ilieva M, 'ADL draft amendments of definitions of "indirect discrimination" and "unfavourable treatment"' (EELN News Report 15 July 2016).

Ilieva M, 'Supreme Administrative Court follow-up in Nikolova/ CHEZ Case (C-83/2014)' (EELN News Report 10 February 2021).

Ionescu I, 'First case of multiple discrimination against Romani women sanctioned by the Romanian national equality body' (EELN News Report 23 January 2018).

Iordache R, 'Report on attitudes and perceptions regarding discrimination in Romania released by the national equality body' (EELN News Report 21 September 2015).

Iordache R, 'National equality body decision on social housing criteria in Bucharest' (EELN News Report 12 August 2016).

Iordache R, 'Draft bill aiming to abrogate Anti-discrimination Law is adopted by the Chamber of Deputies tacitly' (EELN News Report 1 March 2017).

Iordache R, 'The Senate rejects draft bill aiming to abrogate Antidiscrimination Law' (EELN News Report 15 March 2017).

Iordache R, 'National equality body publishes annual activity report for 2016' (EELN News Report 7 June 2017).

Iordache R, 'Court of Appeal maintains NCCD decision on social housing criteria leading to discrimination' (EELN News Report 31 January 2018).

Iordache R, 'The Prime Minister calling political critics pejoratively as "autistic" does not amount to discrimination finds the national equality body' (EELN News Report 6 March 2018).

Iordache R, 'NCCD jurisprudence on ensuring accessibility of public transportation reversed' (EELN News Report 17 May 2018).

Iordache R, 'National equality body publishes annual activity report for 2017' (EELN News Report 28 May 2018).

Iordache R, 'Constitutional Court revokes the mandate of one of the members of the Steering Board of the NCCD' (EELN News Report 21 June 2018).

Iordache R, 'Attacks against the Romanian equality body (NCCD)' (EELN News Report 31 October 2018).

Iordache R, 'The Parliament adopted money laundering provisions which paralyze NGOs, in particular those supporting vulnerable groups' (EELN News Report 31 October 2018).

Iordache R, 'National survey on attitudes and perceptions of discrimination in Romania' (EELN News Report 5 March 2019).

Iordache R, 'Refusal to host conference due to the presence of a trans activist sanctioned by the NCCD' (EELN News Report 10 July 2020).

Irish Human Rights and Equality Commission, 'Amicus Curiae Guidelines' (2016) <https://www.ihrec.ie/app/uploads/2016/12/IHREC-Amicus-Curiae-Guidelines.pdf>.
Irish Human Rights and Equality Commission, 'Annual Report 2015' (2016).
Irish Human Rights and Equality Commission, 'Outline Submission on Behalf of the Irish Human Rights and Equality Commission in the case Ciaran Culkin v. Sligo County Council' (Record no 2015/103, 12 January 2016).
Irish Human Rights and Equality Commission, 'Annual Report 2016' (2017).
Irish Human Rights and Equality Commission, 'Guidelines on applications for legal assistance' (2017) <https://www.ihrec.ie/app/uploads/2017/06/Guidelines-on-applications-for-legal-assistance-April-2017-3.pdf>.
Irish Human Rights and Equality Commission, 'Travellers Denied Service Secure Settlement and Redress' (18 December 2017) <https://www.ihrec.ie/travellers-denied-service-secure-settlement-redress/>.
Irish Human Rights and Equality Commission, 'Annual Report 2017' (2018).
Irish Human Rights and Equality Commission, 'EU Court of Justice Issues Landmark Equality Law Ruling' (4 December 2018) <https://www.ihrec.ie/eu-court-of-justice-issues-landmark-equality-law-ruling/>.
Irish Human Rights and Equality Commission, 'Annual Report 2019' (2020).
Jacobsen BD, *Assistance to Victims of Discrimination by Equality Bodies of the EU Member States: A Scandinavian Perspective* (DJOF Publishing 2010).
Jacobsen BD and Rosenberg Khawaja EO, 'Legal Assistance to Individual. Powers and Procedures of Effective and Strategic Individual Enforcement' in Soraya Obura and Fiona Palmer (eds), *Strategic Enforcement: Powers and Competences of Equality Bodies* (Equinet 2006).
Jacquot S and Woll C, 'Usage of European Integration—Europeanisation from a Sociological Perspective' (2003) 7(12) European Integration online Papers (EIoP).
Kádár A, 'Constitutional Court denies legal standing of NGOs in actio popularis cases' (EELN News Report 14 January 2014).
Kádár A, 'Police ban of LGBTQ demonstration amounts to discrimination and harassment' (EELN News Report 14 October 2014).
Kádár A, 'Ministry of education is also responsible for segregation, but implementation of desegregation plan is not ordered by the court' (EELN News Report 8 January 2016).
Kádár A, 'Roma pupils face difficulties and uncertainties after segregated school closes in Csobánka' (EELN News Report 28 September 2016).
Kádár A, 'Court confirms that refusal by school to admit pupils raised by a lesbian couple amounts to discrimination and awards damages to one of the parents' (EELN News Report 10 January 2017).
Kádár A, 'Curia upholds decision establishing segregation in education and ordering the closing down of segregated school' (EELN News Report 8 November 2017).
Kádár A, 'Discrimination against an LGBTQ sport club through refusing to rent out two lanes of a swimming pool to the club for a sports event' (EELN News Report 2 February 2018).
Kádár A, 'Education ministry found to be in breach of its nondiscrimination obligations for failing to take effective action against segregation in 28 elementary schools' (EELN News Report 6 July 2018).
Kádár A, 'Successful procedure launched by civil society organisation to enforce equality body decision on providing accessibility' (EELN News Report 19 July 2019).
Kádár A, 'Draft Bill on mandatory in-kind compensation for segregation in education submitted' (EELN News Report 5 August 2020).

Kádár A, 'Legislation adopted abolishing the Equal Treatment Authority and transferring its tasks to the Ombudsman' (EELN News Report 10 February 2021).
Kádár T, 'The Standing of National Equality Bodies before the European Union Court of Justice: the Implications of the Belov Judgment' (2013) 11 The Equal Rights Review 13.
Kádár T, 'Equality Bodies: A European Phenomenon' [2018] International Journal of Discrimination and the Law 1–19.
Kelemen D, 'Suing for Europe: Adversarial Legalism and European Governance' (2006) 39(1) Comparative Political Studies 101.
Kelley J, 'International Actors on the Domestic Scene: Membership Conditionality and Socialization by International Institutions' (2004) 58(3) International Organization 425.
Kilpatrick C and de Witte B, 'Introducing the Role of Collective Actors and Preliminary References in the Enforcement of EU Fundamental Rights Law' in Elise Muir and others (eds), *How EU Law Shapes Opportunities for Preliminary References on Fundamental Rights: Discrimination, Data Protection and Asylum* (European University Institute, EUI Working Papers 2017).
Kochenov D, *EU Enlargement and the Failure of Conditionality: Pre-Accession Conditionality in the Fields of Democracy and the Rule of Law* (Kluwer Law International 2008).
Kochenov D, 'The Aquis and Its Principles: The Enforcement of the "Law" versus the Enforcement of "Values" in the EU' in András Jakab and Dimitry Kochenov (eds), *The Enforcement of EU Law and Values: Ensuring Member States' Compliance* (OUP 2017).
Kochenov D and Belavusau U, 'Same-Sex Spouses in the EU After Coman: More Free Movement, But What About Marriage?' [2019] EUI Working Papers 1.
Kochenov D, Magen A, and Pech L, 'The Great Rule of Law Debate in the EU' (2016) 54(5) Journal of Common Market Studies 1045.
Koh HH, 'Why do Nations Obey International Law' (1997) 106 The Yale Law Journal 2599.
Köhler P, 'Promotion of Equal Opportunities between the Sexes, Selection of the Best, Merit System' (2000) 1(1) The European Legal Forum 63.
Krause R, 'Case C-54/07, Centrum voor gelijkheid van kansen en voor racismebestrijding v. Firma Feryn NV, [2008] ECR I-5187' (2010) 47(3) Common Market Law Review 917.
Krstic I, 'Regional conference of equality bodies in South-East Europe' (EELN News Report 2 December 2016).
Lahuerta SB, 'Ethnic Discrimination, Discrimination by Association and the Roma Community: CHEZ' (2016) 53(3) Common Market Law Review 797.
Landman T, 'Measuring Human Rights: Principle, Practice, and Policy' (2004) 26(4) Human Rights Quarterly 906.
Landman T and Carvalho E, *Measuring Human Rights* (Routledge 2010).
Lantschner E, 'Reflexive Governance in the EU Enlargement Process' (2015) 98(2) Kritische Vierteljahresschrift für Gesetzgebung und Rechtswissenschaft 130.
Lantschner E, 'Indicators for Monitoring Implementation of EU Equality Directives' (2020) 45(4) Review of Central and East European Law 444.
Lantschner E, 'Strategic Litigation: Equality Bodies' Strategic Use of Powers to Enforce EU Non-Discrimination Law' [2020] European Equality Law Review 1.
Lantschner E and Marsal S, 'Expert Report Regarding the Protection of Minorities and Cultural Rights in the Republic of Serbia' (Peer review expert mission to Serbia on Chapter 23—Judiciary and fundamental rights, focussing on interim benchmarks on protection of minorities and cultural rights 24 March 2017).
Lawless J, 'Book Review: Reflexive Governance' (2011) 17(3) European Law Journal 429.
Lenoble J and Maesschalck M, *Democracy, Law and Governance* (Ashgate 2010).

Lenoble J and Maesschalck M, 'Renewing the Theory of Public Interest: The Quest for a Reflexive and Learning-based Approach to Governance' in Olivier de Schutter and Jacques Lenoble (eds), *Reflexive Governance: Redefining the Public Interest in a Pluralistic World* (Hart Publishing 2010).

Liddle J, 'Twenty-First-Century Public Leadership Within Complex Governance Systems: Some Reflections' (2010) 38(4) Policy & Politics 657.

Liebowitz DJ and Zwingel S, 'Gender Equality Oversimplified: Using CEDAW to Counter the Measurement Obsession' (2014) 16(3) International Studies Review 362.

Liebscher D, 'Recht als Türöffner für gleiche Freiheit? Eine Zwischenbilanz nach zehn Jahren AGG' (2016) 9 Aus Politik und Zeitgeschichte. www.bpb.de/apuz/221577/eine-zwischenbilanz-nach-zehn-jahren-agg?p=all

Linos K and Pegram T, 'What Works in Human Rights Institutions?' (2017) 112(3) American Journal of International Law 1.

Litigation Association, 'Verbandsklagerecht für den Klagsverband gefordert' (26 September 2017) <https://www.klagsverband.at/archives/12738>.

Litigation Association, 'Verbandsklagerecht für Klagsverband im Nationalrat beschlossen' (13 October 2017) <https://www.klagsverband.at/archives/12792>.

MacKinnon CA, 'Substantive Equality Revisited: A Reply to Sandra Fredman' (2016) 14(3) International Journal of Constitutional Law 739.

MacKinnon CA, 'Substantive Equality Revisited: A Rejoinder to Sandra Fredman' (2017) 15(4) International Journal of Constitutional Law 1174.

Mahlmann M, 'Constitutional complaint in Egenberger case' (EELN News Report 1 July 2019).

Makkonen T, 'European Handbook on Equality Data. 2016 Revision' (European Commission 2016).

Manolakos T and Mayrhofer M, 'Handbook on how to collect equality data targeting public institutions, regional and local units of self-government which collect equality data' (Twinning Project: Establishing a comprehensive system for anti-discrimination protection, Zagreb January 2013).

Marc Bossuyt, 'The concept and practice of affirmative action: Final report submitted by Mr. Marc Bossuyt, Special Rapporteur, in accordance with resolution 1998/5 of the Sub-Commission for the Promotion and Protection of Human Rights' (17 June 2002) UN doc. E/CN.4/Sub.2/2002/21.

March JG and Olsen JP, 'The New Institutionalism: Organizational Factors in Political Life' (1984) 78(3) American Political Science Review 734.

March JG and Olsen JP, 'The Institutional Dynamics of International Political Orders' (1998) 52(4) International Organization 943.

Marín Aís JR, 'Freedom of Religion in the Workplace v. Freedom to Conduct a Business, the Islamic Veil Before the Court of Justice: Ms. Samira Achbita Case' (2018) 3(1) European Papers 409.

Marko J, 'Five Years After: Continuing Reflections on the Thematic Commentary on Effective Participation. The Interplay between Equality and Participation' in Tove Malloy and Ugo Caruso (eds), *Minorities, their Rights, and the Monitoring of the European Framework Convention for the Protection of National Minorities. Essays in Honour of Rainer Hofmann* (Martinus Nijhoff Publishers 2013).

Marko J, 'Einleitende Bemerkungen zur interdisziplinären Perspektive von Politik und Recht in der Rechtsprechung' in Stephan Hinghofer-Szalkay and Herbert Kalb (eds), *Islam, Recht und Diversität* (Verlag Österreich 2018).

Marko J, 'Against Discrimination: The Right to Equality and the Dilemma of Difference' in Joseph Marko (ed), *Human and Minority Rights Protection by Multiple Diversity Governance: History, Law, Ideology and Politics in European Perspective* (Routledge 2019).

Marko J, 'Law and Sociology: The Constructivist and Interpretative Turn' in Joseph Marko (ed), *Human and Minority Rights Protection by Multiple Diversity Governance: History, Law, Ideology and Politics in European Perspective* (Routledge 2019).

McCarthy J, 'Rights watchdog "in the wrong"' *The Times* (14 January 2018) <https://www.thetimes.co.uk/article/rights-watchdog-in-the-wrong-wx8mxwfg7>.

McCrea R, 'Faith at work: the CJEU's headscarf rulings' (EU Law Analysis 17 March 2017) <http://eulawanalysis.blogspot.com/2017/03/faith-at-work-cjeus-headscarf-rulings.html>.

McCrea R, 'Religious discrimination at work: Can employees be fired for getting divorced?' (EU Law Analysis 12 September 2018).

McCrudden C, 'Rethinking Positive Action' (1986) 15(1) Industrial Law Journal 219.

McCrudden C, 'International and European Norms Regarding National Legal Remedies for Racial Inequality' in Sandra Fredman (ed), *Discrimination and Human Rights. The Case of Racism* (OUP 2001).

McCrudden C, 'The New Architecture of EU Equality Law After CHEZ: Did the Court of Justice Reconceptualise Direct and Indirect Discrimination' [2016] European Equality Law Review 1.

McCrudden C and Kountouros H, 'Human Rights and European Equality Law' in Helen Meenan (ed), *Equality Law in an Enlarged European Union: Understanding the Article 13 Directives* (CUP 2007).

McInerney S, 'Equal Treatment between Persons Irrespective of Racial or Ethnic Origin: A Comment' (2000) 25 European Law Review 317.

Mercat-Bruns M, 'A Comparative Study on Collective Redress in France, Norway and Romania: The Challenges of Strategic Litigation' [2020] European Equality Law Review 19.

Mickonyte A, 'Bougnaoui (Rs C-188/15) and G4S Secure Solutions (Rs C-157/15) in European Legal Scholarship' in Stephan Hinghofer-Szalkay and Herbert Kalb (eds), *Islam, Recht und Diversität* (Verlag Österreich 2018).

Mihaylova D and Iordanov M, 'Access to Electricity in Roma Settlements in Bulgaria' (Equal Opportunities Initiative Association 2015).

Mihr A, 'Human Rights Benchmarks for EU's External Policy' (European Parliament, Directorate-General for External Policies, Policy Department, 2011) PE 457.059.

Ministerium für Frauen und Gesundheit and Sozialministerium, 'Evaluierung der Instrumente des Gleichbehandlungsrechts. Weiterentwicklung des Gleichbehandlungsrechts und der Gleichbehandlungsinstrumente—Expert/inn/enbericht' (2016).

Miošić-Lisjak N, 'One Step Forward, Two Steps Back: Anti-discrimination policy in Croatia 2011–2016' (Centre for Peace Studies October 2017).

Moon G, 'Enforcement Bodies' in Dagmar Schiek, Lisa Waddington, and Mark Bell (eds), *Cases, Materials and Text on National, Supranational and International Non-Discrimination Law* (Hart Publishing 2007).

Moravcsik A and Schimmelfennig F, 'Liberal Intergovernmentalism' in Antje Wiener and Thomas Diez (eds), *European Integration Theory* (2nd edn. OUP 2009).

Moravcsik A and Schimmelfennig F, 'Liberal Intergovernmentalism' in Antje Wiener, Tanja A Börzel, and Thomas Risse (eds), *European Integration Theory* (3rd edn. OUP 2019).

Möschel M, 'Race Discrimination and Access to the European Court of Justice: Belov' (2013) 50(5) Common Market Law Review 1433.

Möschel M, 'Litigating Anti-Discrimination Cases in Germany: What Role for Collective Actors?' in Elise Muir and others (eds), *How EU Law Shapes Opportunities for Preliminary References on Fundamental Rights: Discrimination, Data Protection and Asylum* (European University Institute, EUI Working Papers 2017).

Moses J and Knutsen T, *Ways of Knowing: Competing Methodologies in Social and Political Research* (Palgrave Macmillan 2012).

Moumoutzis K and Zartaloudis S, 'Europeanization Mechanisms and Process Tracing: A Template for Empirical Research' (2016) 54(2) Journal of Common Market Studies 337.

Muir E and Kolf S, 'Belgian Equality Bodies Reaching out to the CJEU: EU Procedural Law as a Catalyst' in Elise Muir and others (eds), How EU Law Shapes Opportunities for Preliminary References On Fundamental Rights: Discrimination, Data Protection and Asylum (European University Institute, EUI Working Papers 2017).

Nakrošis V, 'Policy Transfer in the Pre- and Post-Accession Period: Experience of the New EU Member States' [2004] Lithuanian Political Science Yearbook 113.

Niemann A, Lefkofridi Z, and Schmitter PC, 'Neofunctionalism' in Antje Wiener, Tanja A Börzel, and Thomas Risse (eds), *European Integration Theory* (3rd edn. OUP 2019).

Niemann A and Schmitter PC, 'Neofunctionalism' in Antje Wiener and Thomas Diez (eds), *European Integration Theory* (2nd edn. OUP 2009).

Nussbaum M, *Women and Human Development. The Capabilities Approach* (CUP 2000).

Nyitray Z and Cox S, 'Case Watch: Roma Ruling Advances Antidiscrimination Protections in the European Union' (Open Society Foundations—Voices, 16 July 2015).

OHCHR, 'Report on Indicators for Monitoring Compliance with International Human Rights Instruments' (11 May 2006) HRI/MC/2006/7.

OHCHR, 'Report on Indicators for Promoting and Monitoring the Implementation of Human Rights' (6 June 2008) HRI/MC/2008/3.

OHCHR, 'Report of the United Nations High Commissioner for Human Rights to the Economic and Social Council' (26 April 2011) E/2011/90.

OHCHR, 'Human Rights Indicators. A Guide to Measurement and Implementation' (2012) <http://www.ohchr.org/Documents/Publications/Human_rights_indicators_en.pdf>.

Oliveira A, 'What Difference Does EU Law Make? The Added Value of EU Equality Directives on Access to Justice for Collective Actors' in Elise Muir and others (eds), How EU Law Shapes Opportunities for Preliminary References on Fundamental Rights: Discrimination, Data Protection and Asylum (European University Institute, EUI Working Papers 2017).

Ombudswoman of the Republic of Croatia, 'Annual Report 2018' (2019).

Ott K, 'Croatia and the EU: The Catch-Up Issue' (CEPS Commentary 28 June 2013).

Pech L and others, 'An EU Mechanism on Democracy, the Rule of Law and Fundamental Rights' (European Parliament, European Added Value Unit April 2016).

Peers S, 'Love wins in the CJEU: Same Sex Marriages and EU free movement law' (EU Law Analysis 5 June 2018) <http://eulawanalysis.blogspot.com/2018/06/love-wins-in-cjeu-same-sex-marriages.html>.

Pegram T, 'Bridging the Divide: The Merger of the Irish Equality Authority and Human Rights Commission' (2013) 29 Studies in Public Policy, 1.

Peters A, 'The Many Meanings of Equality and Positive Action in Favour of Women under European Community Law—A Conceptual Analysis' (1996) 2(2) European Law Journal 177.

Peters BG and Pierre J, 'Governance Approaches' in Antje Wiener and Thomas Diez (eds), *European Integration Theory* (2nd edn. OUP 2009).

Phinnemore D, 'Beyond 25—The Changing Face of EU Enlargement: Commitment, Conditionality and the Constitutional Treaty' (2006) 8(1) Journal of Southern Europe and the Balkans 7.

Piattoni S, *The Theory of Multi-level Governance: Conceptual, Empirical, and Normative Challenges* (OUP 2010).

Piattoni S, 'Multilevel governance' in Klaus Detterbeck and Eve Hepburn (eds), *Handbook of Territorial Politics* (Edward Elgar 2018).

Poposka Z, 'Shift in the Burden of Proof—Mechanism to Ensure Enforcement of Anti-Discrimination Legislation' (2013) 2 Balkans Social Science Review 133.

Pöschl M, 'Verfassungsrechtliche Gleichheit, arbeitsrechtliche Gleichbehandlung, unionsrechtliche Antidiskriminierung' [2013] DRdA 467.

Pribula L, 'The New Civil Procedure Code in Hungary' (2017) 62(1) Studia UBB Iurisprudentia 79.

Prince R, 'Policy Transfer as Policy Assemblage: Making Policy for the Creative Industries in New Zealand' (2010) 42(1) Environment and Planning A 169.

Regulation (EU) No 231/2014 of the European Parliament and of the Council establishing an Instrument for Pre-accession Assistance (IPA II) 11 March 2014.

Relaño Pastor E, 'Religious Discrimination in the Workplace: Achbita and Bougnaoui' in Uladzislau Belavusau and Kristin Henrard (eds), *EU Anti-Discrimination Law beyond Gender* (Hart Publishing 2018).

Republic of Serbia, 'Action Plan for the Implementation of the Strategy for Prevention and Protection against Discrimination for the Period 2014–2018' (2 October 2014).

Rete Lenford—Avvocatura per i diritti LGBTI, 'Discriminazione delle persone omosessuali in ambito lavorativo: la Corte di cassazione richiede una interpretazione pregiudiziale alla Corte di giustizia in un caso avviato da Avvocatura per i Diritti LGBTI—Rete Lenford' (25 July 2018) <http://www.retelenford.it/1030-discriminazione-delle-persone-omosessuali-in-ambito-lavorativo.html>.

Ringelheim J, 'Du Dialogue aux Assises: heurts et malheurs de l'interculturalité en Belgique' in Emmanuelle Bribosia and Isabelle Rorive (eds), *L'accommodement de la diversité religieuse. Regards croisés—Canada, Europe, Belgique* (Peter Lang 2015).

Risse T, '"Let's Argue!" Communicative Action in World Politics' (2000) 54(1) International Organization 1.

Risse T and Ropp S, 'Introduction and Overview' in Thomas Risse, Stephen C Ropp, and Kathryn Sikkink (eds), *The Persistent Power of Human Rights: From Commitment to Compliance* (CUP 2013).

Risse T, Ropp S, and Sikkink K (eds), *The Power of Human Rights: International Norms and Domestic Change* (CUP 1999).

Risse T, Ropp SC, and Sikkink K (eds), *The Persistent Power of Human Rights: From Commitment to Compliance* (CUP 2013).

Risse T and Sikkink K, 'The Socialization of International Human Rights Norms into Domestic Practices: Introduction' in Thomas Risse, Stephen Ropp, and Kathryn Sikkink (eds), *The Power of Human Rights: International Norms and Domestic Change* (CUP 1999).

Rose R, *Learning From Comparative Public Policy: A Practical Guide* (Routledge 2005).

Rosga A and Satterthwaie ML, 'The Trust in Indicators: Measuring Human Rights' (2009) 27(2) Berkeley Journal of International Law 253.

Sabel CF and Zeitlin J (eds), *Experimentalist Governance in the European Union: Towards a New Architecture* (OUP 2010).

Sabel CF and Zeitlin J, 'Experimentalism in Transnational Governance: Emergent Pathways and Diffusion Mechanisms: Paper presented at the panel on "Global Governance in

Transition", annual conference of the International Studies Association' (Montreal 16 March 2011).
Sabel CF and Zeitlin J, 'Experimentalism in the EU: Common Ground and Persistent Differences' (2012) 6 Regulation & Governance 410.
Sadurski W, *Constitutionalism and Enlargement of Europe* (OUP 2012).
Salinger U, 'Mediation as a Tool for Specialised Equality Bodies' (Equinet 2007).
Sargentini J and Dimitrovs A, 'The European Parliament's Role: Towards New Copenhagen Criteria for Existing Member States?' (2016) 54(5) Journal of Common Market Studies 1085.
Sasse G, 'The Politics of EU Conditionality: The Norm of Minority Protection during and beyond EU Accession' (2008) 15(6) Journal of European Public Policy 842.
Schiek D, '"Kalanke" und die Folgen—Überlegungen zu EG-rechtlichen Anforderungen an betriebliche Gleichstellungspolitik' (1996) 44(4) Arbeit und Recht 128.
Schiek D, 'Sex Equality Law After Kalanke and Marschall' (1998) 4(2) European Law Journal 148.
Schiek D, 'Indirect Discrimination' in Dagmar Schiek, Lisa Waddington, and Mark Bell (eds), *Cases, Materials and Text on National, Supranational and International Non-Discrimination Law* (Hart Publishing 2007).
Schiek D, 'On Uses, Mis-uses and Non-uses of Intersectionality before the European Court of Justice (ECJ). The ECJ rulings Parris (C-433/15), Achbita (C-157/15) and Bougnaoui (C-188/15) as a Bermuda Triangle?' (2018) 7(3) CETLS online paper series 1.
Schiek D, Waddington L, and Bell M (eds), *Cases, Materials and Text on National, Supranational and International Non-Discrimination Law* (Hart Publishing 2007).
Schimmelfennig F, 'Efficient Process Tracing: Analyzing the Causal Mechanisms of European Integration' in Andrew Bennett and Jeffrey T Checkel (eds), *Process Tracing: From Methaphor to Analytical Tool* (CUP 2015).
Schimmelfennig F and Sedelmeier U, 'Governance by Conditionality: EU Rule Transfer to the Candidate Countries of Central and Eastern Europe' (2004) 11(4) Journal of European Public Policy 661.
Schimmelfennig F and Sedelmeier U, 'Introduction: Conceptualizing the Europeanization of Central and Eastern Europe' in Frank Schimmelfennig and Ulrich Sedelmeier (eds), *The Europeanization of Central and Eastern Europe* (Cornell University Press 2005).
Schimmelfennig F and Sedelmeier U (eds), *The Europeanization of Central and Eastern Europe* (Cornell University Press 2005).
Schirmbeck S, 'Normerosion: Zur Schwächung von Tabus in den internationalen Beziehungen. Nukleares Tabu und Folterverbot' (Dissertation, Johann Wolfgang Goethe Universität Frankfurt 2013).
Schlachter M, 'Benachteiligung wegen besonderer Verbindungen statt Zugehörigkeit zu einer benachteiligten Gruppe' [2010] Recht der Arbeit 104.
Schmidt A, 'Artikel 4' in Rainer Hofmann and others (eds), *Rahmenübereinkommen zum Schutz nationaler Minderheiten. Handkommentar* (Nomos, facultas, Dike 2015).
Schröder W (ed), *Strengthening the Rule of Law in Europe: From a Common Concept to Mechanisms of Implementation* (Bloomsbury 2016).
Schuppert GF, 'Governance—auf der Such nach Konturen eines, anerkannt uneindeutigen Begriffs' [2008] Politische Vierteljahresschrift 13.
Sedelmeier U, 'Europeanisation in New Member and Candidate States' (2011) 6(1) Living Reviews in European Governance, 1.
Sedelmeier U, 'Is Europeanisation through Conditionality Sustainable? Lock-in of Institutional Change after EU Accession' (2012) 35(1) West European Politics 20.

Selanec G, 'Forms of Discrimination' in Tena Simonovic Einwalter (ed), *A Guide to the Anti-Discrimination Act* (Government of the Republic of Croatia Office for Human Rights 2009).

Selanec G and Šimonović Einwalter T, 'Scope of the Anti-Discrimination Act' in Tena Simonovic Einwalter (ed), *A Guide to the Anti-Discrimination Act* (Government of the Republic of Croatia Office for Human Rights 2009).

Sen A, *Commodities and Capabilities* (North Holland 1985).

Serban M, 'Rule of Law Indicators as a Technology of Power in Romania' in Sally Engle Merry, Kevin Davis, and Benedict Kingsbury (eds), *The Quiet Power of Indicators: Measuring Governance, Corruption, and Rule of Law* (CUP 2015).

Shrubsall V, 'Article 119, Pensions and Part-time Workers' [1987] Industrial Law Journal 52.

Silvestri E, 'Towards a Common Framework of Collective Redress in Europe? An Update on the Latest Initiatives of the European Commission' (2013) 1(1) Russian Law Journal 46.

Simmons B, *Mobilizing for Human Rights* (CUP 2009).

Škrabalo M, 'Transparency in Retrospect: Preliminary Lessons from Croatia's EU Accession Process' (Discussion paper commissioned by the Greens/EFA in the European Parliament 2012).

Snaith I, 'Two More Equal Pay Cases from the United Kingdom' [1981] European Law Review 193.

Šošić L, 'Croatian Government Called on to stop Attacking Civil Society' (Civil Liberties Union for Europe 8 November 2018) <https://www.liberties.eu/en/news/criminalization-of-solidarity-croatia/16115>.

Spencer S and Harvey C, 'Context, Institution or Accountability? Exploring the Factors that Shape the Performance of National Human Rights and Equality Bodies' (2014) 42(1) Policy & Politics 89.

Stanciu R, 'A disturbing decision by the EU's Court of Justice redefines the term "spouses"' (European Dignity Watch 6 June 2018) <http://www.europeandignitywatch.org/disturbing-decision-by-the-eu-court-of-justice-redefines-the-term-spouses/>.

Starl K and others, 'Human Rights Indicators in the Context of the European Union' (Deliverable within the FP7 Project 'Fostering Human Rights among European Policies', ETC Graz 24 December 2014).

Steering Committee on Anti-Discrimination, Diversity and Inclusion (CDADI), 'COVID-19: An analysis of the anti-discrimination, diversity and inclusion dimensions in Council of Europe member states' (17 July 2020) CDADI(2020)9.

Stein P, 'Diskriminierungsschutz und Kirchenautonomie' [2018] Zeitschrift für europäisches Sozial- und Arbeitsrecht 277.

Suhr O, 'Grenzen der Gleichbehandlung: Zur Vereinbarkeit von Frauenquoten mit dem Gemeinschaftsrecht' (1998) 25(5–6) Europäische Grundrechte-Zeitschrift 121.

Szyszczak E, 'Differences in Pay for Part-time Work' [1981] Modern Law Review 672.

Szyszczak E, 'Positive Action After Kalanke' (1996) 59(6) Modern Law Review 876.

Tobler C, *Indirect Discrimination: A Case Study into the Development of the Legal Concept of Indirect Discrimination under EC Law* (Intersentia 2005).

Tobler C, 'Limits and Potential of the Concept of Indirect Discrimination' (European Network of Legal Experts in the Non-discrimination Field 2008).

Toggenburg GN, 'The Race Directive: A New Dimension in the Fight against Ethnic Discrimination in Europe' (2001) 1 European Yearbook of Minority Issues 231.

Toggenburg GN, 'Discrimination by Association: A Notion Covered by EU Equality Law?' [2008] European Law Reporter 82.

Toggenburg GN and Grimheden J, 'Upholding Shared Values in the EU: What Role for the EU Agency for Fundamental Rights' (2016) 54(5) Journal of Common Market Studies 1093.

Treib O, 'Implementing and Complying with EU Governance Outputs' (2014) 9(1) Living Reviews in European Governance 1.

Treib O, Bähr H, and Falkner G, 'Modes of Governance: Towards a Conceptual Clarification' (2007) 14(1) Journal of European Public Policy 1.

Tryfonidou A, 'Free Movement of Same-Sex Spouses within the EU: The ECJ's Coman Judgment' (European Law Blog 19 June 2018) <https://europeanlawblog.eu/2018/06/19/free-movement-of-same-sex-spouses-within-the-eu-the-ecjs-coman-judgment/>.

Tryfonidou A, 'Case C-507/18 NH v Associazione Avvocatura per i diritti LGBTI—Rete Lenford: Homophobic Speech and EU Anti-Discrimination Law' (2020) 27(4) Maastricht Journal of European and Comparative Law 513.

Tulmets E, 'Experimentalist Governance in EU External Relations: Enlargement and the European Neighbourhood Policy' in Charles F Sabel and Jonathan Zeitlin (eds), *Experimentalist Governance in the European Union: Towards a New Architecture* (OUP 2010).

Tyson A, 'The Negotiation of the European Community Directive on Racial Discrimination' (2001) 3(2) European Journal of Migration and Law 199.

Ubbiali G, 'L'avvocato Taormina sui gay, parola alla Corte europea' *Corriere della sera* (6 August 2018).

Unia, 'Licencié en raison du handicap de sa fille' (12 December 2013) <https://www.unia.be/fr/articles/licencie-en-raison-du-handicap-de-sa-fille>.

Unia, 'La réclamation collective MDAC contre la Belgique devant le CEDS: observations du Centre' (11 March 2015) <https://www.unia.be/fr/legislation-et-recommandations/recommandations-dunia/la-reclamation-collective-mdac-contre-la-belgique-devant-le-ceds-observations-du-centre>.

Unia, 'Evaluation: Loi du 10 mai 2007 modifiant la loi du 30 juillet 1981 tendant à réprimer certains actes inspirés par le racisme ou la xénophobie (MB 30 mai 2007) (loi antiracisme) Loi du 10 mai 2007 tendant à lutter contre certaines formes de discrimination (MB 30 mai 2007) (loi anidiscrimination)' (2017) 97.

Unia, 'The Achbita case: clarity about the headscarf ban in the workplace' (15 March 2017) <https://www.unia.be/en/articles/the-achbita-case-clarity-about-the-headscarf-ban-in-the-workplace>.

Unia, 'Rapport annuel 2017—Refuser l'inertie' (2018).

Unia, 'Le Comité européen suit l'avis d'Unia sur le droit à l'éducation inclusive en Flandres' (29 March 2018) <https://www.unia.be/fr/articles/le-comite-europeen-suit-lavis-dunia-sur-le-droit-a-leducation-inclusive-en-flandres>.

Unia, 'Rapport annuel 2019. Contribuer à une société plus égale pour tous' (2020).

Unia, 'Rapport chiffre 2019' (2020).

United Nations, 'Model National Legislation for the Guidance of Governments in the Enactment of Further Legislation Against Racial Discrimination: Developed in the Context of the Third Decade to Combat Racism and Racial Discrimination (1993–2003)'.

Uzelaz A, 'Proceedings Before the Court' in Tena Simonovic Einwalter (ed), *A Guide to the Anti-Discrimination Act* (Government of the Republic of Croatia Office for Human Rights 2009).

Uzelaz A, 'Why No Class Action in Europe? A View from the Side of Dysfunctional Justice Systems' in Viktoria Harsági and CH van Rhee (eds), *Multi-Party Redress Mechanisms in Europe: Squeaking Mice?* (Intersentia 2014).

van Ballegooij W and Evas T, 'An EU mechanism on democracy, the rule of law and fundamental rights. Interim European Added Value Assessment accompanying the Legislative initiative Report (Rapporteur Sophie in 't Veld)' (European Parliamentary Research Service, European Added Value Unit April 2016).

Venice Commission, 'Compilation of Venice Commission Opinions Concerning the Ombudsman Institutions' (5 February 2016) CDL-PI(2016)001.

Venice Commission, 'Opinion No 897/2017—Principles on the Protection and Promotion of the Ombudsman Institution (Venice Principles)' (3 May 2019).

Vennesson P, 'Case Studies and Process Tracing: Theories and Practices' in Donatella Della Porta and Michael Keating (eds), *Approaches and Methodologies in the Social Sciences* (CUP 2008).

Vidačak I, 'Impact of Europeanization on Interest Groups Access and Representation in the Policy Making Process in Croatia' [2011] Etudes européennes La revue perm@nente des professionnels de l'Europe.

Vidačak I and Škrabalo M, 'Exploring the Effects of Europeanization on the Openness of Public Administration in Croatia' (2014) 14(1) Croatian and Comparative Public Administration 149.

Wagner V and Nowak M, 'Monitoring the Protection of Human Rights in the European Union: An Evaluation of Mechanisms and Tools' in Olivier de Schutter and Violeta Moreno Lax (eds), *Human Rights in the Web of Governance: A Learning-Based Fundamental Rights Policy for the EU* (Bruylant 2010).

Walsh J, 'National equality body instigates equality reviews of Traveller accommodation provision' (EELN News Report 9 July 2019).

Weiler JHH, 'Je Suis Achbita!' (2017) 28(4) European Journal of International Law 989.

Welling JV, 'International Indicators and Economic, Social, and Cultural Rights' (2008) 30(4) Human Rights Quarterly 933–58.

Wiener A, 'Contested Compliance: Interventions on the Normative Structure of World Politics' (2004) 10(2) European Journal of International Relations 189.

Wiener A, 'Making Normative Meaning Accountable in International Politics' [2007] WZB Discussion Papers.

Wiener A, 'The Dual Quality of Norms and Governance beyond the State: Sociological and Normative Approaches to "Interaction"' (2007) 10(1) Critical Review of International Social and Political Philosophy 47.

Wiener A, *The Invisible Constitution of Politics: Contested Norms and International Encounters* (CUP 2012).

Wiener A, *A Theory of Contestation* (Springer 2014).

Wiener A, 'A Theory of Contestation—A Concise Summary of Its Argument and Concepts' (2017) 49(1) Polity 109.

Wilson B, 'Commentary of Article 4 of the Framework Convention for the Protection of National Minorities' in Rainer Hofmann, Tove H Malloy, and Detlev Rein (eds), *The Framework Convention for the Protection of National Minorities. A Commentary* (Brill 2018).

Wladasch K, Hodasz M, and Liegl B, 'Reflexive Governance in the Public Interest: Anti-discrimination' (2008) Working paper series: REFGOV-FR-24.

Woll C and Jacquot S, 'Using Europe: Strategic Action in Multi-level Politics' (2010) 8(1) Comparative European Politics 110.

Wunsch N, 'Beyond Instrumentalisation: NGO Monitoring Coalitions in Croatia, Montenegro, and Serbia' (2015) 31(4) East European Politics 452.

Wunsch N, 'Right Goals, Wrong Tools? Civil Society Empowerment in the EU Accession Process' (February 2015) DGAPanalyse 2.

Wunsch N, 'Coming Full Circle? Differential Empowerment in Croatia's EU Accession Process' (2016) 23(8) Journal of European Public Policy 1199.
Wunsch N, 'Unpacking Differential Empowerment: Civil Society Mobilisation in the EU Accession Process' (PhD thesis in Political Science, University College London 2016).
Wunsch N, *EU Enlargement and Civil Society in the Western Balkans: From Mobilisation to Empowerment* (Palgrave 2018).
Wunsch N, 'Transnational Learning and Civil Society Empowerment in the EU Enlargement Process' [2018] Journal of Common Market Studies 1.
Yesilkagit K and Snijders B, 'Between Impartiality and Responsiveness: Equality Bodies and Practices of Independence' (Equinet, Brussels 2008).
Zimová A, 'Strategic Litigation Impacts: Roma School Desegregation' (Open Society Foundations 2016).

Court of Justice of the European Union/European Court of Justice

Asma Bougnaoui and Association de défense des droits de l'homme (ADDH) v Micropole SA [2017] ECLI:EU:C:2017:204.
Asociația Accept v Consiliul Național pentru Combaterea Discriminării [2013] ECLI:EU:C:2013:275.
Badeck and Others [2000] ECLI:EU:C:2000:163.
'CHEZ Razpredelenie Bulgaria'AD v Komisia za zashtita ot diskriminatsia [2015] ECLI:EU:C:2015:480.
Bilka v Weber von Hartz [1986] ECLI:EU:C:1986:204.
Centrum voor gelijkheid van kansen en voor racismebestrijding v Firma Feryn NV [2008] ECLI:EU:C:2008:397.
Commission v Hungary [2020] ECLI:EU:C:2020:476.
Diskrimineringsombudsmannen v Braathens Regional Aviation AB [2021] ECLI:EU:C:2021:269.
Gabrielle Defrenne v Société anonyme belge de navigation aérienne Sabena [1976] ECLI:EU:C:1976:56.
IR v JQ [2018] ECLI:EU:C:2018:696.
Jenkins v Kingsgate [1981] ECLI:EU:C:1981:80.
Joined cases HK Danmark, acting on behalf of Jette Ring v Dansk almennyttigt Boligselskab and HK Danmark, acting on behalf of Lone Skouboe Werge v Dansk Arbejdsgiverforening, acting on behalf of Pro Display A/S [2013] ECLI:EU:C:2013:222.
Kalanke v Freie Hansestadt Bremen [1995] ECLI:EU:C:1995:322.
Katarina Abrahamsson and Leif Anderson v Elisabet Fogelqvist [2000] ECLI:EU:C:2000:367.
Kommunikationsbehörde Austria (KommAustria) v Österreichischer Rundfunk (ORF) [2007] ECLI:EU:C:2007:613.
Marschall v Land Nordrhein-Westfalen [1997] ECLI:EU:C:1997:533.
NH v Associazione Avvocatura per i diritti LGBTI - Rete Lenford [2020] ECLI:EU:C:2020:289.
Relu Adrian Coman and Others v Inspectoratul General pentru Imigrări and Ministerul Afacerilor Interne [2018] ECLI:EU:C:2018:385.
S. Coleman v Attridge Law and Steve Law [2008] ECLI:EU:C:2008:415.
Samira Achbita and Centrum voor gelijkheid van kansen en voor racismebestrijding v G4S Secure Solutions NV [2017] ECLI:EU:C:2017:203.
Samira Achbita and Centrum voor gelijkheid van kansen en voor racismebestrijding v G4S Secure Solutions NV - opinion of the AG [2016] ECLI:EU:C:2016:382.

Sotgiu v Deutsche Bundespost [1974] ECLI:EU:C:1974:13.
The Minister for Justice and Equality and The Commissioner of the Garda Síochána v Workplace Relations Commission [2018] ECLI:EU:C:2018:979.
V.M.A. v Stolichna Obsthina, Rayon 'Pancharevo' (Sofia municipality, 'Pancharevo' district) referred to the CJEU on 2 October 2020, opinion of the AG presented on 15 April 2021.
Valeri Hariev Belov v CHEZ Elektro Balgaria AD and Others [2013] ECLI:EU:C:2013:48.
Valeri Hariev Belov v CHEZ Elektro Balgaria AD and Others—opinion of the AG [2012] ECLI:EU:C:2012:585.
Vera Egenberger v Evangelisches Werk für Diakonie und Entwicklung e.V. [2018] ECLI:EU:C:2018:257.
Westbahn Management GmbH v ÖBB-Infrastruktur AG [2012] ECLI:EU:C:2012:740.

List of Interview Partners

#	Organization/Function	Place	Date
1	resident twinning adviser in twinning 'Establishing a comprehensive system for anti-discrimination protection'	Phone	11 March 2015
2	staff member of the Office of the Ombudsperson, Regional Office Rijeka, Croatia	Skype	3 and 5 June 2015
3	Deputy Ombudsperson for Gender Equality, Croatia	Zagreb	12 October 2015
4	staff member at the Office for Human and Minority Rights, Croatia	Zagreb	12 October 2015
5	Executive Board Member of Centre for Peace Studies/NGO activist, Croatia	Zagreb	13 October 2015
6	representative of the Croatian Law Centre	Zagreb	13 October 2015
7	Professor of Political Science, University of Zagreb	Zagreb	13 October 2015
8	Professor of Procedural Law, University of Zagreb	Zagreb	13 October 2015
9	Judge at High Misdemeanor Court, Zagreb		
10	Member of the Croatian parliament, President of the Serb National Council	Zagreb	14 October 2015
11	legal adviser at Unia, Belgium	Brussels e-mail	31 May 2018 6 June 2018
12	DG Near, team leader/ policy officer for Fundamental rights, Centre of Expertise for Fundamental Rights and the Rule of Law	Brussels	31 May 2018
13	DG Justice and Consumers, Section D.1 Non-discrimination and Roma coordination	Brussels	1 June 2018
14	Policy Officer at Equinet	Brussels	1 June 2018
15	human rights lawyer I, Romania, EELN legal expert	Skype/ zoom	2 July 2018 2 April 2021

#	Organization/Function	Place	Date
16	Steering Board Member of NCCD, Romania	Phone	10 July 2018 11 July 2018
17	Former Board Member of CFCF and of the Advisory Board of the Equal Treatment Authority, Hungary	Skype	18 July 2018
18	Director, Háttér Society, Hungary	Skype	19 July 2018
19	Director of the Regional Representation Styria, Ombud for Equal Treatment, Austria	Graz	20 July 2018
20	human rights lawyer, Hungary	Skype	24 July 2018
21	human rights lawyer II, Romania, EELN legal expert	Skype	25 July 2018
22	Head of the Legal Department, Equal Treatment Authority, Hungary	e-mail	30 July 2018
23	Director of BUG, Germany	Skype Skype Skype e-mail	26 July 2018 2 August 2018 6 November 2018 31 March 2021
24	staff member, Research and General Affairs Department of FADA, Germany	Phone	26 July 2018
25	Head of unit Analysis, Prevention and International Cooperation, CPAD, Bulgaria	Skype	31 July 2018
26	Executive Board Member of Centre for Peace Studies, Zagreb, Croatia	Skype	1 August 2018
27	Board Member of ACCEPT, Romania	Skype	6 August 2018
28	Director of the Styrian Antidiscrimination Office, Austria	Graz	7 August 2018
29	staff member at the Office of the Ombudsperson, Croatia	Phone/ zoom	26 October 2018 and 26 March 2021
30	President of one of the senates of the Austrian ETC	e-mail	21 November 2018 4 December 2018
31	human rights and equality expert from Ireland	Phone	21 November 2018
32	expert in German anti-discrimination law	Phone	21 November 2018

Index

For the benefit of digital users, indexed terms that span two pages (e.g., 52–53) may, on occasion, appear on only one of those pages.